Using Linux

Bill Ball

Jan Walter

Steve Shah

Sriranga Veeraraghaven

Tad Bohlsen

David Pitts

A Division of Macmillan Computer Publishing, USA
201 W. 103rd Street
Indianapolis, Indiana 46290

Contents at a Glance

Using Linux

FIRST EDITION

International Standard Book Number: 0-7897-1623-2

Library of Congress Catalog Card Number: 97-81344

2001 00 99 98 4 3 2 1

Interpretation of the printing code: the rightmost double-digit number is the year of the book's printing; the rightmost single-digit, the number of the book's printing. For example, a printing code of 98-1 shows that the first printing of the book occurred in 1998.

Composed in Formata and Janson by Macmillan Computer Publishing

Printed in the United States of America

Executive Editor
Jeff Koch

Acquisitions Editor
Tracy Williams

Development Editor
Kate Shoup Welsh

Managing Editor
Sarah Kearns

Project Editor
Tom Lamoureux

Copy Editor
Daryl Kessler

Indexer
Johnna Vanhoose

Technical Editor
Eric Roberts

Production
Cyndi Davis Hubler
Betsy Deeter

Contents

Acknowledgments

Thanks are due to the following people at Macmillan: Theresa Ball, Lynette Quinn, Tracy Williams, Kate Welsh, and Jeff Koch. Thanks also to John Herlig at Gargoyle's in Stafford, Va. for his fresh roast and Yemen mocha. A big note of appreciation is also due to the XFree86 folks in Herndon, Va., without whose efforts many Linux users would not enjoy a graphical interface to the best operating system in the world.

Dedicaton

To Cathy and Nat—it's nice to be home.

About the Author

Bill Ball, author of *Sams Teach Yourself Linux in 24 Hours*, is a technical writer, editor, and magazine journalist. He broke down and bought a PC after using the Macintosh series of computers from Apple for nearly 10 years, but didn't join the Dark Side—he started using Linux! He has published more than a dozen articles in magazines such as *Computer Shopper* and *MacTech Magazine*, and first started editing books for Que in 1986. An avid fly fisherman, he builds bamboo fly rods, and fishes on the nearby Potomac River when he's not driving his vintage MG sports cars. He lives at Aquia Harbor in Stafford County, Virginia.

Jan Walter is a freelance computer consultant living in Vancouver, Canada. He specializes in providing solutions to small and mid-sized businesses, and has supported and worked with Linux, Windows NT, and OS/2 since 1993. Other work includes consulting ISPs on supporting non-Windows based clients, performance optimization of programs, and CGI programming. He can be contacted via email at `jwalter@rogers.wave.ca`.

Steve Shah is a systems administrator at the Center for Environmental Research and Technology at the University of California, Riverside. He received his B.S. in Computer Science with a minor in Creative Writing, and is currently working on his M.S. in Computer Science there as well. Occasionally, Steve leaves his console to pursue analog activities such as DJing and spending time with his better half, Heidi.

Sriranga Veeraraghavan works in the area of network management at Cisco Systems, Inc. He enjoys developing software using Java, C, Perl, and Shell for both Linux and Solaris. His pastimes include playing Marathon and debugging routing problems in his heterogenous network at home. Sriranga graduated from U.C. Berkeley in 1997 with an Engineering degree and is pursuing further studies at Stanford University.

Tad Bohlsen is currently the technology manager for a non-profit organization, and also a consultant on technology issues. In the past he has served as a UNIX system administrator and shell script developer, and worked with companies like Juno Online Services and HBO.

David Pitts is a senior consultant with BEST Consulting. Currently on assignment with The Boeing Company, David is a system administrator, programmer, Webmaster, and author. David can be reached at `dpitts@mk.net` or `kpitts@bestnet.com`. David lines in Everett, Washington, with his wonderful wife Dana.

Tell Us What You Think!

As a reader, you are the most important critic and commentator of our books. We value your opinion and want to know what we're doing right, what we could do better, what areas you'd like to see us publish in, and any other words of wisdom you're willing to pass our way. You can help us make strong books that meet your needs and give you the computer guidance you require.

Do you have access to the World Wide Web? Then check out our site at `http://www.mcp.com`.

As the team leader of the group that created this book, I welcome your comments. You can fax, email, or write me directly to let me know what you did or didn't like about this book—as well as what we can do to make our books stronger. Here's the information:

Fax: 317-581-4669
Email: `cwill@mcp.com`
Mail: Chris Will
Comments Department
Que Corporation
201 W. 103rd Street
Indianapolis, IN 46290

Note: If you have a technical question about this book, call the technical support line at 317-581-3833 or send email to `support@mcp.com`.

INTRODUCTION

THIS BOOK IS FOR RED HAT LINUX USERS and Linux system administrators who don't want to waste time and effort finding the right solution when installing, configuring, using, and maintaining Linux. If you use the Linux operating system, you'll benefit from this book's no-nonsense approach, which gives you explicit direction without long-winded technical discussion on subjects aimed at helping you get work done.

New to Linux? Start at the beginning of the book – I'll introduce you to the basics of getting started. You'll find loads of short-cuts and interesting ways to use basic software tools. You'll also learn how to easily use nearly 100 different programs, and will be up to speed in no time at all.

Part 1 details the basics. However, experienced users will also benefit as each chapter's examples range from the simple to the complex.

Part 2 contains software and hardware configuration information to help you configure your software environment and to make Linux and your hardware work together.

Part 3 covers getting connected to and getting information from the Internet. Electronic mail, web browsing, and news reading are just a few of the subjects outlined in each chapter.

Part 4 spotlights the X Window System – whether it's configuring X, choosing a window manager, or performing common operations, you'll find the information you need.

Seasoned users and budding system administrators with a bit more experience will definitely want to read this book's more advanced chapters. Part 5 contains simple solutions to technical problems, and covers many different tasks required to make Linux more efficient, safe, and secure. You'll get the information you need to build your expertise and real-world savvy as a problem-solving advanced user.

Need answers quickly? This book aims to provide you with the answers you need in the quickest manner possible. It's loaded with cross-references, step-by-step instructions, quick notes on related subjects, and includes a dynamite index. Keep this book handy while you work – you'll reach for it when you need to quickly find a solution to a complex problem.

Inside this book, you'll find get the help you need with a variety of subjects like:

- Installing tape, Zip, and hard drives.
- Configuring Linux for PC cards.
- Sending and receiving faxes.
- Connecting to the Internet.
- Downloading files using FTP or web browsers.
- Watching T.V. and listening to radio over the Internet.
- Reading Usenet news.
- Configuring, using, and getting the most out of the X Window System.
- Managing users, daemons, and the Linux kernel.
- Using the shell and other tools for programming.
- Setting up network, scheduling, and other maintenance services.

I wrote this book to help make your Linux experience easier—to help you accomplish complex tasks in the simplest manner possible. This book was written for Linux users by Linux users – we share a common goal of wanting to help you quickly craft custom solutions to fit your needs - you deserve nothing less.

Conventions Used In This Book

The *Using* series has some conventions that control the formatting of text, and they are used to help you distinguish between generic information and a discussion about a dialog box or menu you're viewing on your screen.

- *Menu and Dialog Box Choices.* Words that appear in a menu or a dialog box are printed in bold type. For example, you might see text that says "choose **Color**, then select a new background color from the palette that appears."
- *Hot-keys.* We underline references to hot-keys, which are underlined letters in menu commands and dialog boxes that you can use with your Alt key instead of employing the mouse.
- *Combination Keys.* We use a plus sign (+) to indicate that keys should be used together. For example, you may see "press **Ctrl+A** to select everything."
- *Cross References.* If there's information that's connected to the topic you're currently reading, we'll tell you which chapter has it. You can use this information to learn more about the subject, or take the next step in building whatever it is you're building at the moment. For example:

SEE ALSO

➤ *To learn how to change the prompt of your command line, see page 96.*

- *Tips, warnings and sidebars.* These new page elements highlight tips, related software news, techniques, and potential traps. By giving these valuable notes explicit titles and placing them in the margin, we've made them handy and easy to find, without breaking up the text that explains the procedure you're currently working your way through.

PART I

Linux Basics

CHAPTER

1

Introducing the Shell

By Bill Ball

What is a shell?

Creating user accounts quickly and easily

Changing user passwords to improve security

How to reboot or shut down Linux

Using multiple logons to work more efficiently

Getting online help

Welcome to Linux

Congratulations on choosing and using Linux, today's newest, most popular, flexible, and powerful free computer operating system. Hang on, because you're riding along the crest of a rising tidal wave of new users as Linux spreads around the globe. While governments and corporations publicly battle one another over commercial software issues, Linux has been steadily gaining worldwide acceptance and respect as a viable alternative computer operating system. Linux quietly sidesteps the restrictions that hold commercial software hostage in the marketplace in a number of ways:

- Linux is distributed under the terms of the Free Software Foundation's GNU General Public License, or GPL. This license preserves software copyrights, but ensures distribution of programs with source code.
- Linux is distributed over the Internet, and is easy to download, upgrade, and share.
- Programmers all over the world create, distribute, and maintain programs for Linux, and much of this software is also distributed under the GPL.

What is Linux?

Linux is the kernel, or core, of a UNIX-like computer operating system. Linux, written by Linus Torvalds, was first released over the Internet in 1991. Since then, Linux has exploded in popularity, maturing with each new version and bug fix. When you install and use Linux, you're installing and using a *distribution*, or collection of associated programs bundled with the Linux kernel. There are a number of popular Linux distributions, including Red Hat Linux, Slackware, Debian, and S.u.S.E.; each distribution has a different installation method and is bundled with different software maintenance tools.

Linux continues to evolve, and major improvements to the last several versions make using, installing, and maintaining this operating system easier than ever. With Linux's increasing popularity, kernel bug fixes and new versions of free software appear every day on more and more Internet servers. New features of the latest versions of the Linux kernel and distributions include the following:

- Support for dynamic code-module loading and unloading. If a printer or sound card is needed, the appropriate code module is loaded from a disk and then released after use as appropriate.
- Increased support for a wide variety of devices such as sound cards, scanners, hard disks, tape drives, printers, digital cameras, and joysticks.
- Increasingly easier installation, configuration, and system maintenance with dozens of different GUI (graphical user

interface) programs, many of which surpass commercial software peers in convenience and ease of use.

There are now versions of Linux for Intel-based PCs, the Apple PowerMacintosh, Digital's Alpha PCs, and Sun SPARC-compatibles. Each version of Linux comes with complete source code, so you can customize, correct bugs, or recompile the operating system.

SEE ALSO

➤ *To learn how to rebuild the Linux kernel, see page 588.*
➤ *To learn how to manage kernel modules, see page 577.*

What Is a Shell?

This chapter, which introduces you to Linux, assumes that you've just booted Linux for the first time after installation. The *shell* is a program started after you log on to Linux; it provides a command-line interface, or *shell*, between you and the Linux kernel. Typed commands are interpreted by the shell and sent to the *kernel*, which in turn opens, closes, reads, or writes files. There are a number of shells for Linux, but the default shell for Red Hat Linux, `bash`, and is found under the `/bin` directory. The shell's internal commands and functions can also be used to write programs.

SEE ALSO

➤ *To learn how to write shell programs, see page 365.*
➤ *To learn about how to use the shell, see page 19.*

Logging On to Linux

Working from the logon and password prompt

1. After you boot Linux for the first time, you'll see a logon and password prompt on your display. To access Linux, type **`root`** at the logon prompt and press Enter.

```
localhost login: root
Password:
```

2. At the password prompt, type the password you chose when you installed Linux.

Running as root can be dangerous!

Before you start using Linux, you should create a user name and password for yourself instead of running as the root operator all the time. You should log in as the root operator only when you need to upgrade Linux, add or partition a new hard drive, perform system maintenance or recovery, or run root-only tools (such as Red Hat's Setup or Control Panel applications. As the root operator, you can create or destroy any file in any directory in your system. Improperly specified unconditional file deletions using wildcards or inadvertent file and directory copying will not only wipe out or overwrite entire directories, but also any other mounted file systems, such as Windows. Always keep a backup of important files!

3. After you press the Enter key, the screen will clear, and you'll be presented with a command line:

```
#
```

Although you can manually edit system files to create, add, edit, or delete users and user information, the Red Hat Linux distribution comes with several command-line and graphical interface tools that make the job a lot easier. However, the first thing you should do after booting Linux following installation is to create your own user account.

Starting to work with Linux

1. Create a user name for yourself or others. Optionally enter user account information.
2. Create a password for yourself or new users.
3. Exit or log out of Linux.
4. Log on to Linux with your new user name and password.

Creating a User Account at the Command Line

When you first log on to Linux, you'll be logged on as the root operator. Create a user name for yourself with the `useradd` command, found under the `/usr/sbin` directory, like so:

```
# useradd fred
```

The `useradd` command creates a user entry in a file called `passwd`, under the `/etc` directory. This entry lists the user's name and password, along with a home directory and default shell:

```
fred:!:501:501::/home/cloobie:/bin/bash
```

The initial password entry will be blank.

Creating a User Account in X11 with the *usercfg* Command

If you're running the X Window System, use the Red Hat `usercfg` command to fill in a form with a user's information and create a new account. In a terminal window, type the following at the command line:

```
# usercfg &
```

This command line runs the User Configurator, shown in Figure 1.1. The User Configurator lists all current users.

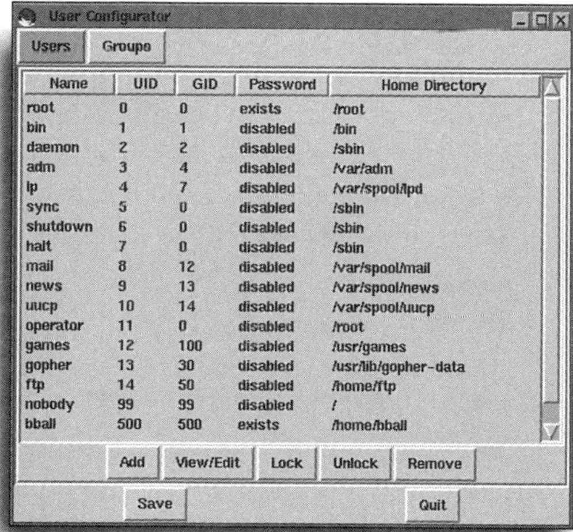

FIGURE 1.1
Using the X11 usercfg client is an easy way to create new user accounts.

Creating a user account in X11

1. Click the Add button to create a user. This invokes the Edit User Definition dialog box, which is shown in Figure 1.2.

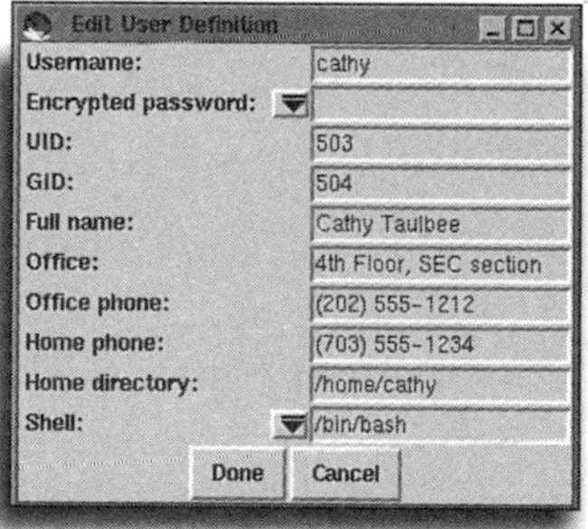

FIGURE 1.2
The Edit User Definition dialog box stores information about a user's account in your system's /etc/passwd file.

2. In the Edit User Definition dialog box, enter the new user name, the user's full name, her office location and phone number, her home phone number, and her home directory, such as `/home/cathy`. This information is used by the finger command, a network user account information utility.
3. Click the Done button to close the dialog box.
4. Click the Save button in the User Configurator dialog box to create your new user account.

SEE ALSO

➤ *To learn how to use the* finger *command, see page 19.*
➤ *To learn how to start the X Window System, see page 260.*

Changing Your Password

As the root operator, you can change the password for any user on your system. After creating a new user account, create a password by using the `passwd` command by specifying the user's name on the command line, as in the following:

```
# passwd fred
New UNIX password:
Retype new UNIX password:
passwd: all authentication tokens updated successfully
```

The `passwd` command, found under the `/usr/bin` directory, prompts for a new password, and then asks you to type it again to verify the change. After you make the change, the `/etc/passwd` entry reflects the password as an encrypted string like so:

```
fred:Qzq/xNwYPy0OU:502:502::/home/fred:/bin/bash
```

SEE ALSO

➤ *To learn more about passwords, see page 422.*

Changing User Account Information with the *chfn* Command

The `/etc/passwd` entries are also used to store information about each user, such as office location or phone numbers. To add more information to the `/etc/passwd` file entry, use the `chfn` command to change finger information, as shown here:

```
# chfn fred
Changing finger information for fred.
Name []: Fred Thomas
Office []: 4th Floor - Computing Services
Office Phone []: (202) 555-1212
Home Phone []: (540) 555-1212
Finger information changed.
```

The `chfn` command, found under the `/usr/bin` directory, prompts for new user information. Existing entries will be echoed between the brackets in the prompts, and overwritten after the changes.

Changing your user information and password in X11

The X11 `usercfg` command can be run only by the root operator to add or change a user's information. Regular users without root access can use Red Hat's X11 GUI clients, `userinfo` and `userpasswd`, discussed in Chapter 25, "Managing Users and Groups," to change their information and passwords.

Running Commands as the Root Operator

After you've logged on under your new user name, you're just like any other user, with one important exception: You know the root password. From now on, whenever you have to accomplish important system tasks or run programs as root, you don't have to exit Linux and log back on as the root operator. Instead, you can use the `su`, or superuser, command to temporarily become the root user. The `su` command can be used by itself or with the `-c` (command) option to run a program:

```
$ whoami
bball
$ su
Password:
# whoami
root
# exit
$ su -c "useradd fred"
Password:
$
```

In this example, the `whoami` command, found under the `/usr/bin` directory, reports on who you are. The `su` command prompts for a password before allowing you to become the root operator.

After you run root commands, use the shell's `exit` command to return to your original shell and identity. When the `su` command is used with the `-c` option, the specified root command, enclosed in quotes, is run and you're immediately returned to your shell. Always use caution when running commands as the root operator.

Using Virtual Consoles

Linux also allows you to log on numerous times and as different users through the use of virtual consoles. *Virtual consoles* offer a way to run two or more shells at the same time. Virtual consoles are handy when you want to run two or more programs simultaneously, or if you must have a root shell open at all times.

Linux supports at least six virtual consoles. When you start Linux, the logon prompt is presented at virtual console number 1. You select virtual consoles by pressing the Alt key along with a Function key (from one to six).

Use a virtual console after starting Linux

1. Type your user name at the login prompt, and then press Enter.
2. Type your password, and then press Enter.
3. After you log in, hold down the Alt key, then press the F2, F3, F4, F5, or F6 function key to start using a new virtual console. A new login prompt will appear.
4. Repeat the login process using your user name, the root operator user name, or another user name.

To switch back to your first, or initial, logon shell, hold down the Alt key and press the F1 function key. Switch between virtual consoles by using the appropriate Alt + function-key combination.

Logging Out of Linux

After you create a new user account and a new user's password, log out of Linux by using the `logout` or `exit` command:

```
# exit
# logout
```

After you enter either of these commands, the display will clear, and the Linux logon prompt will be redisplayed.

Rebooting Linux

Reboot: Controlling the Vulcan nerve pinch: Ctrl+Alt+Del

You can reboot your system by using the Ctrl+Alt+Del key combination. To restrict this keystroke combination for use by only the root operator, create a file called `shutdown.allow` under the `/etc` directory. This can improve security when you're running Linux as a server or if you're worried about someone inadvertently restarting your system. For more details, see the `shutdown` command's manual page.

To reboot your system, always use the `shutdown` command, found under the `/sbin` directory. Just powering off your computer can cause disk errors, and is an unsafe practice. You must be the root operator or use the `su` command to use the `shutdown` command.

The `shutdown` command takes several command-line options. For example, using the `-r`, or *reboot*, option followed by the word `now` will reboot your system immediately:

```
# shutdown -r now
```

Shutting Down Linux

The `shutdown` command's `-h`, or *halt*, command-line option can shut down Linux. As with the `-r` option, a time (in seconds) or the word `now` can be used to specify when Linux should shut down. Using the following command will enable you to shut down your system immediately:

```
# shutdown -h now
```

Getting Help

Linux distributions include documentation about nearly all the programs, commands, and files installed on your hard drive. Each distribution also comes with a number of commands and programs designed to help you learn about your system. These commands are discussed in the following sections.

Getting Help with the *man* Command

The `man` command is a program used to print online help, or documentation called *manual pages*, about a command, file, or other Linux function. To read a manual page, specify a program name on the command line. To learn about the `man` command, follow it with the word `man`, like so:

```
# man man
```

Entering this command sends the manual page to your display; use the less pager to scroll through it. Manual pages (sometimes called *man pages*) are text files written using a special format. To read about the format of these pages, use the `man` command's `section` option to read the `man` manual page under the `/usr/man/man7` directory, as follows:

```
# man 7 man
```

Manual pages and documentation are located under the `/usr/man` directory in several sections organized by task or type. Table 1.1 lists these different sections.

TABLE 1.1 Manual page sections

Section	Type of Documentation
1	Commands (general programs)
2	System calls (kernel functions)
3	Library calls (programming functions)
4	Special files (`/dev` directory files)
5	File formats (`/etc/passwd` and others)
6	Games
7	Macro packages (man page formats, and so on)
8	System management (root operator utilities)
9	Kernel routines (kernel source routines)

Getting Help in X11 with the *xman* Client

To read manual pages while using the X Window System, simply start the `xman` client from the command line of the terminal window:

```
# xman &
```

Figure 1.3 shows a man page viewed within the X Window System.

Getting Help with the *whatis* Command

Use the `whatis` command if you're unsure about what a program does. Using this command prints a short synopsis of each specified command. For example, issuing the command `# whatis cal` returns the following result:

```
cal (1)                 - displays a calendar
```

The synopsis of the specified command is extracted from the command's manual page and is located in a database called `whatis`. The `whatis` database, located under the `/usr/man` directory, is built each day by a `crontab` script run each week by the `makewhatis.cron` script in the `/etc/cron.weekly` directory. This script runs the `makewhatis` command, found under the `/usr/sbin` directory.

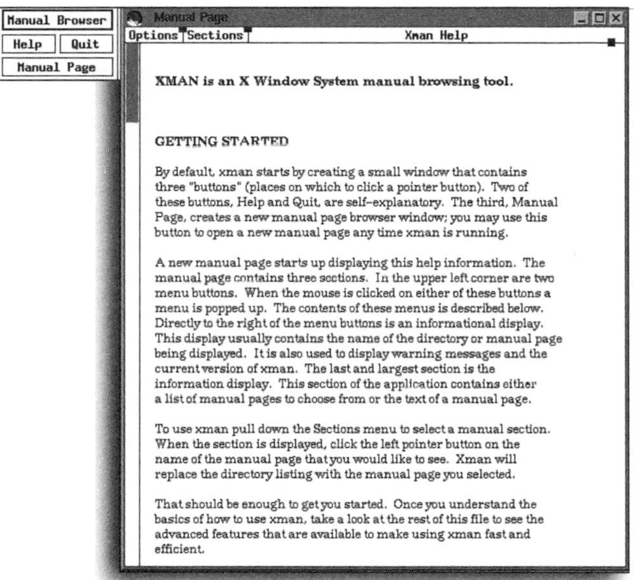

FIGURE 1.3
The xman X11 client displays manual pages in a scrolling window.

Getting Help with the *apropos* Command

The `apropos` command uses the `whatis` database to display all related matches of the command's name. Use this command to find related commands or actions for programs installed on your system. For example, issuing the command `# apropos bell` returns the following result:

```
beep, flash (3)       - Curses bell and screen flash routines
bell (n)               - Rings a display's bell
```

If you do not have `apropos` installed on your system, you can use the `man` command's `-K` option; however, this is a slow way to search for the information because the `man` command must search through each manual page in each manual page section.

CHAPTER

2

Entering Commands

By Bill Ball

Entering Commands at the Shell Command Line

Using Linux means using a command line. Even if you always run the X Window System, you'll need to know how to use the shell at one time or another. By understanding how the shell interprets your keystrokes, you'll learn how to work faster and more efficiently when you enter commands.

Case Sensitivity

All shells for Linux are case sensitive. This means filenames must be specified as they exist, using uppercase, mixed-case, or lowercase letters and characters. Filenames can be as much as 256 characters long, and can contain many different types of characters. For example, the following are valid (but not necessarily good) sample filenames:

```
a_long-filename+a-long=extension
averylongfilenamethatistoolongformostfilenames
pAymEoRyOuWiLlnEvErsEeyOurCaTaGain
a file

a[file]
file:name
 filename
file.txt
file2.txt.extension
~@#^
```

Reserved characters, or characters not to be used in filenames, include the following:

```
"  ,  '  *  &  )  (  ¦  !  `  ?  \  /  <  >  ;
```

Note that it is possible to create a filename with a leading space, an embedded space, or that consists entirely of spaces. Nevertheless, this is not a good practice; it could cause problems later on, especially if you need to manipulate a list of filenames or you want to delete a file.

SEE ALSO

➤ *To learn how to delete files and directories, see page 42.*

Editing the Command Line

Whether you can edit text entered at the command line depends on the shell being used. The default Red Hat Linux shell, `bash`, supports command-line editing. The basic editing commands are listed in Table 2.1, and are entered either by pressing special keys on your keyboard or by using a Ctrl + key combination.

TABLE 2.1 ***bash* shell command-line editing keys**

Action	Key or Keystroke Combination
Forward character	right cursor, Ctrl+F
Forward word	Alt+F
Backward character	left cursor, Ctrl+B
Backward word	Alt+B
Beginning of line	Ctrl+A
End of line	Ctrl+E
Delete character	Ctrl+D
Delete word	Alt+D
Delete to end of line	Ctrl+K
Delete to beginning of line	Ctrl+U

Saving Keystrokes with Shell History

If a shell supports command-line history, you can scroll through previously entered commands. The default shell, `bash`, saves the last 1,000 command lines in a file called `.bash_history` in your `home` directory. To quickly reenter a command line, use the up or down cursor keys to scroll through the list.

SEE ALSO

➤ *To increase or decrease the number of command histories for* `bash`, *see page 90.*

Using the Tab Key to Complete Commands

Another feature of the default shell is command completion. To quickly type or find the name of a command or all commands with similar spellings, type the first few letters of a command's name, and then press the Tab key on your keyboard. For example, type the following:

```
# contr
```

Pressing the Tab key results as follows:

```
# control-panel
```

If you enter enough unique letters of a program's name, the shell will complete the program's name for you. If you enter only the first few letters, you'll have to press Tab twice in succession. For example, type the following:

```
# pi
```

Then press the Tab key twice in succession for the following results:

```
pi1toppm    pic        pick    picttoppm    pilot    ping
pi3topbm    pic2tpic   pico    pidof        pine
```

The shell will print all files with names containing the specified letters.

Entering Multiple Commands

To enter several commands on a single command line, use the semicolon (;), like so:

```
# ls ; cat file.txt
```

This runs the `ls` (list directory) command, followed by the display of the file, `report.txt`, by the `cat` (concatenate) command.

SEE ALSO

➤ *To learn how to create, copy, or delete directories, see Chapter 3, "Navigating the Linux File System."*

Breaking Long Command Lines

Although most shells automatically wrap long command lines when the end of a line is reached, you can use the backslash character (\) with the semicolon to type multiple commands, or single commands on separate lines:

```
# ls /tmp ;\
>ls /boot ;\
>ls /var/log/uucp
```

The shell automatically prints the > character to show that a long command is being entered. Use the backslash to make complex command lines easier to read.

Creating Shell Commands

The shell recognizes a number of special characters on the command line. This section shows how to use these characters to do the following:

- Send a program's output to a file.
- Have a program read text from a file.
- Append a program's output to a file.
- Run a program in the background.

Using the >, >>, and < Redirection Operators

Shell redirection operators are used to direct a program's input and output. The shell can be used to feed a program input from another program, the command line, or even another file. These operators are used to copy, create, or overwrite files, to build reports, or to create databases.

The `cat` (concatenate) command is used to print files to your display; when used with the >, or standard output redirection operator, the `cat` command will copy a file by sending its output to another file:

```
# cat report.txt >newreport.txt
```

This is called *redirecting the standard output*. Through the use of redirection, the output of the `cat` command is sent to a specified file in the current directory.

You can also combine the `cat` command and shell command-line redirection as a method to quickly create and enter text in a file.

Quick text entry

1. Use the `cat` command along with output redirection on the command line to send all typed input from the keyboard directly to a text file:

```
# cat >myfile.txt
>This is a line of text.
>This is the second line of text.
>This is the last line of text.
```

2. When you've finished typing your text, press Ctrl+D to enter an end-of-file mark:

```
>[EOF]
```

3. To check your text, use the `cat` command:

```
# cat myfile.txt
This is a line of text.
This is the second line of text.
This is the last line of text.
```

Output redirection can be dangerous!

Indiscriminately redirecting the output of programs can cause you to lose data because any existing file with the same name as the one on the command line will be overwritten. Make sure you do not redirect output to an existing file. A much safer approach is to use the >> (append redirection) operator to append output. That way, the worst thing that can happen is that data will be appended to the existing file. This is another good reason why you shouldn't run Linux as the root operator—as root, you can overwrite any file on your system, including important configuration files and even the kernel.

The < (standard input) redirection operator feeds information to a program as follows:

```
# cat <report.txt
```

Here, the `cat` command reads the contents of the file `report.txt` and sends its contents to your display. To build a larger report, use the >> append operator to add output to existing files like so:

```
# cat <report.txt >>newreport.txt
```

If the file `newreport.txt` does not exist, it will be created. If the file exists, the contents of the file `report.txt` will be appended to the end of the file `newreport.txt`.

A more obscure redirection operator is the << (here) operator. Use this operator to tell the shell when to stop reading input:

```
# cat <<end
> this is
> the
> end
this is
the
#
```

When the shell reads the specified word following the << operator, it stops reading input. In this case, the `cat` command echoes all entered input until the word `end` is specified, and then properly echoes to the display.

Redirecting Error Output by the Numbers

The standard input and output have assigned file numbers in the shell. The standard input uses the number `0`, and the standard output uses the number `1`. Another type of output is *standard error*, and its number is `2`.

Most commands for Linux report errors using the standard error output, and send the error message to your display as follows:

```
# cat report.txt >newreport.txt
cat: report.txt: No such file or directory
```

By properly redirecting a program's output, you can build a log of any errors. Specify that the standard error output is always sent and appended to a file like so:

```
# cat report.txt >newreport.txt 2>>errors.log
# cat errors.log
cat: report.txt: No such file or directory
```

Because the error output has been redirected to a file, no error message is printed on the display. Although the file `newreport.txt` will be empty, the file `errors.log` will contain a list of errors.

Using Pipes to Build Commands

The vertical bar (or *pipe*) character (`|`) is called a *pipe operator*, and is used to send output from one command to another on the command line. Use input and output redirection with pipes to quickly build custom commands.

Pipes can save time and effort, and work with many commands found under Linux. In order for you to be able to use a command in a pipe, the program must be able to read the standard input and write to the standard output. Such programs are also called *filters*.

Not all programs work the same way

Not all commands for Linux will read from the standard input and write to the standard output. Make sure to read a program's manual page before using the program to build important or complex pipes. See the section "Using Pipes to Build Commands" later in this chapter for more information.

SEE ALSO

➤ *To learn more about text processing filters, see page 66.*

Pipes range from simple to complex, and are used for many purposes. The following are some examples of how pipes can be used:

```
# cat report.txt ¦ wc -l >number_of_lines.txt
```

The preceding example counts the numbers of lines in a file and generates a report.

```
# find / ¦ wc -l >number_of_files.txt
```

This command line counts the number of files on your system, starting at the / or root directory.

```
# find / ¦ sort ¦ uniq -d >duplicate_filenames.txt
```

This example generates a report of your system's duplicate files (files with the same name).

```
# strings /usr/lib/ispell/american.hash ¦ sort ¦ tee upper
➥case.dict ¦
\ tr A-Z a-z >lowercase.dict
```

This example extracts a list of words from the system's dictionary by using the `strings` command. The output is then sorted. The `tee` command is then used to save a copy of the dictionary, still in its original, uppercase form, while the output is converted to lowercase by the `tr` command, and then saved in lowercase. This creates two different dictionaries: one containing uppercase words, and the other containing lowercase words.

Running Programs in the Background

Use an ampersand (`&`) to start and run a program in the background. Although you can use a virtual console to run other programs at the same time, background programs can be started quite easily from a single terminal or command line.

You'll use background processes quite often if you use the X Window System. Most X11 clients do not offer a terminal window or command line, so it is necessary to run the client in the background to free your terminal for further input like so:

```
# xcalc &
#
```

This command starts the X11 `calc` (calculator) client, leaving your terminal free for other command lines.

SEE ALSO

➤ *To learn more about using X11 clients, see page 307.*

Controlling Programs

Most (but not all) shells support some form of control over background processes. Important features include the following:

- Listing current background programs
- Pausing running programs
- Stopping running processes
- Bringing to the foreground programs sent to the background

Controlling background programs is called *job control.*

Using Job Control

Use job control to manage multiple running programs. You can start programs in the background from the `bash` shell command line with the `&` operator, or you can send programs to the background by pressing Ctrl+Z. The shell will respond by printing a job number, followed by a process number of the program:

```
# sc &
[1] 2689
```

Running programs sent to the background with Ctrl+Z will disappear, and the shell will print a job number like so:

```
[2]+ Stopped     sc
```

Many programs or several instances of a single program can be started, suspended, or run. To obtain a list of currently running programs, use the `bash` shell's `jobs` command:

```
# jobs
[2]   Stopped                    sc
[3]-  Stopped (tty output)     pico report.txt
[4]+  Stopped (tty output)     pico newreport.txt
```

The `jobs` command prints each program's job number along with the command line used to start the program. To selectively bring back a program, use the `fg` command followed by the job number, as follows:

```
# fg 3
```

This returns the pico text editor to your display.

Using the *ps* and *kill* Commands

A background program is assigned a unique process number by the Linux kernel. To see the process numbers of currently running programs, use the `ps` (process status) command (not all processes running at the time are listed here to save space). This listing shows that the `su` command is running with a process number of 1658:

```
# ps
...
 1658  p0 S    0:00 su
 1659  p0 S    0:00 bash
 2713  p0 T    0:00 pico report.txt
 2714  p0 T    0:00 pico newreport.txt
...
```

You can stop programs by specifying the process number along with the `kill` command as follows:

```
# kill -9 2714
[4]+  Killed                 pico newreport.txt
```

SEE ALSO

➤ *To learn more about controlling processes and other background programs, see page 581.*

However, stopping programs by killing a process by using a process number is an inconvenient way to stop background programs. Use the `kill` command, followed by the percent sign (%) and the job number or command name, to stop a program like so:

```
# kill %3
[3]+  Terminated                 pico report.txt
# kill %pico
[3]+  Terminated                 pico report.txt
```

Halting programs by job number or name should be used instead of killing processes because you can all too easily enter a wrong process number, and inadvertently bring your system to a halt.

Using Wildcards

Wildcards are used on the shell command line to specify files by name or extension. shells for Linux offer sophisticated forms of wildcards that you can use to perform complex pattern matching. Creating complex wildcards is called building regular expressions.

Building Regular Expressions

Regular expressions are wildcard patterns, built using a special command-line syntax. This syntax uses a number of special characters, some of which are listed in Table 2.2.

TABLE 2.2 **Common regular expressions and characters**

Expression	Action
`*`	Match all characters
`?`	Match a single character
`[a-z]`	Match a range of characters
`[0123]`	Match a range of characters
`\?`	Match the ? character
`\)`	Match the) character
`^abc`	Match pattern abc at beginning of lines
`$abc`	Match pattern abc at end of lines

SEE ALSO

➤ *For more information about using regular expressions with search programs such as* `grep`, *see page 46.*

Use the asterisk (*) to find all matches for leading or trailing patterns:

```
# ls *.txt
```

More regular expressions

Regular expressions are documented in the `bash` shell, `ed`, and `grep` command manual pages. See these pages for additional approaches and characters used to build complex patterns.

The preceding command line lists all files ending in .txt. To list all files in your home directory (normally hidden by the output of the ls command because of a leading period in the filename), you might try the following:

```
# ls *.*
```

Unfortunately, this command lists only files with a period inside the filename. In an attempt to list all hidden files starting with the letter x, you might use the following:

```
# ls *.x*
```

But this won't work either. The way to list these files is to use a leading period, because * matches all *existing* characters:

```
# ls .x*
```

The order of characters in pattern expressions is important. To find characters normally interpreted by the shell as having special meaning, use the backslash (\) character to "escape" the pattern:

```
#  ls *\?*
```

This command lists all files with a ? in the filename.

Selecting a Shell

A number of different shells work with Red Hat Linux, and each has its own features, capabilities, and limitations. Table 2.3 lists shells normally installed on a Red Hat Linux system.

TABLE 2.3 Common shells for Linux

Name	Description
ash	A small shell
bash	The default Red Hat Linux shell
ksh	Public-domain version ksh shell
tcsh	Compatible version of csh shell
zsh	Compatible ksh, csh, and sh shell

Acceptable system shells are listed in a file called `shells` under the `/etc` directory:

```
/bin/bash
/bin/bsh
/bin/sh
/bin/ash
/bin/bsh
/bin/tcsh
/bin/csh
/bin/ksh
/bin/zsh
/usr/bin/pine
```

Some of the shells listed in this file are not actual programs installed on your system, but are symbolic links to existing shells.

SEE ALSO

➤ *To learn about shell programming, see page 365.*
➤ *To learn more about creating or using symbolic links, see page 40.*

Also note that the last entry in the `/etc/shells` file contains the pathname for the pine email program. As the root operator, you can add programs to the `/etc/shells` list, and then restrict a user to running only one or a menu of certain programs after logging on.

Changing Shells with the *chsh* Command

To change the shell run after you log on to Linux, use the `chsh` (change shell) command, found under the `/usr/bin` directory. You can use the `chsh` command by itself on the command line or with the `-s` (shell) option:

```
$ chsh
Changing shell for bball.
Password:
New shell [/bin/bash]: /bin/zsh
Shell changed.
$ chsh -s /bin/bash
Password:
Shell changed.
```

The full pathname, or directory to the desired shell or program, must be provided. Using the previous listing of entries in the `/etc/shell` file, the root operator can also restrict users to running a single program, such as the `pine` email command:

```
# chsh -s /usr/bin/pine fred
Changing shell for fred.
Shell changed.
```

When user `fred` logs on, the pine mailer will run. After quitting the program, `fred` will be logged out. This is a handy way to restrict users, such as children, to certain types of Linux programs. To see a list of acceptable shells for your system, use the `chsh`'s `-l` (list) option:

```
# chsh -l
/bin/bash
/bin/bsh
/bin/sh
/bin/ash
/bin/bsh
/bin/tcsh
/bin/csh
/bin/ksh
/bin/zsh
/usr/bin/pine
```

CHAPTER

3

Navigating the Linux File System

By Bill Ball

Changing Directories

You should know where you are or where you're going when you work with Linux. This section shows you how to navigate your directories at the console or through a terminal window in X11.

Printing the Current Working Directory

Use the pwd (print working directory) command to print the current, or present, working directory (that is, the directory where you are at that moment):

```
# pwd
/home/bball
```

pwd is not always reliable

According to the ash manual page, the built-in pwd command might continue to report the old name of the current directory if the directory's name has been changed. Use the binary version of the pwd command for shell scripts or other commands if you want to be sure of the current working directory.

A binary version of the pwd command can be found under the /bin directory, but nearly all shells have a built-in pwd command.

The built-in pwd command is documented in each shell's manual pages, while the binary version has a manual page found under the /usr/man/man1 directory.

Changing Directories with the *cd* Command

Use the cd (change directory) command to navigate through the Linux file system's directories. Use this command with a directory specification or pathname to move to a specified directory. This command is built in to each Linux shell, and can also be used as a shortcut to quickly move back to your home directory.

```
# pwd
/home/bball
# cd /usr/bin
# pwd
/usr/bin
# cd
/home/bball
```

If you enter the cd command by itself, you'll return to your home directory (specified in the $HOME environment variable). Move up to the next directory by entering two periods (..) with the cd command, like so:

```
# pwd
/home/bball
# cd ..
# pwd
/home
```

SEE ALSO

➤ *To learn more about shell environment variables, see page 90.*

The two periods represent the parent directory. Using a single period represents the current directory, but is not useful for navigating the directory structure. A hyphen, however, can be used as a quick navigation tool:

```
# pwd
/home/bball
# cd /usr/local/bin
# cd -
# pwd
/home/bball
```

Use a hyphen with the `cd` command to quickly navigate between the two most recently visited directories (in the previous example, I navigated from my home directory to the **/usr/local/bin** directory and then back to my home directory). Use a wildcard on the command line to change directories without typing a full pathname:

```
# cd /usr/loc*/lib/say*
# pwd
/usr/local/lib/saytime
```

Use this approach to save typing and time when navigating to known directories.

SEE ALSO

➤ *For information on using wildcards, see page 25.*

The `cd` command is documented in each shell's manual pages.

Listing Directories

Listing the contents of directories, like navigating through your system, is a basic skill you'll quickly master. The following sections describe several directory listing programs that are usually included with Linux distributions.

Listing Directories and Files with the *ls* Command

Use the `ls` (list directory) command to list the contents of one or several directories. This command has more than 40 different command-line options that can be combined to format listings. Wildcards can be used to specify certain files or directories. For example, to list the contents of the `/usr/local` directory, type the following:

```
# ls /usr/local
bin       etc       info      lib      qt       src
doc       games     lesstif   man      sbin
```

By default, the `ls` command lists the contents of directories in columns, sorted vertically. You can use different command-line options and wildcards to view directory contents in different formats. For example, the `-F` (classify) option identifies directories and executable files by appending a forward slash (`/`) and asterisk (`*`) to file or directory names:

```
# ls  -F /usr/local/lib/*
/usr/local/lib/cddb:
eb104910
/usr/local/lib/saytime:
saytime.sh*  sounds/
```

Table 3.1 lists some common command-line options that you can use to view directory contents in different formats.

TABLE 3.1 Common *ls* command-line options

Flag	Description
`-d`	List directories, not files
`-l`	Long format listing
`-m`	List filenames separated by commas
`-x`	Sort filenames in columns horizontally
`-A`	List all files, but not `.` and `..`
`-C`	Sort files in columns vertically
`-F`	Identify directories, links, and executables

Flag	Description
-R	List directory contents recursively
-S	Sort files by size
—color	Use color to identify files

SEE ALSO

➤ *To create* `ls` *command aliases with useful options such as* `-lA`, *see page 97.*

The `ls` command is documented in its manual page, located under the `/usr/man/man1` directory. You should also check out the manual pages for related directory listing commands, such as `dir`, `vdir`, `lsattr`, `tree`, and `dircolors`.

Echoing Directory Contents with the *echo* Command

The `echo` command can also be used to list the contents of directories. This command, built in to each shell, is also a program found under the `/bin` directory. In order to list directories and files, specify a wildcard on the command line like so:

```
# echo /*
/bin /boot /dev /etc /home /lib /lost+found
\/mnt /opt /proc /root /sbin /tmp /usr /var
```

Here's another example:

```
# echo /mnt/z*
/mnt/zip /mnt/zipln
```

The `echo` command prints all matching filenames in alphabetical order, but does not format the listing in columns. Use the `ls` or related ls (list directory) commands for formatted listings.

Changing file and directory listing colors

The default colors for different file types are listed in the file `DIR_COLORS` under the `/etc` directory. To customize the colors for different files when using the `ls` command's `—color` option, copy this file to your home directory (preceding it with a period and making the filename lowercase like so: `.dir_colors`) and then add or change the values. Read the contents of the `DIR_COLORS` file for the different colors or attributes (such as bold, underscore, blink, or reverse) that can be used to identify files and directories.

Viewing Text Files

Linux distributions come with a number of text-viewing programs. The following sections discuss several of these programs, such as the `cat` command and interactive viewers (called *pagers*), that you can use to view text files without running a text editor.

Viewing Text Files with the *cat* Command

Use the `cat` (concatenate) command to print the contents of files to your console display or terminal window. This command is best used to print short files to your display. Use wildcards or other regular expressions to display several files:

```
# cat /etc/issue
Red Hat Linux release 5.0 (Hurricane)
Kernel 2.0.31 on an i586
```

Use the cat command's `-n` (line-numbering) option to have file listings automatically numbered:

```
# cat -n /etc/issue
     1
     2  Red Hat Linux release 5.0 (Hurricane)
     3  Kernel 2.0.31 on an i586
     4
```

Display multiple files either by listing the names on the command line or by using a wildcard. Use output redirection operators, such as `>` or `>>`, to create, copy, overwrite, or append a single file or multiple files. For example, the following command line combines the contents of `file1.txt` and `file2.txt`, and creates `file3.txt`:

```
# cat file1.txt file2.txt >file3.txt
```

The next line appends the contents of `file1.txt` onto `file2.txt`:

```
# cat file1.txt >>file2.txt
```

Finally, the following command line takes the contents of `file2.txt` and either creates or overwrites `file1.txt`:

```
# cat file2.txt >file1.txt
```

By redirecting keyboard input to a file, the `cat` command can be used as a quick text editor:

```
# cat > friends.txt
Joan
Scott
Meredith
Tim
[EOT]
```

The cat command reads characters from the keyboard until Ctrl+D (the end-of-text character) is typed. The cat command will print any type of file, including program binaries. For more details about using the cat command, see its manual page.

SEE ALSO

- *For information about using redirection operators, see page 19.*
- *To change file ownership permissions, see page 418.*

Viewing Text Files with the *less* and *more* Pager Commands

Pager commands such as more and less are used to interactively read text files. Most users will prefer to read files by using the less command, found under the /usr/bin directory, which is generally considered more capable than the more pager, found under the /bin directory. Both more and less are used with a filename on the command line, and both accept wildcards to read multiple files. Following are a few examples:

```
# less file1.txt file2.txt
# less *.txt
# less <file1.txt >file2.txt
```

The less command not only accepts multiple filenames and wildcards, but can also be used with input and output redirection operators. The more and less programs use many of the same keyboard commands (see Table 3.2) to scroll forward and backward while reading documents. However, the less command has many additional features, including the following:

- Using cursor keys to scroll through documents
- Horizontal scrolling for wide documents
- Jumping to document bookmarks
- Keyboard command customization
- Sophisticated searching of multiple documents

Unlike the more command, the less command does not automatically quit when the end of a text file is read. The less pager is usually the default manual page reader, although this option can changed by defining a $PAGER shell environment string.

TABLE 3.2 **Common *more* and *less* pager commands**

Action	more	less
Forward one line	Enter or s	Enter, e, j, or cursor down
Backward one line		y, k, or cursor up
Forward one screen	Space, z, or f	Space, z, or f
Backward one screen	b	b
Help	h or ?	h
Previous file	:p	:p
Next file	:n	:n
Search str	/	/
Quit	q	q

SEE ALSO

➤ *For information on setting environment variables, see page 90.*

Custom keys, or key bindings, for the `less` command can be defined and created in a binary file called `.less` in your home directory. Use the `lesskey` command to read or create this file. See the `lesskey` manual page for more information.

Creating Files and Directories

Creating files and directories is an integral part of organizing your data while using Linux. The following sections show you how to create files and directories, so you can later copy, move, and organize your information.

Using *touch* to Create and Update Files and Directories

The `touch` command is used to create or update files and directories. Use `touch` with a new filename to create a file, or use an existing filename to update the file's access and modification times. For example, the following command line uses `touch` to create three files:

```
# touch file1 file2 file3
```

Use the `ls` command's `-l` (long format) option to check the modification time of a file, like this:

```
# ls -l *.txt
-rw-rw-r--   1 bball    bball    12 Jan 25 12:38 friends.txt
```

In the following lines, the `touch` command is used to update the `friends.txt` file's access and modification time to be four hours more recent:

```
# touch friends.txt
# ls -l *.txt
-rw-rw-r--   1 bball    bball     12 Jan 25 16:14 friends.txt
```

Finally, the following command line resets the time stamp of the file back to the original time:

```
# touch 01251238 friends.txt
# ls -l friends.txt
-rw-rw-r--   1 bball    bball     12 Jan 25 12:38 friends.txt
```

If you don't have the `touch` command installed on your system, use the `>` output redirection operator to create a file, like so:

```
# >file1
```

This command linc creates a file. Be careful not to specify the name of an existing file, or that file might be deleted, if you have write permission to overwrite the file.

The `touch` command is useful to quickly create files, and can be used by other programs during system-management tasks (such as backups). For more information, see the `touch` manual page.

Creating Directories with the *mkdir* Command

The `mkdir` (make directory) command is used to create directories. Use `mkdir` with a directory name on the command line. For example, the following command line creates a directory called `temp`:

```
# mkdir temp
```

`mkdir` can also be used to quickly create a hierarchy of directories. Use the `-p` (parent) command-line option to create each directory required in the structure (existing directories will not be overwritten):

```
# mkdir -p temp/grandparent/parent/child
```

Copying Files and Directories

The ability to quickly and efficiently copy files and directories is important when using Linux. The following sections show you how to copy single or multiple files and directories.

Copying Files with the *cp* Command

The `cp` (copy) command is used to copy files. Use the original filename followed by a new filename on the command line to copy a single file:

```
# cp file1 file2
```

Use wildcards to copy multiple files to a new location:

```
# cp file* /tmp
```

Use the `cp` command with caution. Unless you use the `-i` (interactive) command-line option, the `cp` command overwrites an existing file. When you use the `-i` option, the `cp` command prompts for a `y` or `n` if a file will be overwritten, like this:

```
# cp -i file1 file2
cp: overwrite `file2'? y
```

An even better approach is to use the `-b` (backup) option with the `cp` command. To create a backup of any files that may be overwritten, try the following:

```
# cp -bi file1 file2
cp: overwrite `file2'? y
# ls file2*
file2 file2~
```

Using the `-i` option is a safe way to use the `cp` command. To create a backup of any overwritten files, use the `-b` command-line option. Each backup file has a tilde (~) appended to its name.

Copying Directories with the *cp* Command

The -P (parent) command-line option, along with the -R (recursive) command-line option, not only copies files within one directory to another directory, but also any directories inside. For example, each of the following command lines copy the directory dir1 and any files or directories within to the dir2 directory:

```
# cp -Pr dir1 dir2
# cp -r dir1 dir2
# cp -R dir1 dir2
```

The cp command has nearly 40 command-line options. For details, see the cp manual page.

Moving and Renaming Files and Directories

Moving and renaming files and directories, like file navigation and copying, is a basic skill you'll need when organizing information within Linux. The following sections demonstrate how to use the mv command to move and rename files and directories.

Moving and Renaming Files and Directories with the *mv* Command

The mv (rename) command is used to rename or move files and directories. To rename a file, specify the old filename and the new filename on the command line (unlike the cp command, mv does not leave a copy of the original file):

```
# mv file1 file2
```

To rename a directory, specify the old directory name and new directory name on the command line, like so:

```
# mv mydir newdir
```

Use the mv command with caution. You can easily overwrite existing files unless you use the -i (interactive) command-line option. When you use the -i option, the mv command asks for permission to overwrite an existing file, like this:

```
# mv -i file1 file2
mv: replace `file2'? y
```

A safer way to use the `mv` command is with the `-b` (backup) option. When combined with the `-i` option, the `mv -b` command asks for permission to overwrite a file, and also creates a backup, like this:

```
# mv -bi file1 file2
mv: replace `file2'? y
# ls file*
file2 file2~
```

If you use the `-b` (backup) option, the `mv` command creates a backup of the file being overwritten. The original file remains, with a tilde (~) appended to its filename.

You can also use the `mv` command to move files from one directory to another:

```
# mv file1 /tmp
# mv file1 /tmp/file2
```

Use a new filename when moving a file if you want to rename the file during the move. You might also use this approach when moving directories:

```
# mv dir1 dir3
```

If the destination directory does not exist, `mv` renames the directory. If the destination directory exists, the entire directory, `dir1`, is moved inside the destination directory, `dir3`.

Creating Symbolic Links

Symbolic links are convenient shortcuts used to link existing files or directories to files or directories with recognized path names (such as `/usr/bin` or `/usr/local/bin`), or in more convenient locations. By default, a number of symbolic links are created when Linux is installed:

- Various shells listed under the `/bin` directory, such as `bsh`, `csh`, and `sh`, are actually symbolic links to other shells, such as `bash` or `tcsh`.

- Nearly all the different DOS floppy programs are links to a single program called `mtools`.
- The computer's modem device may be a link to `/dev/modem` instead of `/dev/cua1` or `/dev/ttyS1`.
- The `ex` and `vi` editors are links to the `vim` text editor.

Linking Files with the *ln* Command

Use the `ln` command with the `-s` (symbolic link) command-line option, with the original filename followed by the name of the desired link:

```
# ln -s file file2
# ls -l file*
-rw-rw-r--    1 bball     bball    16821 Feb 10 15:22 file
lrwxrwxrwx    1 bball     bball      4 Feb 10 15:22 file2 -> file
```

Use the `ln` command without the `-s` option to create a hard link:

```
# ln file file3
# ls -l file*
-rw-rw-r--    2 bball     bball        16821 Feb 10 15:22 file
lrwxrwxrwx    1 bball     bball     4 Feb 10 15:22 file2 -> file
-rw-rw-r--    2 bball     bball        16821 Feb 10 15:22 file3
```

Any changes made to the linked file, `file2`, are reflected in the original file, `file`. The hard link, `file3`, is an exact copy of the original file. If the original file is deleted, no data is lost because `file3` remains. However, without the original file, the symbolic link, `file2`, is useless.

Symbolic links can be used for any type of file, including executable scripts:

```
# ln -s /etc/ppp/start-ppp /usr/local/bin/startppp
```

This is a convenient way to save time and keystrokes.

Linking Directories with the *ln* Command

The `ln` command can also be used to create links to often-used directories (this is similar to using shortcuts in Windows 95):

```
# ln -s /dos /mnt/dos/windows/desktop
```

Now, instead of having to type a long pathname when copying files, you can use the following instead:

```
# cp file.txt /dos
```

Deleting Files and Directories

Removing files and directories is another common task when using Linux, but should be performed with care. Deleted files and directories are irrevocably lost. This is a great reason to always maintain backups of important files or directories.

Deleting Files with the *rm* Command

The `rm` (remove) command is used to delete files and directories. You delete files by including a single filename or several filenames on the command line, like so:

```
# rm file1 file2 file3
```

Use wildcards to delete multiple files:

```
# rm file*
```

The `rm` command can also be used to delete files within a specified directory:

```
# rm -r temp
rm: descend directory `temp'? y
rm: remove `temp/file1'? y
rm: remove `temp/file2'? y
rm: remove `temp/file3.txt'? y
rm: remove `temp/file4'? y
rm: remove directory `temp'? y
```

Use the `-r` (recursive) option along with the name of a directory to delete files within a directory. If you attempt to delete a directory without this option, the `rm` command complains and quits.

The `-i` (interactive) command-line option is the safest way to use the `rm` command. In this mode, `rm` interactively queries for a `y` or `n` before it deletes a file:

```
# rm -i file*.txt
rm: remove `file1.txt'? y
rm: remove `file2.txt'? y
rm: remove `file3.txt'? n
```

Deleting Directories with the *rmdir* Command

You can remove directories by using the `rmdir` command.

```
# rmdir temp/grandparent/parent/child
# rmdir temp/grandparent
rmdir: temp/grandparent: Directory not empty
```

However, if any files or directories exist below the specified directory, you must move or delete those first.

Deleting Directories with the *rm* Command

The `rm` command can be used like the `rmdir` command to remove directories, but you must use the `-r` (recursive) option in conjunction with the `-f` (force) option to do so. This combination of options removes files and directories without asking for confirmation. Here is an example:

```
# rm -fr temp
```

Using the `rm` command while root may be dangerous

The `rm` command, used with the `-fr` (recursive and force) options, is especially dangerous to use if you're running as the root operator. A single command line can wipe out your system. Use the `-fr` option with caution; this unconditional delete destroys all files and directories in its path. Avoid using this option while logged on as the root operator unless you're absolutely certain of the files and directories you want to delete.

Finding Files and Directories

Although navigating your disk's directories and listing directory contents can be helpful for finding needed files, Linux comes with several programs that will work much faster. The following sections demonstrate how to use several of these commands to quickly and efficiently find files or directories.

Finding Files with the *find* Command

The `find` command is used to search all mounted file systems for the name or partial name of a file or directory. This powerful command can be used to do much more than simply find files. To search for files or directories, specify a search path and search pattern on the command line, like so:

```
# find  /usr -name pico* -print -xdev
```

As shown in the following, this search of the /usr directory for the pico editor and other files locates the pico program and its manual page. But be warned! Searching a file system, especially in a network environment with remotely mounted filesystems, can take a *long* time.

```
/usr/bin/pico
/usr/man/man1/pico.1.gz
```

To restrict searches to the current file system, use the `-xdev` command-line option. If you don't restrict the search, the `find` command also searches any mounted CD-ROMs or other file systems, such as Windows.

The `find` command reports files by type, date, time, size, or search pattern. Use the `-atime` command-line option to find new or less-often used programs. For example, the following command line locates programs accessed in the last 100 days:

```
# find /usr/bin -type f -atime +100 -print
```

The next command line locates programs that are one or fewer days old:

```
# find /usr/bin -type f -atime -1 -print
```

To search by size, use the `-size` option, followed by a number in blocks (512 bytes), bytes, or kilobytes (1024 bytes). For example, the following command locates all programs in the `usr/bin` directory that are larger than 500,000 bytes:

```
# find /usr/bin -type f -size +500k -print
```

Use the `-exec` option to act on found files. For example, the following command line deletes all core dumps or backup files found in the Linux file system. Without the `-xdev` option, Linux system managers can use this approach to also clean up other file systems.

```
# find / -name 'core *.bak' -xdev -exec rm '{}' ';'
```

This command line works by starting a search at the `/`, or root directory. The `find` command descends through all your directories, looking for any file that is named `core` or that ends in `.bak`. If a file is found, the `rm` command is used to delete the file.

For more details about the `find` command's many different options and search specifications, see its manual page.

SEE ALSO

➤ *For information about using* find *for system-administration tasks, see page 562.*

Finding Files and Directories with the *locate* Command

Use the `locate` command to quickly locate files or directories on your system. This program works very quickly because it uses a database of filenames instead of searching your hard drives, as the `find` program does. Wildcards can be used to either expand or narrow a search. For example, to look for any icons of the emacs text editor, use the `locate` command like this:

```
# locate *icon*emacs*
/usr/share/icons/emacs_3d.xpm
/usr/share/icons/lemacs.xpm
/usr/share/icons/xemacs.xpm
```

The `locate` command searches a database called `locatedb` under the `/var/lib` directory. This database is created with the `updatedb` command. The format of the `locatedb` database is documented in the `locatedb` manual page under the `/usr/man/man5` directory. System managers generally use the `cron` daemon and an update `crontab` entry to keep the `locate` command's database current and accurate.

SEE ALSO

➤ *For details about using the* `cron` *daemon and* `crontab` *file, see page 435.*

Finding Programs and Manual Pages with the *whereis* Command

The `whereis` command is used to list the locations of program binaries, related files, and manual pages. Use this command to verify manual pages and to determine the pathnames of programs or their source files. For example, type the following:

```
# whereis man
```

This command yields the following result:

```
man: /usr/bin/man /etc/man.config /usr/man/man1/man.1
```

The `whereis` command works a lot faster than the `find` command because the pathnames, or directories, searched are built into the program. To search only for manual pages, use the `-m` option. Use the `-b` option for binary searches and the `-s` option to search for sources.

Searching Text Files

Linux also comes with a number of programs that you can use to search files. Some of these commands use regular expressions (introduced in Chapter 2, "Entering Commands"), while others, such as the strings command, offer limited search capabilities.

Using the *grep* Command

The grep command is part of a family of commands: grep, fgrep, and egrep. These commands are closely related, but have different capabilities in the type of expressions or wildcards that can be used on the command line. For example, to look for any reference to the tee command in the file info-dir under the /etc directory, use the grep command like this:

```
# grep -n tee /etc/info-dir
92:* tee: (sh-utils)tee invocation.   Redirect to multiple
files.
```

The grep command returns matches for simple words as patterns on the command line. The -n (number) command-line option prints the line number of the matching line in which the pattern is found. The grep command, by default, recognizes and uses only regular expressions, and reports an error if you try to use an extended regular expression:

```
# grep '\(gp' /etc/info-dir
grep: Unmatched ( or \(
```

Each grep command reads the standard input and writes to the standard output. However, search patterns can also be placed in a text file (as I've done here with the cat command) and used with the -f (file) option:

```
# cat > search.txt
gpm
[EOT]
# grep -f search.txt /etc/info-dir
* gpm: (gpm).                    Text-mode mouse library.
```

The grep command has more than 20 different command-line options, and can be used to emulate the fgrep or egrep commands with the -F and -E options. For details about these programs, see the grep manual page, or use the GNU info program to read the info pages under the /usr/info directory.

zgrep: searching compressed files

A related program called zgrep can be used to search compressed text files by using regular expressions. This program, a shell script, uses the grep or egrep program, along with the gzip command to decompress and search files on the fly.

SEE ALSO

- *To learn how to use regular expressions, see page 25.*
- *To learn more about shell scripts, see page 365.*
- *To learn how to compress or decompress files, see page 542.*

Using the *egrep* Command

The `egrep` command uses extended regular expressions (introduced in Chapter 2) for pattern matching, but also handles regular searches like `grep` and `fgrep`:

```
# egrep -n tee /etc/info-dir
92:* tee: (sh-utils)tee invocation.   Redirect to multiple
files.
```

The difference between `egrep` and the other `grep` commands becomes apparent when regular expressions are used:

```
# egrep '\(gp' /etc/info-dir
* gpm: (gpm).                        Text-mode mouse library.
```

The `egrep` program returns a match, whereas `fgrep` reports nothing, and `grep` reports an error. Apostrophes (') are used to protect expressions from being interpreted by the shell.

The `egrep` command reads the standard input and writes to the standard output. Search patterns can be placed in a text file and used with the `-f` (file) option.

Using the *fgrep* Command

The `fgrep` command uses fixed strings for searching. Patterns and files are specified on the command line like so:

```
# fgrep -n tee /etc/info-dir
92:* tee: (sh-utils)tee invocation.   Redirect to multiple
files.
```

As illustrated by the following, the `fgrep` command does not recognize regular expressions:

```
# fgrep '\(gp' /etc/info-dir
```

Because the `fgrep` command does not recognize expressions other than simple wildcards, no match is reported. Like the other grep commands, fgrep can use search patterns placed in a text file and used with the -f (file) option:

```
# cat > search.txt
gpm
[EOT]
# fgrep -f search.txt /etc/info-dir
* gpm: (gpm).                          Text-mode mouse library.
```

Using the *strings* Command

Use the strings command to extract strings from binary files. This can be useful for peeking inside programs or for finding information inside commands. Combine the output of the strings command with other searching programs by using pipes. For example, the following command line reports on the copyright information of each program under the /usr/bin directory:

```
# find /usr/bin ¦ xargs strings -f ¦ fgrep Copyright ¦ less
```

Without the -f (report files) option, the strings command does not insert the searched file's name in the output fed to the fgrep command.

SEE ALSO

➤ *For details on using pipes, see page 19.*

CHAPTER

4

Using Text Editors

By Bill Ball

Exploring features of text editors for Linux

Using spelling checkers for Linux

Converting text documents

Formatting text documents

Text editors are important tools for Linux users. At one time or another, you'll need to use a text editor to configure your system; although Red Hat Linux continues to mature with each release, not every system-administration tool has point-and-click convenience. To use Linux efficiently and productively, you should choose a text editor best suited to your needs.

Selecting an Editor

Red Hat Linux comes with nearly 20 text editors, if you count all the variations (some editors can emulate other, well-known editors, and also come in versions for the X Window System). This section covers how to use the basic versions of these editors.

Text editors are most often thought of as word processors, or interactive, screen-oriented programs used to open or create text files, to enter or change text, and then to print or save text files. Text editors used for word processing usually support cursor movement through a file and are screen oriented. Some editors, such as those for X11, also have pull-down menus and other convenient user interfaces.

But you can also perform text editing with non-interactive programs, such as text filters or stream editors (discussed later in this chapter). Red Hat Linux also includes more than two dozen different programs you can use to edit text.

Commercial Linux Word Processors

There are nearly 100 different word processors for Linux, including many commercial word processors or office suite applications. Many of these software packages (such as the WordPerfect word processor shown in Figure 4.1, from **www.sdcorp.com**) require the X Window System, and many require the X11 Motif software libraries. If you're interested in trying some of these programs, see the `Commercial-HOWTO` under the `/usr/doc` directory, or check out the following web sites:

```
http://www.sdcorp.com/wpunix.html
http://www.axene.com/english/xclamation.html
http://www.zfc.nl
```

```
http://www.advasoft.com
http://www.caldera.com
http://www.redhat.com
http://www.applix.com
http://www.stardivision.com/
```

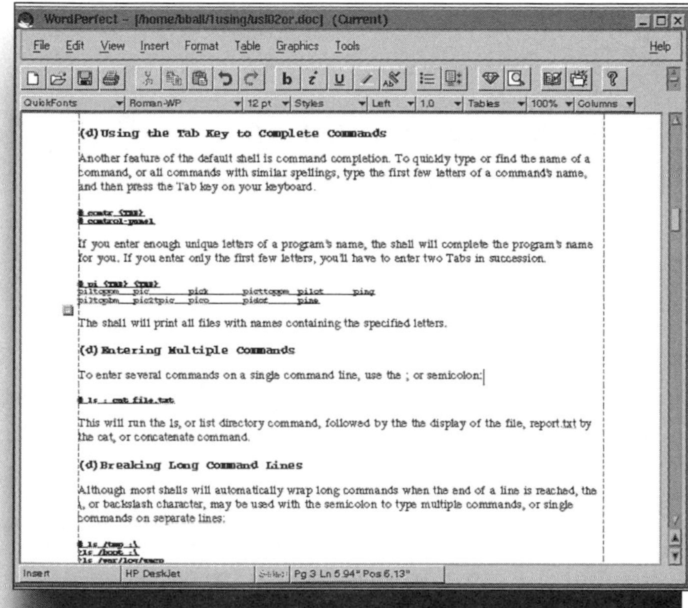

FIGURE 4.1
The WordPerfect word processing program for Linux uses the X Window System.

SEE ALSO

➤ *To learn more about the X Window System, see page 260.*

Using Screen Editors

Screen editors are easy to use, and are usually the preferred tools for programmers, writers, and casual users. Some Linux screen editors work only with the X Window System, while others work from the console or X11. Some important features to look for when choosing a screen editor include the following:

- Support for cursor keys to navigate through a file
- Easily remembered control keys or easy-to-use menus
- The capability to print files
- Crash protection for work in progress, such as automatic backups

- Support for spell-checking of documents
- Easy-to-use search-and-replace features to make changes in a file
- The capability to cut and paste of blocks of text
- The capability to turn word wrap or paragraph justification on or off
- Good documentation, or built-in help

Using the *emacs* Environment

Without a doubt, the most capable (but not the easiest to use) editor included in most Linux distributions is the `emacs`, or editing macros, program. Originally developed by Richard Stallman, this program is much, much more than a text editor. `emacs` can be used as a programming environment and Linux shell; also, emacs contain a Lisp language interpreter, sends electronic mail, reads Usenet news, supports calendar and diary functions, and even plays games!

The `emacs` editor is distributed by the Free Software Foundation as part of the GNU, or GNU's Not UNIX project. The `emacs` distribution included with Red Hat Linux needs more than 35 MB of disk space for a complete installation, but you need only 20 MB if you don't install the `emacs` source files. The X11 version of `emacs` requires nearly an additional 3 MB of disk space.

SEE ALSO

➤ *For more information about electronic mail, see page 183.*
➤ *To learn more about reading Usenet news, see page 227.*

`emacs` has nearly two dozen different command-line options, but is easy to start. To open or create a text file, run `emacs` on the command line, followed the by the name of a new or existing file, like this:

```
# emacs textfile.txt
```

If you're using the X Window System, `emacs` creates or opens your file and displays its main window as shown in Figure 4.2. Note that the X11 version of `emacs` supports menus and the mouse.

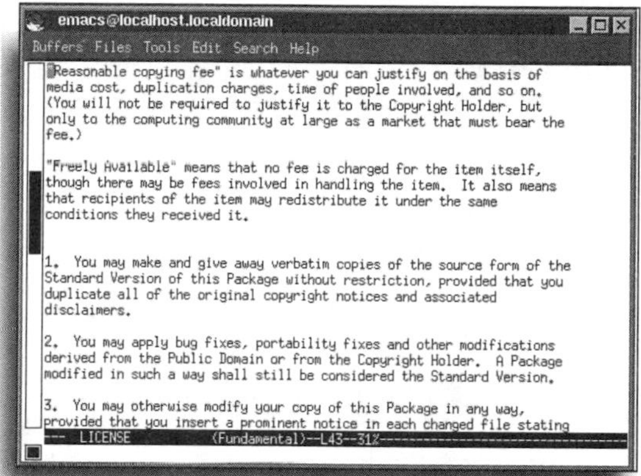

FIGURE 4.2

The emacs editor in the X Window System supports menus and the mouse.

Use X11 toolkit options, such as `-geometry`, `fg`, and `bg`, to set the initial window size, position, and text and background colors:

```
# emacs -geometry 80x25+10+10 -fg blue -bg white
```

This command line starts `emacs` in a window in the upper-left corner of your screen, in an 80-character × 25-line window, with blue text on a white background. `emacs` has more than a dozen different toolkit options that you can use.

To run `emacs` inside the window of an X11 terminal, use the non-X11 version of `emacs`, like this:

```
# emacs-nox textfile.txt
```

This runs `emacs` and opens your file, as shown in Figure 4.3. Learning `emacs` can take some time, but its built-in tutorial will get you started. If you're new to `emacs`, using this tutorial is essential.

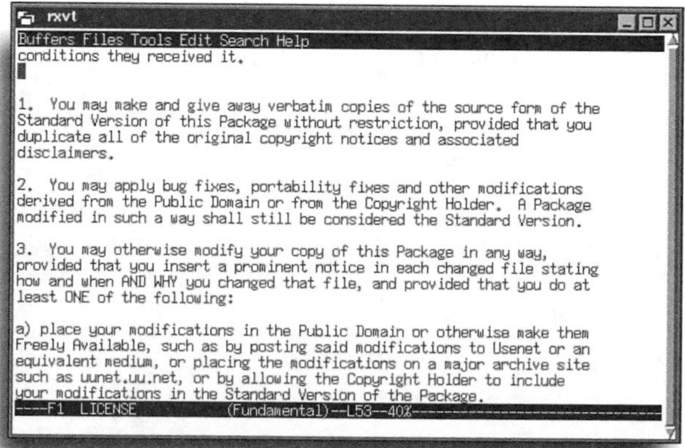

FIGURE 4.3

The emacs editor can also be used inside X11 terminal windows.

SEE ALSO

➤ *To learn more about X11 toolkit options, see page 307.*

Starting the *emacs* tutorial

1. Start `emacs` from the console or the command line of an X11 terminal window:

   ```
   # emacs
   ```

2. Hold down the Ctrl key, and press `H`. You see a prompt at the bottom of the screen:

   ```
   C-h (Type ? for further options)-
   ```

3. Press `T`, and `emacs` starts its tutorial.

`emacs` can take some time to learn. Use the X11 version, which uses menus, to get started. Table 4.1 lists the basic keystrokes you need in order to get started creating and editing files. You can also save the editor's defaults in a file called `.emacs` in your home directory. See the `emacs` manual page for details.

TABLE 4.1 Basic *emacs* commands

Action	Key Command(s)
Move the cursor backward one character	Ctrl+B
Move the cursor down one line	Ctrl+N
Move the cursor forward one character	Ctrl+F
Move the cursor up one line	Ctrl+P
Delete the current character	Ctrl+D
Delete the current line	Ctrl+K
Delete the current word	Alt+D
Go to the beginning of the file	Alt+<
Go to the end of the current line	Ctrl+E
Go to the end of the file	Alt+>
Go to the beginning of the current line	Ctrl+A
Open a file	Ctrl+X, Ctrl+F
Page down one screen	Ctrl+V
Page up one screen	Alt+V
Quit `emacs`	Ctrl+X, Ctrl+C

Action	Key Command(s)
Save the current file	Ctrl+X, Ctrl+S
Save the file as	Ctrl+X Ctrl+W
Show help	Ctrl+H
Start the tutorial	Ctrl+H T
Undo the last operation	Ctrl+_

Documentation for `emacs` is under the `/usr/doc`, `/usr/share/emacs/20.2/etc`, and `/usr/info` directories. See the `emacs` manual page for a complete listing of `emacs` directories.

Editing Text with the *pico* Editor

The `pico` editor, part of the `pine` electronic mail program's software package, is an easy-to-use editor with all the features recommended at the beginning of this chapter. This no-nonsense program is compact, reliable, and efficient (you don't have to use `pine` in order to edit files with `pico`). `pico` even supports your mouse when used with the `-m` command-line option, like this:

```
# pico -m myfile.txt
```

`pico` opens your file, as shown in Figure 4.4. If you're running the X Window System, click one of the commands at the bottom of the screen to progress.

`pico` also protects your work in progress in the unfortunate event of a system crash (a rare event for Linux users), and saves your work with your original file's name with the extension `.save`. If you were working on an original file, the saved file is called `pico.save`.

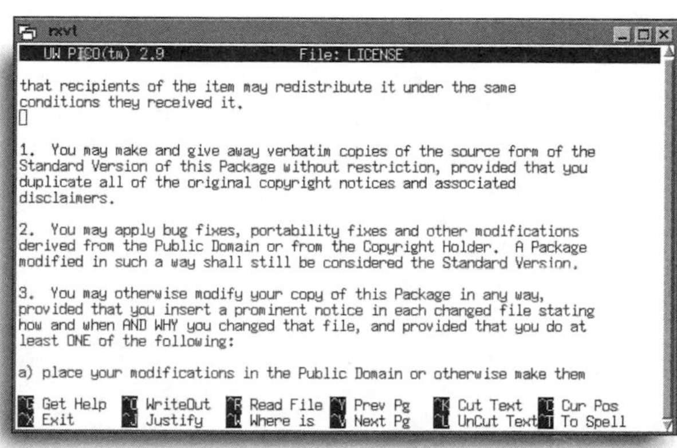

FIGURE 4.4
The `pico` editor is an easy-to-use, compact, and efficient text editor.

Use pico as the default system editor by defining the EDITOR environment variable.

Defining *pico* as the system editor

1. Log on as the root operator. Use pico with the -w (no word wrap) command-line option to preserve long lines, and open the file profile under the /etc directory:

   ```
   # pico -w /etc/profile
   ```

2. Type the EDITOR variable definition, followed by the bash shell's export command:

   ```
   EDITOR=/usr/bin/pico
   export EDITOR
   ```

3. Save the file by pressing Ctrl+X, and then pressing Enter.

4. To use the EDITOR variable right away, use the bash shell's source command to read in the new variable, like this:

   ```
   # source /etc/profile
   ```

SEE ALSO

➤ *To learn more about shell environment variables, see page 90.*

pico recognizes your cursor keys, and has a number of keyboard commands. Table 4.2 lists many of the common commands you can use when editing text.

TABLE 4.2 Basic *pico* commands

Action	Key Command(s)
Move the cursor backward one character	Ctrl+B
Move the cursor down one line	Ctrl+N
Move the cursor forward one character	Ctrl+F
Move the cursor up one line	Ctrl+P
Delete the current character	Ctrl+D
Delete (cut) the current line	Ctrl+K
Display the cursor position	Ctrl+C
Go to the end of the current line	Ctrl+E
Go to the beginning of the current line	Ctrl+A
Insert a file	Ctrl+R

Action	Key Command(s)
Justify the current paragraph	Ctrl+J
Page down one screen	Ctrl+V
Page up one screen	Ctrl+Y
Paste text or unjustify	Ctrl+U
Quit `pico`	Ctrl+X
Search for text	Ctrl+W
Start the spelling check	Ctrl+T
Save the file as	Ctrl+O
Show help	Ctrl+G

Although `pico` supports spell-checking of text documents, you might find that this does not work by default. To spell-check documents with `pico`, use the `pine` mail program to configure `pico`'s spelling program.

Configuring *pico* to check spelling

1. Start the `pine` mail program, like this:

   ```
   # pine
   ```

2. Press the S key. `pine` displays a prompt at the bottom of its screen:

   ```
   Choose a setup task from the menu below :
   ```

3. Press C to start the `Config` option. `pine` displays its configuration screen, as shown in Figure 4.5.

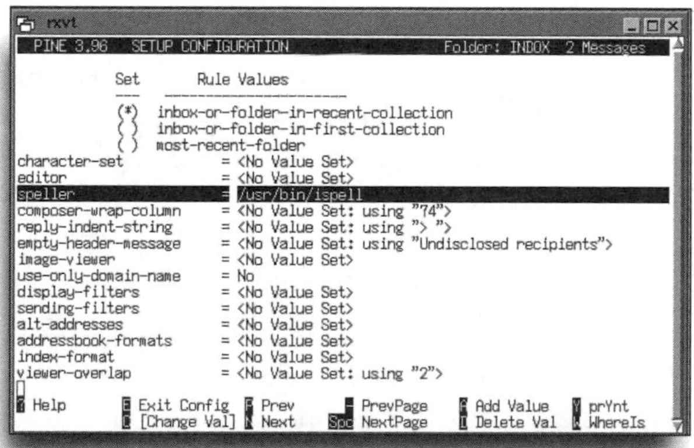

FIGURE 4.5
The `pine` configuration mode is used to set up spell-checking for the `pico` editor.

4. Scroll through the list of configuration items until you see a line like this:

```
speller                       = <No Value Set>
```

5. Using your up or down cursor keys, move your cursor until this `speller` line is highlighted. Press C to change the value. `pine` displays a prompt at the bottom of the screen:

```
Enter the text to be added :
```

6. Type the path for the `ispell` spelling program:

```
/usr/bin/ispell
```

7. Press Enter, followed by the E key. `pine` will ask whether you want to save the changes. Press the Y key to save the changes.

8. Press Q to exit the `pine` program. Press Y to confirm the quit.

   The `pico` editor is now configured to check spelling.

Read the `pico` manual page for more information, or press Ctrl+G to read `pico`'s help screens. For more details about `pico`, use the Lynx web browser to read `pine`'s technical notes (which contain `pico`'s technical details) by typing the following:

```
# lynx /usr/doc/pine-3.96/tech-notes/index.html
```

Features of the *vim* Editor

The `vim` editor is compatible with the original `vi` editor, an enhancement to the early line-oriented editor, `ed`. `vim` also comes in an X11 version called `gvim`, which supports multiple scrolling windows and menus.

`vim` is used with several symbolic links to emulate the `ex`, `vi`, and `view` editors. When used as `ex`, the `vim` editor works as a line or script editor. The `vim` editor has 23 command-line options, which are documented in its manual page. This editor features built-in help, split-screen windows, block moves, command-line editing, horizontal scrolling, and word wrap for word processing.

The X11 version of the `vim` editor, `gvim`, features split-scrollable windows, custom colors, window sizes, scrollbars, and menus you can customize. For details about building custom `vim` menus, see the files `vim_menu.txt` and `vim_gui.txt` under the `/usr/share/vim` directory.

Features of the *joe* Editor

The joe editor software package includes five different editors: jmacs, joe, jpico, jstar, and rjoe. The jmacs version uses many commands similar to the emacs editor. The jpico version emulates the pico text editor. If you remember using the WordStar word-processing program, the jstar editor will be familiar. The rjoe editor edits only files specified on the command line.

To configure the joe editor, copy the file joerc from the /usr/lib/joe directory to your home directory with the name .joerc. Edit .joerc to change joe's help menus, display, and keyboard commands.

Read the joe manual page for details about using each version, or use joe's built-in help (accessed by pressing Ctrl+K, followed by the H key).

Upgrading the joe editor

An upgrade to the joe editor fixes a problem concerning resizing the editor window when using X11. Upgrade by downloading and installing the joe-2.8-10.i386.rpm file from Red Hat's FTP site:

ftp://ftp.redhat.com/pub/redhat/updates/5.0/i386/

It's always a good idea to check the Red Hat web site, as well, for technical bulletins or errata concerning your version of Linux:

http://www.redhat.com

SEE ALSO

➤ *For more information on using FTP to download files from the Internet, see page 198.*

Features of the *jed* Editor

The jed editor, like vim, comes in a version for the console and a version for the X Window System (xjed). To configure the jed editor, copy the file jed.rc from the /usr/lib/jed/lib directory to your home directory with the name .jedrc.

The jed editor has built-in help (you can access it by pressing Esc, the question mark key, and then H). Read the jed documentation under the /usr/doc/jed directory, and the jed manual page for more information.

Using Stream Editors

Using your shell's standard input and standard output is another way to edit text. This practice, called *redirection* (using the < or > operators), also uses shell pipelines (with the ¦ operator) to change streams of the text. Specialized programs, such as sed, are designed to accept redirection and piped text, and are called *stream editors*.

SEE ALSO

➤ *To learn how to use the shell redirection and pipe operators, see page 19.*

Search and Replace Operations with the *sed* Editor

Use the `sed` (stream) editor to quickly edit text from the command line. The `sed` editor has more than two dozen commands, and also uses regular expressions (similar to those of the `egrep` command, discussed in the section titled "Searching for Text Files" in Chapter 3, "Navigating the Linux File System").

The `sed` command can be used to quickly make global changes in a text document without loading a word processor or text editor. For example, if the unfortunate miscreant in the following text is not Mr. Price, but his wife, the phrase `Mr.` would need to be changed:

```
As stated in our previous discussion, Mr. Price has not
responded to our complaints, and has not returned our over-
tures aimed at resolving this credit problem. Mr. Price
knows that we have attempted to make contact, but has
spurned our requests for resolution, even after foreclosure
on the property in question. Mr. Price's whereabouts remain
unknown, but was last seen on St. John's Island.
```

Use the `sed s` (substitute) command to find each instance of the string `Mr.` and replace it with `Mrs.`, as follows:

```
# sed s/Mr./Mrs./ <notice.txt
```

```
As stated in our previous discussion, Mrs. Price has not
responded to our complaints, and has not returned our over-
tures aimed at resolving this credit problem. Mrs. Price
knows that we have attempted to make contact, but has
spurned our requests for resolution, even after foreclosure
on the property in question. Mrs. Price's whereabouts remain
unknown, but was last seen on St. John's Island.
```

Note that each instance of `Mr.` has been changed to `Mrs.`, and that the `sed` command echoes the input back to your display. To create a new file, use the > redirection operator to create a new file:

```
# sed s/Mr./Mrs./ <notice.txt >correctnotice.txt
```

Entering the sed command's -f (script file) command-line option followed by the name of a script file feeds sed a list of changes to perform on a text file.

Using a *sed* script file

1. To make numerous, regular changes to text files, use an editing script with the sed command. For example, using your favorite text editor, create a file called personnel.txt, and enter a paragraph like this:

```
Heretofore, all employees must report in by telephone,
in accordance with the personnel guidebook. Pursuant to
the guide book, this and other regulations are applica-
ble to all employees, and all employees must utilize the
guide book. A new employee must also acquire or procure
the guide book as a draft implementation, or the company
will terminate the employee's position.
```

2. Save the file, and then create a script file with the name grammar.sed. Enter a list of sed commands, like these:

```
s/utilize/use/
s/procure/get/
s/acquire/buy/
s/draft implementation/draft/
s/Heretofore/From now on/
s/in accordance with/according to/
s/thereto/to/
s/Pursuant/According/
s/are applicable/apply/
s/terminate/end/
```

3. Save the file, and exit your text editor. Using the sed command's -f option followed by the name of your script file, use the shell redirection operator to feed the original text file into the sed command, like this:

```
# sed -f grammar.sed <personnel.txt
From now on, all employees must report in by telephone,
according to the personnel guidebook. According to the
guide book, this and other regulations apply to all
employees, and all employees must use the guide book. A
new employee must also buy or get the guide book as a
draft, or the company will end the employee's position.
```

4. The sed command has replaced each word or phrase with the simpler replacement—almost like a grammar-checking program. Experiment with your own scripts to check punctuation or writing style.

Using Linux Dictionaries

Correct spelling is an important part of writing and word processing, and spelling errors can be embarrassing. Most Linux distributions come with several tools to check spelling or look up words in the system dictionary, usually found under the /usr/dict directory (ispell, discussed in the later section "Spell Checking with the ispell Command," uses a different dictionary).

The default system dictionary, words (which could be a symbolic link to the file linux.words under the /usr/dict directory), contains more than 45,000 correctly (I hope) spelled words in an alphabetical list.

Getting the *web2* Dictionary

Not satisfied with 45,000 words? You can get another dictionary, web2, which contains an alphabetized list of more than 234,000 words. The web2 dictionary is usually accompanied by a dictionary of proper names, containing more than 1,300 names, and a word-phrase hyphenation dictionary, called web2a, which contains more than 75,000 phrases.

To get these files, browse to the following web address:

```
ftp://ftp.digital.com/pub/BSD/net2/share/dict
```

Dictionaries: Rolling Your Own

Don't want to use the standard system dictionary? Need to build your own dictionaries containing specialized words for the medical or legal fields? Try using a combination of text filters and shell pipe operators to build your own, with a command line like this:

```
# find *.txt ¦ xargs cat ¦ tr ' ' '\n' ¦ sort ¦ uniq
➥>mydict.txt
```

This command line uses the find command to pipe the names of all files in the current directory to the cat command, which then uses the tr command to translate each space between words to a carriage return, building a single list of words. This list of words is then sorted by the sort command, and any duplicate words are removed with the uniq command. The result won't be perfect, but you'll have a dictionary of all the words in your documents.

SEE ALSO

➤ *To learn more about the* find *command, see page 43.*

Spell Checking with the *ispell* Command

Most Linux distributions come with the interactive spelling program `ispell`. Use this program alone or with your text editor to correct spelling mistakes. Most editors included with Linux distributions can use this program.

Using *ispell* to Check Spelling

1. Use the `ispell` command followed by a filename to check spelling interactively, like this:

   ```
   # ispell document.txt
   ```

2. If no misspelled words are found, `ispell` returns you to the command line. If there are misspellings, the first misspelled word is displayed at the top of your screen, along with the filename. The misspelled word is displayed in context, and a numbered list of suggested replacements is shown, followed by a command-line prompt at the bottom of the screen, (as shown in Figure 4.6).

   Here's how the `ispell` code looks in action:

   ```
   personall                 File: document.txt


   Heretofore, all employees must report in by telephone,
   in accordance with the personall guidebook. Pursuant to
   the guide book, this and other
   ```

```
0: personal
1: personally
2: personals
3: person all
4: person-all


[SP] <number> R)epl A)ccept I)nsert L)ookup U)ncap Q)uit
e(X)it or ? for help
```

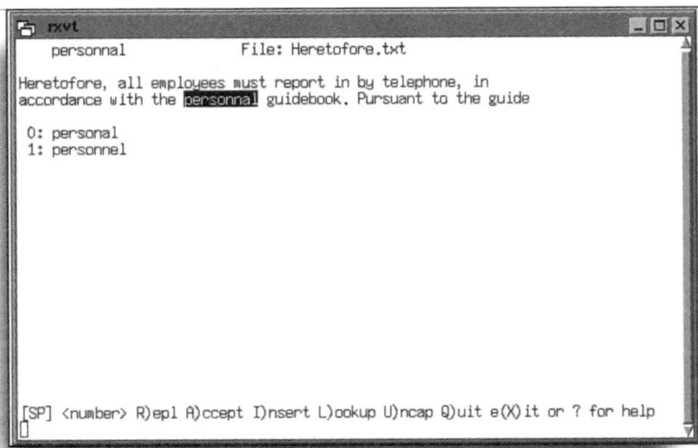

FIGURE 4.6
The `ispell` command is an interactive spelling checker for Linux.

3. Correct the misspelled word by typing the number of the suggested replacement word, or press R to replace the misspelled word. The `ispell` command responds with the following prompt:

   ```
   Replace with:
   ```

4. Enter a correct spelling. `Ispell` replaces the word, and then goes to the next misspelled word. Use the `I` (insert) command to create a personal dictionary, called `.ispell_english`, in your home directory.

To force `ispell` to use the system dictionary (`/usr/dict/words`), use the `-l` (list) option on the command line, followed by the standard input redirection operator and the name of a text file, like so:

```
# ispell -l <document.txt
personall
regurlations
```

The ispell command prints a list of misspelled words found in your document. The ispell software package also includes utilities to build new ispell dictionaries, found under the /usr/lib/ispell directory. For details, read the ispell manual pages and documentation under the /usr/doc/ispell directory.

Saving Paper with the *mpage* Command

Years ago, computer industry wags fatuously predicted that word processing would lead to paperless offices. But as many of us have woefully realized, this revolution has instead lead to the demise of erasable bond and correction fluid, and a perverse *increase* in the use of paper (we had a laser printer in our former office named *tree-eater*).

If you're a serious Linux user, and if you're serious about saving paper, you should not only recycle, but also use the mpage command to print at least two sheets of paper on a single page. The mpage command, followed by a number, will print 1, 2, 4, or 8 pages of text on a single sheet of paper. For example, to print two pages on a single sheet, use the -2 option followed by the -P option and your printer's name, like so:

```
# mpage -2 -o massivedocument.txt -Plp
```

The mpage command creates a PostScript file from your document, and sends the output through your printer. If you have installed your printer using the Red Hat Linux printtool, you'll get a nice printout (at least on laser or inkjet printers) of two side-by-side pages on each sheet of paper. Using the -o command prevents the printing of a line border around your text.

SEE ALSO

➤ *For more information on setting up your printer for Linux, see page 74.*

The mpage command also prints odd- or even-numbered pages, prints page headers, uses different fonts or margins, supports duplex printing, and even reverses a print document by starting at the document's end. See the mpage manual page for more information.

Creating Formatted Documents

Text editors can do basic formatting of text, such as limiting the number of characters or words per line, and justifying paragraphs. But to add page numbering, fancy indenting, or multiple columns and fonts, you must use a formatting or typesetting system. *Formatting* programs, such as the `pr` or `fmt` commands, are usually small text utilities that add headers, footers, margins, and page numbers, usually through command-line options. *Typesetting* systems, such as `groff` or `TeX`, offer a bewildering array of commands that you must insert in your documents before processing, and these software distributions often involve many megabytes of files in several directories.

Using Text-Formatting Filter Commands

Use text-formatting filter programs if you don't want to learn the complicated formatting commands of typesetting systems. Text filters change the output of your documents with several simple command-line options. Use a text-formatting program to quickly format your documents.

Formatting with the *pr* Command

The `pr` command has nearly 20 different command-line options to format documents. For example, to print a document with a page header containing the time and the phrase `Committee Report`, and a left margin of 10 characters, use the `pr` command like so:

```
# pr +2 -h "Committee Report" -o 10 <report.txt ¦ lpr
```

Because the preceding command uses the **+** operator followed by a page number, `pr` starts numbering pages on page 2. The `pr` program also formats text into columns via the `-COLUMN` command-line option. For example, to print the system dictionary in three columns per page, use the `pr` command like this (obviously, I haven't shown the entire output):

```
# pr -3 /usr/dict/words
98-03-15 16:36                         web2
Page     1
A                              Abaris                    abbotnullius
```

```
a                  abarthrosis        abbotship
aa                 abarticular        abbreviate
aal                abarticulation     abbreviately
aalii              abas               abbreviation
aam                abase              abbreviator
```

See the `pr` manual page for more options, such as `-l 1`, which can be used to remove the page header from the output.

Formatting with the *fmt* Command

Use the `fmt` command along with the `pr` command to change the width of your text documents. Use the `fmt` command to format text into the line width you specify, and then send the text through the `pr` command for additional formatting. For example, to format the public-domain license (found under the `/usr/doc/shadow-utils` directory), use the `fmt -w` (width) option followed by a line width (in characters), and then pipe the output to the `pr` command using the `-o` (margin) option followed by a margin (in characters), like so:

```
# fmt -w 40 <LICENSE ¦ pr -o 15
               1.  You may make and give away
               verbatim copies of the source form of
               the Standard Version of this Package
               without restriction, provided that you
               duplicate all of the original copyright
               notices and associated disclaimers.

               2.  You may apply bug fixes,
               portability fixes and other
               modifications derived from the Public
               Domain or from the Copyright Holder.
               A Package modified in such a way
               shall still be considered the Standard
               Version.
```

Obviously, I have not shown all the output here; nonetheless, you should see that this is a convenient way to format text from the command line.

Using Text-Processing Systems

Typesetting documents using text-processing systems, such as `groff` or `TeX`, is usually a three-step process:

1. Use a text editor to create a document. In the text, insert typesetting commands.
2. Process the document through the typesetting program, which then produces a formatted document.
3. Preview the document, checking for errors, or send the document to a printer.

The following sections discuss the formatting of text with the `groff` and `TeX` systems.

Formatting Text with the *groff* Formatter

The GNU `groff` typesetting system uses special formatting commands, called *macros*, to format document. The `man` macro set is used to format your system's manual pages. For example, to format and display the contents of the `cat` manual page, you can use any of the following three command lines (each does the same thing):

```
# man cat
# nroff -man /usr/man/man1/cat.1 ¦ less
# groff -Tascii -man /usr/man/man1/cat.1 ¦ less
```

You can see the `groff` `man` macros if you use the `cat` command to print the `cat` manual page, like this:

```
# cat /usr/man/man1/cat.1
.TH CAT 1 "GNU Text Utilities" "FSF" \" -*- nroff -*-
.SH NAME
cat \- concatenate files and print on the standard output
.SH SYNOPSIS
.B cat
[\-benstuvAET] [\-\-number] [\-\-number-nonblank] [\-\-
➥squeeze-blank]
[\-\-show-nonprinting] [\-\-show-ends] [\-\-show-tabs] [\-\-
➥show-all]
[\-\-help] [\-\-version]
[file...]
.SH DESCRIPTION
```

I have not reproduced the entire contents of the `cat.1` manual page, but if you compare the output from the `man`, `nroff`, or `groff` commands to the original form of the `cat` manual page, you should see that the `man` macros, represented by *dot* commands (such as `.TH` and `.SH`) cause special formatting. These dot commands and other manual page macros are documented in the `man.7` manual page under the `/usr/man/man7` directory.

There are several other sets of typesetting macros for the `groff` formatting system, such as the `me`, `mm`, and `ms` manuscript macros. When you use these macros in a text document, you must specify the macro set used on the `groff` command line, like so:

```
# groff -Tascii -mm mydocument.txt
```

Documentation for these macros is located in various `groff`-related manual pages. Table 4.3 lists some common `groff` macros from the `mm` manuscript macro set.

TABLE 4.3 Common *groff* macros for *mm* manuscript macros

Purpose	Macro Name
Center justify	`.ds C`
End text box	`.b2`
Justification off	`.sa 0`
Justification on	`.sa 1`
Line fill off	`.ds N`
Line fill on	`.ds F`
New paragraph with *x* indent	`.p x`
No indents	`.ds L`
Right justify	`.ds R`
Start bold text	`.b`
Start text box	`.b1`
Use columns	`.mc`
Use one column	`.1c`
Use two columns	`.2c`

If you don't want to use a macro set, try some common `groff` commands, listed in Table 4.4.

TABLE 4.4 Common *groff* typesetting commands

Purpose	Command
Begin new page	`.bp`
Begin new paragraph	`.pp`
Center next *x* lines	`.ce x`
Center text *x*	`.ce x`
Insert (space) *n* inches down	`.sp ni`
Insert *n* inches down	`.sv ni`
Set font bold	`.ft B`
Set font Roman	`.ft R`
Set line spacing to *n*	`.ls n`
Temporary indent *n* inches	`.ti ni`
Turn off line fill	`.nf`
Turn on centering	`.ce`
Turn on indenting *n* inches	`.in ni`
Turn on line fill	`.fi`
Underline next *n* lines	`.ul n`

Saving time previewing `dvi` documents

Previewing `TeX dvi` documents can take several minutes, and is very system-intensive. The best way to preview `TeX dvi` documents is to convert the file to PostScript with the `dvips` command, and then to use the `gv` PostScript previewer, like so:

```
# dvips -f <
➥mytexdoc.dvi >
➥mytexdoc.ps
# gv mytextdoc.ps
```

Use the `groff -T` command-line option followed by an output format specifier to create different document formats, such as PostScript, `TeX dvi`, text, HP printer-control language, or PCL. Preview your documents before printing, and see the `groff` manual pages for more information about this typesetting system.

Formatting Text with *TeX*

The `TeX` typesetting system is a formidable collection of programs, fonts, and other utilities. This sophisticated system includes more than 65 programs, along with related support files such as libraries, macros, and documentation. A typical `TeX` installation requires nearly 50 MB of hard-drive space for the system files, macros, and fonts.

The TeX typesetting system uses formatting commands inserted in text files, a process similar to groff's system. To see how TeX uses its macros, try processing a sample file, such as samples.tex, which is found under the TeX directories.

Processing a sample *TeX* file

1. Use the latex command to typeset the samples.tex file. This process can take up to a minute on some Linux systems. The latex command uses special TeX macros to format documents. Use this command followed by the name of the TeX source document to create a text .dvi file, like this:

```
# latex  /usr/lib/texmf/texmf/doc/generic/pstricks/
samples.tex
```

2. Convert the resulting .dvi file, samples.dvi, to PostScript by using the dvips command. Use the -f command to read the file from the standard input, and redirect the output to a PostScript file:

```
# dvips -f <samples.dvi >samples.ps
```

3. Preview the PostScript document using the gv PostScript previewer (see Figure 4.7):

```
# gv samples.ps
```

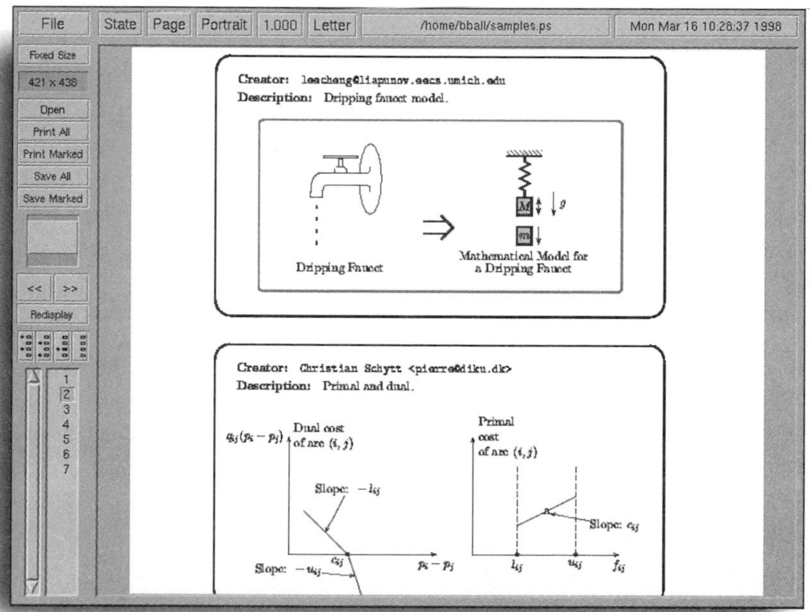

FIGURE 4.7
The gv PostScript previewer can be used to preview or print converted TeX .dvi documents.

4. To print the document, click the File menu and select the Print Document option, or use the `lpr` command followed by the `-P` printer option, like this:

```
# lpr -Plp samples.ps
```

`TeX` can produce complex diagrams and documents, but it takes some effort on your part to learn the system. Read the `TeX` and related manual pages, look at the `/usr/info` directory for `TeX` info files, and browse the `/usr/lib/texmf/texmf/doc` directory. The best way to read about `TeX` and to retrieve sample files is to use the Lynx web browser by entering the following:

```
# lynx /usr/lib/texmf/texmf/doc/index.html
```

Beginners should scroll down to the help section of the `index.html` document and read the `TeX` Frequently Asked Questions (FAQ) file.

SEE ALSO

➤ *To learn how to use the Lynx web browser, see page 212.*

Printing Files

By Bill Ball

- Installing, configuring, and adding printers
- Using the line printer spooling system
- Controlling print jobs
- Sending faxes with the `lpr` command

Adding Printers

If you did not set up a printer when you installed Linux, or if you want to add a different printer to your system, you can do so in at least two ways (both of which are discussed in this chapter):

- Manually
- By using the Red Hat Linux `printtool` command for the X Window System

Printers are described under Linux as character-mode devices. The most common of these devices are for parallel-port printers and are listed under the `/dev` directory, with names similar to `lp`. Here's a sample listing of parallel-port printers:

```
# ls /dev/lp*
/dev/lp0 /dev/lp1 /dev/lp2
```

You should find at least three parallel printer devices listed under the `/dev` directory.

Using a serial printer

Serial printers are serial devices with names similar to your serial or modem ports, such as `/dev/ttyS0`. For information about serial ports or serial printer cables, see the `Serial-HOWTO` under the `/usr/doc` directory. To learn all the details about setting up a serial printer, see the `Printing-HOWTO`, also under the `/usr/doc` directory. Be sure to set your serial port and printer to the same speed. To learn how, read the `setserial` command manual page.

SEE ALSO

➤ *To learn more about the X Window System, see page 260.*
➤ *To learn more about other Red Hat tools, see page 622.*

Checking Your Printer

There are many ways to ensure that a printer you created when you installed Linux is working.

Checking an installed printer

1. Watch the startup messages while Linux is booting; look for a line specifying a found printer device, such as this:

   ```
   lp1 at 0x0378, (polling)
   ```

   This line indicates that Linux found a parallel port device that uses the `/dev/lp1` device.

2. Print a directory listing by sending the output of the `ls` command directly to your printer, or the found device, with a command line similar to the following:

   ```
   # ls >/dev/lp1
   ```

Tip

If the startup messages scroll by too quickly, wait for Linux to boot, log on, and then pipe the output of the `dmesg` command through the `less` pager:

```
# dmesg ¦ less
```

Your printer should activate and print a list of the current directory.

3. If your printer does nothing (make sure it is plugged in and turned on), you can try looking at the contents of the devices file under the `proc` directory by issuing the following command:

```
# cat /proc/devices
```

The `devices` file lists all active devices for your system. Look for the `lp` device under the list of character devices. The device is listed like this:

```
Character devices:
 1 mem
 2 pty
 3 ttyp
 4 ttyp
 5 cua
 6 lp
 7 vcs
10 misc
14 sound
127 pcmcia
```

4. Ensure that parallel printing is available, either as a loadable code module (`lp.o`) under the `/lib/modules/2.0.`*`xx`*`/misc` directory (where *xx* is the version of your kernel), or as code that is compiled into your kernel. Use the `lsmod` command to look for the `lp` module in kernel memory, like this:

```
# lsmod
Module          Pages    Used by
lp                  2           1 (autoclean)
serial_cs           1           0
fixed_cs            1           0
ds                  2    [serial_cs fixed_cs]     4
i82365              4           2
pcmcia_core         8   [serial_cs fixed_cs ds i82365]  5
vfat                3           1 (autoclean)
```

5. If you cannot detect a printer, or if you don't see the lp module, read the `Printing-HOWTO`, found under the `/usr/doc` directory for details about installing a printer.

SEE ALSO

➤ *To learn more about using redirection operators and pipes in the shell, see page 19.*
➤ *To learn more about Linux modules, see page 577.*

Adding a Local Printer by Editing */etc/printcap*

You can add a printer by entering a printer capability definition in the system printer capability database, `printcap`. This file is found under the `/etc` directory, and is a text file that must be changed only by the root operator.

The format, commands, and syntax to use when creating a printer entry in the `/etc/printcap` file are found in the `printcap` manual page. There are more than 40 different commands, but you can quickly create a printer with only the `mx` (maximum size of spooled files) and `sd` (spool directory) commands.

Configuring a simple printer

1. To create a printer called `mylp` for the `/dev/lp1` device, open the `/etc/printcap` file with your preferred text editor. The `sd` command tells the Linux printing daemon, `lpd`, where to temporarily place printed (spooled) files. The `mx` command, used with a value of `0`, places no limit on the size of spooled files. Type an entry such as this:

```
mylp:\
        :sd=/var/spool/lpd/mylp:\
        :mx#0:\
        :lp=/dev/lp1:
```

2. Save the entry, and then create the printer's spool directory by using the `mkdir` command:

```
# mkdir /var/spool/lpd/mylp
```

3. Make sure the directory `lp` has the correct group ownership and permissions by using the `chgrp` and `chmod` commands, as follows:

```
# chgrp lp /var/spool/lpd/mylp
# chmod 755 /var/spool/lpd/mylp
```

4. Test the printer entry with the `lpr` (line printer command):

```
# lpr -Pmylp test.txt
```

5. Your printer should activate and print the test document.

Tip

You might see a "staircase" effect in the printout. This is a common occurrence, indicating that your printer is not completely returning to the beginning of a line before printing another line. Although you can try to set your printer to insert a return after a linefeed, the best solution is to use a printer filter, such as the one installed by the Red Hat `printtool` program, discussed next.

SEE ALSO

➤ *For more information about changing permissions and ownerships by using the* `chown` *and* `chgrp` *commands, see page 417.*

➤ *To learn more about creating directories, see page 36.*

Adding a Local Printer with the Red Hat *printtool* Command

Use the Red Hat `printtool` program whenever you need to install a printer. You must be logged on as the root operator and also run the X Window System in order to use this program. There are two ways to access `printtool`:

- Through the Control Panel client
- Through the command line of an X11 terminal window

Installing a printer by using *printtool*

1. Ensure that your printer is connected to your computer and powered on. Log on as the root operator and start X11.
2. Run the Control Panel client, and then click the `printtool` button or start `printtool` from the command line of a terminal window, like this:

```
# printtool
```

3. The `printtool` main window, shown in Figure 5.1, appears. Any currently defined printers in the `/etc/printcap` database are listed. If you have not defined any printers, the window is blank. Click the Add button.

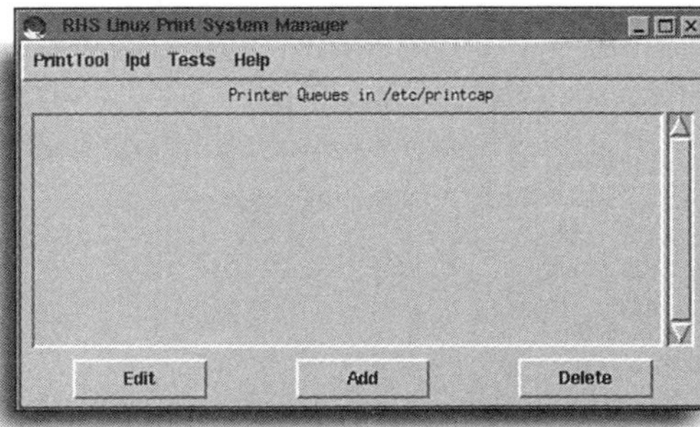

FIGURE 5.1
The `printtool` X11 client is used to add or configure printers for Linux.

4. The window shown in Figure 5.2 appears, asking you to select a local, remote, or LAN Manager printer. To set up a local printer (a printer attached to your computer), click the Local Printer option button, and then click OK.

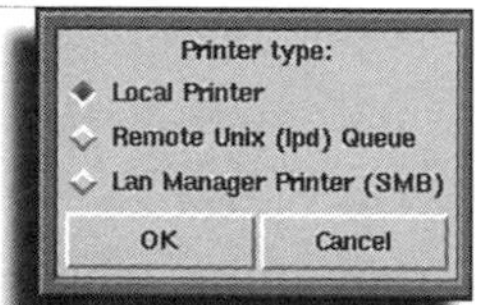

FIGURE 5.2
The `printtool` Printer Type dialog box prompts for a local, remote, or networked printer.

5. You should hear your printer activate when the Autodetection dialog box, shown in Figure 5.3, appears. This dialog box displays the parallel printer device detected on your computer. If no devices are detected, this indicates that your printer is not on or printing support has not been enabled.

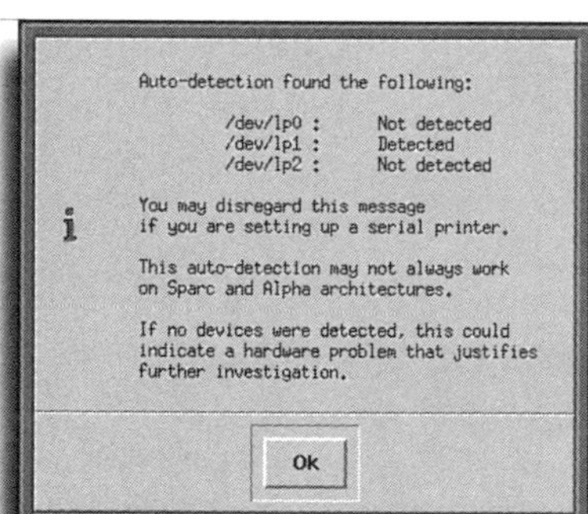

FIGURE 5.3
The `printtool` command automatically detects local printers.

6. Click OK, and a dialog box requesting a printer name appears (see Figure 5.4). Use the default name supplied, or designate a unique name for your printer by typing it in the dialog box's Names field.

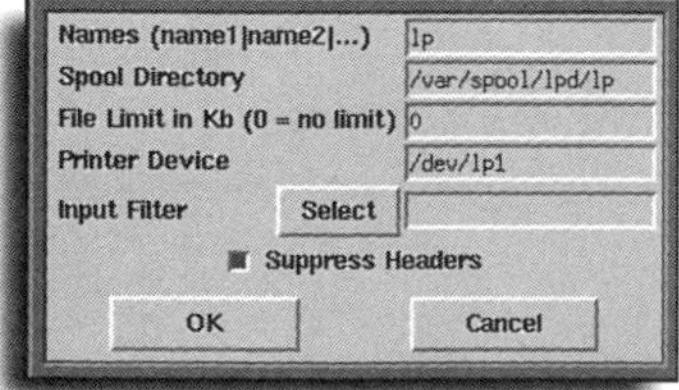

FIGURE 5.4
You can give a printer a unique name or use a default name.

7. Click the Select button next to the Input Filter dialog box entry to invoke the Configure Filter window, shown in Figure 5.5. Select your printer (or a printer similar to yours) from the list of printers. You can also select a printer resolution, paper size, and color depth. The color depth should match your printer's capabilities. Select only black-and-white options if you have a black-and-white printer. When finished, click OK.

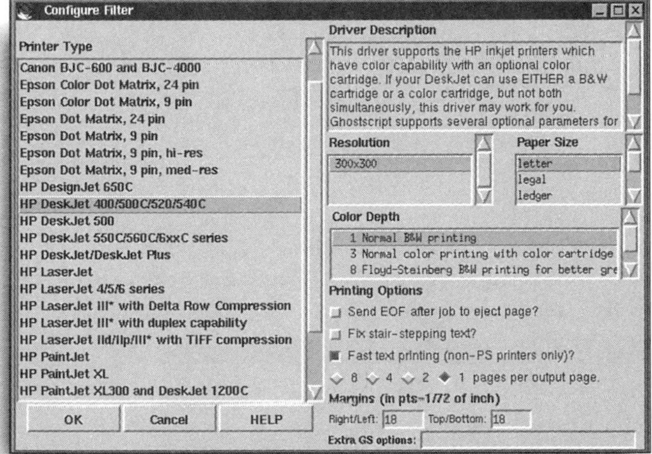

FIGURE 5.5
The `printtool` command offers customized settings for more than two dozen different printers.

8. Click OK in the dialog box shown in Figure 5.6.

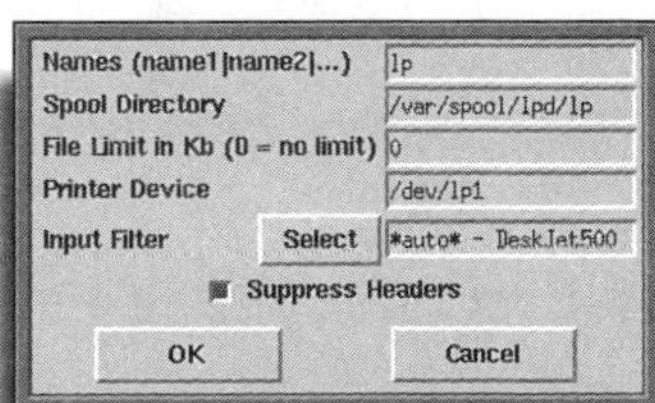

FIGURE 5.6
A print filter has been selected.

9. You should see the main `printtool` window (see Figure 5.7) with the printer you've defined in the list of printers. Test your printer by selecting it, and then selecting the ASCII or PostScript test menu item from the Tests menu. If everything goes well, click the Save button to save your printer's configuration and then exit. You can verify your printer's entry in the `/etc/printcap` database by using the `cat` command to list the entry, as follows:

```
# cat /etc/printcap
# /etc/printcap
#
# Please don't edit this file directly unless you know
what you are doing!
# Be warned that the control-panel printtool requires a
very strict format!
# Look at the printcap(5) man page for more info.
#
# This file can be edited with the printtool in the
control-panel.

##PRINTTOOL3## LOCAL cdj500 300x300 letter {} DeskJet500
8 1
lp:\
        :sd=/var/spool/lpd/lp:\
        :mx#0:\
        :sh:\
        :lp=/dev/lp1:\
        :if=/var/spool/lpd/lp/filter:
```

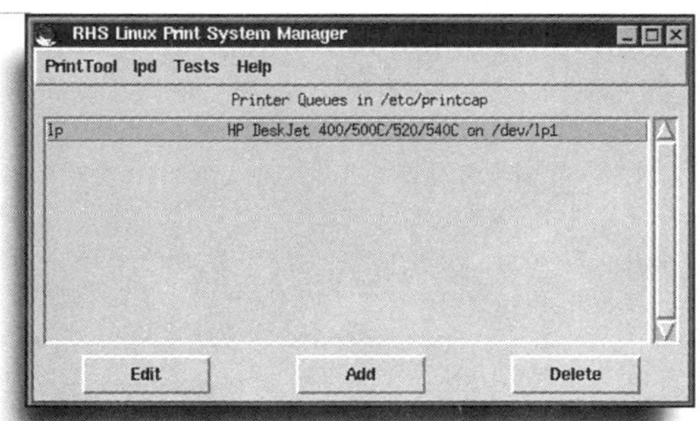

FIGURE 5.7
After configuring a printer, you can print a test page or save your changes and exit the `printtool` program.

Adding a Network Printer with Red Hat's *printtool*

Use the `printtool` command to add a remote printer (a printer that is accessed over a network). When the `printtool` command requests the type of printer, select Remote UNIX and click OK. A dialog box like the one shown in Figure 5.8 appears. Enter the name of the remote computer in the Remote Host field, and enter the name of the printer queue on the remote computer in the Remote Queue field.

SEE ALSO

➤ *To learn more about network connections, see page 444.*

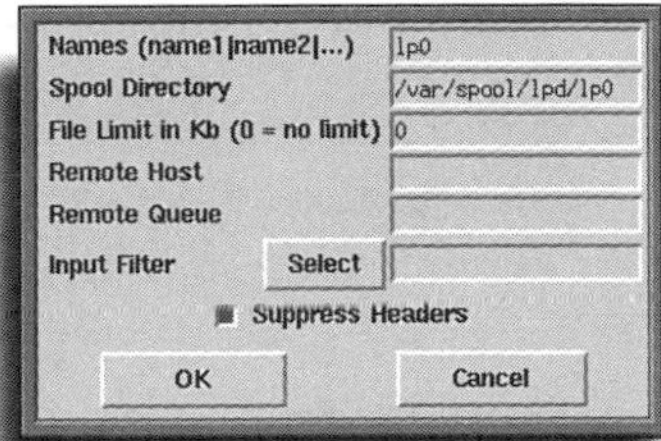

FIGURE 5.8

The `printtool` command will also set up remote printing services.

Limiting Spool File Sizes

The File Limit field (refer to Figure 5.8) is used to limit the size of acceptable printer spool files. Enter a number, such as `1024`, to limit the size of spooled files to 1 MB, or 1,000,000 characters. This is a handy way to avoid printing large files, or to make sure you don't run out of hard-drive space when printing large files. Some documents, especially large text files or graphics, can create enormous spool files, which are sent to your printer a piece at a time (not all printers have enough memory to accept large files).

SEE ALSO

➤ *For information about other ways to save disk space, see page 562.*

Spooling Files to Your Printer

Red Hat Linux uses a modified printing system inherited from the Berkeley Software Distribution (BSD) UNIX operating system. This system is called *line-printer spooling*. Linux starts printing services by running `lpd`, the line printer daemon, after you boot. This daemon runs in the background, and waits for program or command-line print requests.

Documents are printed with the `lpr` command. To print a text document, use the `lpr` command along with the `-P` (printer) option to select a desired printer, like this:

```
# lpr -Plp mydocument.txt
```

The printer name used with the `-P` option will be the name of a printer you've defined with the `printtool` command. The magic of the Red Hat printing system modifications becomes apparent when you print PostScript files, such as the following:

```
# lpr -Plp /usr/share/ghostscript/3.33/examples/tiger.ps
```

Red Hat Linux printing automatically recognizes and prints text and PostScript documents and graphics. (If you have a color printer, you can print color PostScript documents and graphics.)

Printing Files at the Command Line

Spooled documents are sent to a directory with the name of your printer, under the `/var/spool` directory. The `lpr` command, like many Linux programs, can also be used as a filter to print the output of other programs. For example, to quickly print a calendar for a year, pipe the output of the `cal` (calendar) command through the `lpr` command, like this:

```
# cal 1998 ¦ lpr
```

A 12-month calendar will be printed on the default printer. Use this approach to print manual pages or other documents on your printer.

Listing the Print Queue

After you print several documents using the `lpr` command, use the `lpq` (line-printer queue) command to see a list of documents waiting to be printed:

```
# lpq
lp is ready and printing
Rank     Owner     Job    Files                Total Size
active   bball     13     (standard input)     1972 bytes
```

The `lpq` command will report on the status of your printer and spooled documents.

Controlling Printers and Print Jobs

Printers and the order of print jobs can be controlled with the `lpc` (line-printer control) command. The `lpc` command has 14 built-in commands, but, as shown in Table 5.1, only the root operator can use every command. Each command can be used on the command line when you start `lpc`, and some commands require the name of a printer. For example, suppose you're the root operator and want to stop printing. If you simply use `stop` the `lpc` command will complain and quit:

```
# lpc stop
Usage: stop {all | printer}
```

To stop a particular printer, specify the command followed by the printer's name, like this:

```
# lpc stop lp
lp:
        printing disabled
```

The `lpc` command will echo the printer's name, followed by a message verifying that printing is stopped for that printer.

TABLE 5.1 Line printer control program commands

Command	Any User	Root Only	Action
abort		x	Stops the `lpd` daemon and disables printing
clean		x	Removes files from printer queue
disable		x	Turns off a printer's queue
down	x		Stops `lpd` and disables printer
enable		x	Turns on spooling
exit	x		Quits `lpc`
help	x		Help on commands
quit	x		Quits `lpc`
restart		x	Restarts spooling daemon
start		x	Enables printing, starts spooling daemon
status	x		Status of daemon and queue
stop		x	Stops spooling after current job, then disables printing
topq		x	Puts printer job at top of queue
up		x	Enables printers and restarts spooling

Use the status command to get the status of all printers, or if used with a printer's name, to report on the status of a particular printer, like this:

```
# lpc status
lp:
        queuing is enabled
        printing is enabled
        no entries
        no daemon present
```

Reordering Print Jobs

The lpc command can also be used to move print jobs or spooled files to the top of the print queue. In order to see the waiting jobs, use the lpq command, as follows:

```
# lpq
lp is ready and printing
Rank     Owner    Job   Files                  Total Size
active   bball    13    (standard input)        1972 bytes
active   mary     14    (standard input)        4058 bytes
active   fred     15    (standard input)       20103 bytes
```

Root operators can use the topq command followed by a job number or user's name (as reported by the lpq command) to specify that a certain job is to be printed next:

```
# lpc topq 14
```

This command line will move the mary job to the top of the printer queue for the printer lp.

Stopping Print Jobs

To stop a print job, first use the lpq command to see the list of jobs waiting to be printed. Then use the lpq command followed by a job number:

```
# lprm 13
```

This command line will stop job 13. As root operator, you can also stop all the print jobs for a particular user at a particular printer by using the lprm command followed by the -P option (the printer's name) and the user's name, like this:

```
# lprm -Plp bball
```

This command line will stop all print jobs sent to the printer `lp` by the user `bball`.

Sending Faxes with the *lpr* Command

The `lpr` command can also be used to send faxes if you've installed and configured fax service, as outlined in Chapter 11, "Configuring a Modem and Fax Service," in the section titled "Configuring Fax Service." You must first make sure that fax service using the `efax` software package is working properly.

Using *lpr* and *efax* to send faxes

1. Log on as root operator.
2. Using your preferred text editor, open the `/etc/printcap` database.
3. Create a fax printer entry by typing the following:
   ```
   fax:\
             :lp=/dev/null:\
             :sd=/var/spool/fax:\
             :if=/usr/bin/faxlp:
   ```
4. Create a hard link called `faxlp` to the fax command with the `ln` command like this:
   ```
   # ln /usr/bin/fax /usr/bin/faxlp
   ```
5. Create a directory called `/var/spool/fax` with the `mkdir` command, like this:
   ```
   # mkdir /var/spool/fax
   ```
6. Use the `chmod` commands to give the fax directory the correct permissions, as follows:
   ```
   # chmod 775 /var/spool/fax
   ```
7. To send a fax, use the `-P` (printer) and `-J` (job number) options to specify the fax printer and the outgoing fax number, like this:
   ```
   # lpr -Pfax -J 12025551212 myfax.txt
   ```
   This will send the text document, `myfax.txt`, to the fax number specified on the `lpr` command line.

SEE ALSO

➤ *For more information about setting up fax service, see page 159.*

PART

II

Configuring Your System

CHAPTER 6

Configuring Your Environment

By Bill Ball

Setting shell and system environment variables

Customizing your logon, profile, and resources

Customizing your shell

Creating command aliases

Setting Environment Variables

The shell specified in your /etc/passwd entry runs after you log on to Linux. Your shell then loads several files located in different directories on your system. These files, called *resource*, *profile*, or *login* files, are located in your home directory and the /etc directory. For the default Red Hat Linux shell, bash, these files include the following:

- .bashrc—Created by default in your home directory
- .bash_profile—Created by default in your home directory
- .bash_login—Created by default in your home directory
- .bash_history—A list of recently entered commands
- /etc/bashrc—Contains system aliases
- /etc/profile—Contains system environment variables

The profile files contain *environment variables*, which are definitions of values the shell or other programs recognize after you log on. The bash shell recognizes more than 50 different environment variables, and you can also define many of your own.

Displaying Environment Variables with the *printenv* Command

Use the printenv command, found under the /usr/bin directory, to print the value of a particular variable, or a list of currently defined environment variables, like so:

```
# printenv SHELL
/bin/bash
# printenv
USERNAME=
ENV=/home/bball/.bashrc
BROWSER=/usr/local/bin/netscape
HISTSIZE=1000
HOSTNAME=localhost.localdomain
LOGNAME=bball
HISTFILESIZE=1000
MAIL=/var/spool/mail/bball
HOSTTYPE=i386
```

```
PATH=/usr/local/bin:/bin:/usr/bin:.:/usr/sbin:/sbin:/usr/X11R
➥6/bin:
\/usr/local/bin:/usr/bin/mh:/home/bball/bin
HOME=/root
SHELL=/bin/bash
USER=bball
HOSTDISPLAY=localhost.localdomain:0.0
DISPLAY=:0.0
OSTYPE=Linux
NNTPSERVER=news.staffnet.com
SHLVL=5
EDITOR=/usr/bin/pico
```

Not all the environment variables listed here will be present on your system. Many systems have different values (such as USER, ENV, or HOSTNAME). Some commonly defined environment variables are listed in Table 6.1.

TABLE 6.1 Common *bash* and user environment variables

Variable	Description
EDITOR	Default system editor
HISTSIZE	The number of command lines to remember
HOME	Home directory for the current user
HOSTTYPE	The system architecture in use
LOGNAME	Name of the current user
MAIL	The directory to check for incoming mail
OSTYPE	The operating system in use
PATH	Path(s) to search for commands
PS1	Definition of the command-line prompt
PS2	Character used in the secondary command-line prompt
SHELL	Name of the shell currently in use
SHLVL	The number of shells currently running
TERM	The type of terminal in use
USER	Name of the current user

Displaying Environment Variables with the *env* Command

You can also use the env command, found under the /usr/bin directory, to print a list of your currently defined environment variables, as follows:

```
# env
```

Unlike the printenv command, env does not display the value of a single variable.

Setting an Environment Variable on the Command Line

What method you use to set an environment variable from the command line depends on the shell being used. The bash shell requires the use of the built-in export command. Creating a variable on the command line using bash takes the following form:

```
# VARIABLE_NAME="value" ; export VARIABLE_NAME
```

Temporary environment variables

Environment variables set from the command line are only temporary. Although this approach might be useful for testing just-installed software or for entering password keys to run protected software, these variables will last only as long as you're logged on or running a particular terminal. To make this change effective for each logon, add the definition to the proper shell initialization or resource file. See the later section "Customizing Your Logon" for more information.

Creating the *EDITOR* environment variable

1. To create or set an environment variable defining a default text editor (used by many system-administration utilities), export the variable with a command line such as the following:

   ```
   # EDITOR="/usr/bin/pico" ; export EDITOR
   ```

2. This command line creates the environment variable EDITOR. To verify the EDITOR variable, use the printenv command along with the fgrep search utility, like so:

   ```
   # printenv ¦ fgrep EDITOR
   EDITOR=/usr/bin/pico
   ```

   The output of the printenv command is piped through the fgrep command. Only the line containing the word EDITOR is returned, as shows the value of the new EDITOR variable.

SEE ALSO

➤ *To learn more about* fgrep *and other pattern-matching commands, see page 46.*

Environment variables are traditionally named using uppercase letters, although this is not required. The tcsh shell requires the built-in setenv command to define a variable:

```
# setenv VARIABLE_NAME=value
```

Defining a variable using the `ksh` shell requires its built-in `export` command:

```
# export VARIABLE_NAME=value
```

A more convenient way to set environment variables from the command line of any shell is to use the `env` command:

```
# env VARIABLE_NAME=value
```

Deleting an Environment Variable from the Command Line

You cannot delete an environment variable in the current shell unless you know the proper shell command to use. Knowing how to do this is important if you need to create variables to test temporarily installed software.

To delete a variable using `bash`, use the built-in `unset` command:

```
# unset VARIABLE_NAME
```

To delete the variable using the `tcsh` shell, use its built-in `unsetenv` command:

```
# unsetenv VARIABLE_NAME
```

The `ksh` shell, like `bash`, requires the built-in `unset` command:

```
# unset VARIABLE_NAME
```

The `env` command, along with its `-u` (unset) command-line variable, can be used with any shell to delete an environment variable:

```
# env -u VARIABLE_NAME
```

Setting Command *PATHs*

One of the most important environment variables is the `$PATH` variable. `PATH` defines the directory or directories where the shell can find executable programs, much like the DOS version of `PATH`. If the `PATH` variable is not properly set, you must type the complete directory to the name of a program to run the command.

For example, if you're not logged on as the root operator but you want to run the `fuser` command to find existing processes used by a program, the shell reports that the command is not found, as shown in the following:

```
# fuser bash
bash: fuser: command not found
```

However, you know the command exists on your system because the `whereis` command reports the `fuser` pathname, as shown here:

```
# whereis fuser
fuser: /usr/sbin/fuser
```

Although you can run the `fuser` command by typing its complete pathname, a much better approach is to add the `/usr/sbin` directory to your shell's `$PATH` environment variable. To do this temporarily, use the `env` command, like so:

```
# env PATH=$PATH:/sbin
# fuser /bin/bash
/bin/bash:      244e    342e    361e    362e    579e    582m
➥1187m  1277e  1893e
```

SEE ALSO

➤ *To learn how to control processes, see page 23.*

➤ *To learn more about using the whereis command, see page 45.*

Warning: Be careful when editing your PATH

Make changes to your PATH variable carefully. If you make a mistake, the shell won't know where to find commands. Make a copy of any existing PATH definitions, and then cautiously make your changes, especially if you edit the systemwide PATH definition in `/etc/profile` as the root operator.

To add the new directory to your `PATH` environment variable, and to make this change effective for each time you log on, add the path to the file `.bash_profile` in your home directory.

Adding a path to *.bash_profile*

1. Open `.bash_profile` in your favorite text editor and find the `PATH` definition, which will look similar to the following line:
   `PATH=$PATH:$HOME/bin`

2. Change the `PATH` definition line to the following:
   `PATH=$PATH:$HOME/bin:`**`/usr/sbin`**

SEE ALSO

➤ *To learn more about text editors for Linux, see Chapter 4, "Using Text Editors."*

3. To enable this change for all current or future users, make sure you're logged on as the root operator, and make the

change to the PATH definition line in the file profile under the /etc directory:

```
PATH="$PATH:/usr/X11R6/bin:/usr/local/bin:/usr/sbin"
```

Customizing Your Logon

Changes made to shell variables in the .bashrc and profile files under the /etc directory affect all users and are systemwide. Individual users can make changes, or local definitions, to the .bashrc and .bash_profile under their home directories. Local environment variables are defined in .bash_profile like so:

```
# .bash_profile

# Get the aliases and functions
if [ -f ~/.bashrc ]; then
        . ~/.bashrc
fi

# User-specific environment and startup programs

PATH=$PATH:$HOME/bin
ENV=$HOME/.bashrc
USERNAME=""

export USERNAME ENV PATH
```

Lines beginning with a pound sign (#) are comments. When you log on, the bash shell uses this program to first look for a file called .bashrc in your home directory, and then sets some basic environment variables. The .bashrc file in your home directory contains alias definitions (see the later section "Creating Aliases" for more information), as shown in the following:

```
# .bashrc

# User-specific aliases and functions

# Source global definitions
if [ -f /etc/bashrc ]; then
        . /etc/bashrc
fi
```

Both files are read by your shell after you log on, and can be edited to add custom definitions.

Customizing Your Command-Line Prompt

The default `bash` shell prompt variable, `PS1`, is defined in `/etc/profile`. The prompt definition uses special characters recognized by the `bash` shell, as shown here:

```
PS1="[\u@\h \W]\\$ "
```

Copy this line to your `.bash_profile`, and then edit the string to define your own prompt. Don't forget to add `PS1` to the export line in `.bash_profile`:

```
export USERNAME ENV PATH PS1
```

Table 6.2 lists the prompt characters recognized by `bash`.

TABLE 6.2 *bash* shell prompt characters

Character	Definition
`\!`	Print the history number of command
`\#`	Display the number of this command
`\$`	Print a 0, #, or $
`\W`	Print the basename of the current working directory
`\[`	Begin sequence of non-printing characters
`\\`	Print a backslash
`\]`	End sequence of non-printing characters
`\d`	Use the date in prompt
`\h`	Use the computer's hostname in the prompt
`\n`	Print a Newline in the prompt
`\nnn`	Character of octal number *nnn*
`\s`	Print the name of the shell
`\t`	Print the time
`\u`	Print the current user's name
`\w`	Show the current working directory

Test different prompts from the command line by using the bash shell's export command, like so:

```
#  PS1='\d \t: ';export PS1
Wed Feb 11 16:53:32:
```

Use terminal escape codes to create different character effects, such as highlighting, in your prompt, as in the following:

```
# PS1='[\033[4m\u\033[0m@\033[4m\h\033[0m]:';export PS1
```

This definition highlights your name (\u) and the hostname (\h) of your computer at the prompt of your console and an X11 xterm terminal window. In an X11 rxvt terminal window, the name and hostname will be underlined (see the later sidenote "Terminal Definitions").

SEE ALSO

- *To learn more about your computer's hostname, see page 444.*
- *To learn more about the X Window System, see page 260.*
- *To learn how to use X11 terminals, see page 269.*

Creating Aliases

Aliases are redefinitions of commands, usually in shortened form. Systemwide alias definitions are entered by the root operator in the bashrc file under the /etc directory, but you can define your own in your .bashrc file. Several of these aliases are especially useful:

```
alias cp="cp -i"
alias mv="mv -i"
alias rm="rm -I"
```

Redefining the default action of the cp, mv, and rm commands to use interactive querying provides a measure of safety when copying, deleting, moving, or renaming files. Aliases can also be used to craft new commands or variations of often-used commands and command-line options.

Red Hat Linux does not come with an X11 client or program to display the current month's calendar in a small, floating window (although the ical X11 client can be used, the calendar is much

Terminal definitions

Different terminals, such as X11's xterm and rxvt or the Linux console, have different capabilities and respond differently to escape sequences. The terminal definitions for your system are defined in the terminal capability database, called termcap, found under the /etc directory, and additional definitions are found in numerous subdirectories under the /usr/lib/terminfo directory. Do not edit or change the termcap file unless you are absolutely sure about what you're doing; incorrect entries can render your screen useless (make a backup copy first). Documentation for the termcap entries can be found in the /etc/termcap file, and in the terminfo and termcap manual pages.

larger). However, you can create your own by combining the `cal`, or calendar command, and the X11 xmessage client.

Creating a GUI calendar alias

1. Using your favorite text editor, open the file `.bashrc` in your home directory, and add the following line:

```
alias xcal="cal ¦ xmessage -file '-'&"
```

2. Name the alias `xcal`. This alias uses the `cal` command's output piped through the X11 xmessage client. The ampersand background operator (&) will run the program in the background automatically.

3. To use the `xcal` alias right away without the need to log out and then log back on, use the `bash` shell's built-in source command, and then try the `xcal` alias like so:

```
# source .bashrc
# xcal
```

SEE ALSO

➤ *To learn more about the* `cp`, `rm`, *and* `mv` *commands, see Chapter 3, "Navigating the Linux File System."*

➤ *To learn more about X11 clients, see page 294.*

Working with Hard Drives

By Bill Ball

Determining the volume device and partition

Choosing a file system

Formatting a hard drive

Partitioning a hard drive

Configuring mounting options

Take a walk on the technical side

Before installing another hard drive, read the Linux `Disk-HOWTO`, found under the `/usr/doc` directory. This document provides technical details, pointers, and an overview of the Linux file system. Also covered is hard drive technology (how disks are organized), media (such as optical or flash RAM), interfaces (such as IDE or SCSI), file systems (such as Linux `swap`, `minix`, or `ext2fs`), and recommendations about how and where to place different parts of your Linux system for safety, speed, or convenience. The latest version of the `Disk-HOWTO` can be found at the following web address:

`http://www.nyx.net/~sgjoen/disk.html`

Determining the Volume Device and Partition

After installing Linux (follow the instructions in Appendix A, "Installation of Red Hat Linux") you should at least know a little about the hard drive installed on your system. You should also know about Red Hat's `cabaret` program or the `fdisk` command because you created a *partition* on an existing *volume*, or hard drive, to make room for the kernel and software included with your Linux distribution. You might have installed Linux entirely in a single partition, or created several additional partitions to hold different parts of the Linux *file system*, or directory structure.

Linux supports a variety of file systems. If your Linux system shares a hard drive with DOS or Windows, your system uses the `ext2fs`, `msdos`, or `vfat` file system on your hard drive. Table 7.1 lists the file systems recognized by the `mount` command for Linux, which is used to attach a disk device to a specific Linux directory, or *mount point*.

TABLE 7.1 File systems recognized by *mount*

Type	Name
`affs`	Amiga file system
`coherent`	Coherent UNIX file system
`extfs`	Extended file system, successor to the minix file system for Linux
`ext2fs`	The current native Linux, or second extended, file system
`hpfs`	OS/2 file system (read-only)
`iso9660`	CD-ROM file system (read-only)
`minix`	The original Linux file system (no longer used)
`msdos`	DOS file system
`nfs`	Sun Microsystem's network file system
`proc`	Linux Process Information file system
`romfs`	Read-only memory file system (for embedded systems)
`smbfs`	Session message block (network) file system
`swap`	The swap file system used by Linux to temporarily store memory

Type	Name
sysv	UNIX system V file system
ufs	BSD, digital UNIX file system
umsdos	File system to support coexistent DOS and Linux files
vfat	Windows file system
xenix	Xenix file system
xiafs	A Linux file system that is no longer used (not supported by kernel version 2.1.21)

SEE ALSO

➤ *For more information about the Linux kernel and loading modules, see page 577.*

Determining your kernel file system support

1. To find out what file systems are currently supported by your kernel, use the `cat` command to see the contents of the file systems file under the `/proc` directory, like this:

```
#  cat /proc/file systems
        ext2
        msdos
nodev   proc
        vfat
        iso9660
```

   This example shows that your kernel is currently supporting the `ext2`, `msdos`, `vfat`, and `iso9660` file systems. Your system might have a DOS or Windows file system mounted, and an actively mounted CD-ROM.

2. Support for different file systems might come from support compiled into your Linux kernel, or through loadable kernel modules under the `/lib/modules/2.0.xx/fs` directory (where *xx* is your current version of Linux). To see the types of file system support modules available for your version of Linux, use the ls command to look in your module directory:

```
# ls /lib/modules/2*/fs
autofs.o  hpfs.o    minix.o   nfs.o     sysv.o
umsdos.o  xiafs.o
ext.o     isofs.o   ncpfs.o   smbfs.o   ufs.o
vfat.o
```

   The `ls` command lists all modules under the `fs` (file system) module directory.

Hard Drive Devices

Hard drive devices are found under the `/dev` directory, which contains more than 1,400 device names for many different devices (such as serial or printer ports, mice, scanners, sound cards, tape drives, CD-ROM drives, and hard drives). Table 7.2 lists some common devices and device names used as data storage, and explains partition numbers when associated with a storage device.

SEE ALSO

➤ *To learn how to install a PC card, see page 134.*

➤ *For more information about adding other devices (such as a mouse) to your system, see page 144.*

TABLE 7.2 Common storage device names and types

Device name	Type of Media, Volume, or Partition
`/dev/hda`	The first IDE drive
`/dev/hda2`	The second partition on the `/dev/hda` volume
`/dev/hdc`	The third IDE drive
`/dev/hde1`	The first partition on the fifth IDE drive
`/dev/sda`	The first SCSI drive
`/dev/sda4`	The fourth partition on the `/dev/sda` volume

SEE ALSO

➤ *To learn more about managing the Linux file system table, see page 495.*

Your system's current hard drives are listed in the `fstab` (file system table), found under the `/etc/` directory. The `/etc/fstab` file is a map to the storage devices used by Linux for native Linux files, or for mounting of other file systems, and provides directions to the `mount` command about where and how to mount each specified device.

Use the `cat` command to look at your system's `fstab`, like this:

```
# cat /etc/fstab
/dev/hda6       /                    ext2    defaults      1 1
/dev/hda5       swap                 swap    defaults      0 0
```

```
/dev/fd0        /mnt/floppy        ext2     noauto           0 0
/dev/cdrom      /mnt/cdrom          iso9660
user,noauto,dev,exec,ro,suid 0 0
none            /proc               proc     defaults        0 0
/dev/hde1       /mnt/flash         vfat
user,noauto,dev,exec,suid     0 0
/dev/sda4       /mnt/zip            vfat
user,noauto,dev,exec,suid     0 0
/dev/sda4       /mnt/zipext2        ext2
user,noauto,dev,exec,suid     0 0
/dev/hda1       /mnt/dos            vfat
user,noauto,dev,exec,suid     0 0
```

This file system table shows (starting from the left column) the device, where the device can be found if mounted (the mount point), the type of file system, and several mounting options for each device. Note that there are two entries for the same device, `/dev/sda4`, but that each has a different file system specified in the table. This is because the `/dev/sda4` device is a removable SCSI drive that is manually mounted at different times with *media*, or disks, containing different file systems.

Use the `df` (free disk space) command to see the amount of free space left on any currently mounted devices:

```
# df
File system        1024-blocks  Used Available Capacity
Mounted on
/dev/hda6              1443464  985613   383263     72%    /
/dev/hde1                14580   10956     3624     75%
/mnt/flash
/dev/hdc                596900  596900        0    100%
/mnt/cdrom
/dev/hda1               511744  419136    92608     82%
/mnt/dos
/dev/sda4                98078   23176    74902     24%
/mnt/zip
```

The `df` command shows reveals the following information:

- The root Linux partition on `/dev/hda6`, mounted at the `/` directory
- A small storage drive on `/dev/hde1`, mounted at the `/mnt/flash` directory

- A CD-ROM at /dev/hdc, mounted at the /mnt/cdrom directory
- A partition at /dev/hda1, mounted at the /mnt/dos directory
- A hard drive on /dev/sda4, mounted at the /mnt/zip directory

Although the df command is handy for determining how much room can be left on your storage devices, you must use the mount command if you want to know what file system exists for each device. Use the mount command with its -v (verbose) option:

```
# mount -v
/dev/hda6 on / type ext2 (rw)
/dev/hde1 on /mnt/flash type vfat (rw)
/dev/hdc on /mnt/cdrom type iso9660 (ro)
/dev/sda4 on /mnt/zip type vfat (rw)
/dev/hda1 on /mnt/dos type vfat (rw)
```

The mount command reports the following:

- Any mounted devices
- Where the device is mounted in your Linux file system or directory structure
- The file system used on the device
- Whether you can read (r), write (w), or read only (ro) from the device

SEE ALSO

➤ *For information about other ways to mount file systems, see page 488.*

Choosing a File System

When you add a hard drive to your system and want to use Linux and DOS or Windows, use the ext2 and msdos or vfat file systems. Although you can use the msdos file system for a DOS partition, you should use the vfat file system for a Windows 95 partition so you can use larger partitions and get long-filename support. If you mount a vfat partition under a Linux directory, the ls command shows the proper long filenames like this:

```
# ls /mnt/dos/windows/*.bmp
/mnt/dos/windows/Black Thatch.bmp
/mnt/dos/windows/Pinstripe.bmp
```

```
/mnt/dos/windows/Blue Rivets.bmp    /mnt/dos/windows/Red
Blocks.bmp
/mnt/dos/windows/Bubbles.bmp
/mnt/dos/windows/Sandstone.bmp
/mnt/dos/windows/Carved Stone.bmp   /mnt/dos/windows/Setup.bmp
/mnt/dos/windows/Circles.bmp
/mnt/dos/windows/Stitches.bmp
/mnt/dos/windows/Clouds.bmp          /mnt/dos/windows/Straw
Mat.bmp
/mnt/dos/windows/Forest.bmp
/mnt/dos/windows/Tiles.bmp
/mnt/dos/windows/Gold Weave.bmp
/mnt/dos/windows/Triangles.bmp
/mnt/dos/windows/Houndstooth.bmp    /mnt/dos/windows/Waves.bmp
/mnt/dos/windows/Metal Links.bmp
```

A DOS partition does not support long filenames, so if you use an `msdos` file system, mount it, and then copy files from your Linux file system to the DOS partition, the `ls` command would show files from the previous example like this:

```
# ls /mnt/dos/windows/*.bmp
/mnt/dos/windows/blackt~1.bmp  /mnt/dos/windows/pinstr~1.bmp
/mnt/dos/windows/blueri~1.bmp  /mnt/dos/windows/redblo~1.bmp
/mnt/dos/windows/bubbles.bmp   /mnt/dos/windows/sandst~1.bmp
/mnt/dos/windows/carved~1.bmp  /mnt/dos/windows/setup.bmp
/mnt/dos/windows/circles.bmp   /mnt/dos/windows/stitches.bmp
/mnt/dos/windows/clouds.bmp    /mnt/dos/windows/strawm~1.bmp
/mnt/dos/windows/forest.bmp    /mnt/dos/windows/tiles.bmp
/mnt/dos/windows/goldwe~1.bmp  /mnt/dos/windows/triang~1.bmp
/mnt/dos/windows/hounds~1.bmp  /mnt/dos/windows/waves.bmp
/mnt/dos/windows/metall~1.bmp
```

If you add a hard drive to Linux or repartition an existing drive, you can use any file system you want as long as the `cabaret`, `fdisk`, and `mount` commands support the file system. If you're only going to use the new storage for Linux, use the `ext2` file system; if you want to share files between Linux and Windows, stick with `vfat`—Windows will recognize the `vfat` partition, but not one formatted to use `ext2`. This is even more important when using removable devices like flash cards or Zip drives.

File system support does not mean formatting

Although Linux supports many different types of file systems to allow reading and writing of files, you will still need to use another operating system to format a new hard drive. Linux does not come with disk-formatting utilities for other file systems (except DOS). See the `mtools` manual page for more information.

Install your drive properly

Before configuring a drive for Linux, follow your computer manufacturer's instructions for properly installing the hardware. Make sure that all cables are correctly connected, and that any switch configurations are made to match the drive to your existing system. If you've installed a SCSI drive, make sure that all cables are firmly attached and that the SCSI chain is properly terminated.

Getting clues from boot messages

If you installed a new hard drive and boot Linux, carefully examine your system's boot messages. If the screen scrolls by too quickly for you to read, use the `dmesg` command after you boot and log on to Linux to list the bootup messages. Linux should recognize any new devices attached to interfaces supported by your kernel.

Formatting a Hard Drive

Red Hat Linux comes with several programs that you can use to partition and format a hard drive. Although the latest and greatest disk-support tool is Red Hat's `cabaret` command—which provides a graphic interface for configuring, formatting, and mounting storage devices for Linux—you can also use the `fdisk`, `mke2fs`, and `mount` commands.

Using *cabaret* with Hard Drives

Use the `cabaret` command from the command line of your console or an X11 terminal window. This command presents a graphic interface and simplifies the job of installing and configuring hard drives. Press the Tab key or use function keys to navigate through `cabaret`'s dialog boxes. Use your cursor or the Tab key to scroll up and down in dialog lists. Press the Spacebar to select or unselect items in a list.

SEE ALSO

➤ *To read about other ways to use Red Hat's* `cabaret` *command, see page 495.*

Using *cabaret* to format and install a hard drive

1. Log on as the root operator. Start the `cabaret` program from the command line by entering the following:

```
# cabaret
```

The screen clears. `cabaret` reads in your system's file system table and presents its dialog box (shown in Figure 7.1).

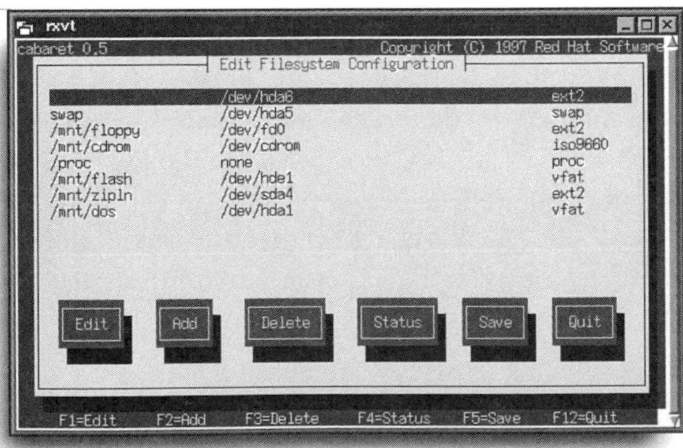

FIGURE 7.1
The `cabaret` command is Red Hat's point-and-shoot file system utility.

2. To add a drive, press the Tab key twice to highlight the Add button, and then press Enter. `cabaret` asks you to choose a file system, as shown in Figure 7.2.

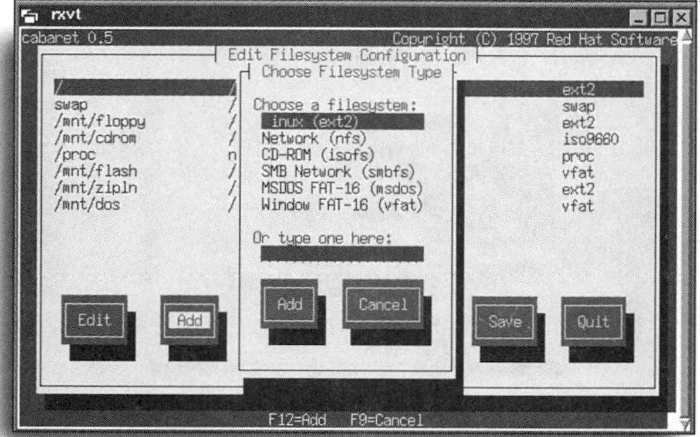

FIGURE 7.2
Choosing a file system is the first step in installing a hard drive with `cabaret`.

3. Use your up or down cursor keys to scroll through the list of file systems, or press the Tab key and enter the name of a file system.

4. After selecting or entering a file system type, press the Tab key until the Add button is highlighted, and then press Enter. `cabaret` asks for a mount point followed by the device name, as shown in Figure 7.3.

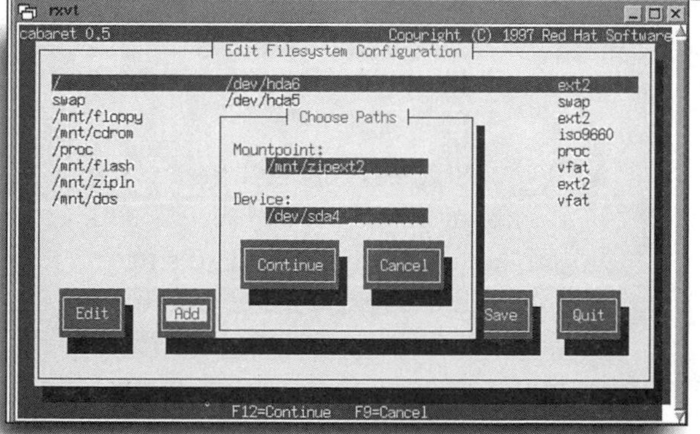

FIGURE 7.3
When adding a new drive, `cabaret` prompts for a mount point in your Linux file system, along with the device name.

5. Type a descriptive directory name (typically under the `/mnt` directory) such as `/mnt/zipext2`, and press Enter. Then type the device name—`/dev/sda4`, for example. Press the Tab key to highlight the Continue button, and press Enter.

6. As shown in Figure 7.4, `cabaret` presents a list of options to use when mounting the device. These options are inserted into your system's file system table, `/etc/fstab`.

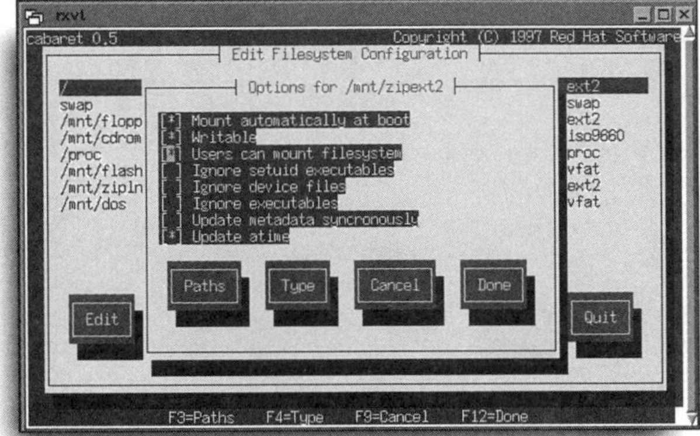

FIGURE 7.4
`cabaret` lets you configure a device's mounting options from a scrolling list in a mounting configuration dialog box.

7. Scroll through the list of options by using your up and down cursor keys, selecting or unselecting an option by pressing the spacebar. Three important options are as follows:
   - Mount Automatically at Boot—If you select this option, Linux automatically tries to mount the device when booting.
   - Writable—If you select this option, you will be able to write or delete files on the device.
   - Users Can Mount Filesystem—If you select this option, other users will be able to mount or unmount the device.
8. If you decide to change where you'd like to mount the device, or if you want to specify a different device, press the Tab key to highlight the Paths button (as shown in Figure 7.4), and then press Enter. You'll see a dialog box similar to the one in Figure 7.3. If you decide to change the file system type, select the Type button and press Enter. When finished, select the Done button and press Enter.
9. The dialog box disappears. `cabaret` again lists the file system table, but with your new device in the list (see Figure 7.5). Scroll down the list until your defined device is highlighted, then press the Tab key until the Status button is highlighted.

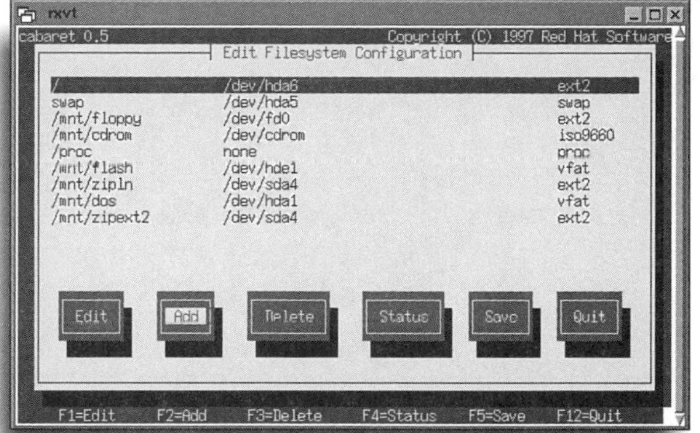

FIGURE 7.5
Newly defined devices in the file system table are listed in `cabaret`'s main dialog box.

10. Select the Status button, and `cabaret` presents a dialog box that offers you a choice about whether you want to mount or format the device (see Figure 7.6).

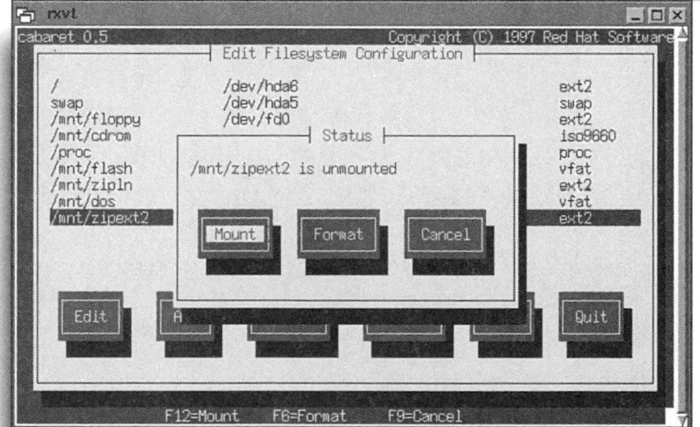

FIGURE 7.6
New volumes or partitions must be formatted before use.

11. If you select the Mount button, `cabaret` attempts to mount the device, but the mount fails. Instead, press the Tab key until the Format button is highlighted, and then press Enter.

12. The dialog box shown in Figure 7.7 appears; here you select what type of file system to use for the new device. Make sure you enter the same file system type you entered in step 3, or the new drive will not be mounted correctly.

13. Scroll through the list of file systems and select the desired type by pressing the spacebar. Then press the Tab key until the OK key is highlighted.

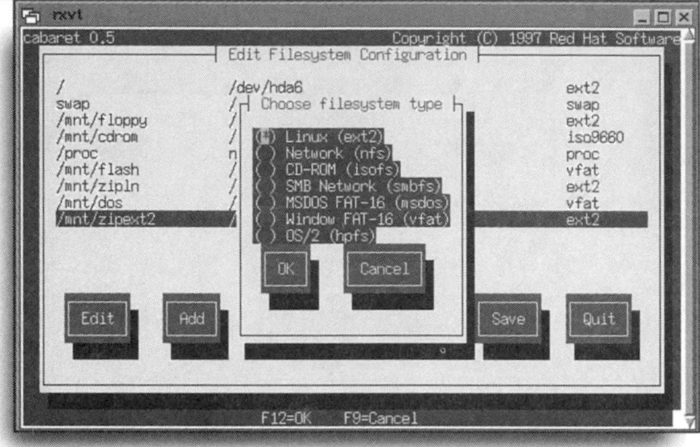

FIGURE 7.7
Before formatting a device, `cabaret` prompts you for the type of file system to use.

14. Linux formats the device. When the device is formatted, press the Tab key until the Status button is highlighted, and then press Enter.
15. The dialog box shown in Figure 7.6 appears, informing you that the device is not mounted. Press Enter to mount the device. To verify whether the device is mounted, select the Status button. This time, `cabaret` should inform you that the device is mounted at the mount point you've specified, as shown in Figure 7.8.

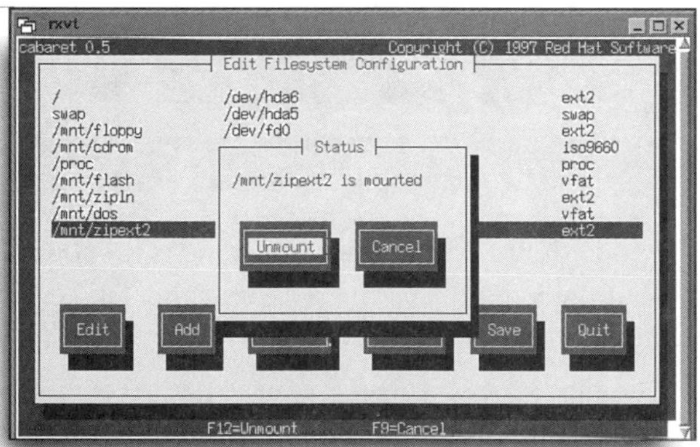

FIGURE 7.8
`cabaret` can also be used to unmount devices from your Linux file system.

16. Press Enter to unmount the new device, or press the Tab key followed by the Enter key to cancel unmounting.
17. In `cabaret`'s main dialog box, press the Tab key until the Save button is highlighted, and then press Enter. A confirmation dialog box like the one shown in Figure 7.9 appears.

Press Enter when the Save button is highlighted to save your new file system table.

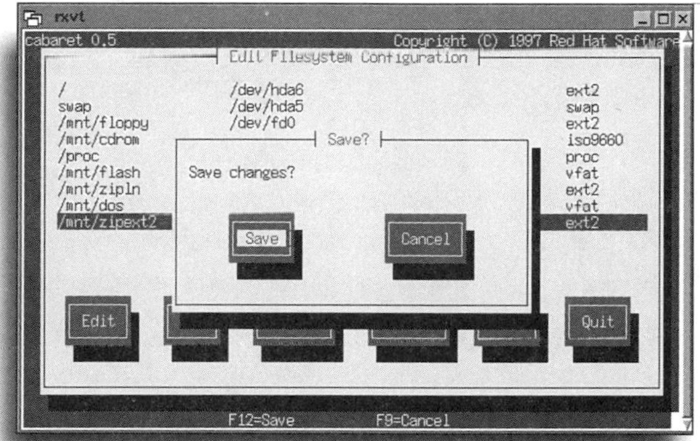

FIGURE 7.9
`cabaret` verifies whether to save new file system tables in `/etc/fstab`.

18. After saving your changes, tab to the Quit button and press Enter, or press F12 to exit `cabaret`.

Partitioning a Hard Drive with the *fdisk* Command

Use the `fdisk` command to prepare a new hard drive with one or more partitions. If you do not need to partition a new drive, use the `cabaret` command as outlined in the previous section. `fdisk` is not the most intuitive Linux command (much like the DOS `fdisk` command) but can be used to quickly prepare a hard drive for use.

Partitioning a hard drive with *fdisk*

1. Log on as the root operator. Use the `fdisk` command to prepare and partition a hard drive by specifying the drive's device name on the command line (I've used the drive from the `cabaret` example):

```
# fdisk /dev/sda4
Command (m for help): m
```

2. `fdisk` prints a prompt after recognizing your device. Press M for a list of `fdisk` commands. The program responds like this:

```
Command action
   a   toggle a bootable flag
   b   edit bsd disklabel
   c   toggle the dos compatibility flag
   d   delete a partition
   l   list known partition types
   m   print this menu
   n   add a new partition
   p   print the partition table
   q   quit without saving changes
   t   change a partition's system id
   u   change display/entry units
   v   verify the partition table
   w   write table to disk and exit
   x   extra functionality (experts only)
```

3. Press N to add a new partition table. The `fdisk` program responds as follows:

   ```
   Command (m for help): n
   Command action
      e   extended
      p   primary partition (1-4)
   ```

4. You're only going to use one primary partition on this drive, so press P for a primary partition. The `fdisk` program responds as follows:

   ```
   p
   Partition number (1-4):
   ```

5. Type the number **1**, and press Enter. The `fdisk` responds with the following:

   ```
   Partition number (1-4): 1
   First cylinder (1-96):
   ```

6. Note that this is a small hard drive (less than 100 MB), as indicated by the small number of cylinders. Type the number **1** and press Enter. The `fdisk` command then asks for the ending cylinder number for the partition:

   ```
   First cylinder (1-96): 1
   Last cylinder or +size or +sizeM or +sizeK ([1]-96):
   ```

7. Type **96**, and press Enter (if you'd entered **50**, you'd still have 46 cylinders on the device and could create a new

partition to run from cylinder 51 to 96—about half the storage capacity of the drive).

```
Last cylinder or +size or +sizeM or +sizeK ([1]-96): 96
```

8. Press P to print the partition table:

```
Command (m for help): p
Disk /dev/sda4: 64 heads, 32 sectors, 96 cylinders
Units = cylinders of 2048 * 512 bytes

    Device Boot    Begin     Start       End    Blocks
Id  System
/dev/sda41              1         1        96     98288
83  Linux native
Command (m for help):
```

9. To change the partition's type, press T.

```
Command (m for help): t
```

10. `fdisk` asks for the partition to change. Type **1**.

```
Partition number (1-4): 1
```

11. `fdisk` asks for a hex code, representing a type of file system. To see the types of file systems you can use, press L, and `fdisk` prints a list like this:

```
Hex code (type L to list codes): L

 0  Empty              9  AIX bootable     75  PC/IX
b7  BSDI fs
 1  DOS 12-bit FAT    a  OS/2 Boot Manag 80  Old MINIX
b8  BSDI swap
 2  XENIX root        b  Win95 FAT32      81  Linux/MINIX
c7  Syrinx
 3  XENIX usr        40  Venix 80286      82  Linux swap
db  CP/M
 4  DOS 16-bit <32M 51  Novell?          83  Linux
native     e1  DOS access
 5  Extended         52  Microport        93  Amoeba
e3  DOS R/O
 6  DOS 16-bit >=32 63  GNU HURD         94  Amoeba BBT
f2  DOS secondary
 7  OS/2 HPFS        64  Novell Netware  a5  BSD/386
ff  BBT
 8  AIX              65  Novell Netware
Hex code (type L to list codes):
```

12. To use the new partition for Linux, type the number **83** and press Enter:

```
Hex code (type L to list codes): 83
Changed system type of partition 1 to 83 (Linux native)

Command (m for help): p

Disk /dev/sda4: 64 heads, 32 sectors, 96 cylinders
Units = cylinders of 2048 * 512 bytes

    Device Boot    Begin     Start       End    Blocks
Id  System
/dev/sda41             1         1        96     98288
83  Linux native
Command (m for help):
```

13. fdisk prints a short message, informing you of the new file system type. Use the p command to confirm this, and use the w command to save your changes and exit. The fdisk command prints the following short message and then quits:

```
Command (m for help): w
The partition table has been altered!

Calling ioctl() to re-read partition table.
Syncing disks.

WARNING: If you have created or modified any DOS 6.x
partitions, please see the fdisk manual page for
additional information.
```

After partitioning a drive and specifying a file system, you still must format the drive. To format the drive for use by Linux, use the mke2fs command. This command has several command-line options; the most important is -c, which you use to check for any bad blocks during formatting. To format this chapter's sample drive, use the mke2fs command with -c option, followed by the device name, like so:

```
# mke2fs  mke2fs -c /dev/sda4
mke2fs 1.10, 24-Apr-97 for EXT2 FS 0.5b, 95/08/09
Linux ext2 file system format
File system label=
24576 inodes, 98288 blocks
4914 blocks (5.00%) reserved for the super user
```

```
First data block=1
Block size=1024 (log=0)
Fragment size=1024 (log=0)
12 block groups
8192 blocks per group, 8192 fragments per group
2048 inodes per group
Superblock backups stored on blocks:
        8193, 16385, 24577, 32769, 40961, 49153, 57345,
        65537, 73729, 81921, 90113
Checking for bad blocks (read-only test):  2240/   98288
```

The `mke2fs` command starts checking your drive before formatting (which can take at least several minutes), and then formats your drive:

```
Writing inode tables: done
Writing superblocks and file system accounting information:
done
```

Hidden space on Linux drives?

Note that by default (and for safety reasons) the `mke2fs` command reserves 5% of a drive's space for use by the root operator. This means that a 1 GB hard drive might have nearly 50 MB of free drive space available, even though disk utilities such as `df` report that the drive is nearly full. To use all available space on a Linux `ext2` file system, use `mke2fs`' `-m` option followed by the number `0` when formatting a drive.

Mounting a Hard Drive or Other Device

After partitioning and formatting a new drive, you must mount the drive. To mount a new drive, you must have a mount point, know the drive's file system type, and know the drive's device name.

Mounting a newly partitioned and formatted drive

1. Log on as the root operator. Use `mkdir` to create a mount point for the new drive, like this:
   `# mkdir /mnt/zipext2`

2. Use the `mount` command, and specify the type of file system using the `-t` option, the device name, and the mount point:
   `# mount -t ext2 /dev/sda4 /mnt/zipext2`

3. Use the `df` command to verify that the new drive has been mounted:
   `#df`

```
File system          1024-blocks  Used Available
Capacity Mounted on
/dev/hda6              1443464 1011187   357689      74%
/
/dev/sda4                95167      13    90240       0%
/mnt/zipext2
```

4. To unmount the drive, use the `umount` command followed by the mounting point:

```
# umount /mnt/zipext2
```

The final step in installing a new drive is to make an entry in the file system table. This will ensure that the device is available the next time you boot Linux, and simplifies the job of mounting the file system. For example, with a proper `fstab` entry, mounting the sample hard drive would be as simple as the following:

```
# mount /mnt/zipext2
```

Although using Red Hat's `cabaret` command is the preferred and safer method for editing the system's file system table, you manually edit the `/etc/fstab` file using a text editor. Be warned! Make a copy of this file before proceeding, and have an emergency boot disk handy. If you screw up `fstab`, you might not be able to boot properly or mount your Linux file system.

Adding an entry to the sample drive

1. To add an entry to the sample drive, log on as the root operator. Use your text editor, such as `pico`, to edit `fstab`:

```
# pico -w /etc/fstab
```

2. Add a line to the file, specifying the device name, the mount point, the file system type, and mounting options:

```
/dev/sda4       /mnt/zipext2      ext2
user,noauto,dev,exec,suid 0 0
```

3. These mounting options specify that the drive will not be automatically mounted when Linux boots but will allow anyone to mount or unmount the drive. To have the drive automatically mounted, and to restrict unmounting or mounting to the root operator only, use an entry like the following:

```
/dev/sda4       /mnt/zipext2      ext2    defaults 0 0
```

Table 7.3 lists common mounting options that you can use in a file system table entry. For complete details, see the `mount` command's manual page.

TABLE 7.3 Common mounting options in */etc/fstab*

Option	Keyword
Allow programs to run from device	`exec`
Allow users to mount the device	`user`
Device must be specified to mount	`noauto`
Do not allow programs to run from device	`noexec`
Do not allow users to mount the device	`nouser`
Mount automatically at boot	`auto`
Mount the device read-only	`ro`
Mount the device read-write	`rw`

SEE ALSO

➤ *For more information about using the* `pico` *editor, see page 50.*

CHAPTER

8

Adding Tape and Zip Drives

By Bill Ball

Adding a tape drive

Retensioning, rewinding, and erasing tapes

Adding a SCSI or parallel-port Zip drive

Mounting a Zip drive

Printing with a parallel-port Zip drive

Ejecting and password-protecting a Zip disk

This chapter describes how to install and use a tape and Iomega Zip drive with Linux. Tape drives and removable drives are often used for system backups and archiving of important software. Removable drives can also be used to store a Linux file system.

SEE ALSO

➤ *To learn how to back up your system, see page 542.*

Adding a Tape Drive

Numerous tape drives are supported by Linux through the `ftape.o` and `st.o` tape modules, found under the `/lib/modules/2.0.xx/misc` directory (where *xx* represents your kernel's version). The `ftape` module is a device driver used to support floppy controller tape or removable backup devices, whereas the `st.o` module supports SCSI tape devices. Both modules are automatically loaded and unloaded by the `kerneld` system daemon when needed during tape operation.

Generally speaking, although nearly all SCSI and floppy controller tape drives should work with modern Linux kernels, version 2.0 and up, many high-speed or parallel-port tapes may not. Check the `Hardware-HOWTO` or `Ftape-HOWTO` pages found under the `/usr/doc/HOWTO` directory to see whether your tape drive and interface are supported.

Installing a Tape Drive

SCSI tape drives are either attached directly to an installed SCSI adapter or added to the current SCSI device chain. Make sure that a free device number is used, and that the SCSI chain is properly terminated. The devices used to support SCSI tape drives are found under the `/dev` directory and begin with the letters `st`:

```
/dev/st0   /dev/st1   /dev/st2   /dev/st3
/dev/st4   /dev/st5   /dev/st6   /dev/st7
/dev/nst0   /dev/nst1   /dev/nst2   /dev/nst3
/dev/nst4   /dev/nst5   /dev/nst6   /dev/nst7
```

There are two types of tape drive devices:

- Rewinding—Rewinding devices automatically rewind after tape operation.
- Nonrewinding—Devices with names starting with `n` are nonrewinding tape devices, and will not rewind after tape operation.

For more information about these SCSI tape devices, see the `st` manual page, or see Section 8, "Tapes," of the `SCSI-HOWTO`, found under the `/usr/doc/HOWTO` directory.

Floppy controller tape drives are attached to the spare floppy controller port. You cannot use your floppy drive when using a floppy tape drive. The devices used to support tape drives are found under the `/dev` directory and have the letters `ft` in their filenames:

```
/dev/nrft0   /dev/nrft2   /dev/rft0    /dev/rft2
/dev/nrft1   /dev/nrft3   /dev/rft1    /dev/rft3
```

Creating a tape drive device symbolic link

1. Choose the device names, such as `/dev/st0` or `/dev/rft0`, that match your SCSI or floppy tape drive.
2. As the root operator, use the `ln` command to create symbolic links for your devices, like so:

   ```
   # ln -s /dev/nrft0 /dev/nftape
   # ln -s /dev/rft0 /dev/ftape
   ```

   This command creates easily remembered names of your tape drive. Tapes must be purchased preformatted or must be formatted by using another operating system's utilities; at the time of this writing, no Linux utilities were available to format magnetic tapes.

Using the *mt* Command

The `mt` (magnetic tape) command is used to control tapes in your tape drive. These operations include the following:

- Rewinding the tape
- Retensioning the tape

- Erasing the tape
- More than two dozen SCSI-specific tape operations

The mt command can also be used by backup scripts, such as taper, or other backup utilities, such as the tar or cpio commands, to archive Linux directories and files. The mt command has several different command-line options, but is usually used with the -f option to specify the tape device followed by a command:

```
# mt -f /dev/nftape command
```

Tape drives, unlike other file systems, are not mounted or unmounted for read or write operation.

SEE ALSO

➤ *To learn more about mounting file systems and using the mount command, see page 115.*

➤ *To learn how to use the* tar *and* cpio *commands, see page 542.*

Retensioning Tapes

The general consensus among Linux tape users is that it is a good idea to retension new tapes before use. Tapes should be retensioned before use to take up any existing slack, and to make sure the tape conforms to your tape drive's tension strength. This will help to reduce the risk of errors during backups. To retension a tape, insert the tape into the tape drive, then use the mt command with the nonrewinding tape drive device and the retension command:

```
# mt -f /dev/nftape retension
```

Rewinding Tapes

Although some tape drives automatically rewind inserted tapes, you might occasionally need to rewind a tape yourself, especially if a backup operation has been halted by software or operator intervention. To rewind a tape, use the mt command with the nonrewinding tape drive device and the rewind command:

```
# mt -f /dev/nftape rewind
```

Preparing Tapes for Linux Backups

Before using a formatted tape for backups, you must generally use the mt command to erase the tape and prepare it for Linux.

To erase a tape, use the `mt` command with the nonrewinding tape drive device and the `erase` command:

```
# mt -f /dev/nftape erase
```

Adding a Zip Drive

Current Linux distributions and software utilities available for the Zip drive only support the original Zip drive, and not the Zip Plus drive. This is especially true for the parallel-port version of the Zip drive; at the time of this writing, work on a driver for the plus version had not even started.

The Zip drive is an affordable alternative to removable hard drives, although the current hardware and format limits disk capacity to a little less than 100 MB of storage. If you need a larger removable drive, consider other drives from Iomega or Syquest. Support exists for the SCSI version of the Zip drive because it is treated like any other SCSI disk (check the `Hardware-HOWTO` page to see whether your SCSI adapter is supported). The parallel-port Zip drive is also supported if you either recompile the kernel or use a loadable software module.

For more information about Iomega Zip drives, use your favorite Web browser to visit the following site:

http://www.iomega.com

SEE ALSO

➤ *For details about recompiling the Linux kernel, see page 588.*
➤ *For details about using modules with the Linux kernel, see page 577.*

Before Installing a Zip Drive

Although most Linux distributions come with the required drivers and file-system utilities to support Zip drives, you must ensure the following before installation:

- For all Zip drives, the kernel must have SCSI support either compiled in or available as loadable modules.
- Parallel-printer support must not be compiled into the Linux kernel, but instead should be available as a loadable

module. This module, called `lp.o`, is found in the `/lib/modules/2.0.xx/misc` directory (where *xx* is the version of the Linux kernel).

- For parallel-port Zip drives, the `ppa` driver must be compiled into the kernel or, if you are using a kernel supporting loadable modules, must be available as the file `ppa.o` under the `/lib/modules/2.0.xx/scsi` directory.
- A copy of Grant Guenther's Zip drive `mini-HOWTO` page should be on hand; this document, which is usually found under the `/usr/doc/HOWTO/mini` directory, contains technical details of kernel configuration and driver customization and provides pointers to the latest drivers.

Installing Linux on a Zip disk

For details about how to install Linux on a Zip disk, read John Wiggins' `mini-HOWTO` called "Putting Linux on a Zip Disk." This document, found under the `/usr/doc/HOWTO/mini` directory, outlines the basic steps required to set up, format, and mount a Zip disk for use as a root file system. This procedure requires, among other things, crafting a custom kernel with SCSI support and the `ppa` driver, creating a boot disk, and selecting various rpm packages to build a file system that will use less than 100 MB.

SEE ALSO

➤ *To install a hard drive, see page 106.*

Installing a SCSI Zip Drive

Installing a SCSI Zip drive is much the same as installing a regular SCSI disk.

Installing a SCSI Zip drive

1. Install the SCSI adapter card and Zip drive according to the manufacturer's instructions.
2. Make the proper cable connections between the adapter card and the Zip drive.
3. Make sure the SCSI chain is properly terminated (on both ends of the chain). See the manufacturer's instructions for details.
4. Follow the directions detailed in the later section "Installing and Mounting the Parallel-port Zip Drive" for details on creating a file system table entry and mounting the drive.

For details about installing SCSI support for the Linux kernel and about troubleshooting SCSI device detection while Linux is booting, read Drew Eckhardt's `SCSI-HOWTO`, usually found under the `/usr/doc/HOWTO` directory. This document contains details about device recognition (how to configure a particular SCSI interface card at boot time by using LILO to pass kernel messages).

Linux SCSI drive devices are found under `/dev` directory, and have the following names, usually starting with the letters `sd`:

```
/dev/sda      /dev/sda11    /dev/sda14    /dev/sda3     /dev/sda6
/dev/sda9
/dev/sda1     /dev/sda12    /dev/sda15    /dev/sda4     /dev/sda7
/dev/sda10    /dev/sda13    /dev/sda2     /dev/sda5     /dev/sda8
```

If you use a preformatted DOS Zip disk, the Zip drive will use the `/dev/sda4` device (partition 4 on the `/dev/sda` volume). According to Bob Willmot's `JAZ-drive mini HOWTO`, this usage ensures compatibility for preformatted Zip disks on PC and Macintosh computers. For more details, read the file `Jaz-Drive` under the `/usr/doc/HOWTO/mini` directory.

SEE ALSO

➤ *For directions on using LILO, see page 382.*

Installing and Mounting the Parallel-Port Zip Drive

The parallel-port Zip drive has two DB-25 male connectors on its back. Plug one end of the supplied cable into the back of the Zip drive, and the other into the parallel port of your computer. Then plug your printer's cable into the remaining connector on the back of the Zip drive. Make sure the Zip drive is powered up.

Installation

1. Ensure that the kernel has SCSI support, and that the `ppa` module is installed under the `/lib/modules/2.0.xx` directory.
2. While logged on as the root operator, open the file `conf.modules`, found under the `/etc` directory, and enter the following:

   ```
   alias block-major-8 ppa
   ```

   This line tells the `kerneld` daemon to autoload the parallel-port driver, `ppa.o`, when the drive device, `/dev/sda`, is requested after Linux is running.
3. Load and edit either the `rc.local` or the `rc.sysinit` file under the `/etc/rc.d` directory, and enter the following line:

   ```
   /sbin/insmod ppa
   ```

   This line loads the `ppa` driver while Linux boots. Save the file.
4. Insert a Zip disk into the drive, and restart Linux.

5. When Linux reboots, look for the SCSI device to be detected. If the boot messages scroll by too quickly, use the `dmesg` command to read the system startup messages:

```
# dmesg ¦ less
```

   Look for lines similar to the following:

```
scsi0 : PPA driver version 0.26 using 4-bit mode on port
0x378.
scsi : 1 host.
  Vendor: IOMEGA    Model: ZIP 100        Rev: D.17
  Type:   Direct-Access                   ANSI SCSI
revision: 02
Detected scsi removable disk sda at scsi0, channel 0, id
6, lun 0
SCSI device sda: hdwr sector= 512 bytes. Sectors= 196608
[96 MB] [0.1 GB]
sda: Write Protect is off
sda: sda4
```

6. Decide what type of file system to install on the Zip disk.
   - If you prefer to use a preformatted Zip disk for DOS, create an entry in the Linux file system table database for either `msdos` or `vfat`. The file `fstab`, found under the `/etc` directory, contains a database of the different file systems, and specifies how the `mount` command should handle different storage devices, such as the type of file system used, or where to mount the device on the file system.

     Use two different entries if you use different file systems on your Zip disks (you don't have to, but it may be easier to remember what type of file system is mounted where). For example, a preformatted DOS Zip disk may have an entry like the following:

```
/dev/sda4         /mnt/zip          vfat
defaults,noauto 0 0
```

     This entry tells the `mount` command to mount the Zip disk using the `vfat` file system at the `/mnt/zip` directory.
   - To use a Linux native file system, first make sure you're logged on as the root operator, then eject the currently inserted Zip disk and insert a new disk into the drive.

Format the Zip disk by executing the following command:

```
# mke2fs /dev/sda
```

The `mke2fs` command formats the disk for Linux, using the `ext2` file system. After the disk has been formatted, create an entry in the `/etc/fstab` file, specifying the device, mount point, file system, and other options, as shown here:

```
/dev/sda4          /mnt/zipln        ext2
defaults,noauto 0 0
```

This `fstab` entry tells the `mount` command to mount the Zip disk as a native Linux partition at the `/mnt/zipln` directory.

7. After saving the changes to the `fstab` file, restart Linux. After booting, make sure the Zip drive was recognized during startup. To mount the disk with the `ext2` file system, use one of the following command lines:

```
# mount /mnt/zipln
# mount -t ext2 /dev/sda4 /mnt/zipln
```

Either command will mount the disk. To mount the DOS Zip disk, first `unmount` the Linux Zip disk like so:

```
# umount /mnt/zipln
```

Eject the disk, and then mount the DOS Zip disk with one of the following:

```
# mount /mnt/zip
# mount -t vfat /dev/sda4 /mnt/zip
```

Either command line will mount the Zip disk at the `/mnt/zip` directory.

SEE ALSO

- *For details on using the* `mount` *command, see page 115.*
- *For details on using a graphical interface to the file system table, read about the* `cabaret` *utility on page 106.*

File systems: Use `vfat` for Windows 95

Linux users with a Windows 95 partition will probably want to use the `vfat` file system type for DOS-formatted Zip disks. You'll benefit by being able to use 32-character filenames either for Linux or Windows 95 files copied to the Zip disk.

Power and printing

The Zip drive must be plugged in to allow use of the printer. The printer pass-through port is active only when the power is on. See your Zip drive manual or technical documentation for other requirements.

Printing with a Parallel-Port Zip Drive

If you use the parallel-port Zip drive, you cannot print and use the Zip drive at the same time, even though the printer might be attached to the drive. However, you can alternate between the two devices by using the `rmmod` and `insmod` module utilities to unload or load the `ppa` and `lp` kernel modules.

Printing with a parallel-port Zip drive

1. To print while using a Zip disk, first unmount the Zip disk. Then remove the `ppa` driver from the kernel, and activate the printer by using the `insmod` command:

   ```
   # umount /mnt/zip
   # rmmod ppa
   # insmod lp
   ```

2. To return to using the Zip drive after printing, unload the line-printer module, reload the `ppa` driver, and remount the drive:

   ```
   # rmmod lp
   # insmod ppa
   # mount /mnt/zip
   ```

These sequences can be combined into a shell script for convenience (I've called the script in Listing 8.1 `Zip` because there is a Linux file-compression utility called *zip*, and Linux recognizes case in filenames). The script works by mounting or unmounting a Zip disk and then loading or unloading the printer or `ppa` drivers according to the print or disk command-line options.

LISTING 8.1 Zip drive shell script

```
#!/bin/bash
option=$1
if [ $option  = "h" ]
then /bin/echo "usage: Zip [h]¦[print]¦[disk]"
fi

if [ $option = "print" ]
then
     /bin/echo "unmounting Zip disk"
     /bin/umount /mnt/zip
     /bin/echo "unloading ppa driver"
```

```
        /sbin/rmmod ppa
        /bin/echo "loading line-printer driver"
            /sbin/insmod lp
        /bin/echo "done"
fi
if [ $option = "disk" ]
then
        /bin/echo "unloading line-printer driver"
        /sbin/rmmod lp
        /bin/echo "loading ppa driver"
        /sbin/insmod ppa
        /bin/echo "mounting Zip disk"
        /bin/mount /mnt/zip
        /bin/echo "done"
fi
```

Enter this script by using your favorite text editor, and then make the script executable by using the `chmod` command:

```
# chmod +x Zip
```

SEE ALSO:

➤ *For details on installing a printer, see page 74.*

➤ *For details about writing your own shell programs, see page 365.*

After you copy this file to the `/usr/local/bin` directory, alternate between printing or using a Zip disk by using the disk or print command-line options, as follows:

```
# Zip disk
unloading line-printer driver
loading ppa driver
mounting Zip disk
done
# Zip print
unmounting zip disk
unloading ppa driver
loading line-printer driver
done
```

Feel free to expand or customize this script, but remember that the mount point for the `/dev/sda4` partition listed in the shell script should match the mount point specified in the Zip drive's `/etc/fstab` entry.

Ejecting Zip Disks and Password- and Read-Write-Protecting Zip Disks

Use the `ziptool` command to take advantage of some of the unique features of the Zip drive, such as read-write or password protection. Several versions of this program exist for Linux—and go by the same name—but all perform these basic functions:

- Eject an unmounted Zip disk.
- Report on read-write protection of an unmounted Zip disk.
- Toggle read-write protection of a unmounted Zip disk.
- Enable or disable password protection of an unmounted, write-enabled Zip disk

For a copy of one of the `ziptool` programs, browse the following Web sites:

http://www.cnet.com/~bwillmot

http://www.torque.net/ziptool.html

ftp://ftp.funet.fi/pub/Linux/images/RedHat-contrib/i386

Mirko Kraft's version of `ziptool` (which also handles Iomega Jaz drives) has five command-line options. To use `ziptool`, specify one of the options followed by the device volume name (`/dev/sda`), not the device partition name (`/dev/sda4`).

Ejecting a Zip disk

1. Unmount the Zip disk by using the `umount` command followed by the pathname of the Zip disk's mount point:
   ```
   # umount /mnt/zip
   ```
2. To eject the disk, use `ziptool`'s `-e` (eject) option:
   ```
   # ziptool -e /dev/sda
   ```
   Use this `ziptool` option to physically eject a Zip disk.

Password-protecting a Zip disk

1. Password-protecting a Zip disk requires that a disk be inserted into the Zip drive but not mounted. If the drive is mounted, first unmount the disk with the `umount` command.
2. To check on the status of the disk, and to get a report on the password or read-write status, use `ziptool`'s `-s` (status) option:

```
# ziptool -s /dev/sda
ziptool: medium is not protected.
```

3. To password-protect and enable read-only protection of a Zip disk, use the `-rp` option, like so:

```
# ziptool -rp /dev/sda
Password: mypasswd
ziptool: medium is password write-protected.
```

To delete password protection and enable writing to the disk, use the `-rw` (read-write) option:

```
# ziptool -rw /dev/sda
Password: mypasswd
ziptool: medium is not protected.
```

Remember your Zip disk's password

If you forget the password when you protect a Zip disk with `ziptool`, the disk will have to be reformatted before it can be used again for storage (otherwise, it makes a nice—but expensive—coffee-table coaster).

Read-write protecting a Zip disk

1. To make the Zip disk write-protected, use the `-ro` (read-only) option:

```
# ziptool -ro /dev/sda
ziptool: medium is write-protected.
```

2. To toggle the read-write protection, use the `ziptool` command with the `-rw` option:

```
# ziptool -rw /dev/sda
ziptool: medium is not protected.
```

CHAPTER 9

Enabling a PC Card Device

By Bill Ball

Adding PC cards to your computer

Enabling PC card service in Linux

Configuring PC cards for Linux

Using the `cardmgr` command to control PC cards

Enabling PCMCIA Services

Newer Linux kernels with support for loadable and unloadable code modules have made life a lot easier for laptop users with special devices such as a PCMCIA, or PC card. Linux laptop users are a special breed and depend on hardware-specific built-in interfaces that cannot be changed on the computer's motherboard. Fortunately, Linux supports many of these devices through the `kerneld` and `cardmgr` daemons, started after bootup, which automatically load and unload needed modules as devices are inserted or reinserted.

SEE ALSO

➤ *To learn more about the Linux kernel and module control, see page 577.*

To use PC cards or services with Red Hat Linux, you should install the `pcmcia` package, which is found under your CD-ROM's `Redhat/RPMS` directory. Use the `rpm` command and the `-i` (install) command-line option to install the package, like so:

```
# rpm -i pcmcia-cs-2.9.11-7
```

This command line installs the following:

- The `pcmcia` configuration files and database under the `/etc/pcmcia` directory
- A directory containing loadable PC card modules under the `/lib/modules` directory
- Specialized startup scripts under the `/etc/rc.d` directory, used to load the PC card drivers
- Several different PC card programs
- Nearly 30 documentation files and manual pages

Some of the PC cards supported by the `cardmgr` daemon include the following:

- Ethernet cards
- Fast Ethernet adapters
- Token-ring adapters
- Wireless network adapters
- Modem and serial cards

- Memory cards
- SCSI interface adapters
- ATA/IDE CD-ROM interface adapters
- Multifunction cards, such as LAN/modem cards
- ATA/IDE drive cards
- Miscellaneous cards, such as Trimble's Mobile GPS (Global Positioning Service) card

SEE ALSO

➤ *To learn more about Linux and using serial ports and modems, see page 152.*
➤ *To learn about Linux networking services, see page 444.*

Determining Your PCMCIA Controller

In order to set up Linux for PC card service, first determine both the number of slots available for PC cards and the type of PC card controller installed on your computer. Use the `probe` command, found under the `/sbin` directory, to report the number of slots:

```
# probe
PCI bridge probe: Cirrus PD6729 found, 2 sockets.
```

Use the `probe` command's `-m` command-line option to find the type of controller chip used in your computer:

```
# probe -m
i82365
```

The type of controller chip should be either tcic or i82365; this information will be used to configure the `cardmgr` daemon.

Enabling PC card service

1. To enable PC card services for Linux, make sure you're logged on as the root operator, and then navigate to the `/etc/sysconfig` directory.
2. Open the file `pcmcia` using your favorite text editor. Enter the word **yes**, along with the type of PC card controller used in your computer (either i82365 or tcic; see the `probe -m` output):
   ```
   PCMCIA=yes
   PCIC=i82365
   ```

Will my PC card work with Linux?

To determine whether Linux supports your PC card, read the file `SUPPORTED.CARDS` in the `/usr/doc/pcmcia` directory. If you don't see your card listed, try it anyway! Many cards are supported even though they are not listed; even if your card is not recognized at startup, you might be able to configure it to enable it to work.

Details about configuring unrecognized cards are found in the `PCMCIA-HOWTO` page under the `/usr/doc/HOWTO` directory. For the latest version of the `PCMCIA-HOWTO`, a Linux PCMCIA programmer's guide, or a list of the latest supported PC cards, browse David Hinds' web pages at the following address:

`http://hyper.stanford.edu/HyperNews/get/pcmcia/home.html`

```
PCIC_OPTS=
CORE_OPTS=
```

3. Save the file after making your changes.
4. Make sure your PC card(s) is properly inserted, and restart Linux.
5. While rebooting, listen for a series of beeps, which indicate whether your PC cards are recognized and configured by the `cardmgr` daemon. See Table 9.1 for the codes.

SEE ALSO

➤ *To find out how to reboot Linux, see page 10.*

TABLE 9.1 *cardmgr* daemon beep codes

Number/Type of Beep	Indication
One beep	PC card ejected
Two high beeps	PC card identified and configured during booting
High beep, lower beep	PC card identified, not configured during booting
Low beep	PC card not identified
Two high beeps	PC card inserted
Two high beeps	PC card service uninstalled during reboot or shut down

Note that some cards, such as flash memory, drive cards, or CD-ROM adapters, also require proper entries in the Linux file system table, `/etc/fstab`, before you can use the device.

SEE ALSO

➤ *To learn how to use the* `/etc/fstab` *database or file system table, see page 115.*

Using the *cardmgr* Command

The `cardmgr` daemon is used to monitor your computer's PC card sockets for inserted or removed cards and will load or unload the device needed for your PC card. The proper driver is found in the `cardmgr`'s database of PC cards, in the file `config` under the `/etc/pcmcia` directory. The database entry for your card tells the cardmgr daemon which code module (code modules are found under the /lib/modules directory) to load or unload.

Listing Your PC Card and Drivers

The cardmgr daemon creates and updates a system table called stab under the /var/run directory, when starting up or when PC cards are inserted or ejected. To see a list of the current PC cards and drivers in use, look in this stab system table like so:

```
# cat /var/run/stab
socket 0: empty
socket 1: Serial or Modem Card
1       serial  serial_cs       0       ttyS1   4       65
```

This particular stab file shows that two PC card sockets are available (socket 0 and 1) and that socket 1 contains a serial or modem card that uses the serial_cs code module (found under the /lib/modules directory) to provide serial service for the /dev/ttyS1 device. If another card is inserted, the cardmgr daemon does the following:

1. It notes the insertion.
2. It looks up the card in the /etc/pcmcia/config database.
3. It attempts to load the appropriate module.
4. It beeps twice if the card is recognized and configured.

The /var/run/stab file is then updated with this new information, and might look like the following:

```
# cat /var/run/stab
socket 0: ATA/IDE Fixed Disk Card
0       fixed   fixed_cs        0       hdc     22      0
socket 1: Serial or Modem Card
1       serial  serial_cs       0       ttyS1   4       65
```

This shows that a fixed disk card in socket 0 was detected, recognized, and configured as a hard drive, using the /dev/hdc volume, while the serial or modem card, using the /dev/ttyS1 serial port, still resides in socket 1.

Disabling *cardmgr* Command Event Notification

After you've determined that your PC cards are being properly recognized, you can silence any cardmgr beep notification by editing the file `pcmcia`, found under the `/etc/rc.d/init.d` directory. Use the `-q` (quiet) command-line option, where the `cardmgr` command is used in the `pcmcia` script. After this change, you won't hear any beeps when the `cardmgr` command is used to recognize and configure your PC card(s) while booting Linux.

Disabling PC card notification

1. Make sure you're logged on as the root operator. If you use the pico text editor, use the `-w` (disable word wrap) command-line option (so as not to disturb script structure).
2. Open the file `/etc/rc.d/init.d/pcmcia` for editing by executing the following command:
```
# pico -w /etc/rc.d/init.d/pcmcia
```
3. Look for the portion of the script containing the `cardmgr` command, like so:
```
/sbin/cardmgr $CARDMGR_OPTS
```
4. Add the `-q` (quiet) option to the `cardmgr` command line:
```
/sbin/cardmgr -q $CARDMGR_OPTS
```
5. Save the changes and exit.
6. Restart Linux.

SEE ALSO

➤ *To learn how to use the pico text editor, see page 50.*

Using the *cardctl* Command

Use the `cardctl` (card control) command to control your PC card slots. You can also use this command to gather information about your PC cards or to load a PC card *scheme* to change the types of cards that are installed in your computer. The default scheme, located under the `/var/run` directory, is named `pcmcia-scheme`. Details about using PC card schemes are found in `PCMCIA-HOWTO`, under the `/usr/doc/HOWTO` directory.

Obtaining the Status of PC Cards

To get the status of your PC card(s), use `cardctl`'s `status` option and, optionally, a card socket number, like so:

```
# cardctl status
socket 0:
  Function 0:
  card present, ready, battery low
socket 1:
  Function 0:
  card present
```

The `cardctl` command reports on the number of sockets and the status of any cards currently inserted and in use in each socket.

Listing Your PC Card Configuration

To see your PC card's configuration, use the `cardctl` command with the `config` option, as follows:

```
# cardctl config
socket 0:
  Vcc = 5.0, Vpp1 = 0.0, Vpp2 = 0.0
  Card type is memory and I/O
  IRQ 3 is exclusive, level mode, enabled
  Function 0:
    Config register base = 0x0200
      Option = 0x41, status = 0000, pin = 0000, copy = 0000
    I/O window 1: 0x0100 to 0x010f, auto sized
socket 1:
  Vcc = 5.0, Vpp1 = 0.0, Vpp2 = 0.0
  Card type is memory and I/O
  IRQ 9 is exclusive, level mode, enabled
  Speaker output is enabled
  Function 0:
    Config register base = 0x0300
      Option = 0x61, status = 0x08
    I/O window 1: 0x02f8 to 0x02ff, 8 bit
```

This information can be handy if you need to see power settings, interrupts, or other registry information about inserted, configured, or active cards. For specific details about configuring PC cards, see the section titled "Overview of the PCMCIA Configuration Scripts" in David Hinds' `PCMCIA-HOWTO`, found under the `/usr/doc/HOWTO` directory. For the latest PC card support information, check out the following site:

http://hyper.stanford.edu/HyperNews/get/pcmcia/home.html

Ejecting a PC Card

Although the cardmgr daemon will automatically unload the required software modules needed to configure and use a PC card after the card is physically ejected, you can also use the cardctl command to perform a software eject of the card and then cut power to the PC card's socket. This is a handy way for laptop users to save battery power without resorting to physical removal of the PC card.

To eject a PC card using socket 0, use cardctl's eject command, like this:

```
# cardctl eject 0
```

This command will eject and power off socket 0 of your PC card interface.

Inserting a PC Card

Although the cardmgr daemon automatically recognizes and configures a supported PC card after physical insertion, you can also use cardctl's insert command to restore the card's socket after you perform a software eject. This saves you the trouble of physically removing and then reinserting the PC card to get the cardmgr daemon to configure and reinstall the card.

To perform a software PC card insert for socket 0, use the insert command, like so:

```
# cardctl insert 0
```

This command line performs a software insert of a card in the PC card socket 0.

Suspending and Restoring PC Card Power

Another method of saving battery power for laptop users with PC cards is to suspend and restore power to a card. The cardctl command allows you to shut down and disable a socket with the suspend command, like this:

```
# cardctl suspend 0
```

This shuts down and powers off socket 0. To restore this socket for use after you've executed the `suspend` command, use the `resume cardctl` command-line option, as follows:

```
# cardctl resume 0
```

Do not disable sockets while in use!

Do not use the `eject` or `suspend cardctl` command option while a PC card device is in use. You can scramble the structure of a memory disk or cause your computer to hang (although you can kill the offending processes). Use the `cardctl` command judiciously, and make sure no other applications are using your device before you eject or power off a PC card's socket.

CHAPTER

10

Adding a Pointing Device

By Bill Ball

Adding a Mouse

Mouse support for Linux is fairly extensive. A wide variety of devices is supported. Although you can use a keyboard to control your mouse pointer when using the X Window System, a mouse or other hardware device to control the pointer is indispensable. You'll use your mouse to pull down menus, press buttons in dialog boxes, and copy and paste text between programs.

When you install Red Hat Linux, you're asked to confirm the creation of a symbolic link, called /dev/mouse, that points to the correct pointing device. To see the device that /dev/mouse points to for your system, use the `ls`, or list directory, command like this:

```
# ls -l /dev/mouse
lrwxrwxrwx    1 root      root              5 Mar  9 07:54
/dev/mouse -> psaux
```

This shows that /dev/mouse points to the `psaux`, or PS/2 mouse device. However, you can install other pointing devices, or configure your mouse in many ways.

SEE ALSO

➤ *To learn more about the X Window System, see page 260.*

➤ *To learn more about copying and pasting text in X11, see page 317.*

Configuring a Mouse with the *mouseconfig* Command

The `mouseconfig` command, shown in Figure 10.1, automatically determines the type of mouse installed on your system (if it is connected), and configures your mouse by creating the necessary links to the required mouse device. The program looks for a mouse attached to any available serial, SCSI, IDE, or PS/2 port. You must be logged on as the root operator to run the `mouseconfig` command.

This program has two different operating modes and four different command-line options. You can also use the name of a mouse with `mouseconfig` to automatically set your mouse type. `mouseconfig` recognizes the following mouse names: microsoft, mouseman, mousesystems, ps/2, msbm, logibm, atibm, logitech, mmseries, and mmhittab. For example, to automatically create a PS/2 mouse, use `mouseconfig` like this:

```
# mouseconfig ps/2
```

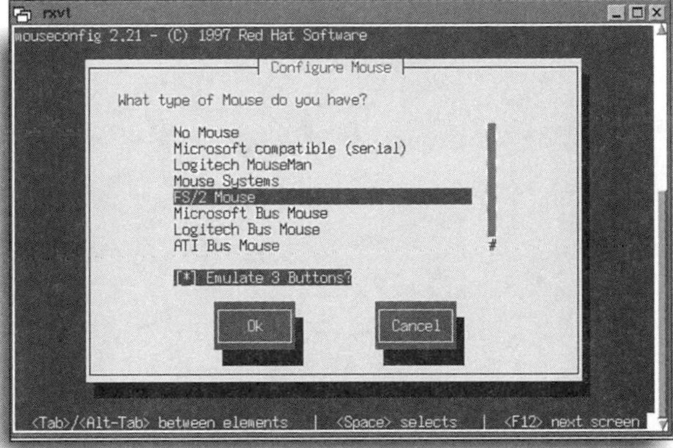

FIGURE 10.1
The `mouseconfig` command probes your system automatically for a mouse.

Configuring a mouse

1. Log on as the root operator.
2. To automatically detect an installed mouse, use the `mouseconfig`:

   ```
   # mouseconfig
   ```

   If you have a PS/2 mouse, `mouseconfig` reports a probe result as shown in Figure 10.1. (The result will look different if you have a different device, such as a serial mouse.)
3. Press Enter to configure your mouse, and `mouseconfig` quits.
4. Use `mouseconfig` with the `--noprobe` and `--expert` options to manually set your mouse type, like this:

   ```
   # mouseconfig --noprobe --expert
   ```

   `mouseconfig` program presents a scrolling list of different pointing devices, as shown in Figure 10.2.
5. Choose your mouse by highlighting its type.
6. If you use the X Window System and your mouse has only two buttons, press the Tab key to move the cursor to the `Emulate 3 Buttons` item.

   If you want your two-button mouse to emulate three buttons, press the spacebar to select or unselect three-button emulation (in which simultaneously pressing the left and right buttons simulates a middle-button press).

Otherwise, press the Tab key to move the cursor to the OK button, and press Enter to save your configuration.

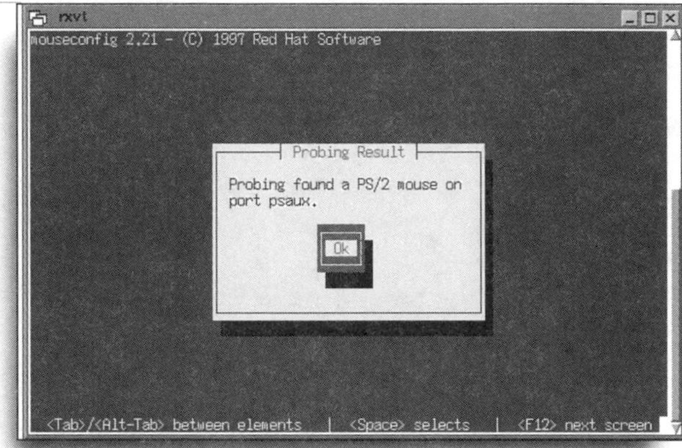

FIGURE 10.2
The `mouseconfig` command can be used to automatically probe and configure or manually configure your system for a pointing device.

Configuring a Synaptics Touchpad

If you use a laptop for Linux and have a Synaptics touchpad, use the `tpconfig` command to configure your touchpad. The `tpconfig` program, by C. Scott Ananian, can be found by browsing to the following web address:

http://www.pdos.lcs.mit.edu/~cananian/Synaptics/

Use the `tpconfig` program to configure your touchpad button mode, taps, tap mode (such as no taps for left mouse-button presses), or pressure sensitivity.

Installing and configuring the *tpconfig* command

1. Download the tpconfig archive. Log on as the root operator and uncompress the archive using the `tar` command:
   ```
   # tar xvzf synaptics-latest.tar.gz
   ```
2. Change directory to the software's directory:
   ```
   # cd syn*
   ```
3. Run the included configure shell script:
   ```
   # configure
   ```

4. Use the `make` command followed by the word `install` to compile, build, and install the `tpconfig` command in the `/usr/local/bin` directory:

```
# make install
```

5. To configure your touchpad, you must not be running X11 or the `gpm` mouse daemon (which supports cut and paste for console displays). To stop the `gpm` daemon, search for the process number of the `gpm` daemon by using the `ps` and `fgrep` programs in a pipe:

```
# ps aux ¦ fgrep gpm
root        220  0.0  0.1   732    40  ?  S   11:21
0:00 gpm -t PS/2
```

Then use the `kill` command with the `gpm` process number (returned from our example above), like this:

```
# kill -9 220
```

6. To get information about your touchpad, use the `-i`, or info option:

```
# tpconfig -i
Synaptics Touchpad, firmware rev. 3.5 [Standard OEM]
Sensor: Standard-size module
Geometry: Standard module
Rightside-up/Landscape New-style abs-mode packets.
Corner taps disabled. Tap mode: Tap and non-locking drag
Edge motion only during drag.      Z-threshold 3 of 7
Relative mode                            Low  sample rate.
2 button mode            Corner tap is right button click
```

7. The `tpconfig` command has 11 different command-line options, but it is easy to use. For example, to turn off the tap mode, use the `-t` option, followed by the number `0`:

```
# tpconfig -t0
```

SEE ALSO

➤ *To learn more about file compression and archiving, see page 542.*

➤ *For more information about using the* `make` *command or other programming utilities, see page 382.*

Installing a Joystick

A *joystick* is a handy pointing device, especially when playing arcade-style games or using flight simulators, such as the *fly8* simulator (shown in Figure 10.3).

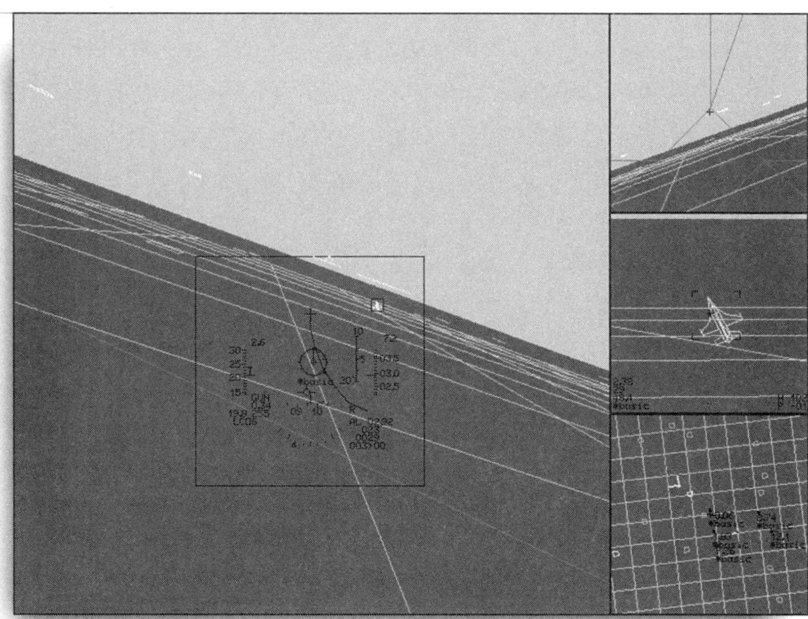

FIGURE 10.3
Using a joystick in the X Window System under Linux makes using the fly8 flight simulator easier.

In order to use a joystick with Linux, your computer must support the joystick hardware, usually indicated by a mini-plug on the back of the main box. You also need to download and install software support for your joystick, found in the compressed archive `joyfixed.tgz`, which can be found at the following web address:

`ftp://sunsite.unc.edu/pub/Linux/kernel/patches/console/joyfixed.tgz`

Getting the joystick driver in `rpm` format

Red Hat Linux users do not have to go through the previously described process; a compiled module that can be installed by using the **`rpm`** command can be found at the following web address:

`ftp://sunsite.unc.edu/pub/Linux/distributions/redhat/contrib/i386/joystick-0.8.0-1.i386.rpm`

Installing the joystick module and utilities

1. Download the joystick `rpm` file.
2. Log on as the root operator.
3. Use the `rpm` command's `-i`, or install, option, to install the joystick module, `joystick.o`, the `js` manual page, and the `js`

and jscal utilities:

```
# rpm -i joystick-0.8.0-1.i386.rpm
```

SEE ALSO

- *For more information about using the* rpm *command, see page 520.*
- *For details about downloading files, such as* rpm *archives, see page 198.*
- *To learn more about copying and pasting text in X11, see page 317.*

Building the Joystick Module

Before you can use your joystick, you must build the joystick kernel module, joystick.o. This module is usually loaded when Linux is booted.

Building the *joystick.o* module

1. Log on as the root operator and download the joyfixed.tgz archive.
2. Uncompress the archive using the tar command:
   ```
   # tar xvzf joyfixed.tar
   ```
3. Navigate to the new joystick directory with the cd command:
   ```
   # cd joy*
   ```
4. Use the make command to compile the joystick.o kernel module:
   ```
   # make joystick.o
   ```
5. Use the mknod command (used to create devices) to create two joystick devices for use by the joystick.o module:
   ```
   # mknod /dev/js0 c 15 0
   # mknod /dev/js1 c 15 1
   ```
6. Copy the joystick.o module to the /lib/modules directory:
   ```
   # cp joystick.o /lib/modules
   ```
7. To use the joystick modules, use your favorite text editor, such as pico, to open the rc.local file under the /etc/rc.d directory:
   ```
   # pico -w /etc/rc.d/rc.local
   ```
8. Insert a line to tell Linux to use the insmod command to load your joystick module:
   ```
   insmod /lib/modules/joystick.o
   ```

9. Save the file and restart Linux. When Linux reboots, you should see a message similar to the following:

```
js_init: found 2 joysticks
```

SEE ALSO

➤ *To learn more about the* `pico` *editor, see page 50.*
➤ *For more information about loadable kernel modules, see page 577.*

Configuring a Joystick

Two programs, `js` and `jscal`, are included with the joystick driver. Use the `js` program followed by a number corresponding to your joystick device (in this case `0`) to test your joystick:

```
# js 0
```

The program runs continuously, reporting on button presses and the location of your cursor while you move the joystick. Press Ctrl+C to quit the program.

Use the `jscal` command to adjust your joystick by specifying the joystick number on the command line, like this:

```
# jscal 0
```

The `jscal` program asks you to move your joystick to the lower-right corner, and then press a joystick button. Press Ctrl+C to quit the program.

CHAPTER

11

Configuring a Modem and Fax Service

By Bill Ball

Selecting a modem and modem port

Creating the `/dev/modem` device

Configuring a modem with the `ln` and `modemtool` commands

Getting serial port information with the `setserial` command

Configuring for dial-in and fax service

Sending and receiving a fax

Selecting a Modem for Linux

Many different types of modems work with Linux. In order to use a modem, you must first determine which serial port is connected to your modem. Serial ports can be found on the back of a desktop computer or internal PC serial board, or as a PC card or RJ-11 jack on the back of a laptop. Serial port devices for Linux are found in the `/dev` directory, with filenames containing `cua` or `tty`. Table 11.1 lists the eight most common serial devices, along with the corresponding "traditional" DOS port names and addresses. If you're concerned about your modem, check the Red Hat Linux Support Area at the following address:

`http://www.redhat.com`

PC card serial ports and modems

PC card owners must first enable PCMCIA services to get Linux to recognize and configure a PC card. Fortunately, most serial and modem PC cards work under Linux with few problems. For details about how to install PCMCIA services, refer to Chapter 9, "Enabling a PC Card Device," and read the `PCMCIA-HOWTO`, found under the `/usr/doc` directory.

Will my modem work with Linux?

Although nearly any modem works with Linux, there are at least two types to avoid: WinModems and Mwave. Both of these modems require special drivers for Windows that are not available for Linux. Although you can use the Mwave board to support sound by booting Linux from DOS, you should avoid any type of modem or serial board that requires special drivers (at least until manufacturers recognize that Linux is a part of mainstream computing). "Plug-and-Pray" devices might also work, but in general, you should stick with "normal" modems to avoid trouble.

TABLE 11.1 **Linux serial devices and DOS port addresses**

Linux Device	DOS Port and Address
`/dev/cua0, /dev/ttyS0`	COM1, 0x3F8 IRQ 4
`/dev/cua1, /dev/ttyS1`	COM2, 0x2F8 IRQ 3
`/dev/cua2, /dev/ttyS2`	COM3, 0x3E8 IRQ 4
`/dev/cua3, /dev/ttyS3`	COM4, 0x2E8 IRQ 3

Looking at Table 11.1, you'll notice that the `cua` and `tty` devices with the same number correspond to the same serial port. These devices are nearly the same, but the `cua` devices allow you to call out with a communications program while another program (such as `ugetty`, discussed later in this chapter in the section "Enabling Dial-In Service") monitors the modem port for incoming calls.

Using the *dmesg* Command to Check Serial Port Status

Use the `dmesg` command to determine whether your serial ports are enabled. The `dmesg` command displays the `dmesg` startup log, found under the `/var/log` directory. Look for lines in the `dmesg` output that list any recognized serial drivers and ports, such as the following:

```
Serial driver version 4.13 with no serial options enabled
tty00 at 0x03f8 (irq = 4) is a 16550A
tty03 at 0x02e8 (irq = 3) is a 16550A
```

This output shows that Linux found two serial ports at COM1 and COM4. If a serial driver or port is not listed, make sure that serial-line support is enabled for your Linux kernel, or that the proper serial devices exist under the `/dev` directory. Read the `MAKEDEV` manual page for details on how to create serial devices.

SEE ALSO

➤ *For the details about enabling serial support, see Chapter 32, "Managing the Kernel."*

Testing Your Modem with the *echo* Command

You can test your modem by using the `echo` command to send a command string through a serial port.

Testing your modem

1. Log on as the root operator.
2. Make sure your modem is switched on, or if you have a modem card, that it is plugged in.
3. Check any serial cable connections for your external modem.
4. Make sure your phone lines are properly connected to the modem or modem card.
5. Choose the proper `cua` serial device corresponding to your modem port. If necessary, find the DOS COM port used, and then choose the device listed in Table 11.1.
6. Type the following at the console or terminal window, replacing *X* with the serial port you want to test:
   ```
   echo "ATDT/n" >/dev/cuaX
   ```
7. Wait at least 10 seconds; you should then hear a dial tone.

SEE ALSO

➤ *To learn more about the echo command, see page 33.*

Your modem's AT commands

Not all modems possess the same AT command set, and minor variations exist between modems from different manufacturers. The best reference to use is your modem manual, which should specify your modem's AT command set in detail.

Creating the */dev/modem* Device

You don't have to always remember which serial port is connected to your modem. An easy way to determine what port your modem is attached to is to create a device called `/dev/modem`. You'll find a GUI utility that you can use with Red Hat Linux to create this device, or you can create one from the command line using the `ln` command.

Creating */dev/modem* with the Control Panel Client

The Red Hat X11 Control Panel client has a button you can click to set up your modem. This button uses the `modemtool` client, which you can also run from the command line of a terminal window.

Using the Control Panel client

1. Log on as the root operator. You must also run the X Window System.
2. From the command line of a terminal window, start the Control Panel client:
   ```
   # control-panel &
   ```
3. Click the `modemtool` button in the Control Panel (see Figure 11.1).

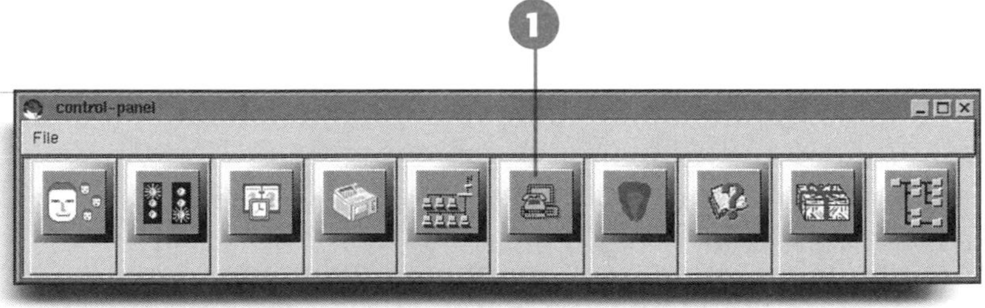

FIGURE 11.1
Click the `modemtool` icon.

1 modemtool

4. The `modemtool` client creates a window with a list of serial ports, as shown in Figure 11.2. Select the port connected to your modem, and then click OK.

SEE ALSO

➤ *To learn more about symbolic links and how to use the* `ln` *command, see page 40.*

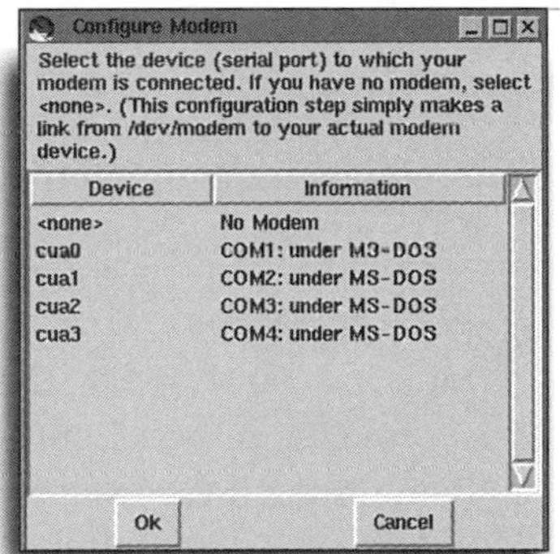

FIGURE 11.2
The `modemtool` dialog box, run from the X11 Control Panel client, creates a symbolic link called `/dev/modem`.

The `modemtool` client creates a symbolic link, or file, called `/dev/modem`, which points to your modem's serial port.

Creating */dev/modem* with the *ln* Command

You can also create the `/dev/modem` device from the command line by using the `ln` (link) command. To create `/dev/modem` if your modem is connected to COM1, log on as the root operator and enter the following:

```
# ln -s /dev/cua0 /dev/modem
```

This command line creates a symbolic link, `/dev/modem`, which points to the COM1 serial port. Check this link with the `ls` (list directory) command, like so:

```
# ls -l /dev/modem
lrwxrwxrwx   1 root     root            9 Feb 19 07:56
/dev/modem -> /dev/cua1
```

Getting Serial Port Information with the *setserial* Command

The `setserial` command, found under the `/bin` directory, reports on the status, type, and configuration of the four default serial ports. This command can also be used to configure how the kernel recognizes additional serial ports or to alter how the kernel acts with an existing port.

To get information about a specified port, use the `-a` (all available information) option followed by the port's device name, like so:

```
# setserial -a /dev/modem
/dev/modem, Line 1, UART: 16550A, Port: 0x02f8, IRQ: 2
        Baud_base: 115200, close_delay: 50, divisor: 0
        closing_wait: 3000, closing_wait2: infinte
        Flags: spd_normal skip_test
```

This information shows the device, line, hardware chip, port, and interrupt used by the specified port. The highest speed supported by the serial port, along with other operational features such as the delay used before closing a connection, is also listed.

Serial port technical details

For technical information regarding Linux and serial ports, see the `Serial-HOWTO` and `Serial-Programming-HOWTO` under the `/usr/doc` directory.

Enabling Dial-In Service

Linux supports dial-in service. This means that you can call in from another computer and log on over the phone. If you have two modems and phone lines for your computer, you can log on and then either dial out on the spare phone line or use Internet services if the spare line maintains an active Internet connection.

Setting up Linux for dial-in service requires the following:

- A phone line
- A serial port and attached modem

It also requires that you do the following:

- Configure the modem.
- Edit the system initialization table.
- Restart Linux.

Use caution when editing system files

To set up your system to accept incoming calls, you must edit the system's initialization table, `/etc/inittab`. If you edit this file incorrectly, you might hang your system. Keep a boot disk handy, and copy the `/etc/inittab` file before making changes. For details about creating an emergency boot disk, see the section titled "Performing Hard Drive Recovery" in Chapter 29, "Managing the File System."

Configuring Linux for Dial-in Service

Configuring Linux for dialing in is easy. You can perform one of the first steps, configuring the modem, while running Linux (if you're familiar with the kermit or minicom communications programs) or by using DOS or Windows communications programs.

Creating dial-in service

1. Attach your modem to a recognized serial port. Make sure the modem is connected properly and turned on.

2. Start a communications program. Use the AT command &V to display your modem's profile, like this:

```
AT&V
ACTIVE PROFILE:
B1 E1 L1 M1 N1 Q0 T V1 W0 X4 Y0 &C1 &D2
&G0 &J0 &K3 &Q5 &R1 &S0 &T5 &X0 &Y0 ~Z0
S00:000 S01:000 S02:043 S03:013 S04:010
S05:008 S06:004 S07:045 S08:002 S09:006
S10:014 S11:095 S12:050 S18:000 S25:005
S26:001 S36:007 S37:000 S38:020 S44:020
S46:138 S48:007 S51:012 S52:012 S53:010
S54:010 S95:000
```

3. If your modem is set to the following, you're all set:

```
E1 Q0 V1 S0=0 &C1 &S0
```

If not, set your modem by using the following AT command string:

```
ATE1Q0V1S0=0&C1&S0&W
```

This command string configures your modem with the proper settings and then saves the configuration by using the &W command. Make sure your modem echoes an OK string.

4. Ensure that you're logged on as the root operator.

5. Using your favorite text editor, create a file called conf.uugetty.ttyS*X* in the /etc directory, in which *X* matches the device number of your modem's serial port (if your modem is connected to /dev/ttyS0, create the file conf.uugetty.ttyS0). Type the following:

```
ALTLOCK=cua0
ALTLINE=cua0
# line to initialize
INITLINE=cua0
# timeout in seconds before disconnect
TIMEOUT=60
# initialize modem
INIT="" AT\r OK\r\n
WAITFOR=RING
# modem connect
CONNECT="" ATA\r CONNECT\s\A
# delay in seconds before sending contents of /etc/issue
DELAY=1
```

Make sure values for ALTLOCK, ALTLINE, and INITLINE match your modem's serial port.

Set the TIMEOUT value to the amount of time in seconds you want your modem to wait for a carriage return from the caller before disconnecting.

Set the DELAY value to the amount of time in seconds you want before the file /etc/issue, or welcome text, is echoed to the caller.

6. Save the file and exit your text editor.
7. Open your system's initialization table, inittab, under the /etc directory. Look for these lines:

```
# Run gettys in standard runlevels
1:12345:respawn:/sbin/mingetty tty1
2:2345:respawn:/sbin/mingetty tty2
3:2345:respawn:/sbin/mingetty tty3
4:2345:respawn:/sbin/mingetty tty4
5:2345:respawn:/sbin/mingetty tty5
6:2345:respawn:/sbin/mingetty tty6
```

Specifically, locate this line:

```
3:2345:respawn:/sbin/mingetty tty3
```

Change it to the following:

```
3:2345:respawn:/sbin/uugetty -d /etc/conf.uugetty.ttyS0
\ttyS0 38400 vt100
```

This change to inittab makes Linux run the uugetty command when you boot your system. The uugetty command uses the configuration file you created, watches for an incoming call on the specified serial port, and then answers when a modem is detected. If you'd like to support faster dial-in speeds, enter 57600 instead of 38400.

8. Save the file, exit the text editor, and restart your system.

SEE ALSO

➤ *To learn more about using the* /etc/inittab *file for the X Window System and the* xdm *chooser client, see page 260.*

After you restart Linux, the uugetty command constantly checks the /dev/ttyS1 serial port for incoming calls. When you call in, wait for the modem to connect, and then press Enter. Linux then echoes back a logon prompt.

Configuring Fax Service

If you have a fax modem, you should be able to send and receive faxes using Linux. Fax transmission and reception requires a fax modem and graphics translation of files to be sent and received. You should have your modem's technical documentation on hand, along with the `efax` software package. This software package includes the software and documentation shown in Table 11.2.

TABLE 11.2 The efax software package

File	Purpose
`/usr/bin/fax`	Comprehensive shell script to create, send, receive, view, and print faxes
`/usr/bin/efax`	Driver program to send and receive faxes
`/usr/bin/efix`	File conversion program
`/usr/man/man1/fax.1`	Fax script manual page
`/usr/man/man1/efax.1`	`efax` manual page
`/usr/man/man2/efix.1`	`efix` manual page
`/usr/doc/efax-0.8a`	Directory containing a README file

Fax service packages

You can use a number of other fax software packages to set up fax service for your Linux system, such as mgetty+sendfax, or the Hylafax network fax package. For more information about these software packages, look under the `/usr/doc` directory, or check your favorite Linux Internet web site. The following is one good place to look:

`ftp://sunsite.unc.edu/pub/Linux/apps/serialcomm/fax/`

Make sure to read the `fax`, `efax`, and `efix` manual pages, along with the README documentation before you start configuring your Linux system for fax service.

Configuring the *fax* Shell Script

Setting up for sending and receiving faxes involves editing the `/usr/bin/fax` shell script. You'll need to check some of the configuration lines, and you must edit other lines to customize your fax headers and specify your modem. The script contains easy-to-follow instructions, but the basic changes are outlined here.

Editing the *fax* shell script

1. After you've made sure you're logged on as the root operator, open the /usr/bin/fax shell script with your favorite text editor.
2. The /usr/bin/fax shell script lists the pathnames for the FAX, EFAX, and EFIX commands. Make sure the script has the correct pathnames for the efax programs, like this:
   ```
   FAX=/usr/bin/fax
   EFAX=/usr/bin/efax
   EFIX=/usr/bin/efix
   ```
3. Edit the entry specifying your modem's serial port:
   ```
   DEV=cua0
   ```
   Use the word modem if you've created the symbolic link /dev/modem. If your system is configured for dial-in use, enter the actual name of the device, such as cua0.
4. Specify the fax CLASS type your modem supports. Comment out the undesired CLASS by using the pound sign (#), and uncomment the desired CLASS by removing the pound sign:
   ```
   # CLASS=1
   CLASS=2
   # CLASS=2.0
   ```
   Make sure only one CLASS is selected, or uncommented.
5. Specify your phone number:
   ```
   FROM="1 202 555 1212"
   ```
6. Enter your name:
   ```
   NAME="William Ball"
   ```
7. Specify the default fax page size, again using the pound sign to comment out the undesired sizes, and by removing the pound sign in front of the proper size:
   ```
   PAGE=letter
   # PAGE=legal
   # PAGE=a4
   ```
   Ensure that only one size is specified.
8. Save the file and exit your text editor.

Testing Your Fax Configuration

Test your fax configuration and fax modem by using the fax script's `test` command-line option, like so:

```
# fax test
```

The `fax` script prints three pages of information to your display. A better way to see the test results is to redirect the output of the test to a file, like this:

```
# fax test > test.txt
```

Look for error messages in the output file. Common errors include specifying the wrong serial port for your fax modem and having more than one fax `CLASS` or default `PAGE` size specified.

Sending a Fax Using the *fax* Shell Script

Fax a text document using the `fax` script's `send` and `-l` command-line options, followed by a fax number and filename, like so:

```
# fax send -l afaxphonenumber test.txt
```

This command line sends a low-resolution fax to the specified fax number using the specified file. High-resolution faxes are sent by default if you don't use the `-l` command-line option.

Setting Up to Wait for Incoming Faxes

You can use the `fax` script to have your computer automatically wait for incoming faxes. Use the `fax` script's `wait` command-line option:

```
# fax wait &
```

The `fax` command uses your fax modem to answer incoming fax calls and then saves incoming faxes under the `/var/spool/fax` directory.

Checking the Status of Incoming or Outgoing Faxes

To make sure the `fax` script is waiting for faxes, use the `fax` command's `status` command-line option:

```
# fax status
```

To see if you've received any faxes, use the `fax` script's `queue` command:

```
# fax queue
```

This command line causes the `fax` script to list the contents of the `/var/spool/fax` directory.

Viewing Received Faxes

After checking the fax queue, use the `fax` script's `view` option along with a received fax's filename to read a fax:

```
# fax view 1204164646*
```

The `fax` command automatically runs the X11 xv graphic program to view or print your incoming faxes.

Printing a Received Fax

Although the X11 xv client can be used to print faxes while viewing, you can also use the `fax` script's `print` command-line option as an alternative way to print a fax:

```
# fax print 1204164646*
```

SEE ALSO

➤ *For more information about setting up your printer for Linux, see page 74.*

Deleting a Received Fax

To delete a fax, use the `fax` script's `rm` command-line option, like so:

```
# fax rm 120417243*
```

SEE ALSO

➤ *For more information about deleting files, see page 42.*

Be careful when deleting faxes

Always specify a fax filename, as returned by the `fax` script's `queue` option, when deleting a fax using the `rm` command-line option. This command can be dangerous, and can unnecessarily delete critical files, especially if used with the wildcard character (`*`). Use specific filenames when deleting faxes.

PART

III

Connecting to Your Internet Service Provider

CHAPTER

12

Connecting to Your Internet Service Provider

By Bill Ball

Setting up for a Point-to-Point Protocol (PPP) connection

Configuring PPP for your Internet service provider (ISP)

Starting a PPP connection

Closing a PPP connection

Checking PPP connections

Creating a PPP connection in X11

If you use the X Window System, you can use `netcfg`, the GUI system administration tool, to create a PPP connection network interface. The `netcfg` client is part of the Red Hat Linux Control Panel client, used by the root operator. For step-by-step details on using `netcfg`, see the section "Using the `netcfg` Tool" in Chapter 27, "Managing Network Connections."

Configuring a PPP Connection

Connecting to the Internet by using Linux and the serial-line Point-to-Point Protocol (PPP) is easy. If you follow the steps outlined in this chapter, you'll be able to quickly connect to and disconnect from the Internet through your Internet service provider (ISP). After you are connected, you can send and retrieve email, download files, read Usenet news, or use a web browser to surf World Wide Web sites.

SEE ALSO

➤ *To learn more about email, see page 180.*

➤ *To learn more about Web browsers, see page 212.*

➤ *For details about reading Usenet news, see page 227.*

In this chapter, you find the basic steps for checking your hardware, configuring your software, and connecting to your ISP, and commands that you can use to check your connection. You'll need the basic hardware required for modem connections, several standard Linux programs, and some technical information from your ISP in order to begin. These hardware and software items include the following:

- A working serial port and attached modem
- A Linux kernel supporting the PPP and TCP/IP protocols
- The ppp-2.2 software package, which includes the `pppd` daemon, the chat dialer program, associated scripts, and the `pppstats` command
- The minicom communications program (optional)
- An active account with an ISP supporting PPP (nearly all use PPP)

Setting up PPP and then connecting to your ISP involves several steps, including the following:

1. Check your serial port and modem.
2. Check your kernel for PPP and TCP/IP support.
3. Edit and customize the PPP connection scripts.

4. Edit or create required system configuration files.
5. Dial out and establish a PPP connection.
6. Check the connection.
7. Disconnect and shut down the PPP connection.

Checking Your Serial Port and Modem

To check your serial port and modem, you need a phone line, modem, and modem cable (if you have an external modem). If you know your modem works under Linux, you can skip to the next section, "Checking Your Linux Kernel and File System for PPP Support."

Checking the modem connection

1. Make sure your phone line is attached to your modem and that your modem is connected to your computer.
2. Pipe the output of the `dmesg` command through the `less` pager to determine whether your serial port is enabled and working:

   ```
   # dmesg ¦ less
   ```

3. Look for lines detailing serial driver information similar to these:

   ```
   Serial driver version 4.13 with no serial options
   enabled
   tty00 at 0x03f8 (irq = 4) is a 16550A
   tty03 at 0x02e8 (irq = 3) is a 16550A
   ```

4. If you don't find serial support, refer to Chapter 11, "Configuring a Modem and Fax Service," for details about configuring your modem. If you have defined a symbolic link called `/dev/modem` that points to your modem's serial port, test the modem and phone-line connection by using the `echo` command like this:

   ```
   # echo "ATDT\n" >/dev/modem
   ```

   You should hear a dial tone after a few seconds. If not, reread Chapter 11 to find out how to create the `/dev/modem` symbolic link.

SEE ALSO

➤ *To learn more about pipes, see page 21.*
➤ *For more details about installing and configuring a modem, see page 152.*

Checking Your Linux Kernel and File System for PPP Support

Your Linux kernel must support PPP in order to connect to your ISP. Support can be compiled into your kernel or loaded as a code module. The PPP module, `ppp.o`, is found under the `/lib/module/2.0.xx/net` directory (where *xx* is your kernel's version).

Checking for PPP support

1. Use the output of the `dmesg` command, piped through the `less` pager, to determine whether PPP support is enabled for your kernel:

```
# dmesg ¦ less
```

2. Look for lines detailing TCP/IP and PPP support similar to these:

```
Swansea University Computer Society TCP/IP for NET3.034
IP Protocols: IGMP, ICMP, UDP, TCP
PPP: version 2.2.0 (dynamic channel allocation)
PPP Dynamic channel allocation code copyright 1995
Caldera, Inc.
PPP line discipline registered.
```

3. If you do not see this support enabled, you must enable the TCP/IP and PPP networking support. This means that you must either ensure that the required modules or network services are enabled or rebuild the kernel with built-in support. See Chapter 27, "Managing Network Connections," and the section titled "Recompiling the Kernel" in Chapter 32, "Managing the Kernel," for details.

SEE ALSO

➤ *To learn more about the* `less` *pager, see page 33.*
➤ *To learn more about kernel modules, see page 577.*

SEE ALSO

➤ *For more details about installing networking support, see page 444.*

You also must ensure that the required PPP connection software and directories are installed on your system.

Checking for PPP software

1. Ensure that the `pppd` daemon, the `chat` dialing command, and the PPP connection scripts are installed by using the `ls` (list directory) command:

```
# ls /usr/sbin/pppd
/usr/sbin/pppd
# ls /usr/sbin/chat
/usr/sbin/chat
# ls /etc/ppp
chap-secrets      options        ppp-on-dialer
connect-errors    pap-secrets    ppp-on
ip-up             ppp-off
```

2. If you don't find these programs and scripts on your system or on your CD-ROM, you must find and download the PPP software (try **http://www.redhat.com**).

3. After you find the software, install the PPP package using the X11 `glint` client. If you're not running X11, use the Red Hat `rpm` (software package manager) like this:

```
# rpm -i ppp-2.2.0f-5.i386.rpm
```

4. If the PPP scripts `ppp-on`, `ppp-on-dialer`, and `ppp-off` are not found in the `/etc/ppp` directory after installation, copy them from the `/usr/doc/ppp-2.2.0f-5/scripts` directory by issuing the following command:

```
# cp /usr/doc/ppp-2.2.0f-5/script/* /etc/ppp
```

SEE ALSO

➤ *To learn more about Linux software package management, see page 520.*

➤ *To learn more about (shell) scripts, see page 365.*

Configuring PPP for Your ISP

You must have a PPP account with a service provider to connect to the Internet. At a minimum, you'll need the following information about your account:

- The user name and password.
- The phone number for your ISP's modem.
- The Internet Protocol (IP) addresses of your ISP's domain name servers, and the ISP's domain name. The addresses will look something like `205.198.114.1` or `205.198.114.20`, and the domain name might be the name of the ISP with `.com`, `.org`, or `.edu` appended.

After you have this information, the next step is to create or edit the resolver configuration file, `/etc/resolv.conf`. This file contains the DNS addresses used by email, newsreaders, or web browsers to look up valid Internet addresses. The DNS addresses are the Internet addresses of your ISP's computer running the domain name system, which translates a text address, such as `staffnet.com`, to its numerical address (in this case, `207.226.80.14`).

Creating */etc/resolv.conf*:

1. Make sure you're logged on as the root operator. Using your favorite text editor, create or edit the file `/etc/resolv.conf`:
   ```
   # touch /etc/resolv.conf
   # pico /etc/resolv.conf
   ```
2. Add the search path for DNS searches by entering the resolver keyword search, followed by your ISP's domain name:
   ```
   search myisp.com
   ```
3. Add the IP addresses of the DNS server or servers, preceding each address with the `nameserver` keyword:
   ```
   nameserver 205.198.114.1
   nameserver 205.198.114.20
   ```
4. Save and close the file.

SEE ALSO

➤ *For details about domain name service, see page 444.*

Configuring Your PPP Connection Scripts

In order to dial out and connect with your ISP, you must configure the PPP connection script `ppp-on`, found under the `/etc/ppp` directory. This script contains all the necessary information needed to connect to your ISP. When started, `ppp-on` uses the `/etc/ppp/ppp-on-dialer` script to make the call. Use your account information from your ISP, and enter the correct user name, phone number, password, and addresses to make the `ppp-on` script work correctly.

Editing the *ppp-on* Connection Script

Customizing the *ppp-on* script

1. Make sure you're logged on as the root operator.
2. Using your favorite text editor, open the `ppp-on` file in the `/etc/ppp` directory.
3. Enter the phone number for your ISP's modem in the `TELEPHONE` field:

   ```
   TELEPHONE=555-1212 # The telephone number for the
   connection
   ```

4. Enter your user name in the `ACCOUNT` field (where *`myusername`* is the user name assigned by your ISP):

   ```
   ACCOUNT=myusername    # The account name for logon
   ```

5. Enter your password in the `PASSWORD` field (where *`mypassword`* is your password):

   ```
   PASSWORD=mypassword  # your assigned password
   ```

6. If your ISP has assigned you an IP address, enter it in the `LOCAL` field. If your IP address is assigned dynamically when you log on, enter the address as follows:

   ```
   LOCAL_IP=0.0.0.0    # Local IP address
   ```

7. If you've created a symbolic link for your modem's serial port, use /dev/modem followed by the highest speed supported by your modem in the pppd command line (if you do not have a dynamically assigned IP number, see the sidenote "Dynamic Addresses and the pppd Daemon"):

```
exec /usr/sbin/pppd lock modem crtscts /dev/modem 57600\
        asyncmap 20A0000 escape FF $LOCAL_IP:$REMOTE_IP \
          noipdefault netmask $NETMASK defaultroute
          connect \
             $DIALER_SCRIPT &
```

8. Make both the ppp-on and ppp-on-dialer scripts executable by using the chmod program and its +x command-line option:

```
# chmod +x /etc/ppp/ppp-on*
```

SEE ALSO

➤ *For more information about changing file permissions, see page 418.*

Dynamic addresses and the pppd daemon

If you have a permanently assigned IP address (also called a *static IP address*), remove the `noip default` option from the `pppd` command line in the `ppp-on` script (see step 7 of "Customizing the `ppp-on` script") and change the `$REMOTE_IP` string to the IP address provided by your ISP. If your ISP uses dynamic addressing, you don't have to make this change; your IP address will be different every time you log on.

Starting a PPP Connection

There are at least two ways to start a phone-line PPP connection. In this section, you learn how to start your Internet session using the minicom communications program, and how to start a PPP connection with the ppp-on script.

Starting a PPP Connection Using the minicom Program

The minicom communications program, found under the /usr/bin directory, can be used to establish a PPP connection with your ISP. Although using this approach is not as convenient as using the ppp-on script, it is a good method to verify that your user name, password, and PPP connection work with your ISP.

This approach works because you can quit minicom without hanging up and resetting your modem (not always a good idea, especially if making long-distance connections—even at a rate of five cents a minute!).

Connecting to the Internet with the minicom command

1. Log on as the root operator; make sure your modem is plugged in and turned on.
2. Run the minicom program from the command line, like this:

   ```
   # minicom
   ```

3. Use the modem ATDT command followed by your ISP's modem number, and then press Enter to dial out:

   ```
   ATDT555-1212
   ```

4. Wait for the connection. Your ISP's computer should present a logon prompt. Enter your user name and your password.
5. Press Ctrl+Q to exit minicom without hanging up and resetting your modem.
6. Start your PPP connection from the command line, using the `pppd` daemon on the command line, and type the following:

   ```
   # pppd -d detach /dev/modem &
   ```

7. Test your connection by using the `ifconfig` command (see the later section "Checking Your PPP Connection").

Starting a PPP Connection with the *ppp-on* Script

After you've verified that your PPP connection works, you can use the `ppp-on` script to start your Internet sessions. Using this script is a lot easier than using the minicom program.

Starting Internet sessions by using the *ppp-on* script

1. Make sure you're logged on as the root operator.
2. Either copy the `ppp-on` script to a recognized program directory, such as `/usr/local/bin`, or create a symbolic link in a recognized directory, like this:

   ```
   # ln -s /etc/ppp/ppp-on /usr/local/bin/ppp-on
   ```

3. To let all users of your system start PPP connections, use the `chmod` command to change the execute permissions of the `ppp-on` script:

   ```
   # chmod 4711 /etc/ppp/ppp-on
   ```

4. Start a PPP connection using the script:

   ```
   # ppp-on
   ```

5. After a few seconds, you should hear your modem dial out and then connect with your ISP's modem. After several seconds, test or close the connection.

Closing Your PPP Connection

Use the `ppp-off` script, found under the `/etc/ppp` directory, to stop your PPP connection:

```
# /etc/ppp/ppp-off
```

Unlike the `ppp-on` script, the `ppp-off` script must be run by the root operator. This is not a problem unless your system's users must dial long distance to make a connection; most ISPs configure their systems to hang up after a set period of inactivity.

Checking Your PPP Connection

Most Linux distributions come with a number of commands that you can use to check your PPP connection. Many of these commands are network utilities. You can also look at system logs to diagnose or troubleshoot a bothersome connection.

Checking PPP Connections with the *ifconfig* Command

Although usually used by network administrators to configure network interfaces, the `ifconfig` command, found under the `/sbin` directory, can be used to gather a report on the status of your PPP connection. The `ifconfig` command lists information about active network interfaces. The first PPP connection started on your system is represented by the `ppp0` device. To see the status of your PPP connection, start a PPP session and use the `ifconfig` command with the `ppp0` device command-line option:

```
# ifconfig ppp0
ppp0      Link encap:Point-to-Point Protocol
           inet addr:207.226.80.155  P-t-P:207.226.80.214
Mask:255.255.255.0
```

```
UP POINTOPOINT RUNNING  MTU:1500  Metric:1
RX packets:109 errors:0 dropped:0 overruns:0
TX packets:117 errors:0 dropped:0 overruns:0
```

Along with IP address of your computer and the connected computer, using the `ifconfig` command shows the number of characters received (`RX`) and transmitted (`TX`) over your PPP interface. See the `ifconfig` manual pages for more details.

SEE ALSO

➤ *For more details about configuring network services, see page 482.*
➤ *For more information about other network services, see page 444.*

Getting PPP Statistics with the *pppstats* Command

Use the `pppstats` command, found under the `/usr/sbin/` directory, to print short reports about the statistics (such as incoming and outgoing data) of a specified PPP device connection (such as `ppp0`, as returned by the `ifconfig` command). To use the `pppstats` command, specify the unit number of the PPP interface on the command line, like this:

```
# pppstats 0
    in    pack    comp uncomp     err  |     out    pack    comp
    uncomp      ip
285567     281     143      91       0  |   9472     282     126
111       45
```

The `pppstats` command displays a line of information every five seconds while your connection is active. This information includes the number of 512-byte packets received and sent, along with some technical packet-compression information. The `pppstats` program is most useful to at least verify your PPP connection. Change the update rate by setting the `-i` (interval) command-line option to the desired number of seconds between report updates. See the `pppstats` manual page for more information.

Testing PPP Connection Speed with the *ping* Command

Use the `ping` command to verify an Internet host name or address and to test response times of your host servers. This command sends small test packets of data to the specified computer, and then measures the time it takes for the computer to send back the information. Use the `ping` command, followed by a host computer's name or address, as follows:

```
# ping staffnet.com
PING staffnet.com (207.226.80.14): 56 data bytes
64 bytes from 207.226.80.14: icmp_seq=0 ttl=254 time=4296.3 ms
64 bytes from 207.226.80.14: icmp_seq=1 ttl=254 time=3900.0 ms
64 bytes from 207.226.80.14: icmp_seq=2 ttl=254 time=2940.0 ms

--- staffnet.com ping statistics ---
6 packets transmitted, 3 packets received, 50% packet loss
round-trip min/avg/max = 2940.0/3712.1/4296.3 ms
```

The `ping` command will continuously send and receive information until you tell it to quit by pressing Ctrl+C.

Getting PPP Interface Information with the *route* Command

Use the `route` command, found under the `/sbin` directory, to get additional information about your active PPP interface. Although the `route` command is usually used as a network-administration tool to set up or delete networking routes for interfaces, `route`'s report, especially the `Flags` column, can be useful in showing your PPP interface status. Use the `route` command as shown in Figure 12.1.

FIGURE 12.1
The route report.

```
# route
Kernel IP routing table
Destination      Gateway          Genmaks         Flags Metric Ref    Use Iface
pm0.staffnet.co  *                255.255.255.255 UH    0      0      0   pppo
127.0.0.0        *                255.0.0.0       U     0      0      2   lo
default          pm0.staffnet.co  0.0.0.0         UG    0      0      2   ppp0
```

In this report, the `U` flag shows that the interface is up (running). See the `route` command's manual page for more information.

Troubleshooting PPP Connections with Your System Log

Use your Linux system's logs to troubleshoot problems in establishing a PPP connection. Some of these problems include the following:

- PPP kernel services not available
- `pppd` kernel not loading
- Modem not dialing out
- Abrupt disconnects from your ISP
- Problems logging on to your ISP
- Unrecognized Internet addresses or host names

To see what's going on in detail when you start a PPP connection, read the file called `messages` found under the `/var/log` directory. Make sure you're logged on as the root operator, and then pipe the contents of the `messages` file through the `less` pager:

```
# less /var/log/messages
```

The output, shown in Listing 12.1, shows the details of starting a PPP connection, including PPP code module loading, dialing out with the `chat` command (started by the `ppp-on` script), connecting, logging on, and assigning a dynamic IP address for your computer after logon.

LISTING 12.1 PPP connection details in */var/log/messages*

```
Feb 24 09:26:15 localhost kernel:
PPP: version 2.2.0 (dynamic channel allocation)
Feb 24 09:26:15 localhost kernel:
PPP Dynamic channel allocation code copyright 1995 Caldera, Inc.
Feb 24 09:26:15 localhost kernel: PPP line discipline registered.
Feb 24 09:26:15 localhost kernel: registered device ppp0
Feb 24 09:26:15 localhost pppd[5147]: pppd 2.2.0 started by bball, uid
    ➥500
Feb 24 09:26:16 localhost chat[5148]: timeout set to 3 seconds
Feb 24 09:26:16 localhost chat[5148]: abort on (\nBUSY\r)
Feb 24 09:26:16 localhost chat[5148]: abort on (\nNO ANSWER\r)
```

continues...

LISTING 12.1 Continued

```
Feb 24 09:26:16 localhost chat[5148]: abort on
    ➥(\nRINGING\r\n\r\nRINGING\r)
Feb 24 09:26:16 localhost chat[5148]: send (rAT^M)
Feb 24 09:26:16 localhost chat[5148]: expect (OK)
Feb 24 09:26:16 localhost chat[5148]: rAT^M^M
Feb 24 09:26:16 localhost chat[5148]: OK — got it
Feb 24 09:26:16 localhost chat[5148]: send (ATH0^M)
Feb 24 09:26:16 localhost chat[5148]: timeout set to 30 seconds
Feb 24 09:26:16 localhost chat[5148]: expect (OK)
Feb 24 09:26:16 localhost chat[5148]: ^M
Feb 24 09:26:16 localhost chat[5148]: ATH0^M^M
Feb 24 09:26:16 localhost chat[5148]: OK — got it
Feb 24 09:26:16 localhost chat[5148]: send (ATDT102881540555-1212^M)
Feb 24 09:26:17 localhost chat[5148]: expect (CONNECT)
Feb 24 09:26:17 localhost chat[5148]: ^M
Feb 24 09:26:37 localhost chat[5148]: ATDT102881540555-1212^M^M
Feb 24 09:26:37 localhost chat[5148]: CONNECT — got it
Feb 24 09:26:37 localhost chat[5148]: send (^M)
Feb 24 09:26:37 localhost chat[5148]: expect (ogin:)
Feb 24 09:26:37 localhost chat[5148]:  57600^M
Feb 24 09:26:45 localhost chat[5148]: ^M
Feb 24 09:26:45 localhost chat[5148]: ^M
Feb 24 09:26:45 localhost chat[5148]: Staffnet PM0 login: — got it
Feb 24 09:26:45 localhost chat[5148]: send (bball^M)
Feb 24 09:26:46 localhost chat[5148]: expect (assword:)
Feb 24 09:26:46 localhost chat[5148]: bball^M
Feb 24 09:26:46 localhost chat[5148]: Password: — got it
Feb 24 09:26:46 localhost chat[5148]: send (mypasswd^M)
Feb 24 09:26:46 localhost pppd[5147]: Serial connection established.
Feb 24 09:26:47 localhost pppd[5147]: Using interface ppp0
Feb 24 09:26:47 localhost pppd[5147]: Connect: ppp0 <—> /dev/modem
Feb 24 09:26:49 localhost pppd[5147]: local  IP address 207.226.80.155
Feb 24 09:26:49 localhost pppd[5147]: remote IP address
    ➥207.226.80.214
```

Examine your log for modem or logon errors. Common problems include use of the incorrect phone number, user name, or password.

Troubleshooting PPP connections

Still having trouble making a connection? Read Robert Hart's **PPP-HOWTO**, along with Al Longyear's **PPP-FAQ** (he's the author of the `ppp-on` and `ppp-on-dialer` scripts). These documents, found under the `/usr/doc` directory, contain loads of valuable tips about setting up and troubleshooting PPP connections and discuss other issues, such as security.

CHAPTER

13

Using Electronic Mail

By Bill Ball

Downloading electronic mail for PPP

Sending and receiving electronic mail

Reading electronic mail

Using Netscape Messenger to send and retrieve mail

Managing mail and spam with the `procmail` command

Retrieving Electronic Mail

Configuring Linux for sending and retrieving electronic mail can be a complex task but, fortunately, most Linux distributions automatically configure and set up the main email software and directory components during installation. In simple terms, the two types of programs involved in email are as follows:

- Transport agents—Programs, such as the `sendmail` daemon, which send mail files from one computer to another.
- User agents—Programs, also called *mail readers*, such as mail, pine, or Netscape Messenger, used to compose and manage messages.

The `sendmail` daemon is started when you boot Linux. Its job is to send, not retrieve, email. To retrieve mail over a Point-to-Point Protocol *interface*, or connection, you must use a retrieval program.

The basic approach to handling mail over a PPP connection is to log on, connect with your Internet service provider's computer, retrieve your waiting mail, and then either disconnect or stay connected to browse the Web, read news, or download files.

`sendmail`–A black art?

Thanks to the efforts of the individuals who prepared your Linux distribution, you won't have to suffer the heartache of configuring the `sendmail` electronic mail transport agent, a task that can make even the most experienced system administrators tremble. This also means that you should never edit the `sendmail` configuration file (`sendmail.cf`, found under the `/etc` directory) unless you absolutely know what you're doing. For details about Linux mail handling and for other sources of information, see the `Mail-HOWTO` under the `/usr/doc/HOWTO` directory.

Using *fetchmail*

To get your email, you'll need the IP address or name of your ISP's mail server (such as `mail.myisp.com`), the mail-retrieval protocol used by your ISP, and a retrieval program such as `fetchmail`. Most ISPs use the Post Office Protocol, or POP2 or POP3 protocols, which are supported by the `fetchmail` command, found under the `/usr/bin` directory.

There are a number of ways to configure the `fetchmail` program to retrieve mail. Retrieving mail from a remote computer usually involves passwords. Following is the simplest and most secure way to get your mail.

Retrieving mail with *fetchmail*

1. Dial out and establish your PPP connection.
2. Use the `fetchmail` program, along with your ISP's mail protocol and domain name, like this:
   ```
   # fetchmail -POP3 staffnet.com
   ```

3. After you press the Enter key, the `fetchmail` program prompts for a password:

```
Enter password for bball@staffnet.com:
```

Enter the password used to establish your PPP connection, not the system password for your computer. The `fetchmail` command does not echo back your password, so be sure to enter it correctly.

4. `fetchmail` retrieves any waiting mail messages from your ISP. Incoming mail is stored in a file with your username under the `/var/spool/mail` directory.

The `fetchmail` program works only one way: It retrieves your mail, and, by default, tells your ISP's mail server to delete the retrieved mail messages. Table 13.1 lists some of the common `fetchmail` command-line options that you can use to manage waiting or retrieved mail. See the `fetchmail` manual page for more options.

TABLE 13.1 Common *fetchmail* POP3 retrieval options

Option	Specifies
`-B n`	Do not retrieve more than *n* messages.
`-F`	Delete previously retrieved messages before retrieving new messages on the remote mail server.
`-K`	Delete retrieved messages on the remote mail server.
`-a`	Retrieve all messages from remote mail server.
`-c`	Check only for mail (no retrieval).
`-d n`	Daemon mode: Check for mail and retrieve every *n* seconds.
`-e`	Delete waiting messages.
`-k`	Keep retrieved messages on the remote mail server; do not delete them.
`-l n`	Do not retrieve messages larger than *n* characters.
`-s`	Operate silently; do not print status messages.
`-t secs`	Abort retrieval if you receive no response in `secs` from the mail server.

continues...

TABLE 13.1 Continued

Option	Specifies
`-u name`	Retrieve mail for the user with the username *name*.
`-v`	Operate verbosely; print all status messages.

The `fetchmail` program also recognizes a resource, or configuration file, called `.fetchmailrc`, if present in your home directory. Using keywords documented in the `fetchmail` manual pages, you can configure `fetchmail` to automatically retrieve your mail without requiring you to type numerous options on the command line.

Configuring *.fetchmailrc*

1. Use your favorite text editor to create a file called `.fetchmailrc` in your home directory.
2. Enter the `poll` keyword, followed by your ISP's domain name, like this:
   ```
   poll staffnet.com
   ```
3. On the same line, enter the `protocol` keyword, followed by the mail protocol supported by your ISP's mail server:
   ```
   poll staffnet.com protocol pop3
   ```
4. Again, on the same line, add the `user` keyword followed by your username, like this:
   ```
   poll staffnet.com protocol pop3 user bball
   ```
5. If you don't want to enter your mail service password each time you use `fetchmail`, use the `password` keyword followed by your mail server's password:
   ```
   poll staffnet.com protocol pop3 user bball password
   mon6key
   ```
6. Save and close the file.
7. Use the `chmod` command to change the file permissions of the `.fetchmailrc` file to user read-write, or `-rw------` (as returned by the command `ls -l`), like this:
   ```
   # chmod 600 .fetchmailrc
   ```
8. To retrieve your mail, start your PPP connection, then use the `fetchmail` command:
   ```
   # fetchmail
   ```

SEE ALSO

➤ *To learn more about the* chmod *command to change file ownership and permissions, see page 418.*

You can also use command-line options in conjunction with your .fetchmailrc settings. For example, to retrieve your mail but not erase retrieved messages, and to retrieve only short messages, use the -k (keep) option along with the -l (limit) option, like so:

```
# fetchmail -k -l 32000
```

This command line won't erase retrieved messages from your ISP's mail server, and won't download files larger than 32,000 characters.

Selecting a Mail Program

After you've retrieved your messages, a user agent, or mail program, is used to list, read, delete, forward, or create new messages to send. Selecting a mail program is primarily a matter of taste; some are easy to use, whereas others might offer more complex functions such as address books or file attachments. In this section, you are introduced to several simple and popular mail programs that work with Linux.

Using *mail*

The simplest mail program is called mail, and is usually found under the /bin directory. This program does not have a full-screen editor, and does not require the X Window System. The mail command, similar to the mailx program distributed with other versions of UNIX, supports the basic features needed to compose, send, list, and read messages.

Creating and sending mail by using *mail*

1. At the command line, enter the word mail followed by an email address, like this:

   ```
   # mail bball@staffnet.com
   ```

2. The mail command will respond with the prompt Subject. Enter a short subject line:

   ```
   Subject: 1999 Solar Eclipse
   ```

3. Press Enter and type the text of your message:

```
This is to let you know about the next solar eclipse!
You should be able to see it next August. Don't forget
to use a projection viewer or #14 Welder's glass to
➥watch it!
Have fun, and enjoy!
bball@staffnet.com
```

4. After you finish typing your text, enter a period (.) on a line by itself to send the message:

```
.
EOT
```

5. The `mail` program responds by printing the letters `EOT` (end of text), and sends the message.

Use the `mail` command to retrieve your mail from the `/var/spool/mail` directory. To read your mail, use the `mail` command on the command line, as follows:

```
# mail
Mail version 5.5-kw 5/30/95.  Type ? for help.
"/var/spool/mail/bball": 1 message 1 new
>N  1 bball@localhost.loca  Wed Feb 25 15:34  17/610   "1999
➥Solar Eclipse"
&
```

When you use the `mail` command, it prints a short version message, and then lists your messages. The ampersand (`&`) is a command-line prompt. Use a single-letter command (see Table 13.2) to read, delete, save, or reply to the current mail message, which is denoted by a greater than character (`>`). By default, saved messages are stored in a file called `mbox` in your home directory. Table 13.2 lists the most common `mail` program commands; for a complete list of `mail` commands, see the `mail` manual page.

TABLE 13.2 **Common *mail* program commands**

Key	Specifies
+	Move to the next message and list it.
-	Move to the previous message and list it.
?	Print a helpful list of mail commands.
R	Reply to sender.

Key	Specifies
d	Delete the current message.
h	Reprint the list of messages (after listing a message).
n	Go to the next message and list it.
q	Quit, and save messages in the default mailbox, mbox.
r	Reply to the sender and all recipients.
t	Type, or list, the current message.
x	Quit, and don't save messages in mbox.

SEE ALSO

➤ *To learn more about using pipes and redirection in the shell, see page 19.*

The mail command also supports command-line redirection operators and pipes of your shell. This is an easy way to quickly send program output or large files as messages. To use a pipe, use the mail command along with the -s (subject) command-line option followed by an email address. For example, to quickly mail a copy of the current month's calendar, pipe the output of the cal command through mail, as follows:

```
# cal ¦ mail -s "This Month's Calendar" bball@staffnet.com
```

To quickly send a large file, redirect the contents of a file using the standard input, like this:

```
# mail -s "This is a big file" bball@staffnet.com
</usr/dict/words
```

Be careful when mailing from the command line

Use redirection with care. It's not a good idea to mail someone the contents of your system's spelling dictionary!

Using *pine*

The pine mail program, developed by The University of Washington, is a software package consisting of a mail program and a nifty text editor called pico (pico is discussed in Chapter 4, "Using Text Editors," in the section titled "Using Screen Editors"). The pine and pico commands do not require the X Window System, and work especially well if you have set up Linux to support dial-in logons. These easy-to-use programs are favorites among Linux users because of their compact size and numerous features, such as spell checking and built-in help.

SEE ALSO

➤ *To learn more about the* pico *editor, see page 50.*

Using the *pine* mail program

1. Start the `pine` program from a command line:

   ```
   # pine
   ```

   The program automatically creates a directory called `mail` in your home directory, along with a configuration file called `.pinerc`.

2. Configure `pine` by entering your username, your ISP's domain name, and your ISP mail server's name (listed as `smtp-server` in Figure 13.1). Do this by typing an `s`, and then type a `c` to get to the configuration screen.

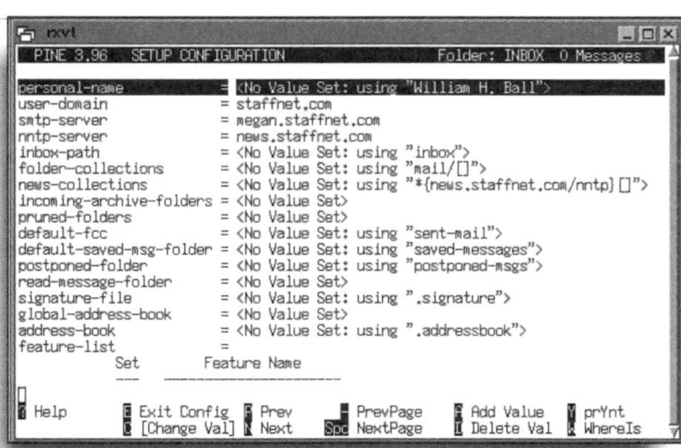

FIGURE 13.1
The `pine` mailer configuration screen specifies your username and mail server name.

3. After you enter your username, the domain of your ISP, and the name of your ISP's mail server, type an `e`. The `pine` program asks whether you want to save the changes in the `.pinerc` file. Press Y to save the changes.

4. Press C to compose a message; `pine` enters compose mode, shown in Figure 13.2.

5. Type the name of the addressee in the To: field, and press Enter. If you want to copy the message to someone else, enter another addressee in the Cc: field. After you've entered all the addressees, press Enter. To send a file as an attachment with the message, enter a valid pathname for a file and press Enter:

   ```
   /mnt/dos/windows/desktop/report.doc
   ```

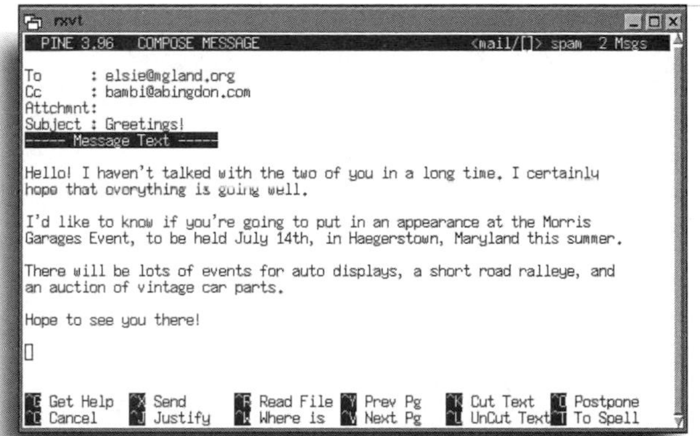

FIGURE 13.2

The `pine` compose mode is used to create a mail message.

6. Enter a subject line in the Subject: field, and press Enter. Now compose your message. Lines automatically wrap when you reach the far right margin.
7. After you finish, send the message by pressing Ctrl+X. To cancel the message, press Ctrl+C. To postpone sending the message, press Ctrl+O. Table 13.3 summarizes the `pine` commands that are supported for creating or editing a message.

TABLE 13.3 *pine* keyboard motion, action, and editing commands

Command	Specifies
Ctrl+@	Go to the next word.
Ctrl+A	Go to the beginning of the line.
Ctrl+B	Go back one character.
Ctrl+C	Cancel the message.
Ctrl+D	Delete one character.
Ctrl+E	Go to the end of the line.
Ctrl+F	Go forward one character.
Ctrl+G	Show the help screen.
Ctrl+H	Backspace one character.
Ctrl+J	Justify the paragraph.
Ctrl+K	Delete the current line.
Ctrl+N	Go down one line.

continues...

TABLE 13.3 Continued

Command	Specifies
Ctrl+O	Postpone sending and save the message.
Ctrl+P	Go up one line.
Ctrl+R	Insert a file.
Ctrl+T	Spell check the message.
Ctrl+V	Page down.
Ctrl+W	Search for a word.
Ctrl+X	Send the message.
Ctrl+Y	Page up.

Like the `mail` command, `pine` extracts your messages from the `/var/spool/mail` directory. Incoming messages are displayed in a list, as shown in Figure 13.3; you can select messages by scrolling up and down with the cursor keys. From the main list of messages, you can delete, undelete, save, read, and export messages to your home directory. To read a message, move your cursor to the desired message and press Enter.

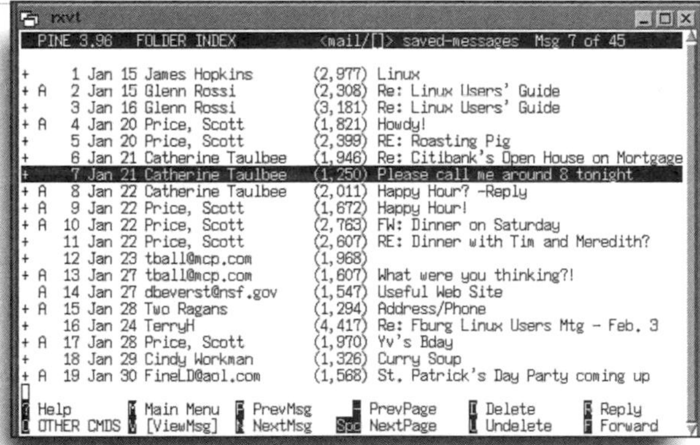

FIGURE 13.3
The `pine` mail program displays messages in a scrolling list.

Using Netscape Messenger to Create, Send, and Read Mail

Netscape Communicator, perhaps best known as a web browser, also supports electronic mail through the Netscape Messenger component. Netscape Messenger must be configured before you can use it to send or retrieve email. You must run the X Window System in order to use Netscape.

SEE ALSO

➤ *To learn more about using Netscape, see page 216*

➤ *To learn more about PPP connections, see page 166.*

Configuring Netscape Messenger

1. Start Netscape Messenger from the command line of a terminal window by typing the following:

```
# netscape -mail &
```

2. This launches Netscape; the Netscape component bar will appear (see Figure 13.4), along with the main window for Netscape Messenger (as shown in Figure 13.5).

FIGURE 13.4
The Netscape component bar.

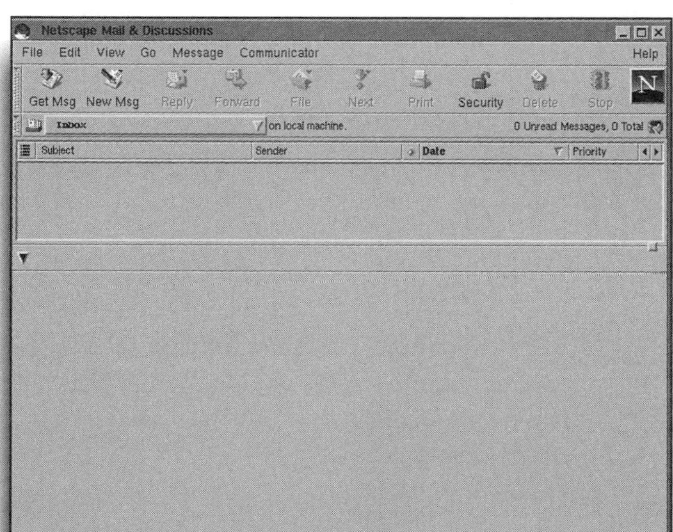

FIGURE 13.5
The Netscape Messenger application supports email for X11 Linux users.

3. Pull down the Edit menu and select Preferences. This displays the Messenger Preferences dialog box (shown in Figure 13.6).

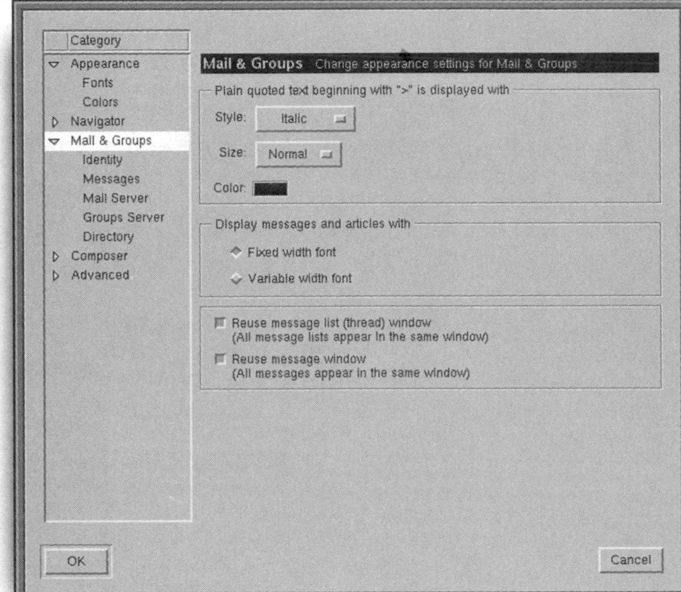

FIGURE 13.6
Configure Netscape Messenger through its Preferences dialog box.

4. Move the cursor to the Identity item in the Category list and click it to display the Identity dialog box. Type your name in the Your Name field and type your email address in the EmailAddress field, as shown in Figure 13.7.

5. Move the cursor to the Mail Server item in the Category list, and click it to display the Mail Server dialog box, shown in Figure 13.8. Enter your username (assigned to you by your ISP) in the Mail Server User Name field. Enter the name of your outgoing mail server in the Outgoing Mail (SMTP) Server field. Enter the name of your incoming mail server (the name of your ISP's mail server) in the Incoming Mail Server field.

6. If your ISP's mail server uses the POP3 mail protocol, make sure the diamond next to POP3 is selected, and then press Enter. Netscape automatically creates a directory called `nsmail` in your home directory. This directory contains the following files:

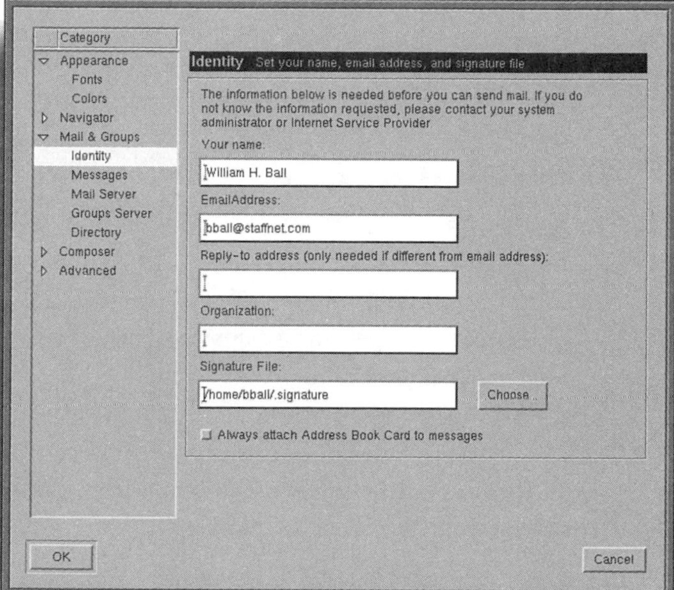

FIGURE 13.7

The Netscape Messenger Identity Preference dialog box contains email identification information, such as your name and email address.

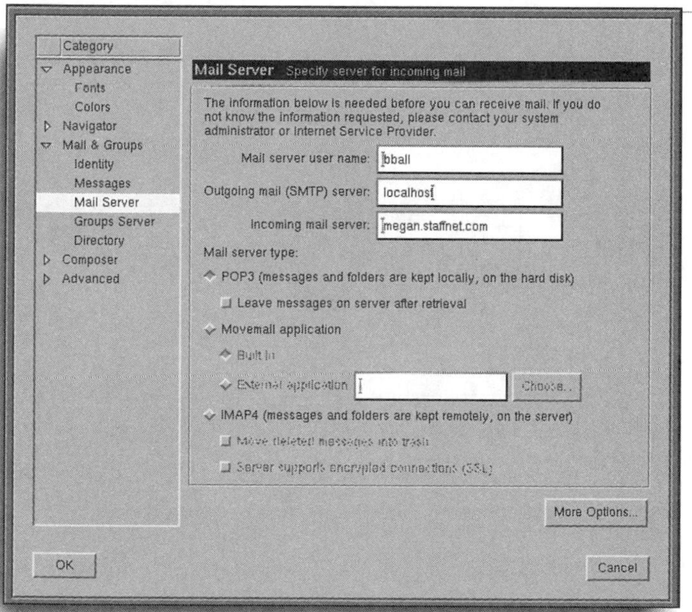

FIGURE 13.8

The Netscape Messenger Mail Server dialog box contains information about your username as well as incoming and outgoing mail services and protocols.

```
Drafts          Sent           Unsent Messages
Inbox           Trash
```

These files represent email you create, edit, send, or postpone while using Netscape Messenger.

Retrieving and creating mail

1. Launch Netscape Messenger. Start your PPP connection with your ISP.
2. Click the Get Msg button (refer to Figure 13.5). Netscape Messenger prompts you for your ISP mail server's password. Enter the password and press Enter.
3. Netscape Messenger downloads waiting mail messages from your ISP's mail server, and then displays the list of messages in the Messenger window (see Figure 13.9). To view a message, double-click it in the message list.

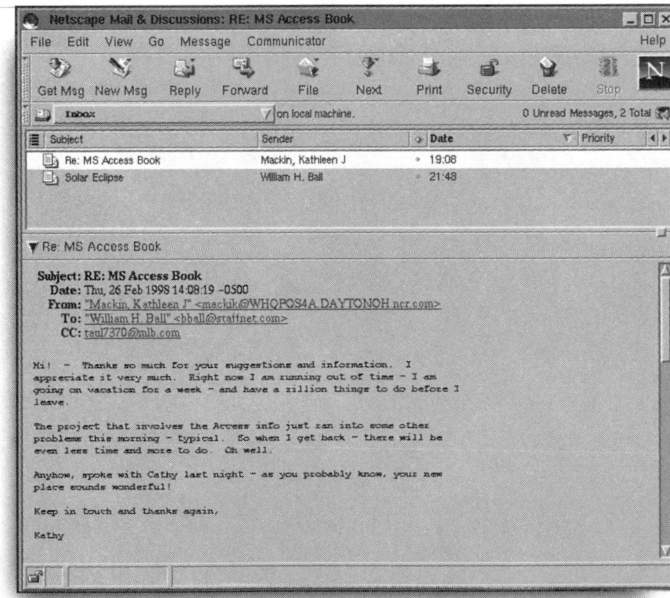

FIGURE 13.9
Read received messages by double-clicking them in the message list of Netscape Messenger's main window.

4. After you read the message, you can reply to, forward, or file it by selecting the appropriate button in Netscape Messenger's toolbar (refer to Figure 13.9).
5. To create a message, click the New Msg button. Netscape Messenger displays its Message Composition window, shown in Figure 13.10.

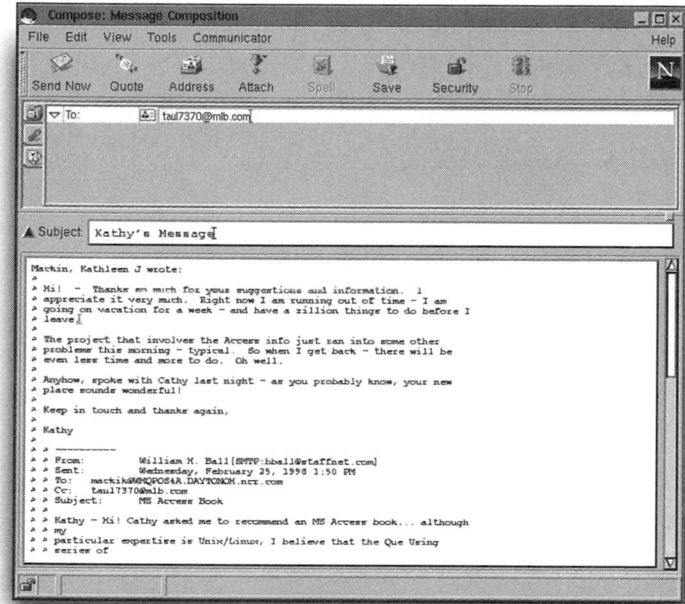

FIGURE 13.10

Create new messages in Netscape Messenger's Message Composition window.

6. Move your mouse cursor to the To line and type an email address.
7. Move the cursor to the Subject line, and enter a subject. Press Enter and start typing your message.
8. When finished, click the Send Now button on the Message Composition window toolbar (refer to Figure 13.10) to send the message right away. To save the message as a draft, click the Save button on the toolbar.

Bug fix: Can't get help with Netscape?

Netscape Communicator 4.04 has comprehensive built-in help for each included component, including Netscape Messenger. However, Netscape's installation script, `ns-install`, does not create required directories or links for Netscape's built-in help files. If you click Netscape's Help button, you'll get an error message dialog box indicating that required files and directories are not available. You can fix this problem by creating a symbolic link (symbolic links are discussed in Chapter 3, "Navigating the Linux File System," in the section titled "Creating Symbolic Links") with the following:

```
# ln -s /opt/netscape
/usr/local/lib/netscape
```

After you create this symbolically linked directory, Netscape 4.04 will know where to find its help files.

Managing Electronic Mail

Junk email, also known as *spam*, is annoying. These insipid messages are mass mailings sent out by pseudo-entrepreneurial idiots who hawk their unwanted drivel by bombarding millions of electronic mailboxes with banal Get-Rich-Quick schemes. Spam wastes your time and money, especially if you make a long-distance call to your ISP to retrieve your messages only to wade through lists of intrusive, flimflam trash from these boneheads (who usually use counterfeit, or forged, return email addresses routed illegally through innocent mail servers).

What can you do about spam? I list some general rules to follow, but not all may be effective:

- Unless you know and trust the company or vendor, never enter your email address in a request form on a web site.
- If you regularly post or reply to Usenet newsgroup messages, configure your mail program to send your real user name accompanied by an embedded string that can be easily removed. This clues in the truly concerned, but foils email villains who use extraction software to harvest email addresses from newsgroup postings to build bulk emailing lists. Try an email address like the following:
  `bball@_FIGHT_ALL_spam_staffnet.com`
- If you receive particularly obnoxious email, complain in writing to pertinent local, state, or federal authorities, and include a printed copy of the message.
- At the end of the body text of any posted Usenet message, include valid email addresses of your state attorney general or of pertinent federal postal or commerce fraud-reporting authorities. This will help ensure that these addresses, if harvested, are included in future spam mailings.
- Complain to your ISP about unwanted email from bulk emailers.
- Don't bother complaining to spammers: These worms are scofflaws of dubious lineage. Don't fall for any encouraged procedures, such as the TO BE REMOVED, REPLY TO: bait, as this will certainly ensure more spam because you've verified your email address!
- Use mail filters to delete or organize all incoming email from unwanted sources.

SEE ALSO

➤ *To learn more about reading Usenet news or using newsreaders, see page 227*

Configuring *procmail* to Filter Mail

`procmail`, a mail-processing program, is a first-line-of-defense weapon in the war against spam. This command, found under the `/usr/bin` directory, filters incoming mail so that you can automatically delete or organize messages by sender, subject, recipient, or text. Mail handling is accomplished by using procmail's command syntax to write short filters, or *recipes*.

Writing *procmail* recipes

1. Using your favorite text editor, create a text file called .procmailrc in your home directory. Specify the name of your mail directory (mail, if you use pine), the location of the .procmail directory, and the name of your procmail filter file, like this:

```
MAILDIR=$HOME/mail
PMDIR=$HOME/.procmail
INCLUDERC=$HOME/rc.mailfilter
```

2. Save this file, and then create a text file called .forward in your home directory, with the following line (replace *username* with your user name):

```
"¦IFS=' ' && exec /usr/bin/procmail -f- ¦¦ exit 75
#username"
```

3. Save the .forward file, then use the chmod command to change the permissions of the .forward file and your home directory, as follows:

```
# chmod 644 .forward
# chmod a+x /home/bball
```

4. Use the mkdir command to create a directory called .procmail:

```
# mkdir .procmail
```

5. Switch to the .procmail directory by entering the following:

```
# cd .procmail
```

6. Create a text file called rc.mailfilter, and enter three procmail recipes, like this:

```
:0:
*^From:.*aol.com
AOL
:0:
*^From:.*hotmail.com
/dev/null
:0:
*^Subject:.*CASH
/dev/null
:0:
```

7. Save the file `rc.mailfilter`.
8. Connect to your ISP and retrieve your mail. From now on, `procmail` will filter all incoming mail (the `.forward` file specifies that all your incoming mail be forwarded through the `procmail` program). The first recipe saves mail messages from anyone at `aol.com` into a mail folder called `AOL`. The next recipe sends all messages from the domain `hotmail.com` to a place where they rightfully belong: the 'ol bit bucket, `/dev/null`. This means that as you receive a message with the string `hotmail.com` in the From: field, `procmail` won't even save it on your hard drive. The last recipe sends all messages with the word `CASH` on the Subject: line to the same boneyard.
9. As you receive additional spam, enter new recipes to filter unwanted mail.

To add more features to your `procmail` recipes, read the `procmailrc` manual page. For a great selection of `procmail` recipe examples, see the `procmailex` manual page.

Sick of Spam?

I mean spurious email, not the delightful food product trademarked by Hormel, Inc. Nonetheless, if you want to learn more about what you can do to protect yourself against these despicable bulk emailers, browse to the following sites to learn how to protect yourself, write more complex `procmail` recipes, and complain to the proper authorities in case of suspected fraud:

`http://spam.abuse.net/spam`

`http://www.cauce.org`

`http://www.elsop.com/wrc/`

`http://members.aol.com/macabrus`

CHAPTER

14

Using FTP

By Bill Ball

Features of the `ftp` and `ncftp` commands

Downloading with the `ftp` command

Downloading with the `ncftp` command

Using Netscape to download files

Using the *ftp* Command

Use the `ftp` (file transfer) command to download files directly to your computer from another computer on the Internet. `ftp` supports the standard File Transfer Protocol, or FTP, and was originally designed to transfer files to and from other networked computers on the Internet.

`ftp`, found under the `/usr/bin` directory, has five command-line options and 53 built-in commands. Use this program from the command line of the console or a terminal window, followed by a name of a remote computer, like this:

```
# ftp ftp.mcp.com
Connected to ftp.mcp.com.
220 iq-mcp FTP server (Version wu-2.4(4) Sun Dec 21 13:01:32
➥EST 1997) ready.
Name (ftp.mcp.com:bball):
```

You can also use an Internet (IP) address to connect to a remote computer, like this:

```
# ftp 206.246.150.88
Connected to 206.246.150.88.
220 iq-mcp FTP server (Version wu-2.4(4) Sun Dec 21 13:01:32
➥EST 1997) ready.
Name (206.246.150.88:bball):
```

Both command lines connect you to the same remote computer. You don't even have to specify a hostname on the command line when using `ftp`; you can run the program interactively—repeatedly connecting to and disconnecting from different computers—by using `ftp`'s `open` and `close` commands:

```
# ftp
ftp> open ftp.mcp.com
Connected to ftp.mcp.com.
220 iq-mcp FTP server (Version wu-2.4(4) Sun Dec 21 13:01:32
➥EST 1997) ready.
Name (ftp.mcp.com:bball): anonymous
331 Guest login ok, send your complete e-mail address as
➥password.
Password:
230 Guest login ok, access restrictions apply.
Remote system type is UNIX.
Using binary mode to transfer files.
```

```
ftp> close
221 Goodbye.
```

After using the close command, you can then open a new connection to another computer by using the open command, followed by the name of an FTP server:

```
ftp> open ftp.tenon.com
Connected to toady.tenon.com.
220-
220-Welcome to ftp.tenon.com, Tenon Intersystem's FTP
➥server.
220-              - Thanks, Tenon Tech Support
220-                        support@tenon.com
220 toady FTP server (Version wu-2.4(2) Wed May 10 19:20:08
➥GMT-0800 1995) ready.
Name (ftp.tenon.com:bball): anonymous
331 Guest login ok, send your complete e-mail address as
➥password.
Password:
230-Please read the file README
230-  it was last modified on Wed Jan 18 14:54:20 1995 -
1167 days ago
230 Guest login ok, access restrictions apply.
Remote system type is UNIX.
Using binary mode to transfer files.
ftp> bye
221 Goodbye.
```

In this example, I first connected to the FTP server at Macmillan Computer Publishing by using the open command. After logging on, I disconnected from MCP's server by using the close command, connected to Tenon's FTP server, and then closed the connection by using the bye command. Most of the commands you'll use with ftp are listed in Table 14.1.

TABLE 14.1 Common *ftp* commands

Command name	Action
!	Run a shell command.
ascii	Specify text file downloads.
binary	Specify binary file downloads.

continues...

TABLE 14.1 Continued

Command name	Action
`bye`	Close the open connection and exit `ftp`.
`cd` *`nnn`*	Change to directory *`nnn`*.
`close`	Close the open connection.
`exit`	Close any open connection and quit.
`get` *`file`*	Download *`file`* from the current directory of the remote computer.
`help`	List help topics for `ftp`'s commands.
`help` *`str`*	List help for specific topic *`str`*.
`ls`	List files or directories in the current directory of the remote computer.
`mget` *`nnn`*	Download multiple files according to pattern *`nnn`*.
`mput` *`nnn`*	Send (upload) multiple files to remote computer according to pattern *`nnn`*.
`open`	Open a connection to a remote computer.
`prompt`	Turn off prompting during multiple file transfers.
`pwd`	Print the current working directory on the remote computer.
`put`	Send (upload) a file from your computer to the remote computer.

Using *ftp* to Download Files

After `ftp` connects to a remote computer, the remote computer usually presents a logon prompt. If you do not have an account on the remote computer system (such as a user name or password), type `anonymous` at the `Name` prompt and press Enter. At the `Password` prompt, type your email address. Your email address will not be echoed back to your screen.

SEE ALSO

➤ *To learn more about changing directories using the* `cd` *command, see page 30.*
➤ *To learn more about using electronic mail, see page 180.*
➤ *To learn more about the Internet network services and Linux, see page 444.*

Logging on, navigating, and downloading files

1. Start your Internet connection—a PPP connection, for example. At the command line of the console or a terminal window, use the `ftp` command followed by the name of a remote computer, like so:

```
# ftp sunsite.unc.edu
Connected to sunsite.unc.edu.
220-                    Welcome to the SunSITE USA ftp
➥archives!
220-
220-You can access this archive via http with the same
➥URL.
220-
220-example:     ftp://sunsite.unc.edu/pub/Linux/ becomes
220-             http://sunsite.unc.edu/pub/Linux/
220-
220-For more information about services offered by
➥SunSITE,
220-go to http://sunsite.unc.edu.
220-
220-WE'RE BACK TO USING WUFTPD.
220-You can still get tarred directories if you issue
➥the following command:
220-    get dirname.tar
220-You can also get gzipped or compressed tarred
➥directories by following
220-the .tar with .gz or .Z, respectively.
220-
220-Have any suggestions or questions? Email
➥ftpkeeper@sunsite.unc.edu.
220-
220 helios.oit.unc.edu FTP server (Version wu-2.4.2-
➥academ[BETA-13]/
(6) Thu Jul 17 16:22:52 EDT 1997) ready.
Name (sunsite.unc.edu:bball):
```

2. Type `anonymous` at the `Name` prompt:

```
Name (sunsite.unc.edu:bball): anonymous
331 Guest login ok, send your complete e-mail address as
➥password.
Password:
```

Linux and `ftp`

When you install Red Hat Linux, a user named `ftp` is created, along with a directory called `ftp` under the `/home` directory. (You can check this by looking at the contents of your system's `/etc/passwd` file.) To enable FTP access for your system, log on as the root operator, start X11, and use Red Hat's `tksysv` Control Panel tool to start `inet` services. To test your system to see whether FTP access is available, use the `ftp` command followed by the name of your computer, like this:

```
# ftp localhost
```

If you get a logon prompt, FTP has been enabled. For more information about Internet network services for Linux, see the `services` manual page.

3. Enter your email address at the `Password` prompt—for example, `bball@staffnet.com`:

```
Password:
230 Guest login ok, access restrictions apply.
Remote system type is UNIX.
Using binary mode to transfer files.
ftp>
```

Remember: You won't see any text entered at the `Password` prompt!

4. To see the contents of the current directory, use `ftp`'s `ls` (list directory) command:

```
ftp> ls
200 PORT command successful.
150 Opening ASCII mode data connection for /bin/ls.
total 28797
dr-xr-xr-x    9 root     other          512 Feb 16 16:22.
dr-xr-xr-x    9 root     other          512 Feb 16 16:22..
-r--r--r--    1 root     other     29428182 Mar 31 07:26
➥IAFA-LISTINGS
lrwxrwxrwx    1 root     other            7 Jul 16  1997
➥README -> WELCOME
-r--r--r--    1 root     other          608 Jan 13  1997
➥WELCOME
dr-xr-xr-x    2 root     other          512 Jul 16  1997
➥bin
dr-xr-xr-x    2 root     other          512 Jul 16  1997
➥dev
dr-xr-xr-x    2 root     other          512 Jul 18  1997
➥etc
drwxrwxrwx    6 root     other        18944 Mar 30 01:48
➥incoming
dr-xr-xr-x   17 root     root           512 Mar 19 22:13
➥pub
dr-xr-xr-x    3 root     other          512 Jul 16  1997
➥unc
dr-xr-xr-x    5 root     other          512 Jul 16  1997
➥usr
226 Transfer complete.
➥ftp>
```

5. To navigate to a different directory, use `ftp`'s `cd` (change directory) command followed by the name of a directory:

```
ftp> cd pub
```

```
250 CWD command successful.
ftp>
```

6. To navigate to a specific subdirectory, use a more complete path specification with the `cd` command:

```
ftp> cd pub/Linux/games/arcade
250 CWD command successful.
ftp>
```

7. To list specific files, use `ftp`'s `ls` command along with a wildcard pattern:

```
ftp> ls xcen*
200 PORT command successful.
150 Opening ASCII mode data connection for /bin/ls.
-rw-rw-r--   1 67       1002          6884 Aug 01  1996
➥xcentipede-0.01.ELF.gz
-rw-rw-r--   1 67       1002          1595 Aug 01  1996
➥xcentipede-0.01.README
-rw-rw-r--   1 67       1002          1104 Aug 01  1996
➥xcentipede-0.01.lsm
-rw-rw-r--   1 67       1002         10016 Aug 01  1996
➥xcentipede-0.01.src.tgz
226 Transfer complete.
ftp>
```

8. To prepare to download a binary file, such as a compressed Linux `gzip` archive, use `ftp`'s `binary` command:

```
ftp> binary
200 Type set to I.
ftp>
```

9. To download a single file, use `ftp`'s `get` command followed by the filename:

```
ftp> get xcentipede-0.01.ELF.gz
local: xcentipede-0.01.ELF.gz remote: xcentipede-
➥0.01.ELF.gz
200 PORT command successful.
150 Opening BINARY mode data connection for xcentipede-
➥0.01.ELF.gz (6884 bytes).
226 Transfer complete.
6884 bytes received in 2.37 secs (2.8 Kbytes/sec)
ftp>
```

10. If you can't remember the current directory of the remote computer, use `ftp`'s `pwd` (print working directory) command:

```
ftp> pwd
```

```
257 "/pub/Linux/games/arcade" is current directory.
ftp>
```

11. To prepare to download text files, use `ftp`'s `ascii` command:

```
ftp> ascii
200 Type set to A.
ftp>
```

12. To download multiple files, use `ftp`'s `mget` command followed by a filename pattern:

```
ftp> mget xb*.lsm
mget xbattle.patch.lsm? y
200 PORT command successful.
150 Opening ASCII mode data connection for
➥xbattle.patch.lsm (286 bytes).
226 Transfer complete.
295 bytes received in 0.0602 secs (4.8 Kbytes/sec)
mget xbill-2.0.lsm? y
200 PORT command successful.
150 Opening ASCII mode data connection for xbill-2.0.lsm
➥(606 bytes).
226 Transfer complete.
623 bytes received in 0.131 secs (4.6 Kbytes/sec)
mget xblast-2.2.1.lsm? y
200 PORT command successful.
150 Opening ASCII mode data connection for xblast-
➥2.2.1.lsm (858 bytes).
226 Transfer complete.
879 bytes received in 0.161 secs (5.3 Kbytes/sec)
mget xboing-2.3.lsm? y
200 PORT command successful.
150 Opening ASCII mode data connection for xboing-
➥2.3.lsm (465 bytes).
226 Transfer complete.
479 bytes received in 0.111 secs (4.2 Kbytes/sec)
ftp>
```

Before retrieving each file, `ftp` prompts and asks for a **Y** or an **N**. Press Y to download the file; press N to skip the file and go to the next file.

13. To download multiple files without a prompt, use `ftp`'s `prompt` command to toggle interactive downloads:

```
ftp> prompt
```

```
Interactive mode off.
ftp> mget xb*.lsm
local: xbattle.patch.lsm remote: xbattle.patch.lsm
200 PORT command successful.
150 Opening ASCII mode data connection for
➥xbattle.patch.lsm (286 bytes).
226 Transfer complete.
295 bytes received in 0.0602 secs (4.8 Kbytes/sec)
local: xbill-2.0.lsm remote: xbill-2.0.lsm
200 PORT command successful.
150 Opening ASCII mode data connection for xbill-2.0.lsm
➥(606 bytes).
226 Transfer complete.
623 bytes received in 0.121 secs (5 Kbytes/sec)
local: xblast-2.2.1.lsm remote: xblast-2.2.1.lsm
200 PORT command successful.
425 Can't create data socket (152.2.254.81,20): Address
➥already in use.
local: xboing-2.3.lsm remote: xboing-2.3.lsm
200 PORT command successful.
150 Opening ASCII mode data connection for xboing-
➥2.3.lsm (465 bytes).
226 Transfer complete.
479 bytes received in 0.0906 secs (5.2 Kbytes/sec)
ftp>
```

14. To use a shell command from inside `ftp`, use the exclamation-point character (`!`) followed a command line:

```
ftp> ! ls -l xb*.lsm
-rw-rw-r--    1 bball    bball         286 Mar 31 12:41
➥xbattle.patch.lsm
-rw-rw-r--    1 bball    bball         606 Mar 31 12:41
➥xbill-2.0.lsm
-rw-rw-r--    1 bball    bball         858 Mar 31 12:39
➥xblast-2.2.1.lsm
-rw-rw-r--    1 bball    bball         465 Mar 31 12:43
➥xboing-2.3.lsm
ftp>
```

15. To close the connection without quitting `ftp`, use the `close` command:

```
ftp> close
221 Goodbye.
ftp>
```

Return to `ftp` with the `exit` command

Using `ftp`'s shell prompt can be handy but confusing, especially if you type the exclamation character and press the Enter key without a trailing command. You'll find yourself at your shell prompt, and might think you've disconnected and quit the program. Type the word `exit` to return to the `ftp` program.

16. To quit and exit `ftp`, use the `quit` or `exit` command:

```
ftp> quit
```

SEE ALSO

➤ *To learn more about using a shell with Linux, see page 16.*

Using *ftp* Help Commands

`ftp` has built-in help that you can use as a quick reminder about its different commands. This help system can be used before or during a remote connection; simply type help to print a list of all built-in commands:

```
# ftp
ftp> help
Commands may be abbreviated.  Commands are:

!           debug       mdir        sendport    site
$           dir         mget        put         size
account     disconnect  mkdir       pwd         status
append      exit        mls         quit        struct
ascii       form        mode        quote       system
bell        get         modtime     recv        sunique
binary      glob        mput        reget       tenex
bye         hash        newe        rstatus     tick
case        help        nmap        rhelp       trace
cd          idle        nlist       rename      type
cdup        image       ntrans      reset       user
chmod       lcd         open        restart     umask
close       ls          prompt      rmdir       verbose
cr          macdef      passive     runique     ?
delete      mdelete     proxy       send
ftp> help prompt
prompt force interactive prompting on multiple commands
ftp> help exit
exit terminate ftp session and exit
ftp>
```

Typing `help` and then the name of a command will print a short description of the command.

Use `ftp`'s built-in help to supplement its manual page. More extensive documentation can be found under the `/usr/doc/wu-ftpd` directory.

Using the *ncftp* Command

The `ncftp` command is similar to the `ftp` command, but has additional features, including the following:

- Three visual (screen) modes
- 15 command-line options
- A command line separate from a main scrolling window
- A status line showing download progress with elapsed and remaining time to completion
- An editor for bookmarks (abbreviated hostnames of remote computers)

The `ncftp` command also features a built-in help facility that is similar to `ftp`'s. You can read more about `ncftp` by browsing to this address:

http://www.probe.net/~mgleason

Downloading with the *ncftp* Command

The `ncftp` command features several command-line options that can save you time and typing.

Downloading files with the *ncftp* command

1. Start your PPP connection. Use the `ncftp` command followed by the `-a` (anonymous) option to quickly log on to a remote computer, like so:

   ```
   # ncftp -a ftp.ncftp.com
   ```

2. Your screen clears, and `ncftp` automatically logs you on to the remote computer, sending information to your display that is similar to the following:

   ```
   Trying to connect to ftp.ncftp.com...
   ```

```
You are user #2 of 50 simultaneous users allowed.

Welcome to ftp.ncftp.com
Logged in anonymously.
```

3. If you know the complete path to a desired file on a remote computer, use `ncftp`'s `-a` option followed by the name of the FTP server, a colon, and the complete path or directory specification to the desired file:

   ```
   # ncftp -a sunsite.unc.edu:/pub/Linux/NEW
   ```

   This command line retrieves a list of the newest software for Linux at the `sunsite.unc.edu` FTP server (with the very latest files at the bottom of the list).

4. To save even more time, use `ncftp`'s `-c` command to pipe the retrieved file through the `tail` and `less` commands, like so:

   ```
   # ncftp -ac sunsite.unc.edu:/pub/Linux/NEW | tail | less
   ```

   After a pause, following `ncftp`'s automatic logon and retrieval, you should see something like the following:

   ```
   system/network/serial/ppp/gppp-1.0.tar.gz (183724 bytes)
      ppp setup program with a similar user interface to
   windows' Internet Wizard (
   Mar 30, 1998 16:38:13 EST)

   kernel/patches/cdrom/linux-2.0.30-cm205ms-0.10.tgz (41435
   ➥bytes)
      new cdrom device driver Philips/LMS cm205ms/cm206
   ➥(Mar 30, 1998 20:59:44 EST)

   system/mail/mua/mr0721beta.tar.gz (71392 bytes)
      mr is a colorful mailreader (Mar 31, 1998 2:29:3 EST)
   ```

SEE ALSO

➤ *To learn more about using the* `less` *pager command, see page 33.*

Use `ncftp` to get a new version of `ncftp`

To get the latest version of the `ncftp` command, type the following:

```
# ncftp -a
➥ftp.ncftp.com:/nc
ftp/ncftp-2.4.3.tar.gz
```

Using Netscape to Download Files

Netscape Communicator not only interactively browses the Web, but can be directed to retrieve files from remote computers through the command line of a terminal window. Netscape Navigator, a component of the Netscape Communicator distribution for Linux, recognizes a uniform resource locator (URL) specification of the FTP protocol (`ftp://`). This is handy for quickly downloading known files from familiar places on the Internet.

SEE ALSO

➤ *For more information about Netscape Communicator for Linux, see page 216.*

➤ *To learn more about the X Window System, see page 260.*

Downloading from the command line with Netscape

1. Start an X Window System session. On the command line, use the `netscape` command followed by the `ftp://` URL specification, the name of a remote server, and the complete pathname to a desired file, like this:

```
# netscape ftp://sunsite.unc.edu/pub/Linux/NEW
```

This command line produces a list of the latest Linux files (refer to the previous example). Netscape loads, connects, and retrieves the file, as shown in Figure 14.1.

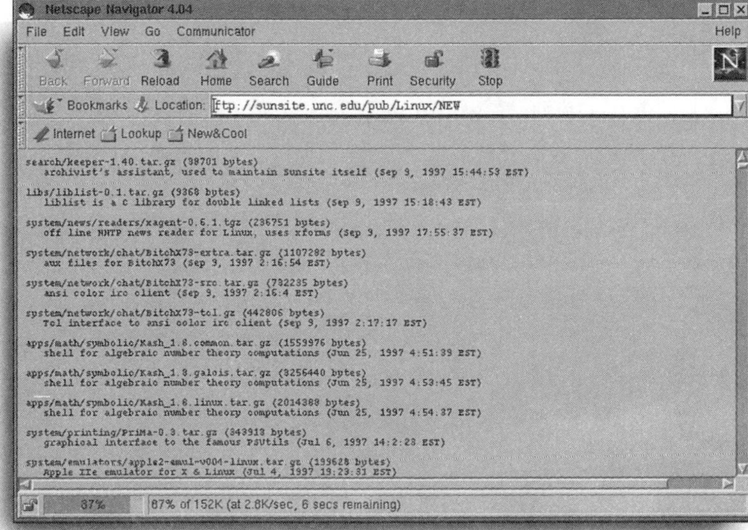

FIGURE 14.1
Netscape can be started from the command line of a terminal window to directly navigate to a desired file on a remote computer.

2. To save time when directly downloading a binary file, such as a compressed archive, you should know the name of the remote server and the complete pathname of the file. For example, to download a great arcade game for Linux and X11, use `netscape` on the command line like this:

```
# netscape
ftp://sunsite.unc.edu/pub/Linux/games/arcade/Terroid-
1.4-486-elf.tar.gz
```

Netscape connects to the remote computer and attempts to retrieve the file. If the file is found, Netscape presents a save dialog box, as shown in Figure 14.2. Although the dialog box offers a wildcard field (normally used to selectively view a list of files to open by using wildcards), go to the next step.

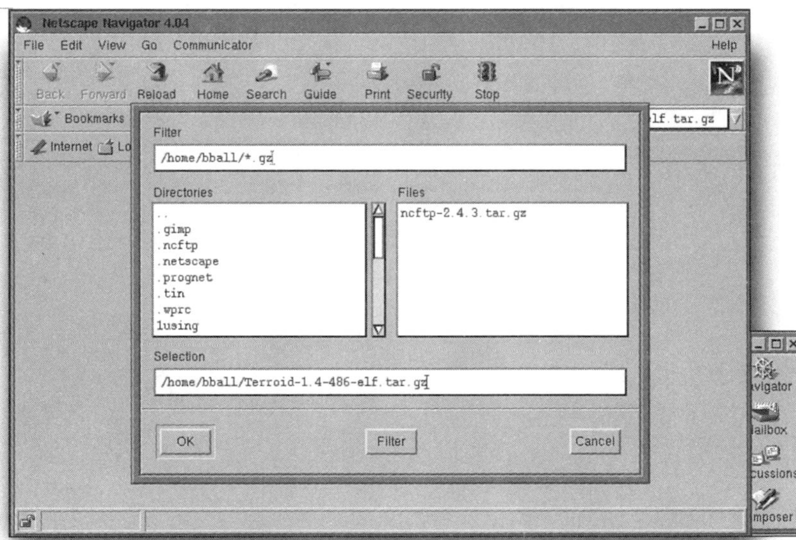

FIGURE 14.2
Netscape presents a save dialog box before downloading and retrieving files from remote computers.

3. Click OK to start retrieving your file. Netscape then presents a download progress window, showing the filename, size, and estimated time to complete the download.

CHAPTER

15

Using Web Browsers

By Bill Ball

Configuring and using the lynx web browser

Downloading and installing Netscape Communicator

Configuring and using Netscape Communicator

Using the lynx Browser

The lynx web browser, hosted at the University of Kansas, is a text-only browser. This program will not load web page graphics, play sound or use any of the plug-in features of today's modern web browsers. However, lynx is fast and efficient and does not take up much disk space (around 500,000 bytes versus nearly 22 megabytes for Netscape).

You don't need to use X11 to browse the Web; use lynx from the command line:

```
# lynx http://www.mcp.com
```

The lynx browser will connect to Macmillan Publishing's web page and will show it on your display or in a terminal window, as shown in Figure 15.1.

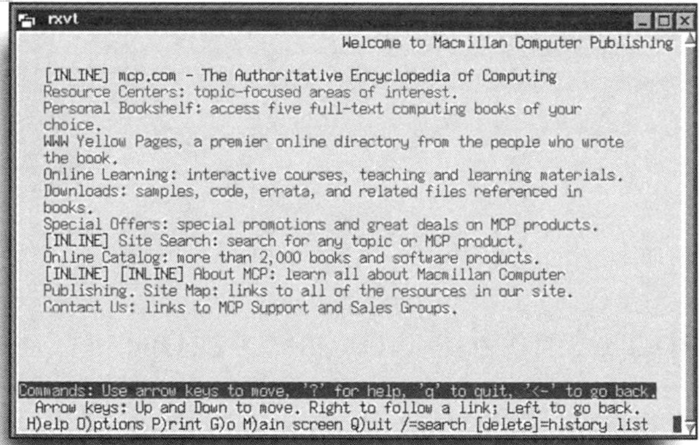

FIGURE 15.1
The lynx program is a text-only web browser.

If you're using the X Window System, you can also use lynx to browse the Web in the window of an X11 terminal client. Use lynx to quickly browse web pages without the delay, or "World Wide Wait," of advertisements, large graphics, or animations that can get in the way of getting information.

The lynx browser has 66 different command-line options but is easy to use. The most common keystroke commands used to navigate web pages are listed in Table 15.1.

TABLE 15.1 **Common lynx keyboard commands**

Action	Keystroke
Add page to bookmark file	a
Download highlighted file	Enter key or d key
Edit current URL before jump	G
Get help	? key or h key
Jump to an URL	g
Jump to topic	Enter key or Cursor right
Mail current page	p, followed by cursor down, Enter key
Next topic	Cursor down
Previous page	Cursor left
Previous topic	Cursor up
Save link to bookmark file	a
Save page to a file	p, followed by Enter key
Scroll backward one page	PageUp key
Scroll backward one-half page	(
Scroll forward one page	Spacebar key
Scroll forward one-half page	)
Search page	/

SEE ALSO

➤ *To learn more about PPP connections, see page 166.*

➤ *To learn more about the X Window system and X11 terminals, see page 260.*

Using lynx command lines

1. Start your PPP connection. To browse to a specific page on the Internet, enter the web address (also known as a Uniform Resource Locator, or URL):

```
# lynx http://www.mcp.com
```

2. To go to a File Transfer Protocol (FTP) server, use an FTP URL address:

```
# lynx ftp://sunsite.unc.edu/pub/Linux
```

   This command line will log you on to the specified ftp server, and display a list of available files, as shown in Figure 15.2.

```
rxvt
                                   /pub/Linux directory (p1 of 4)

Mirrors are better!  Look at the MIRRORS file to find one near you.

Email linuxguys@sunsite.unc.edu with comments/complaints about this archive.

Please see HINTS for information on how to get most effective use out of
this archive.  HINTS was last updated on 17 March 1997.
 ------------------------------------------------------------------------
Sep 19  1997  text/plain        !INDEX  2Kb
Sep 19  1997  text/html         !INDEX.html  6Kb
Sep 19  1997  text/html         !INDEX.short.html  3Kb
Mar 23 05:04  text/plain        .du-s  20 bytes
Mar 23 05:15  gunzip            .du.gz  19Kb
Jan 18  1995  Directory         .html-icons
Jul  9  1993  text/plain        .link  739 bytes
Mar 23 05:00  gunzip            00-find.Linux.gz  4Kb
Mar 16 22:03  Directory         ALPHA
Mar 11 18:40  Directory         GCC
May 27  1997  text/plain        HINTS  1Kb
Sep  8  1997  text/plain        HOW.TO.SUBMIT  1Kb
-- press space for next page --
  Arrow keys: Up and Down to move. Right to follow a link; Left to go back.
 H)elp O)ptions P)rint G)o M)ain screen Q)uit /=search [delete]=history list
```

FIGURE 15.2
The lynx browser lists and retrieves files from FTP servers.

3. To use lynx browser to retrieve text files without browsing, enter a known URL and then use the `-dump` option, followed by the shell's standard output redirection operator, like this:

```
# lynx http://www.yahoo.com/headlines/news/summary.
html -dump >news.raw
```

This command line will dump the text of the requested page into a text file on your disk (note that the URL might be outdated by the time you read this).

Save time and effort downloading files

If you frequently use the `ftp` command to retrieve files from remote computers, try using the lynx browser instead. Many FTP sites now include index files in `.html` format that makes listings much easier to read. To download a file, hold down the Shift key and click on the filename.

Configuring the lynx Browser

To configure the `lynx` command, log on as the root operator and edit the file `lynx.cfg` under the `/etc` directory. Make a backup copy first if you want (but you'll find an original copy under the `/usr/doc/lynx` directory). The `/etc/lynx.cfg` file contains systemwide settings for the lynx browser's features.

Configuring the lynx browser

1. Using your favorite text editor, such as pico, open the lynx.cfg file and turn off line-wrapping:

```
# pico -w /etc/lynx.cfg
```

2. To change the default web address used when starting lynx from the command line without an URL, change the default address used with the `STARTFILE` variable, from

```
STARTFILE:http://lynx.browser.org/
```

to a different address (Red Hat Linux users will find `STARTFILE` defined as "`/usr/doc/HTML/index.html`"):

```
STARTFILE:http://www.yahoo.com/
```

3. To configure lynx to use its help files installed on your disk in the `/usr/doc/lynx/lynx_help` directory, change the `HELPFILE` variable, from its default web address:

```
HELPFILE:http://www.crl.com/~subir/lynx/lynx_help/lynx_
help_main.html
```

to the location of the `lynx_help_main.html` file:

```
HELPFILE:localhost/usr/doc/lynx-
2.7.1/lynx_help/lynx_help_main.html
```

After making this change, lynx will read in the help files installed on your system following a question mark (?) key press, as shown in Figure 15.3, instead of browsing to its home page for help information. (Check your `/usr/doc` directory to make sure that you enter the correct path for the lynx help file.)

SEE ALSO

➤ *For more information about text editors, see page 50.*

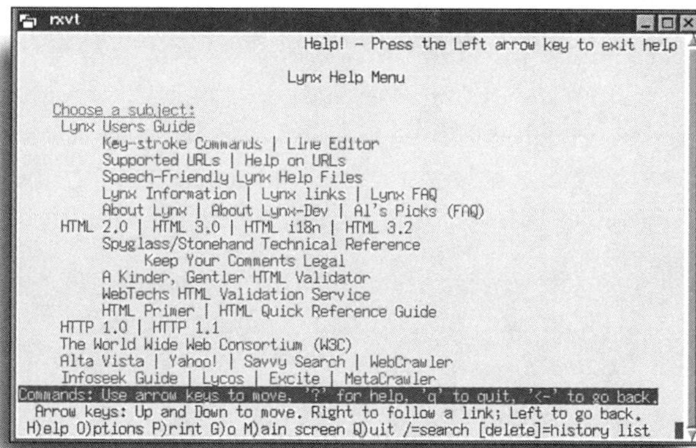

FIGURE 15.3
The lynx program can display online help from files on your hard drive, or through links to web pages on the Internet.

4. To configure lynx to work as a Usenet newsreader, find the `NNTPSERVER` line and enter the name of your Internet Service Provider's (ISP) news server:

```
NNTPSERVER:your.ISPnewserver.com
```

5. To read articles in newsgroups specified in your `.newsrc` file in your home directory, use the news URL prefix, followed by your news server name:

```
# lynx news://your.ISPnewserver.com
```

6. To download files while using lynx, navigate to the filename on the display web page and press either Enter or the d key.

Using Netscape Communicator

This section details how to install, configure, and use some basic features of Netscape Communicator. This program is much more than a web browser and includes a suite of four tools: Navigator for web browsing; Messenger for electronic mail; Collabra for reading local and Usenet news; and Composer, for creating and editing web pages.

For the latest information about Netscape Communication for Linux, browse to Netscape's home page at:

`http://home.netscape.com`

SEE ALSO

➤ *To learn more about reading Usenet news, see page 227.*

➤ *For more information about electronic mail, see page 183.*

Downloading and Installing Netscape Communicator

The Netscape Communicator web browser, by Netscape Communications, is one of the most popular browsers for all computer systems, including Linux. Thanks to Netscape, Linux users will continue to enjoy this browser for a long time (see the following sidenote, "Freely Licensed Netscape Communicator Source"). Netscape is destined to become the standard web browser for Linux.

Navigate to the Netscape home page, `http://home.netscape.com`, to download the proper version of Netscape Communicator for your version of Linux (there are versions for the 1.x or 2.x kernels).

Be prepared for a long download if you're getting Communicator over a 33.6KB PPP connection—the latest version is more than 10MB in compressed form and will require nearly 22MB of disk space when installed. Also consider that the installed default `.netscape` directory in your home directory can grow to more than 10MB after using Netscape for awhile.

Installing and configuring communicator

1. Log on as the root operator. Start your PPP connection, navigate to Netscape's home page—

Freely licensed Netscape Communicator source

Along with Netscape Communications' decision to make Netscape Communicator 4.0 free for all users, the company shocked and delighted many Linux software developers by announcing plans "to make the source code for the next generation of its highly popular Netscape Communicator client software available for free licensing on the Internet."

What does this mean for you? Expect to see rapid development of the Netscape Communicator suite of Internet tools, with many enhancements. Expect to see this program become a standard part of nearly all Linux distributions in the future. (Itś currently included with all new Red Hat Linux CD-ROM distributions.) For Netscape, one of the first large commercial software companies to endorse and credit the power of the Free Software Foundation's GNU Public License, this means that the company will benefit from seeing rapid enhancements, improvements, and variations to its browser tools.

Kudos to Netscape for taking this bold step. You can be sure that the worldwide community of Linux software developers will repay this generosity tenfold with some "insanely great" improvements to your favorite browser in the near future. For more information about Netscape's source licensing of Communicator and related programs, see:

`http://developer.netscape.com`

http://home.netscape.com, and download Netscape Communicator for Linux.

2. Use the mkdir command to create a temporary directory and copy the file into it. Then change directory into the temporary directory and use the tar command to decompress and extract the Netscape package:

```
# tar xvzf *
```

3. Begin installing Netscape Communicator by using its installation script:

```
# ./ns-install
```

4. The installation script will ask some simple questions and then extract required files, create any necessary directories, and install the browser. By default, Communicator and its files are installed into the /opt/netscape directory.

5. Check out the README file in the netscape directory for information on release notes, features, or known problems.

6. To start Netscape from the command line of a terminal window, specify its full path:

```
# /opt/netscape/netscape
```

7. A much better way to configure Netscape is to create a symbolic link, called netscape, in the /usr/local/bin directory:

```
# ln -s /opt/netscape/netscape /usr/local/bin/netscape
```

8. Netscape's installation script does not create a required symbolic link to use the client's built-in help. If you try to use Netscape help, you'll get an error message. You can configure Netscape in two different ways. One way is to create the required link with the ln command:

```
# ln -s /opt/netscape /usr/local/lib/netscape
```

The other way is to create an environment variable, NS_NETHELP_PATH, which points to the /opt/netscape/nethelp directory, and add the /opt/netscape directory to your shell's PATH environment variable. Open the bash shell's Startup file, /etc/profile, and enter the following:

```
NS_NETHELP_PATH=/opt/netscape/nethelp
PATH=$PATH:/opt/netscape
export NS_NETHELP_PATH PATH
```

Save the file. To use this variable right away, use the bash shell's source command:

```
# source /etc/profile
```

SEE ALSO

➤ *For more information about symbolic links and using the* `ln` *command, see page 40.*
➤ *To learn more about shell environment variables, see page 90.*

Working with Netscape Communicator

Netscape Communicator has nearly 30 different command-line options. Like most well-behaved X11 clients, this program also supports several X11 Toolkit options, such as geometry settings. For example, if you want a smaller initial window, specify a smaller starting window using geometry settings.

Starting Netscape from the command line

1. Use Navigator's `--help` option to see a list of supported command-line options:

   ```
   # netscape --help
   ```

   If the list is too large for your terminal window, redirect the standard error output to a file:

   ```
   # netscape --help 2>netscape.options
   ```

   The file `netscape.options` will contain the output from the `--help` option.

2. To start Netscape with a specific window size, use the X11 Toolkit `-geometry` setting, followed by a window size in horizontal and vertical pixels:

   ```
   # netscape -geometry 600x400 &
   ```

SEE ALSO

➤ *For more information about X11 Toolkit options, see page 307.*
➤ *To learn more about input or output redirection, see page 19.*

3. The Navigator window will appear, as shown in Figure 15.4. To start Communicator without an initial window, and to have a convenient floating toolbar of the four basic Communicator components available without using a lot of screen real estate, use the `-component-bar` option:

   ```
   # netscape -component-bar &
   ```

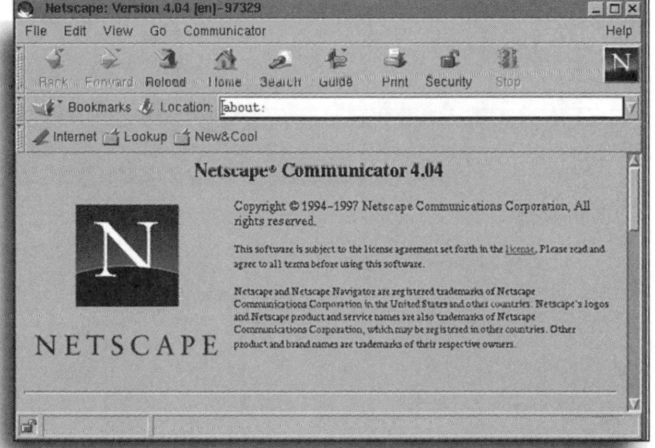

FIGURE 15.4
The Navigator window size can be specified with X11 `-geometry` settings.

4. The toolbar will appear, as shown in Figure 15.5. Run a desired component by clicking on the Navigator, Mailbox, Discussions, or Composer icons on the toolbar.

FIGURE 15.5
The Netscape Communicator toolbar is a handy way to access four different Communicator components.

Setting Navigator preferences

1. To set preferences for Navigator, move your mouse cursor to the Navigator Edit menu and select the Preferences menu item. The Preferences dialog box will appear, as shown in Figure 15.6.
2. To configure Communicator to launch a specific component, select one of the components under the Appearance setting. To configure the appearance of Communicator's component bar, select a Show Toolbar As setting.
3. Click on the Fonts or Colors settings to customize the font size of menus and the background or foreground colors used by Communicator.
4. Move your mouse cursor to the Navigator item under the Category menu (as shown in Figure 15.6). Click on the

Navigator item. The Navigator settings appear, as shown in Figure 15.7.

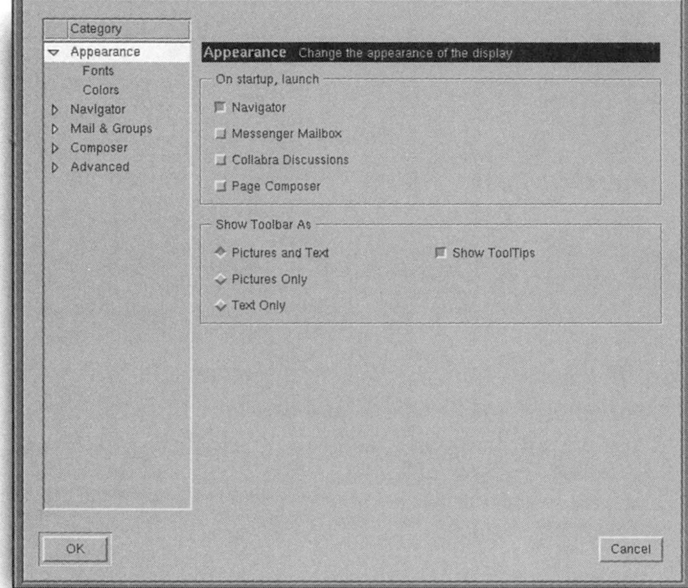

FIGURE 15.6
Numerous Communicator preferences are set through the Navigator Preferences dialog box.

SEE ALSO

➤ *To learn more about configuring your mouse for the X Window System, see page 269.*

5. Select your preference for how Communicator should start, the default home page, and the cache or history settings. Then move your mouse cursor to the Navigator menu item under the Category list. Click your left mouse button on the small triangle next to the word *Navigator*. The preferences dialog box will then list the Languages and Applications menu items. Click on the Applications menu item, and the Navigator Preferences dialog box will change as shown in Figure 15.8.

Netscape Communicator supports *plug-ins*, or additional programs that can add features to the browser. One of these is the RealPlayer plug-in named rvplayer, which you can use to listen to audio or video broadcasts through the Internet (audio or video will be played automatically when you click on audio or video links on a web page).

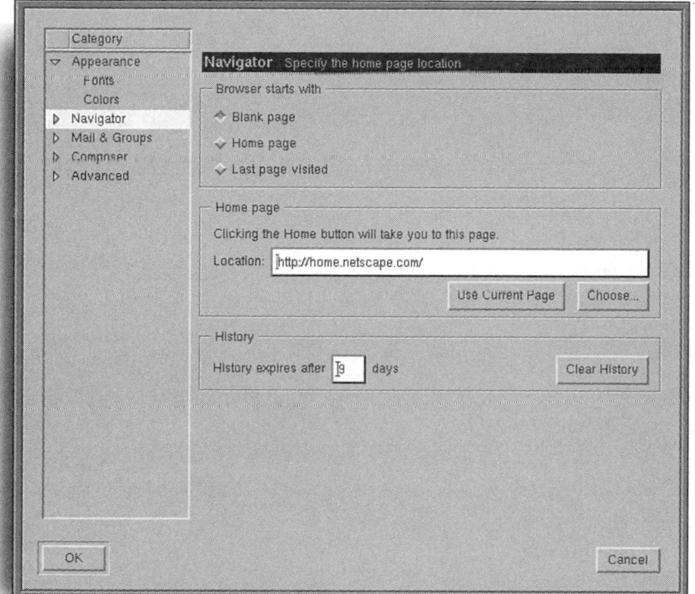

FIGURE 15.7
The Navigator settings determine how Navigator works upon starting, what the default home page is, and how long Navigator retains its cache list of visited web pages.

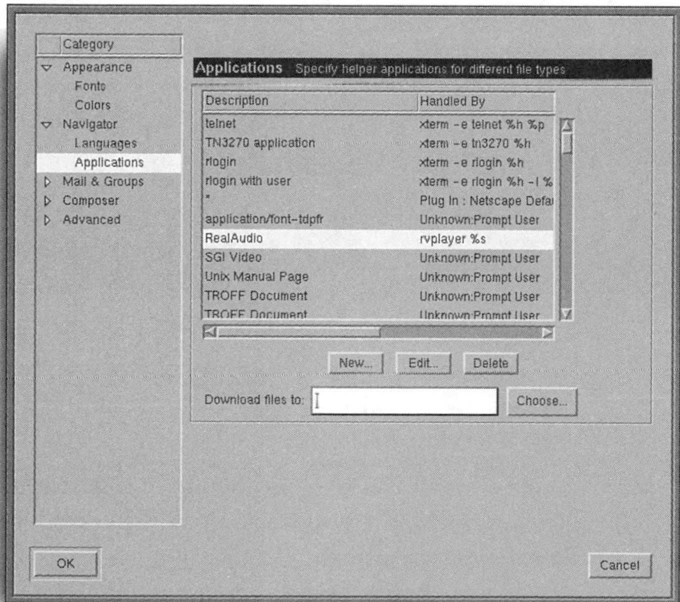

FIGURE 15.8
The Navigator Applications setting is used to add support for external programs or plug-ins, such as the RealVideo Player.

Installing Internet video support for Netscape

1. To add support for the RealPlayer plug-in, continue from the previous step-by-step and scroll through the list of Applications. Select the RealAudio application and then click on the Edit button with your mouse's left mouse button. A dialog box will appear, as shown in Figure 15.9.

SEE ALSO

➤ *To learn about more multimedia tools for Linux, see page 358.*

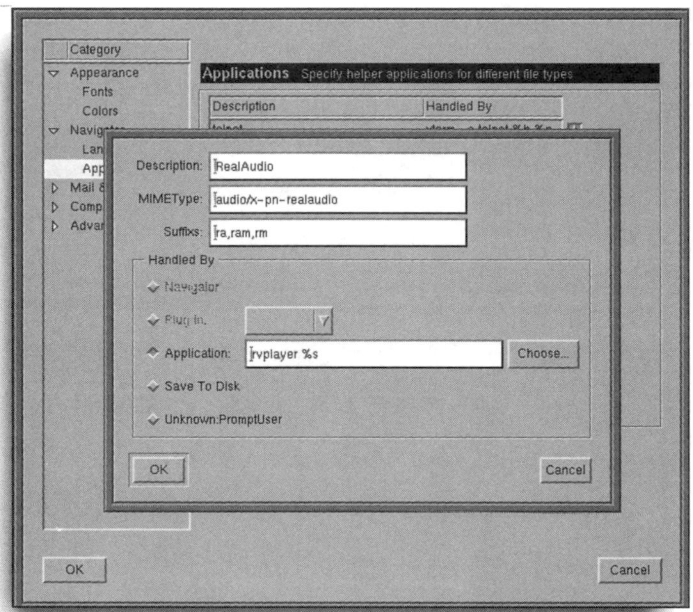

FIGURE 15.9
Use the Navigator Application Edit dialog box to add specific support for the RealAudio Player.

2. Add the filename extension `.rm` to the list, edit the Handled by Application: field to read rvplayer %s, and then click on the OK button. Click the OK button again to exit and save your Navigator Preferences.

3. To test the rvplayer plug-in, first make sure that it is installed on your system (look under the `/usr/bin` directory for the rvplayer program), and then use Navigator to read in the rvplayer sample video from your hard drive:

```
# netscape file:/usr/lib/rvplayer/welcome.rm
```

After Navigator displays its initial window, the RealVideo Player will start and will play a short music and video clip, as shown in Figure 15.10.

FIGURE 15.10
The RealVideo Navigator plug-in will play audio and video clips during your Internet sessions when you use Netscape Navigator.

Look under the `/usr/doc/rvplayer` directory for information about the RealVideo Player. To get the latest RealVideo plug-in for Linux, browse to:

`http://www.real.com`

For more information about using Communicator plug-ins, browse to:

`http://home.netscape.com`

Red Hat Linux users can also find more specific information about Netscape Communicator and plug-ins in Red Hat package manager format by browsing to:

`http://www.redhat.com`

CHAPTER

16

Reading Usenet News

By Bill Ball

Specifying NNTP service

Using newsreaders for Linux

Configuring newsreaders for Linux

Specifying NNTP Service

At last count, there were more than 30,000 Usenet newsgroups, with more being created each day. In order to read Usenet news, you must have access to a network news server. These are the computers that send, receive, and store the thousands of Usenet Internet messages exchanged daily. Chances are your Internet service provider (ISP) provides access to a Usenet news server.

You'll also need a news-reading program, or *newsreader*, that understands the Network News Transfer Protocol (NNTP). Newsreaders generally work by retrieving lists of messages, or articles, sorted by newsgroup, from your ISP's news server through a network connection. Newsgroups to which you are subscribed are usually contained in a text file called `.newsrc` in your home directory. Before you can begin to read Usenet news, you must create your `.newsrc` file.

What newsgroups should I start with?

I've recommended a list of initial Linux newsgroups to get you started, but the quickest way to set up your `.newsrc` file is to use the `newsetup` command, found under the `/usr/bin` directory. This command is part of the `trn` newsreader software, and simply creates a `.newsrc` file in your home directory with the default newsgroup `news.announce.newusers`. This newsgroup is the best place to start learning about reading Usenet news. You'll find tips, pointers, and lists of Frequently Asked Questions (FAQs) that will help you avoid problems as a new Usenet news reader.

Creating your *.newsrc* file

1. Using your favorite text editor, create a file called `.newsrc` in your home directory. This file will contain your initial list of newsgroups from which you'd like to read articles.
2. Enter the following list of initial newsgroups for Linux:
```
comp.os.linux.advocacy:
comp.os.linux.announce:
comp.os.linux.development.apps:
comp.os.linux.development.system:
comp.os.linux.hardware:
comp.os.linux.misc:
comp.os.linux.networking:
comp.os.linux.setup:
comp.os.linux.x:
```
3. Save the file and exit your editor.

SEE ALSO

➤ *For more information about connecting to the Internet, see page 166.*
➤ *To learn how to use text editors, see page 50.*

For your newsreader to be able to retrieve your newsgroups' articles, you must tell the newsreader the name of your ISP's news server. Although most Linux newsreaders use the `NNTPSERVER` environment variable, you can also place the server's name in a file called `nntpserver` under the `/etc` directory. News server environment variables can be defined for all users on your system or for individual users.

Creating your system's *NNTPSERVER* environment variable

1. To create the `NNTPSERVER` variable for all users on your system, log on as the root operator and, using your favorite text editor, open the file profile under the `/etc` directory. This file defines default variables for all users.
2. Enter the name of your news server in the file:
   ```
   NNTPSERVER=news.staffnet.com
   ```
3. Don't forget to include a following `EXPORT` statement (used by the bash shell) in the file:
   ```
   export NNTPSERVER
   ```
4. Save the file and exit your editor. To use this variable right away, use the `source` shell command (if you're using the `bash` shell) to read the new variable in the profile file:
   ```
   # source /etc/profile
   ```
5. To verify that your news server variable has been defined, pipe the output of the `printenv` command through the `fgrep` search program:
   ```
   # printenv ¦ fgrep NNTPSERVER
   NNTPSERVER=news.erols.com
   ```
   The `fgrep` command displays the value of your `NNTPSERVER` variable.

If you'd prefer to allow your users to use different news servers, follow the previous steps, but edit the file `.bash_profile` in your home directory rather than in the system's `/etc/profile`.

SEE ALSO

➤ *To learn more about using shell commands such as* `export` *or* `source`, *see page 90.*

➤ *To learn more about using pipes on the command line, see page 19.*

Selecting a Newsreader

Choosing a newsreader is a matter of personal preference. You might be surprised to learn that most Linux distributions include at least a half dozen newsreaders, including the following:

- lynx—Although it is usually considered a text-only Web browser, lynx can also be used to read Usenet news. See the lynx manual page for more information.
- Netscape—The latest version of this X11-based Web browser, Communicator, includes Netscape Collabra, a newsreader.
- `pine`—Although it is usually considered a mail-transport agent or mail reader, `pine` also reads Usenet news.
- `slrn`—This capable console newsreader with mouse and color support also works under X11 in a terminal window.
- `tin`—This console newsreader also works under X11 in a terminal window.
- `trn`—This console newsreader also works under X11 in a terminal window.
- `xrn`—This X11-only newsreader has only bare-bones features for reading news.

Choose the newsreader that most easily allows you to subscribe or unsubscribe to newsgroups, as well as to browse, save, reply to, or post messages. If you use the X Window System, you might want to choose a newsreader such as `slrn` or Netscape if color and mouse support is important. Other newsreaders, such as `tin` or `trn`, work well over remote logons, such as dial-in service, because they do not require the graphics overhead of X11.

SEE ALSO

➤ *To learn more about using the lynx Web browser, see page 212.*
➤ *For more information on using the X Window System, see page 260.*

Using the *tin* Newsreader

The `tin` newsreader reads your list of newsgroups from the `.newsrc` file in your home directory. This reader, found under the `/usr/bin` directory, displays your newsgroups and newsgroup articles in lists you can browse with your cursor keys (see Figure 16.1). You can read one of the listed articles by selecting the newsgroup and then pressing Enter.

```
rxvt
                 Group Selection (news.erols.com  9)                      h=help

  1 1550 comp.os.linux.advocacy          Benefits of Linux compared to other operating systems.
  2   70 comp.os.linux.announce          Announcements important to the Linux community. (Modera
  3 1662 comp.os.linux.development.apps  Writing Linux applications, porting to Linux.
  4 2254 comp.os.linux.development.system Linux kernels, device drivers, modules.
  5  630 comp.os.linux.hardware          Hardware compatibility with the Linux operating system.
  6 2042 comp.os.linux.misc              Linux-specific topics not covered by other groups.
  7 3437 comp.os.linux.networking        Networking and communications under Linux.
  8 5401 comp.os.linux.setup             Linux installation and system administration.
  9  494 comp.os.linux.x                 Linux X Window System servers, clients, libs and fonts.

         <n>=set current to n, TAB=next unread, /=search pattern, c)atchup,
     g)oto, j=line down, k=line up, h)elp, m)ove, q)uit, r=toggle all/unread,
      s)ubscribe, S)ub pattern, u)nsubscribe, U)nsub pattern, y)ank in/out

                             *** End of Groups ***
```

FIGURE 16.1

The `tin` newsreader displays lists of newsgroups in its main window.

To retrieve your newsgroups' articles remotely from your ISP's news server, start `tin` with the `-r` (remote) option on the command line, like this:

```
# tin -r
```

This command line checks for new newsgroups and retrieves the current list of all active newsgroups on your ISP's news server. This can take a long time! To speed things up, use the `-n` option (to retrieve articles only for newsgroups in your `.newsrc` file) along with the `-q` option (to disable checking for new newsgroups), like this:

```
# tin -nqr
```

Use the `-f` option to read articles in newsgroups appearing in files other than the default `.newsrc` file. (Creating files other than the default `.newsrc` file is a good way to organize your newsgroups by interest.) Follow the `-f` option with the name of your specific newsgroup resource file:

```
# tin -nqrf .myaltnewsrc
```

This command causes `tin` to retrieve articles only from newsgroups listed in the `.myaltnewsrc` file (which can look the same as `.newsrc`, but contains a list of different newsgroups, such as `alt.barney.die.die.die`).

The `tin` reader has a number of different keyboard commands that you can use while reading news, as shown in Table 16.1.

TABLE 16.1 **Common *tin* keyboard commands**

Key(s)	Action
/	Search forward through articles.
?	Search backward through articles.
Enter	List articles in the current group, or read a message.
C	Mark all articles as read.
H	Get built-in help.
Q	Quit the current newsgroup or `tin`.
S	Save the current message in the default news folder (when reading a message).
S	Subscribe to the current group (when listing news groups, such as in Figure 16.1).
U	Unsubscribe to the current group.
W	Post an article to the current group.

Using the *slrn* Newsreader

The `slrn` newsreader works much like the `tin` newsreader, but features several improvements, such as support for color and a mouse, simultaneous display of articles and article lists, and the capability to designate a NNTP server on the command line.

Although the `slrn` newsreader uses an `NNTPSERVER` variable, you can enter the `-h` option followed by the name of a different news server to read news from a different computer:

```
# slrn -h news.erols.com
```

Use the `-f` option to read articles in newsgroups listed in a different `.newsrc` file, like this:

```
# slrn -f .myautonewsrc
```

This command line instructs `slrn` to read articles from newsgroups defined in `.myautonewsrc` in your home directory. This can be handy for separating your news-reading sessions according to different interests (such as `rec.autos` or `rec.autos.antiques`).

When you run `slrn`, your newsgroups will appear in a list. To read articles for a particular newsgroup, move your cursor to the newsgroup and press Enter. The `slrn` newsreader displays the article list. To read an article, move your cursor to it, and then press Enter. As shown in Figure 16.2, the `slrn` program features a split display, showing not only the current article, but also other articles in the newsgroup.

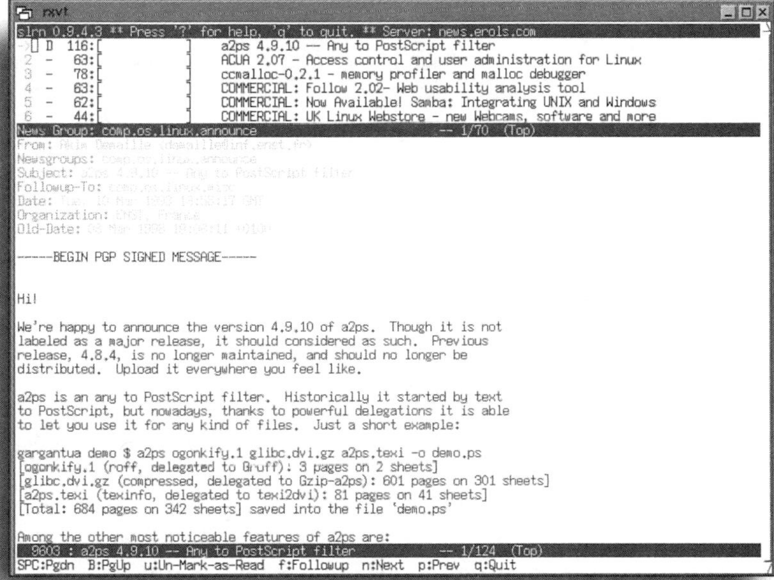

FIGURE 16.2
The slrn newsreader features a handy split screen to view article lists while reading articles.

Like `tin`, `slrn` supports many keyboard commands, the most common of which are shown in Table 16.2.

TABLE 16.2 Common *slrn* keyboard commands

Key(s)	Action
/ *str*	Search for *str* in newsgroup names.
/ *str*	Search for *str* in article while reading.
?	Search backward.
F	Forward an article by email.
H	Hide the current article.
N	Go to the next newsgroup.

continues...

TABLE 16.2 Continued

Key(s)	Action
P	Post an article to the current newsgroup.
c	Mark newsgroup articles as read.
f	Post a follow-up to the current article.
h	Hide the article window.
n	Read the next article.
o	Save the article to a file.
p	Post the article to the current newsgroup.
q	Quit.
r	Reply to the article author by email.
s	Subscribe to the current newsgroup.
u	Unsubscribe from the current newsgroup.

Using the *trn* Newsreader

The `trn` newsreader works much like the `tin` newsreader, and retrieves newsgroup articles for newsgroups defined in your `.newsrc` file in your home directory. This program has more than 45 command-line options as well as numerous features—too many to document here (see the `trn` manual page for details).

The `trn` reader recognizes the `NNTPSERVER` environment variable, or the name of the server defined in the file server, under the `/usr/local/lib/rn` directory. To read your newsgroups' articles, start `trn` like this:

```
# trn
```

The `trn` newsreader retrieves messages for your newsgroups, but asks whether you want to read messages in each group, as shown in Figure 16.3.

Using the *xrn* Newsreader

Like many of the newsreaders in this chapter, the `xrn` newsreader uses your `.newsrc` file as the default list of newsgroups to read, and also recognizes the `NNTPSERVER` environment variable. You must run the X Window System in order to use this newsreader.

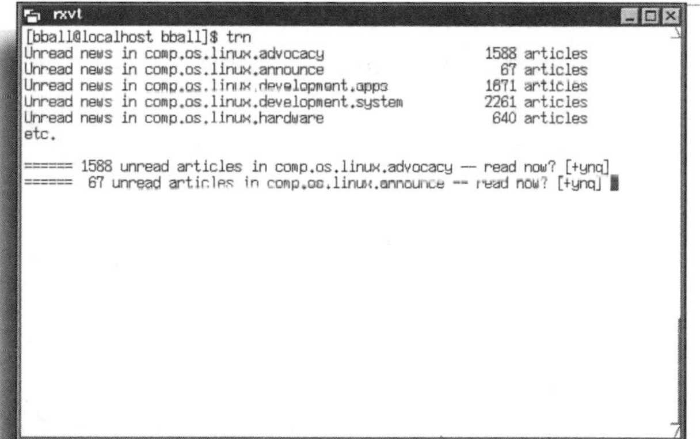

FIGURE 16.3
The trn newsreader asks whether you want to read articles in a subscribed newsgroup.

The xrn default window size is too large for 800×600-pixel displays. Fortunately, xrn, like several other X11 clients, also recognizes many X11 Toolkit options. Use the X11 -geometry command-line option to start xrn in a window small enough for your display, like so:

```
# xrn -geometry 640x480
```

The xrn newsreader features a split window for viewing lists of articles and newsgroups at the same time. To read an article, click a newsgroup and then an article listing.

Unfortunately, the version of xrn distributed with recent releases of Red Hat Linux does not include documentation or manual pages for its more than 70 command-line options. However, you can learn about these options by feeding xrn a question mark on the command like this:

```
# xrn -?
```

The list of options scrolls down your screen. If your X11 terminal window is too small, use the shell redirection operator to redirect the output to a text file that you can later read:

```
# xrn -? >xrn.help
```

Using the *pine* Mailer to Read Usenet News

The pine program, discussed in the section titled "Selecting a Mail Program" in Chapter 13, "Using Electronic Mail," is a capable mail-transport agent, but it also functions as a Usenet newsreader. When you use pine, reading news articles is as easy as reading your email messages.

Reading Usenet news with *pine*

1. Start your Internet connection, and then start `pine` from the command line by entering the following:
   ```
   # pine
   ```
2. Press Enter to go to the folder list.
3. Press the down-arrow key to move your cursor to the News Collection list, and press Enter. The list of newsgroups defined in your `.newsrc` file in your home directory is displayed, as shown in Figure 16.4.

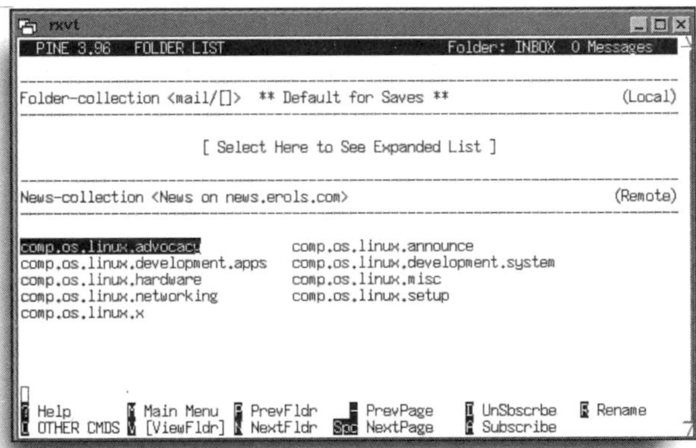

FIGURE 16.4
The `pine` mailer can be used to retrieve articles from subscribed newsgroups.

4. To read articles in a particular newsgroup, move your cursor to the desired newsgroup and press Enter. The `pine` program retrieves articles for that newsgroup and displays them in a list exactly like your email messages.

SEE ALSO

➤ *To learn more about the* `pine` *email program, see page 183.*

Reading News with Netscape Communicator

Although many users think of Netscape as a web browser, experienced Linux and X11 users know that the latest versions of Netscape Communicator do much more, including providing support for reading newsgroups.

Reading Usenet news with Netscape Communicator

1. From the Netscape Navigator window, select the Communicator menu, and then select the Collabra

Discussions menu item. The Netscape Messenger window, shown in Figure 16.5, appears. Double-click the news server to display your newsgroups.

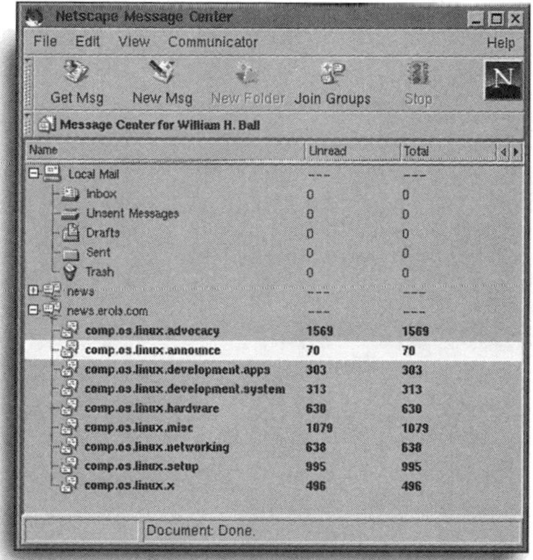

FIGURE 16.5
Netscape's main Messenger window displays each subscribed newsgroup, along with the number of unread articles.

2. From the command line of a terminal window, start Netscape in the component bar mode by typing the following:

```
# netscape -component-bar &
```

The Communicator component bar, shown in Figure 16.6, appears. Click the Discussions button to open the Netscape Messenger window (refer to Figure 16.5).

FIGURE 16.6
Netscape's component bar can be used to start reading Usenet news.

3. From the Netscape Messenger window, open the Inbox drop-down list to view a list of mail folders, including news (see Figure 16.7). Notice that the list of newsgroups, defined in your `.newsrc` file in your home directory, also appears.

Select the newsgroup from which you'd like to read articles.

4. From the command line of a terminal window, start

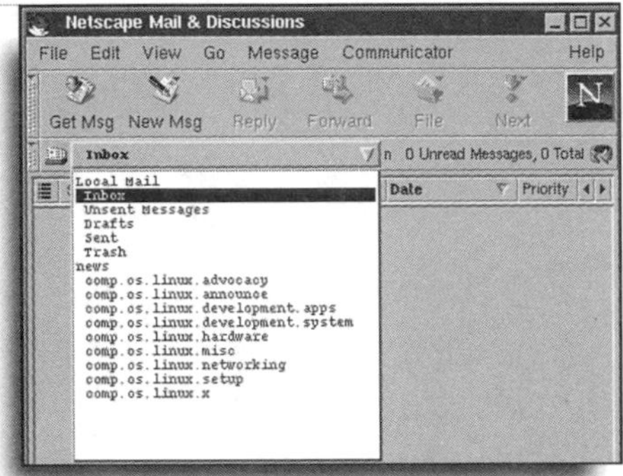

FIGURE 16.7

Netscape's Messenger window features a drop-down list of newsgroups to which you subscribe.

Netscape with the `-news` command-line option, like so:

```
# netscape -news &
```

SEE ALSO

➤ *For more information about Netscape Communicator, see page 216.*

Configuring Newsreaders

After you've defined your `NNTPSERVER` environment variable and created your `.newsrc` file, most of the work of configuring your system for reading Usenet articles is done. Nonetheless, your newsreader might provide various features designed to make it easier to read news. Configuring a specific newsreader can become quite complicated because of the number of features.

Many newsreaders, such as `tin`, `trn`, and `slrn`, have supplementary documentation (including tips and hints) under the `/usr/doc` directory. Use the information from these documents, along with information from the programs' manual pages, to configure your newsreader.

The easiest way to read Usenet news?

For background information about Usenet news or NNTP, and for details about setting up your system to distribute newsgroup articles, see Olaf Kirch's *Linux Network Administrator's Guide*, usually found under the `/usr/doc/LDP/nag` directory in Red Hat Linux distributions. Details about how to set up Linux to get news feeds can be found in Kirch's chapter titled "A Description of NNTP," and you can read the "Netnews" chapter to learn how to set up your own NNTP server. You'll find lots of great information, including this jewel, perhaps the simplest newsreader (which uses the `find` command to pipe news articles through the `cat` and `more` commands):

```
$ find /var/spool/news -name '[0-9]*' -exec cat {} \; | more
```

Configuring the *tin* Newsreader

The `tin` newsreader can be configured in a number of different ways, for different reasons—such as to create a signature file for newsgroup postings, or to retrieve and save articles while you're away from your computer. Most of `tin`'s resource files are located in the .tin directory in your home directory. This directory, and two files, attributes and posted, are created when you first run tin.

Customize tin by pressing M while running the program. You'll see a menu, shown in Figure 16.8, in which you can set 18 different options. When you save your options, the file tinrc is created and saved in the .tin directory.

Edit the tinrc file directly if you'd like to see 19 more options.

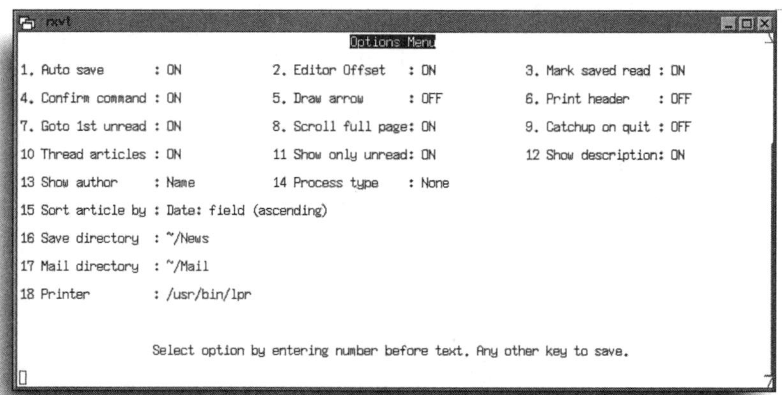

FIGURE 16.8
The tin newsreader features a convenient configuration screen.

For details about these options, see the "Global Options Menu" and "Tinrc Configurable Variables" sections of the tin manual page.

Configuring the *slrn* Newsreader

The slrn newsreader reads systemwide defaults from a file called slrn.rc, found under the /usr/lib/slrn directory. To customize slrn for all users on your system, log on as the root operator and edit this file. To customize slrn for yourself, copy this file to your home directory and name the file .slrnrc. Then follow these steps to customize just some of slrn's features.

Customizing the *slrn* newsreader

1. Copy the file /usr/lib/slrn/slrn.rc to your home directory, renaming it to .slrnrc, like this:

```
# cp /usr/lib/slrn/slrn.rc .slrnrc
```

2. Using your favorite text editor, open the file. Look for lines similar to the following:

```
% SERVER to NEWSRC mapping
%server "hsdndev.harvard.edu" ".jnewrc-hsdndev"
%server "news.uni-stuttgart.de" ".jnewsrc-stuttgart
```

Note that these entries have a percent sign (%) at the beginning of each line. This symbol indicates the presence of a comment, and slrn ignores an entry if you place this symbol at the beginning of that line. If you have access to different news servers and want to use a customized list of newsgroups to read from each, specify the server names along with the name of the file containing the lists of newsgroups, omitting the percent sign, like this:

```
server "news.staffnet.com" ".staffnetnewsrc"
server "news.erols.com" ".erolsnewsrc"
```

3. Look for the username and replyto entries, similar to these:

```
%set username "jd"
%set realname "John Doe"
%set replyto  "jd@somthing.com"
```

Enter your username, realname, and replyto settings:

```
set username "bball"
set realname "William Ball"
set replyto "bball@erols.com"
```

If you want to protect yourself from getting junk email from idiot spammers (who electronically harvest email addresses from Usenet newsgroup articles), insert a bogus phrase in these settings like this:

```
set username "bball_REMOVE_TO_REPLY_"
set replyto "bball_REMOVE_TO_REPLY_SPAM@erols.com"
```

This ensures that spammers reap a bad email address, but clues responders to remove the phrase to email a reply.

4. One of slrn's great features is its capability to support the selection and scrolling of messages with your mouse. Look for the mouse configuration section, which has lines like the following:

```
% Enable xterm mouse support: 1 to enable, 0 to disable
  set mouse 0
```

Change `set mouse 0` to `set mouse 1` to enable mouse support.

5. The `slrn` newsreader supports customized colors. You can change the colors of different parts of articles by editing the `Colors` section of your `.slrnrc` file. Look for the color configuration section, which has lines like the following:

```
%-----------------------------------------------------
% Colors
%-----------------------------------------------------
color header_number      "black"        "white"
color header_name        "black"        "white"
color normal             "black"        "white"
color error              "red"          "white"
color status             "yellow"       "blue"
color group              "blue"         "white"
color article            "blue"         "white"
color cursor             "black"        "white"
color author             "blue"         "white"
color subject            "black"        "white"
color headers            "black"        "white"
color menu               "yellow"       "blue"
color menu_press         "blue"         "yellow"
color tree               "red"          "white"
color quotes             "red"          "white"
color thread_number      "blue"         "white"
color high_score         "red"          "white"
color signature          "red"          "white"
color description        "blue"         "white"
color tilde              "black"        "white"
color response_char      "green"        "white"
```

Each line lists a part of the `slrn` window, newsgroup, or article. For example, the default colors used to display the subject line of an article are black text on a white background. Available color entries include

```
black                  gray
red                    brightred
green                  brightgreen
brown                  yellow
blue                   brightblue
magenta                brightmagenta
```

```
cyan            brightcyan
lightgray       white
```

Be careful! You can make it impossible to read postings by changing the color of the text and background of articles to a setting like this:

```
color article              "white"              "white"
```

Configuring the *trn* Newsreader

The trn newsreader has many different command-line options, but unlike other newsreaders, does not have a default resource file, such as .trnrc, to read settings upon startup. However, you can create your own resource file and enter different settings to customize how trn works.

Creating and editing a *.trnrc* resource file

1. Using your favorite text editor, open the file .bash_profile (if you use the default Red Hat Linux shell bash), and enter the following environment variable and export statement:
   ```
   TRNINIT=$HOME/.trnrc
   export TRNINIT
   ```
2. Save your .bash_profile file. To use this variable right away, use the bash shell's source command, like this:
   ```
   # source .bash_profile
   ```
3. Again using your text editor, create a file called .trnrc. You can include any number of trn's command-line options, such as the -q (quick check) option, which instructs trn not to request any new newsgroups, but instead to retrieve articles for newsgroups in your .newsrc file. Enter this option like this:
   ```
   -q
   ```
4. To use a REPLYTO line to foil spammers, enter a line like this:
   ```
   -EREPLYTO="bball_REMOVE_TO_REPLY_@erols.com"
   ```
5. See the trn manual pages and the file HINTS.TRN, found under the /usr/doc/trn directory, for more options and details about how to use a resource file.

Configuring the *pine* Mailer to Read Usenet News

The `pine` email program automatically reads your `.newsrc` file of newsgroups. To configure `pine` to read Usenet news, you must start `pine`, and then use its Setup and Config menus.

Configuring *pine* to read news

1. Start `pine` by entering the following at the command line:
   `# pine`

2. Press S, then C. `pine` displays its configuration screen, as shown in Figure 16.9.

FIGURE 16.9
The `pine` mailer configuration screen is used to specify the NNTP server used to read Usenet news.

3. Move the cursor down to the `nntp-server` line and press C. Type the name of your ISP's news server and press Enter.

4. Scroll down the list of `pine`'s other options. Look for a line similar to the following:

   ```
   [ ]  news-read-in-newsrc-order
   ```

   If you want `pine` to display your newsgroups in the same order as entered in your `.newsrc` file, press X to set this variable. An `X` appears between the brackets in front of the option, like this:

   ```
   [X]  news-read-in-newsrc-order
   ```

5. When you're finished making changes, press E to exit `pine`'s configuration. `pine` asks whether you want to "Commit changes." Press Y to save your changes.

Configuring Netscape Collabra to Read News

Netscape Communicator automatically uses your `.newsrc` file to read Usenet news, but you must first configure Netscape to use your ISP's news server.

Specifying your news server for Netscape Communicator

1. Connect to your ISP and start a PPP connection.
2. Start Netscape from the command line of a terminal window by typing the following:
   ```
   # netscape &
   ```
3. From the Navigator Edit menu, select the Preferences menu item. The Preferences dialog box, shown in Figure 16.10, appears.

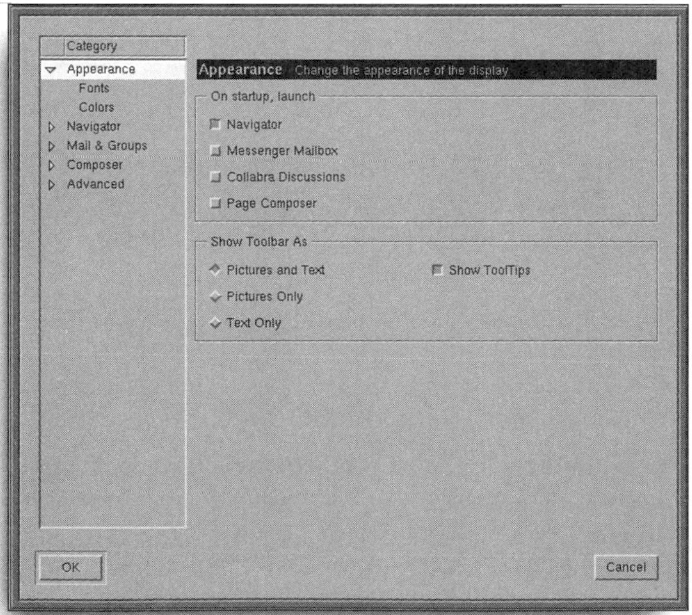

FIGURE 16.10
Configure Netscape Navigator through its Preferences dialog box.

4. Click the Mail & Groups item in the Preferences dialog box to reveal a list of five additional settings (see Figure 16.11).

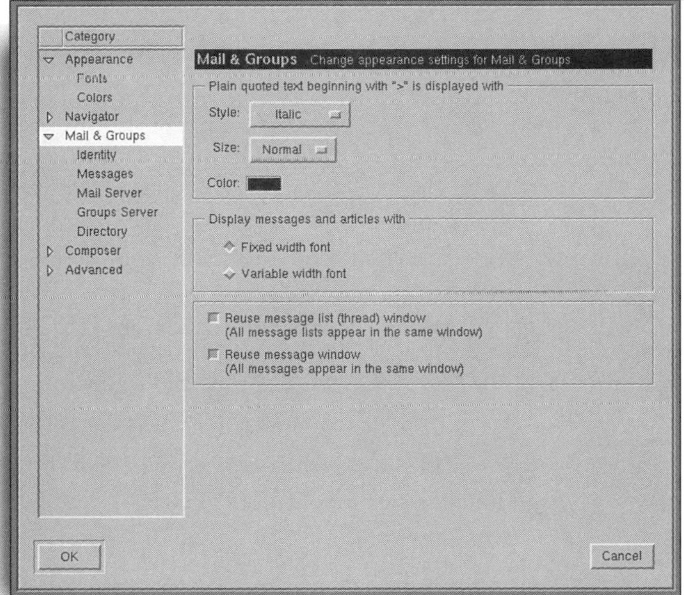

FIGURE 16.11
The Preferences dialog box offers a Mail & Groups settings to configure news server settings.

5. Click the Groups Server entry. The Groups Server dialog box, shown in Figure 16.12, appears.

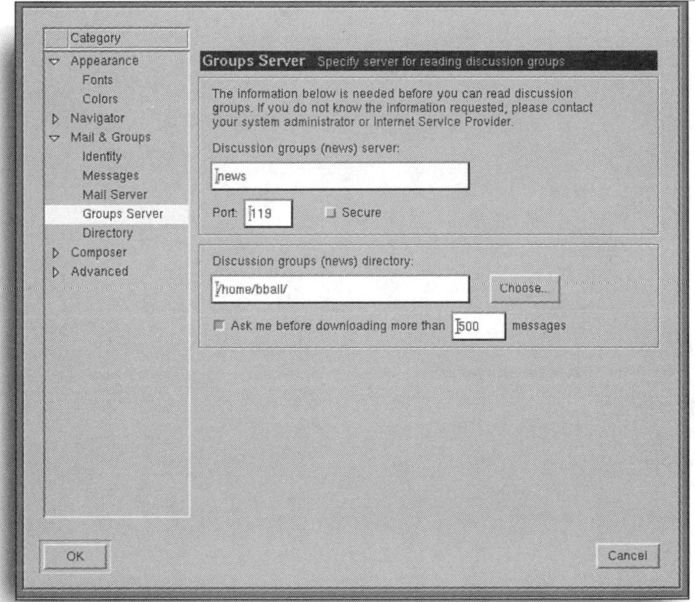

FIGURE 16.12
Specify the desired NNTP server by entering the name of your ISP's news server in the Groups Server dialog box.

6. In the Discussion Groups (News) Server field, enter the name of your ISP's news server, like this:
   `news.erols.com`

7. Click OK to save your preferences.

As described in the earlier section, "Reading News with Netscape Communicator," you can use Netscape Messenger to read Usenet news articles. And although you can manually add newsgroups to your `.newsrc` file, you can also use Netscape Messenger to add new newsgroups or servers.

Adding newsgroups and news servers to Netscape

1. Connect to your ISP and start a PPP connection.
2. Start Netscape in the news-reading mode from the command line of a terminal window by typing the following:
   ```
   # netscape -news &
   ```

   This command displays Netscape Messenger (refer to Figure 16.5). Click the Join Groups button or select Add Discussion Group from the File menu. The dialog box shown in Figure 16.13 appears, listing your current news server.

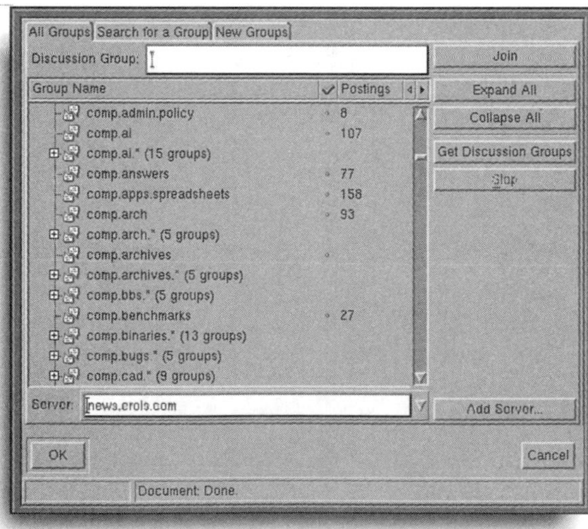

FIGURE 16.13
Netscape Messenger retrieves and displays a list of current newsgroups that you can subscribe to.

4. To add a news server, click the Add Server button. A dialog box like the one shown in Figure 16.14 appears. Enter the name of your new server, like so:
```
nws.staffnet.com
```

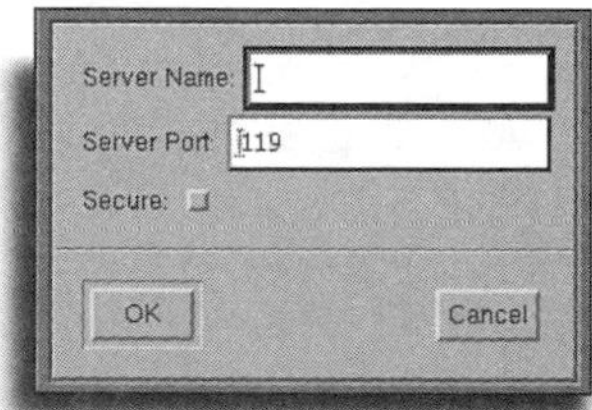

FIGURE 16.14
Add a news server.

5. Click OK. To add more groups, click the All Groups, Search for a Group, or New Groups tab at the top of dialog box shown in Figure 16.14.
6. Click the Search for a Group tab. This tab, shown in Figure 16.15, provides a Search For field, in which you can enter a search string (including wildcards). For example, to search for all Linux newsgroups, use a search line like the following:
```
comp.os.linux*
```

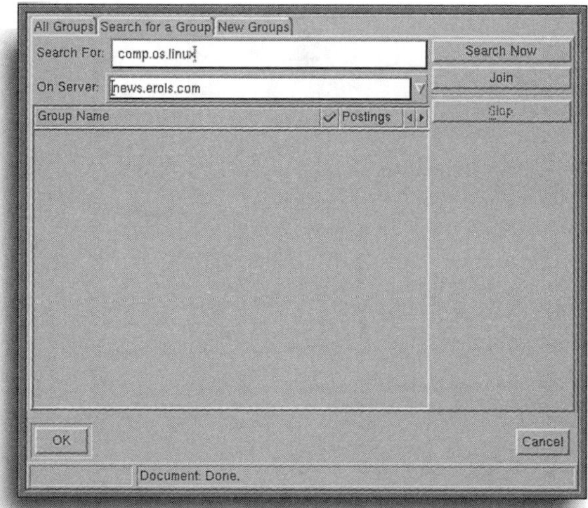

FIGURE 16.15
Search for newsgroups via the Search for a Group tab.

7. After you enter your search string, click the Search Now button. A list of matching newsgroups appears in the Group Name section, as shown in Figure 16.16. To join a

newsgroup, select it, and then click the Join button. Click OK to exit the Join Groups dialog box.

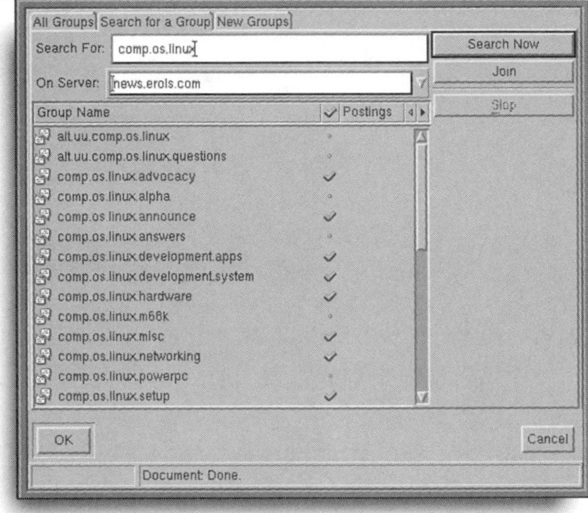

FIGURE 16.16
Netscape Messenger returns a list of all matching newsgroups from your search entry.

CHAPTER

17

Using *telnet* and Internet Relay Chat

By Bill Ball

Connecting to remote computers

Logging on with the `telnet` command

Downloading files during `telnet` sessions

Finding Internet chat groups

Joining Internet chat groups

Chatting on the Internet with Internet Relay Chat

Using the *telnet* Command

The `telnet` command is used to log on to remote computers on the Internet. Use `telnet` to log on, usually with a user name and password, and run programs, view files, or download data. The `telnet` command is on the command line, followed by a hostname, or remote computers system's name to start a `telnet` session.

For example, to connect to the U.S. Environmental Protection Agency (which runs open information services on several remote computer systems), use the `telnet` command, like this:

```
# telnet ttnbbs.rtpnc.epa.gov
```

This command connects you to the EPA's remote computer, and you receive a logon prompt (as shown in Figure 17.1).

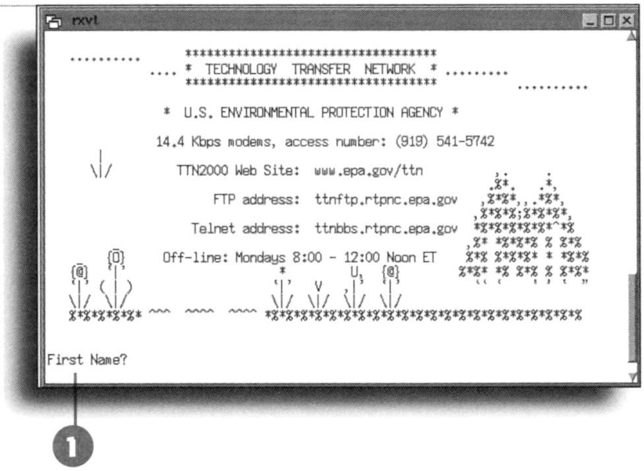

FIGURE 17.1
Log on to remote federal government or other computer systems by using the `telnet` command.

1 Login prompt

SEE ALSO

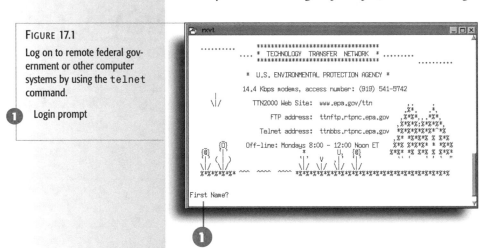

➤ *For more information on using Netscape Communicator, see page 216.*

Connecting to Other Computers

You usually need an active username and password on the remote computer in order to log on to the remote system using the `telnet` program. This means that you generally need an account on the remote computer system to get in. Few system administrators allow anonymous `telnet` access, although you can find a list of computer systems with open `telnet` access (such as those that run bulletin-board systems, or BBSs) by using a search engine through a favorite Web search site (such as `http://www.yahoo.com`).

The `telnet` command, like the `ftp` command, can also be used in an interactive mode, so you can open and close sessions to different remote computers without exiting the program. The `telnet` command also has built-in help (accessed by the keyword help without an active session). Table 17.1 lists many of `telnet`'s built-in commands.

TABLE 17.1 Common *telnet* commands (accessed by Ctrl+] during an active session)

Command	Action
!	Run a shell from `telnet`.
?	Show help.
close	Close the current connection.
display	Display control characters.
environ	List or change environment variables.
logout	Log off remote system and close the connection.
open	Connect to a remote computer.
quit	Exit the `telnet` program.
send	Send special characters to remote computer.
set	Set various operating parameters status. Print connection status.
toggle	Toggle various operating parameters.
unset	Unset various operating parameters.
z	Suspend `telnet`.

Starting a *telnet* session

1. Start your Internet session (such as through a Point-to-Point-Protocol, or PPP, account with your Internet Service Provider).
2. From the command line of the console or an X11 terminal window, use the `telnet` command, followed by the name or Internet Protocol, or IP, address, like this:

   ```
   # telnet fbminet.ca
   ```

Netscape does it all—`telnet` too!

The Netscape Navigator component of Netscape's Communicator can also be used to `telnet` to remote computers, because it recognizes a Uniform Resource Locator (URL) specification of the `telnet` protocol, such as `telnet://ttnbbs.rtpnc.epa.gov`. If you enter a `telnet` address in Netscape's Location field or click on a `telnet` link on a Web page, a separate program (the X11 terminal client, `xterm`) is launched by Netscape to start your `telnet` session.

3. The `telnet` program prints the IP address of the remote computer, like this:

```
Trying 199.214.6.227...
```

4. The `telnet` program then (hopefully) connects, informs you of the escape character you can use to run `telnet` commands (Ctrl+]), and presents the logon screen for the remote computer:

```
Connected to fbminet.ca.
Escape character is '^]'.
MAXIMUS/2 v2.02MAXIMUS/2 v2.02
±±±±±±±±±Ü ±±±±±±±±±Ü  ±±±±±±±±±±Ü  ±±±±Ü
±±ÛBBB±±Û  ±±ÛBBB±±Û  ±±ÛB±±ÛB±±Û   ±±ÛB
±±Û    BB  ±±Û    ±±Û  ±±Û ±±Û ±±Û    ±±Û  ±±±±±Ü±±Ü ±±±±±±Ü
➥±±±±±±±±±Ü
±±±±±Ü      ±±±±±±±ÛB  ±±Û ±±Û ±±Û    ±±Û  ±±Û±±Û±±Û ±±ÛBBBB
➥BB±±ÛBBB
±±ÛBBB      ±±ÛBBB±±Û  ±±Û ±±Û ±±Û    ±±Û  ±±Û±±Û±±Û ±±±±Ü
➥±±Û
±±Û         ±±Û    ±±Û  ±±Û  BB ±±Û    ±±Û  ±±Û±±Û±±Û ±±ÛBB
➥±±Û
±±±±Û       ±±±±±±±±±Û ±±±±Û    ±±±±Û ±±±±Û ±±Û±±±±±Û ±±±±±±Ü
➥±±Û
BBBB        BBBBBBBBB  BBBB     BBBB  BBBB  BB BBBBB  BBBBBB
➥BB
            Farm Business Management Information Network
            A project of the Canadian Farm Business
            Management Council

         National Internet Telnet Site --
    ➥Telnet://FBMInet.ca
                     FBMInet Node 2001:1/101   Telnet Line 4

    If your Telnet client does not support ANSI emulation,
    Zmodem file transfers, and IBM boxdraw characters, we
    suggest you try NetTerm.You can download a shareware
    version of NetTerm from this BBS or directly from the
    FBMInet web site at http://FBMInet.ca
```

5. Log on to the remote computer. (Note that some remote computers use logon prompts much different than your Linux system's!)

```
William Ball [Y,n]?
Password: ******

Hi there, and welcome back to FBMInet-CFBMC Telnet Site
Telnet://FBMInet.ca!

We're glad that you called back, and we hope that you'll
call again in the future.  Enjoy your stay!
```

6. When you finish with the `telnet` session (by using the `logout`, `exit`, or `close telnet` commands, or through the remote computer's commands—refer to Table 17.1), the `telnet` program quits and prints a message like this:

```
Connection closed by foreign host.
```

Use *ping* to test your session

If you have trouble connecting to the remote computer with the `telnet` command, make sure you're using the correct name of the computer or Internet Protocol (IP) address. To see if the name is correct, use the `ping` command, followed by the computer's name:

```
# ping staffnet.com
PING staffnet.com (207.226.80.14): 56 data bytes
64 bytes from 207.226.80.14: icmp_seq=0 ttl=249 time=315.7
➥ms
64 bytes from 207.226.80.14: icmp_seq=1 ttl=249 time=179.8
➥ms
64 bytes from 207.226.80.14: icmp_seq=2 ttl=249 time=167.2
➥ms

--- staffnet.com ping statistics ---
3 packets transmitted, 3 packets received, 0% packet loss
round-trip min/avg/max = 167.2/220.9/315.7 ms
```

The ping command continues until you press Ctrl+C. You can also use the computer's IP address with the ping command like this:

```
# ping 207.226.80.14
PING 207.226.80.14 (207.226.80.14): 56 data bytes
64 bytes from 207.226.80.14: icmp_seq=0 ttl=249 time=161.6
➥ms
64 bytes from 207.226.80.14: icmp_seq=1 ttl=249 time=150.1
➥ms
64 bytes from 207.226.80.14: icmp_seq=2 ttl=249 time=150.5
➥ms

--- 207.226.80.14 ping statistics ---
3 packets transmitted, 3 packets received, 0% packet loss
round-trip min/avg/max = 150.1/154.0/161.6 ms
```

Downloading Files During *telnet* Sessions

Downloading programs from a remote computer during a telnet session can present a problem. The telnet command is not an FTP connection, so you must use programs on each end of the telnet connection to transfer files. To download a program from the remote computer, the remote computer should have a program, such as sz, or send ZMODEM, communications program. To download files from the remote computer, use the rz, or receive ZMODEM, communications program. The sz and rz commands are included in the Red Hat Linux, and most other Linux distributions.

Downloading a file with the *sz* and *rz* commands

1. To retrieve a file called program.tgz from a remote computer, start your telnet session, and then use the sz command from the command line of the remote computer. Start the file transfer by using sz like so:

   ```
   # sz -w 2048 filename.tgz
   ```

   This command sends the file filename.tgz using the ZMODEM communications protocol.

2. Immediately after starting the sz command on the remote computer, press Ctrl+] to escape to the telnet prompt, which looks like the following:

   ```
   telnet>
   ```

3. Type the `telnet` shell command (the exclamation character), followed by the `rz` command and a press of the Enter key to start receiving the file:

   ```
   telnet> ! rz
   ```

   The file starts transferring from the remote computer to your computer. See the `sz` and `rz` manual pages for more information.

SEE ALSO

➤ *To learn more about the shell, see page 19.*

Chatting with Internet Relay Chat

Use the `irc`, or Internet Relay Chat, command, to converse with other people on the Internet. When you run `irc`, use its built-in commands to connect to chat servers, to see who is chatting, and to set other options. The `irc` command's built-in help documents more than 110 commands and topics. To use `irc`, you should have an active Internet connection.

Starting an *irc* Session

Starting a chat session with *irc*

1. Start your Internet connection. To start an `irc` session, use `irc` on the command line of the console or an X11 terminal window like this:

   ```
   # irc
   ```

   The `irc` program connects to a default chat server, or other computer supporting `irc`, as shown in Figure 17.2.

2. If you're using `irc` for the first time, use the `/HELP` command, followed by the keyword `newuser`, as shown:

   ```
   > /HELP newuser
   ```

   A screen or two of helpful information is printed to your display. You can also browse through the `irc` command's help facility and read introductory information by using the `/HELP` command followed by one of these keywords, or topics: `basics`, `commands`, `etiquette`, `expressions`, `intro`, `ircII`, `menus`, `news`, `newuser`, and `rules`.

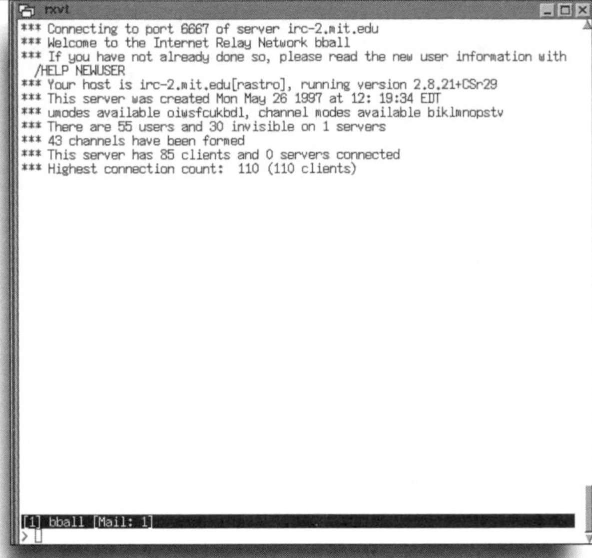

rxvt
*** Connecting to port 6667 of server irc-2.mit.edu
*** Welcome to the Internet Relay Network bball
*** If you have not already done so, please read the new user information with /HELP NEWUSER
*** Your host is irc-2.mit.edu[rastro], running version 2.8.21+CSr29
*** This server was created Mon May 26 1997 at 12: 19:34 EDT
*** umodes available oiwsfcukbdl, channel modes available biklmnopstv
*** There are 55 users and 30 invisible on 1 servers
*** 43 channels have been formed
*** This server has 85 clients and 0 servers connected
*** Highest connection count: 110 (110 clients)
[1] bball [Mail: 1]
>

FIGURE 17.2
The irc command displays a scrolling screen with a command line at the bottom of the screen.

3. To see a list of active chat groups on the server, use the `/LIST` command on the `irc` command line, like this:

   > **/LIST**

   After a slight pause, the screen scrolls a list of current discussion groups, as shown in Figure 17.3.

4. To see details about the members of a particular group, use the `/WHO` command, followed by the name of the group, like this:

   > **/WHO #giggles**

   The `irc` command lists the names of any current members.

5. To become a member of a discussion group, use the `/JOIN` command, followed by the name of the group, like this:

   > **/JOIN #giggles**

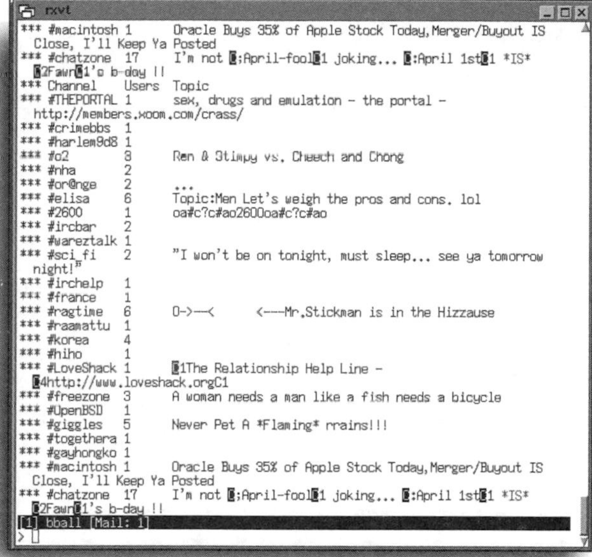

FIGURE 17.3

The irc /LIST command displays a list of current discussion groups.

Your screen starts scrolling messages as member of the group talk (as shown in Figure 17.4). From now on, all text you type followed by the Enter key, is broadcast to all members of the group. See the ircII manual page (found under the /usr/doc/irc/doc directory) for more information about using irc.

6. To quit the irc program, use irc's /QUIT command and press Enter. The irc program exits and severs your connection.

SEE ALSO

➤ *For more information about starting PPP connections, see page 172.*

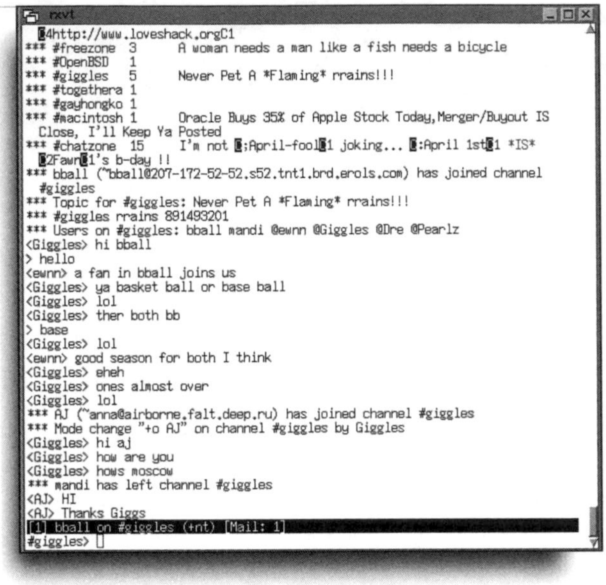

FIGURE 17.4
Group discussions continuously scroll up the screen after you've joined an `irc` chat session.

```
rxvt
  4http://www.loveshack.orgC1
*** #freezone  3      A woman needs a man like a fish needs a bicycle
*** #OpenBSD   1
*** #giggles   5      Never Pet A *Flaming* rrains!!!
*** #togethera 1
*** #gayhongko 1
*** #macintosh 1      Oracle Buys 35% of Apple Stock Today,Merger/Buyout IS
  Close, I'll Keep Ya Posted
*** #chatzone  15     I'm not ;April-fool1 joking... :April 1st1 *IS*
  2Fawn1's b-day !!
*** bball (~bball@207-172-52-52.s52.tnt1.brd.erols.com) has joined channel
  #giggles
*** Topic for #giggles: Never Pet A *Flaming* rrains!!!
*** #giggles rrains 891493201
*** Users on #giggles: bball mandi @ewnn @Giggles @Dre @Pearlz
<Giggles> hi bball
> hello
<ewnn> a fan in bball joins us
<Giggles> ya basket ball or base ball
<Giggles> lol
<Giggles> ther both bb
> base
<Giggles> lol
<ewnn> good season for both I think
<Giggles> eheh
<Giggles> ones almost over
<Giggles> lol
*** AJ (~anna@airborne.falt.deep.ru) has joined channel #giggles
*** Mode change "+o AJ" on channel #giggles by Giggles
<Giggles> hi aj
<Giggles> how are you
<Giggles> hows moscow
*** mandi has left channel #giggles
<AJ> HI
<AJ> Thanks Giggs
[1] bball on #giggles (+nt) [Mail: 1]
#giggles>
```

PART

IV

The X Window System

CHAPTER

18

Running and Configuring X11

By Bill Ball

Starting the X Window System

Logging on with the `xdm` chooser

Customizing `xdm` banner screens

Customizing the `.xinitrc` startup script

Stopping X11 sessions

Using virtual consoles with X11

Customizing your workspace

Bad news for free X11?

The XFree86 distribution is a good deal, considering that the software works with many different computers, more than 30 operating systems, and many video cards. However, recent news from The Open Group concerning new licensing requirements for the next version of X11, X11R6.4, might spell bad news for continued free distributions of X11, the distributors of X11, and independent X developers (check out **http://www.opengroup.org** for more information).

How the new licensing requirements will affect development of new X11 software for Linux remains uncertain. Although you might still be able to develop software for noncommercial use for new versions of X, companies such as Red Hat Software and independent Linux developers might have to pay thousands of dollars to distribute or develop new versions of X11 or X11 software (this was one of the greatest fears of X11 software developers, and was realized after the X Consortium gave all rights to the Open Software Foundation, now known as The Open Group).

The good news is that the XFree86 folks say they will "remain committed to providing a free X11 implementation for UNIX and UNIX-like OSs." Check the XFree86 web site (**http://www.xfree86.org**) for the latest developments.

Starting X11

The default graphic interface for Linux is the X Window System, usually the port of X11 from the XFree86 Project, Inc. This collection of software includes nearly 3,500 files, almost 200 programs (or clients), more than 500 fonts, and more than 500 graphics in nearly 50MB of software.

SEE ALSO

➤ *To learn how to install the X Window System, see page 641.*

There are other sources for distributions of the X Window System for Linux. A commercial distribution, which can cost from $50 to several hundred dollars, can be especially helpful if you can't get X running on your computer, if you want specialized technical support, or if the distribution includes commercial programs—such as a word processor or database manager. For information about other sources of X for Linux, check out the following sites:

http://www.caldera.com

http://www.xig.com

http://www.redhat.com

http://www.metrolink.com

Using the *startx* Command

After installing Linux and the X Window System, use the `startx` shell script to start an X session, like so:

```
# startx
```

The `startx` script is used to feed options to the `xinit` (X initializer) command, which is discussed later in this chapter in the section titled "Customizing the `.xinitrc` Startup Script."

If you've configured X to use different color depths (such as 8, 16, 24, or 32 bits per pixel), use the `-bpp` option followed by the color depth you'd like to use for your X session:

```
# startx — -bpp 16
```

This command line starts X and tells the X server to use 16-bits-per-pixel color.

Using *xdm* for X11 Logons

Using the startx script is only one way to start an X11 session. If you've installed the Common Desktop Environment (CDE), you should be familiar with xdm, the X display manager command. The xdm client is used to display a logon screen before running CDE (note that you don't have to use xdm to run CDE—for details, see the section titled "Starting a Window Manager" in Chapter 19, "Using a Window Manager."

Be careful editing /etc/inittab!

Make a backup copy of your systemís /etc/inittab file before making any changes. Incorrect settings in this file can render your system inoperable by not supporting the boot process correctly (but can be easily fixed by using an emergency boot disk).

The xdm client provides a logon prompt similar to the console prompt. In order to use xdm (as shown in Figure 18.1), you must configure Linux to boot directly to X11.

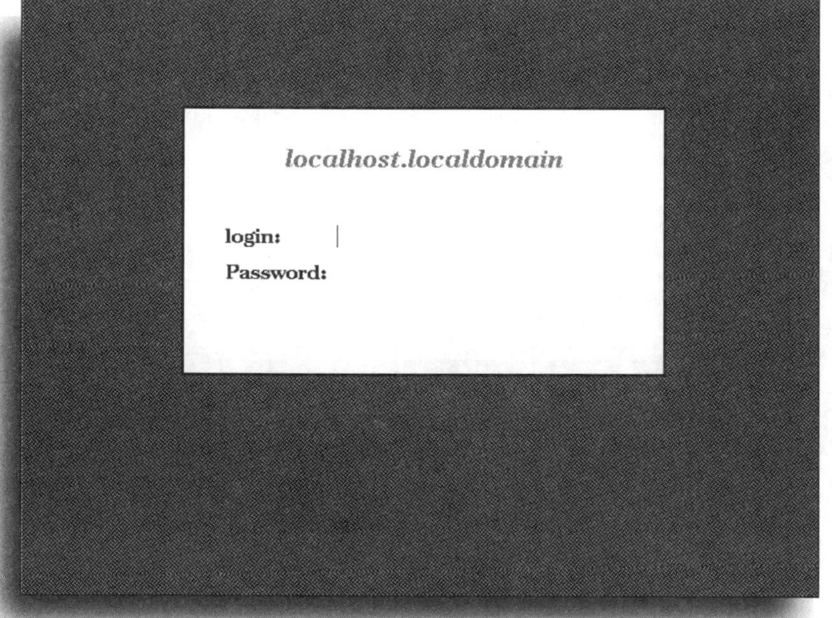

FIGURE 18.1
The xdm client displays a logon console to start an X session.

Configuring Linux to use *xdm*

1. To configure Linux to boot directly to X11 through the xdm client, first log on as the root operator.
2. Use your favorite text editor (such as pico), and open the file inittab under the /etc directory by entering the following:
   ```
   # pico /etc/inittab
   ```

3. Move your cursor to the default initialization entry, which looks like this:

```
id:3:initdefault
```

4. Change the number 3 to the number 5:

```
id:5:initdefault
```

5. Save and close the file.
6. Restart Linux, using the `shutdown -r` (reboot) command:

```
# shutdown -r now
```

7. After Linux restarts, you are presented with the default Red Hat `xdm` logon screen, shown in Figure 18.2.

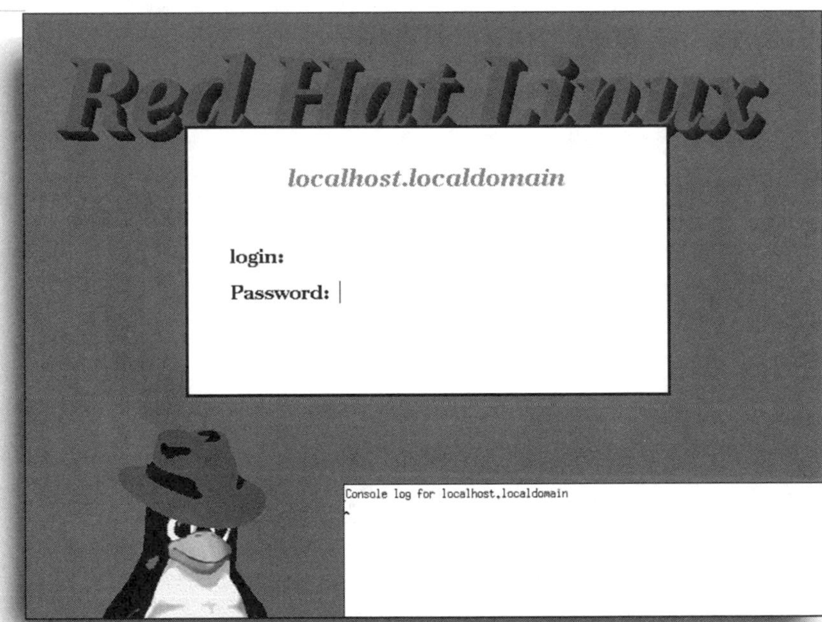

FIGURE 18.2
The Red Hat Linux `xdm` logon display uses the `xbanner` command for a custom look.

If you just want to try `xdm` between Linux reboots, first make sure you're not running X11, and then log on as the root operator. Use `xdm` and the `-nodaemon` option, like this:

```
# xdm -nodaemon
```

Your display clears, and the `xdm` screen appears (refer to Figure 18.2).

SEE ALSO

➤ *To learn about the* `/etc/inittab` *file and starting Linux, see page 474.*

Running Root Commands During *xdm* X11 Sessions

Starting an X client with the su command from an X11 terminal window after starting X through xdm might not work because of an extra level of security used by your X server and how your server was started. For example, if you start X after logging on through xdm, and then try to use the su command to run the Control Panel, you might get an error like the following:

```
# su -c "control-panel"
Password:
Xlib: connection to ":0.0" refused by server
Xlib: Client is not authorized to connect to Server
** ERROR **: cannot open display: :0.0
```

Use the xhost command to temporarily authorize the desired command's access to the X server by adding the hostname of your computer to the X server's access list. Also include the desired root command by using the su command, like this:

```
# xhost +localhost; su -c "control-panel"
```

SEE ALSO

➤ *To learn more about using the* su *command, see page 5.*

Customizing the *xdm* Banner Screens

The Red Hat Linux distribution includes a custom xdm configuration, and uses the xbanner command to spiff up the display with a title, graphic, and background color. The xbanner command, used by xdm's setup function, is defined in the Xsetup_0 file (found under the /usr/X11R6/lib/xdm directory) with an entry such as the following:

```
/usr/X11R6/bin/xbanner
```

To change the title, or to insert your own graphic into the xdm logon screen, edit the file Xbanner, found under the /usr/X11R6/lib/X11/app-defaults directory. Xbanner is an X11 resource file (discussed later in this chapter in the section "Using X11 Resources"), and contains settings that you can change to personalize your xdm logon screen.

Creating a custom logon screen

1. Log on as the root operator. Using a text editor such as pico, open the Xbanner resource file under the

/usr/X11R6/lib/X11/app-defaults directory by entering the following:

```
# pico -w /usr/X11R6/lib/X11/app-defaults/XBanner
```

2. Scroll through the document until you reach the Xbanner.Label section, which looks like the following:

```
! The text that will appear! This gets parsed for
➥environment variables
! as in the shell. So $HOSTNAME and ${HOSTNAME} will
➥work!
XBanner.Label:          Red Hat Linux
```

3. Typing over the default .Label entry, enter your own title:

```
XBanner.Label           Laptop Linux
```

4. Scroll through the file until you reach the effects section. Select an effect from the list of effects, shown here:

```
! Type of effect to render the text with. Allowed key-
words:
! None                 : Draw the text in the Foreground
                        ➥color
! Shadow               : Add shadow under the text using
                        ➥the ShadowColor
! Outline              : Add an outline to the text.
! Shadowed-Outline    : Outline with a shadow.
! 3D-Shadow            : Outline in a 3D fashion
! Thick                : Shows text with thick letters
! StandOut             : 3D thing standing out of the
                        ➥screen.
! StandIn              : Opposite of StandOut...
! PopArt               : Alternating HiColor/ShadowColor
! Coin                 : Somewhat like a coin.
! Fade                 : Shadow/Thickness along a color
                        ➥gradient
! Backlight            : Text with a color gradient
! FatText              : Text fat and with a shadow.
! StandOut2            : Different way to do it.
! StandIn2             : Same here...
! FunnyOutline        : The wider areas of text filled
                        ➥with HiColor
! FgGrad               : Color gradient on text and
                        ➥shadow.
! FgPlasma             : Foreground oftext is PlasmaCloud
! Shake                : 'Nervous? Tense? Tired?' sign
                        ➥XBanner.Effect:          Fade
```

5. Set the desired effect (in this case, `PopArt`) by typing the following:

```
XBanner.Effect:              PopArt
```

6. To change the default penguin graphic, scroll down to the image section, which looks like the following:

```
! *** PASTE PIXMAP OPTIONS ***


! XBanner can put an image on the screen. Currently only
➥.XPM!
! If your filename starts with '@', then it is a file
➥containing a list
! of pixmaps of the format:
! <pathname> <x> <y>
! And the PixmapX/PixmapY have no effect.
XBanner.DoPixmap:          True
XBanner.PixFile:
➥/usr/X11R6/include/X11/pixmaps/rhpenguin.xpm
XBanner.PixmapX:           30
XBanner.PixmapY:           400
```

7. Enter the location of your new graphic (which must be in XPM format) by changing the `PixFile` entry, like so:

```
XBanner.PixFile
➥/usr/X11R6/include/X11/pixmaps/escherknot.xpm
```

   Note that the `Xbanner`, `.PixmapX`, and `.PixmapY` settings are used to place the graphic on the display at specified x and y coordinates (0,0 being the upper-left corner of your display).

8. Save the changes and exit your text editor. If you're running X, quit your session. To see your changes, start `xdm` by entering the following:

```
# xdm -nodaemon
```

   The new `xdm` logon screen appears as shown in Figure 18.3.

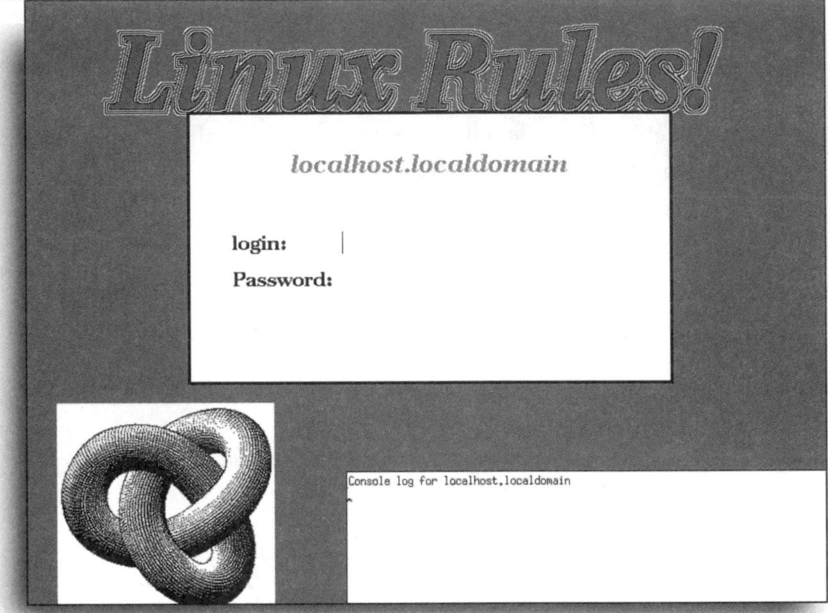

FIGURE 18.3
Customize the xdm logon screen by using the xbanner command.

The xbanner program has nearly 80 command-line options, but curiously, no manual page. To read all the xbanner documentation, use the Lynx web browser to reach the following:

```
# lynx /usr/doc/xbanner-1.31/index.html
```

Customizing the *.xinitrc* Startup Script

The .xinitrc, or X initialization script, is a file used by the xinit command (started by the startx command) to configure your X session, or to start other window managers and clients. The default initialization script is found under the /etc/X11/xinit directory. If you customize this file as the root operator, any changes are systemwide and affect all users. To make individual changes, copy xinitrc to your home directory with .xinitrc as the file's name by entering the following:

```
# cp /etc/X11/xinit/xinitrc $HOME/.xinitrc
```

SEE ALSO

➤ *To learn how to use* .xinitrc *to start different window managers for X, see page 288.*

Customizing *.xinitrc* with *AnotherLevel*

The AnotherLevel configuration of the fvwm2 window manager features a handy Save Desktop to new.xinitrc menu item under the desktop's Preferences menu, which you can use to build custom desktops.

Creating a custom *.xinitrc*

1. Start an X11 session.
2. Start various terminal windows or X11 clients.
3. Resize or move the windows until your desktop is arranged to your satisfaction.
4. Click a blank area of the desktop. Scroll to the Preference menus, and then to the Save Desktop to new.xinitrc menu item.
5. Release your mouse button. A file called new.xinitrc is created in your home directory. This file contains command lines with geometry settings and other options you've used to start the programs running in your desktop. Use these settings as entries in your existing .xinitrc file, or to configure your window manager's startup functions. (For details, see the section "Configuring Window Managers" in Chapter 19, "Using a Window Manager.")

Using the *wxininfo* Client to Configure *.xinitrc*

Use the wxininfo client, or window information utility, to help create custom command lines for entry in your .xinitrc file.

Using *wxininfo*

1. Start wxininfo from the command line of a terminal window by entering the following:

   ```
   # xwininfo
   ```

   The wxininfo client prints a short message, asking you to click on a desired window:

   ```
   xwininfo: Please select the window about which you
             would like information by clicking the
             mouse in that window.
   ```

2. After you click a window, information about the window appears in the original terminal window. This information resembles the following:

```
xwininfo: Window id: 0x1c00002 "rxvt"

  Absolute upper-left X:  10
  Absolute upper-left Y:  28
  Relative upper-left X:  0
  Relative upper-left Y:  0
  Width: 574
  Height: 340
  Depth: 8
  Visual Class: PseudoColor
  Border width: 0
  Class: InputOutput
  Colormap: 0x21 (installed)
  Bit Gravity State: ForgetGravity
  Window Gravity State: NorthWestGravity
  Backing Store State: NotUseful
  Save Under State: no
  Map State: IsViewable
  Override Redirect State: no
  Corners:  +10+28  -216+28  -216-232  +10-232
  -geometry 80x24+5+5
```

This information (in this case, about an `rxvt` terminal window) can be used to record the window's geometry settings or color depth for custom `.xinitrc` entries.

Stopping X11

Always shut down properly!

Anytime you want to stop your X11 session or shut down Linux, use the proper keystrokes or commands. Never, *never* simply turn off your computer. This can wreak havoc with the file structure of your Linux partition!

There are several ways to stop an X11 session. You can use the Exit menu of your window manager to properly exit X11, or if you are using an Xfree86 X server, press Ctrl+Alt+Backspace to return to your console shell prompt.

Using Virtual Consoles with X11

Unless something is seriously wrong with your computer, or unless X appears to be hung (an extremely rare occurrence), you can exit X11 to a virtual console and return by using Linux virtual-console keyboard commands through the Ctrl, Alt, and function keys on your keyboard.

Switching between X11 and the console

1. Start an X11 session. To move to the first virtual console, press Ctrl+Alt+F1.
2. If you started X from the first virtual console (the default console) with the `startx` command, you won't be able to use this console. Press Alt+F2 to go to the second virtual console.
3. You should see a logon prompt. Log on to get to another shell prompt. To return to your X session, press Alt+F7. By default, Red Hat Linux supports six virtual consoles, available through the F1–F6 function keys.

SEE ALSO

➤ *To learn more about virtual consoles, see page 5.*

Customizing Your Workspace

The XFree86 X Window System distribution comes with a variety of clients that you can use as screen savers, to set background colors and patterns, or to configure your cursor and mouse. You can also load pictures and even animated screen savers into your root desktop display. Insert particularly pleasing screen savers or desktop color settings into your `.xinitrc` file so you can use them during your X sessions.

Setting a Screen Saver

Screen savers for X11 are not only fun to watch, but can also be used to password-protect your computer while you're using X. Red Hat Software's Linux distribution includes several screen-saving clients, such as `xset`, `xscreensaver`, and `xlock`.

`xset`

The `xset` client manages the screen-saving facilities of your X server, and can be used to set, turn on, test, and turn off screen savers.

Screen saving with the *xset* client

1. Start the xset client with the s command-line option, followed by a timeout interval (in seconds):

   ```
   # xset s 30
   ```

   This command sets the time that passes before a screensaver kicks in.

2. In order to turn on screen saving, use xset with the s option, followed by on, like this:

   ```
   # xset s on
   ```

3. To test screen saving right away instead of waiting for your timeout, follow the s option with activate, like so:

   ```
   # xset s activate
   ```

4. All you get is a blank screen. Not much fun, huh? To use a graphic and background pattern, use the s option with noblank, like this:

   ```
   # xset s noblank
   ```

5. Repeat step 3. You should see a light gray screen with a black X logo.

6. To turn off screen saving, follow the s option with off:

   ```
   # xset s off
   ```

xscreensaver

For a more animated display, use the xscreensaver and xscreensaver-command clients. The xscreensaver client has 16 command-line options, but is easy to use.

Screensaving with *xscreensaver*

1. Start the xscreensaver client as a background process with the -timeout option, followed by a number (in minutes), like so:

   ```
   # xscreensaver -timeout 5 &
   ```

2. After five minutes of no keyboard or mouse activity, xscreensaver runs a screen saver. Use the xscreensaver-command client to control xscreensaver. For example, to immediately test xscreensaver, use the -activate option, like this:

   ```
   # xscreensaver-command -activate
   ```

Your screen slowly fades, and a screen saver starts.

3. To lock your screen saver and require a password to return to your X session, use the -lock option, like so:

```
# xscreensaver-command -lock
```

4. To turn off xscreensaver, use xscreensaver-command followed by the exit option, like so:

```
# xscreensaver-command -exit
```

5. To run a demonstration of xscreensaver, use the -demo option, like so:

```
# xscreensaver-command -demo
```

Your screen fades, and a dialog box appears, from which you can select a screen saver. An easier way to see an individual screen saver is to enter the screen saver's name from a command line, because each screen saver is a standalone client. For example, to see the shade sphere screen saver (©1988 by Sun Microsystems) program, use a command line like the following:

```
# sphere
```

The screen saver runs in an X11 window, as shown in Figure 18.4.

FIGURE 18.4
Sun Microsystems' sphere drawing program can be used with the xscreensaver command.

6. Another option is to run the animated screen saver in your root desktop, like an animated wallpaper. To work with X11 clients in the foreground while your background display is filled with movement and color, use the name of a screen saver, followed by the `-root` option, like this:

```
# forest -root &
```

For a list of screen savers for the `xscreensaver` client, see the `xscreensaver` manual page or the file `Xscreensaver` in the `/usr/X11R6/lib/X11/app-defaults` directory.

xlock

The `xlock` client is a sophisticated terminal-locking program with nearly 50 command-line options and more than 50 built-in screen savers. Use this client to password-protect your X session while you're away from your desk.

You can use `xlock` as a simple screen saver without password protection by using the `-nolock` option. For example, to see a random selection of `xlock`'s screen savers every 15 seconds, use the `-duration` option, followed by a number (in seconds), the `-nolock` and `-mode` options, and the word `random`, like so:

```
# xlock -duration 15 -nolock -mode random
```

Like `xscreensaver`, `xlock` offers animation in your root display. Use the `-inroot` command-line option, like this:

```
# xlock -inline -mode random &
```

Setting the Background Desktop Color

Use `xsetroot` to change the color of your root display. For example, to use the color `LavenderBlush3`, use the `xsetroot` command's `-solid` option followed by the color's name (from the file `rgb.txt` under the `/usr/X11R6/lib/X11 directory`), like so:

```
# xsetroot -solid LavenderBlush3
```

Setting the Background Desktop Pattern

Use the `xsetroot` client along with the `-bitmap` option and the name of an X11 bitmap to set a pattern for your root display.

You'll find nearly 90 bitmap graphics in the `/usr/include/X11/bitmaps` directory. To set a blue basket-weave pattern for your desktop, use the `-bitmap` option followed by the path to a graphic, and the `-bg` (background) option, followed by a color's name, like this:

```
# xsetroot -bitmap /usr/include/X11/bitmaps/wide_weave -bg
➥blue
```

Using a Desktop Wallpaper

Using a wallpaper, or graphic image, in the root display of your desktop can enhance how your screen looks during your X sessions. The clients `xloadimage` and `xv` support many different graphics formats, and can be used to load pictures onto your desktop.

xloadimage

Use the `xloadimage` client to display a picture on your desktop. This program supports a number of graphics file formats, which are listed in Table 18.1.

TABLE 18.1 *xloadimage*-supported file formats

File Type	Description
`cmuraster`	CMU WM raster
`faces`	Faces project
`fbm`	FBM image
`gem`	GEM bit image
`gif`	GIF image
`jpeg`	JFIF-style JPEG image
`macpaint`	MacPaint image
`mcidas`	McIDAS area file
`niff`	Native image file format (NIFF)
`pbm`	Portable bit map (PBM, PGM, PPM)
`pcx`	PC paintbrush image
`rle`	Utah RLE image

continues...

TABLE 18.1 Continued

File Type	Description
`sunraster`	Sun rasterfile
`vff`	Sun visualization file format
`vicar`	VICAR image
`xbm`	X bitmap
`xpm`	X pixmap
`xwd`	X window dump

For example, to load a GIF graphic as a wallpaper graphic, use `xloadimage` with the `-onroot` option, followed by the graphic's name, like this:

```
# xloadimage -onroot /usr/lib/tk8.0/demos/images/earth.gif
```

This command line displays the earth in a tiled format in the background display. Use `xloadimage` with the `-fullscreen` option along with the `-onroot` option to fit the graphic to the size of your display, like this:

```
# xloadimage -onroot -fullscreen
➥/usr/lib/tk8.0/demos/images/earth.gif
```

Note that you might have to experiment with different graphics to get the best effect.

XV

The `xv` client (usually used as an image viewer, editor, or conversion program) displays an image in the root window. Use the `-root` option followed by name of the graphic, like so:

```
# xv -root /usr/lib/tk8.0/demos/images/earth.gif
```

SEE ALSO

➤ *To learn more about the* `xv` *client, see page 341.*

Setting the Mouse Pointer

Use the `xsetroot` command to change the mouse pointer for X. If you use Red Hat's `AnotherLevel` window manager for X, use the Set Root Cursor menu, found under the Root Cursor section of the Preferences menu.

Changing cursors with *xsetroot*

1. To use the `xsetroot` client to change your cursor, first use the `less` pager to read the `cursorfont.h` file under the `/usr/X11R6/include/X11` directory, like this:

   ```
   # less /usr/X11R6/include/X11/cursorfont.h
   ```

2. You'll see a list of nearly 80 cursor definitions that will resemble the following:

   ```
   ...
   #define XC_box_spiral 20
   #define XC_center_ptr 22
   #define XC_circle 24
   #define XC_clock 26
   #define XC_coffee_mug 28
   #define XC_cross 30
   #define XC_cross_reverse 32
   #define XC_crosshair 34
   #define XC_diamond_cross 36
   #define XC_dot 38
   ...
   ```

3. To set your cursor to `coffee_mug`, use the `xsetroot` client along with the `-cursor_name` option and the name of the cursor, like so:

   ```
   # xsetroot -cursor_name coffee_mug
   ```

4. To reset your cursor to the normal X11 cursor, use `xsetroot` with `X_cursor name`, like so:

   ```
   # xsetroot -cursor_name X_cursor
   ```

5. To see a character grid of the available cursors, use the `xfd` (X11 font display) client with the `-fn` command-line option followed by the name of the cursor font, like so:

   ```
   # xfd -fn cursor
   ```

   A window containing a small graphic of each cursor appears, as shown in Figure 18.5.

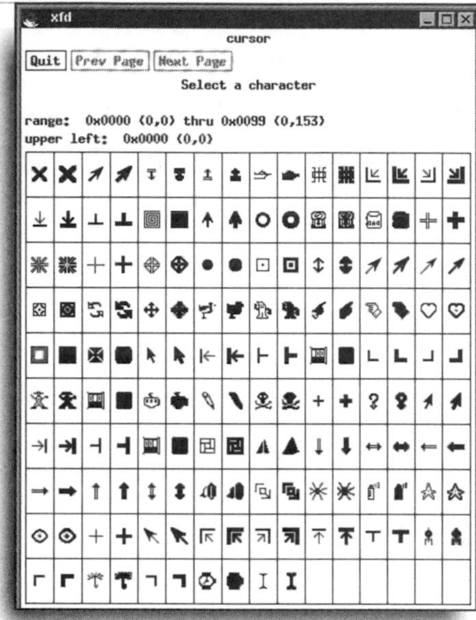

FIGURE 18.5
The `xfd` client can display pictures of available X11 cursors in the cursor's font.

Configuring the Mouse

Use the `xmodmap` and `xset` clients to configure how your mouse works with X11. The `xmodmap` client can change the order of your mouse buttons, while the `xset` client can set your mouse acceleration.

Setting your mouse with *xmodmap* and *xset*

1. Use `xmodmap` with the `-e` (expression) option followed by the pointer specification to switch your mouse buttons. For example, to reverse the order of the buttons, use `xmodmap` like so:

```
# xmodmap -e "pointer 3 2 1"
```

2. Use the `xset` client with the `m` (mouse) option followed by two numbers to set the acceleration of your pointer. For example, to slow down your mouse, use `xset` like so:

```
# xset m "1 5"
```

Too slow? Try the following:

```
# xset m "40 20"
```

Too fast? Try the following:

```
# xset m "4 8"
```

3. To reset your mouse, use `xset` with the `m` option followed by the word `default`, like this:

```
# xset m "default"
```

SEE ALSO

➤ *For more information about using a mouse with Linux, see page 144.*

Configuring the Terminal Window

Terminal emulator clients such as `rxvt` or `xterm` display an open window with a shell command line. Terminal windows are resizable, and can be moved, minimized (iconified), or maximized. A minimized terminal window can appear on the desktop or, if you're using the `AnotherLevel` configuration of the `fvwm2` window manager, is placed in an icon dock or taskbar at the bottom of your screen.

Chapter 20, "Performing Common X11 Operations," discusses many of the X Toolkit command-line options that you can use to configure terminal windows. However, some terminal emulators, such as `nxterm`, can be configured via a combination of the keyboard and your mouse.

Configuring *nxterm*

1. To use a larger or smaller font in the terminal window, right-click the terminal window while holding down the Ctrl key. This invokes the VT Fonts menu, shown in Figure 18.6.

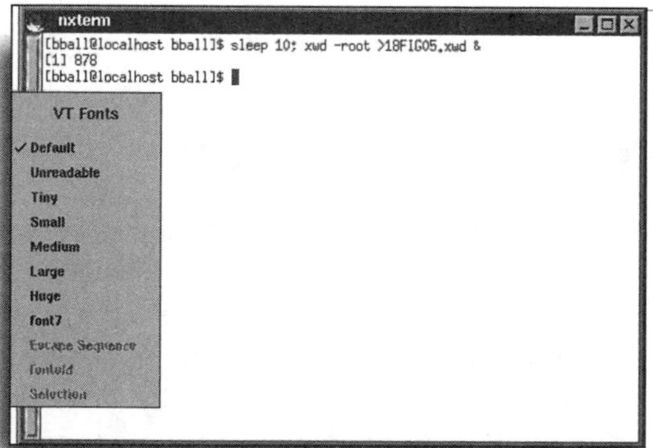

FIGURE 18.6
The VT Fonts menu of the `nxterm` X11 terminal client lets you configure terminal fonts with the keyboard and mouse.

2. To select a different font for your terminal, use the VT Fonts menu Selection option and the `xfontsel` client. Start the `xfontsel` client from the command line like so:

```
# xfontsel &
```

3. The `xfontsel` window appears. Select a different font by clicking the font line below the Quit and Select buttons, as shown in Figure 18.7.

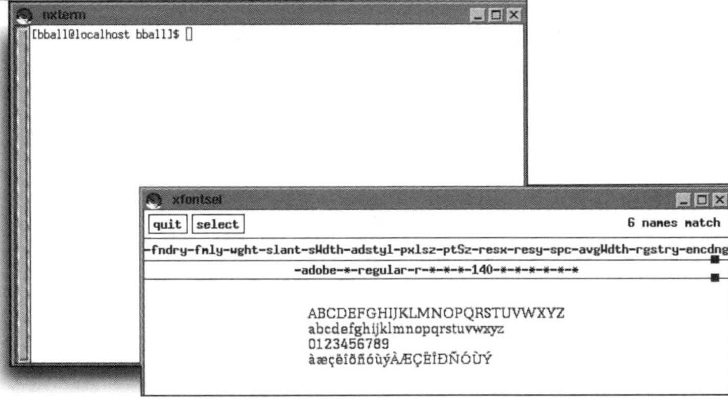

FIGURE 18.7
The `xfontsel` client displays X11 fonts, and can be used to configure the `nxterm` terminal font.

4. Click the Select button at the top of the `xfontsel`'s window.
5. Hold down the Ctrl key, right-click the `nxterm` window, and choose Selection from the VT Fonts menu (refer to Figure 18.6). The `nxterm` window now uses the selected font.

SEE ALSO

➤ *To learn how to configure terminal windows from the command line, see page 307.*
➤ *To learn more about the* `xfontsel` *client, see page 313.*

Using X11 Resources

Many X Window System clients use a configuration, or resource, file. This is a text file that contains line-item settings, or resource strings, used to determine how the client looks or runs. Many of these settings can be specified by using the `-xrm` X11 Toolkit option followed by a resource string, but most programs use only a resource file.

To change resource settings for an X11 client, first read the program's manual page. Alternatively, look for a resource file in the `app-defaults` directory under `/usr/X11R6/lib/X11` by entering the following.:

```
# ls -A /usr/X11R6/lib/X11/app-defaults
Beforelight    RXvt         XGammon       XRn              Xgopher
Bitmap         Seyon        XGetfile      Xscreensaver     Xgopher color
Bitmap-color   Seyon-color  XLoad         XSm              Xloadimage
Chooser        Viewres      XLock         XSysinfo         Xmag
Clock-color    X3270        XLogo         XSysinfo-color   Xman
Editres        XBanner      XLogo-color   XTerm            Xmessage
Editres-color  XCalc        XMailbox      XTerm-color      Xmh
Fig            XCalc-color  XMdb          Xditview         Xvidtune
Fig-color      XClipboard   XMixer        ditview-chrtr    xosview
GV             XClock       XPaint        Xedit
GXditview      XConsole     XPat          Xfd
KTerm          XDbx         XPlaycd       Xfm
Nxterm         XFontSel     Playmidi      Xgc
```

Each resource file (usually with the name of the corresponding client, but with a leading capital letter) contains resource strings that not only determine how a program is displayed, but also the contents and handling of menus, buttons, and other parts of a program.

Read the X manual page to learn how to define resource strings. As an example, the resource settings for the `xcalc` calculator client are defined in the `Xcalc` resource file.

Changing resource settings

1. Log on as the root operator. Using your text edit (`pico`, for example), open the resource file `Xcalc` for the `xcalc` calculator by entering the following:

   ```
   # pico -w /usr/X11R6/lib/X11/app-defaults/XCalc
   ```

2. Scroll through the resource file. You see definitions for the title, cursor, icon name, and other settings, such as the font used for the calculator keys. To change the calculator to use words instead of numbers for the calculator keys, look for

the `*ti.buttonxxLabel` resource definitions, which resemble the following:

```
*ti.button22.Label:                 7
```

3. Change the numeral `7` to the word `seven`:

```
*ti.button22.Label:                 seven
```

4. Change the labels for the other keypad numerals, save the file, and exit. To see your changes, run the `xcalc` client by entering the following:

```
# xcalc &
```

Your new calculator should look like the one on the right in Figure 18.8.

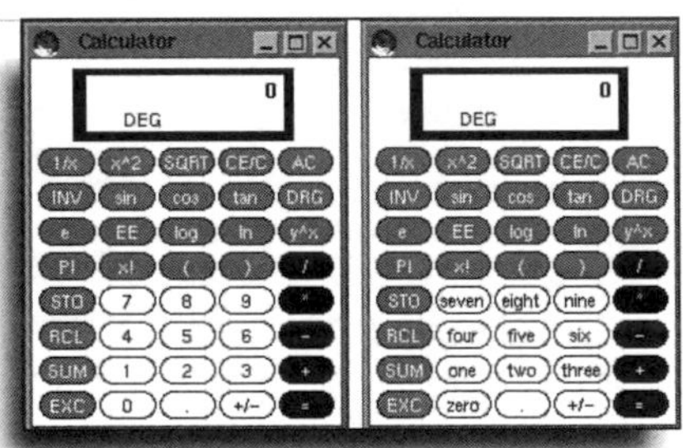

FIGURE 18.8
Change resource settings for X11 clients, such as `xcalc`, to alter the client's appearance.

Always make a backup copy of the original file before committing changes to a resource file. Also, make sure that any changes to a program's default window size work with your display. (In other words, don't create a default 1024×786 window for a program if you use only an 800×600 display.)

CHAPTER

19

Using a Window Manager

By Bill Ball

Features of selected X11 window managers

Installing selected window managers for X

Starting a window manager

Configuring window managers and window manager menus

Selecting an X11 Window Manager

There are more than 50 different window managers for Linux and the X Window System. Although choosing a window manager may be a matter of personal preference, many Red Hat Linux users happily use Red Hat Software's `AnotherLevel` configuration of the popular `fvwm2` window manager for its convenience and features, such as the following:

- Automatic installation of existing applications in desktop menus (such as the Applixware office suite and Netscape Communicator)
- Convenient menus for controlling background color, mouse, and scrollbar settings
- Comprehensive window control operations through menus or the keyboard
- Screen saving or screen locking with 60 different effects
- Easily configured desktop application menus

Window managers vary in ease of use, convenience, size (from fewer than 70,000 characters to more than 40MB), style, and price. Although you can use only one window manager at a time on a single display, you might have several installed on your system. Window managers demonstrate the graphic flexibility of the X Window System, and show that there is no such thing as a "standard" graphical user interface for X.

Building and installing window managers

Compiling and installing a window from scratch might seem like a formidable task, but don't be intimidated! The job is usually made easy by shell scripts or `make` files that automate the process. After you download the window manager software, read the `INSTALL` or `README` file before you begin. Look for other X11 window managers by browsing the following site:

`http://www.sunsite.unc.edu/pub/Linux/X11/window-managers`

For a more comprehensive listing of the latest window managers for X11 and Linux, along with links to the source code for many different X11 window managers, try the following:

`http://www.gaijin.com/X/links/x.apps.html#WindowManagers`

SEE ALSO

➤ *For more information about using the X Window System, see page 260.*
➤ *To learn more about Linux programming tools and compiling programs, see page 382.*

One great feature of X11 is that it provides the freedom to choose how to manage the windows or programs on your screen. But this freedom can have a downside—you might be overwhelmed by the array of configuration files, scripts, or resource settings required to make a window manager work the way you want (some window managers are poorly documented).

`AnotherLevel` is the default window manager for Red Hat Linux, and is a special configuration of the `fvwm2` window manager. Red Hat Linux also includes the older `fvwm` and `twm` managers if you do a full (or "everything") installation. These window managers, and others, such as the CDE, KDE, and Motif's `mwm`, are discussed throughout this chapter.

Using X11 and the Common Desktop Environment

The *Common Desktop Environment*, or *CDE*, is a commercially sold and licensed graphical interface for X11. A sophisticated and complex GUI (see Figure 19.1), CDE hosts many advanced features, such as the following:

- An included suite of personal productivity tools, supporting data exchange and context-sensitive help
- Built-in help for nearly all programs and desktop actions
- Control-panel configuration of the desktop's display colors, window borders, and themes
- Drag-and-drop (such as dragging and dropping a document's icon onto a printer icon to print the file)
- Graphic dialog boxes to configure your system's keyboard, mouse, and sound
- Icons for all programs, directories, and other data types on the desktop
- Safer deletes with a desktop trash can
- Double-clicking with the mouse pointer to run clients, so users don't have to use a terminal command line to run programs

CDE is based on the latest version of Motif, a commercial set of software libraries. You must purchase CDE from a licensed vendor, such as Red Hat Software, Inc., or Xi Graphics, Inc. A full installation requires nearly 50MB of hard disk space and at least 32MB of RAM. For more information about CDE for Red Hat Linux, browse these sites:

http://www.redhat.com
http://www.triteal.com

Installing and Using the K Desktop Environment

The *K Desktop Environment*, or *KDE*, is one of the newest and most popular window managers for Linux and X11. Like CDE,

KDE is a complete graphical environment for X11 (see Figure 19.2), and provides similar features, including the following:

FIGURE 19.1
The CDE is a complete graphic environment for X11, and it features a suite of integrated personal productivity tools.

- An integrated suite of more than 100 programs and games
- Configuration of window scrollbars, fonts, color, and size using graphic dialog boxes
- Mounting of filesystems, such as CD-ROMs, using the mouse pointer
- *Network Transparent Access*, or *NTA*, in which clicking on a graphic file in an FTP listing results in an automatic download and display of the graphic
- Support for background (desktop) wallpaper graphics in JPEG format
- Support for session management (applications and window positions are remembered between sessions)

To use KDE, you must download and install the QT graphic software libraries and then download and install the KDE distribution.

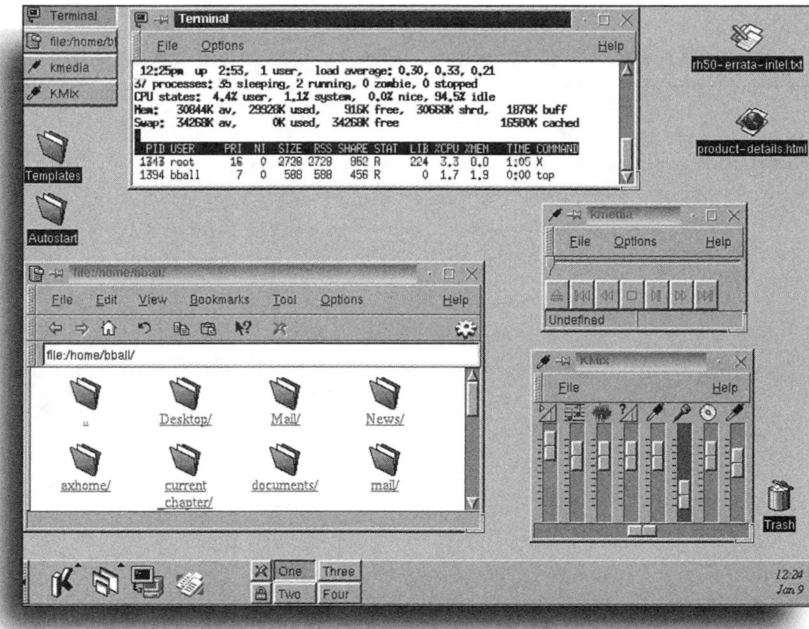

FIGURE 19.2
The KDE comes with nearly 100 programs, and is one of the newest and most popular X11 window managers for Linux.

Installing KDE

1. Download the latest QT software libraries for Linux from the following site:
   `http://www.troll.no/dl`
2. Install the QT libraries (follow the directions included with the libraries).
3. Download the current KDE distribution (a full installation requires eight different compressed archives) from the K Desktop site (or one of its mirrors):
   `http://www.kde.org`

   Red Hat Linux users will want KDE's files in RPM package format.
4. Log on as the root operator, and install the KDE `rpm` files using the `rpm` command, like this:
   ```
   # rpm -i kde*.rpm
   ```
   This installs KDE in the `/opt/kde` directory. KDE requires nearly 13MB of hard drive space.

5. Use your text editor to edit the system's /etc/profile file. Edit the PATH environment variable to include the path for the KDE binary files and the directory under /opt/kde, like this:

```
PATH=/opt/kde/bin:$PATH
KDEDIR=/opt/kde
```

6. Save the file and exit your text editor.

Read the KDE documentation under the /opt/kde/share/doc/HTML/en directory, or use the desktop's or application's built-in help. Remember, though, that KDE is a work in progress, so don't be surprised if documentation is missing or if some programs work incorrectly. Nonetheless, the recent release (Beta 3 as of this writing) shows continued improvement, and you can use KDE to get work done.

SEE ALSO

➤ *For more information about downloading files from the Internet, see page 200.*

Using X11 and the Motif Window Manager, *mwm*

The mwm, or Motif window manager, is part of the commercial Motif software library, distributed and sold, like CDE, by licensed vendors. Unlike X11, you must pay for a Motif distribution. Although you need to buy Motif to get the mwm window manager, you'll also receive software libraries to support other Motif applications, more than 30 additional Motif clients, hundreds of icons, and nearly 600 pages of documentation. You can get Motif for Red Hat Linux from Red Hat Software, Inc., at the following address:

http://www.redhat.com

Other companies that sell Motif for Linux include the following:

- Xi Graphics, Inc. (**http://www.xig.com**)
- Metro Link Incorporated (**http://www.metrolink.com**)
- InfoMagic (**http://www.infomagic.com**)
- Linux Systems Labs (**http://www.lsl.com**)
- Caldera (**http://www.caldera.com**)

Red Hat's Motif distribution requires at least 20MB of hard drive space. If you install only mwm and the required libraries, you'll need 5MB of space. Follow the instructions included with your Motif distribution for a proper installation.

Emulating Motif's *mwm* with the LessTif *mwm* Window Manager

LessTif is an alternative software library designed to be compatible with Motif version 1.2, and includes a Motif-workalike window manager, shown in Figure 19.3. LessTif is distributed under terms of the GNU General Public License, so you don't have to spend money to use LessTif with X11 to get Motif's features. LessTif's software libraries also allow you to run many Motif programs, and new versions of LessTif are released regularly. You can download LessTif from the following address:

`http://www.lesstif.org`

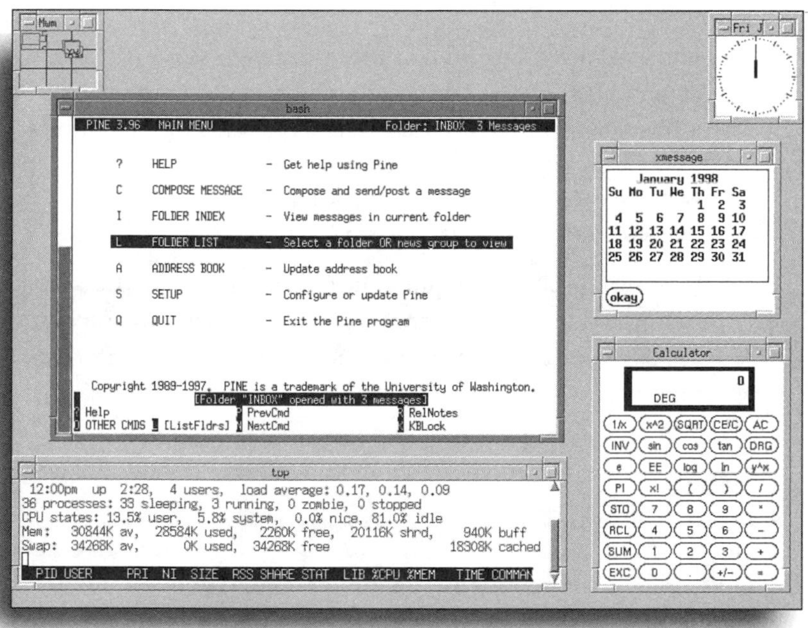

FIGURE 19.3
The LessTif software library distribution features the mwm window manager.

Installing LessTif

1. Log on as the root operator. Use your favorite web browser and navigate to the following address:
   `http://www.lesstif.org`

2. Create a temporary directory and download the binary versions of LessTif for Linux into that directory.

3. Uncompress the LessTif archive, using the `gunzip` and `tar` commands:

```
# gunzip lesstif-0.81-linux.tar.gz
# tar xf  lesstif-0.81-linux.tar
```

4. Use the `cd` (change directory) command to switch to the resulting LessTif directory:

```
# cd less*
```

5. Use the `mkdir` command to create a directory called `lesstif` under the `/usr/local` directory:

```
# mkdir /usr/local/lesstif
```

6. Use the `mv` command to move the contents of the LessTif directory to the new `/usr/local/lesstif` directory:

```
# mv * /usr/local/lesstif
```

7. Use your text editor to edit the systemwide `bash` shell file, `/etc/profile`, and add the LessTif binary path to your `PATH` environment variable. Also create a `LIBRARY_PATH`, pointing to the LessTif software library, with the following lines:

```
PATH=/usr/local/lesstif/bin:$PATH
LIBRARY_PATH=/usr/local/lesstif/lib
```

8. Save `/etc/profile`, and quit your text editor. To use LessTif right away, use the `bash` shell's `source` command (if you don't use bash, see the LessTif documentation for more information):

```
# source /etc/profile
```

SEE ALSO

➤ *For more information about using file compression and archiving utilities such as* `gzip` *and* `tar`*, see page 542.*

➤ *To learn more about using shell and environment variables, see page 90.*

Starting a Window Manager

Most window managers are started by line entries in a file called `.xinitrc` in your home directory. The systemwide default `.xinitrc` file is found under the `/etc/X11/xinit` or `/usr/X11R6/lib/X11/xinit` directory. When you first start X (as detailed in the section "Starting X11" in Chapter 18, "Running and Configuring X11"), the `xinit` program (started by the `startx` command) first looks for the initializer file `.xinitrc` in your home directory. If it is not found, `xinit` then looks for `.xinitrc` in the `/usr/X11R6/lib/X11/xinit` directory.

You do not have to use the default `.xinitrc` system file, but if you want to experiment, use the `cp` command to copy and create your own `.xinitrc` file, like this:

```
# cp /usr/X11R6/lib/X11/xinit/xinitrc $HOME/.xinitrc
```

SEE ALSO

➤ *To learn more about using* `.xinitrc`, *see page 266.*

Starting *AnotherLevel*

Because `AnotherLevel` is the default window manager used by Red Hat Linux, you can start `AnotherLevel` by using the `startx` command like so:

```
# startx
```

`AnotherLevel`, shown in Figure 19.4, is started by the `xinit` command (`xinit` is run by `startx`), which uses a file called `Xclients` under the `/usr/X11R6/lib/X11/xinit` directory. The `Xclients` file is a shell script that looks for `AnotherLevel`'s configuration files in the `/etc/X11/AnotherLevel` directory.

To start `AnotherLevel` from a line in your own `.xinitrc` file, use your text editor to create a `.xinitrc` file in your home directory, and then add a line like this:

```
fvwm2 -cmd 'FvwmM4 -debug /etc/X11/AnotherLevel/fvwm2rc.m4'
```

This command line forces the `fvwm2` window manager to read AnotherLevel's configuration files. Save the `.xinitrc` file, and then use the `startx` command to start your X session.

Starting *fvwm2*

To use `fvwm2` and its default settings instead of the `AnotherLevel` configuration, use your text editor to open your `.xinitrc` file. Then use the pound (#) character to comment out the `fvwm2` `AnotherLevel` entry, and insert the `fvwm2` command, like so:

```
# fvwm2 -cmd 'FvwmM4 -debug
/etc/X11/AnotherLevel/fvwm2rc.m4'
fvwm2
```

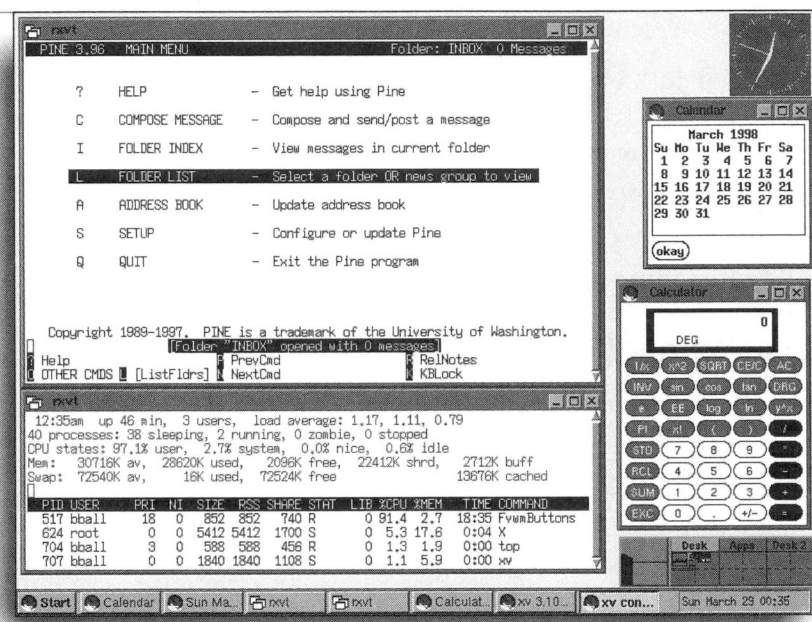

FIGURE 19.4
AnotherLevel is Red Hat Software's custom configuration of the fvwm2 window manager, and is the default window manager for Red Hat Linux.

Save the .xinitrc file, and use the startx command to run fvwm2, which is shown in Figure 19.5.

Starting *fvwm*

To use the fvwm window manager (shown in Figure 19.6) instead of fvwm2, use your text editor to open your .xinitrc file. Then use the pound (#) character to comment out fvwm2, and insert the fvwm command like so:

```
# fvwm2 -cmd 'FvwmM4 -debug
/etc/X11/AnotherLevel/fvwm2rc.m4'
#fvwm2
fvwm
```

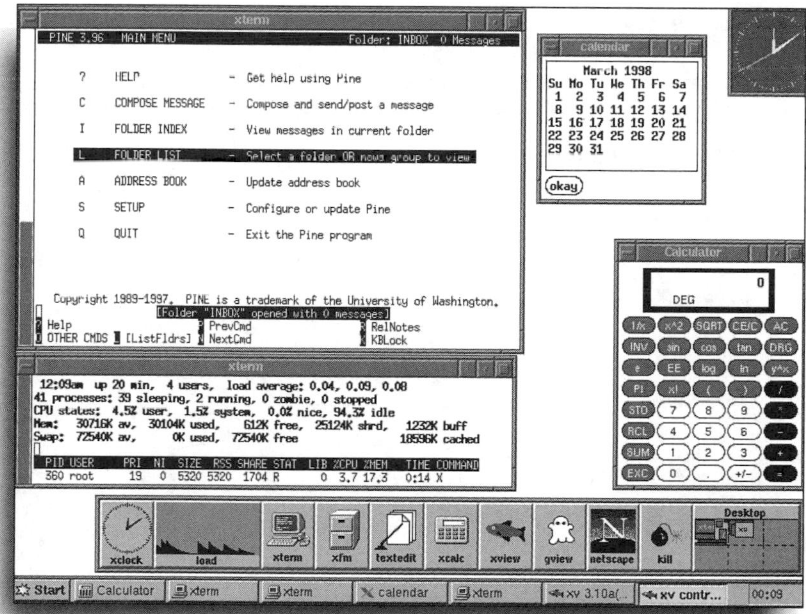

FIGURE 19.5

The fvwm2 window manager for X11 is an improved version of the fvwm window manager.

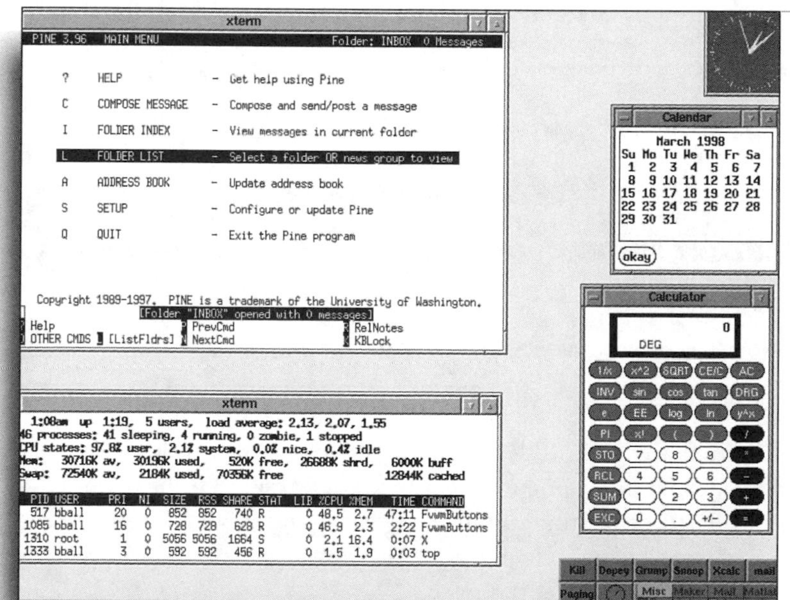

FIGURE 19.6

The fvwm window manager is an earlier version of fvwm2, but features virtual desktops, icon docks, and many features required by today's Linux X11 users.

Save the `.xinitrc` file, and use the `startx` command to run `fvwm`.

Starting *twm*

To use the `twm` window manager (shown in Figure 19.7) instead of `fvwm`, use your text editor to open your `.xinitrc` file. Use the pound (`#`) character to comment out `fvwm`, and insert a command to run a terminal client, such as `xterm`, followed by the `twm` command, like so:

```
#fvwm2 -cmd 'FvwmM4 -debug /etc/X11/AnotherLevel/fvwm2rc.m4'
#fvwm2
#fvwm
exec xterm &
twm
```

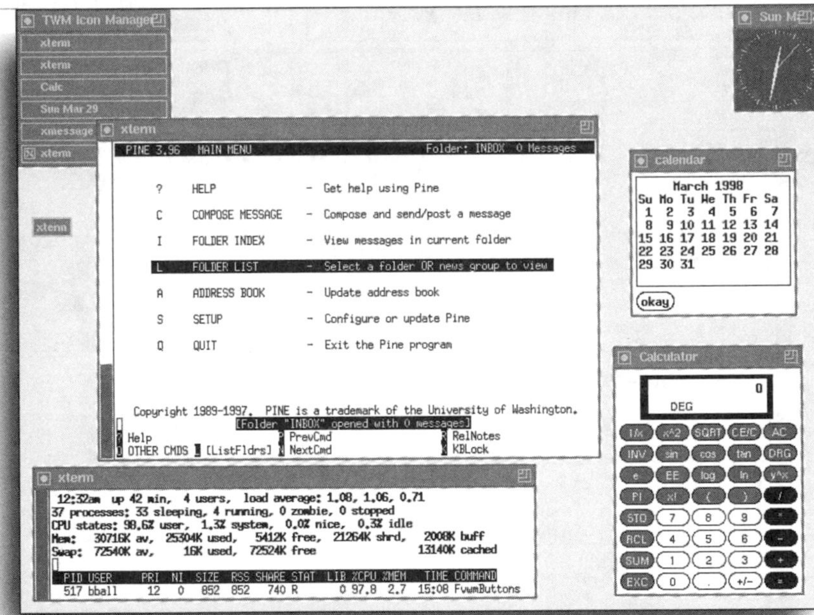

FIGURE 19.7
The `twm`, or Tab window manager, supports only basic desktop operations for window movement and decoration.

You must start at least one terminal window if you use the default `twm` configuration file: `system.twmrc`. This is because the default configuration file does not define any programs or clients in `twm`'s desktop menu. Save the `.xinitrc` and use the `startx` command to run `twm`.

Starting CDE

Although other window managers can be started by using the window manager's name in your `.xinitrc` file in your home directory, CDE generally requires you to start your X session by logging on to X through the `xdm`, or X Display Manager, client. This means that after you install and configure CDE, your system automatically starts X11 after you start Linux, and displays the `xdm` host chooser (see Figures 18.1 or 18.2 to see what the `xdm` chooser looks like).

To start Red Hat's distribution of CDE from a console or non-X11 display, create a text file containing the following line:

```
xinit /usr/dt/bin/Xsession
```

Save this with a filename like `startcde`, and then use the `chmod` command to make it executable, like this:

```
# chmod +x startcde
```

To start CDE, use **`startcde`** on the command line, like so:

```
# startcde
```

Running as root with CDE

You might not be able to run programs as the root operator from a terminal window if you use CDE and X after logging on through `xdm`. (`xdm` offers a small measure of security, and running clients as another user requires authorization.) To get around this problem, use the `xhost` command to temporarily add the hostname of your computer to the access list of your X server, and include the root command by using the `su` command, like this:

```
# xhost +localhost; su
➥-c "desired_root_
➥command"
```

`desired_root_command` is the name of the client or program you want to run as the root operator (such as `mount`, `umount`, or Red Hat's Control Panel clients).

Starting KDE

Use your text editor to create or edit your `.xinitrc` file in your home directory. Comment out any previous window managers, and insert the `startkde` command in your `.xinitrc` file, like this:

```
#fvwm2 -cmd 'FvwmM4 -debug /etc/X11/AnotherLevel/fvwm2rc.m4'
#fvwm2
#fvwm
#exec xterm &
#twm
startkde
```

Save your file, and then use the `startx` command to start X11 and run KDE, like this:

```
# startx
```

Starting Motif's *mwm* Window Manager

To use the `mwm` window manager, use your text editor to open your `.xinitrc` file. Use the pound (#) character to comment previous window managers, and insert the `mwm` command like so:

```
#fvwm2 -cmd 'FvwmM4 -debug /etc/X11/AnotherLevel/fvwm2rc.m4'
#fvwm2
#fvwm
```

```
#exec xterm &
#twm
#startkde
mwm
```

Save the `.xinitrc` file and use the `startx` command to run `mwm`.

Starting LessTif's *mwm*

Start LessTif's `mwm` window manager just as you do Motif's `mwm`: by using a Motif-like `mwm` entry in your `.xinitrc` file. If you have Motif and LessTif installed, rename `mwm`, the Motif window manager, to `Mwm`. The next time you use the `startx` command, your X session will use the LessTif `mwm` window manager.

Configuring Window Managers

The `fvwm2`, `fvwm`, and `twm` window managers use systemwide configuration files, usually found under the `/etc/X11` directory in a directory with the window manager's name. For example, a directory listing of the `/etc/X11` directory shows the configuration file directories for `AnotherLevel`, `fvwm2`, `fvwm`, and `twm`:

```
# ls /etc/X11
AnotherLevel    fs       twm        xinit
TheNextLevel    fvwm     wmconfig   xsm
X               fvwm2    xdm
```

Changes made to configuration files under these directories affect all users. Window managers such as `fvwm2`, `fvwm`, `twm`, or `mwm` also use custom settings in a file in a user's home directory. To find out how to make custom changes to a specific window manager's file, read the appropriate window manager's manual pages.

Configuring *AnotherLevel*

`AnotherLevel`, shown in Figure 19.8, is Red Hat's special configuration of the `fvwm2` window manager. Unlike other window managers, such as `fvwm` or `twm`, `AnotherLevel` has more than a dozen configuration files, found under the `/etc/X11/AnotherLevel` directory. These files include

```
# ls -A /etc/X11/AnotherLevel
decors              fvwm2rc.functions    fvwm2rc.menus
fvwm2rc.apps        fvwm2rc.hostmenus    fvwm2rc.modules
fvwm2rc.decors      fvwm2rc.init         fvwm2rc.mouse
fvwm2rc.defines     fvwm2rc.keys         fvwm2rc.xlock
fvwm2rc.defstyles   fvwm2rc.m4           scripts
fvwm2rc.forms       fvwm2rc.macros
```

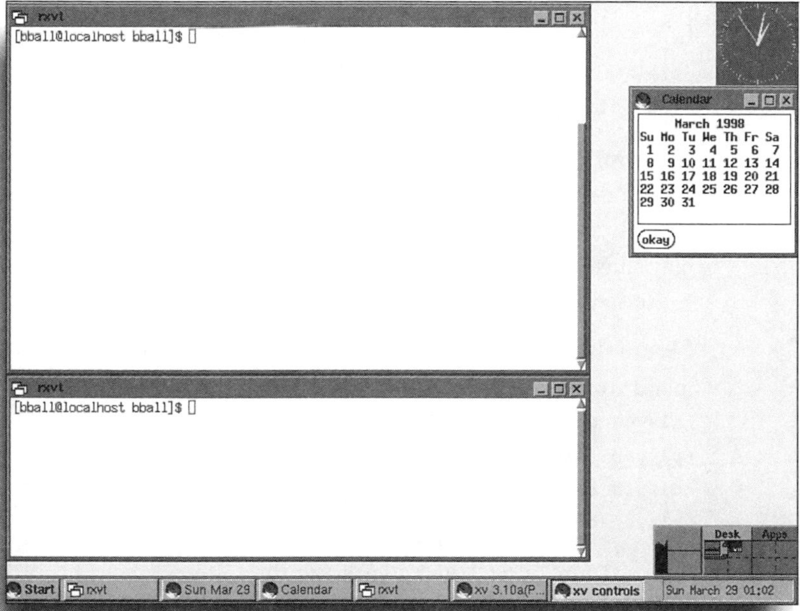

FIGURE 19.8
The AnotherLevel window manager features advanced window controls, a taskbar, and scrollbars for X11 windows.

The root operator can make changes to these files to customize how this window manager works for the system. Many of these files automatically determine the screen size and availability of different X11 clients installed on your system in order to set the following:

- Window sizes and placement
- Color options for client windows
- Fonts used in window titles or menus
- Names of programs in desktop menus
- Default clients for web browsing
- Sounds for system events

- Icons for programs in desktop menus
- Support for a number of virtual desktops
- Options for tear-off menus

To customize the list of clients in `AnotherLevel`'s menus, create or edit configuration files in the `/etc/X11/wmconfig` directory. You do not have to run X11 to create menu items.

Configuring *AnotherLevel*'s desktop menu

1. Log on as the root operator, then navigate to the `/etc/X11/wmconfig` directory, like so:

   ```
   # cd /etc/X11/wmconfig
   ```

2. Use your favorite text editor to create a text file with the name of the client you want to install. For example, to create a Music menu category with the X11 client `xplaycd` (used to play music CDs), create a file called `xplaycd`, like this:

   ```
   # pico xplaycd
   ```

3. Create the menu entry, program menu item, and client command to run by entering the following text:

   ```
   xplaycd name "Xplaycd"
   xplaycd description "Play Music CDs"
   xplaycd exec "xplaycd &"
   xplaycd group "Music"
   ```

4. Save the file. Start X11 by entering the following:

   ```
   # startx
   ```

   If you're already running X, select the Restart menu item from the Exit Fvwm menu, as shown in Figure 19.9. Reach this menu from the window manager's Start button on the taskbar at the bottom of the screen, or by clicking a blank area of the desktop.

5. Use the Start menu on the taskbar or click a blank area of the desktop. Navigate through the Program menu, and you'll see the `xplaycd` menu item under a new menu called Music, as shown in Figure 19.10.

SEE ALSO

➤ *For more information about using the* `pico` *editor, or other text editors for Linux, see page 50.*

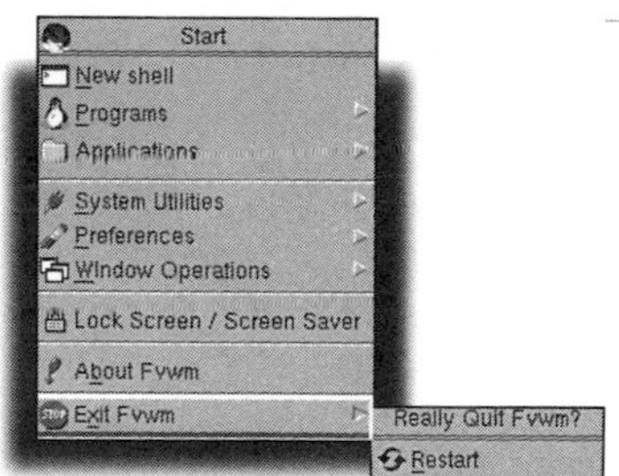

FIGURE 19.9

Use AnotherLevel's Restart menu item to force the fvwm2 window manager to recognize menu changes without exiting your X11 session.

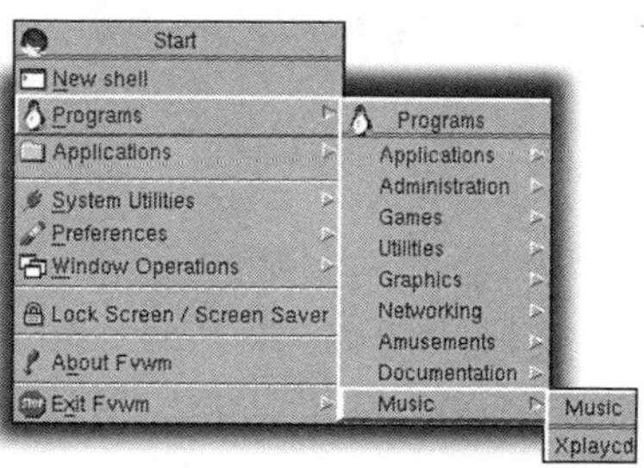

FIGURE 19.10

AnotherLevel's desktop (root) menu can be customized by adding new X11 clients, such as the CD music player, xplaycd.

To customize the main menu of the desktop menu, you must edit the file fvwm2rc.menus in the /etc/X11/AnotherLevel directory. Creating menu items in the main menu makes it easy to quickly start often-used X11 clients or other programs. You do not need to run X11 to customize this menu.

Adding menu items to the main desktop menu

1. Log on as the root operator, and navigate to AnotherLevel's configuration directory by entering the following:

   ```
   # cd /etc/X11/AnotherLevel
   ```

2. Using your favorite text editor, open the fvwm2rc.menus file and disable line wrapping. If you're using the pico editor, enter the following:

   ```
   # pico -w fvwm2rc.menus
   ```

3. The fvwm2rc.menus file contains many lines of instructions; you can add programs under the BasicStartMenu section. For example, if you frequently use the X11 calculator client, xcalc, look for a section of text like this:

   ```
   # This is for the Start menu of the FvwmTaskBar
   define(`BasicStartMenu',`dnl
   + "&New shell MiniTitleIcon(sh1)"       Exec  RXVT -fg
   ➥black -bg white
   ```

```
+ "&Programs MiniTitleIcon(penguin)"   Popup ROOT_MENU
')
```

To add the xcalc client to the Start menu, type a menu entry, specifying the name of menu item (Calculator), its icon (calc, which is found under the /usr/share/icon directory), and the X11 command, xcalc, to start the calculator:

```
# This is for the Start menu of the FvwmTaskBar
define(`BasicStartMenu',`dnl
+ "&New shell MiniTitleIcon(sh1)"         Exec  RXVT -
➥fg black -bg white
+ "&Calculator MiniTitleIcon(calc)"       Exec xcalc &
+ "&Programs MiniTitleIcon(penguin)"      Popup
➥ROOT_MENU
')
```

4. To create a menu entry to run a non-X11 or console program, such as the pico text editor, use the rxvt terminal client, along with the -e (execute) option:

```
+ "&Text Editor MiniTitleIcon(edit)"      Exec rxvt -e
➥pico &
```

5. Save and close the file. Then start an X11 session using the startx command, like so:

```
# startx
```

If you're already running X, restart fvwm2 from the Exit Fvwm menu. After you restart, the desktop menu has the Calculator entry, along with an icon, as shown in Figure 19.11.

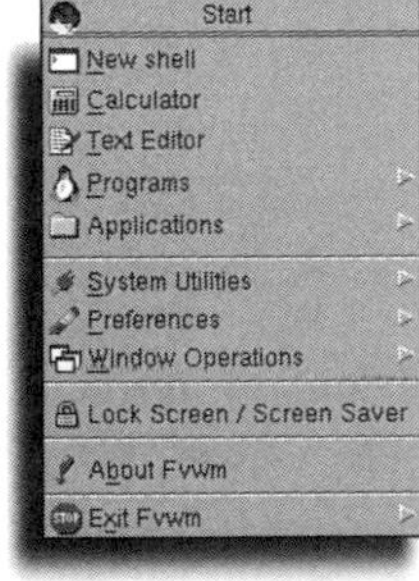

FIGURE 19.11
The top level of AnotherLevel's Start menu can be customized.

The taskbar at the bottom of AnotherLevel's desktop is a convenient place to access minimized windows or clients running on adjacent desktops. But if you need screen real estate, the taskbar can get in the way. To make the taskbar disappear when you're not using it, you must uncomment (remove the pound (#) character in front of) the pertinent line in the file `fvwm2rc.modules`.

Autohiding *AnotherLevel*'s taskbar

1. Log on as the root operator. Navigate to the `/etc/X11/AnotherLevel` directory or, using your favorite text editor, open the file `fvwm2rc.modules` and disable line wrapping. If you're using a `pico` text editor, your command will look something like this:

   ```
   # pico -w /etc/X11/AnotherLevel/fvwm2rc.modules
   ```

2. Look for the `FvwmTaskBar` section, which begins like this:

   ```
   ##### FvwmTaskBar
   ```

3. Scroll to the end of the section, and look for the `AutoHide` entry, which looks like this:

   ```
   #*FvwmTaskBarAutoHide
   ```

4. Enable autohide by removing the pound (#) character, so that the entry looks like this:

   ```
   *FvwmTaskBarAutoHide
   ```

5. Save the file, exit your editor, and restart `AnotherLevel`. After restarting, your taskbar disappears until you move your mouse pointer to the bottom of your screen.

Although you can organize your desktop by starting programs with line entries in the `.xinitrc` or `.Xclients` files in home directories, root operators can configure a systemwide default X11 desktop that presents a standard layout of clients—such as a clock, a calendar, or terminal windows—whenever a user starts an X11 session. This configuration can be entered in the `fvwm2rc.init` file under the `/etc/X11/AnotherLevel` directory, and can be accomplished without running X. The `fvwm2rc.init` file defines default startup procedures for `AnotherLevel`.

Configuring default desktop layouts

1. Log on as the root operator. Use a text editor such as `pico`, to open the `fvwm2rc.init` file, like so (don't forget to disable line wrap):

   ```
   # pico -w /etc/X11/AnotherLevel/fvwm2rc.init
   ```

2. Scroll through the file and look for the `StartupFunction` section, which should resemble the following:
   ```
   AddtoFunc "StartupFunction"
   ```

3. To add a clock, calendar, and two terminal windows, type the following four entries below the `AddtoFunc` line. Consider what default resolution your users can use (my suggested configuration is for an 800×600-pixel display). Type the entries, specifying any X Toolkit options, and use `geometry` settings to place the clients on the desktop, like so:
   ```
   + "I" Exec rxvt -fg black -bg white -geometry 80x24+5+5
   + "I" Exec rxvt -fg black -bg white -geometry
   ➥80x11+5+373
   + "I" Exec cal ¦ xmessage -title Calendar -file –
   ➥-geometry +627+86
   + "I" Exec rclock -bg red -fg yellow -update 1 -geometry
   ➥80x80-3+3
   ```

4. Save the file, and then start an X11 session. The desktop should appear as shown in Figure 19.12: with two terminal shell windows, a handy calendar window, and a clock.

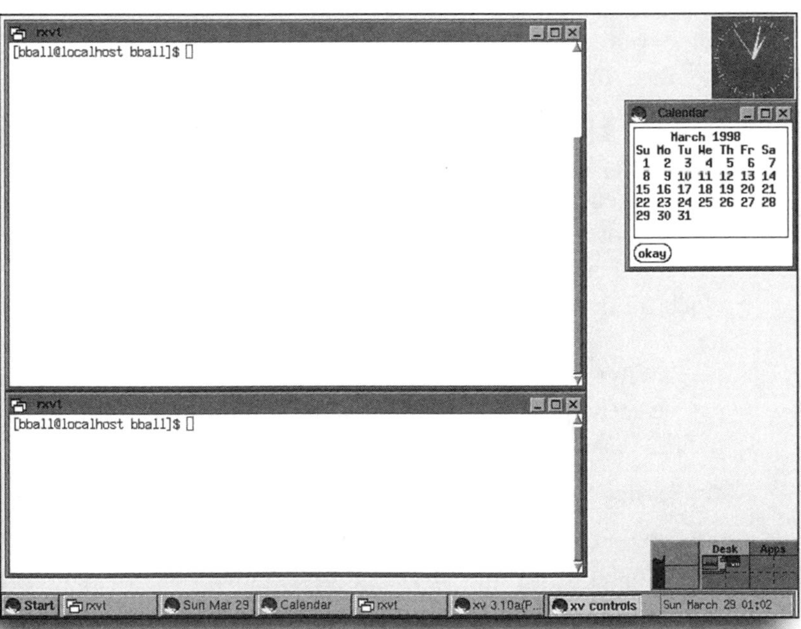

FIGURE 19.12
The `fvwm2rc.init` file can be used to configure system wide default desktops with correctly placed windows and X clients for users starting an X11 session.

SEE ALSO

➤ *For more information about using terminal programs for X11, such as* `rxvt` *or* `xterm`*, see page 269.*

The default `AnotherLevel` configuration requires you to click in a window to make it active, or to bring a window to the top level of the display. Activating a window with your mouse is called *pointer focus*. You can configure `AnotherLevel` to have the focus follow your mouse pointer, which activates the window when you merely move the pointer over a window.

Another configurable feature of this window manager is its capability to interactively place a client window when the X11 client starts. When you use `AnotherLevel` and start an X11 client, the program's window automatically appears on your desktop by default. This is not always convenient, especially if you haven't used `geometry` settings, or if the client's window is too large for your display (such as with `xfig`, which requires a screen resolution of at least 1024×768 pixels). By configuring `AnotherLevel` to allow interactive placement, a client's window is attached to your mouse pointer; the window doesn't become active until you press the left mouse button.

You can also set the number of virtual desktops, or extra screens, to use during your X11 sessions. You access the desktops by clicking the Desk square in `AnotherLevel`'s pager window (shown in the bottom-right corner of the desktop in Figure 19.12), or through the appropriate keyboard navigation command listed in Table 20.2 of Chapter 20, "Performing Common X11 Operations."

Setting *AnotherLevel* pointer focus, window placement, and desktops

1. Log on as the root operator. Using a text editor, open the `fvwm2rc.defines` file under the `/etc/X11/AnotherLevel` directory. If you're using `pico`, your command will look something like this:

   ```
   # pico -w /etc/X11/AnotherLevel/fvwm2rc.defines
   ```

2. To enable the focus-follows–pointer feature (which makes a window become active simply when your mouse pointer moves to the window), first look for the section dealing with pointer focus. The section should look like this:

```
# If defined, the focus follows the pointer. Otherwise
focus is set by clicking on a window. Undefined this
#  implements "ClickToFocus". Please note
# that AutoRaise does not work with ClickToFocus...
#define(`FOCUS_FOLLOWS_POINTER')
```

3. Remove the pound (#) character from the beginning of the feature definition. The line should look like this after you finish:

   ```
   define('FOCUS_FOLLOWS_POINTER')
   ```

4. To enable the interactive placement feature (in which a new client window appears only when you click an area of the desktop), first look for the section that looks like this:

   ```
   # Define this for interactive placement (InteractivePlacement),
   # which forces the window manager to allow manual
   # placement of all windows on the desktop
   # define (`INTERACTIVE_PLACEMENT')
   ```

5. Remove the pound (#) character in front of the feature definition:

   ```
   define('INTERACTIVE_PLACEMENT')
   ```

6. To set the number of desktops for X11 sessions, look for the `NUM_DESKTOP` section:

   ```
   # NUM_DESKTOPS is number of desktops -- each desktop is
   # DESKTOP_SIZE panes
   define(`NUM_DESKTOPS',2)

   # DESKTOP_SIZE is a geometry specifying horizontal desk#
   # top x vertical desktops  So 3x3 gives 9 panes per # #
   # desktop
   define(`DESKTOP_SIZE',2x2)
   ```

   This configuration shows that the default pager displays eight different virtual desktops (two pager windows of four desktop panes each).

7. To create an additional four virtual desktops, change the number following the `'NUM_DESKTOPS'` setting to `3`:

   ```
   define('NUM_DESKTOPS',3)
   ```

8. Save the file, exit your text editor, and start X11. Your pager block should look like the one shown in Figure 19.13. You now have an additional pager window with four new pager

panes, for a total of 12 different desktops for your X sessions.

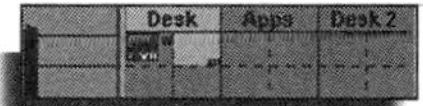

FIGURE 19.13
You now have 12 different desktops for your X sessions.

Configuring the *fvwm2* Window Manager

The fvwm2, or virtual window manager, found under the /usr/X11R6/bin directory, is a descendant of the twm, or tab window manager. Fvwm2 builds on the initial features of the twm and fvwm window managers, and offers several improvements, such as virtual desktops, three-dimensional window decorations (scrollbars, borders, and so on), and code modules to support pagers or icon docks.

Configuring the fvwm and fvwm2 window managers is very similar (they're closely related). To configure fvwm, copy the file system.fvwmrc from the /etc/X11/fvwm directory to your home directory, with .fvwmrc as the file's name.

Configuring *fvwm2* pointer focus, desktops, and menus

1. Copy the file system.fvwm2rc from the /etc/X11/fvwm2 directory to your home directory by entering the following:

   ```
   # cp /etc/X11/fvwm2/system.fvwm2rc $HOME/.fvwm2rc
   ```

   Note that you changed the file's name to .fvwm2rc.

2. Use your favorite text editor to open the .fvwm2rc file.

3. To change the pointer focus, look for fvwm2's focus section, which should look like this:

   ```
   Style "*" ClickToFocus
   # Comment the above and uncomment one of the following
   # if you prefer focus follow mouse.
   #Style "*" MouseFocus
   #Style "*" SloppyFocus
   ```

4. The default focus setting requires you to click on a window to activate it. To change the pointer focus so that a window becomes active when you simply move your mouse pointer to a window, insert a pound character (#) at the beginning of

the `ClickToFocus` line, and remove the pound character from the beginning of the `MouseFocus` line, like so:

```
#Style "*" ClickToFocus
# Comment the above and uncomment one of the following
# if you prefer focus follow mouse.
Style "*" MouseFocus
#Style "*" SloppyFocus
```

5. To use SloppyFocus—which is similar to MouseFocus, but lets you type in the previously active window—insert and remove comment characters, like this:

```
#Style "*" ClickToFocus
# Comment the above and uncomment one of the following
# if you prefer focus follow mouse.
#Style "*" MouseFocus
Sytle "*" SloppyFocus
```

6. To change the number of virtual desktops, scroll to the `DesktopSize` section, which looks like this:

```
#
# Set the desk top size in units of physical screen size
#
DeskTopSize 3x2
```

7. The default configuration is six virtual desktops. To change this to nine desktops, change the `DeskTopSize` setting like so:

```
DeskTopSize 3x3
```

8. To add menu items to the top level of `fvwm2`'s Start menu, scroll to the taskbar's Start menu section, which looks like this:

```
# This is for the Start menu of the FvwmTaskBar
AddToMenu "StartMenu"
+ "New shell        %mini-sh1.xpm%"          \
Exec     color_xterm -ls -sb -fn 8x1$
+ "Manual pages     %mini-book1.xpm%"        Exec
➥xman &
+ "Magnifying glass %mini-zoom.xpm%"         Exec xmag &
```

9. To add the X11 `xcalc` calculator client to this menu (displayed when you press the Start button on the taskbar), for

example, insert an entry with the name of the menu item, followed by an icon name and command line, like so:

```
# This is for the Start menu of the FvwmTaskBar
AddToMenu "StartMenu"
+ "New shell         %mini-sh1.xpm%"     \
Exec color_xterm -ls -sb -fn 8x1$
+ "Calculator        %mini-calc.xpm%"   Exec xcalc &
+ "Manual pages      %mini-book1.xpm%"  Exec xman &
+ "Magnifying glass %mini-zoom.xpm%"    Exec xmag &
```

10. Save the .fvwm2rc file. To use these changes, start an X11 session.

Configuring the *twm* Window Manager

The twm, or tab window manager, is one of the original window managers for the X Window System, and provides rudimentary window-management features, such as window titles, icons, root or desktop menus, and custom mouse and keyboard commands.

Like the fvwm and fvwm2 window managers, twm's configuration file, system.twmrc, is found in the /etc/X11/twm directory. Changes made to twm's configuration files under the /etc/X11 directory are systemwide; users can customize twm by copying the system.twmrc file to a home directory as .twmrc. See the twm manual page for more details about configuration options.

Configuring Motif's *mwm*

After installing Motif, customize mwm by copying the file system.mwmrc from the /usr/lib/X11 directory to your home directory. Rename the file .mwmrc. Edit this file to change settings for your mouse, mwm windows, or the mwm desktop menu. The Motif mwm manual page offers details about how to customize the .mwmrc file.

Configuring LessTif's *mwm*

The LessTif version of mwm, like Motif's mwm, also uses a resource file called .mwmrc in your home directory. Edit this file to customize the root or desktop menu (which you display by right-clicking a blank area of the desktop).

Edit the file `mwm`, found in `app-defaults` under the `/usr/local/lesstif` directory, to customize other features of LessTif's `mwm`. See the LessTif documentation and `mwm` manual page for more details.

CHAPTER

20

Performing Common X11 Operations

By Bill Ball

Using X11 Toolkit options

Moving and resizing windows

Viewing fonts

Viewing font characters

Navigating windows with the keyboard

Cutting and pasting text

Capturing windows and the desktop

Using X11 Toolkit Command-Line Options

Nearly all X Window System clients, or programs, accept a set of similar command-line options, known as X11 Toolkit options. These options provide a range of choices for the window size, placement, colors, window title, or fonts used when a client starts. Most of the standard X11 Toolkit options are discussed in the `X` manual page.

SEE ALSO

➤ *To learn more about the X Window System, see page 260.*

Using Geometry Settings to Set Window Size

Use the `-geometry` option followed by `width`, `height`, and `xoffset` or `yoffset` values to start your program with a specific window size, in a specified area of your display, or in a virtual desktop.

Placing *rxvt* terminal windows by using *-geometry*

1. Use the `-geometry` setting with the `rxvt` terminal emulator to place the initial window in the upper-right corner of your display. Assuming you have an 800×600-pixel desktop, start `rxvt` with an 80-character wide by 24-line window by typing the following at the command line:

   ```
   # rxvt -geometry 80x24+216+0 &
   ```

   The value `216` is the `xoffset` value, and forces the `rxvt` window to start 216 pixels from the left side of the screen. A `yoffset` value of `0` forces the `rxvt` window to the top of screen.

2. Use the `-geometry` setting again, but this time, start `rxvt` in the lower-right corner of your screen by entering the following at the command line:

   ```
   # rxvt -geometry 80x24+216+232&
   ```

3. Use geometry offset settings greater than your desktop size to start the `rxvt` client offscreen in an adjacent virtual desktop. If your screen size is 800×600 pixels, use an `xoffset` value slightly greater than `800` to place the terminal window in the desktop to the right, like this:

   ```
   # rxvt -geometry 80x25+801+0
   ```

Using geometry to place a window

You can also use `-geometry -0+0` to place a client window in the upper-right corner of your display. This saves you the effort of manually moving the window or performing subtraction of a client's window size from your desktop's size.

Automatically placing windows in the lower-right corner

`-geometry -0-0` does the same thing, and places any clientís window in the lower-right corner of your desktop!

This command line starts rxvt in the upper-left corner of the desktop that is located to the right of your screen.

4. To start rxvt in a desktop below your current screen, use a yoffset slightly greater than your screen's height, like so:

```
# rxvt -geometry 80x25+0+601
```

This command line starts rxvt in the upper-left corner of the desktop that is located below your screen. Be careful not to use negative values, or you might not be able to use your desktop pager or virtual window manager to retrieve your client!

Use geometry settings to start clients in each of your desktops. For example, one desktop could be dedicated to web browsing or email, another could be dedicated to a sports graphics program, and a third could be occupied by your word processor or text editor.

SEE ALSO

- *For more information about the* AnotherLevel *configuration of the* fvwmw *X11 window manager, see page 282.*
- *To learn more about using and configuring virtual desktops, see page 294.*

Setting up X11 desktops

X11 Toolkit geometry settings are handy for building organized desktops. Red Hat Linux fans using the AnotherLevel fvwmw window manager configuration will also appreciate AnotherLevel's convenient Save Desktop to new.xinitrc feature, found under the Start menu's Preferences menu. When you use this feature, a file called new.xinitrc is created in your home directory. This file contains a starting command line for each active client, along with the client's geometry settings. Copy these command lines to your .xinitrc file in your home directory to automatically configure your desktops.

Setting Foreground and Background Colors

Use the -bg and -fg X11 Toolkit options to set the background and foreground colors of an X11 client's window. The list of colors supported by the XFree86 256-color servers are in the file rgb.txt under the /usr/X11R6/lib/X11 directory, or you can use the showrgb client to display the list of colors by typing the following at the command line:

```
# showrgb
```

To start the rxvt terminal emulator with a BlanchedAlmond background and MidnightBlue text for the foreground, for example, use the -bg and -fg options:

```
# rxvt -bg BlanchedAlmond -fg MidnightBlue &
```

If you must use the XF86_VGA16 server for your X11 sessions, only 16 colors are available. Use the xcmap client to display the available colors, like this:

```
# xcmap &
```

The available colors will be displayed in a grid, as shown in Figure 20.1. Users of black-and-white–display servers, such as the monochrome server XF86_Mono, might want to experiment with the -rv and +rv reverse video modes to invert the display of terminal windows or text editors.

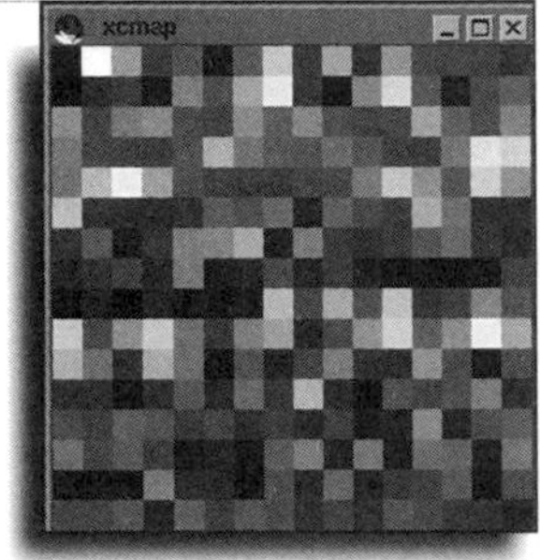

FIGURE 20.1
The xcmap client displays a grid of available colors for your X11 desktop.

SEE ALSO

➤ *To learn more about using the* XFree86 *series of X11 servers, see page 260.*

Moving, Resizing, and Managing Windows

The types and features of windows used by X11 clients depend on the X11 window manager used during your X Window System sessions. Because this book concentrates on the Red Hat Linux distribution, window-management features and windows created and used with the AnotherLevel configuration of the fvwmw window manager are discussed. (Other window managers might offer fewer or more window features, such as borders, scrollbars, and Maximize, Minimize, or Close buttons.)

The anatomy of an X11 window is shown in Figure 20.2. Note that the AnotherLevel window manager provides vertical and horizontal scrollbars, so that the contents of the window, such as a terminal emulator, can be scrolled vertically or horizontally.

Specifying an X11 Window Title

The topmost portion of an X11 window is called the *title bar*, and usually contains the name of the X11 client. You can change the name that appears on the title bar by using the X11 Toolkit

-title option. For example, to start the rxvt X11 terminal emulator with a custom title bar, enter a command line such as the following:

```
# rxvt -title "Welcome to Red Hat Linux! Have a nice day!
➥:-)"
```

FIGURE 20.2
A typical AnotherLevel X11 window, showing common window features, such as a title bar, scrollbars, and window control buttons.

SEE ALSO

➤ *For more information about configuring X11 terminal emulators, such as* rxvt *or* xterm, *see page 269.*

Minimizing, Maximizing, or Closing Windows

In the upper-right portion of each window there are three buttons: Minimize, Maximize, and Close. If you click the Minimize button, the window will shrink, appearing only as a button in the AnotherLevel taskbar (shown in Figure 20.3). If you click the Maximize button, the window will enlarge to fill your display, or will be restored to a previous size (note that you can also double-click the window's title bar to maximize or restore a window's size). Although you should usually use an X11 client's documented method to quit, you can close the client or window by clicking the Close button.

There are several ways to resize a window. To resize a window horizontally using your mouse, move your cursor to right or left edge of the window, and click and drag the window until it reaches the desired width. To resize a window vertically using your mouse, move your cursor to the top or bottom of the window, and click and drag the window until it reaches the desired height. To resize vertically and horizontally at the same time, move your mouse cursor to one of the window's four corners, and click and drag the window until it reaches the desired size. These operations are also available through a shortcut menu displayed when you click the upper-left corner of a window.

FIGURE 20.3
The `AnotherLevel` desktop taskbar provides a Start menu, placement for minimized X11 windows, and the current date and time.

Using Window-Management Keyboard Commands

The `AnotherLevel` window manager offers keyboard support for various actions, such as managing which window is active and which windows are inactive (this is known as *window focus*). These keyboard commands, which are listed in Table 20.1, are defined in the file `fvwmwrc.keys` found in the `/etc/X11/AnotherLevel` directory. Create a backup copy of this file before making any changes!

TABLE 20.1 ***AnotherLevel* window management keyboard commands**

Action	Keyboard Command
Move window	Ctrl+Shift+F7
Resize window	Ctrl+Shift+F8
Make next window active	Alt+Tab
Make previous window active	Shift+Alt+Tab
Display window list (menu)	Alt+Esc
Maximize window vertically	Ctrl+Shift+up arrow
Maximize window horizontally	Ctrl+Shift+right arrow
Raise window to top	Ctrl+Alt+Return
Lower window to bottom	Ctrl+Alt+Return
Minimize (iconify) window	Ctrl+Shift+down arrow
Move to last virtual desktop	Ctrl+Shift+Alt+End
Move to first virtual desktop	Ctrl+Shift+Alt+Home

Action	Keyboard Command
Delete current window	Ctrl+Shift+Alt+Backspace
Destroy current window	Ctrl+Shift+Alt+Decimal Point
Display window operations menu	Ctrl+Shift+Alt+W
Display desktop preferences menu	Ctrl+Shift+Alt+P

Viewing X11 Fonts

Use the `xlsfonts` program to list the fonts recognized by the X Window System. Use wildcards or patterns to match font names to find specific fonts. For example, to list all bold fonts from the Adobe Utopia family, use `xlsfonts` with the `-fn` (font) option and a wildcard, like so:

```
# xlsfonts -fn *utopia*bold*
-adobe-utopia-bold-i-normal—0-0-0-0-p-0-iso8859-1
-adobe-utopia-bold-r-normal—0-0-0-0-p-0-iso8859-1
```

Use the `xlsfonts` program to find font names for the `-fn` X11 Toolkit option, or with the `xfontsel` or `xfd` clients discussed in this section.

SEE ALSO

➤ *To learn how X uses fonts, see page 260.*

Viewing X11 Fonts with the *xfontsel* Client

The `xfontsel` client provides an easy way to see samples of each font available during your X11 session. By default, `xfontsel` attempts to read the names of every available font, but when used with the `-pattern` option, displays fonts matching a wildcard pattern. For example, to force `xfontsel` to use all Adobe fonts, use the `-pattern` option followed by a wildcard pattern:

```
# xfontsel -pattern *adobe*
```

The `xfontsel` client presents a window, as shown in Figure 20.4, along with a sample of the first font found. To display different fonts, click any of the `fmly`, `wght`, or `slant` names, and then select an option from the ensuing shortcut menu.

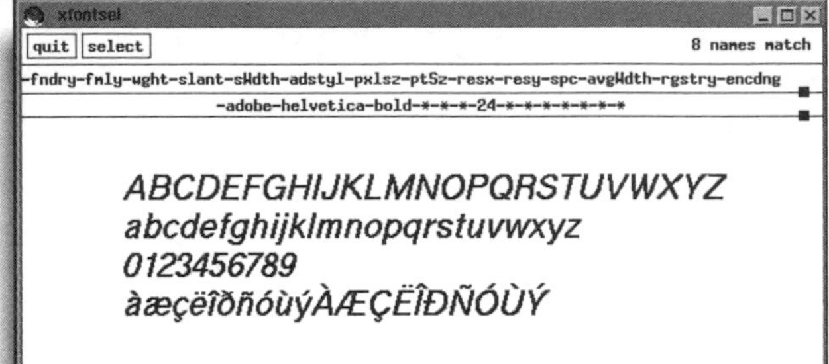

FIGURE 20.4
The `xfontsel` client displays a character-set sample of a selected font.

Using the *xfd* Client to View Font Character Maps

Use the X11 `xfd` (X font display) client to see all the characters in a font. The font must be made available to your X11 server through the `Files` section of your system's `XF86Config` file (described in Chapter 18, "Running and Configuring X11," in the section "Starting X11"). If you're not sure about what font to display, use the `xfontsel` client or look under the `/usr/X11R6/lib/X11/fonts` directory. For example, to display all the available miscellaneous fonts, use the `ls` command, as follows:

```
# ls /usr/X11R6/lib/X11/fonts/misc
10x20.pcf.gz         8x16rk.pcf.gz        deccurs.pcf.gz
12x24.pcf.gz         9x15.pcf.gz          decsess.pcf.gz
12x24rk.pcf.gz       9x15B.pcf.gz         fonts.alias
3270-12.pcf.gz       clB6x10.pcf.gz       fonts.dir
3270-12b.pcf.gz      clB6x12.pcf.gz       gb16fs.pcf.gz
3270-20.pcf.gz       clB8x10.pcf.gz       gb16st.pcf.gz
3270-20b.pcf.gz      clB8x12.pcf.gz       gb24st.pcf.gz
3270.pcf.gz          clB8x13.pcf.gz       hanglg16.pcf.gz
3270b.pcf.gz         clB8x14.pcf.gz       hanglm16.pcf.gz
3270d.pcf.gz         clB8x16.pcf.gz       hanglm24.pcf.gz
3270gt12.pcf.gz      clB8x8.pcf.gz        heb6x13.pcf.gz
3270gt12b.pcf.gz     clB9x15.pcf.gz       heb8x13.pcf.gz
3270gt16.pcf.gz      clI6x12.pcf.gz       hex20.pcf
3270gt16b.pcf.gz     clI8x8.pcf.gz        jiskan16.pcf.gz
3270gt24.pcf.gz      clR4x6.pcf.gz        jiskan24.pcf.gz
3270gt24b.pcf.gz     clR5x10.pcf.gz       k14.pcf.gz
```

```
3270gt32.pcf.gz      clR5x6.pcf.gz      nil2.pcf.gz
3270gt32b.pcf.gz     clR5x8.pcf.gz      olcursor.pcf.gz
3270gt8.pcf.gz       clR6x10.pcf.gz     olgl10.pcf.gz
3270h.pcf.gz         clR6x12.pcf.gz     olgl12.pcf.gz
5x7.pcf.gz           clR6x13.pcf.gz     olgl14.pcf.gz
5x8.pcf.gz           clR6x6.pcf.gz      olgl19.pcf.gz
6x10.pcf.gz          clR6x8.pcf.gz      vga.pcf
6x12.pcf.gz          clR7x10.pcf.gz
6x13.pcf.gz          clR7x12.pcf.gz
6x13B.pcf.gz         clR7x14.pcf.gz
6x9.pcf.gz           clR7x8.pcf.gz
7x13.pcf.gz          clR8x10.pcf.gz
7x13B.pcf.gz         clR8x12.pcf.gz
7x14.pcf.gz          clR8x13.pcf.gz
7x14B.pcf.gz         clR8x14.pcf.gz
7x14rk.pcf.gz        clR8x16.pcf.gz
8x13.pcf.gz          clR8x8.pcf.gz
8x13B.pcf.gz         clR9x15.pcf.gz
8x16.pcf.gz          cursor.pcf.gz
```

Note that each font is compressed (with the `.gz` extension). This is a feature of X Window System release X11R6.3, which can use compressed fonts to save disk space. If you're using an earlier release of X11 (such XFree86 3.1.2), the fonts are not compressed.

SEE ALSO

➤ *To learn more about compressed files, see page 542.*

Displaying X11 font characters

1. Use the `xfd` client from the command line of a terminal window, followed by the `-fn` (font) option and the name of the desired font. The `xfd` client also supports many standard X11 Toolkit options, so you can use geometry, foreground, or background settings to customize how the characters are displayed. For example, to display the characters contained in a tiny font, use the `xfd` client like this:

```
# xfd -geometry 500x400 -fn 5x7
```

The `xfd` client displays a window like the one shown in Figure 20.5.

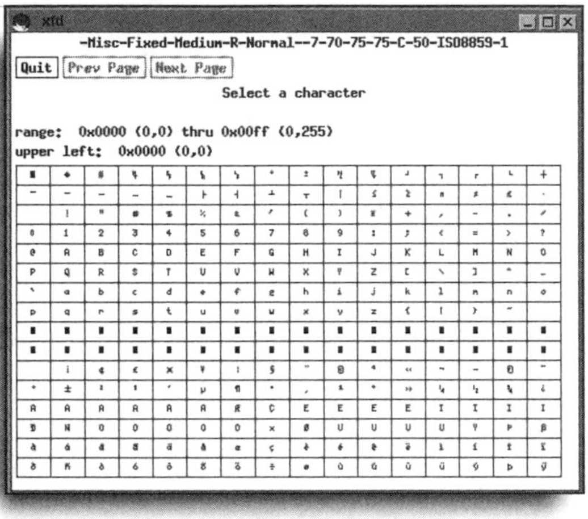

FIGURE 20.5
The `xfd` client displays characters defined in a specified X11 font.

2. To see the available X11 cursors, use the `xfd` client along with geometry settings for size and color and the `-center` option to center each character in the display:

```
# xfd -geometry 500x400 -bg blue -fg white -center -fn
➥cursor
```

This displays a 500×400-pixel window, with each X11 cursor in white on a blue background.

SEE ALSO

➤ *For more information about using compression programs, see page 542.*

Using the Keyboard to Control and Navigate Windows

Don't want to use a mouse? Use the `fvwm` X11 window manager's mouse keys to move around the X11 desktop or through virtual screens, or to control windows. Table 20.2 lists many of the common keyboard commands defined in the `fvwmrc.keys` configuration file under the `/etc/X11/AnotherLevel` directory.

TABLE 20.2 ***fvwm's AnotherLevel* keyboard navigation**

Action	Keyboard Command
Next desktop to right	Ctrl+Shift+Alt+right arrow
Next desktop to left	Ctrl+Shift+Alt+left arrow
Next desktop up	Ctrl+Shift+Alt+up arrow
Next desktop down	Ctrl+Shift+Alt+down arrow
Mouse up 5% of display's size	Ctrl+Shift+F11
Mouse down 5% of display's size	Ctrl+Shift+F10
Mouse right 5% of display's size	Ctrl+Shift+F12
Mouse left 5% of display's size	Ctrl+Shift+F9
Mouse up 10% of display's size	Ctrl+Alt+F11
Mouse down 10% of display's size	Ctrl+Alt+F10
Mouse right 10% of display's size	Ctrl+Alt+F12
Mouse left 10% of display's size	Ctrl+Alt+F9

SEE ALSO

➤ *For more information about configuring your window manager, see page 294.*

Copying and Pasting Text

Copying and pasting text between terminal windows is a common X11 operation, and involves using your mouse to select, drag, and then paste selected portions of text. Your keyboard can also play a part in these operations, especially for selecting large areas of text.

Copying and pasting text is handy for quickly copying complex command lines for later use in shell scripts, for duplicating text blocks, or for moving chunks of text from a program's output in a terminal window into a text editor window.

Copying and pasting words, lines, and blocks

1. To copy a word from text in a terminal window, double-click the word. Move to another window, and press the middle mouse button (or both left and right mouse buttons simultaneously if you use a two-button mouse) to paste the word.

2. To copy a line of text, triple-click the line, and then paste using the same technique as described in step 1. Note that if you copy a command line from a terminal window, you might also get a carriage return in your pasted text.

3. To copy a large chunk of text, you must first highlight it. Move your cursor to the beginning of the text area, and then drag to the end of the area with the left mouse buttons held down. Alternatively, you can click at the beginning of the text and then, holding down the Shift key, click at the end of the text.

   To paste the highlighted selection, click the middle mouse button (or simultaneously click the left and right mouse buttons if you use a two-button mouse). Alternatively, hold down the Shift key, and then press the Insert key.

SEE ALSO

➤ *To learn how to configure your mouse for X11, see page 276.*

Using the *xcutsel* Client to Copy Text

Use the `xcutsel` client to copy text from one window to another. This client offers a convenient way of copying text from one application to another through the use of buttons in dialog boxes, and can serve as a temporary holding place for copied text.

Copying text with *xcutsel*

1. Start the `xcutsel` client from the command line of a terminal window by typing the following:

```
# xcutsel &
```

2. The `xcutsel` client window, shown in Figure 20.6, appears. Two buttons (`copy PRIMARY to 0` and `copy 0 to PRIMARY`) are used to copy text.

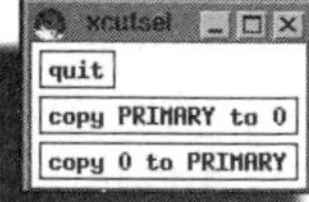

FIGURE 20.6
The `xcutsel` client supports the copying and pasting of text between X11 clients.

3. Highlight a word, line, or block of text in a terminal window.
4. Click the `copy PRIMARY to 0` button.
5. Click the `copy 0 to PRIMARY` button.
6. Move your mouse cursor to the terminal or client window where you want to paste the text.
7. Paste the text by clicking the middle mouse button or by pressing Shift+Insert.

Copying Text with the *xclipboard* Client

Use the `xclipboard` client to copy and paste text. This client works just like the `xcutsel` client, but in addition to copying large sections of text and serving as a temporary holding place, it displays the copied text before your paste operation, supports multiple buffers of copied text, and can save buffers or copied text into text files.

Copying, saving, and pasting text with *xclipboard*

1. Start the `xclipboard` client from the command line of terminal window by typing the following:
   ```
   # xclipboard &
   ```
2. A small window appears (see Figure 20.7). Note the Quit, Delete, New, Save, Next, and Prev buttons.

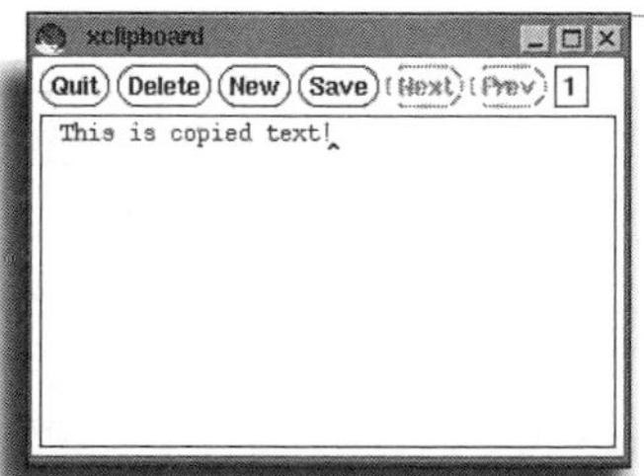

FIGURE 20.7
The `xclipboard` client offers multiple buffers for copied text, and enables you to save copied text to disk.

3. Highlight the desired word, line, or block of text in a terminal or client window.
4. Move your mouse cursor to the `xclipboard` window.
5. Paste the highlighted text into the `xclipboard` window. Unlike with normal cut-and-paste operations, you must use

your middle mouse button (or a simultaneous left- and right-button press if using a two-button mouse) to paste.

6. To save the text to a file, click the Save button. A small dialog box with the default name (`clipboard`) will appear.
7. If you don't wish to use the default name, enter a new filename. Click the Accept button.
8. To save multiple buffers, click the New button. The Prev button should become active, and a `2` should appear next to it.
9. Repeat step 3 to highlight text, and then paste the text into the `xclipboard` window. You now have two buffers of copied text.
10. To paste the first buffer, click the Prev button. Your previously copied text appears.
11. Highlight the text displayed in the `xclipboard` window.
12. Move your mouse to the desired terminal or client window, and click your middle mouse button (or press Shift+Insert) to paste the text.

Capturing Windows and the Desktop

Use the `xwd`, `xmag`, or `xv` client, found under the `/usr/X11R6/bin` directory, to capture a window picture, a portion of the X11 display, or the entire desktop. This is a handy way to capture, copy, or print graphics from your X11 sessions. Some of the techniques and X11 clients described in this section might come in handy if you use any of the graphics programs described in Chapter 21, "Using Graphics and Multimedia Tools."

Using *xwd* to Capture Windows

Use the `xwd` (X11 window dump) program to take snapshots of your desktop or of a desired terminal or client window.

Saving window dumps with *xwd*

1. Start the `xwd` client from the command line of a terminal window, using the standard output redirection operator (>) to create a file with an `.xwd` extension:

```
# xwd >dump1.xwd
```

2. By default, xwd sends its output, a special text graphics format, to the standard output. Alternatively, you can use the -out option followed by a filename to save the graphic, like so:

```
# xwd -out dump1.xwd
```

3. When you start xwd, your cursor turns into a cross-hair (+). To capture a window, click the window or its border. The window graphic is saved to the specified filename. Even if a selected window is overlapped by another window, the contents of the selected window are captured.
4. To capture the entire screen, click the root desktop or display.

SEE ALSO

➤ *To learn more about using shell redirection operators, see page 19.*

Using *xwud* to Display Window Dumps

Use the xwud (X11 window undump) client to view your captured graphic.

Viewing window dumps

1. Start the xwud client from the command line of a terminal window, using the -in option followed by the name of your window dump, like so:

```
# xwud -in dump1.xwd
```

2. Alternatively, you can use the shell's standard input redirection operator (<) to read in your captured graphic:

```
# xwud <dump1.xwd
```

3. By default, the xwud client quits when you click the displayed window (shown in Figure 20.8). If you want to disable this feature, use the -noclick option. If you want to distort the graphic or rescale the window, use the -scale option, which allows you to resize the graphic's window. These options can be combined as follows:

```
# xwud -in dump1.xwd -noclick -scale
```

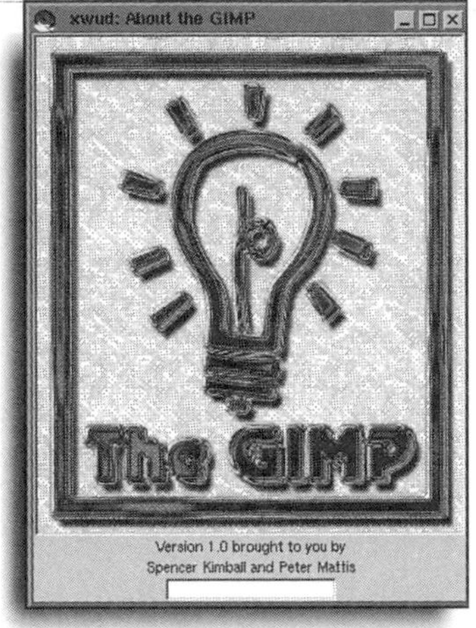

FIGURE 20.8
The xwud client displays graphics captured by the xwd command.

Using the *xloadimage* Client to View Captures

Use the `xloadimage` client, found under the `/usr/X11R6/bin` directory, to view graphics captured by the `xwd` command. To view a captured window dump, use `xloadimage` followed by the name of the dumped graphic, like so:

```
# xloadimage dump1.xwd
```

The `xloadimage` client displays a series of screen dumps one at a time after each press of N when you use the `-goto` option, like so:

```
# xloadimage dump1.xwd dump2.xwd dump3.xwd -goto dump1.xwd
```

This command line causes `xloadimage` to repeat the sequence of graphics on your display until you press Q to quit. See the `xloadimage` manual page for more information about this program, such as graphics file format conversion.

SEE ALSO

➤ *To learn more about converting graphics formats, see page 341.*

Capturing and Viewing Screens with the *xv* Client

Use the `xv` client to capture or display X11 windows or desktops. This command has a bewildering array of more than 100 command-line options, but you can read the `xv` documentation by using the `gv` client (which is in PostScript format) like this:

```
# gv /usr/doc/xv-3.10a/xvdocs.ps
```

SEE ALSO

➤ *For more information about the* gv *PostScript previewer, see page 347.*

Capturing X11 windows by using the *xv* client

1. Start the xv client from the command line of terminal window like so:

   ```
   # xv &
   ```

2. The xv title screen appears. Right-click the title screen to display the main xv dialog box, shown in Figure 20.9.

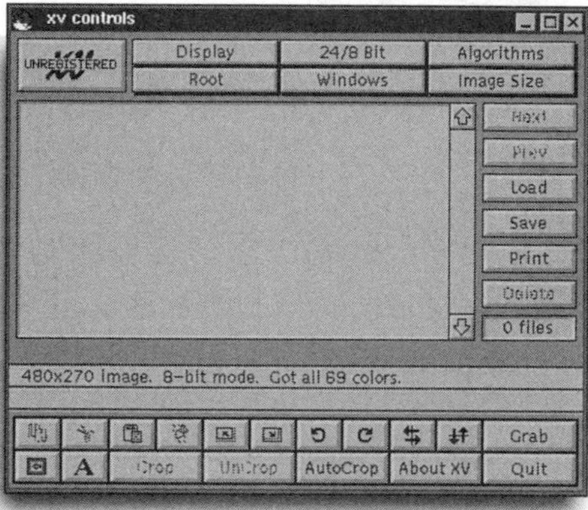

FIGURE 20.9
The xv graphics utility client offers an array of features, including screen captures.

3. To capture a window, click the Grab button.
4. The xv Grab dialog box, shown in Figure 20.10, appears. Click the dialog box's Grab button, and then click the desired window.

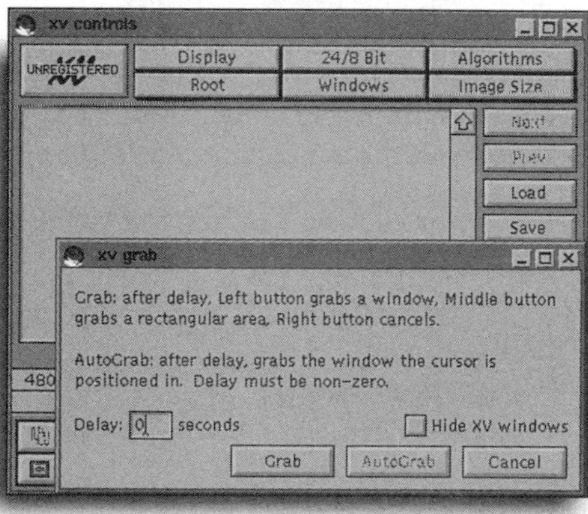

FIGURE 20.10
The xv Grab dialog box is used to capture all or portions of your X11 desktop.

5. The xv client beeps once, and then again after it displays the captured graphic in a window (see Figure 20.11).

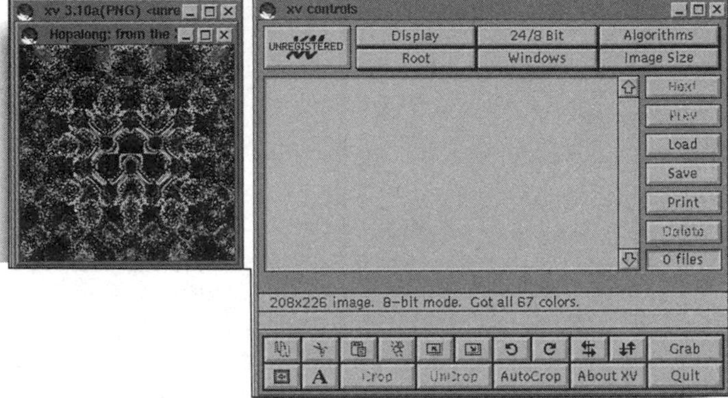

FIGURE 20.11
After a screen capture, the xv displays the graphic in a separate window.

6. To capture a portion of a window, hold down your middle mouse button (or both mouse buttons if you're using a two-button mouse), and drag to create a rectangle. To capture a window using a time delay, move your mouse to the Delay field, enter the number of seconds for the delay, click the AutoGrab button, and then move your mouse to the desired window (or select the rectangular area to grab). Use the Hide XV Windows button to make the xv client disappear when performing the graphics capture.
7. After capturing your graphic, click xv's Save button. A Save dialog box, shown in Figure 20.12, appears. Select the desired graphics output format by clicking the Format button. To save the graphic as a grayscale or black-and-white image, click the Colors button.

Although the xv command-line options (detailed starting on page 74 of xv's 128-page manual) might at first be confusing, the xv client is simple to use when displaying window dumps. Use the xv command followed by the name of your dumped graphic like this:

```
# xv dump1.xwd
```

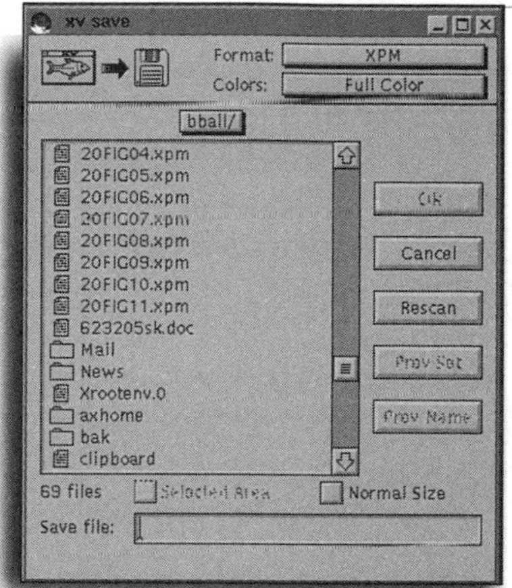

FIGURE 20.12

Use the xv client's Save dialog box to save your screen capture to disk in different graphics formats.

Use the handy -expand command-line option followed by a positive or negative number to display captured images as larger or smaller. For example, to display a small window graphic at three times its original size, use the -expand option:

```
# xv -expand 3 dump1.xwd
```

To display a full-screen image capture at one-half its original size, use -expand -2 like so:

```
# xv -expand -2 dump1.xwd
```

Using the *xmag* Client to Capture Magnified Images

You can use the xmag client to capture or magnify portions of your display, such as window buttons or icons.

Capturing images with the *xmag* client

1. Start the xmag client from the command line of a terminal window like this:

   ```
   # xmag &
   ```

2. To specify a level of magnification to use when capturing magnified images, use the -mag option followed by a positive number (xmag will not capture reduced images). For example, to capture a graphic at three times its original size, use the -mag option like this:

   ```
   # xmag -mag 3 &
   ```

3. After you start the xmag program, your cursor changes to a character that resembles a rotated L. To capture the default 64×64-pixel area, click a desired portion of the window. The main xmag window, shown in Figure 20.13, appears.

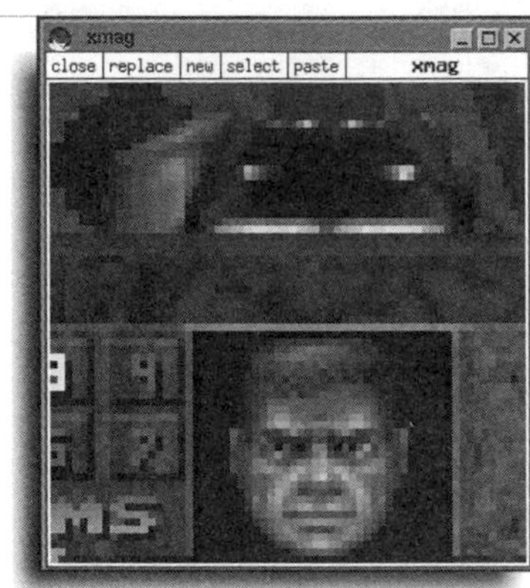

FIGURE 20.13
The xmag client captures magnified portions of your X11 desktop.

4. To capture an area larger or smaller than the default, hold down your middle mouse button and drag to select a larger rectangular area before releasing the button. You can also use the -source option followed by an X11 Toolkit geometry setting to specify a custom area. For example, to capture a 200×200-pixel area, use the -source option:

```
# xmag -source 200x200 &
```

5. The xmag window (refer to Figure 20.13) has five buttons: Close, Replace, New, Cut, and Paste. Click the Close button to quit the xmag client. Click the Replace button to select a new area to be displayed in the original xmag window. Click the New button to select a new area to be displayed in a new xmag window.
6. To copy the currently captured area, click the Select button.
7. To paste the graphic, move your mouse cursor to an open window of an X11 graphics program, such as xpaint or Gimp (discussed in Chapter 21), and paste the image.
8. The xmag Paste button can be used to paste a selected image from one xmag window to another. To scale an xmag image, hold down the Shift key, move your mouse to a corner of an xmag window, and drag (with your left mouse button held down) to make the xmag window smaller or larger.

Handling areas larger than your desktop

Be careful! By using this option with the default magnification level 5, the resulting xmag window will cover the entire desktop of an 800×600 display, and you won't be able to use the program (press the Q key or Ctrl+C to quit). The best approach is to use the -mag and -source options to find the optimum results for your screen display. (-mag 2 at 200×200 works well with an 800×600 display, for example.)

CHAPTER 21

Using Graphics and Multimedia Tools

By Jan Walter

Selecting graphics programs

Translating or converting graphics

Previewing graphics and PostScript documents

Creating graphic slide shows

Playing music CDs

Watching and listening to Internet TV and radio

Playing animations and movies

Selecting a Graphics Program

Linux is distributed with many different programs, and many distributions include a wealth of graphics programs for creating, editing, and converting graphics images. These programs range from simple to complex. Some programs work only on the command line for translating graphics file formats, whereas others rival commercial-quality graphics software applications.

Using the GIMP Client

One of the best and newest graphics tools for Linux is GIMP, the GNU Image Manipulation Program. This X11 client, shown in Figure 21.1, is a full-feature image-editing program with many menus, tools, and filters. The GIMP features include

- Floating menus (which you access by right-clicking an image window)
- Graphics layers (so that effects can be superimposed)
- More than 100 plug-in filters and tools
- More than 20 editing tools
- Multiple image windows (for cutting and pasting graphics, or for multiple views of a file)
- Multiple undo levels
- Scripting language to automate image processing or to create new filters
- Six floating tool, brush, colors, and pattern windows
- Support for the importing and exporting of 24 graphics formats

GIMP requires nearly 23MB of hard drive space for its software libraries, support files, and related directories, which are installed under the `/usr/share/gimp/x.xx` directory (where `x.xx` is the current version). A library of GIMP plug-ins is installed in the `/usr/lib/gimp/x.xx/plug-ins` directory. *Plug-ins* are compiled modules, or programs, run by GIMP from different menus.

FIGURE 21.1
The GIMP image editor has features that rival commercial image-manipulation programs.

Starting the GIMP

1. First, start an X11 session. Then start the GIMP from the command line of a terminal window, with the name of a graphic file:

   ```
   # gimp rhpenguin.gif &
   ```

2. When you use GIMP for the first time, the program will present a dialog box like the one shown in Figure 21.2. This dialog box contains various details, such as version number, required resources, and installation procedures. To proceed, click the Install button.
3. A dialog box like the one shown in Figure 21.3 will appear after GIMP creates its `.gimp` directory in your home directory.
4. Click the Continue button. GIMP will load and present the graphics image you specified in step 1, as shown in Figure 21.4.
5. To open the Brush Selection dialog box, shown in Figure 21.5, press Shift+Ctrl+B. This dialog box boasts 115 brush patterns, 15 drawing modes, and sliding controls to change the size or opacity of the brush.

X Toolkit options and the GIMP

Although you must run the X Window System to use the GIMP, it does not support any X11 Toolkit options such as geometry settings.

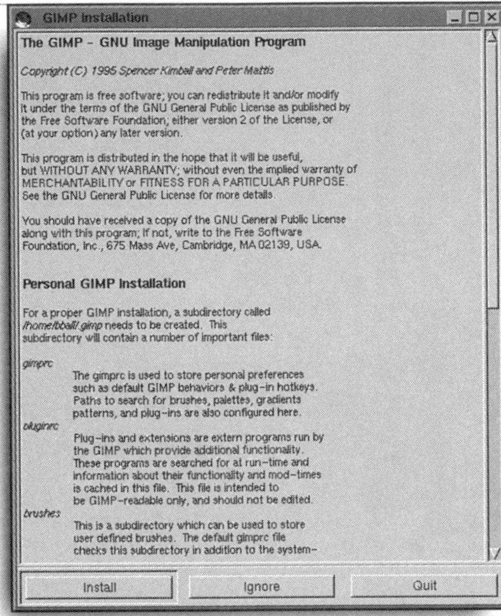

FIGURE 21.2

The first time you use the GIMP editor, it will ask whether you want to configure itself in your home directory.

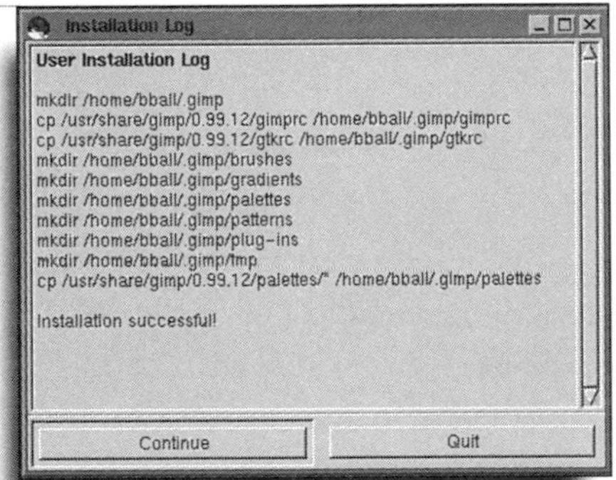

FIGURE 21.3

After installing its resources in your home directory, the GIMP will summarize what it has done.

Use your keyboard or mouse with the GIMP

GIMP's floating toolbar (refer to Figure 21.4) provides access to a number of drawing, painting, and selection tools. You can also use a number of keyboard commands, as listed in Table 21.1.

6. Click a brush to select it. Click the Mode pop-up menu to select a drawing mode, and drag the slider controls to change the opacity or spacing of the brush pattern.
7. To view GIMP's Pattern Selection dialog box, shown in Figure 21.6, press Shift+Ctrl+P. This dialog box boasts 168 patterns that you can select for painting or filling image areas.
8. Click a pattern to select it, or use the scrollbar to view more patterns.

FIGURE 21.4

GIMP loads your images into a floating window, with a separate operations menu.

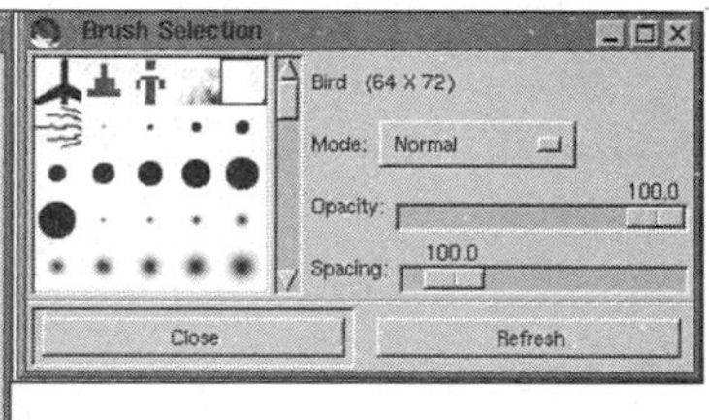

FIGURE 21.5

GIMP's brushes window offers 115 different brush patterns to use when creating or editing images.

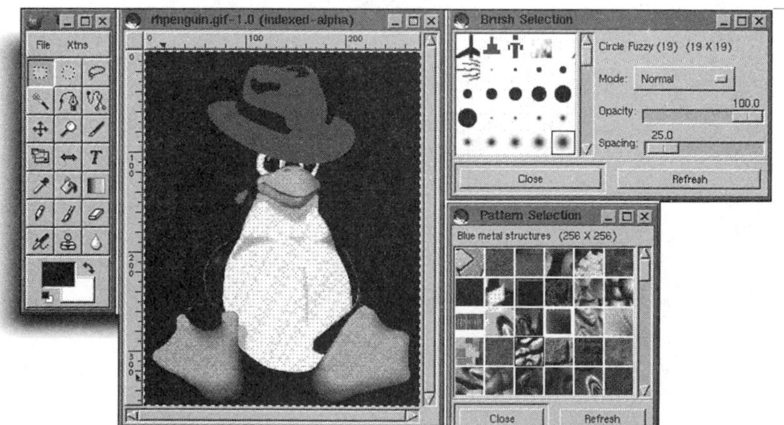

FIGURE 21.6

The GIMP Pattern Selection dialog box offers 168 patterns that you can use when editing images.

9. There are several ways to quit the GIMP: Click the File menu and select Quit; press Ctrl+Q; or right-click the graphic's window and select Quit from the shortcut menu.

SEE ALSO

➤ *For more information about X11 Toolkit options, such as geometry settings, see page 307.*

TABLE 21.1 Common GIMP keyboard commands

Command	Description
Ctrl+K	Clear selection
Ctrl+W	Close file
Ctrl+C	Copy selection
Ctrl+N	Create new file
Ctrl+X	Cut selection
Ctrl+.	Fill selection
Ctrl+B	Lower layer
Ctrl+M	Merge layer
Ctrl+O	Open file
Ctrl+V	Paste Clipboard
Ctrl+Q	Quit GIMP
Ctrl+F	Raise layer
Ctrl+R	Redo last action
Ctrl+S	Save file
A	Select Airbrush tool
Ctrl+A	Select all
Shift+B	Select Bucketfill tool
Shift+E	Select Eraser tool
F	Select Free-selection tool
Z	Select Fuzzy selection tool (magic wand)
P	Select Paintbrush tool
Shift+P	Select Pencil tool
R	Select Rectangular selection tool
Shift+Ctrl+H	Sharpen selection

Command	Description
Shift+Ctrl+B	Show Brushes dialog box
Ctrl+G	Show Gradient editor
Ctrl+L	Show Layer Channel editor
Ctrl+P	Show Palette dialog box
Shift+Ctrl+P	Show Patterns dialog in active window
Shift+Ctrl+T	Show Tool Options dialog box from main menu
Shift+Ctrl+T	Show guides
Shift+Ctrl+R	Show rulers
Ctrl+Z	Undo last action
=	Zoom in
-	Zoom out

After starting GIMP, you might want to configure some of its default settings. To configure the GIMP, edit the file `gimprc` in the `.gimp` directory under your home directory.

Configuring GIMP

1. The `.gimp` directory contains tool resources and settings, along with your GIMP preferences. Use the `ls` command to see the installed GIMP files:

```
# ls -l .gimp
total 15
drwxrwxr-x 2 bball bball 1024 Apr 6 13:21 brushes
-rw-r--r-- 1 bball bball 7277 Apr 6 13:21 gimprc
drwxrwxr-x 2 bball bball 1024 Apr 6 13:21 gradients
-rw-r--r-- 1 bball bball 379 Apr 6 13:21 gtkrc
drwxrwxr-x 2 bball bball 1024 Apr 6 13:21 palettes
drwxrwxr-x 2 bball bball 1024 Apr 6 13:21 patterns
drwxrwxr-x 2 bball bball 1024 Apr 6 13:21 plug-ins
drwxrwxr-x 2 bball bball 1024 Apr 6 13:21 tmp
```

2. The `gimprc` file contains settings for defaults, such as brushes, patterns, palettes, measurements, number of undo levels, and temporary directories. For example, one way to change the number of GIMP's undo levels is to use your favorite

Another way to set the GIMP's undo levels

You can also change the number of undo levels while GIMP is running through its Preferences menu.

text editor, such as pico, and edit the gimprc file (disabling line-wrapping):

```
# pico -w $HOME/.gimp/gimprc
```

3. Scroll though the gimprc file until you come to the undo default section, which looks like this:

```
# Set the number of operations kept on the undo stack
(undo-levels 5)
```

4. Change the number following undo-levels to the number you want. For example, to change the number of actions you can undo to 2, edit the line to look like this:

```
# set the number of operations kept on the undo stack
(undo-levels 2)
```

5. If you don't have a lot of memory, such as 32MB, configure GIMP for stingy-memory-use. If you try to edit graphics as large as 640×480 pixels, GIMP will use nearly 16MB of your system memory. Scroll through the gimprc file until you come to the memory section, which looks like this:

```
# There is always a tradeoff between memory usage and
➥speed. In most
# cases, the GIMP opts for speed over memory. However,
➥if memory is
# a big issue, set stingy-memory-use
# (stingy-memory-use)
```

6. To use this feature, remove the pound (#) character in front of the memory setting like so:

```
# There is always a tradeoff between memory usage and
➥speed. In most
# cases, the GIMP opts for speed over memory. However,
➥if memory is
# a big issue, set stingy-memory-use
(stingy-memory-use)
```

7. If you try to edit a large graphics file such as a full-page, color, TIFF document, you can also run out of disk space. GIMP creates large temporary files during editing sessions, typically three times the memory required to load an image. A little math can show you that editing a 20MB graphic can translate to a lot of used disk space. Scroll to the swap file section, which looks like this:

```
# Set the swap file location. The gimp uses a tile based
➥memory
# allocation scheme. The swap file is used to quickly and
➥easily
# swap files out to disk and back in. Be aware that the
➥swap file
# can easily get very large if the gimp is used with
➥large images.
# Also, things can get horribly slow if the swap file is
➥created on
# a directory that is mounted over NFS. For these
➥reasons, it may
# be desirable to put your swap file in "/tmp".
(swap-path "${gimp_dir}")
```

If your system has a second hard drive or a little-used partition, say at `/d2`, use the `mkdir` command to create a swap file directory for GIMP:

```
# mkdir /d2/tmp
```

To configure GIMP to use this new directory, change the `swap-path` from the default `${gimp_dir}` directory (`tmp` under `.gimp` in your home directory) to the path of your second drive or partition:

```
(swap-path "/d2/tmp")
```

8. Save the `gimprc` file and exit your text editor.

SEE ALSO

➤ *For more information about text editors, see page 50.*
➤ *For details about using* `mkdir`, *see page 36.*

GIMP's floating tool, pattern, and brush windows are convenient to use when editing an image. Access the complete GIMP menu system by right-clicking over your image; GIMP's menus will cascade.

GIMP does not come with a manual page or much documentation, although you might find some documentation (out of date) under the `/usr/doc/gimp` directory after you install the program. The best source of documentation may be found by browsing to:

`http://www.gimp.org/docs.html`

For a series of tutorials to learn how to use the GIMP, browse to:

`http://abattoir.cc.ndsu.nodak.edu/~nem/gimp/tuts/`

To read a series of Frequently Asked Questions (FAQs), browse to:

`http://www.rru.com/~meo/gimp`

For the latest tools, or plug-ins, go to:

`http://registry.gimp.org`

SEE ALSO

➤ *For more information about using a web browser to download files from the Internet, see page 209.*

Using ImageMagick

The ImageMagick software package is a collection of seven graphics-manipulation programs for the X Window System, although several of these programs, such as the `convert` command, can be used from the command line of the console. Table 21.2 describes each ImageMagick component.

TABLE 21.2 ImageMagick program requirements and descriptions

Name	X11 Required	Description
`animate`	X	Display a series of graphics
`combine`		Combine, or overlay multiple images
`convert`		Translate, or convert graphics file formats
`display`	X	Interactive image-editing, manipulation program
`import`	X	Window capture utility
`montage`		Create tiled images, combine graphics files
`mogrify`		Convert, overwrite multiple graphics files

Using ImageMagick's *display* client

1. Use the `display` command, an X11 client, to edit or modify graphics. First, start an X11 session. Then, from the command line of a terminal window, use the `display` command, followed by a graphics filename:

```
# display rhpenguin.gif &
```

The `display` command will show the ImageMagick splash screen and then load your graphic. Click the image window to view the `display` command's menu, as shown in Figure 21.7.

FIGURE 21.7
ImageMagick's `display` command for X11 uses a menu system and separate window for manipulating graphic images.

2. Another feature of the `display` command is a visual directory view of all specified graphics in a directory. To use a visual directory, click the ImageMagick File menu and select Visual Directory. A File dialog box will appear, as shown in Figure 21.8.

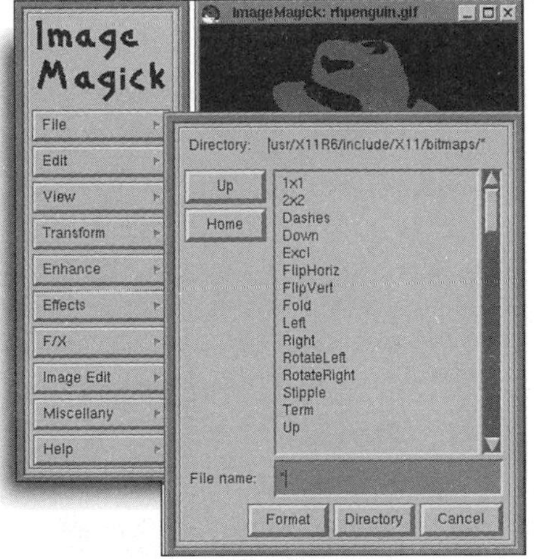

FIGURE 21.8
ImageMagick's `display` command uses file dialog boxes to open, save, or create a visual directory.

3. To create a visual directory of all files in the current directory, click the Directory button. To display only certain files—

such as those with filenames beginning with the letter m—type a wildcard pattern in the Filename field:

`m*`

4. Press Enter, and the `display` command will build a visual directory of the selected files (see Figure 21.9).

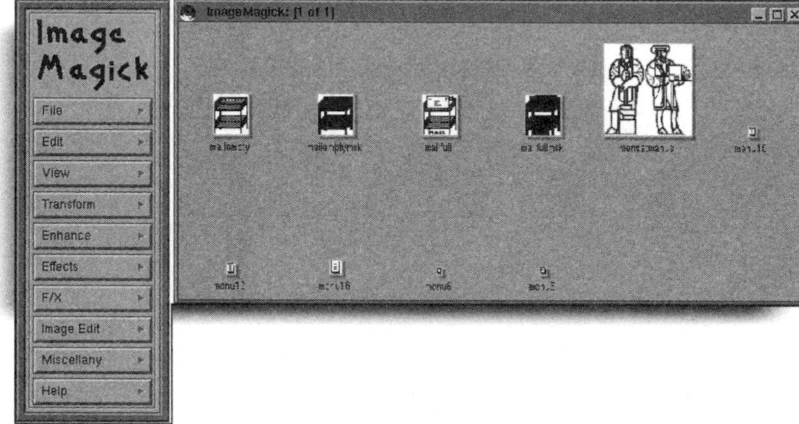

FIGURE 21.9
ImageMagick's visual directory is a convenient way to display and open graphics files.

5. To open a file from the visual directory, right-click the file's thumbnail graphic, and select Load from the shortcut menu. The `display` command will load the file.
6. Use `display`'s View menu to resize your image. To reverse, flip, or rotate the image, use the Transform menu. To change the brightness, contrast, or other qualities of the image, use the Enhance menu. For special effects, use the F/X menu. For example, to distort the image, click F/X on `display`'s menu and select Swirl. A dialog box like the one shown in Figure 21.10 will appear.
7. Enter a number, such as **60**, and click the Swirl button. ImageMagick will distort the image, as shown in Figure 21.11.
8. To save your image, click the File menu, and select the Save menu item. A save dialog box will appear, as shown in Figure 21.12. If you click the Save button to save your image, the `display` program will quit.

FIGURE 21.10
Many of ImageMagick's special effects offer controls, such as numeric settings.

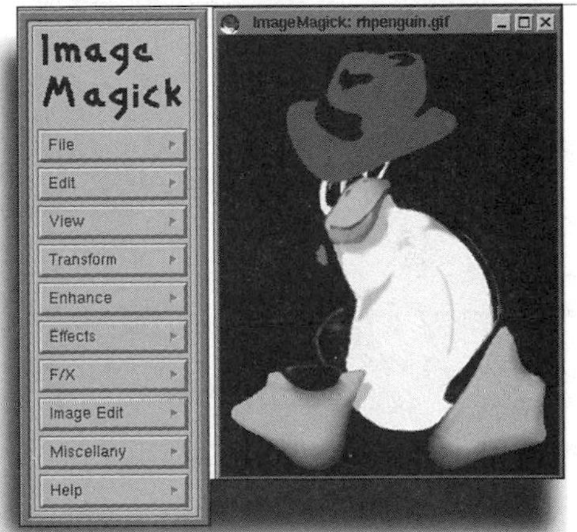

FIGURE 21.11
ImageMagick comes with a number of special effects, such as swirl, that you can apply to images.

9. To save your image in a different graphics format, such as JPEG, click the Format button instead of the Save button to open the Format Selection dialog box (shown in Figure 21.13).

10. Scroll through the list of formats and click JPEG to select it. Click the Select button to return to the Save dialog box. The selected extension of the graphic's type will be appended to your image's name. Click the Save button to save your image and exit the `display` program.

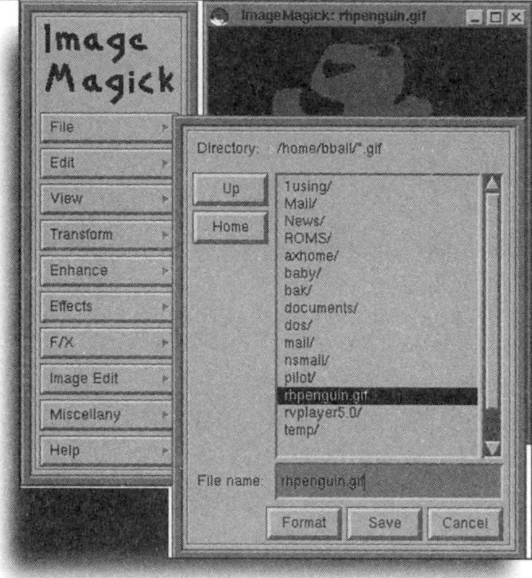

FIGURE 21.12
ImageMagick's Save dialog box offers the choice of saving your image in a different graphics format.

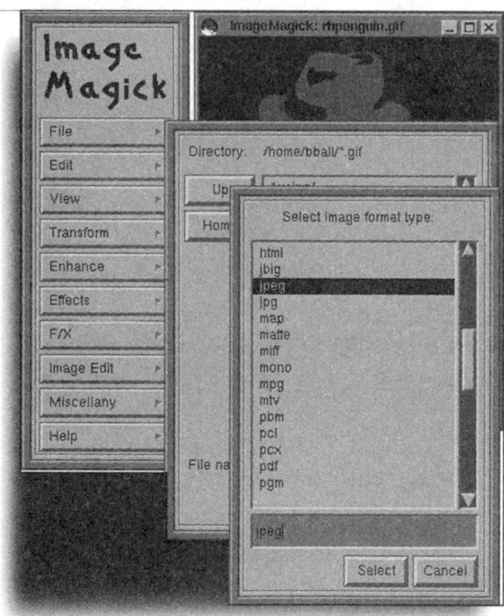

FIGURE 21.13
ImageMagick can save your image in 60 different graphics formats.

Much of the "magic" of the ImageMagick software distribution is through the `convert` command. Use this program from the command line to change your image with more than 70 different effects, and to then save your graphic into more than 70 different file formats.

For example, to convert your sample file, originally a GIF (graphics interchange format) to a JPEG (joint photographics expert group), use the convert command with the original file's name, followed by the new file's name:

```
# convert rhpenguin.gif rhpenguin.jpeg
```

The convert command automatically translates the original graphic to a new format based on the new filename's extension. To apply the swirl effect demonstrated previously, use the convert command with its -swirl option followed by the number 60. You can also convert the file at the same time:

```
# convert rhpenguin.gif -swirl 60 rhpenguin.jpeg
```

For more information about ImageMagick, see its manual page and the manual pages for its component programs (refer to Table 21.2). Use your favorite web browser to load and read ImageMagick's hypertext documentation, found in the /usr/doc/ImageMagick directory.

Translating or Converting Graphics

Using ImageMagick's convenient and capable convert command is only one way to translate graphics. Most Linux distributions include a host of programs in the Portable Bitmap (pbm) and Portable Anymap (pnm) series. Many (but not all) of these programs can be combined with other commands to work as conversion filters in piped commands.

Table 21.3 lists many different graphics file formats, along with pertinent conversion programs you'll find for Linux. Chances are good that if you're faced with the task of converting a graphics file to a readable format, you'll find a program for Linux that will help you!

TABLE 21.3 Linux graphics formats and conversion programs

Extension	Format Type	Conversion Program
.10x	Gemini 10X	pbmto10x
.3d	Red/Blue 3D pixmap	ppm3d
.asc	ASCII text	pbmtoascii
.atk	Andrew Tookit raster	atktopbm pbmtoatk

continues...

TABLE 21.3 Continued

Extension	Format Type	Conversion Program
`.avs`	AVS X image	`convert`
`.bie`	Bi-level image expert	`convert`
`.bg`	BBN BitGraph graphic	`pbmtobg`

`.bmp`	Windows, OS/2 bitmap	`bmptoppm`
		`convert`
		`ppmtobmp`

`.bmp24`	Windows 24-bit bitmap	`convert`
`.brush`	Xerox doodle brush	`brushtopbm`
`.cgm`	Computer graphics metafile	`convert`
`.cmu`	CMU window manager bitmap	`cmuwmtopbm` `pbmtocmuwm`
`.dcx`	ZSoft Paintbrush	`convert`
`.ddif`	DDIF image	`pnmtoddif`
`.dib`	Windows bitmap image	`convert`
`.dxb`	AutoCAD database file	`ppmtoacad` `sldtoppm`

`.dvi`	TeX printer file	`dvips`
		`dvilj4`
		`dvilj4l`
		`dvilj2p`
		`dvilj`

`.eps2`	Encapsulated PostScript Level II	`convert`
`.epsi`	PostScript preview bitmap	`pbmtoepsi` `convert`
`.epsf`	Encapsulated PostScript	`convert`
`.epson`	Epson printer graphic	`pbmtoepson`
`.fax`	Group 3 fax	`convert`
`.fig`	TransFig image	`convert`

`.fits`	FITS file	`fitstopnm`
		`pnmtofits`
		`convert`

`.fpx`	FlashPix file	`convert`
`.g3`	Group 3 fax file	`g3topbm` `pbmtog3`

Extension	Format Type	Conversion Program
.gif	Graphics Interchange	giftopnm gif2tiff ppmtogif convert
.gif87	Graphic Interchange	convert
.go	Compressed GraphOn	pbmtogo
.gould	Gould scanner file	gouldtoppm
.icn	Sun icon	icontopbm pbmtoicon
.ilbm	IFF ILBM file	ilbmtoppm ppmtoilbm
.img	GEM image file	gemtopbm pbmtogem imgtoppm
.icr	NCSA ICR raster	ppmtoicr
.jbig	Joint Bi-level image	convert
.jpeg	JPEG	cjpeg djpeg jpegtran convert
.lj	HP LaserJet data	pbmtolj
.ln03	DEC LN03+ Sixel output	pbmtoln03
.mgr	MGR bitmap	mgrtopbm pbmtomgr
.miff	MNG multiple-image network	convert
.mitsu	Mitsubishi S340-10 file	ppmtomitsu
.mpeg	Motion Picture Group file	convert
.mtv	MTV ray tracer	mtvtoppm convert
.pbm	Portable bitmap	pbm*
.pcd	Photo CD	convert
.pcl	HP PaintJet PCL	ppmtopjxl convert
.pcx	PCX graphic (PC Paintbrush)	pcxtoppm ppmtopcx convert

continues...

TABLE 21.3 Continued

Extension	Format Type	Conversion Program
.pgm	Portable graymap	pbmtopgm pgmtoppm ppmtopgm convert
.pi1	Atari Degas file	pi1toppm ppmtopi1
.pi3	Atari Degas file	pbmtopi3 pi3topbm
.pict	Macintosh PICT file	picttoppm ppmtopict convert
.pj	HP PaintJet file	pjtoppm ppmtopj
.pk	PK format font	pbmtopk pktopbm
.plasma	Plasma fractal	convert
.plot	UNIX plot file	pbmtoplot
.png	Portable network graphic	pngtopnm pnmtopng convert
.pnm	Portable anymap	pnm* convert
.pnt	MacPaint file	macptopbm pbmtomacp
.ppm	Portable pixmap	ppm* convert
.ps	PostScript (lines)	pbmtolps pnmtops convert
.ptx	Printronix printer graphic	pbmtoptx
.qrt	QRT ray tracer	qrttoppm
.rad	Radiance image	convert
.ras	Sun rasterfile	pnmtorast rasttopnm
.rla	Alias/Wavefront image	convert (read only)

Extension	Format Type	Conversion Program
.rle	Utah run-length encoded	convert (read only)
.sgi	Silicon Graphics image	pnmtosgi sgitopnm convert
.sir	Solitaire graphic	pnmtosir sirtopnm
.sixel	DEC sixel format	ppmtosixel
.spc	Atari Spectrum file	spctoppm
.sun	Sun rasterfile	convert
.spu	Atari Spectrum file	sputoppm
.tga	TrueVision Targa file	ppmtotga tgatoppm convert
.tiff	Tagged file format	pnmtotiff tifftopnm ppmtotiff tiff2ps convert
.tiff24	Tagged file format (24-bit)	convert
.txt	Text file bitmap	pbmtext convert (read only)
.uil	Motif UIL icon	ppmtouil convert
.upc	Universal Product Code	pbmupc
.uyvy	16-bit YUV format	convert
.vicar		convert
.viff	Khoros Visualization image	convert
.x10bm	X10 bitmap	pbmtox10bm
.xbm	X11 bitmap	pbmtoxbm xbmtopbm convert
.xim	Xim file	ximtoppm
.xpm	X11 pixmap	ppmtoxpm xpmtoppm convert
.xv	xv thumbnail	xvminitoppm

continues...

TABLE 21.3 **Continued**

Extension	Format Type	Conversion Program
.xvpic	xv thumbnail file	xvpictoppm
.xwd	X11 window dump	pnmtoxwd xwdtopnm convert
.ybm	Bennet Yee face file	pbmtoybm ybmtopbm
.yuv	Abekas YUV file	ppmtoyuv yuvtoppm convert
.zeiss	Zeiss confocal file	zeisstopnm
.zinc	Zinc bitmap	pbmtozinc

Using the *pbm*, *ppm*, and *pnm* Utilities

The Portable bitmap, pixmap, and anymap series of commands can be combined to translate and even change graphics. These commands are meant to be used from the command line of the console or an X11 terminal window but do not require you to run X.

However, if you are running X11, you can take an instant screen shot of your X11 desktop from the command line of a terminal window using several of these programs. Use the `xwd` (X window dump) command with its `-root` option in a shell pipe with the `xwdtopnm` (X window dump to Portable anymap) command. This will capture your entire display and translate the output of the `xwd` client, which is the X Windows dump format, to the Portable anymap format.

The output of the `xwdtopnm` command can then be piped through other commands, such as `pnmflip`, to flip the image upside down using its `-tb` (top-to-bottom) option. Finally, the graphic can be converted to a third format, such as TIFF, using the `pnmtotiff` command, which translates Portable anymap graphics to Tagged File Format. Construct the pipe like this:

```
# xwd -root | xwdtopnm | pnmflip -tb | pnmtotiff >xwd.tiff
```

SEE ALSO

➤ *For more information about using pipes with the shell, see page 19.*

Previewing Graphics and PostScript Documents

Linux distributions include a number of programs for the X Window System that you can use to preview or print a variety of graphics, such as PostScript or Portable Document Format, also known as `pdf`.

Using the *gv* PostScript Previewer

The `gv` command is a PostScript previewer for the X Window System. Use `gv` to read PostScript documents or to print PostScript graphics. This command is an improved version of the earlier `ghostview` client for X.

Using the *gv* client

1. The `gv` command, like many X11 clients, obeys X11 Toolkit options, such as geometry settings. To read the PostScript documentation for the `xv` X11 graphics client, use `gv` with the `-geometry` option, followed by a window size and the name of the document, like so:

   ```
   # gv -geometry 750x550 /usr/doc/xv-3.10a/xvdocs.ps
   ```

   The `gv` client will load the file. After a slight pause, the first page of the document will appear as shown in Figure 21.14, in a window 750 pixels wide by 550 pixels high.

2. To scroll the document window, click the rectangular button below the Save Marked button. The displayed page will shift inside `gv`'s main window.

3. To move to the next page, click the Next button, which is the one with two greater-than symbols (>>). The next page of the document will be displayed.

4. To jump several pages, scroll through the list of page numbers below the Next button and click the desired page number. The `gv` command will then display that page. Note that the Previous button—marked with two less-than symbols (<<)—will become active as soon as you jump past the first page of a PostScript document.

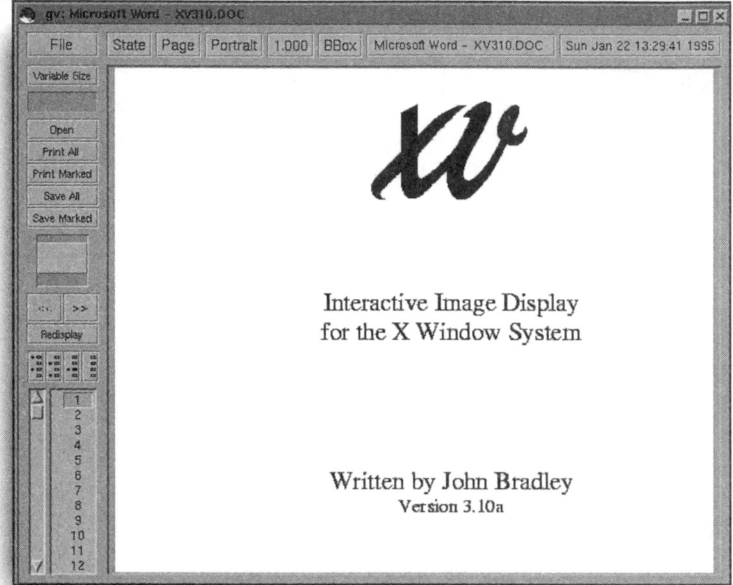

FIGURE 21.14
Use the gv program to read PostScript documents during your X Window session.

5. To view your document in a different size, use gv's Scales button at the top of its main window. This button is a number, 1.000 by default. Click the button, and a menu of percentages will appear. Select a number less than 1.000 to reduce the PostScript window's size. Select a number greater than 1.000 to enlarge the displayed page. For example, selecting a value of 8.000 will enlarge the view 800 percent, as shown in Figure 21.15.

   Note that the Scroll button has automatically reduced in size. This is because the gv window is much smaller relative to the viewing size of the displayed graphic.

6. To print a graphic or pages of a PostScript document, pages must first be marked. There are four marking buttons, located beneath the Redisplay button (which is used to redisplay draft documents). Clicking the first button marks all odd-numbered pages. Clicking the second button marks all even-numbered pages (this is a handy feature for printing double-sided documents—simply mark and print all odd pages and then reinsert the printed pages in your printer and mark and print all even pages). Clicking the third button

marks the currently displayed page, whereas clicking the last button will unmark all marked pages.

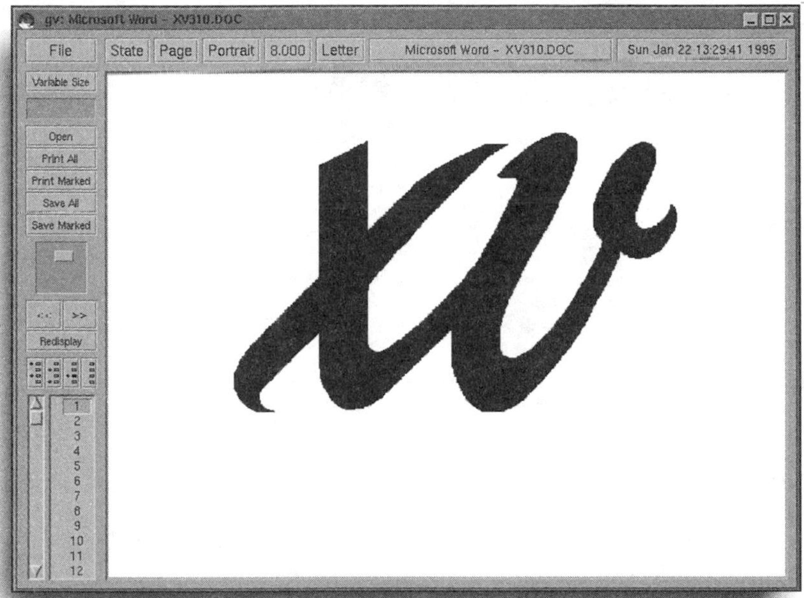

FIGURE 21.15
The gv X11 client can be used to view PostScript graphics or documents in different sizes.

7. After marking the desired pages, click the File button and select Print Document (alternatively, you can press the P key). The Print dialog box, shown in Figure 21.16, will appear.
8. To use the default printer, click the Print button. To use a different printer, use the `lpr` command's `-P` option followed by a printer's name (as found in the `/etc/printcap` database):

```
lpr -Pmycolorprinter
```

9. To exit the `gv` client, select Quit from the File menu, or press the Q key.

SEE ALSO

➤ *For more details about printing documents or graphics, see page 74.*
➤ *For more information about using geometry settings with X11 clients, see page 307.*

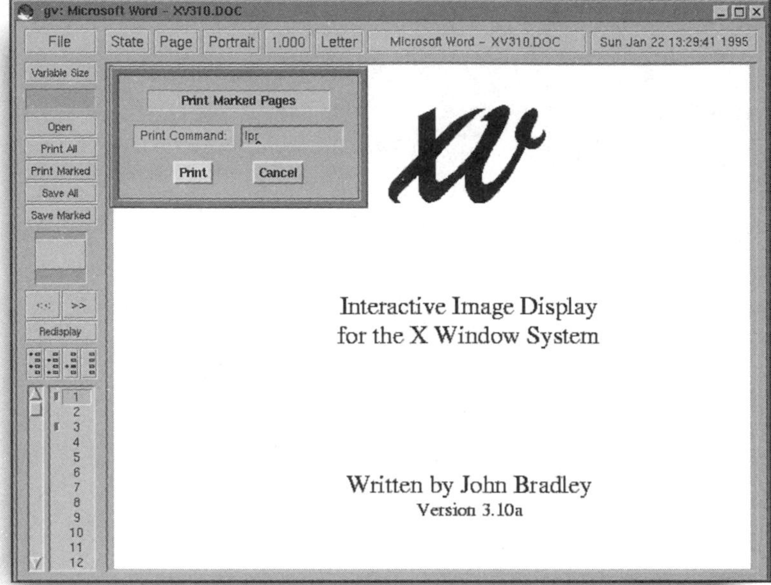

FIGURE 21.16
To print from the gv client, specify a print command in its print dialog box.

For more details about using gv, see its manual page or browse its hypertext documentation under the /usr/doc/gv directory. For example, to use the lynx web browser, use a command like this:

```
# lynx /usr/doc/gv-3.5.8/gv.html
```

Using Adobe Acrobat

The Adobe Acrobat Reader, from Adobe Systems, Inc., is an X11 client that you can use to read Portable Document Format (PDF) files. To obtain the latest copy for Linux, browse to this address:

```
http://www.adobe.com/prodindex/acrobat/readstep.html
```

If you'd rather retrieve the file using the ftp command, try the following:

```
ftp.adobe.com/pub/adobe/acrobatreader/unix/3.x/acroread_linux
_301.tar.gz
```

After downloading the compressed Acrobat archive (which is nearly 4MB), use the tar command with the xvzf option to decompress and unarchive the file:

```
# tar xvzf acroread_linux_301_tar.gz
```

Follow the instructions in the file `INSTGUID.TXT` to install Acrobat. After you install the `Acrobat3` directory under `/usr/local`, `/usr/local` will contain more than 8.5MB of the Acrobat software. The Acrobat application is named `acroread` and is found under the `/usr/local/Acrobat3/bin` directory. To create a symbolic link to a known directory, log on as the root operator and use the `ln` command:

```
# /usr/local/Acrobat3/bin/acroread /usr/local/bin/acroread
```

Your Linux system should have at least 32MB of memory to use Acrobat. To read a PDF file, use the `acroread` command from the command line of a terminal window, followed by the name of a file (in this case its user manual), like so:

```
# /usr/local/Acrobat3/bin/acroread
➥/usr/local/Acrobat3/Reader/Acrobat.pdf
```

The Acrobat reader will start and display its main window with the first page of the document, as shown in Figure 21.17. Acrobat can also be configured as a helper application for use by the Netscape web browser.

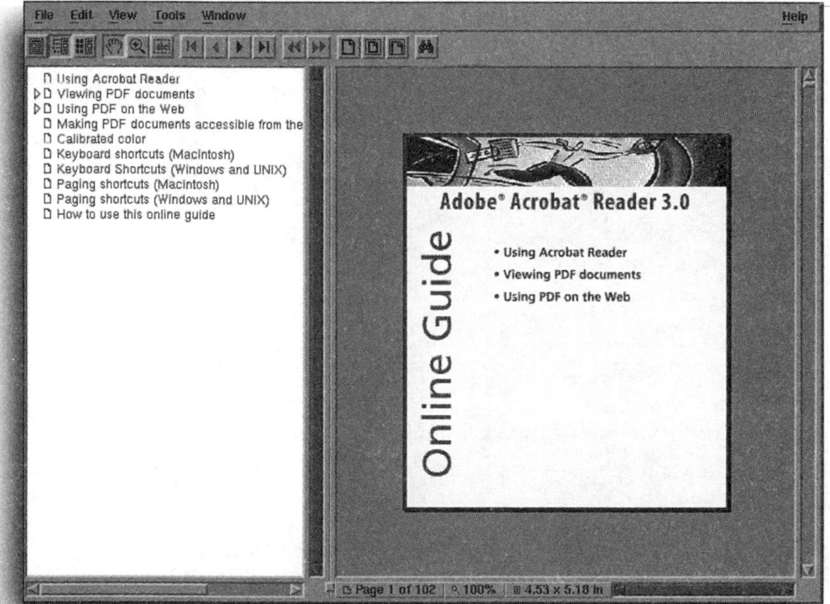

FIGURE 21.17
The Adobe Acrobat reader for Linux displays Portable Document Format, (PDF) files in an X11 window.

Installing Acrobat as a Netscape helper application

1. Start the Netscape browser from the command line of a terminal window:
   ```
   # netscape &
   ```
2. Select the Preferences menu item from Netscape's Edit menu.
3. Click the triangle next to the Navigator Category item in the Preferences dialog box.
4. Two new items, Languages and Applications, will appear below the Netscape item. Click Applications to open the Applications preferences dialog box, shown in Figure 21.18.

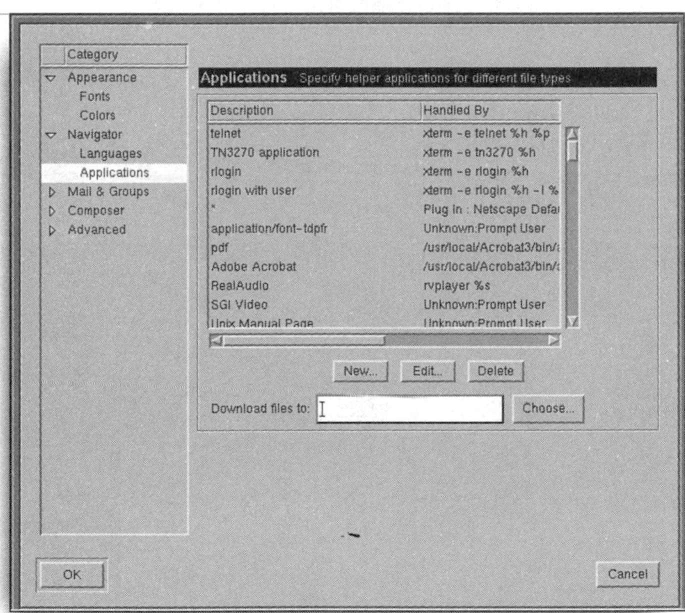

FIGURE 21.18
Netscape's Applications preferences dialog box is used to configure Netscape to start external applications when encountering foreign documents.

5. Click the New button, found beneath the Applications list in the dialog box. A blank dialog box will appear, as shown in Figure 21.19.
6. In the Description field, enter the following:
   ```
   Adobe Acrobat
   ```
   In the MIMEtype field, enter the following:
   ```
   application/pdf
   ```

In the Suffixs field, enter the following:

```
pdf
```

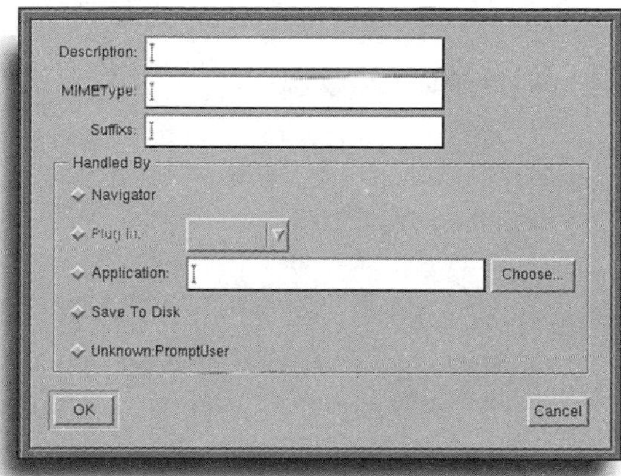

FIGURE 21.19
Configure external applications for Netscape, such as Adobe Acrobat, by entering a description, type, suffix, and pathname to the program.

7. Click the Application field and type the pathname to the Acrobat reader:

   ```
   /usr/local/Acrobat3/bin/acroread
   ```

8. Click the check box to the left of the Application field and then click the OK button.
9. Click the Applications preferences dialog box's OK button to save your preferences. Netscape will now use Acrobat if it encounters PDF files when browsing the Internet; Netscape can even be used to open a PDF file, like so:

   ```
   # netscape myfile.pdf
   ```

For more information about Adobe Acrobat, select the Reader Online Guide from Acrobat's Help menu.

Playing Music CDs

To play music CDs while working with Linux, your system's kernel must be configured to use your sound card. Sound support must either be installed in your kernel or available as a loadable module.

If your sound card works with Linux and you have a CD-ROM drive, you should be able to play music CDs. Most Linux distributions come with music CD programs for the console and X11.

Singing the sound card configuration blues?

Having a hard time configuring your system for sound? If you don't want to waste the time and effort by recompiling your Linux kernel, or if Red Hat's `sndconfig` program does not work for you, take heart. A much easier way to configure Linux for sound is to use the Open Sound System from 4Front Technologies. The OSS software package is easy to install and use, and could solve your sound-configuration problems. The software uses self-configuring, loadable kernel modules, and contains support for many types of sound cards not found in Linux distributions. For more information, browse to: `http://www.4front-tech.com`

To play a CD from the command line of the console or a terminal window, use the `cdp` command.

SEE ALSO

➤ *To learn how to configure Linux to use your sound card, see page 573.*

Playing music using *cdp*

1. Log on as the root operator. Make sure that there is a device named `cdrom` under the `/dev` directory by using the `ls` command :

   ```
   # ls -l /dev/cdrom
   lrwxrwxrwx 1 root root 3 Mar 9 07:55 /dev/cdrom -> hdc
   ```

2. If the `/dev/cdrom` device is not found, use the `ln` command to create a symbolic link from your CD-ROM's device to `/dev/cdrom`:

   ```
   # ln -s /dev/XXX /dev/cdrom
   ```

   where *XXX* is the name of your CD-ROM drive, such as `hdb`, `hdc`, and so on.

3. Make sure that the `/dev/cdrom` device is publicly readable by using the `chmod` command:

   ```
   # chmod 666 /dev/cdrom
   ```

4. Insert a music CD into your CD-ROM drive.
5. Start the `cdp` command from the command line:

   ```
   # cdp
   ```

6. Before pressing the Enter key, activate the Num Lock feature by pressing the Num Lock key on your keyboard. The `cdp` command will start and display a list of the tracks on your CD, as shown in Figure 21.20.

SEE ALSO

➤ *To learn more about creating and using symbolic links, see page 40.*

7. Use the keypad controls, listed in Table 21.4, to control the `cdp` player (you can also use the regular numbers on your keyboard).

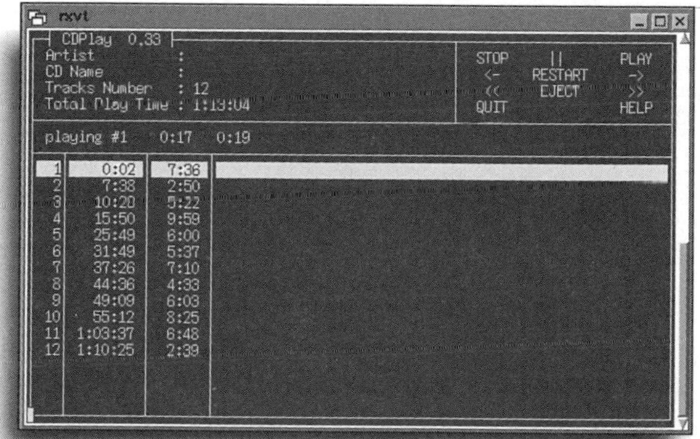

FIGURE 21.20
The cdp music CD player displays a list of your CD's tracks when playing music.

TABLE 21.4 Keypad controls for the *cpd* command

Control	Keypad Key
Back 15 seconds	1
Eject CD from drive	2
Exit, but continue music	0 or Q
Forward 15 seconds	3
Help	.
Next track	6
Play	9
Previous track	4
Replay CD	5
Stop	7
Toggle pause/resume	8

The `cdp` command's companion program, a symbolic link called `cdplay`, can be used to play music without an interactive screen. For example, to start playing a music CD at track number four, use `cdplay` followed by the `play` option and a track number:

```
# cdplay play 4
```

Use the `xplaycd` client to play music CDs during your X11 session. Start `xplaycd` from the command line of a terminal window:

```
# xplaycd &
```

The xplaycd client will display a small window with CD controls, horizontal stereo volume bars, and a list of buttons representing the tracks on the CD, as shown in Figure 21.21.

FIGURE 21.21
The X11 xplaycd client features CD controls and music track resequencing.

You can also rearrange the order of tracks to be played from the music CD. Click a track number to select it, and drag the number to the front or back of the list of track numbers. To play the same track several times, select a track number with your middle mouse button (hold down the left and right mouse buttons if using a two-button mouse), and drag the track along the CD track sequence. When you release your mouse button(s), the track number will be duplicated.

The xplaycd also supports a music CD database to create play lists of tracks for your favorite CDs. Read the xplaycd manual page for more details about creating its CD database.

Watching and Listening to Internet TV and Radio

One of the most exciting aspects of getting connected to the Internet is that you can listen or watch live radio and TV broadcasts. The program of choice for this is RealNetwork's RealPlayer 5.0 for Linux, shown in Figure 21.22. To get a copy of rvplayer for your system, browse to:

```
http://www.real.com
```

To configure the Netscape web browser to use the rvplayer client, see section titled "Using the Netscape Browser" in Chapter 15, "Using Web Browsers."

FIGURE 21.22
RealNetwork's Internet video client, `rvplayer`, plays live radio or TV broadcasts during your Internet and X11 sessions.

Using RealPlayer

The `rvplayer` X11 client is usually used as a Netscape Communicator plug-in, or external program that adds features to the browser. After you properly configure Netscape, the `rvplayer` will automatically play audio or video when you click an audio or video link on a web page.

You can also use `rvplayer` to play video clips downloaded from remote computers. These video clips must be in RealVideo format and usually have `.rm` as a filename extension. For example, to play a clip of one of the infamous dancing baby animations, start an X11 session and use the `rvplayer` client from the command line of a terminal window, like so:

```
# rvplayer bluesuede.baby &
```

The `rvplayer` program loads the video clip and starts playing, as shown in Figure 21.23.

FIGURE 21.23
RealNetwork's `rvplayer` will not only load and play video clips without an Internet connection, it can make a baby dance!

Picture this: more colors!

The `rvplayer` client requires an 8-bit, or 256-color, display. When you use X, other applications can use many of the available colors needed to provide good-looking video. If your computer's graphics chip and X11 configuration support X sessions with more than 256 colors, `rvplayer`'s video display will look much better. Start your X session at a greater color depth by using the `startx` command's `-bpp` (bits-per-pixel) option, followed by a color depth. For example, to start an X11 session using 16 bpp, use `startx` from the console command line like so:

```
# startx -- -bpp 16
```

For details about how to use your X11 server and computer graphics card, see the various READMEs under the `/usr/X11R6/lib/X11/doc` directory, the `startx` manual page, or the documentation for your distribution of X11. For XFree86 users, different color depths are supported in your X11 configuration file, `XF86Config` (found under the `/etc` directory).

SEE ALSO

➤ *For more information about starting the X Window System, see page 260.*
➤ *For details about configuring Netscape Communicator to use* `rvplayer`, *see page 216.*

After downloading and installing `rvplayer`, look under the `/usr/doc/rvplayer` directory for information about how to use the RealVideo Player.

Playing Animations and Movies with the *xanim* Client

Another X11 client you can use to play sound or video clips is the `xanim` program. The `xanim` client will play a variety of audio and video clips in different formats. Some of the formats supported by this program are listed in Table 21.5.

TABLE 21.5 Audio and video clips supported by *xanim*

Type	Description
AU	Audio track of animation
AVI	Windows animations (not all types supported)
DL	Animation
FLC	Animation
FLI	Animation
GIF	Single, multiple images
IFF	Animation
JFIF	Single images
MOV	QuickTime animations (not all supported)
MPEG	Animation (not all supported)
MovieSetter	Amiga animation
PFX	Amiga PageFlipper Plus
RLE	Utah Raster Toolkit animations, images
WAV	Audio track of animation

By default, `xanim` does not play audio tracks of specified video clips. To configure `xanim` to use sound and display video, use its

+Ae (audio-enable) command-line option and the name of the video clip, like so:

```
# xanim +Ae blownaway.avi &
```

This will run xanim, as shown in Figure 21.24, with a floating controls window and a video window. The xanim controls allow you to stop, start, set the volume, or play the video clip frame by frame. For more information, see the xanim manual page.

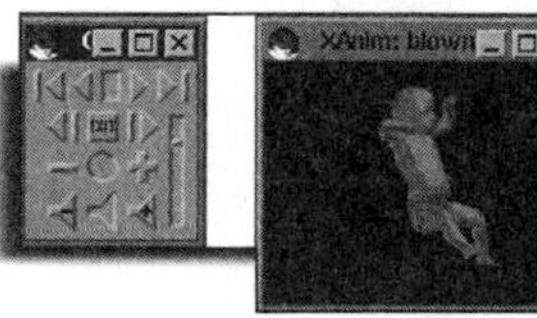

FIGURE 21.24
Oh no! Another dancing baby, courtesy of the xanim X11 video player client.

PART V

System Administration

CHAPTER

22

Basic Shell Programming

By Jan Walter

What shell scripts are used for

Writing shell programs

Using shell variables

Using shell constructs

Writing shell functions

The part of any system that interprets keyboard or mouse commands is called the *shell*. Under MS-DOS, for example, the shell is called `COMMAND.COM`; under Windows 95, the graphical shell is called `EXPLORER.EXE`. Under most UNIX systems, users have their choice of shells in both the graphical and text-mode environments.

The most popular Linux shell is `bash`. This stands for *Bourne-Again Shell*, and is named after one of the original UNIX shell designers. `bash` has a lighter relative, `ash`, which lacks some features such as command-line histories, but requires substantially less memory and is therefore found on things like the Red Hat installation and emergency recovery disks. Clones of the standard UNIX shells, `sh` (the Bourne shell), `csh` (the c shell), and `ksh` (the Korn shell) are also available.

Another point to remember is that a shell under Linux (as well as under other UNIX systems, and interestingly enough, under DOS and OS/2) is just another program. You can start another shell from the shell you're in, just like you can start the program `ls` to get a directory listing. This is significant because many shell scripts are not interpreted by the shell in which you type the command; instead, another shell is started to process the command.

What Shell Scripts Are Used For

Shell scripts are actually one of the most common types of programs on all UNIX systems. They are relatively easy to write and maintain, and they can tie together other programs (for example, other shell scripts) to get a lot of work done with one simple command.

Every time you log on to your Linux system, the system executes a shell script before you even see the first `$` prompt. Almost all aspects of system startup and network configuration are controlled by shell scripts. For a regular Linux system user, shell scripts can make work easier and more productive. For the Linux system administrator, a basic understanding of shell scripts makes all the difference between a well-run and trouble-free Linux system and one that can get really ugly, really fast.

Writing Shell Programs

Shell programs are closely related to batch files in the DOS world. Unlike DOS batch files, however, shell programs have much more advanced functionality; they are akin to conventional programming languages. Entire books have been written about most available shells; this chapter covers only `bash` because it is the most popular, and because it is used by default on Red Hat Linux systems.

Good Programming Practice

Good shell programs are easy to read and understand. This is vital if someone else must modify your work, or if you come back to it months later to fix or extend something. Badly written code is very difficult to work with and understand. Don't kid yourself about being able to remember what you've written (let alone understand what someone else has written) if the code is not formatted and commented properly. I hate preaching, but remind yourself when looking at the examples that the indentations and so on are there to help you understand the code. Give others who have to work with your code the same courtesy.

A simple shell script consists of regular shell commands, like the ones that would be typed interactively at the shell command line. Because it's handy to document what you're doing in a shell script for when you need to modify or fix it, comment lines can be included in a script by preceding the line with a `#` character. `bash` then treats the rest of the line as a comment.

Indentation is an important tool to help make your code readable when things get complicated. Blank lines can be used as well. Too many blank lines, indents, and comments, however, can make the code look just as jumbled as if it all had been crammed on one line.

A Sample Program

The last thing the world needs is another "Hello, World!" program. Instead, I want to show you something useful. For example, suppose you want a nicely formatted printout of what is in the current directory. The code shown in Listing 22.1 provides a means to do just that (the numbers at the beginning of each line are for your use; they do not actually appear in the code).

LISTING 22.1 *printdir* sends an appropriately paginated list of files and directories to the printer

```
1   #!/bin/bash
2   #Sample Program for Using Linux
3   # Jan Walter jwalter@rogers.wave.ca
4   # Using Linux, Chapter 22
5   # Copyright 1998 Macmillan Computer Publishing and Jan Walter
6   # All rights reserved.
7   # This code comes without warranty of any kind. If it breaks you
➥get
8   # to keep both pieces.
9   ls -l > /tmp/lstemp
10  pr /tmp/lstemp ¦ lpr
11  rm /tmp/lstmp
12  #end of script
```

This script works best when you're logged on as a regular user rather than system administrator; it assumes that you have a printer installed and correctly configured. Simply put, it executes the commands in the file in sequence. The more interesting aspects of this listing are as follows:

- Line 1 tells the system which shell the system should start to execute the script. This is vital because different shell programs use different commands.
- Line 9 executes the program `ls -l` and redirects output to a file in the system temporary directory.
- Line 10 feeds the contents to `pr` (which breaks the file into pages and, depending on the arguments, numbers the pages, adds a nice header, and so on) and feeds the output of `pr` to `lpr`, the system print spooler. The important point here is the redirection of the output of commands, not the commands themselves.
- Line 11 removes the temporary file created in line 3. (Just a reminder: Make sure your programs are polite to other users on the system and clean up after themselves.)

Try the script out

1. Start an editor, such as `joe`, like this:
   ```
   joe printdir
   ```
2. After the editor starts, enter the script text in Listing 22.1.
3. If you are using `joe`, press Crtl+K, and then press X to save the file and quit.
4. You still need to tell Linux that this file is indeed something it can execute. To do this, use the `chmod` command:
   ```
   chmod a+x printdir
   ```
5. Try out your creation by issuing the following command:
   ```
   ./printdir
   ```
   Your printer should spit out a long listing of the contents of your directory.

I admit that all of this can be done easily at the command line with the following command:

```
ls -l | pr | lpr
```

All this really does is create a long directory listing, along with file permissions, sizes, and so on, and uses a `bash` pipe to redirect the output of the program. In this case, the output gets sent to `pr`, which formats the text into nice 60-line pages, with page numbers, time and date, and the output of `pr` gets passed on to `lpr`.

Nonetheless, the point is that you can now do all this with the simpler command `./printdir`. The idea also carries on to the bigger scripts that actually do something significant, such as add a new user to the system. Every expression you use in a shell script can also be used interactively.

In Listing 22.2, I've tweaked the script in Listing 22.1 to provide what programmers call instrumentation. *Instrumentation* is the process of indicating to the user of the program what is actually happening. This prevents users from prematurely terminating the program (possibly while the program is in the middle of doing something critical) because the system appears to be sitting there and doing nothing.

Note

You can look up these commands in the system manual by using the command `man`.

Tired of typing ./ to start your scripts?

You can put your frequently used scripts into a directory called `bin` in your home directory. This directory's contents are always in your application path (the directories the system searches when looking for a program whose name was not preceded by a directory name), which allows you use the script without using the path just as with a regular system program.

LISTING 22.2 ***printdir2*** **sends the nicely paginated list of files in the current directory to the printer and provides feedback to the user while doing so**

```
#!/bin/bash
# printdir2
# Jan Walter jwalter@rogers.wave.ca
# Using Linux, Chapter 22
# Copyright 1998 Macmillan Computer Publishing and Jan Walter
# All rights reserved.
# This code comes without warranty of any kind. If it breaks you
➥get
# to keep both pieces.
echo -n "Getting Directory listing ..."
ls -l > /tmp/lstmp
echo " done."
echo -n "Formatting and printing Directory listing ..."
pr /tmp/lstmp ¦ lpr
echo " done."
echo -n "Cleaning up ..."
rm /tmp/lstmp
echo " done."
# end of script
```

The output of the program looks something like this:

```
[jwalter@jansmachine samples_22]$ ./printdir2
Getting Directory listing ... done.
Formatting and printing Directory listing ... done.
Cleaning up ... done.
[jwalter@jansmachine samples_22]$
```

If the directory listing is large or the system that's being used is heavily loaded, the first step might take some time; it's nice to see what's happening as a program proceeds through the work it's doing. This is, of course, much more useful when many more steps are involved.

The command `echo` is just another program (type `man echo` to view `echo`'s man page), and the `-n` parameter simply tells `echo` to not output a newline character after printing something on the display. In this case, I use `echo -n` to keep progress information on a single line, which, in my opinion, looks nicer.

Using Shell Variables

Variables are temporary placeholders for information, either numbers or sequences of characters (called *strings*). The system (that is, the shell) has a number of useful predefined variables, such as the user name, home directory, and system name. Using the env command generates a listing of all *persistent* variables (meaning that they don't stop existing when the current command or script ends) defined in your shell.

Listing 22.3 is the output generated by the env command on my machine. This will vary somewhat from machine to machine, of course.

LISTING 22.3 Sample output listing of the *env* command

```
[jwalter@jansmachine samples_22]$ env
USERNAME=
ENV=/home/jwalter/.bashrc
BROWSER=xterm -font 9x15 -e lynx
HISTSIZE=1000
HOSTNAME=jansmachine.censvcs.net
LOGNAME=jwalter
HISTFILESIZE=1000
MAIL=/var/spool/mail/jwalter
TERM=xterm
HOSTTYPE=i386
PATH=/usr/local/bin:/bin:/usr/bin:/usr/X11R6/bin:/opt/kde/bin:
    ➥/usr/bin/mh:
/home/jwalter/bin
KDEDIR=/opt/kde
HOME=/home/jwalter
SHELL=/bin/bash
USER=jwalter
MANPATH=/usr/man:/usr/X11R6/man:/usr/local/man
DISPLAY=:0.0
OSTYPE=Linux
MM_CHARSET=ISO-8859-1
SHLVL=5
=/usr/bin/env
[jwalter@jansmachine samples_22]$
```

Modifying variables in your login shell

It's not a good idea to mess with the predefined shell variables in your system unless you know exactly the effect you're trying to achieve. If `PATH` or some other vital variable is filled with invalid data, you will have difficulty executing normal commands—even `exit`, which you need to log out. If you modify your login script (the `.bash_profile` script in your home directory), you might not even be able to log on.

Be sure to keep this in mind when you modify root's login scripts! I find it best to keep another root logon on another terminal to ensure that I have a usable shell if the new login script does not work.

The majority of the environment variables are used for library and application pathnames, and things like the OS type and platform.

Using Variables in Scripts

Unlike most conventional programming languages, variables in `bash` shell scripts are *optionally* typed (that is, classified as to whether they contain integers, characters, or floating point numbers). Some numerical operations are faster when `bash` is informed that a variable contains only a number. Variables are not required to be declared before they are used, but it does make the code more readable.

After a variable is *referenced* (that is, used by having something assigned to it), you can use the value of the variable in expressions by prefixing the variable name with a `$` character.

To make a variable persistent, use the `export` command. This command is useful for modifying shell variables that already exist (like the ones you see when the `env` command is executed) because changes made to the values of the variables already declared will otherwise be lost after the script finishes.

A Sample Script

The script in Listing 22.4 uses shell variables, decision-making constructs, and some more advanced shell techniques to clear all files owned by the current user from the `/tmp` directory. This is a common operation done by system administrators because some programs don't clean up after themselves properly, and some users like to use the `/tmp` directories for other things. As an option, if the user is root, the script accepts a user name argument and clears that user's files instead.

LISTING 22.4 Use *cleantmp* to clean up files in the */tmp* directory left by the current user (or if the user of the script is root, the name specified on the command line)

```
#!/bin/bash
# cleantmp
# bash script that cleans up the files left in /tmp by a user
# usage: cleantmp <user>
```

```
# the user argument is only valid if the script is run as root
# Jan Walter jwalter@rogers.wave.ca
# Using Linux, Chapter 22
# Copyright 1998 Macmillan Computer Publishing and Jan Walter
# All rights reserved.
# This code comes without warranty of any kind. If it breaks you
➥get
# to keep both pieces.

#check to see if root executed this
if [ $LOGNAME = 'root' ]; then
    if [ $1 ]; then
        DELNAME=$1
    else
        DELNAME=$LOGNAME
    fi
else
    if [ $1 ]; then
        echo "Only root is allowed to specify another user id."
        exit 1
    else
        DELNAME=$LOGNAME
    fi
fi
echo "User's files to remove: " $DELNAME
echo "Proceeding with this script can cause problems if other
➥applications"
echo "still require access to those files."
echo -n "Proceed with clearing the files? [y/N]"
read

if [ $REPLY ]; then
        if [ $REPLY = 'y' -o $REPLY = 'Y'  ]; then
            echo "You pressed yes."
        else
            echo "You pressed no."
        exit 0
        fi
else
    echo "You did not press anything."
    exit 0
fi

# all this leads up to one big finale ...
```

continues...

LISTING 22.4 Continued

```
47  echo -n "Deleting files in /tmp directory tree belonging to "$DEL
    ➥NAME" ... "
48  rm -f $( find /tmp -user $DELNAME )
49  echo "done."
50
51  # end of script
```

Following is a review of the use of variables and the more complex parts of the script:

- Line 14 introduces the `if` expression and the test expression (more about these later), and references your first variable. This variable is also listed in the output of the program `env` and, as you might have guessed by the output there, contains the name under which the user is currently logged on. The `if` executes all statements immediately following the `then` if the expression that immediately follows it is true (or equal to `1`). In this case, it compares the variable `LOGNAME` to the string `root` to determine whether the user who typed the command is root.

Command-line arguments in `bash`

Command-line arguments are defined by `bash` as anything following the first word of a command. These arguments are separated from the command by a space. For example, with `ls -l`, `ls` is the command and `-l` is an argument.

- Line 15 uses the `if` expression and the test expression to determine whether the program has a command-line argument. Command-line arguments are referenced by their position on the command line, `$1` being the first, `$2` being the second, and so on. If you want to use all command-line arguments in a list, for example to document what's happening, you can use `$@` to use them all as one string. A single variable in a test expression is evaluated by `bash` to determine whether the variable actually contains anything.

- Line 16 assigns a value to the variable `DELNAME`. Note that there are no spaces between the equal sign (=) and the value being assigned to the variable. If you must have spaces in the value you're assigning, make sure to enclose the value in single quotes, with no space between the quote and the equal sign.

- Lines 14–27 essentially check the user ID and command-line arguments according to the following logic:

```
If the user is root
    then
```

```
    if there is a command line argument
        accept another name as a command line argument
and set
        ➥DELNAME to that argument
    else
        set DELNAME to root
    end if
else
    if there is a command line argument
        then tell the user they are not allowed to do
➥this and exit
    else
        set DELNAME to the user's name
    end if
end if
```

The only other thing to note here is that, unlike with most other programming languages, `if` statements in `bash` are ended with `fi` instead of with `endif` or `end` (refer to line 27 of Listing 22.4).

- Lines 28–30 basically provide documentation and a warning to users that what they are about to do can have potentially undesirable effects. It's important to tell users this; otherwise, you, the system administrator, are likely to get a lot of complaints or service calls about weird things happening on the system.
- Line 31 uses the `echo -n` command that was introduced earlier to provide a prompt for confirmation from the user, and to ensure that the cursor stays on the same line as the question to underscore to the user that the program requires a response.
- Line 32 introduces the `read` command. This command reads a line of input from the user, and then puts each word into the variable names that follow, one per variable, placing any remaining words (if applicable) into the last variable. If no variable is given, as in this case, the `read` command places everything that was read into the `REPLY` variable.
- Lines 34–44 check whether there is something in the `REPLY` variable (if there is nothing, this indicates that the user simply hit the Enter key), and if there is, check for a lowercase

A word about warnings

It's especially important to notify users when a script is about to delete any data that might belong to them, and to give them the opportunity to abort the operation!

or a capital Y. The only way the program can proceed is if the REPLY variable contains y or Y; all other conditions cause the script to terminate (note that the echo statements provide documentation to users to make sure they understand why the program did not continue).

- Line 48 does all the work of the program—it calls rm -f for all files found with the name contained in DELNAME's user ID. This is all wrapped up in another echo statement to give the user some idea of the completion status. Note that the find command contained in the $(...) expression is executed first, and the output of the program used as input for the rm -f statement.

You must wonder whether all this is really necessary to execute what essentially boils down to one command. I would argue that the extra checks, and moreover the ease of use of the script, will make it more likely for someone to complete the task successfully. Most shell programs are not full-blown applications, but helpers in everyday tasks. It's relatively easy to make them somewhat interactive, and so they are very useful if you want to prompt users as to whether they are certain they want to do something.

Using Shell Constructs

bash provides the following constructs:

- Decision constructs—These are statements that cause code to be executed depending on a decision.
- Repetitive constructs—These are statements that repeat the themselves a given number of times.

As stated before, this chapter is not intended to teach you how to program, but only to introduce you to the most commonly used parts of shell programming so that if you're confronted with a shell script, you'll be able to figure out what's happening.

Decision Constructs: The *if* Statement

The if statement executes lines of code depending on whether the conditional expression following the keyword if evaluates to a true result. The code following the `else` keyword (if any) is executed if the condition evaluates to false. The syntax of the `if` statement is shown in Listing 22.5.

LISTING 22.5 ***if* expression syntax**

```
if <expression>
then
     <code executed if expression true>
else
     <code executed if expression false>
fi
```

The `else` statement and subsequent code is unnecessary if nothing needs to be done when the expression evaluates to a false result.

How `bash` interprets `true` and `false`

Conventional programming languages (specifically C and C++) interpret true and false as numerical values, where `0` is false, and any other result is true. In `bash`, however, true and false values are reversed: `bash` interprets `0` as true and `1` as false. This is because `if` expressions were designed to test the return codes of actual programs and commands, and a `0` typically indicated success, not failure, of the program.

All `bash` constructs and expressions automatically handle this for you; you need only worry about whether the expression is true or false without worrying about the actual numerical values. But remember to take this into account when dealing with programs that donít follow the conventions for return values

Testing Expressions with *test*

`test` provides the other half of the functionality of `if`. Test expressions perform mathematical, Boolean, and other tests and return true or false depending on the outcome.

Test expressions can appear in two forms:

- With the keyword `test`, like so:
  `test $LOGNAME = 'root'`
- With square brackets, like so:
  `[ $LOGNAME = 'root' ]`

Both forms of test expressions work in the same way.

Integer Expressions

Test expressions are remarkable compared to other programming languages' comparison expressions because they do not use operators such as >, <, >=, and so on for greater-than and less-than comparisons. Instead, integer expressions, which are discussed in Table 22.1, are used.

TABLE 22.1 Integer test expressions

Expression	True If:
`x -eq y`	x equals y
`x -ne y`	x is not equal to y
`x -ge y`	x is greater than or equal to y
`x -gt y`	x is greater than y
`x -le y`	x is less than or equal to y
`x -lt y`	x is less than y

String Expressions

String expressions, on the other hand, can test to determine whether strings are identical, not identical, zero or non-zero lengths, or null values (that is, empty or not initialized). Note that `bash` discriminates between zero-length strings and empty ones. Table 22.2 illustrates how string expressions operate.

TABLE 22.2 String test expressions

Expression	True If:
`-z` *`string`*	*`string`* has a length of zero
`string`	*`string`* is not null, (that is, it is uninitialized)
`-n` *`string`*	*`string`* has a non-zero length
`string1` `=` *`string2`*	*`string1`* is identical to *`string2`*
`string1` `!=` *`string2`*	*`string1`* is not identical to *`string2`*

File-Testing Expressions

File-testing expressions test for information about files, and are typically used by scripts to determine whether the file should be backed up, copied, or deleted. There are numerous file-testing expressions, so I will list only some of the more common ones in Table 22.3. See the `bash(1)` manual page, or more specifically, the `test(1)` manual page for more of these expressions.

TABLE 22.3 **File-testing expressions**

Expression	True If:
`-e` *file*	*file* exists
`-r` *file*	*file* is readable
`-w` *file*	*file* is writable
`-d` *file*	*file* is a directory
file1 `-nt` *file2*	*file1* is newer than *file2*
file1 `-ot` *file2*	*file1* is older than *file2*

Negation and Boolean Operators

Test expressions support the basic AND, OR, and NOT Boolean operators. Table 22.4 illustrates how these expressions operate.

TABLE 22.4 **Boolean test expressions**

Expression	Effect:
!expression	Reverses the evaluation of *expression* (that is, it changes the evaluation to true if *expression* is false, and vice versa)
expression1 `-a` *expression2*	True if both expressions are true (*expression1 AND expression2*)
expression1 `-o` *expression2*	True if either expression is true (*expression1 OR expression2*)

Repeating Commands with *while*

`while` is used to repeat commands until a given condition evaluates to false. It's used when it cannot be predicted or calculated how many iterations the loop will go through. Listing 22.6 shows the `while` syntax.

LISTING 22.6 ***while* syntax**

```
while expression
do
    <code executed while the expression is true>
done
```

Repeating Commands with *for*

`for` works differently in `bash` than it does in any other programming language: It is used to traverse lists of words, and to process each word in sequence. This is useful because so much work deals with handling lists. Command-line arguments are lists of separate strings, as are multiple words that can be returned from `readline`.

Writing Shell Functions

Shell functions are one of the more advanced features of the `bash` shell programming language. In most programming languages, programmers accumulate snippets of code that are useful in more than one program. To make the reuse of code easier between programs, these snippets of code were grouped into functions. They are essentially subprograms that your shell programs can call. BASIC calls these *subroutines*, Pascal and Modula-2 call them *procedures*, and C, C++, and `bash` call them *functions*.

Note

I tend to put my `bash` functions in a directory called `include` in my home directory's `bin` directory, because `include` directories are conventionally used for containing header files that programs written in C and C++ use. I do plenty of programming in all of these languages, and so the less I have to change my way of working, the better.

I also group my functions into separate categories, and keep them in different files according to category –such as `fileman` (short for file management), which I use for the finding and handling files. I admit that my procedure libraries are pretty sparse–I spend too much time moving from system to system to really accumulate a comprehensive function library.

Functions usually take an argument or more to pass to them the data they are supposed to work on. The idea is that the code in a function should be packaged in such a way as to make it useful in more than one circumstance. To allow more than one shell program to use the same function library, and to prevent multiple copies of these functions from littering the `bin` directories of hapless shell programmers, `bash` introduces the concept of including files in your script.

Consider for a moment the advantages of doing this. There would be one file (or different files containing groups of functions useful for different things) that contains functions that any other script can use. When a problem is discovered in one of those functions and fixed, all scripts using this function automatically use the updated—and hopefully less problematic—code. This reduces the time spent maintaining scripts, and frees the shell programmer to do other things.

Using functions in a single script can make programming easier and less likely to contain errors. Using functions in multiple scripts has the same advantages, but also requires some forethought. Different files containing functions scattered all over the place tend to make reusing code difficult.

A Simple Shell Function

From bash's point of view, a shell function is essentially a script within a script. Functions can do anything that scripts can do, with the added benefit that properly designed functions can be reused in other scripts.

To declare a function, use the (appropriately named) `function` keyword. Functions, just like scripts, take arguments, and these are treated the same way in the code. All code contained within a function is enclosed in curly braces ({ }). As an example, the following function would print the words `function called` on the screen and list the arguments given.

```
function test_functions()
{
    echo "This function was called with the following
➥arguments:"
    echo  $@
}
```

Note that `$@` means "all arguments" in bash.

The function would be called in the script like this:

```
... (preceding code)
test_function argument1 argument2 and so on
... (code afterwards)
```

The output on the screen (excluding anything else the script might put up, of course) would look like this

```
This function was called with the following arguments:
argument1 argument2 and so on
```

All in all, functions don't behave much differently from separate scripts, but because they are in the same file, the additional overhead of starting yet another instance of bash to process the script is not incurred.

Using a Library

By definition, a library contains only functions. To load a library of functions (you need to do this before using the function in the library), you must execute the file containing the library. Because the file does not contain any code that bash will immediately execute, bash will load only the functions from the file. After this, you can use all the functions just as though they were in the local file.

Libraries follow the same conventions as regular scripts and executable files in most respects—including the PATH environment variable. For example, this technique provides one single point of maintenance for the init scripts on your system for functions dealing with process control. To include a file of functions (this example is from the init scripts in your /etc/rc.d/init.d directory), type the following at the command line:

```
. /etc/rc.d/init.d/functions
```

The . indicates that the file following the space should be loaded and executed. Because library files contain nothing but functions, they are simply loaded and then available for use. bash also has another keyword that does the same thing: source. The . is easier, and most people use this to get bash to load a file full of functions.

CHAPTER

23

Using Basic Programming Tools

By Jan Walter

Building programs with the `make` command

Getting started quickly with new programs

Specifying different makefiles

Building X11 makefiles with the `xmkmf` script

Compiling programs with `gcc`

Linking programs with the `ld` linker

One of the greatest strengths of Linux is that it can run almost any UNIX program. But many UNIX machines don't use the Intel (or Digital Alpha) processors. What's more, when UNIX was designed, binary emulation of different machine architectures was prohibitive in terms of hardware requirements and was unworkable in business environments in which UNIX was deployed. Nonetheless, UNIX systems are, for the most part, *source-code compatible*, so a program's source code (typically in C) can be recompiled on a different platform and will usually work. Of course, this is not guaranteed, so sometimes minor changes are required.

Even DOS and Windows programmers have reason to give thanks to UNIX systems: The standard C libraries are part of the ANSI C standard. This means that code complying with the standard will also compile and run on any platform that complies with this standard. The standard is superficial, but it enables most programs to *port* (to attain a new platform) with minimal changes—or none at all.

This chapter covers compiling programs that are available in their source-code form. The Linux project people have been busy, and just about every available free program—certainly every program from the GNU project—has been both ported and confirmed to work with Linux.

Building Programs with the *make* Command

The `make` utility provides a scripting capability to automate the compilation and linking of programs. If the program's source code comes with a `makefile`—and if the documentation says the program supports Linux—making the program work on your system should be quite easy.

The syntax of the `make` command is as follows:

```
make <options> <make target>
```

Because `make` works based on *targets*, it is often used to automate not only the building of programs but also other tasks such as program installation and object file maintenance. `make` runs based on *dependencies*, which means that a certain action must be completed successfully before the system can carry out another action. This process is usually implemented to force `make` to build the program before initiating the install script, which makes sense.

`make` also has built-in defaults that are, for a UNIX program, relatively sane. I would suppose this to be the case because UNIX is one of the most common utilities used by programmers, and programmers certainly are in a position to modify programs to do exactly what is required. `make` calls these sane defaults the *default rules*, which state, for instance, that a file ending with `.c` should be compiled with the system's C compiler, files ending in `.cc`, `.cpp`, and `.c++` should be compiled with the C++ compiler, and so on. Most of these work pretty much as a programmer would expect.

For instance, the command to compile the C program `myprogram.c`

```
gcc -o my program my program.c
```

can get pretty tedious, even if you consider the functionality that a shell such as `bash` provides with regard to command-line histories to repeat commands easily. Instead, typing `make myprogram` would be a lot easier. `make` looks for any compilable file of that name and then compiles and links it for you. The programmer does not have to think about the language in which his program is written because `make`—having been configured correctly by the system administrator—knows about most, if not all, compilers installed on the system. If you're the system administrator, don't worry too much about configuring `make` because the installation script in most cases does this.

The only drawback to using `make` in this way is that it provides little facility for programs composed of multiple files, which unfortunately covers the majority of programs. The other disadvantage is that `make` offers little control over the optimizations the compiler uses to compile your program, which can have some impact on overall program performance.

`make` does support optimizations, as well as the building of multiple source file programs; this, in fact is the capability for which `make` was intended. All the programmer has to do is write his or her own `makefile`.

make Options

Typing the make command is often all that is needed to prepare a program to run on your system. When you type **make** at the command line, make looks for a file called Makefile (note the case) in the current directory to decipher what actions to perform. make performs the first action it finds in the file. By convention, this builds the program but does not install it for everyone to use on the system. The reason for this is simple: If you're logged on as root and type make, the last thing you want is for your directories to be littered with new programs that might not be working yet.

The typical program installation

Typically, you would run make first and then try the program to make sure it works and is configured correctly. You would then use make install to first ensure that the program files generated by make are up to date and then to copy them to their intended locations in the system.

Be sure to read the documentation to make sure that programs are configured with the defaults you want. Otherwise, the programs you install might not work as expected—and could even damage data.

make install

To build and install the program, use the make install command. This tells make to build the program and, if everything is successful, to install its executable and configuration files in the appropriate directories, with the correct permissions, ready for users on your system to use.

configure

Large programs with numerous configuration options often come with a configure target. This option usually walks you through a script to establish the program's configuration and to configure other files before you run make and make install. I appreciate the programs that come with a configure script because this tends to take care of the really minor version differences between Linux systems if they are at issue with the program with which I am working. If the documentation says the program supports the configure option, you can run it by typing make configure or make config, depending on the program.

Constants

The make command also enables you to define constants for the program. In beta distributions (or in distributions in which not much time was spent on the makefile), you might have to define a constant to ensure that compilation and linking completes successfully. Usually, this takes the form of make -D__LINUX_ to define the constant LINUX to the preprocessor of the code.

clean

Finally, most makefiles provide the option to clean up after themselves. Large programs often leave a substantial number of intermediate files lying about in their source directories, which can consume a significant amount of space. To make sure that these are cleaned up, or to clean up after a failed build of the program, try using the command `make clean`. This should also be run after the configuration of the program is changed, such as after `make config` has been run.

Getting Started Quickly with New Programs

This section is intended to help you get started quickly with programs that were downloaded as source code. The text assumes that the source distribution of the program already supports Linux.

Security precautions

When you first compile and test new programs, make sure you're logged on as a regular user to ensure that the program does not affect your system integrity. Although there is a great deal of trust in the Linux community, you'll want to make sure that you don't trip up your system by missing something important in the program's configuration.

Checking for documentation

1. The first thing you'll want to do is extract the program's source directory tree. Some programmers use a fairly intricate directory structure to manage their programs and distribute everything, but this depends on the program complexity as well as the number of programmers who worked on the project.
2. Look for files with names such as `readme.1st`, `readme.install`, or `readme`. As the names imply, these contain additional information that might not have made it into the program's primary documentation in time. They usually document peculiarities in the configuration, installation, and running of the program.
3. The next place to check for additional hints or documentation is a subdirectory in the source tree that is usually called `doc` or `Documentation` (remember that directory names are case sensitive).
4. The root of the distribution directory should contain a file called `Makefile`. This is the file that `make` reads by default, and it contains all the rules and targets `make` follows when

making the program. You should peruse the file for comments (as with shell scripts, the comments begin with #) indicating that certain things should be commented, filled in, or commented out.

At this point, you're ready to try making the program for the first time.

Making the program

1. Unless the documentation states otherwise, type **`make`**. The source code begins to compile, link, and sometimes run text processors (such as `TeX` to make printable manuals) or other commands to make `man` or `info` pages. If the program stops with an error message, you have overlooked some configuration option in the `makefile`, the `make` target, or another file. Reread the documentation on making the program and what you need to configure. You might have to edit header files, or run `make config` or a configuration script. Make sure that you run the cleanup script (usually called `make clean`) after rerunning `make config`.
2. Assuming that the `make` process completed successfully, you should now have some programs in the source tree that you can try out. Most `make` scripts generate or copy the final programs to the root directory of the source tree, but this might vary—the readme and other files tell you where to look for the program.
3. Try the program. Verify that the program works to your satisfaction and that everything behaves as expected.
4. When you finish testing the program—or when selected users on your system confirm that the program works as expected—you are ready to install the program for everyone's use. You can use the `make install` command or run an installation script mentioned in the program documentation. This is the only step for which you're required to log on as root because only root can put new programs in the `/bin`, `/usr/bin`, and `/usr/local/bin` directories, where programs are normally installed.

The point I want to emphasize is that you must read the documentation to make sure you get all this right. It's not as difficult as it sounds when you have done it a few times.

Specifying Different Makefiles

You have the option of copying or renaming the `makefile` you want to use, but often it's just as fast to specify the `makefile` by giving the command `make -f <makefile>`.

Different makefiles for different platforms

Some programs' source distributions come with different makefiles for different platforms. This is often the case with older programs, which had to support platforms in which the `make` program was not as functional as the one included with Linux or most other UNIX systems. This is also often the case for programs that support DOS as well as Linux.

These programs usually have `makefiles` with the platform name as the extension, such as `Makefile.linux`, `Makefile.borland` (indicating this would be a `makefile` for Borland's C/C++ compilers on the DOS, OS/2, and Win32 platforms), `Makefile.msc` (`makefile` for Microsoft compilers on DOS and Win32 platforms), `Makefile.sco` or `Makefile.sunos` (for SCO UNIX and Sun SunOS systems, respectively).

Building X11 Makefiles with the *xmkmf* Script

The X11 system is much more complicated than the conventional Linux text mode. Many more configurations and quirks must be accounted for, as must differences between XFree86 and commercial X11 distributions. Most X11 source distributions come with a file called the `Imakefile`, which contains detailed information about how the program should be configured for various platforms running various X11 systems. This is not a file you want to feed directly to `make` because the contents and format are quite different.

Instead of feeding this file to `make`, the file is fed to a program that generates a `makefile` specifically for your system and other information for `make` (called *dependencies*). The script `xmkmf` does all this for you and ensures that the program generating the makefile (called `imake`) is called with all the appropriate options for your system. Optionally, the script can call `make` a few times to finish the configuration and make the dependencies.

Compiling an X11 program

1. To generate the correct configuration to compile an X11 program, go into the source's root directory (where the `Imakefile` is located), and enter the following command:
   `xmkmf`

2. Optionally, if you want `xmkmf` to also call `make makefiles` to process the `makefiles` for the subdirectories (if any) and to call `make include` and `make dep` (which generate additional

information that the complete make process needs to complete), you would use the following:

```
xmkmf -a
```

Whether you use xmkmf or xmkmf -a depends on the documentation you received with your X11 program.

3. When xmkmf is finished, you can run make to build the program.

Compiling Programs with *gcc*

The C and C++ compiler included with Linux is gcc. This compiler supports all the latest features that would be expected from a commercial compiler, including a very good code optimizer (better than some compilers costing a significant amount of money), support for ANSI C and C++, C++ templates and template classes, and the C++ Standard Template Library. The gcc compiler is part of a complete development system, including a debugger (gdb), a profiler (gprof), various code-processing tools (such as make), and the runtime library itself.

The actual gcc compiler is used to compile programs written in C; g++ is used to compile programs written in C++. These commands run the same program but with different settings. For all other purposes, they are equal.

The gcc compiler is the equivalent of cc on other UNIX systems. In fact, Linux sets a symbolic link so that all programs (such as make, when compiling programs actually written for other UNIX systems) that are told to call cc will call gcc instead. make calls gcc to compile all source files written in the C and C++ languages.

The gcc compiler can call ld and link your program for you, and it also can produce intermediate files. To compile a program with a single C file, use the following command:

```
gcc -o <program name> <sourcefile>
```

If you need to debug the program...

This command does not include the additional information for the debugger. To use the debugger on the program, give gcc the -ggdb switch, in addition to any others.

Using this command, gcc produces an executable file with the name <program name> from the source file given. The source files for gcc usually end in .c. If you don't specify an output file, gcc assumes the file a.out.

By default, gcc does not use its built-in code optimizer. To use the optimizer, you can use the -O2 switch to make the compiler do everything it can to increase the performance of the program. Note that when you enable optimizations, you should make sure the compiler is not producing debugging information as well. Unless you have a lot of experience with the GNU tools and debugging code, trying to debug optimized code can be frustrating. To instruct the program to produce output that the code profiler can read and from which it can generate reports, add the -pg switch to the compiler's command line.

Often, the programs will be modular, which means that they are comprised of several C modules that must be linked together. The gcc compiler can handle more than one source file at a time, but more than a few will begin to result in a lot of typing, and it's not worth the trouble for use on a regular basis. To automate this process, you use makefiles and usually process C files one at a time; then you link together the object files with ld at the end. The gcc compiler provides a command-line option specifically for this: -c. For example, you use the following command to generate a file called greeting.o from the C file greeting.c:

```
gcc -c greeting.c
```

The gcc compiler automatically uses the same filename in this case to generate a file with the .o extension.

Linux uses dynamic linking, too

Shared code uses dynamic linking to reduce the amount of memory a program takes. For example, many programs use the same code to put text on the screen; shared code enables many programs to use this code at the same time while keeping only one copy in memory. This is the same idea used for .dll files on Windows and OS/2 systems. However, differences in the versions of the shared code libraries can cause programs to malfunction. When you compile your programs, you can optionally tell the linker to include the versions of the libraries it has statically instead of using shared libraries. Although this prevents version conflicts, it wastes memory on the system.

Linking Programs with the *ld* Linker

The ld linker links object files (the intermediate files that gcc generates) to system library files to produce executable files. Because most programs that Linux runs are based on shared code, incompatibilities sometimes occur when moving programs between different releases or distributions of Linux.

The ld linker knows about the standard libraries on your system and attempts to link these with the object files of the program. For example, if you have an object file called greeting.o that you have compiled with gcc, you would use the following command to produce an executable file with the same name:

```
ld -o greeting greeting.o
```

The `ld` linker would take the standard library files and dynamically link everything it could to reduce the memory your program takes. If you wanted to make sure this code runs on all systems, or that versioning of the dynamic libraries did not affect the program, you would use the following command to link the program:

```
ld -Bstatic -o greeting greeting.o
```

This file would naturally be quite a bit larger than the dynamically linked version.

CHAPTER

24

Using LILO and LOADLIN

By Jan Walter

Both LILO and LOADLIN provide a vital service to Linux: They load the kernel (the part of the operating system that does all the work) into memory and then *boot* it. You will need one of these programs to get Linux going.

Configuring LILO

LILO (short for LInux LOader) is the standard Linux loader. This program is the most flexible of the Linux boot loaders. LILO can be configured to reside in either the main boot record of your hard disk or the boot sector of a partition of a hard disk. You will have made this decision when installing Linux; depending on your system, one or the other will work best for you.

If your mind stalled when reading the previous paragraph, you're not alone. The most modern PC today boots very much like a PC did in 1982. However, the hardware has changed so much that the boot process requires the operating system and the loader for the operating system to be aware of the various workarounds that have been implemented on PCs to support, such as larger hard disks.

The boot procedure for every PC is relatively straightforward when viewed from a distance. It works like this:

1. When the PC is turned on, the processor begins executing the code in the BIOS. This code sizes the memory, tests the processor and hardware, and initializes the hardware to a known state.
2. The BIOS then looks for the boot drive (usually either a floppy disk or a hard disk); if it's a hard disk, BIOS reads the main boot record and executes it. This main boot record (usually installed by DOS a k a Windows 95) looks for the first active partition and then attempts to load this boot record.
3. The partition's boot record contains instructions on how to load the boot loader. Size limitations are in effect here, so the boot loader must be very small. DOS itself is small enough to fit there, so for a DOS system, the boot process is

finished. Other systems will have a program here that loads the operating system kernel and boots it, such as LILO loading the Linux kernel, decompressing it, and then booting it. The memory the boot loader uses is then usually reclaimed by the operating system that has been booted.

LILO's options are set and configured while Linux is running, which means that if LILO won't boot Linux, you must use your emergency boot disks to access the system's hard disk and then configure LILO. You may need to experiment to determine whether LILO works best for you in the hard disk's MBR or in the boot sector of your boot partition.

Using other boot loaders in conjunction with LILO

If you're using System Commander or IBM's Boot Manager (this ships with OS/2, as well as the latest versions of Partition Magic by Powerquest) to boot multiple operating systems, you can also use it to boot Linux. Simply configure LILO to install itself into the boot record of the Linux partition, and then configure your boot loader to boot that partition like a DOS one.

LILO reads its configuration from a file in your systems `/etc` directory called `lilo.conf`. This file tells LILO the operating systems for which to configure and where to install itself. At its most basic is the `lilo.conf` file, which tells LILO to boot only one operating system, as shown in Listing 24.1.

LISTING 24.1 A typical *lilo.conf* file

```
boot=/dev/hda4
map=/boot/map
install=/boot/boot.b
prompt
timeout=50
image=/boot/vmlinuz-2.0.32
        label=linux
        root=/dev/hda4
        read-only
```

This file tells LILO to place itself in the boot sector of the partition `/dev/hda4`, to wait for five seconds for user input at the `LILO:` prompt, and to boot the kernel `vmlinuz-2.0.32` in the `/boot` directory of the `/dev/hda4` partition. LILO puts up a prompt and waits for five seconds for input before booting the first image in the `lilo.conf` file. Note the timeout value for five seconds is `50`—LILO measures time in .10 second increments.

Why is the kernel called `vmlinuz`?

The "z" at the end is there because the kernel image is compressed to reduce the amount of disk space it takes by using a method similar to `gzip`; the image is uncompressed when booted. The name has been the convention for some time, and the installation script for the kernel assumes this name. If you really want to, you can change it–just make sure that you point LILO to the right file!

It's also possible to have a choice of several different Linux kernels to boot; this is handy if you're trying out the latest one but want to have the option of booting the old one just in case. It's worth the effort to set this up because it can save you—and those who depend on your system—a lot of frustration if a new kernel has problems.

Changing the Default Boot

The first entry in the `lilo.conf` file is the default boot configuration, which LILO starts when the timeout value has been reached. Changing the boot order is a simple matter of cutting and pasting, using your preferred text editor, and then rerunning LILO to install the new boot sector. If it is not convenient to make these changes to the `lilo.conf` file, add the directive `default = <label>` (where `<label>` is the text on the label of the image you want LILO to boot by default).

LILO uses labels to allow the booting of multiple operating systems or different Linux kernels. In Listing 24.2, typing the word `dos` at the `LILO:` prompt instructs LILO to boot DOS on your system.

Passing Kernel Parameters

The Linux kernel can take command-line arguments, much like a regular program. LILO supports this and can pass parameters from either the `LILO` prompt or the configuration file. Generally, the command line for the kernel is used to tell the kernel to expect more than one network card or device address. These options can be manually entered at boot time to permit experimentation or one-time modifications to the way the system or kernel loads. Alternatively, the options can be hard-coded into the `lilo.conf` file.

To pass a parameter from the `LILO` prompt, you first must give the name of the image to which you want to pass the parameter, and then you must give the parameters. For example, if you have a system with more than one network card, you must tell the kernel to keep looking for a second network card, or it will stop looking after finding and initializing the first one. The following command tells the stock kernel to do this:

```
LILO: linux ether=0,0,eth0 ether=0,0,eth1
```

The two `ether` parameters tell the kernel that there should be two auto-detectable ethernet cards in the system. The order in which they are found depends on the network card driver(s) involved. If you need to have specific cards assigned to certain ethernet device names, you must determine the card parameters by using this method, then note the interrupt number and the IO Address that the Linux kernel reports (these also are in the kernel log file (`/var/log/messages`) after the system comes up), and then set those parameters in your `lilo.conf` file.

This `lilo.conf` file lists three boot images:

- `/vmlinuz`
- `/vmlinuz.old`
- A DOS partition

Note how the kernel parameters are attached via the `append` command, as shown in Listing 24.2.

LISTING 24.2 A *lilo.conf* file is set up to boot either of two Linux kernels, as well as a DOS partition

```
boot=/dev/hda2
map=/boot/map
install=/boot/boot.b
prompt
timeout=50
image=/vmlinuz
        label=linux
        append="ether=0,0,eth0 ether=0,0,eth1"
        root=/dev/hda2
        read-only
image=/vmlinuz.old
        label=old
        root=/dev/hda2
        read-only
other=/dev/hda1
        label=dos
        table=/dev/hda
```

Booting to a Specific Run Level

You can override the run level to which Linux boots by passing a command-line argument to the kernel at the LILO prompt. For example, to boot Linux into single-user mode, enter the following command at the LILO prompt:

```
lilo: linux single
```

Single-user mode is a maintenance mode for UNIX systems and does not start any daemons, networking, or logon programs. This basically ensures that the system boots successfully (as long as the hard disk, kernel files, and so on, are okay). To boot another run level (for example, to test whether it's configured correctly), make the run level number the last item on the kernel command line at the LILO prompt.

You can make such a change to the `append` command in the `lilo.conf` file, but I don't suggest that you do so. Instead, modify your `initrc` file, as described in Chapter 27, "Managing Network Connections."

There are some things you don't really want to do at the LILO command prompt. For example, don't set the system to run level 0 or 6 (which are shutdown and reboot, respectively) because the system will happily boot up—only to shut down immediately afterward.

Using LOADLIN

LOADLIN is designed to boot Linux from a DOS prompt, which means that it is possible to boot Linux from DOS without actually rebooting the machine. This has inherent advantages, because it requires no modifications to the hard-disk structure to work, other than the creation of the Linux data and swap partitions.

One other advantage exists, which relates to unsupported hardware. Sound cards, in particular, often have SoundBlaster emulation modes, and these modes can be reached only by using DOS programs. Because LOADLIN does not reboot the machine, the sound card stays in a mode compatible with SoundBlaster and allows the regular Linux sound driver to work with it. I don't recommend doing this, but it *is* an option if nothing else works. For me, LOADLIN is just plain convenient.

Booting from DOS to Linux

Setting up LOADLIN is somewhat simpler than using LILO because LOADLIN is run as a regular DOS program and takes all the information it needs to boot Linux from its command line. For example, the following command causes LOADLIN to load the Linux kernel image `vmlinuz` and point it at partition `/dev/hda4`, initially read-only:

```
loadlin vmlinuz /dev/hda4 ro
```

Setting Up LOADLIN

LOADLIN is archived at the main Linux software distribution point, `sunsite.unc.edu`. If you purchased Linux as a CD set, it will be worth your while to look through those disks first because the Sunsite Linux Archive is usually quite busy. The distribution of LOADLIN as of this writing is version 1.6, and the file is called `lodlin16.tgz`. The latest version can be found in the `/pub/Linux/system/boot/dualboot/` directory at Sunsite (accessible via FTP or HTTP) or on the equivalent directory on your CD distribution. When you have the file, you can extract it to its own directory by issuing the following command:

```
tar xzf lodlin16.tgz
```

The .tgz extension

Some extraction programs for DOS enable you to extract the contents of this file. A good place to look for utilities is in the wc archive at `ftp://ftp.cdrom.com/pub`.

LOADLIN comes with a sample batch file that you can use to boot Linux. This file must be modified for your particular setup.

Setting up LOADLIN and the batch file

1. You'll need to know the partition on which Linux is installed. To do so, type the following:

   ```
   $ mount
   ```

   This is the result:

   ```
   /dev/hda4 on / type ext2 (rw)
   /proc on /proc type proc (rw)
   /dev/hdb7 on /mnt/f type vfat (rw)
   /dev/sda4 on /mnt/zip type vfat (rw,nosuid,nodev)
   ```

   This shows you the partitions Linux has mounted and the location of those partitions. The root partition (that is, the one mounted at the `/` mount point) is the partition from which Linux boots. In this case, `/dev/hda4` is the root partition. You also may have noted this information when you installed your system, in which case you can skip this step.

2. You'll need to know any kernel parameters that your system requires (for example, whether you have two network adapters in your machine). The best way to check the parameters for your kernel is to check the `append` command in the `lilo.conf` file from your current installation. Most systems do not require parameters for anything vital, except for the multiple network card switch.

3. You'll need to know the name of the kernel file itself, which is `/boot/vmlinuz`.

4. Determine whether your machine requires the initial ramdisk (`initrd`) to boot. The initial ramdisk is loaded by the boot loader and contains the device drivers that Linux needs to access the actual device(s) from which Linux boots. Most SCSI adapters, for example, allow simple DOS access without a device driver, but 32-bit operating systems cannot use this method. The boot loader (as with LILO and LOADLIN) uses the DOS method to load the ramdisk and the kernel, and the kernel then loads the device driver modules from the ramdisk to continue booting the system.

   If you have an SCSI adapter, the answer will generally be yes.

5. Get the ramdisk file, `/boot/initrd-2.0.31.img`. Make sure that the version number of the file is the same as the version of the kernel you're using!

Setting up a LOADLIN boot disk

1. Using DOS or Windows 95, format a bootable floppy disk. From the DOS or Windows 95 command prompt, type the following:

   ```
   format a: /u /s
   ```

   The `/u` parameter prevents DOS 6.*x* from saving unformat information to the disk, and it also speeds up the operation. The unformat information that DOS puts on the disk, in theory, would enable you to recover data from the disk if it were formatted accidentally. However, it's impossible to unformat a disk after a significant amount of data has been written to it.

2. Copy the files `loadlin.exe` (the program itself), `vmlinuz` (the Linux kernel), and `initrd-2.0.31.img` (the initial ramdisk, if you need one) to the floppy disk. You will want to rename `initrd-2.0.31.img` to `initrd.img` to get a short filename that DOS supports.

3. Using your favorite text editor, create a DOS batch file on the floppy disk. If you want to boot Linux automatically, name the file `autoexec.bat`. Otherwise, call it `linux.bat`. This file will call LOADLIN with the correct list of arguments. You could do it manually every time, but using a batch file is probably more convenient. You might want to add DOS sound drivers, a boot-up menu, or other objects to the floppy's `autoexec.bat` and `config.sys` files (either now or later). However, don't add the driver `EMM386.EXE` because this driver can cause you lots of grief when booting Linux with LOADLIN.

   The command line that tells LOADLIN to boot your system without an inital ramdisk is as follows:

   ```
   loadlin vmlinuz root=/dev/hda2 ro
   ```

   If you had to use an inital ramdisk, you'd use the following:

   ```
   loadlin vmlinuz initrd=initrd.img root=/dev/hda2 ro
   ```

   This example assumes that your system boots from the partition `/dev/hda2`. Be sure to specify the correct partition for your installation. The `ro` at the end tells the Linux kernel to initially mount the root file system as read-only. This enables you to check the file system if necessary.

4. Try it out. Remember that if you did not put the `loadlin` command in the `autoexec.bat` on the disk, you must issue the command `linux` to run the `linux.bat` batch file.

Text files, DOS, and Linux

When editing text files, remember that the DOS text-file convention includes a line feed as well as a carriage return in the file, whereas Linux and other UNIX systems use only the line-feed character. This is why text files often appear stair-stepped when sent directly to the printer from Linux. Although Linux usually understands DOS text files with the carriage-return characters in them, DOS does not extend Linux the same courtesy. Thus, when editing text files intended to be read on a DOS (or Windows, Windows NT, or OS/2) system, add the carriage-return character manually by pressing Crtl+M, or by using conversion utilities such as `fromdos` and `todos` afterward. These utilities can be downloaded in the easy-to-use `rpm` format from `ftp://ftp.redhat.com/pub/contrib/`.

Passing Kernel Parameters with LOADLIN

LOADLIN interprets everything after the first argument (which it expects to be the kernel name) as a kernel argument.

Therefore, to boot Linux to run level 5 with LOADLIN, use the following command:

```
loadlin vmlinuz root=/dev/hda2 ro 5
```

The previous command assumes that your Linux root partition is /dev/hda2. If you are booting from a floppy disk and LOADLIN sees some of the LOADLIN header and copyright information or some information about your current operating system (such as DOS), LOADLIN begins to load the ramdisk and kernel image, displaying dots as it proceeds. The system then boots the kernel. If you're running LOADLIN from a hard disk, this all happens too quickly to see—unless you have an older machine, of course.

CHAPTER

25

Managing Users and Groups

By Steve Shah

Users, groups, and their relation to the system

Creating, editing, and removing users with `usercfg`

Creating, editing, and removing users from the command line

Understanding the user and group configuration files

The Password Authentication Module (PAM)

Users, Groups, and Their Relation to the System

How does this compare to Windows NT?

Linux is similar to Windows NT in regards to the concept of users. Each user has a designated set of permissions, which allows them to run certain programs, save files in a certain place, and read files owned by other users provided that other users have set their file permissions accordingly.

Unlike many other operating systems currently available on the market, Linux supports the concept of multiple *users* and *groups*. A *user* is someone who has a unique identifier on the system, both a name and a number. This information allows the system to control how access is granted to the system and what the person may do after he or she has been allowed in. Users' activities are tracked by the system using their unique user identification number.

A *group* is a collection of users. Every group also has a unique identification number as well as a unique name by which it can be referenced. Systems administrators often control access by groups. (For example, all users in the group "undergrad" may not log in to the server "insoc.")

Every user and group has some peripheral information attached to it. The information is listed in Table 25.1.

TABLE 25.1 What makes up a user

Field	Description
Login	The user's unique name in the system.
Password	The password by which the user may access the system (encrypted).
UID	Short for User IDentification. This number pairs up with the login name. Every login/uid combination must be unique.
GID	Short for Group IDentification. This number pairs up with the group the user belongs to by default. All users must belong to at least one group. (See Table 25.2 for more information.)
Comment	A free-form entry used to describe the user. Usually this is the user's full name. This entry does not have to be unique.
Home Directory Path	The directory where the user's files are stored. Each user's personal configuration files are kept here. When the user logs in, his or her default directory will be here as well.

Field	Description
shell	The program that is run automatically when the user logs in. This is usually a shell program such as `/bin/bash`, which gives the user a UNIX prompt (much the same way the `command.com` program gives users access to DOS under Windows).

TABLE 25.2 What makes up a group

Field	Comment
Name	The group's name. Every group name must be unique.
Password	If a group has a password to control access to it, this must be set. In most instances, you do not need to worry about setting this.
GID	Short for Group IDentification. This associates a number to the group name. All group name/group number combinations must be unique.
User list	A comma-delimited list of users who are part of this group—for example, the list `sshah, hornbach,jnguyen` indicates that the three users, sshah, hornbach, and jnguyen are in this particular group.

These two tables are stored in the files `/etc/passwd` and `/etc/group`, respectively. The programs that manage users in one way or another essentially edit these files for you. If you are feeling adventurous, take a look at the password file in its raw format with the command:

```
[root@insoc /root]# more /etc/passwd
```

Table 25.1 explains each field, but don't worry if it doesn't make too much sense. All you *need* to know is that they are there.

The following sections use this information to establish, edit, and remove users using the tools built into Red Hat Linux.

Using the *usercfg* Tool

The `usercfg` tool is an all-in-one package for manipulating user and group information. Because of its graphical interface, it is easy to use.

To start the program, simply run `usercfg` like so:

Starting the User Configurator

1. Log in as the root user.
2. Start the X Window System with the **`startx`** command.
3. Open up an `xterm` and run the command **`usercfg`**.

The opening window should look something like Figure 25.1.

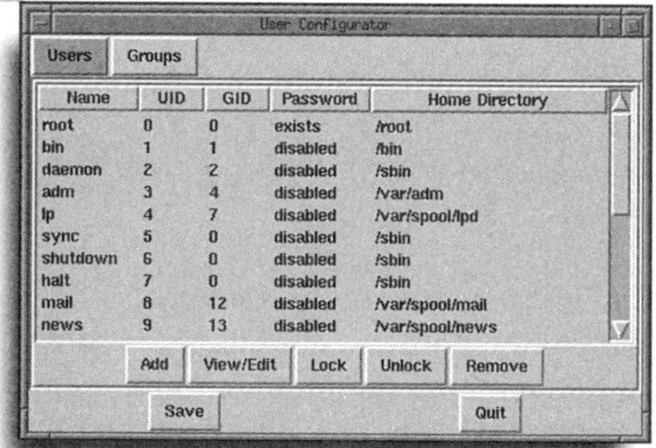

FIGURE 25.1
The User Configurator window as it appears when first started.

At the top of the window you see two buttons, one for Users and one for Groups. On startup, the Users button is always highlighted. Below those two buttons is the list of the current users in the system. The first column is the login name; then the User IDentification (UID); the Group IDentification (GID); whether the user's password exists, is disabled, or empty; and finally, the location of the user's home directory.

If you click the Groups button at the top of the window, you can see what the group configuration currently looks like. A stock configuration should look something like Figure 25.2.

Adding a User with *usercfg*

How to add a new user

1. Click the top button labeled Users to bring the user list back. The list of buttons on the bottom two rows show which functions are available. click the Add button to bring up a new Edit User Definition dialog box, as shown in Figure 25.3.

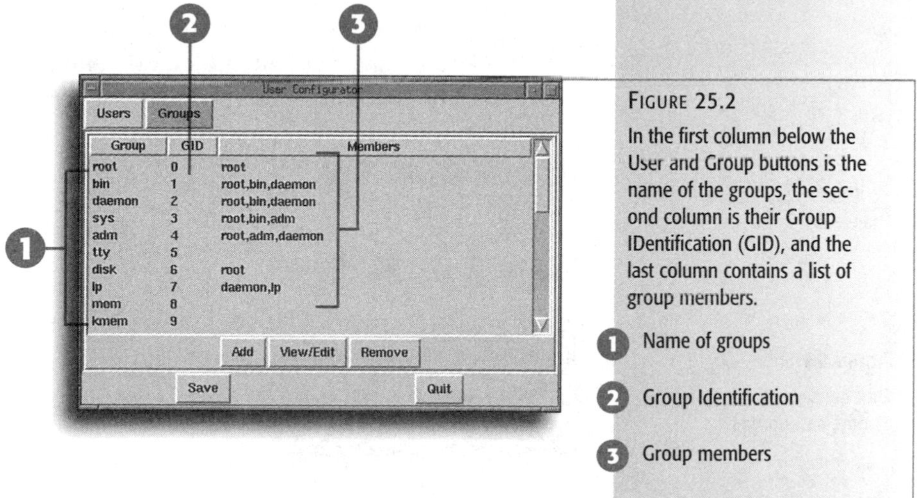

FIGURE 25.2

In the first column below the User and Group buttons is the name of the groups, the second column is their Group IDentification (GID), and the last column contains a list of group members.

1. Name of groups
2. Group Identification
3. Group members

Edit User Definition
Username:
Encrypted password:
UID: 514
GID: 514
Full name: Red Hat Linux User
Office:
Office phone:
Home phone:
Home directory:
Shell: /bin/bash
Done Cancel

FIGURE 25.3

The Edit User Definition dialog box. Notice the defaults set by the system.

`usercfg` will automatically fill in the UID and GID for you. In our example, that is UID 514 and GID 514. In addition, `usercfg` fills in the Full Name field with a default string `Red Hat Linux User`. Finally, `usercfg` gives you the default shell setting to `/bin/bash`.

2. Select a new login name. The login name should not be greater than eight characters. This should consist of only letters and numbers.
3. Click the down arrow button next to the password entry. Select the second option, Change. This will bring up a dialog box like the one shown in Figure 25.4.
4. Enter the password you want to assign to the user and press Enter. The dialog box will then prompt you to verify the password by reentering it. (The system wants to be sure that

The difference between *login* and *username*

You will often find that people use the terms *login* and *username* interchangeably. Within most contexts, they mean the same thing.

you haven't made a typing mistake.) Enter the password again and press Enter. The first line of the dialog box will show the encrypted version of the string as in Figure 25.5.

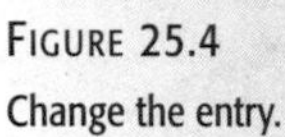

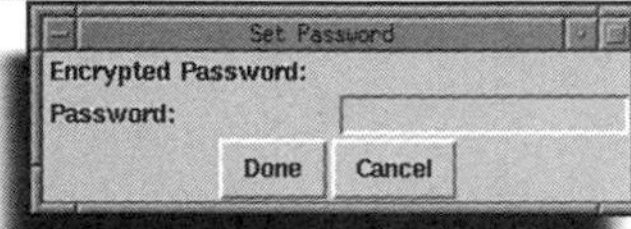

FIGURE 25.4
Change the entry.

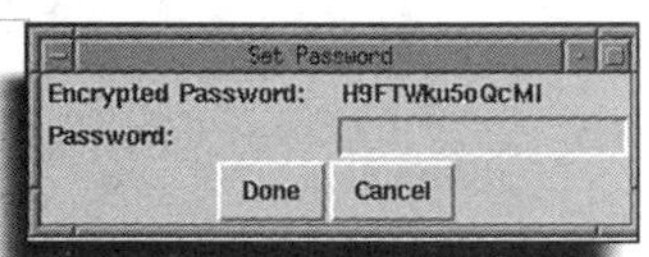

FIGURE 25.5
Click the Done button to make that the password entry.

5. `usercfg` will have already filled in a UID and GID for you. If you want the user to be part of an existing group, provide that group number instead of the suggested one. Of course, you can always add that user to the group by editing the groups file, as you will see shortly.
6. In the Full Name entry, fill in the complete name of the user. If the user wants to go by an alias, for example "Steveoid," enter the alias here.
7. The entries for Office, Office Phone, and Home Phone are optional. They are only used when the user is queried by other people using the `finger` command.
8. In the Home Directory entry, specify where the user's home directory will be. By default, the home directory will be `/home/`*`login`* where *`login`* is the user's login name. For most systems, this is acceptable and can be left alone. If you maintain a different home directory structure, replace this entry with the appropriate directory.
9. In the default shell entry, specify which shell the user will use when he logs in. The default shell is `/bin/bash`, which is fine for most users. If the user wants a different shell, you can click the down arrow button to see a listing of available shells based on the contents of the `/etc/shells` file. If you want to give the user a shell not listed, simply erase the entry and enter whatever shell you want to assign them.

Password information

Accounts should always have passwords. It is bad practice to leave accounts open to login without passwords, especially if your machine attaches to a network in any way. Furthermore, you need to use a good password–one that cannot be guessed using any of the automated password guessing programs available on the Internet.

A good password is at least six characters long, contains a mixture of uppercase letters, lowercase letters, punctuation, and numbers. One good technique is to pick a phrase and use the first letter of each word in the phrase. This makes the password easy to remember but difficult to crack. For example, "Always remember, It's a great big disco world" would be Arlagbdw.

10. After you have completed the dialog box, click the Done button. You should see your new entry in the main User Configurator window.

View/Edit Users

After a user has been added, you might find it necessary to go back and edit his information. To bring up the Edit User Definition dialog box, follow these steps:

Editing user settings

1. Either double-click the user or click once on the user and click the View/Edit button at the bottom of the window. The Edit User Definition window looks just like the Add User window without the option to change the login name (see Figure 25.6).

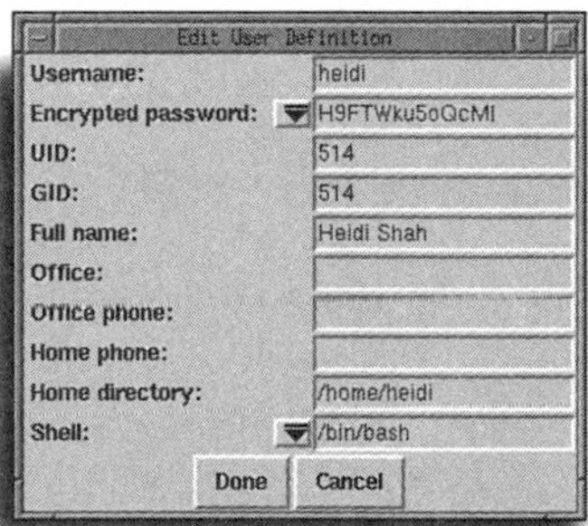

FIGURE 25.6
The Edit User Definition dialog box. Note the striking similarity to the Add User dialog box.

2. Each field containing the user's current information will be available for you to edit, except for the login name. You may change any of the other fields as you deem necessary.
3. When you have finished making changes, click the Done button at the bottom of the active window. This will commit your changes to the system.

Don't change the User Identification (UID)

As mentioned earlier, you cannot change a user's login name in the View/Edit dialog box. You have the option, however, to change the User ID (UID). *DON'T.* Changing a user's ID number will cause a great deal of confusion because Linux associates file ownership to UID's, not login names. Thus, changing a person's UID will cause him to lose ownership of all of his files.

If for whatever reason you need to do this, be sure you read the section later in this chapter on how to use the `chown` command to reassign ownership to files.

Locking a User

There eventually will come a time when a user on your system has become so troublesome that you need to lock him out of the system until you've had a chance to talk with him and set him straight. For example, you've just found out that the user vector has formed the Internet Terrorist Task Force and is attacking other sites. To lock him out, do the following:

Locking out a user

1. At the top of the `usercfg` window, click the Users button. This should bring up the list of users on the system.
2. Click once on Vector's entry.
3. Click the Lock button at the bottom of the `usercfg` window. This will bring up the Archive User window, as shown in Figure 25.7.

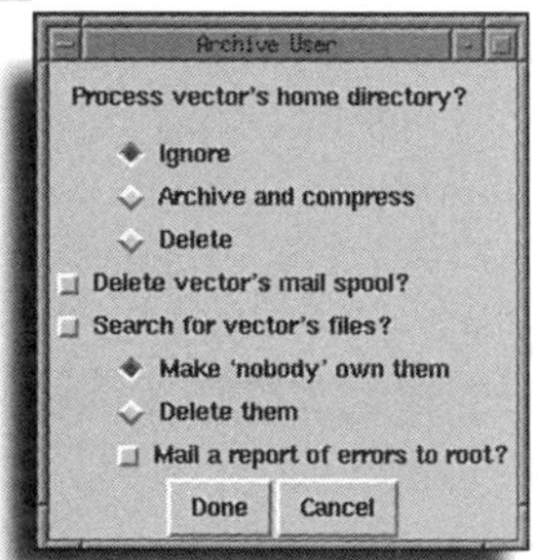

FIGURE 25.7
Open the Archive User window.

4. The first choice is what you want to do with Vector's home directory. The three options are to either ignore it, archive and compress it, or delete it altogether. Ignoring it will leave his home directory intact. Archiving and compressing will cause his home directory to be combined into one large file and compressed with the `tar` and `gzip` commands. (Together, they work similarly to the way WinZip works under Windows.) The last option to is delete his files altogether. In most instances, you will only want to disallow access to your system until you've had a chance to talk to your user about inappropriate behavior; thus, select the first option, Ignore.
5. The second option is whether you want to delete the user's undelivered mail. Unless you have a specific reason to remove it, leave it alone.
6. The last option is whether you want to change the ownership of all the user's files to the user `nobody`. In most instances, you will not want to do so. Select the option accordingly.

7. Click Done. Another dialog box will appear warning you that locking out a user will cause any changes made so far to be written to disk. click Really Archive if you want to proceed; otherwise, you can cancel the operation.

After the home directory is dealt with, the password entry is locked by placing an asterisk character in it, thereby preventing the user from logging in.

Unlocking a User

After you've had a chance to talk with your user and you feel that he should have access to the system once again, you will want to unlock his account. To do so, follow these directions:

Unlocking a user

1. Click once on the user's login name in the User Configurator. This will highlight his entry.
2. Click the Unlock button at the bottom of the window. A dialog box will inform you that unlocking a user will cause any changes made so far to be written to disk. If you are sure that you want to unlock the account, click Really Unlock; otherwise, click Cancel.

With the home directory back in place, the password entry will have the asterisk character removed, thereby allowing him to enter the system.

Removing a User

Occasionally, you will need to remove a user from the system. To remove the user vector from the system, follow these directions:

Removing a user

1. Click vector's login name in the User Configurator dialog box. This will highlight his entry.
2. Click the Remove button at the bottom of the User Configurator dialog box. This will bring up the Delete User dialog box, as shown in Figure 25.8.

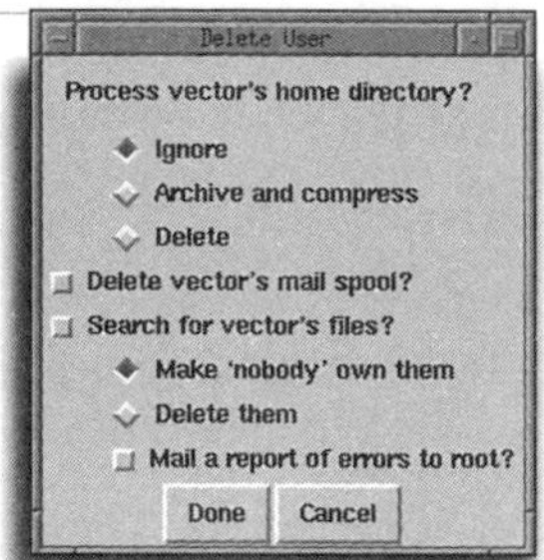

FIGURE 25.8
The Delete User dialog box. Note the similarity to the Lock User dialog box shown in the preceding section.

The menu options in this window are identical to the ones in the Lock User window. Here, however, you will want to take more drastic options if you're looking to completely remove him from the system. In most cases, you do want all traces of him remoed.

3. The first option allows you to specify how you want the contents of Vector's home directory dealt with. You will probably want to remove it. click the Delete button.
4. Click the button to delete vector's mail spool.
5. Click the button to Search for vector's files to tell the system that you want to find files outside vector's home directory that he owns (for example, files stored in `/tmp`).
6. Click the radio button to Delete Them under the Search for vector's Files button. This will cause any files owned by vector found outside vector's home directory to be deleted.
7. Just to be on the safe side, click the button to Mail a Report of Errors to Root.
8. The Delete User window should look like Figure 25.9 for the options you have selected.

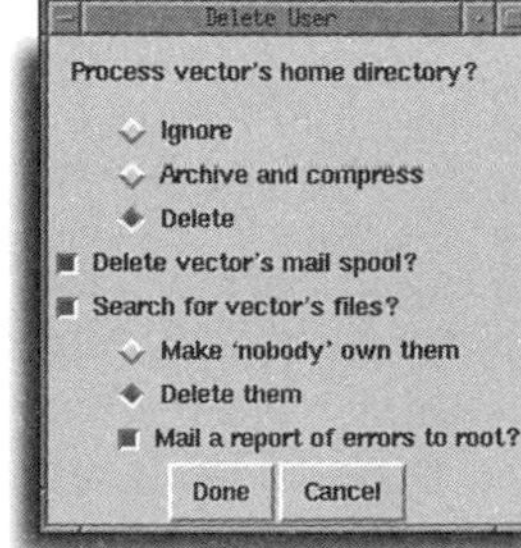

FIGURE 25.9
The Delete User dialog box after it has been filled out.

9. Click Done to indicate that you are happy with the selections you have made. You will get a warning about this operation not being undoable. Click Really Delete if you are sure; otherwise, click Cancel.

Adding a Group

To add a new group, do the following:

Adding a group

1. Click the Groups button at the top of the User Configurator window. The window will show the current listing of groups in the system, similar to Figure 25.10.

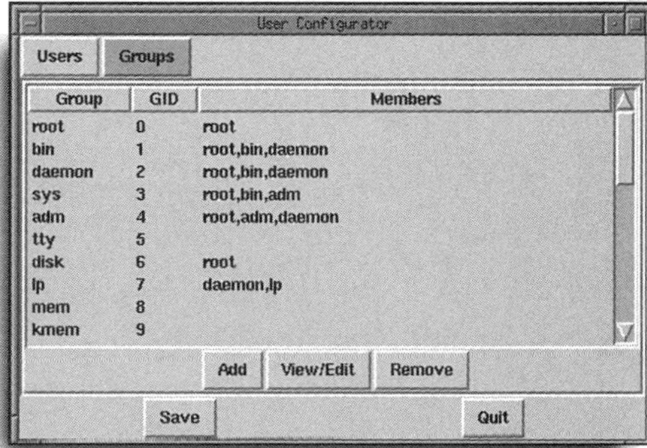

FIGURE 25.10
The User Configurator when listing groups.

2. Click the Add button at the bottom of the window. This will bring up the Edit Group Definition window similar to the one shown in Figure 25.11.

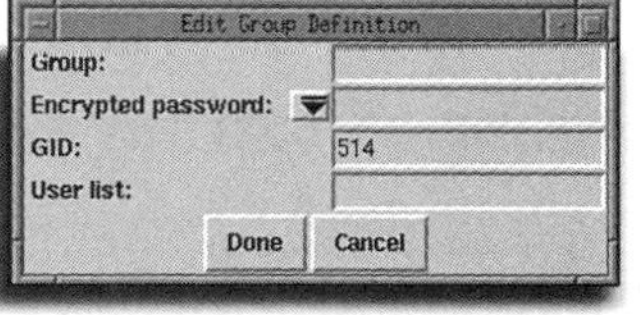

FIGURE 25.11
The Edit Group Definition dialog box.

3. Enter the name you want to call your new group. Like a login name, group names cannot be longer than eight characters and can only consist of letters and numbers.

Note: The next two steps are identical to the steps used to set the password when adding a user. The figures used to describe this process in the "Adding a User" section (Figures 25.4 and 25.5) apply here as well.

4. Click the down arrow button next to the password entry. Select the second option, Change.
5. Enter the password you want to assign the user and press Enter. The dialog box will then prompt you to verify the password by reentering it. (The system wants to be sure that you haven't made a typing mistake.) Enter the password again and press Enter. The first line of the dialog box will show the encrypted version of the string. Remember! Linux is case sensitive! You *must* enter the password exactly the same way both times, with the exact same mix of capital and lowercase letters!
6. Click the Done button to make that the password entry.
7. The GID entry will be prefilled in with the next available GID and can be left alone.
8. The user list is a comma-separated list of the users whom you want to be part of this group. For example, if the users sshah, heidi, and jnguyen are working on a new project, you could create a group for them and have each login listed as a member. When they use the `newgrp` command to switch into that group, they will not have to give a password to gain access.
9. After you have completed the form, click the Done button. The new group should appear in the User Configurator window.

Editing an Existing Group

To edit an existing group, do the following:

Editing groups

1. Click the Groups button at the top of the User Configurator window.
2. Click once on the group's entry to highlight it and then click the View/Edit button at the bottom of the User Configurator window.

3. Make the changes you want to the group's information. It should be noted that changing the value of the GID will cause confusion because files will need their group ownership reset. In general, the only changes you need to make to a group after it is created is to either add or delete users who are members of the group. Remember that the list of users who are members of a group must be comma separated.
4. Click Done to finalize changes.

Removing a Group

Removing a group is even simpler than removing a user.

Removing groups

1. Click the Groups button at the top of the User Configurator window.
2. Click the group you want removed.
3. Click the Remove button at the bottom of the User Configurator window. The group will be removed immediately.

Finishing Up with *usercfg*

Unless otherwise mentioned, the changes you make with the `usercfg` program will not take effect until you explicitly click the Save button at the bottom of the User Configurator window. After you have saved your changes, you can click Quit to exit the User Configurator.

Adding, Editing, and Deleting Users Using the Command Line

Unfortunately, it isn't always possible to use a graphical tool such as `usercfg` to manipulate users. In these instances, you should be familiar with the command-line versions of these tools called `useradd`, `usermod`, and `userdel` for adding, modifying, and deleting users, respectively.

Adding Users with *useradd*

To add a user with the useradd command, log in to the root account and enter the following command:

```
[root@insoc /root]# useradd -d homedir -s /bin/tcsh [ic]
                    -c "User's Real Name" newlogin
```

where *homedir* is the home directory of the user being created, *User's Real Name* is the real name of the user. (Be sure to have the user's name inside the double quotation marks.) And finally, *newlogin* is the login name of the user being added.

Study this example:

```
[root@insoc /root]# useradd -d /home/sshah -s /bin/tcsh [ic]
            -o "Steve Shah" sshah
```

See the `man` page regarding `useradd` for the complete details on all the options available.

Modifying Users with the *usermod* Command

The `usermod` command allows you to change all the parameters you set for a user when adding him or her to the system. Note that the user cannot be logged in when you are changing his or her login, UID, GID, or home directory because the system will get very confused.

To change a user's configuration information, log in as the root user and enter the following command:

```
[root@insoc]# usermod -c "New Name" -d homedir -m -g
➥groupname -s shell -l newlogin currentlogin
```

where *New Name* is the user's new real name (for example, if a user named Kurt Valaquen wanted to change his name to Kurt Harland), *homedir* is the new home directory for the user, *groupname* is the name of the default user group he will belong to, *shell* is the desired shell of the user, *newlogin* is the new login name the user wants, and finally *currentlogin* is the login name of the user you want to change.

For example, if a user wants to set his name to "Kurt Harland" with a home directory of `/home/vector`, a default group setting to ittf, using the shell /bin/bash and using the login name vector, you would use the following command:

```
[root@insoc /root]# usermod --o "Kurt Harland" --d /home/
➥vector --m --q ittf --s /bin/bash --l vector vector
```

See the man page regarding usermod for a list of all the available command-line options.

Deleting Users with the *userdel* Command

To remove a user from your system, use the userdel command. Note that the user must be logged out of the system before removing him. To use userdel, log in as the root user and enter the following command:

```
[root@insoc /root]# userdel --r login
```

where *login* is the login name of the user you want to remove.

For example, if you want to remove the user vector, you would use userdel as follows:

```
[root@insoc /root]# userdel --r vector
```

See the man page for userdel of a list of all the command-line options.

Adding, Editing, and Deleting Groups

Similar to the user commands, there are commands for controlling groups as well. They are

groupadd	Add groups
groupmod	Modify groups
groupdel	Delete groups

Adding Groups with the *groupadd* Command

The groupadd command allows you to add groups to the system from the command line. To do so, log in as the root user and enter the following command:

```
[root@insoc /root]# groupadd groupname
```

where *groupname* is the name of the group you want to add to the system.

What am I typing?

If the preceding command appears cryptic to you, don't worry. Its design was geared toward functionality over readability. Let's dissect the preceding command to see what it is doing.

The usermod portion simply specifies the command we are running. This program will interpret the remainder of the line.

The first thing that will be interpreted is the string -o "Kurt Harland". The -o tells the program that we want to change the comment field of the password entry to "Kurt Harland". Quotation marks are placed around his name so that the program doesn't get confused and think the string "Harland" is the next parameter.

Each of the parameters works in a similar way where strings that start with a dash character tell usermod that we want to change an aspect of the user's settings and the string that immediately follows is the desired value. The last parameter is the user's login, which is required for this command.

For example, to add the group www to your system, you would use the command:

```
[root@insoc /root]# groupadd www
```

See the man page regarding groupadd for a full list of all the command-line options available.

Modifying Groups with the *groupmod* Command

To modify the name of a group after it has been created, use the groupmod command. To make the change, log in as the root user and enter the following command:

```
[root@insoc /root]# groupmod --n newgroup currentgroup
```

where *newgroup* is the new name you want to give the group, and *currentgroup* is the current name of the group.

For example, to change a group name from admin to sysadmin, you would use the following command:

```
[root@insoc /root]# groupmod --n sysadmin admin
```

See the man page regarding groupmod for a full list of all the command-line options available.

Deleting Groups with the *groupdel* Command

To remove an existing group, use the groupdel command as described here. Log in as the root user and enter the following command:

```
[root@insoc /root]# groupdel groupname
```

where *groupname* is the group you want to delete. There is one catch, however. You cannot delete a group if it is the primary group of any users. You either need to remove the users or change their primary group using the usermod command first.

For example, to remove the group ittf, you would use the command:

```
[root@insoc /root]# groupdel ittf
```

Changing User and Group Ownership

Linux provides two programs to help you manage user and group ownership from the command line. The first, `gpasswd`, allows you to administer a group with relative ease. `chgrp`, the second program, allows users to change the group of particular files.

Managing Groups with *gpasswd*

To add users to an existing group, log in as the root user and enter the following command:

```
[root@insoc /root]# gpasswd -a loginname groupname
```

where *loginname* is the login name of the user you want to add to the group *groupname*.

For example, to add the user vector to the group ittf, you would use the command:

```
[root@insoc /root]# gpasswd -a vector ittf
```

To remove a user from an existing group, log in as the root user and enter the following command:

```
[root@insoc /root]# gpasswd -d loginname groupname
```

where *loginname* is the login that you want to remove from the group *groupname*.

For example, if you wanted to remove the user yoko from the group beatles, you would use the command:

```
[root@insoc /root]# gpasswd -d yoko beatles
```

For a full list of command-line options available for the `gpasswd` command, see the related `man` page.

Using the *chgrp* Command

To change the group of a file, use the `chgrp` command. Log in as the root user and enter the following command:

```
[root@insoc /root]# chgrp groupname filename
```

where *groupname* is the name of the group you want to change the file's group setting to, and *filename* is the name of the file for which you want the group changed.

For example, if you wanted to change the group for the file index.html to www, you would use chgrp as follows:

```
[root@insoc /root]# chgrp www index.html
```

To change the group of a directory and all its subdirectories and files, you can use the chgrp command with the -R option. For example, to change the group on all the files in the htdocs directory to www, you would use:

```
[root@insoc /root]# chgrp -R www htdocs
```

Changing File Ownership and Permissions

Two programs in the command-line arsenal help change file ownership and permissions. chown, or Change Ownership, lets you change a file (or group of files) to another owner. chmod lets you change the access permissions to individual files.

Using the *chown* Command

To change the owner of a file, you use the chown command. Log in as the root user and enter the following command:

```
[root@insoc /root]# chown ownername filename
```

where *ownername* is the login name of the user you want to change the file's owner setting to, and *filename* is the name of the file for which you want the owner changed.

For example, if you wanted to change the owner for the file index.html to sshah, you would use chown as follows:

```
[root@insoc /root]# chown sshah index.html
```

To change the owner of a directory and all its subdirectories and files, you can use the chown command with the -R option. For example, to change the owner on all the files in the htdocs directory to sshah, you would use:

```
[root@insoc /root]# chown -R sshah htdocs
```

Using the *chmod* Command

Before we can explain the usage of the chmod command, you need to first understand file permissions.

In Linux, every file and directory has three sets of access permissions: those applied to the owner of the file, those applied to the group the file has, and those of all users in the system. You can see these permissions when you do an `ls -lg`. For example:

```
drwxr-xr-x    2 sshah     sysadmin      1024 Feb 14 15:49
➥wedding_plans
-rw-------    1 sshah     sysadmin      2465 Feb  5 19:22
➥index.html
```

The first column of the listing is the permissions of the file. The first character represents the type of file (ëd' means directory, ël' means symbolic link, and so on), and the next nine characters are the permissions. The first three characters represent the permissions held by the file's owner, the second three are for the group the file is in, and the last three represent the world permissions.

The following letters are used to represent permissions:

Letter	Meaning
r	Read
w	Write
x	Execute

Each permission has a corresponding value. The read attribute is equal to 4, the write attribute is equal to 2, and the execute attribute is equal to 1. When you combine attributes, you add their values. See the following examples.

The most common groups of three and their meanings are:

Permission	Values	Meaning
---	0	No permissions
r--	4	Read only
rw-	6	Read and write
rwx	7	Read, write, and execute
r-x	5	Read and execute
--x	1	Execute only

Although other combinations do exist (for example: -wx), they are nonsensical, and the likelihood you'll ever run across them is almost nil.

When you combine these values, you get three numbers that make up the file's permission. Common permission combinations are:

Permission	Value	Meaning
-rw-------	600	The owner has read and write permissions. This is what you want set on most of your files.
-rw-r--r--	644	The owner has read and write permissions. The group and world has read only permissions. Be sure you want to let other people read this file.
-rw-rw-rw-	666	Everybody has read and write permissions on a file. This is bad. You don't want other people to be able to change your files.
-rwx------	700	The owner has read, write, and execute permissions. This is what you want for programs that you wish to run.
-rwxr-xr-x	755	The owner has read, write, and execute permissions. The rest of the world has read and execute permissions.
-rwxrwxrwx	777	Everyone has read, write, and execute privileges. Like the 666 setting, this is bad. Allowing others to edit your files is a cookbook formula for disaster.
-rwx--x--x	711	The owner has read, write, and execute privileges. The rest of the world has execute only permissions. This is useful for programs that you want to let others run, but not copy.

drwx------	700	This is a directory created with the `mkdir` command. Only the owner can read and write into this directory. Note that all the directories must have the executable bit set.
drwxr-xr-x	755	This directory can be changed only by the owner, but everyone else can view its contents.
drwx--x--x	711	A handy trick to use when you need to keep a directory world readable, but you don't want people to be able to see a directory listing via the ls command. Only if the person knows the filename they wish to retrieve will they be allowed to read it.

Now that you're fluent with permissions, learning `chmod` is easy. To change the permissions on a file, log in as the root user and enter the following command:

```
[root@insoc /root]# chmod permissions file
```

where *`permissions`* is a numeric value (three digits), which we discussed above, and *`file`* is the name of the file for which you want this to affect.

For example, to set the `index.html` file to be changeable by the owner, but only readable by the file's group and the world, the command would be:

```
[root@insoc /root]# chmod 644 index.html
```

To recursively change the permissions on all the files in a specific directory, use the `-R` option in `chmod`. For example, to make all the files in `/usr/bin` set to the permissions 755, you would use:

```
[root@insoc /root]# chmod -R 755 /usr/bin
```

Advanced Concepts: Password Authentication Module

The Password Authentication Module (PAM) is for those who want to modify the security model that comes with Red Hat. By

What are SetUID programs?

SetUID is a special permission applied to programs. Remember how everything in Linux has an owner? This concept of ownership applies to programs in execution (processes) as well. Each process is owned by the person who invoked it. For example, if you log in as yourself, start the program `xtetris`, and then list the running processes using the `ps` command, you'll see that you are the owner of the `xtetris` process. But if you do a directory listing on the `xtetris` program using `ls -l`, you'll see that the file itself is owned by the root user.

Under normal circumstances, this is good. You want to make programs available to your users to run without giving away the privilege to change them. However, you occasionally run across a need for the program to run not as the user who invokes it, but as the user the file is owned by. The `ping` command is a common instance of this. For `ping` to work, it must be run as the root user. To allow normal users of the system to use `ping`, you can make it SetUID.

To make a file SetUID, prefix the permissions with the number 4. For example:

```
[root@insoc /root]# chmod 4755 /bin/ping
```

default, the model is reasonably strict about who may enter the system and in most instances, does not need to be adjusted. Like the password and group configuration files, though, understanding this subsystem will better prepare you for troubleshooting problems.

Improving System Security Using PAM

In an effort to separate authentication techniques from applications, the Linux development community took hints from the Solaris operating system and created its own implementation of PAM, Pluggable Authentication Modules. By separating the method of authentication from applications, it is possible for system administrators to implement their own authentication techniques and have application software automatically use them.

This section explains the key components of the PAM system, its installation, configuration file, and some modules that come with Red Hat Linux.

Installing PAM

If you chose a standard installation procedure with Red Hat Linux, you probably have PAM already installed. If you don't have it installed, don't worry, it's very straightforward.

Begin by acquiring the RPM package for PAM. This should be on the distribution you installed with. If not, you can always download it from Red Hat's Web site at `http://www.redhat.com`. Our distribution for this section is version 0.57 with configuration file version 0.51. We would use the following commands to install the RPMs:

```
[root@insoc /root]# rpm -i pam-0.57-2.i386.rpm
[root@insoc /root]# rpm -i pamconfig-0.51-2.i386.rpm
```

If you already had the packages installed, `rpm` should have told you. If they are older versions, be sure to specify the `-U` option with `rpm` so that it will upgrade.

The PAM Configuration Files

As of version 0.56, PAM prefers to use the directory-based approach for managing its configuration files. These files are located in the /etc/pam.d directory, and each filename represents a particular service. For example, ftpd and login are considered services.

Each file consists of lines in the following format:

```
module_type     control_flag     module_path     arguments
```

where *module type* represents one of four types of modules, auth, account, session, or password. Comments must begin with the hash (#) character.

auth — Instructs the application program to prompt the user for a password and then grants not only user privileges but group privileges too.

account — Performs no authentication, but determines access based on other factors, such as time of day or location of the user. For example, the root login can be given only console access this way.

session — Specifies what, if any, actions need to be performed before or after a user is logged in—for example, logging the connection.

password — Specifies the module that allows users to change their password (if appropriate).

control_flag — Allows you to specify how you want to deal with the success or failure of a particular authentication module.

required — The module must succeed in authenticating the individual. If it fails, the returned summary value must be failure.

requisite — Similar to required; however, if this module fails authentication, modules listed after this one in the configuration file are not called, and a failure is immediately returned to the application. This allows you to require that certain conditions hold true before even accepting a login attempt. (For example, the user must be on the local area network and cannot come in from over the Internet.)

sufficient — If the module returns a success and there are no more required or sufficient control_flags in the

SetGID

SetGID works similarly to SetUID. Programs that are SetGID are executed with the permissions of the group that owns the program rather than the group of the user. You can set a file to be SetGID by prefixing the permissions with the number 2. For example:

```
[root@insoc /root]#
chmod 2755
/usr/local/backups/
backup_level_0
```

When listing a file with the ls -l command, you can visually see whether a file is SetUID or SetGID. SetUID files have an ës' where the first ëx' should be, and setGID files have an ës' where the second ëx' should be.

	configuration file, PAM returns a success to the calling application.
`optional`	This flag allows PAM to continue checking other modules even if this one has failed. You will want to use this when the user is allowed to log in even if a particular module has failed.

The *`module_path`* specifies the actual directory path of the module that performs the authentication task. For a full list of modules that came with PAM, check out the file `/usr/doc/pam-0.59/html/pam-6.html` using your favorite web browser. Text versions of the document are also available in the `/usr/doc/pam-0.59` directory.

`arguments` are the parameters passed to the authentication module. Although the parameters are specific to each module, some generic options can be applied to all modules. They are

`debug`	Send debugging information to the system logs. (Usually located at `/var/log`—check `/etc/syslog.conf` for details.)
`no_warn`	Do not give warning messages to the calling application.
`use_first_pass`	Do not prompt the user for a password a second time. Instead, use the password entered the first time to determine the user's eligibility to enter the system.
`try_first_pass`	Similar to `use_first_pass` where the user is not prompted for a password the second time; however, if the existing password causes a failure to be returned from the module, the user is then asked to enter a second password.
`use_mapped_pass`	Passes the password from a previous module into the current one much like `use_first_pass`; however, the password is then used to generate an encryption or decryption key.

Cryptography by law

Due to the cryptography laws of the United States, this module is currently not supported by any of the modules in the Linux-PAM distribution. (The U.S. Government considers cryptography a type of munitions, which cannot be exported.)

One special feature of PAM is its "stackable" nature. That is, every line in the configuration file is evaluated during the authentication process (with the exceptions shown later). Each line specifies a module that performs some authentication task and returns either a success or failure flag. A summary of the results is returned to the application program calling PAM.

Let's examine a sample PAM configuration file, /etc/pam.d/login.

```
#%PAM-1.0
auth        required    /lib/security/pam_securetty.so
auth        required    /lib/security/pam_pwdb.so shadow
➥nullok
auth        required    /lib/security/pam_nologin.so
account     required    /lib/security/pam_pwdb.so
password    required    /lib/security/pam_cracklib.so
password    required    /lib/security/pam_pwdb.so shadow
➥nullok use_authtok
session     required    /lib/security/pam_pwdb.so
```

You can see that the first line begins with a hash symbol and is therefore a comment. You can ignore it.

Now go through the rest of the file line by line:

```
auth        required    /lib/security/pam_securetty.so
```

specifies that the `module_type` is `auth`, which means it will want a password. The `control_flag` is set to `required`, so this module must return a success or the login will fail. The module itself is the `pam_securetty.so` module, which verifies that logins on the root account can only happen on the terminals mentioned in the `/etc/securetty` file.

```
auth        required    /lib/security/pam_pwdb.so shadow
➥nullok
```

Similar to the previous line, this line wants to use a password for authentication, and if the password fails, the authentication process will return a failure flag to the calling application. The `pam_pwdb.so` module behavior is based on the `module_type`. In this case, the `auth` type allows `pam_pwdb.so` to do basic password checking against the `/etc/passwd` file. The shadow parameter tells it to check the `/etc/shadow` file if it is there, and the `nullok` parameter tells the module to allow users to change their password from an empty one to something. (Normally, it treats empty passwords as an account locking mechanism.)

```
auth        required    /lib/security/pam_nologin.so
```

The pam_nologin.so module checks for the /etc/nologin file. If it is present, only root is allowed to log in, and others are turned away with an error message. If the file does not exist, it always returns a success.

```
account     required    /lib/security/pam_pwdb.so
```

Because the module_type is account, the pam_pwdb.so module will silently check that the user is even allowed to log in (for example, has his password expired?). If all the parameters check out okay, it will return a success.

```
password    required    /lib/security/pam_cracklib.so
```

The password module_type account means that we will be using the pam_cracklib.so module during a password change. The pam_cracklib.so module performs a variety of checks to see whether a password is "too easy" to crack by potential intruders.

```
password    required    /lib/security/pam_pwdb.so shadow
➥nullok use_authtok
```

This is another example of the versatility of the pam_pwdb.so module. With the module_type set to password, it will perform the actual updating of the /etc/passwd file. The shadow parameters tell it to check for the existence of the /etc/shadow file and update that file if it does exist. nullok allows users to change their passwords from empty entries to real passwords. The last option, use_authtok, forces pam_pwdb.so to use the password retrieved from a previous module_type entry of password.

```
session     required    /lib/security/pam_pwdb.so
```

This is the fourth and final usage of the pam_pwdb.so module. This time it sends login successes and failures to the system logs because the module_type is set to session.

The *other* File

What happens when you need to authenticate someone for a service, but you don't have a PAM configuration file for him? Simple. Use the /etc/pam.d/other configuration file—a sort of catch-all type of setup.

In this situation, if a user tries to authenticate himself using a PAM-aware application (for example, the FTP server) but the configuration file for it is not there (in the case of the FTP server, the `/etc/pam.d/ftp` file got accidentally removed), PAM will default to using the configuration file `/etc/pam.d/other`.

By default, the other configuration file is set to a paranoid setting so that all authentication attempts are logged and then promptly denied. It is recommended that you keep it that way.

Oh No! I Can't Log In!

In the immortal words of Douglas Adams, "don't panic." Like many other configuration errors that can occur under Linux, this one can be fixed by either booting into single user mode or booting off a floppy. (See Chapter 24, "Using LILO and LOADLIN," for details on booting into single user mode.)

After you are back into the system in single user mode, simply edit the `/etc/pam.d/login` file so that it contains only the following lines:

```
auth          required     /lib/security/pam_unix_auth.so
account          required     /lib/security/pam_unix_acct.so
password      required     /lib/security/pam_unix_passwd.so
session          required     /lib/security/pam_unix_session.so
```

This simplified login configuration will stick to the original UNIX authentication method, which should hopefully work well enough to get you back into the system in multiuser mode.

After you are back in multiuser mode, be sure to go back and fix the login configuration file to reflect what you really wanted to do instead of what it did—lock you out!

Debugging/Auditing

While you are debugging the PAM configuration files, be sure to keep an eye on the system log files. (Usually in `/var/log`.) Most of the error logging will occur there.

When you have things working the way you like, be sure to check those files for auditing information from PAM. It reports not only authentication successes but failures as well. Multiple failures for a particular person or for a range of people in a short time could indicate trouble.

CHAPTER

26

Managing Scheduling Services

By David Pitts

Configuring `inittab` and `rc` files

Configuring `crontab` scheduling service

Configuring the at command service

Scheduling resources is a management process. Whether you are scheduling a workforce, a tournament, or class load, you are required to look at each piece from the perspective of the whole. For example, it is good to take English and math in high school, but it is not good to schedule them both at 9:00 in the morning. Part of scheduling, then, is making sure that there are enough resources for all the work. There is only one you, and you can be in only one class at a time.

Scheduling a computer's resources is also a management process. Certain processes, by their very nature, use more of the computer's resources than other processes. Some require dedicated time or dedicated access, whereas other processes manage regardless. As the system administrator, it is your job to manage all the processes so that maximum efficiency is achieved, and so that the users can get their work done with as little interruption as possible. Fortunately, there are tools that allow you to manage your resources, and even start and stop processes when you are not around. Scheduling services are broken down into three areas:

- Processes that run all the time (or once, but always at startup)
- Processes that run repeatedly, at a specific time or on a specific day
- Processes that run only occasionally

For processes that run all the time, you have two tools: `inittab` and the `rc` files. For processes that run repeatedly, at a specific time or on a specific date, you have the `crontab` tool. For processes that need to be run only occasionally, you have the `at` tool.

Configuring *inittab* and *rc* Files

Before discussing the ins and outs of `inittab` and `rc` files, a brief discussion is needed on `init`, the parent process of `inittab`. When `init` is kicked off, it reads the file `/etc/inittab`, which tells `init` what to do. Usually, it tells `init` to allow user logons (`gettys`), and controls autonomous processes and other "at boot time" processes.

The `init` process can run at one of 15 levels. The run level is changed by having a privileged user (root) run `/sbin/telinit`, which sends appropriate signals to `init`, telling it which run level to change to.

After it has spawned all its processes, `init` waits for one of its child processes to die, for a power fail signal, or for a signal from `/sbin/telinit` to change the system's run level. When one of these changes occurs, the `/etc/inittab` file is reexamined. Although new entries can be added to this file at any time, `init` does not read them until one of these three events occurs.

The *inittab* File

Understanding the contents of the `inittab` file

Lines beginning with a pound sign (#) are comments, and are ignored. Any other lines define processes to be run.

The `inittab` file, which tells `init` what to do, is a list of colon-delimited entries that use the following format:

`id:runlevels:action:process`

Table 26.1 examines and describes each of these entries.

TABLE 26.1 The makeup of each line in the *inittab* file

Entry	Description
`id`	Identifies a unique sequence of 1–4 characters, which identifies an entry.
`runlevel`	Describes at which run level this action should occur.
`action`	Dictates which action is to be taken.
`process`	Specifies the process to be executed. If the process field starts with a `+`, `init` does not do `utmp` and `wtmp` accounting for that process.

`action` and *`process`* are easily confused. The action is what `init` does, not what the process does. There are 14 possible actions, as illustrated in Table 26.2.

TABLE 26.2 Possible actions *init* can take

Action	Description
`respawn`	`init` restarts the process whenever the process terminates.

continues...

TABLE 26.2 Continued

Action	Description
`wait`	`init` starts this process, and waits for it to complete before continuing to the next process.
`once`	`init` starts this process and moves on. If/when this process terminates, it is not restarted.
`boot`	This process runs during system boot. The *`runlevel`* field is ignored.
`bootwait`	`init` starts this process at system boot, and waits for it to complete before continuing. The *`runlevel`* field is ignored.
`off`	This does not run.
`ondemand`	This process is run whenever the specified `ondemand` run level is called. No actual run level change occurs. `ondemand` run levels are a, b, and c.
`initdefault`	This entry specifies the run level that should be entered after system boot. If none exists, `init` asks for a run level on the console. The *`process`* field is ignored. The default value is 3.
`sysinit`	This process is executed during system boot, and before any `boot` or `bootwait` entries. The *`runlevel`* field is ignored.
`powerwait`	This process is executed when `init` receives the `SIGPWR` signal, indicating that there is something wrong with power. `init` waits for the process to finish before continuing.
`powerfail`	This process is executed when `init` receives the `SIGPWR` signal, indicating that there is something wrong with power. `init` does not wait for the process to finish before continuing.
`powerokwait`	`init` executes this command when it receives the `SIGPWR` signal, provided that there is a file called `/etc/powerstatus` containing the word OK. This indicates that the power has come back on again.
`ctrlaltdel`	`init` executes this process when it receives the `SIGINT` signal. This means that someone on the system console has pressed the Ctrl+Alt+Del key combination. Typically, this is either a shutdown command or a boot to single-user mode.
`kbrequest`	This is one of the newer actions. When `init` receives a signal from the keyboard handler that a special key combination was pressed on the console keyboard, then this command is executed. See documentation found in the `kbd-x.xx` package for more information.

Listing 26.1 shows an example `inittab` file from a machine running Red Hat Linux 5.0.

LISTING 26.1 A sample *inittab* file from a system running Red Hat Linux 5.0

```
#
# inittab       This file describes how the INIT process should set up
#               the system in a certain run-level.
#
# Author:       Miquel van Smoorenburg, <miquels@drinkel.nl.mugnet.org>
#               Modified for RHS Linux by Marc Ewing and Donnie Barnes
#

# Default run level. The run levels used by RHS are:
#   0 - halt (Do NOT set initdefault to this)
#   1 - Single user mode
#   2 - Multiuser, without NFS (The same as 3, if you do not have
➥networking)
#   3 - Full multiuser mode
#   4 - unused
#   5 - X11
#   6 - reboot (Do NOT set initdefault to this)
#
id:3:initdefault:

# System initialization.
si::sysinit:/etc/rc.d/rc.sysinit

l0:0:wait:/etc/rc.d/rc 0
l1:1:wait:/etc/rc.d/rc 1
l2:2:wait:/etc/rc.d/rc 2
l3:3:wait:/etc/rc.d/rc 3
l4:4:wait:/etc/rc.d/rc 4
l5:5:wait:/etc/rc.d/rc 5
l6:6:wait:/etc/rc.d/rc 6

# Things to run in every run level.
ud::once:/sbin/update

# Trap CTRL-ALT-DELETE
ca::ctrlaltdel:/sbin/shutdown -t3 -r now

# When our UPS tells us power has failed, assume we have a few minutes
```

continues...

LISTING 26.1 Continued

```
# of power left.  Schedule a shutdown for 2 minutes from now.
# This does, of course, assume you have powerd installed and your
# UPS connected and working correctly.
pf::powerfail:/sbin/shutdown -f -h +2 "Power Failure; System Shutting
   ➥Down"
# If power was restored before the shutdown kicked in, cancel it.
pr:12345:powerokwait:/sbin/shutdown -c "Power Restored; Shutdown
   ➥Cancelled"


# Run gettys in standard run levels
1:12345:respawn:/sbin/mingetty tty1
2:2345:respawn:/sbin/mingetty tty2
3:2345:respawn:/sbin/mingetty tty3
4:2345:respawn:/sbin/mingetty tty4
5:2345:respawn:/sbin/mingetty tty5
6:2345:respawn:/sbin/mingetty tty6

# Run xdm in run level 5
x:5:respawn:/usr/bin/X11/xdm -nodaemon
```

A number of the lines should now be familiar. It is good to point out that the `id` of each of these entries corresponds with the entry itself (for example, `pf` = power fail). This is a good habit to get into. Also, from the `lilo` line, you can specify a level by entering the following (in which `#` is the runtime level you want to use):

```
linux #
```

The *rc* Files

This section focuses particular attention on the lines in the `inittab` file that call the `rc` files (refer to Listing 26.1):

```
l0:0:wait:/etc/rc.d/rc 0
l1:1:wait:/etc/rc.d/rc 1
l2:2:wait:/etc/rc.d/rc 2
l3:3:wait:/etc/rc.d/rc 3
l4:4:wait:/etc/rc.d/rc 4
l5:5:wait:/etc/rc.d/rc 5
l6:6:wait:/etc/rc.d/rc 6
```

What is actually being called is the `/etc/rc.d/rc` file. This file is receiving an argument for the run level. At the end of this file, the following commands are called:

```
# Now run the START scripts.
for i in /etc/rc.d/rc$run level.d/S*; do
# Check if the script is there.
[ ! -f $i ] && continue
# Check if the subsystem is already up.
subsys=${i#/etc/rc.d/rc$run level.d/S??}
[ -f /var/lock/subsys/$subsys ] && \
[ -f /var/lock/subsys/${subsys}.init ] && continue
# Bring the subsystem up.
$i start
done
```

This loop is checking for a directory associated with that particular run level. If the directory exists, each process in that directory is initiated. After all other `rc` files are run, `/etc/rc.d/rc.local` is initiated. This is the best place to put your changes to the system. Note that this file overwrites the `/etc/issue` file at every bootup. So if you want to make changes to the banner that is displayed at logon, make your changes in the `rc.local` file rather than in the `/etc/issue` file.

With `inittab` and `rc` files, you have an excellent set of tools for starting processes at boot time, capturing keystroke events (such as Alt+Ctrl+Delete), and reacting in a proactive manner.

Configuring *crontab* Scheduling Service

Certain processes must be run at a specific time, over and over again. An example of this might be a backup process that is kicked off each night, or a log analyzer that must be run every minute. These processes are run at specific times or on specific days; the rest of the time, they are not running.

`cron` is started from either `rc` or `rc.local` and returns immediately, so there is no need to background this command. `cron` searches `/var/spool/cron` for entries that match users in the `/etc/passwd` file; found entries are loaded into memory. `cron` also searches `/etc/crontab` for system entries.

cron "wakes up" once a minute and does several things:

- It checks the entries that it knows about and runs any commands that are scheduled to run.
- It determines whether the modtime on the cron directory has changed.
- If the modtime on the cron directory has changed, cron checks each of the files and reloads any that have changed.

Do I need to restart cron after a change?

Since cron checks for changes every minute, it is unnecessary to restart cron when the cron files are changed.

Enabling *crontab* Service

It is crontab's job to schedule these services. The cron daemon reads the crontab file; each user can have his or her own version of this file. Flags associated with the crontab application specify whether to open crontab for listing, editing, or removal.

The syntax for the crontab program is as follows:

```
crontab [-u user] file
crontab [-u user] -l -e -r
```

These parameters indicate the following:

- The -u option tells the system the name of the user whose crontab file is about to be used. If the -u option is omitted, the system assumes that you are editing your crontab. The switch user (su) command can confuse crontab, so if you are su'ing to someone else, be sure to use the -u option.
- The -l option tells crontab to list the file to standard output (in other words, to list the file).
- The -e option tells crontab to edit the file. cron uses the editor defined by EDITOR or by VISUAL. If neither is defined, it defaults to vi. When the file is exited, it is immediately placed in the correct location and the time stamp is updated.
- The -r option removes the specified crontab file. If no file is specified, it removes that user's crontab file.

crontab Entries

Two types of entries are allowed in the crontab file:

- Environment settings

- Command settings

These entries are discussed in the following sections.

Environment Settings

Environment settings use the following form:

```
name = value
```

`cron` already knows about several environment settings. For example, `SHELL` is set to `/bin/sh`. Other environment variables, such as `LOGNAME` and `HOME`, are associated with the owner of the file. `SHELL` and `HOME` can be overridden in the script; `LOGNAME` cannot. If `MAILTO` is defined (that is, `MAILTO` actually appears in a line in the `crontab` file and is not set to `""`), it mails any messages to the specified user. The following shows `MAILTO` set to a specific user:

```
# mail any output to 'paulc', no matter whose crontab this
➥is MAILTO=paulc
```

Command Settings

Command settings use a standard format: Each line starts with five time/date fields. If this is the system `crontab`, the next field is the username associated with the entry. Following this entry is the command to be executed. The command is executed only when the current date and time meet all five of the time/date field criteria.

Table 26.3 shows the available time/date fields and the ranges of values for each field. A time/date field can contain an asterisk instead of a number or a name; an asterisk indicates that any valid value should be matched.

Field	Allowable Values
minute	`0–59`
hour	`0–23`
day	`0–31`
month	`0–12` (alternatively, three-letter, not case sensitive abbreviations of names can
be	used)

continues...

Using ranges to specify starting times

Ranges can be specified through the use of a hyphen. A value of `1-5` indicates that this field is valid for numbers `1` through `5`. If you use a name instead of a number, you cannot specify a range.

Using step values to specify starting times

Step values can be used in conjunction with ranges. To specify a step value, follow the range with a forward slash (`/`) and a number. The number specified is the step value. For example, the following specifies that every third value (in this case, `2`, `5`, `8`, and `11`) should be matched:

```
0-12/3
```

Step values can also be used with asterisks. The value `*/3` in the hour field would match every third hour (`0`, `3`, `6`, `9`, `12`, `15`, `18`, and `21`).

Using lists to specify starting times

Lists are also acceptable; each item in a list is separated by a comma. It is common to use lists in conjunction with ranges, like so:

```
1-15,31-45
```

This example matches all numbers from 1 through 15 and from 31 through 45. If you use a name instead of a number, you cannot specify a list.

...continued

Field	Allowable Values
day of the week	`0`–`7` (with `0` and `7` being Sunday; alternatively, three-letter, not case sensitive abbreviations of names can be used)

Listing 26.2 shows the default `/etc/crontab` that comes with Red Hat Linux version 5.0.

LISTING 26.2 An example of a *crontab* file

```
SHELL=/bin/bash
PATH=/sbin:/bin:/usr/sbin:/usr/bin
MAILTO=root
# run-parts
01 * * * * root run-parts /etc/cron.hourly
02 1 * * * root run-parts /etc/cron.daily
02 2 * * 0 root run-parts /etc/cron.weekly
02 3 1 * * root run-parts /etc/cron.monthly
```

Notice that this `crontab` actually calls four different `crontabs`:

- One associated with hourly events
- One associated with daily events
- One associated with weekly events
- One associated with monthly events

If you are using a system that switches between Linux and another operating system, such as Windows 95, you might want to kick off some of these `cron` jobs yourself (if, for example, their scheduled time lapsed while you were in another operating system). Remember: The system does not go back and "pick up" `cron` jobs; it executes them only if the current date/time matches the entry.

Allowing and Preventing Access to the *crontab* Service

Two files enable root to allow or deny `crontab` service to users:

- `/etc/cron.allow`—This file does not exist by default; you must create it. Any entries you place in this file override entries placed in /etc/cron.deny. If the /etc/cron.allow file exists, only those users specified in that file can use the crontab service.

- /etc/cron.deny—This file exists by default. In it, you enter the usernames of users who are not allowed to use the crontab service.

It is important that only root be allowed to edit or add these files to the system.

If a user attempts to use cron (crontab -e), but his or her user name has been placed in the /etc/cron.deny file, the following error occurs:n

```
You (account name) are not allowed to use this program
➥(crontab).
See crontab(1) for more information.
```

Specifying a day

The day that a command runs is specified by two fields; day of the week and day. The command runs if either of these is true. For example, the following entry specifies that the command be executed at 5:00 p.m. on the 1st and 15th of the month, and on every Friday:

```
0 17 1,15 *, 5
```

Configuring the *at* Command Service

crontab is great for processes that must be run on a regular schedule, but is a poor tool for something you want to run only once. The at tool enables you to specify a command to run at a certain time; the time can be the current time or it can be a specified time in the future.

To go along with the at command is the batch command, which executes commands when system load levels permit—that is, when the load average (measured by /proc/loadavg) drops below 1.5 or some other value specified at the invocation of atrun.

Enabling *at* Command Service

The at command service (as well as the batch command service) reads commands from standard input or a specified file that is to be executed at a later time via /bin/sh. The syntax for the at command is as follows:

```
at [-V] [-q queue] [-f file] [-mldbv] TIME
at -c job [job...]
atq [-V] [-q queue] [-v]
atrm [-V] job [job...]
batch [-V] [-q queue] [-f file] [-mv] [TIME]
```

Table 26.4 briefly describes what each command does.

TABLE 26.4 **The *at* commands**

Command	Description
at	Executes commands at a specified time
atq	Lists the user's pending jobs (unless the user is the superuser, in which case it lists everyone's pending jobs)
atrm	Removes at jobs
batch	Executes commands when system load levels permit

Options for the at command include the following:

- -b An alias for batch.
- -c Shows jobs listed on the command line to standard output (the monitor).
- -d An alias for atrm.
- -f Reads the job from a file rather than standard input.
- -l An alias for at.
- -m Mails the user when the job is complete. This sends mail to the user specified (even if there is no output).
- -q Uses a specified queue. A queue designation consists of a single letter, with c being the default for at, and E for batch. Valid designations are a..z and A..Z. Queues with letters closer to Z (A is closer to Z than z is) run with increased performance. If a job is submitted to a queue with an uppercase designation, the job is treated as a batch job. If atq is given a specific value, it shows jobs pending for only the specified queue.
- -v Shows jobs that are complete, but not yet deleted.
- -V Prints the version number to standard output.

Common Problems with the *at* Command

Several people have had problems with at jobs, some to the point where they would prefer to make the job a cron job, and then go back after the fact and remove the cron job.

Most of the problems with `at` jobs are in defining them. A straight `at` job is simple enough if you are calling a single word for a command, but it can easily get confusing. For example, I tried to run the following simple at job:

```
at now + 2 minutes touch ~/touch_file
```

When I pressed Enter, I got an error with the time:

```
parse error.  Last token seen: touch
Garbled Time.
```

Using the `echo` command, you can turn this at job around, and thus avoid the problems with "garbled time." Following is the same command, except I have turned it around with an `echo` command:

```
echo touch ~/touch_file ¦ at now + 2 minutes
```

Sure enough, this one worked without a problem, and two minutes later my file in my home directory (`touch_file`) had its access date set to the current time.

The same problem occurs when you try to configure a `shutdown` command to run at a specific time:

```
echo shutdown -fr now ¦ at now + 4 hours
```

This shuts down the system exactly four hours after this `at` job is initiated.

`at` jobs can accept the standard `hh:mm` time, but if the specified time has already passed, the system assumes that you mean that time tomorrow. You can use some common words with `at` jobs to specify time, including `NOON`, `MIDNIGHT`, `TEATIME` (4:00 p.m.), `TODAY`, `TOMORROW`, and `NOW`. The use of `am` and `pm` is also allowed. Days in the future can also be specified, and months can be designated with their three-letter abbreviations. For example, if you wanted to execute something at 4 a.m. two days from now, the command would look like this:

```
at 4am + 2 days
```

To run a job at noon on my birthday (November 25th), you would use the following:

```
at noon Nov 25
```

Determining who can use the `at` command

Root can always use the `at` command. All others depend upon the `at.allow` and the `at.deny` files.

Finally, to shut down the system at 1 a.m. tomorrow, you would use the following:

```
echo shutdown -fr now ¦ at 1am tomorrow
```

Allowing and Preventing Access to the *at* Command Service

By default, an empty `/etc/at.deny` file exists. Because it is empty, every user is allowed to use the `at` command. If there are usernames (as defined in the `/etc/passwd` file) in this file, then those users are *not* allowed to use the `at` command.

By default, `/etc/at.allow` does not exist. If it does exist, only users whose usernames are entered in this file can use the `at` command. This means that `/etc/at.allow` has precedence over `/etc/at.deny`. If both exist, only the `/etc/at.allow` file is checked, and only those entries are allowed to use the `at` command. If neither file exists, then only root can run `at` commands.

If a user attempts to run the `at` command, but his or her user name appears in the `/etc/at.deny` file (or an `/etc/at.allow` file exists and his or her username is not one of the entries), the following error occurs:

```
You do not have permission to use at.
```

CHAPTER

27

Managing Network Connections

By Sriranga Veeraraghaven

Setting the hostname

Enabling the loopback interface

Adding a PPP interface

Adding a SLIP interface

Adding a PLIP interface

Adding an ethernet interface

Configuring Network Connections

Managing network connections with Red Hat Linux is straightforward, thanks to the user-friendly Network Configuration tool `netcfg`. This tool provides for the enabling and configuring of network connections in a graphical interface.

Using the Network Configuration Tool

To launch `netcfg`, type the following at root's prompt:

```
# netcfg
```

Run `netcfg` as root

It is important that root run `netcfg`; otherwise, the modifications made to the network will not be applied.

When `netcfg` launches, the following is displayed in the terminal window:

```
Red Hat Linux netcfg 2.13
Copyright (C) 1996 Red Hat Software
Redistributable under the terms of the GNU General Public
➥License
```

After the program finishes loading, the Network Configurator window (shown in Figure 27.1) is displayed.

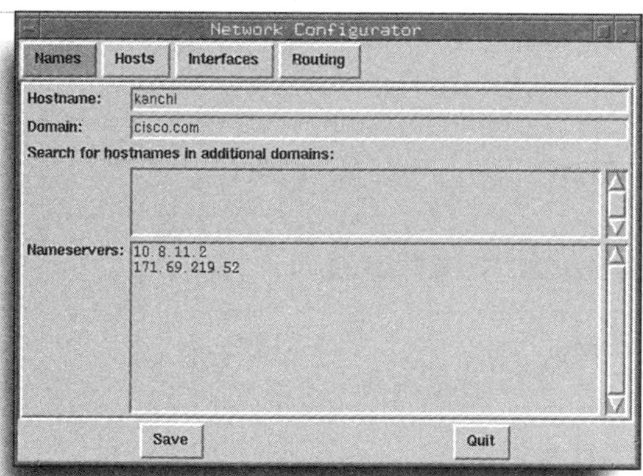

FIGURE 27.1
This screen shows the main netcfg window.

Setting the Hostname and the Domain Name

When `netcfg` is running, setting a machine's hostname is simple. Just click in the Hostname text field and type the name you want to give the machine. To save the hostname, click the **Save** button.

To set the domain name, click in the Domain text field and type your domain. To save the domain name, click the **Save** button.

In addition to setting the hostname and the domain name, the main window enables you to set the name servers that the local machine uses to translate hostnames into IP addresses. To add a name server, click in the Nameservers text area and type the IP address of your name server (this address should be given to you by your ISP or company).

Set the hostname and domain name correctly

For most people, hostnames and domain names are provided by their Internet service provider or their school/business. In such cases, it is important that the name entered in the Hostname and the Domain field is the same as the name provided by the ISP or other entity.

Enabling the Loopback Interface

The loopback interface is used by the computer to make connections to itself. Information requests made by computers using the Internet Protocol go through interfaces. If a computer wants to get information from itself, the fastest way to obtain this information is to have a software interface.

The easiest way to set up this interface is to use the `ifconfig` and `route` commands, like so:

```
# ifconfig lo 127.0.0.1
# route add -host 127.0.0.1 lo
```

The `ifconfig` command tells the computer to enable the interface `lo` (short for loopback) with an IP address of 127.0.0.1. The `route` command tells the computer to add a route to the host 127.0.0.1 through the interface `lo`. When these commands have been executed, you can test whether the loopback address is working by typing the following:

```
# ping 127.0.0.1
```

This results in the following output:

```
127.0.0.1 is alive
```

Make sure the loopback interface has the right IP address

The loopback interface is always assigned the IP address 127.0.0.1. This standardization means you can be sure that connections made to the IP address 127.0.0.1 are always made to the local computer, not some other computer.

When the loopback interface has been configured, it must be named.

Naming the interface

1. Launch `netcfg` and click the **Hosts** button in the main window. You'll see the screen shown in Figure 27.2.

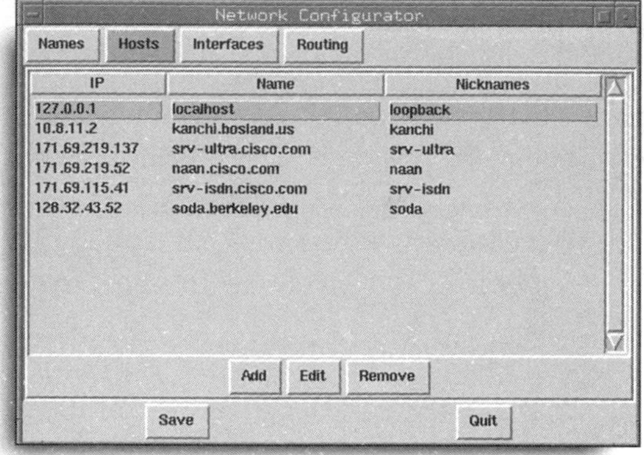

FIGURE 27.2
This `netcfg` window is used to configure Host attributes.

2. Click the entry for `127.0.0.1`. The Edit/etc/hosts Window, shown in Figure 27.3, appears.

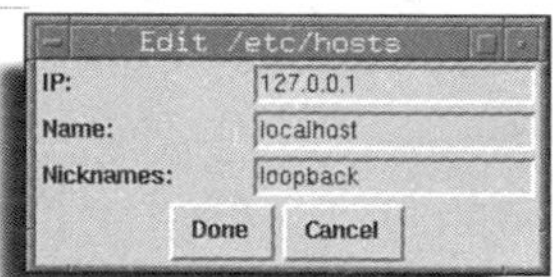

FIGURE 27.3
Give the loopback interface a name.

3. Type **localhost** in the Name field. Optionally, type **loopback** in the Nicknames field.
4. Click **Done**, and then click the **Save** button. The changes you made will be saved.

This process can be used to give names to other IP addresses as well, but very few IP addresses need to be named on systems using name servers.

Adding a PPP Interface

The Point-to-Point Protocol (PPP) is a method of creating and running IP over a serial link made using modems and phone lines. With PPP, a client connects to a PPP server. When connected, the client can access resources on the PPP server's network as though it were connected directly to the network. PPP is one of the most common ways for personal computers to connect to the Internet.

Configuring PPP on a Linux machine

1. The first step is to use the `modemtool` program to create the modem device in the `/dev` directory. To launch `modemtool`, type the following (as root) from the command line:
   ```
   # modemtool
   ```
2. This opens the window shown in Figure 27.4. Click the COM port to which the modem is connected and then click the **OK** button to create the appropriate `/dev/modem` file.
3. Launch `netcfg` and click the **Interfaces** button. You'll see the screen shown in Figure 27.5.
4. Click the **Add** button to open the Choose window (see Figure 27.6).
5. Select **PPP** and click **OK**. This opens the Create PPP Interface, shown in Figure 27.7.
6. Click the Phone Number field and type the phone number that the modem will dial.
7. Click the PPP logon name field and type the name that PPP should use to log on. This is your user name on the machine that is being called.
8. Click the PPP password field and type the password that PPP should use for the logon you gave. Because the password is entered as clear text, make sure that no one who should not know your password is present when you enter it.
9. Click the **Customize** button to open the Edit PPP Interface dialog box, shown in Figure 27.8.

TCP/IP connections over serial lines

The three common protocols for running TCP/IP on serial or parallel lines are the Point-to-Point Protocol (PPP), the Serial Line Internet Protocol (SLIP), and the Parallel Line Internet Protocol (PLIP).

Of these, SLIP is the oldest and has problems dealing with noisy low-speed telephone lines. SLIP predates the standardization process for protocols, so it is not considered one of the Internet standard protocols.

The Internet standard replacement for SLIP is PPP. This protocol provides similar functionality to SLIP, but in a reliable manner over all types of phone lines. Currently, PPP is the most widely used protocol for running TCP/IP over phone lines.

PLIP is a variant of SLIP, which enables TCP/IP to be run over the parallel port of a computer. PLIP is faster than PPP or SLIP but is not widely used for connecting computers over phone lines.

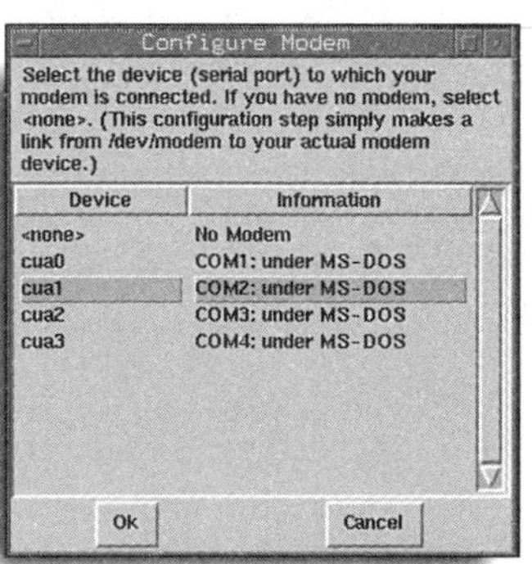

FIGURE 27.4

Use the `modemtool` to configure your modem.

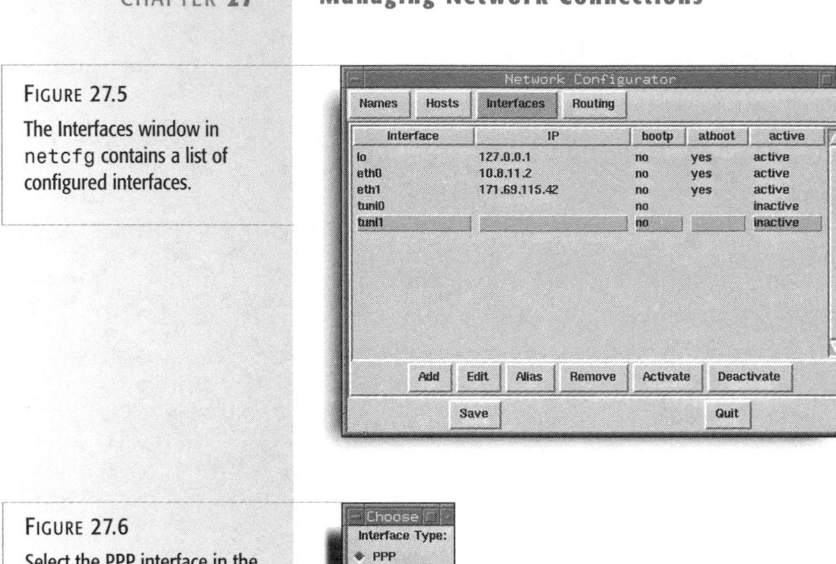

FIGURE 27.5

The Interfaces window in `netcfg` contains a list of configured interfaces.

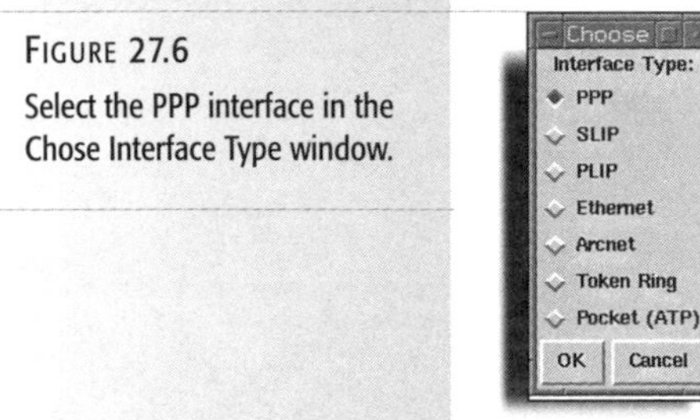

FIGURE 27.6

Select the PPP interface in the Chose Interface Type window.

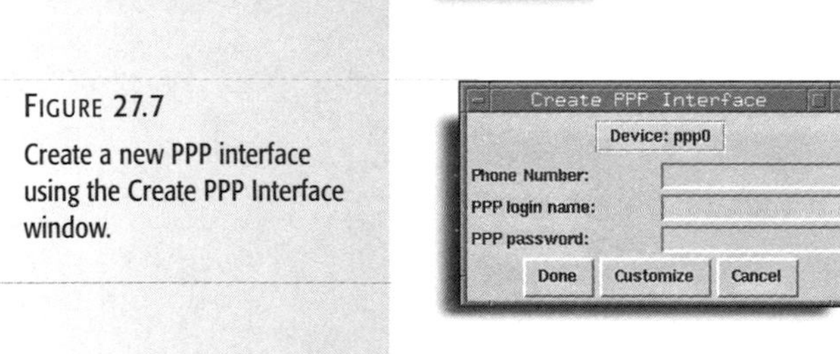

FIGURE 27.7

Create a new PPP interface using the Create PPP Interface window.

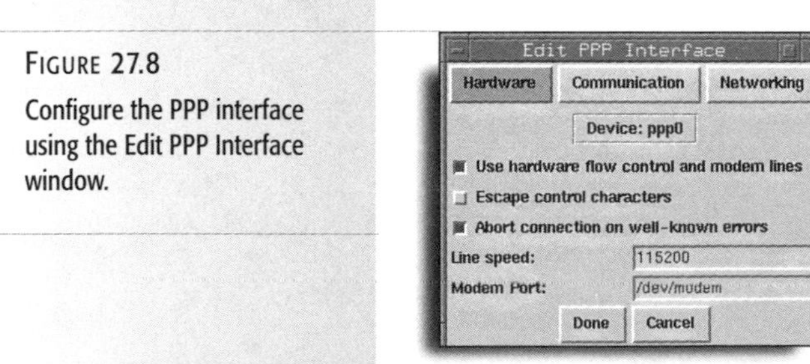

FIGURE 27.8

Configure the PPP interface using the Edit PPP Interface window.

10. Select the **Use hardware flow control and modem lines** option and use the Abort connection on well-known errors option.

11. Set the value in the Line speed to the maximum speed which the computer can communicate with the modem. For most modems, this will be the default value (115200). If a different value for the line speed is given in your modem's manual, usc that valuc for optimal performance.
12. Make sure the default modem port is configured to `/dev/modem`.
13. Your PPP interface is now configured. If you want a more advanced configuration, click the **Networking** button. Otherwise, click **Done**.
14. If you click the **Networking** button, you'll see the Edit PPP Interface dialog box, shown in Figure 27.9. In this window, you can set the following parameters:
    - *Activate interface at boot time*. This means that when your computer boots up, it will dial your modem and establish a PPP link. This is useful if your service provider grants you unlimited connection time.
    - *Set default route when making connection*. This means that all packets requested by your machine for addresses other than the local host will be sent to the PPP interface. This is useful when PPP is the main network connection for your machine.
    - *Restart PPP when connection fails*. This useful option prevents you from having to restart PPP every time the connection fails.
    - *MRU*. The maximum receive unit is the maximum size in bytes of a packet that can be sent and received by your machine. The allowable range is 296 bytes to 1,500 bytes. The value you enter depends on the quality of your phone line. Noisy lines require smaller numbers, and clean lines can use larger numbers.
    - *Local IP address and Remote IP address*. These options are useful only for machines with static IP addresses. If you have a static IP address, these values will be provided to you by your company or service provider.

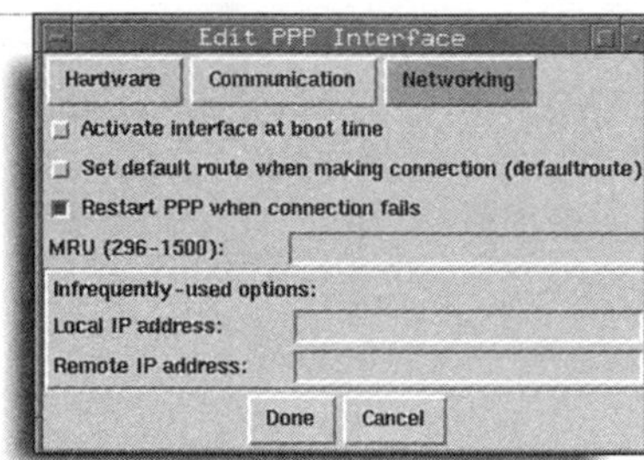

FIGURE 27.9
Set the appropriate PPP options using the Networking options window.

15. After these configuration options are entered, click the **Done** button. In the dialog box that asks whether you want to save the configuration, click **Yes**. The Edit PPP Interface dialog box disappears, and a new entry (`PPP0`) is added to the Interfaces screen (refer to Figure 27.5). Click on the **Save** button in the Interfaces screen to save the changes.

After your PPP interface is configured, you'll want to test it to make sure it works the way you want.

Testing the PPP interface

1. Click the **Activate** button in the Interfaces screen. You should hear your modem dialing and connecting to your service provider.
2. After the connection is established, ping a well-known host (for example, try pinging `192.31.7.130`, which is `www.cisco.com`):

```
kanchi 1555$ ping -c 3 192.31.7.130
PING 192.31.7.130 (192.31.7.130): 56 data bytes
64 bytes from 192.31.7.130: icmp_seq=0 ttl=248
➥time=38.5 ms
64 bytes from 192.31.7.130: icmp_seq=1 ttl=249
➥time=32.5 ms
64 bytes from 192.31.7.130: icmp_seq=2 ttl=249
➥time=30.7 ms

--- 192.31.7.130 ping statistics ---
3 packets transmitted, 3 packets received, 0% packet
➥loss
round-trip min/avg/max = 30.7/33.9/38.5 ms
```

If your output is similar to this, your connection is working correctly.

To easily activate and deactivate a PPP interface, bash and ksh users can add the following aliases to their profile:

```
alias activate-ppp=î/etc/sysconfig/network-scripts/ifup-PPPî
alias deactivate-ppp=î/etc/sysconfig/network-scripts/ifdown-
➥PPPî
```

Users of csh and tcsh can add the following aliases to their .cshrc, to easily activate and deactivate the PPP interface:

```
alias activate-ppp î/etc/sysconfig/network-scripts/ifup-PPPî
alias deactivate-ppp î/etc/sysconfig/network-scripts/ifdown-
PPPî
```

Activating and deactivating an interface

If the `netcfg` Interfaces window shows an interface as inactive, the window can be made active by clicking on the **Activate** button. Activating an interface is referred to as bringing up an interface.

Similarly, if the Interfaces window shows an interface as active, the interface can be made inactive by clicking the **Deactivate** button in the Interfaces screen. Deactivating an interface is referred to as bringing an interface down.

Adding a SLIP Interface

The Serial Line Internet Protocol (SLIP) is another way of connecting two computers using IP. Setting up a SLIP interface is similar to setting up a PPP interface.

Creating a SLIP interface

1. Launch `netcfg` and click the **Interfaces** button to view the Interfaces screen (refer to Figure 27.5).
2. Click the **Add** button to open the Choose Interfaces dialog box (refer to Figure 27.6).
3. Select **SLIP** and click the **OK** button. This opens the Create SLIP Interface screen, shown in Figure 27.10.

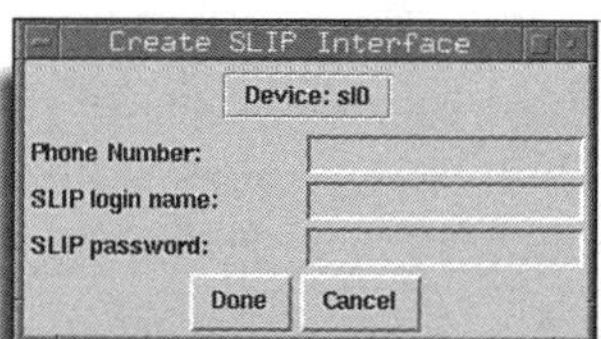

FIGURE 27.10
Create a new SLIP interface using the Create SLIP Interface window.

4. Click the Phone Number field and type the phone number that the modem will dial.
5. Click the SLIP logon name field type the name SLIP should use to log on. This is your username on the machine that is being called.

6. Click the SLIP password field and type the password that SLIP should use for logon. The password is entered as clear text, so make sure that no one who should not know your password is present when you enter it.
7. Click the **Done** button. The Edit SLIP Interface dialog box, shown in Figure 27.11, appears.

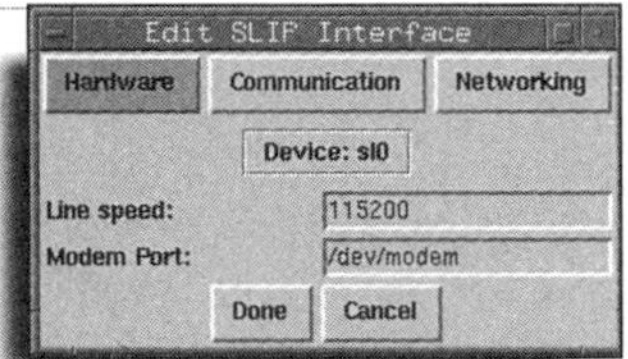

FIGURE 27.11
Configure a new SLIP interface using the Edit SLIP Interface window.

8. Set the line speed option to the maximum speed the computer can use to talk to the modem. This value is usually specified in the modems manual. For most modems, the default value (115200) is sufficient.
9. The Modem Port should be set to `/dev/modem`, your modem device. If you have not configured your modem, see the previous section for directions on using `modemtool` to do this.
10. Your SLIP connection is now configured. If you want to customize the SLIP connection's network properties, click the **Networking** button. Otherwise, click **Done** to view the screen shown in Figure 27.12. You can enable the following options in this window:
    - *Activate interface at boot time*. If you select this option, it means that when your computer boots up, it will dial your modem and establish a SLIP connection. This is useful if your service provider grants you unlimited connection time.
    - *Set default route when making connection*. If you set this option, all packets requested by your machine for addresses other than the local host will be sent to the SLIP interface. This is useful when SLIP is the main network connection for your machine.

- *Restart SLIP when connection fails*. This useful option prevents you from having to restart SLIP every time the connection fails.
- *MRU*. The maximum receive unit is the maximum size in bytes of a packet that can be sent and received by your machine. Allowable sizes range from 296 bytes to 1,500 bytes. The value you set depends on the quality of your phone line. Noisy lines require smaller numbers, and clean lines can use larger numbers.
- *Local IP address and Remote IP address*. These options are useful only for machines with static IP addresses. If you have a static IP address, these values will be provided to you by your company or service provider.
- Mode (SLIP/CSLIP). This field enables you to change the mode in which SLIP runs: standard (SLIP) or compressed (CSLIP). CSLIP is sometimes slower than SLIP because each packet must be decompressed as it is received. For this reason, many Internet service providers do not have CSLIP set up. Check with your ISP to determine which mode you should use. If in doubt, use the default mode SLIP.

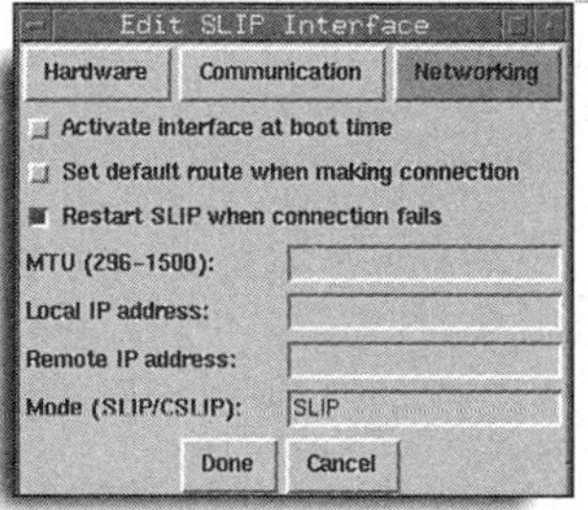

FIGURE 27.12
Configure a new SLIP interface using the Edit SLIP Interface Networking options window.

11. After you finish setting the Networking options, click **Done**. Click **Yes** in the window that asks whether you want to save the configuration; the Edit SLIP window disappears. A new entry, `sl0`, appears in the Interfaces window.
12. To activate the SLIP interface, click the **Activate** button. You should hear the modem dialing and connecting.

13. After a connection has been established, ping a well-known host to test the connection.

Adding a PLIP Interface

The Parallel Line Internet Protocol (PLIP) is very similar to SLIP because it provides a point-to-point connection between two machines. The difference between the two is that PLIP uses the parallel ports on the computer to provide higher speeds.

Configuring a PLIP interface

1. Launch `netcfg`.
2. Click the **Interfaces** button in the Network Configurator main window (refer to Figure 27.1).
3. Click the **Add** button in the Interfaces screen to open the Choose Interface dialog box (refer to Figure 27.6).
4. Select **PLIP** and click **OK**. This opens the Edit PLIP Interface dialog box, shown in Figure 27.13.

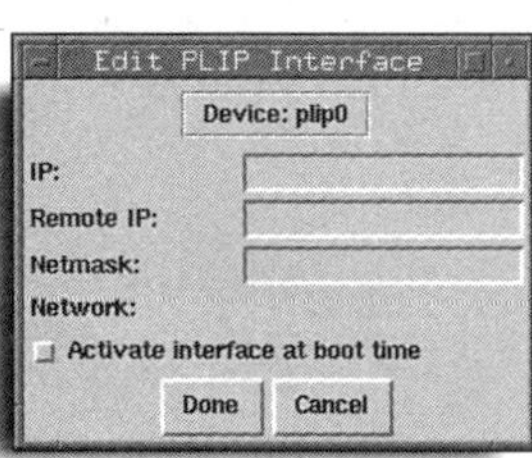

FIGURE 27.13
Configure a new PLIP interface using the Edit PLIP Interface window.

5. Click the IP field and type the local machine's IP address.
6. Click the Remote IP field and type the remote machine's IP address.
7. Click the Netmask field and enter the network mask for the local machine's IP address.
8. If you want the PLIP interface to be active when your machine boots, select the **Activate interface at boot time** option.
9. Click **Done**. In the window that asks whether you want to save the current configuration, click **Yes**.

10. A new entry, `plip0`, should appear in the Interface screen. To activate it, click the **Activate** button.
11. Test the PLIP interface by pinging the remote machine. For example, if the remote machines IP address is `10.8.11.5`, ping would produce the following output:

```
kanchi 1572$ ping -c 3 10.8.11.5
PING 10.8.11.5 (10.8.11.5): 56 data bytes
64 bytes from 10.8.11.5: icmp_seq=0 ttl=255 time=1.7 ms
64 bytes from 10.8.11.5: icmp_seq=1 ttl=255 time=1.7 ms
64 bytes from 10.8.11.5: icmp_seq=2 ttl=255 time=1.7 ms

--- 10.8.11.5 ping statistics ---
3 packets transmitted, 3 packets received, 0% packet
➥loss
round-trip min/avg/max = 1.7/1.7/1.7 ms
```

If your output looks similar, your PLIP interface is working properly.

Adding an Ethernet Interface

Ethernet is by far the most used type of hardware for local area networks because it is cheap, fast, and reliable. Configuring an ethernet interface is similar to configuring a PLIP interface.

Configuring an Ethernet interface

1. Launch `netcfg`.
2. Click the **Interfaces** button in the Network Configurator main window (refer to Figure 27.1).
3. Click the **Add** button.
4. In the Choose Interface window, click **Ethernet** to open the Edit Ethernet dialog box (see Figure 27.14).
5. Click the IP field and type the IP address of the interface. If ethernet is your machine's primary interface, type the machine's IP address.
6. Click the Netmask field and enter the network mask for the IP address entered in step 5.

8. Click the **Activate interface at boot time** option.
9. Unless you need the capability of booting remote machines using this interface as the address of the boot server, leave the Configure interface with BOOTP option unselected.

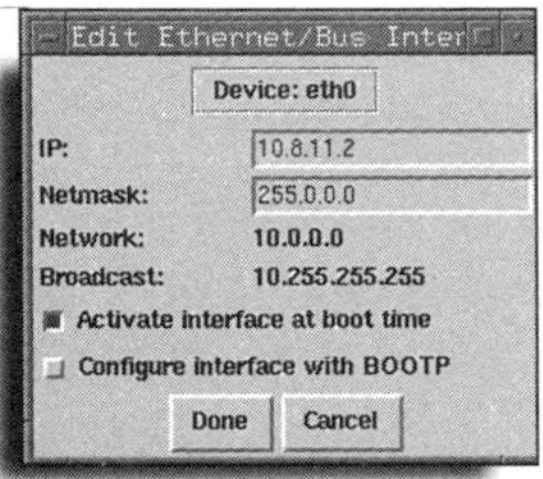

FIGURE 27.14
Configure a new ethernet interface using the Edit Ethernet Interface window.

Setting Up a Router

The previous steps configure your ethernet interface, but for your machine to be able to talk to other machines, the routing must be set up. The following example covers setting up a machine to be a *router*. Client setups for Linux, Windows, and MacOS are covered in separate subsections.

For the purposes of the following examples, assume that the local network is the one shown in Figure 27.15 and that the `eth0` interface for `kanchi` has been configured with the parameters shown in Figure 27.14.

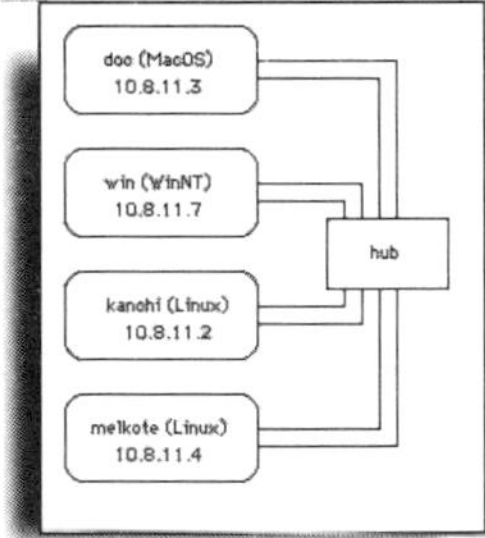

FIGURE 27.15
This is a sample network, used to illustrate connecting hosts to a Linux machine.

The network illustrated in Figure 25.15 boasts four hosts, which will be used to demonstrate the process of configuring different types of machines to talk to a Linux machine acting as a router.

- *doc*. This is a Macintosh running system 8.1 with open transport. Its local IP address is 10.8.11.3.
- *win*. This is an x86 machine running Windows NT Workstation 4.0. Its local IP address is 10.8.11.7.
- *kanchi*. This main Linux machine is the router for all the other machines in the network. Its IP address is 10.8.11.2.
- *melkote*. This is a client Linux machine. Its local IP address is 10.8.11.4.

To configure `kanchi` to route packets for all machines, several routes must be added to the routing table, which helps the kernel keep track of where packets should be sent. The routing table is used to track three main types of routes:

- Host routes
- Network routes
- Default routes

Setting up routes

1. The first type of route you must set up is a host route to yourself. To do this, use the route command (while acting as root), as follows:

   ```
   # route add -host 10.8.11.2 netmask 255.255.255.255 dev
   ➥lo
   ```

   This creates a route to the host 10.8.11.2 through the interface `lo` (loopback).

2. Add a route to all hosts with IP addresses starting with `10.`:

   ```
   # route add -net 10.0.0.0 netmask 255.0.0.0 dev eth0
   ```

   The route that is created enables the computer to use the ethernet interface eth0 to communicate with all hosts that have an IP address of the form 10.*x.x.x*, where x is a number between 1 and 254. Some examples of valid IP address starting with 10. are 10.0.0.1 and 10.8.11.2.

3. For all packets going to hosts without 10.*x.x.x* addresses, you must add the default route. In the case of this machine, the default route runs through itself, so you add it as follows:

```
# route add default gw 10.8.11.2 dev eth0
```

Now that the main Linux machine, `kanchi`, is configured, you can configure the other machines.

Connecting Two Linux Systems

Connecting two Linux machines is easy. This is usually referred to as configuring one Linux machine to be the client of another. In this case, `melkote` as is configured to be a client of `kanchi`.

Configuring *melkote*

1. Make sure that `melkote`'s `lo` and `eth0` interfaces have been configured properly.
2. Add a route to the `kanchi` (10.8.11.2). This route will be used by the local machine for sending and receiving packets from `kanchi`. Entering the following at the command line adds a route to `kanchi` via the `eth0` interface:

```
# route add -host 10.8.11.2 netmask 255.255.255.255 dev
eth0
```

3. For the local machine (`melkote`) to communicate with the other computers on the network, you must add the default route. The default route is used to communicate with hosts that do not have explicit entries in the routing table. To add the default route for `melkote` via `kanchi`, enter the following:

```
route add default gw 10.8.11.2 dev eth0
```

This adds a default route for all packets to be sent to the router at 10.8.11.2 on your `eth0` interface. A program such as Telnet or PING will confirm if the routing is working properly.

Connecting a MacOS Machine to a Linux System

Connecting the machine `doc`, which runs MacOS as a `kanchi`, is straightforward under Open Transport.

Configuring *doc*

1. Click the **Apple** menu and select **Control Panels**.
2. In the Control Panels window, select the TCP/IP icon. The TCP/IP screen shown in Figure 27.16 appears.

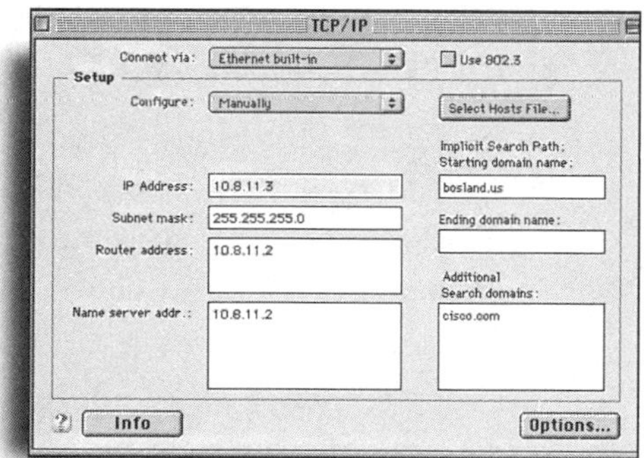

FIGURE 27.16
Configure TCP/IP on a computer running MacOS using the TCP/IP control panel.

4. Click **Connect via drop-down list** and select the **Ethernet built-in** option.
5. Click **Configure drop-down list** and select the **Manually** option.
6. In the IP Address field, enter `doc`'s IP address (in this example, the IP address is 10.8.11.3).
7. In the Subnet mask field, enter the network mask for the IP address entered in step 6.
8. In the Router Address field, enter `kanchi`'s address (10.8.11.2).
9. Close the window to initialize the network by clicking the Close box in the upper-left side of the window.

Testing the connection

To test the connection between `doc` and `kanchi`, try using the NCSA Telnet program.

Connecting a Windows Machine to a Linux System

Configuring a Windows machine is similar to configuring a Macintosh. This example demonstrates how to configure

Windows NT; configuring Windows 95 (and, presumably, Windows 98) works in exactly the same way.

Configuring *win*

1. Click the **Start** menu, click **Settings**, and then choose **Control Panel** to open the Control Panel window.
2. Click the **Network** icon to open the Network window.
3. Click the **Identification** tab.
4. Click the Computer Name field and type the name of the computer (I've typed `win` in this example).
5. Click the **Protocols** tab.
6. If TCP/IP Protocol is displayed in the list of network protocols, double-click it. If not, click the **Add** button and select **TCP/IP Protocol**. Return to the **Protocols** tab, and then double-click the newly added **TCP/IP Protocol** entry.
7. In the ensuing Microsoft TCP/IP Properties dialog box, click the **Specify an IP address** option.
8. Click the IP Address field and type the computer's IP address (in this case, I entered 10.8.11.7).
9. Click the Subnet Mask field and type the computer's subnet mask. (in this case, I entered 255.255.255.0).
10. Click the Default Gateway field and type the computer's gateway, which is the machine through which all packets are routed (I entered 10.8.11.2 because win's gateway is `kanchi`).
11. Click **OK** in the Microsoft TCP/IP Properties window, and then click **OK** in the Network window.
12. Click **Yes** in the window that asks whether you want to reboot the machine for the new network configuration.

After the machine reboots, the network will be properly configured (I used the `dos` shell and the PING program to test this).

Enabling the Network File System Service

The Network File System (NFS) provides for the mounting of directories across a network. Directories on a remote machine mounted via NFS on the local machine appear to be part of the local machines file system.

Configuring the NFS service involves two parts:

- *Configuring the NFS server*. This is the machine from which a directory is mounted. In my sample network, the NFS server is `kanchi`.
- *Configuring the NFS client*. This is the machine mounting the directory. In my sample network, the NFS client is `melkote`.

This example demonstrates how to mount the `kanchi`'s `/home` directory on `melkote` so that users have the same `/home` directory on both machines.

Configuring an NFS server

1. As root, open the file `/etc/exports` in your editor. If the file existed prior to opening it in the editor, its contents will be displayed in your editor's window. If the file did not exist when you opened it, your editor will create the file and display a blank screen.
2. A shorthand for allowing everyone to mount a directory is to simply give the permissions and not list any host names. Let's take a look at a sample:

   ```
   # exports file for kanchi
   /mnt/cdrom       (ro)
   /mnt/zip         (rw)
   /store/pub       (rw)
   ```

   This is the `/etc/exports` file on `kanchi`; the three entries in it correspond to directories that can be mounted by NFS clients. In this case, all three directories are mountable by everyone. The permissions are clearly seen in this file:

- (ro) This indicates read-only permissions.
- (rw) This indicates read and write permissions.

3. Make the /home directory available for NFS mounting on melkote by entering the following line:

```
/home              melkote(rw)
```

   This indicates that melkote can mount /home with read and write permissions.

Now that you have configured the NFS server kanchi, you can configure the NFS client melkote. To the client, mounting an NFS directory is the same as mounting any other type of device, such as a hard drive or CD-ROM.

The syntax of /etc/exports

The syntax of the /etc/exports file is simple. The directories available for NFS mounting are specified one per line. On each line, the first entry is the directory that you want to mount. The next two entries are a pair. The first entry in this pair is the name of a machine that should be capable of mounting this directory; the second entry in this pair is the permissions with which this machine can mount the directory. As many host and permission pairs can exist as you want.

Configuring an NFS client

1. For melkote to mount /home properly, you must add an entry to its /etc/fstab file. In this case, the entry is as follows:

```
kanchi:/home     /home     NFS
```

2. After you have added this entry, you can mount kanchi's /home directory as root by typing the following:

```
mount kanchi:/home
```

3. Now anyone who logs on to melkote will get the same /home directory as on kanchi.

Enabling Dial-In Service

Enabling dial-in service on a Linux system requires two programs:

- The PPP daemon (PPPD), which is used to detect incoming connections and to shut down active PPP links when a connection terminates.
- The getty program, which handles modem communications intelligently. This chapter gives an overview of the format of the file, /etc/gettydefs, used to handle logon process for a dial-up user.

These programs are available on every Red Hat Linux installation.

The process in which a user establishes a PPP link is as follows:

1. The phone number of the modem connected to the Linux system (the PPP server) is dialed from a remote host (the PPP client).

   The user logs on to the server with a valid username and password.

2. At the shell prompt, the user issues the following command to start PPP on the server:

   ```
   exec /usr/sbin/pppd ñdetach
   ```

3. The user starts PPP on the client.

Setting Up the PPP Options Files

Two files must be present to grant PPP access to a Linux system. The first file, `/etc/ppp/options`, contains the common PPP options required for modem connections. These options are listed one per line in the file as shown here:

```
asyncmap 0
netmask 255.255.255.0
proxyarp
lock
crtscts
modem
```

The line for `netmask` should be modified to be the netmask for your Linux system's IP address.

The second file that must be created is the `/etc/ppp/options.tty01` file. This file contains a list of IP addresses or hostnames and the PPP interfaces with which they are associated. For example, if the `/etc/ppp/options.tty01` file contained the following line

```
srv-ss2:ppp0
```

when a PPP client connects to the ppp0 interface, it is automatically given the name srv-ss2 along with the IP address of srv-ss2.

Multiple modem

If a Linux system has more than one modem connected to it, each modem on which users can dial up should have a separate file `/etc/ppp/options.tty`*XX*, where *XX* corresponds to the modem's number (starting with 01).

Configuring Getty Devices

When a user dials into a Linux system, three actions must be performed before the user can log on:

1. Open tty lines and set their modes.
2. Print the logon prompt.
3. Initiate the logon process for the user.

These actions are handled by the `getty` program, which keeps a list of tty lines and their modes and sets the mode of dial-up connection to the appropriate entry in the list. Each individual entry in the list is referred to as a `getty` device. After the line has been set up, `getty` prints the logon prompt and initiates the logon process.

The process of configuring `getty` devices is done by adding entries to the `/etc/gettydefs file`. The default version of this file is fine for most installations, but occasionally, entries for newer or faster modem types must be added.

`gettydefs` file format

The `/etc/gettydefs` file has the same convention as most UNIX configuration files, in that lines starting with the # character or completely blank lines are ignored. All other lines are treated as configuration entries.

Usually a configuration entry consists of two lines. The first line is a description of the entry, and the second is the entry itself. Strictly speaking, only the configuration lines are required, but it is a good idea to include a description for each entry.

Entries are made up of five values separated by the # character.

A sample entry in the `/etc/gettydefs` files looks like this:

```
# 19200 fixed-baud modem entry
F19200# B19200 CS8 # B19200 SANE -ISTRIP HUPCL #@S ➥login:
#F19200
```

The first and the last value in each entry describe the speed of the modem. These must always be the same. In this case, we see that the speed is 19200, which corresponds to a 19.2Kb modem.

The second and third values are called the init flags and the final flags. These are given in this format:

```
B[speed] [options]
```

Because the speed for this entry is 19200, the init flags are set as `B19200 CS8` and the final flags arc sct as `B19200 SANE -ISTRIP HUPCL`. Usually the only option specified for init flags is `CS8`. The options that can be specified for the final flags are covered in great detail in the `getty man` page, but the most common options used are the ones listed in this entry.

The fourth entry is the prompt to be issued for the user to log on. This can be set to any value, but the standard is either `login:` or `username:`.

CHAPTER

28

Managing Daemons

By Jan Walter

Editing and creating run levels

Editing `inittab`

Using `chkconfig`

Editing startup and shutdown scripts

Customizing the logon greeting

Enabling and customizing the MOTD

Using the `tksysv` tool

Using the `ntsysv` tool

Enabling FTP access

Enabling a web server

Linux, and all other UNIX variants, start a number of services at system startup. It is these services—called *daemons*—that the users, and you, the administrator, interact with. To increase flexibility, all these systems give you the option of starting the system in different modes, called *run levels*, each of which configures the system to operate in a certain way. Understanding how the entire process works is fundamental to successfully managing a Linux system.

The two UNIX camps

The UNIX world is divided into two differing camps–Berkeley and AT&T. Because Linux straddles the ground between the two, each distribution has a lot of leeway as to how to implement the run-level mechanism.

Many beginning administrators have trouble understanding *parent processes*. All processes on the system have a parent process, which starts the actual program. For example, every time you type `ls` at the command line, your shell starts the program `ls`—in this case, the shell is the parent process. *Login* is the parent process of the shell you get when you log on. The parent of all processes is called `init`; this process controls what happens when the system starts, and controls how the system runs.

Because Linux is a multiuser system, it must have several modes of operation. For example, the `halt` and `reboot` modes of operation make the system do things not typically associated with a valid state for an operating system. UNIX and Linux call the state of the operating system a run level. As shown in Table 28.1, six run levels are implemented for a stock Red Hat Linux system:

TABLE 28.1 **Linux system run levels**

Run Level	Name	Purpose
0	Halt	When the system is at this run level, nothing is running, and the disk volumes are not mounted. The only things you can do at this level are to turn off the system or press Crtl+Alt+Delete.
1	Single User Mode	This is the systems maintenance mode. This mode guarantees that only the person at the console of the system is able to use the system. This mode is used for checking disks or for serious system-maintenance work that cannot be done when users are on the system or when processes are accessing the disk.

Run Level	Name	Purpose
2	Multi-User Mode Without Networking	This allows multiple logons via the console sessions or via serial ports, but does not configure the network, or anything that relates to it, such as the Web and samba servers. Typically, this run level is not used, but some sysadmins use it to make changes to network configurations without having to kick all the users off the system. On some other systems, this run level only disables `nfs`, the network file system.
3	Multi-User Mode	This is the normal operating mode for which Linux is configured. All services required for the full capability of the system are started.
4	Multi-User Mode, Spare	This mode is a spare multiuser mode. On Red Hat systems, it does pretty much the same things that level 3 does. Since it's a spare, you can test new configurations with this run level before rolling out a configuration to run level 3.
5	XDM Mode	This mode keeps XDM, the X11 logon manager, running. Its most notable change is that you now get a graphical logon prompt, and the user's X11 configuration starts up immediately after logon. This is great for systems that are used as workstations rather than network servers, since workstations are not normally running (many) other services that may need the extra memory this takes. Take my advice: For high-load servers, you don't want to start at this run level.

continues…

TABLE 28.1 **Continued**

Run Level	Name	Purpose
6	Reboot	This run level's ultimate goal is to reboot your Linux computer. No services should be running when the computer finally reboots.

The point to remember for both run levels 0 and 6 is this: It's not the run level itself that is significant, it's *getting there* that matters. In the process of switching run levels, `init` starts and stops the services to make the system conform to the specification of that run level. This is a complicated way of saying that if a process is called for at the run level where the system is (or is going to), `init` makes sure that it's running. The opposite also applies—if a service is not called for at the run level the system is going to, `init` stops it.

Editing and Creating Run Levels

`init` reads its configuration from the file `/etc/inittab`, which contains a number of pieces of information for `init`. It outlines what processes `init` should keep running (and restart if necessary) at each run level. Your logon prompts (called `getty` processes) are started and restarted by `init`. `init` reads the names of scripts to run when the system changes run level. This is probably the most confusing point about `init` and how the system starts: The scripts can (and usually do) also start processes. These are very different from the processes directly controlled by `init`, because they are not absolutely vital to the operation of the system (*vital* being defined here as being necessary to prevent the system from being completely inaccessible, as in not being able to log on at the console). The script that `init` calls, as well as exactly how it operates, is very much distribution dependent.

Red Hat Linux's set of `init` scripts (so named because they are called by `init`, not because they are the initialization scripts) are kept in the `/etc/rc.d` and `/etc/rc.d/init.d` directories. The scripts in `/etc/rc.d` are there primarily for backward compatibility with other Linux distributions. The most noteworthy file is called `rc.local`, which is a shell script in which modifications specific to the particular Linux system would go on other systems. The standard installation's `rc.local` script sets the `/etc/issue` file only to the version of Red Hat Linux that's being used.

The more interesting directory is called the `init.d` directory. This directory holds a number of scripts that control the non-vital system services. If none of the services in this directory start, your system won't do much, but hopefully `init` will have managed to start a logon prompt.

These directories are pretty vital to your system. In fact, I recommend that the entire `/etc/` directory tree appear in every backup you do. Thank me later for reminding you.

Where should I start?

Most system services are not absolutely vital. If you need `init` to baby-sit the process to make sure it's always running, it would be worthwhile for the daemon to be started from the `inittab` file. Thankfully, the vast majority of daemon programs do not require this sort of attention, and for ease of maintenance are best started from a script in `/etc/rc.d/init.d` and managed through the `tksysv` tool.

However, if the daemon is started from the `inittab` file and `init` needs to *respawn* (the term used for restarting a daemon process) the program too often, it disables the program for a while. You'll see a message like the following in the kernel message file (/var/log/messages):

```
init: process
➥respawning too fast.
➥disabled for 5
 minutes
```

Editing *inittab*

Adding a process to the `inittab` file is pretty easy. Like many of the system files in Linux, this file is delimited by the colon (:) character. Each line has the following format:

```
[ID]:[Runlevels to be running at]:[Action]:[program name and
➥arguments]
```

Table 28.2 describes each field in the preceding code.

TABLE 28.2 *Inittab* file layout

Field Name	Description
ID	This is a short description of the line or event. For example, pressing Crtl+Alt+Delete causes `init` to look for the `crtl-alt-del` event in the `inittab` file. There are events for power failure as well, and along with the proper service process (also called daemon) this

continues...

TABLE 28.2 **Continued**

Field Name	Description
	mechanism can provide for UPS monitoring (look up `powerd` in the `man` pages if you want to see how to do this). Services that are attached to terminal devices (virtual terminals or serial ports) use the name of the port after the letters `tty` as their ID (for example, `ttyS1` becomes `S1`), since the `tty` prefix is implied.
`Runlevels`	This section contains the numbers for the run level on which the command should be executed (for example, 345).
`Action`	This tells `init` what action to take. A whole list of actions is documented in the `inittab(5) man` page, but the most commonly used actions are `wait`, `respawn`, and `boot`.
`Program name and arguments`	The last part of the `inittab` line contains the name of the program and the command-line arguments.

Remember the 3 B's of system administration: back up, back up, and back up again

Make sure you have a backup copy of the `inittab` file before you start editing it.

Using *chkconfig*

`chkconfig` is an automated `init` script-management tool. It acts as a sanity checker to make sure that the system will stop a service when leaving a run level.

`chkconfig` requires some additional comment lines in the actual `init` script to tell it in which run levels the service should be started, and when, relatively, the service should be started during the initialization of the run level. (`init` scripts are processed in a specific order to ensure that services dependent on others are started after the services they depend on.) These lines, taken from the `httpd init` script, are as follows:

```
# chkconfig: 345 85 15
# description: Apache is a World Wide Web server.  It is
➥used to serve
# HTML files and CGI.
```

The first line, which is a marker for `chkconfig`, tells it that the given script should be run for run levels 3, 4, and 5, with a start order of 85, and a stop order of 15. This means that `http` is one of the last services to start when entering one of these run levels, and one of the first ones to get stopped when leaving one of them.

Listing Services by Using *chkconfig*

To get a list of which services are started at which run level, use the command `chkconfig --list`. Optionally, you can add a name as an additional argument, and `chkconfig` will list only the information for that service. Following is the output of `chkconfig --list httpd` on my system:

```
[jwalter@jansmachine jwalter]$ /sbin/chkconfig --list httpd
httpd 0:off 1:off 2:off 3:on 4:on 5:on 6:off
```

In this case, `chkconfig` reports that the `httpd` service is to be started for run levels 3, 4, and 5.

Removing a Service Using *chkconfig*

To remove a service from a certain run level, use the following command:

```
chkconfig --level <runlevel> <servicename> off
```

`runlevel` is the run level number you want to modify, and *`servicename`* is the name of the service. The commands `on` and `off` enable and disable the service, respectively. For example, to turn off `httpd` for run level 3, you would issue the following command:

```
chkconfig --level 3 httpd off
```

This command removes the service only for a specific run level, which is the most common operation. You can list multiple run levels (for example, you could type `345` on the command line to change the settings for multiple run levels). If you need to remove a service altogether, you would use the following command:

```
chkconfig --del httpd
```

This command has the effect of removing `httpd` from all `rcX.d` directories. It does not remove the service's script from the `/etc/rc.d/init.d` directory; it just removes the symbolic links to the file from the directories that the `init` scripts search.

What's a sanity checker?

Tools that have solved—or that at least help you solve—particularly irritating problems for programmers and systems administrators have become known as *sanity checkers*. In particular, setting up `init` scripts has caused systems administrators significant amounts of grief since the early days of the UNIX operating system. Many systems administrators have whiled away days (and nights!) looking for a problem with their system configuration or trying to configure things. Frustration over extended periods of time, combined with lack of sleep, too much coffee, and probably heartburn from pizza, has been known to make even the most level-headed systems administrators behave irrationally.

More uses for `chkconfig`

The `chkconfig` program also provides a means to add and remove services from run levels from the shell command line without having to manipulate symbolic links.

Stopping the service before removing it

When you remove or disable a service, you have no guarantee that the system will stop the service gracefully the next time the system changes run levels. To make sure a service is stopped properly, do it manually before removing the service from the run levels.

You can use `tksysv` or `ntsysv` to manually stop a service—these are graphical front ends to manage the services on the system for X11 and text mode, respectively.

You can also simply call the script that manages the service by employing the `stop` command-line argument. For example, you would use the following command to stop `httpd` before disabling it:

```
/etc/rc.d/init.d/httpd
➥stop
```

Incidentally, you can use this method to start services outside of their normal run level or before adding them by using the `start` command line argument instead. This is useful for determining whether the services are running properly.

Adding a Service by Using *chkconfig*

To add a service to a specific run level, use the following command:

```
chkconfig --level <runlevel> <servicename> on
```

To add `httpd` back to run level 3, use the following command:

```
chkconfig --level 3 httpd on
```

To add a new service to all run levels according to the recommendations given to `chkconfig`, use the following command:

```
chkconfig --add <servicename>
```

`chkconfig` sets all the links for the service in the correct directories in one swoop.

Resetting Service Information

Playing with services is educational, as long as you have a backup of your `/etc/rc.d` directory tree and a way to get back into the system to restore it. However, this type of drastic action is usually not necessary. Instead, you can restore the service's startup priority and other information to the recommended settings by issuing the following command

```
chkconfig <servicename> reset
```

This command returns everything to a (hopefully) "sane" default.

Editing Startup and Shutdown Scripts

The startup and shutdown scripts reside in the `/etc/rc.d` directory subtree. These are generally `bash` scripts that start daemons. Each run level has its own subdirectory of `/etc/rc.d`, which contains the run level number (as in `/etc/rc.d/rc0.d` for run level 0, `/etc/rc.d/rc3.d` for run level 3, and so on). These subdirectories contain *symbolic links* to actual scripts in `/etc/rc.d/init.d`. This ensures that all run levels read from the same set of scripts. There is something else to account for, however: Certain processes and daemons must start before other processes. For example, it makes little sense for the system to start the web server (`httpd`) before having started the networking on the system because the web server needs a network interface on which to initialize.

So this is how it happens: Depending on whether the script is designed to start a service or to ensure that a service is stopped, the first letter of the script name is either `S` (for start) or `K` (for kill). Then comes a (by convention) two-digit number, and then the name of the script in the `init.d` directory. When the system changes to a different run level, the `K` scripts are run first, in numerical order, and then the `S` scripts, again in numerical order.

The `chkconfig` utility checks the recommended numbers for the script you're using, for both start and kill scripts (the example in the previous section using `httpd`'s `init` script lists `85` as the start-up number and `15` as the kill number). You should, for the most part, use these numbers unless you have a good reason to do otherwise.

The `init` scripts do make things easy for you, however—the difficult scripting has been done for you and packaged into functions that your script can call to do most of the dirty work.

A Sample *init* Script

The `init` script in Listing 28.1 is for `httpd`, the Apache web server that comes packaged with Red Hat Linux. I use this as an example because the majority of additional services out there work very similarly to thisw

LISTING 28.1 Listing of */etc/rc.d/init.d/httpd*, the *init* script for the web server

```
#!/bin/sh
#
# Startup script for the Apache Web Server
#
# chkconfig: 345 85 15
# description: Apache is a World Wide Web server.  It is used to
➥serve \
```

continues...

LISTING 28.1 Continued

```
# HTML files and CGI.
#
#


# Source function library.
. /etc/rc.d/init.d/functions

# See how we were called.
case "$1" in
  start)
    echo -n "Starting httpd: "
    daemon httpd
    echo
    touch /var/lock/subsys/httpd
    ;;
  stop)
    echo -n "Shutting down http: "
    kill `cat /var/run/httpd.pid`
    echo httpd
    rm -f /var/lock/subsys/httpd
    rm -f /var/run/httpd.pid
   ;;
  status)
    status httpd
    ;;
  restart)
    $0 stop
    $0 start
    ;;
  *)
    echo "Usage: httpd.init {start|stop|restart|status}"

    exit 1
esac

exit 0
```

The easiest way to set up another program as a daemon in your system is to copy an existing script to a new file, and edit the file to suit your needs. The only lines in the script shown in Listing 28.1 that are specific to `httpd` are lines 3–7, 18–21, 24–28, 31, and 33. These lines either provide feedback while the script is executing, or actually start the program.

Lines 25 and 28 are specific to Apache because Apache stores its process ID numbers in a file in the `/var/run/httpd.pid` file to make stopping the process easier. If the daemon you want to add cannot be configured to do this, the script called `functions` that is included at the beginning contains a function to automatically find the PID(s) of the daemon in question and to kill the process. For example, if your program were called `mydaemon`, lines 24–28 would look like the following:

```
24:      echo -n "Shutting down mydaemon : "
25:      killproc mydaemon
26:     echo mydaemon
27:      rm -f /var/log/subsys/mydaemon
28:     ;;
```

Note that the line to remove the PID file in `/var/run` is not there (of course, you could leave it in if `mydaemon` were to support it).

init script checklist

Using this short checklist should ensure that all necessary features are present to make working with the script you created easy and painless for both you and other systems administrators.

- The script supports `start` and `stop` command-line arguments.
- The script has appropriate lines for `chkconfig` to manage the script. If you're in doubt of the order the program should be started, start it with a high number and stop it with a low number.
- Make sure that the script handles creating the lock files in `/var/lock/subsys` and the PID files in `/var/run`; the `status` command-line argument and the `killproc` function for the script use these. A status check is nice to have for a daemon process.

- Make sure that the script provides appropriate feedback to make clear to the user what is happening. Be especially sure of this if the daemon that's starting needs to start connections that need some time to initialize. Otherwise, observers might get the impression that the system has hung, and take some drastic actions that might not be warranted.

Customizing the Logon Greeting

The `getty` programs that manage logons over terminals and network connections print a message to the screen before asking for the logon ID. The default message is as follows:

```
Red Hat Linux release 5.0 (Hurricane)
Kernel 2.0.32 on an i586
```

Many organizations dealing with computer security recommend that there be no information about the operating system, or about the company whose machine is in the logon message. All operating systems have potential security holes that system crackers can exploit if they know which version of the system they are working with. Making this information more difficult to obtain goes a long way toward thwarting an attack. On a more upbeat note, it's nice to be able to modify this to put either amusing or informative messages at the logon prompt.

Red Hat Linux generates its `issue` file at every system boot by default, and this should be the first thing that gets turned off if you want to customize the logon greeting. The code that does this is in the file `/etc/rc.d/rc.local`. The lines look like this on my system (I included the comments as well):

```
# This will overwrite /etc/issue at every boot.  So, make
➥any changes you
# want to make to /etc/issue here or you will lose them when
➥you reboot.
echo "" > /etc/issue
echo "Kernel $(uname -r) on $a $(uname -m)" >> /etc/issue

cp -f /etc/issue /etc/issue.net
```

Putting the # character before each of the offending lines will comment them out and render them harmless to your system's issue file. Then, feel free to edit the /etc/issue file with any message that pleases you and, hopefully, your users.

Customizing the Logon Greeting for Network Connections

Linux copies the /etc/issue file to the greeting file for network connections (aptly named /etc/issue.net), so I refer you to the previous section for information on where to disable this. Once this is complete, feel free to edit the /etc/issue.net file to say the same thing, or anything else.

It is common—and recommended—for corporate Linux systems to have different messages for network and local connections. Most crackers use networks, not local terminals, so on network connections it is especially important not to give out any information that these individuals may be able to use against you.

Disclaimers and other legal notifications

It is possible that some states, countries, or provinces require system administrators to make sure that people logging on to the system understand that their actions or transmissions may be monitored. It can be argued that this possibility is implied in the use of any computer or data network (including public phone systems!), but some people may not feel the same way about this. In this case, the best place to put a message like this is in the /etc/issue and /etc/issue.net files. If you really want to be safe, mention this in the motd (Message of the Day) file as well.

Enabling and Customizing the MOTD

MOTD stands for Message of the Day, and has long been something that administrators use to convey important information, like scheduled shutdowns or maintenance to users. The MOTD should be provided for users after they log on but before they come to the shell prompt.

The file the message of the day is kept in is /etc/motd. The contents of this file are displayed every time a user logs on. It's that simple. When you first install the system, the file is empty.

Changing the message of the day

1. Start your favorite editor to edit /etc/motd. In this case, I use vi, so the command vi /etc/motd will do the trick.
2. Press the I key on your keyboard to begin inserting text.
3. Type your message.
4. Press the Esc key to stop inserting text.
5. Type the command :wq to save the file and quit vi.

Using the *tksysv* Tool

tksysv is the X11 manager for system services. This program allows you to start and stop services and reorganize them for various run levels.

To start tksysv, start X11, open an XTerm, and type tksysv &. Make sure that you're logged on as or su'd to root.

Adding a Service with *tksysv*

The left pane in Figure 28.1 lists which services are currently available for use in the system. The right pane lists the services that are started and stopped for each run level.

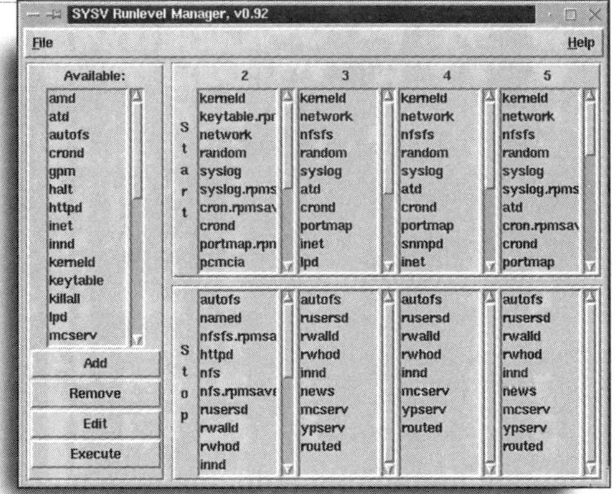

FIGURE 28.1
Don't worry about the frills on the windows—these vary depending on the X11 window manager that's installed.

To add a service to a run level, select the service and click the Add button (see Figure 28.2).

Choose whether to start or stop the service, specify the run level you wish to modify, and then click Done (see Figure 28.3).

tksysv then asks for the starting number (order) for the service. If the service has a chkconfig entry, tksysv reads it and fills in the order number for you—stick with the recommendations unless you have a very good reason not to. Click Add. To cancel, click Done.

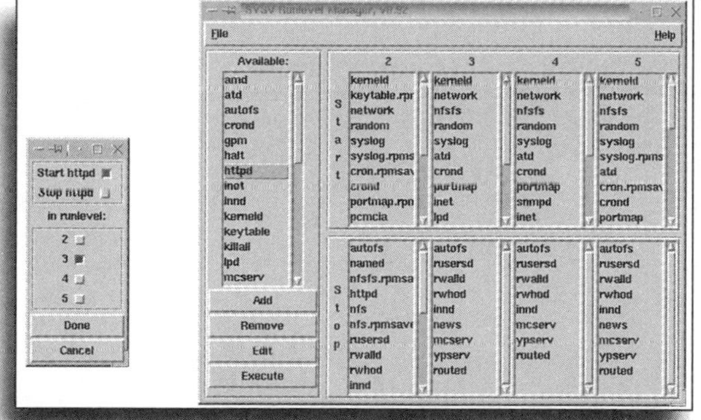

FIGURE 28.2
Choose which run level to add a service to.

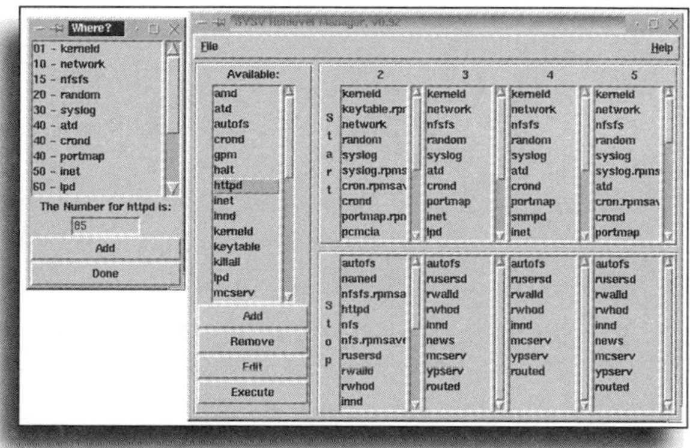

FIGURE 28.3
Choose the starting order for the service.

Removing a service with *tksysv*

1. With `tksysv` running, click on the service on the run level side that you want to remove.
2. Click Remove.

Starting and stopping a service

1. Choose from the left pane the service you want to start or stop (see Figure 28.4).
2. Click Execute.

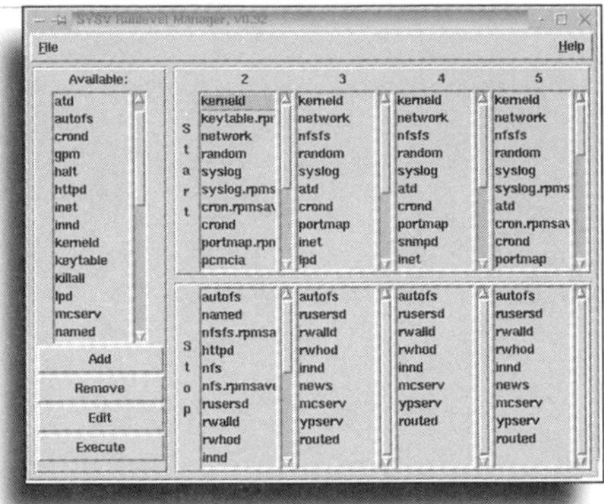

FIGURE 28.4
The service start/stop dialog box.

3. Click on Start or Stop to start or stop the service, respectively.

Don't count on a confirmation request

`tksysv` does not request confirmation when removing a service from a run level, so pause a moment and ask yourself whether you really want to remove the service before clicking that Remove button.

Make it a habit to ask yourself each time you prepare to perform a serious action as root if that action is really what you want to do. Most system commands, as you will likely have discovered by now, don't require confirmation.

Starting and Stopping Network Services

When starting and stopping network services, make sure that you stop all network-related services first. For the most part, these services continue to run if not stopped, generating errors and filling up log files. Furthermore, stopping the services properly ensures that all network connections have had the time to close down properly.

Using the *ntsysv* Tool

`ntsysv` is the text-mode service manager for Red Hat Linux. It is quite a bit simpler to use than `tksysv`, mainly because it deals with things one run level at a time.

To start `ntsysv`, type the command `ntsysv --level <runlevel>`, in which `<runlevel>` is the run level you want to edit. To edit multiple run levels with `ntsysv`, list them all (for example, `234`).

Run a chkconfig

When editing multiple run levels, `ntsysv` marks a service as being started if it is started on any run level that is currently being edited. You should confirm that any changes made did not have any undesirable effects by running `chkconfig` after running `ntsysv` this way.

Adding or removing a service to a run level by using *ntsysv*

1. Log on as root.
2. Issue the command `ntsysv --level <runlevel>` in which `<runlevel>` is the number of the run level you wish to edit.

3. Use the up and down arrow keys to move to the service that you want to modify.
4. Press the Spacebar to turn the service on or off for the run level.
5. Repeat steps 3 and 4 to turn any additional services on or off, as you need.
6. Press the Tab key to highlight the OK button.
7. Prcss Enter while OK is selected to save your work.

Enabling FTP Access

The FTP network service is controlled by the Internet service daemon, `inetd`. To ensure that `inetd` knows how to respond to FTP connection requests, you must edit `/etc/inetd.conf` to ensure that the FTP service is enabled.

There are two types of FTP access—one type for regular users of your system (who have user accounts), and the other for *anonymous* user access. Anonymous user access allows anyone to download files from a set of defined directories on your system by logging on as user *anonymous* and by convention, leaving his email address as a password.

Determining whether FTP is enabled on your system

1. Make sure you have the FTP server installed on your system. Issue the command `rpm -q wu-ftpd`. If the system responds with the message `package wu-ftpd is not installed` then you must install the package before continuing.
2. Ensure that the FTP service line in `/etc/inetd.conf` exists and not commented out. Issue the command `less /etc/inetd.conf` and then make `less` perform a forward search for the word ftp by using the command `/ftp`. `less` should stop at a line like the following:

   ```
   ftp      stream  tcp      nowait  root     /usr/sbin/tcpd
   ➥in.ftpd -l -a
   ```

   If this line starts with a `#` you need to remove this before continuing.

3. If you had to edit the `inetd.conf` file, you must notify `inetd` of the change to the file. Issuing `/etc/rc.d/init.d/inet restart` should do this for you.

Your system is now configured to accept incoming FTP connections.

To enable anonymous FTP access, first follow the preceding steps. The `wu-ftpd` server included with Red Hat Linux provides anonymous FTP server capabilities immediately upon installation, but the additional directories are not installed with the server. You will need the package `anonftp` for this.

To check if you have `anonftp` installed, type **`rpm -q anonftp`** at the command line, and install the file if necessary.

The anonymous FTP server directories are in `/home/ftp`. Anything in the `/home/ftp/pub` directory can be downloaded by anonymous users.

Provide support for anonymous uploads

1. Log on as root.
2. Change directories to `/home/ftp`.
3. Create a directory called `incoming`.
4. Change the write permissions to all everyone write access to the `chmod a+w /home/ftp/incoming` directory.

Test your FTP server before letting other users onto it

1. FTP to your server with the command `ftp localhost`.
2. Log on as user anonymous. Enter a password when prompted. If the password was not a valid email address, the server should issue a warning but still let you in.
3. Change to the incoming directory.
4. Set your FTP client's binary mode by typing the command `bin` at the `ftp>` prompt.
5. Attempt to upload a file to the server using the command `<filename>` where `filename` is the name of the file you want to upload.
6. Try to download a file from your FTP server to make sure that everything works as expected.

Enabling a Web Server

The stock web server that Red Hat Linux ships with is Apache. This is the most popular web server used on the Internet by a large margin, and is fast and relatively efficient. It's not unreasonable to use Linux as a high-volume web server with Apache, and a great many sites on the Internet run this combination.

To set up Apache on your system, ensure that you have the correct package installed:

1. Confirm that Apache is installed on your system by issuing the command `rpm -q apache` at the command line. If the system reports that the package is not installed, you must install it before proceeding.
2. Although Apache can be run under the auspices of `inetd`, this is not common. Web clients are an impatient bunch, and the added time it takes for `inetd` to start Apache to handle a request for each connection adds too much wait time for all but the least-loaded web servers. Apache is usually started as a regular daemon, and is left to manage itself after that. Use `chkconfig` to see if the service `httpd` (the generic name for web services) is started: `chkconfig --list httpd`. If the service is listed as `on` for the run level where your system is (probably 3), then Apache starts for this run level.
3. If `httpd` is not configured to start for your run level, typing `chkconfig httpd reset` should set up Apache to run in the run levels in which it should be running.
4. If you're sure that Apache was not started when the system last entered your current run level, you can start it manually by giving the command `/etc/rc.d/init.d/httpd start`. Watch for error messages.
5. Test your web server by starting a web client on your machine, such as `lynx` for text mode, or Netscape for X11, and going to address `http://localhost`. You should get the page entitled "It Worked!"

The files that your web server reads by default are in `/home/httpd/html`.

Configuring the Apache Web Server

Apache's configuration files are kept in `/etc/httpd/conf`.

`httpd.conf` contains the main server configuration. You may need to change the `ServerName` directive for the server if, when started, the server responds with the message `Unable to resolve host name` or `Unable to determine local host name`. This file typically contains other server-specific settings used to fine-tune the server, such as the minimum and maximum number of servers processes to run at the same time, and the number of requests each server should process before terminating. Each server process services one request at once, so it's important to keep these numbers appropriate to the load on the server.

`srm.conf` contains information for Apache on how to handle different file types, and which directory to treat as the root directory for the server.

`access.conf` contains all the access control options for all the directories on the server. With `access.conf` it is possible, for example, to exclude certain addresses from accessing the server, or certain directories on the server.

These files are very well commented and each setting is documented in detail. If you point your web browser at `localhost` (or if you are on another machine, the Linux machine's host name) and follow the links to Apache Documentation, you see the most current documentation that shipped with the version of the server that is installed.

CHAPTER

29

Managing the Filesystem

By James Youngman

Mounting hard drives and other filesystems

Mounting disks with Red Hat's `usermount` command

Mounting filesystems with the `mount` command

Preparing and mounting filesystems with Red Hat's `cabaret` tool

Setting up filesystems with Red Hat's `fstool` command

Editing the filesystem table `/etc/fstab`

Repairing damaged filesystems

Restoring Linux system files

Mounting and Unmounting Filesystems

The filesystems on your hard disk drives are mounted for you automatically when the system boots. The removable devices (for example, floppy disks and CD-ROM drives) are not.

All of the people using a Linux machine see the same view of the filesystem (although many of them are unable to access all parts of it). This means that mounting a filesystem is an action reserved for the superuser. The superuser can indicate that some filesystems can be mounted and unmounted by ordinary users (the `user` option in the file `/etc/fstab` is used for this).

The superuser sets up the `/etc/fstab` file to specify what filesystems are used on each device, using either the `cabaret` command, the Red Hat control panel, or by using a text editor directly on the `/etc/fstab` file.

SEE ALSO

➤ *To learn more about being a superuser and using the* `su` *command with Linux, see page 5.*

Using the *usermount* Command

Red Hat Linux comes with a command called `usermount` that provides a GUI interface for mounting and unmounting filesystems. The `usermount` command must be run during an X11 session. When you start `usermount`, it shows you what filesystems you can *mount* (or format). The `usermount` program is shown in Figure 29.1.

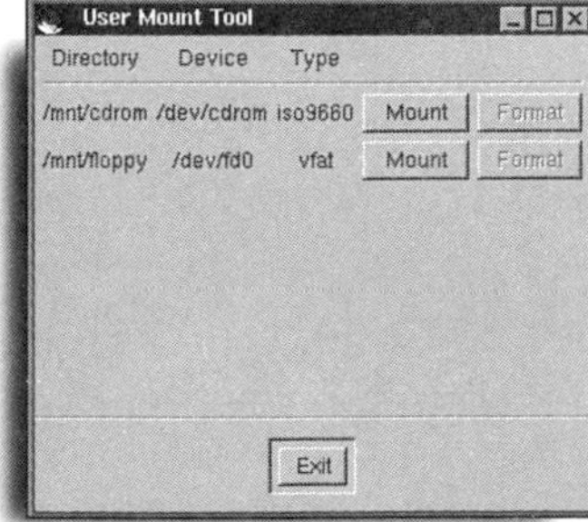

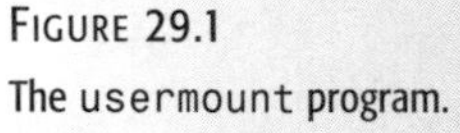
FIGURE 29.1
The `usermount` program.

SEE ALSO

➤ *To learn more about the X Window System, see page 260.*

The buttons for `/mnt/cdrom` (the CD-ROM drive) and `/mnt/floppy` (the floppy disk drive) are labeled Mount and Format. If you click the Mount button with a disk in the drive, the disk is mounted and the button changes to Unmount, as shown in Figure 29.2.

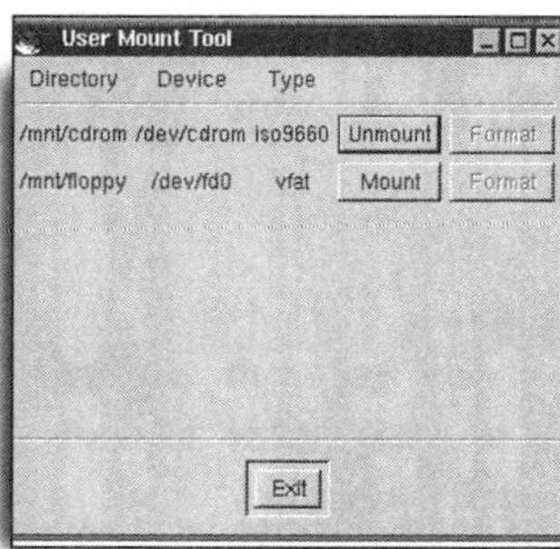

FIGURE 29.2
The disk is mounted and the button changes to Unmount.

If you try to mount the floppy disk (`/dev/fd0`) without having a disk in the drive, you receive an error message in a dialog box similar to the one shown in Figure 29.3.

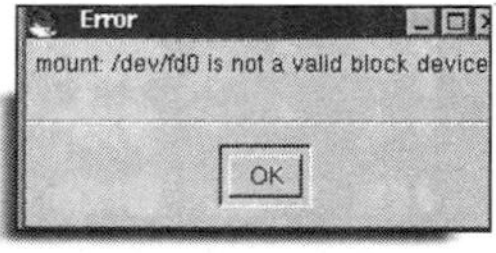

FIGURE 29.3
Mounting without the disk in the drive results in this dialog box.

Formatting a floppy disk with *usermount*

1. To format a floppy disk with the `usermount` command, your system must be set up so that you are allowed (have permission) to write to the floppy disk drive.
2. Insert a blank disk in your disk drive, and start the `usermount` command from the command line of a terminal window like this:

```
# usermount
```

3. The Format button is active for the floppy drive. Ensure that there is no data that you want to keep in the drive before clicking this button.
4. Click the Format button. A dialog box appears, asking if you are sure. There is also a checkbox on the dialog box that asks if you want to do a low-level format (as shown in Figure 29.4).

   If you don't elect to do the low-level format because the disk has already been formatted, Linux builds a new, clean filesystem on the disk, which takes a second or so. A low-level format, on the other hand, takes quite a while.

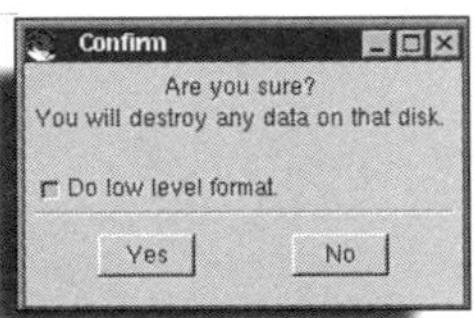

FIGURE 29.4
Specify whether you want to do a low-level format.

Although you can reformat your hard disk partitions by using Linux's `fdisk` and `mkfs` programs, they are omitted from the `usermount` program in the interests of safety.

SEE ALSO

➤ *For more information about using or setting permissions, see page 418.*

Using the *mount* Command

To mount a block device into the file system, use the `mount` command. You must specify what device contains the filesystem, what type it is, and where in the directory hierarchy to mount it.

A `mount` command looks like this:

```
mount [-t type] [-o options] device mount-point
```

`device` must be a block device; or, if it contains a colon, it can be the name of another machine from which to mount a filesystem. *`mount-point`* should be an existing directory; the filesystem appears at this position (anything previously in that directory is

hidden). The filesystem type and options are optional, and the variety and meaning of options depend on the type of filesystem being mounted. If the filesystem you want to mount is specified in the `/etc/fstab` file, you need to specify only the mount point or the device name; the other details will be read from `/etc/fstab` by `mount`.

Mounting a floppy with the *mount* command

1. Use the `mount` command, followed by the device name, the `-t` (filesystem type) option, the name of a filesystem, and the mount point in your system's directory structure. For example, to mount a floppy disk, first log on as the root operator, and then use the `mkdir` command to create a mount point like this:

```
# mkdir /mnt/floppy
```

2. Use the `mount` command, specifying your floppy drive's device name, and the type of filesystem (such as DOS), like this:

```
# mount /dev/fd1 -t vfat /mnt/floppy
mount: block device /dev/fd1 is write-protected,
➥mounting read-only
```

3. The disk's contents become available at the specified mount point (directory). Use the `ls` (list directory) command to verify that the disk is mounted, like this:

```
# ls /mnt/floppy
grub-0.4.tar.gz
```

4. After you have finished reading, copying, or deleting files on the disk, use the `umount` command, followed by the mount point, or pathname, to unmount the filesystem, like this:

```
# umount /mnt/floppy
```

SEE ALSO

➤ *To learn more about drivers, code modules, and the magic of the Linux kernel, see page 577.*

Is it magic, or the Linux `kerneld` daemon?

Mounting a `vfat` floppy disk causes the Linux kernel to automatically load the `vfat` driver into the kernel while it is needed. These (and other) drivers are loaded by the system daemon `kerneld`; when the drivers are no longer being used, such as after a filesystem is unmounted, the drivers are unloaded to recover the memory.

Don't forget the mount point

In order to mount a filesystem, the point at which it is to be mounted (that is, the mount point) must be a directory. This directory doesn't have to be empty but after the filesystem is mounted, any files "underneath" it will be inaccessible. Be careful when mounting disks or other media!

Any one of several things can cause the `mount` command to fail. It is possible to specify an incorrect device name (that is, to specify a device file that does not exist, one for which a driver is not available in the kernel, or one for which the hardware is not present). Other error conditions include unreadable devices (for example, empty floppy drives or bad media) and insufficient permissions (`mount` commands other than those sanctioned by the administrator by listing them with the option `user` in `/etc/fstab` are forbidden to ordinary users). Trying to mount a device at a mount point that does not already exist also will not work.

Still more error conditions are possible but unlikely (for example, exceeding the compiled-in limit to the number of mounted filesystems) or self-explanatory (for example, most usage errors for the `mount` command itself).

Linux provides a *singly rooted* filesystem, in contrast to those operating systems that give each filesystem a separate drive letter. Although this might seem less flexible, it is actually *more* flexible, because the size of each block device (that is, the hard disk, or whatever) is hidden from programs, and things can be moved around.

For example, if you have some software that expects to be installed in `/opt/umsp`, you can install it in `/big-disk/stuff/umsp` and make `/opt/umsp` a symbolic link. There is also no need to edit a myriad of configuration files that are now using the wrong drive letter after you install a new disk drive, for example.

There are many options governing how a mounted filesystem behaves; for example, it can be mounted read-only. There are options for filesystems such as `msdos`, and others, such as the `nfs` filesystem, which has so many options that it has a separate manual page (`man nfs`).

Table 29.1 contains options useful for `mount`, given in alphabetical order. Unless otherwise indicated, these options are valid for all filesystem types, although asking for asynchronous writes to a CD-ROM is no use! Options applicable only to `nfs` filesystems are not listed here; refer to the `nfs` manual page for those.

TABLE 29.1 ***mount* options**

Option	Description
`async`	Write requests for the filesystem normally should wait until the data has reached the hardware; with this option, the program continues immediately instead. This does mean that the system is slightly more prone to data loss in the event of a system crash, but, on the other hand, crashes are very rare with Linux. This option speeds up `nfs` filesystems by a startling extent. The opposite of this option is `sync`.
`auto`	Indicates to `mount` that it should mount the device when given the `-a` flag. This flag is used by the startup scripts to make sure that all the required filesystems are mounted at boot time. The opposite of this option is `noauto`.
`defaults`	Turns on the options `rw`, `suid`, `dev`, `exec`, `auto`, `nouser`, and `async`.
`dev`	Allows device nodes on the system to be used. Access to devices is completely determined by access rights to the on-disk device node. Hence, if you mount an `ext2` filesystem on a floppy and you have previously placed a writable `/dev/kmem` device file on the disk, then you've just gained read/write access to kernel memory. System administrators generally prevent this from happening by mounting removable filesystems with the `nodev` `mount` option.
`exec`	Indicates to the kernel that it should allow the execution of programs on the filesystem. This option is more frequently seen as `noexec`, which indicates to the kernel that execution of programs on this filesystem shouldn't be allowed. This is generally used as a security precaution or for `nfs` filesystems mounted from another machine that contain executable files of a format unsuitable for this machine (for example, intended for a different CPU).
`noauto`	Opposite of `auto`; see `auto` table entry.
`nodev`	Opposite of `dev`; see `dev` table entry.
`noexec`	Opposite of `exec`; see `exec` table entry.
`nosuid`	Opposite of `suid`; see `suid` table entry.

continues...

TABLE 29.1 Continued

Option	Description
`nouser`	Opposite of `user`; see `user` table entry.
`remount`	Allows the `mount` command to change the flags for an already-mounted filesystem without interrupting its use. You can't unmount a filesystem that is currently in use, and this option is basically a workaround. The system startup scripts, for example, use the command `mount -n -o remount,ro /` to change the root filesystem from read-only (it starts off this way) to read/write (its normal state). The `-n` option indicates to `mount` that it shouldn't update `/etc/fstab` because it can't do this while the root filesystem is still read-only.
`ro`	Mounts the filesystem read-only. This is the opposite of the option `rw`.
`rw`	Mounts the filesystem read/write. This is the opposite of the option `ro`.
`suid`	Allows the set user ID and set group ID file mode bits to take effect. The opposite of this option is `nosuid`. The `nosuid` option is more usual; it is used for the same sorts of reasons that `nodev` is used.
`sync`	All write operations cause the calling program to wait until the data has been committed to the hardware. This mode of operation is slower but a little more reliable than its opposite, asynchronous I/O, which is indicated by the option `async` (see preceding).
`user`	Allows ordinary users to mount the filesystem. When there is a `user` option in `/etc/fstab`, ordinary users indicate which filesystem they want to mount or unmount by giving the device name or mount point; all the other relevant information is taken from the `/etc/fstab` file. For security reasons, `user` implies the `noexec`, `nosuid`, and `nodev` options.

Options are processed by the `mount` command in the order in which they appear on the command line (or in `/etc/fstab`). Thus, it is possible to allow users to mount a filesystem and then run set user ID executables by using the options `user, suid`, in that order. Using them in reverse order (`suid, user`) doesn't work because the `user` option turns the `suid` option off again.

SEE ALSO

➤ *For more information about using the* `mount` *command, see page 115.*

There are many other options available, but these are all specific to particular filesystems. All the valid options for `mount` are detailed in its manual page. An example is the `umask` flag for the `vfat` and `fat` filesystems, which allows you to make all the files on your MS-DOS or Windows partitions readable (or even writable if you prefer) for all the users on your Linux system.

Setting Up New Filesystems

When the kernel boots, it attempts to mount a root filesystem from the device specified by the kernel loader, LILO. The root filesystem is initially mounted read-only. During the boot process, the filesystems listed in the filesystem table `/etc/fstab` are mounted. This file specifies which devices are to be mounted, what kinds of filesystems they contain, at what point in the filesystem the mount takes place, and any options governing *how* they are to be mounted. The format of this file is described in `fstab`.

Using Red Hat's *cabaret* Tool

There are times when it is not possible to use Red Hat's filesystem manager (`fstool`, discussed later in this chapter) under the X Window System—for example, when X doesn't run because it wasn't installed, or when X does run but too slowly, such as when you are on the wrong end of a slow Internet link. In these cases, it is useful to implement Red Hat's `cabaret` program, which runs on any kind of text display (the text-mode console, or a terminal emulator on another computer, for example).

Importance of the `/etc/fstab` table

Always make a backup copy of the filesystem table, `/etc/fstab`, before making changes to your system, such as adding additional hard drives, or editing the table. If you make a mistake in the file, your system may not boot properly or at all. With a backup copy you can easily restore your system's settings.

Starting *cabaret*

`cabaret` resides in the `/usr/sbin` directory with many of the administration programs (the others are stored in `/sbin`). You start it by typing the following:

```
..../usr/sbin/cabaret
```

Filesystem mount points

If you mount a filesystem on a directory, this hides anything that was previously there. When you unmount the filesystem, it is again visible.

Adding a New Local Filesystem by Using *cabaret*

If you want to add a filesystem on an unused part of a hard disk, you must make an empty partition first. Please see Chapter 7, "Working with Hard Drives," for instructions on this. If the partition already exists, either because it belongs to another operating system, or because you just finished following the instructions in Chapter 7, please continue.

Adding a filesystem to an existing partition

1. Press the Tab key until the Add button is highlighted and then press Enter. (Alternatively, just press F2.)
2. Choose from the provided list the type of the filesystem that you want to add.
3. Select Add (as in step 1).
4. Type in the name of the directory in which you want to mount the filesystem (this directory must already exist; if you need to create it, you can back out of the current procedure by selecting Cancel).
5. In the Device text box, enter the name of the device containing the filesystem (for example, `/dev/fd0` is the first floppy disk). Select Continue.
6. The Options dialog box that appears next allows you to change certain options for this filesystem. The defaults are usually appropriate. Click Done when you are finished.
7. Select Save and confirm that you want to save these changes to the `/etc/fstab` file by selecting Save in the Confirmation dialog box.

SEE ALSO

➤ *For additional information on partitioning, formatting, and mounting other filesystems with Red Hat's* `cabaret` *command, see page 106.*

Adding a New Network Filesystem by Using *cabaret*

If you want to mount a network filesystem, you must first ensure that you can communicate over the network to the server machine. For more information about this, please see Chapter 27, "Managing Network Connections." You also need to ensure that the remote machine permits you to mount its shared filesystems. You may need to consult with the administrator of that machine to confirm this.

Ensuring that you can communicate with the server

1. Start the `cabaret` command. Select Add from `cabaret`'s main menu.
2. Select the appropriate filesystem type (`smb` for a Windows share, or `nfs`, for example).
3. For `nfs`, give the name of the server in the Choose Remote System dialog box. Select one from the list of available filesystems provided.

   For `smb`, you must instead give the name of the remote system, the name of the share, and where the filesystem should be mounted on your machine.
4. Select any options you require from the Options dialog box. The defaults are usually appropriate; for `nfs`, however, there is a separate Options dialog box, some of which it is useful to change. Select Done when you are finished.
5. Select Save from the main menu, and then confirm that you want to save these changes to the `/etc/fstab` file by selecting Save in the Confirmation dialog box.

SEE ALSO

➤ *For hints on partitioning your system during the installation process, see page 632.*
➤ *To add or delete partitions on your hard disks, see page 106.*
➤ *For instructions on adding Zip drives, see page 123.*
➤ *For more information on networked filesystems, see page 461.*

Filesystem Options

When you create a new entry for a filesystem using `cabaret`, as described in the preceding sections, you are given the opportunity to change the options pertaining to it. Many options are possible, but only some of them are commonly used.

The options fall fairly neatly into those suitable for removable devices and those suitable for nonremovable ones.

Options Useful for Removable Devices

Removable devices like floppy disks must be mounted and unmounted in order to be used (unless you use the `mtools` package for floppy disks). The Users Can Mount Filesystem option (which appears as `user` in `/etc/fstab`) is required for this to happen. Conversely, for nonremovable devices like hard disk partitions, allowing just anybody to unmount the `/usr` filesystem would pretty much be a disaster. The various Ignore options are listed in Table 29.2.

TABLE 29.2 **Removable device mounting options**

Long Name	Short Name
Ignore setuid executables	`nosuid`
Ignore device files	`nodev`
Ignore executables	`noexec`

The first two options, `nosuid` and `nodev`, are security features, which prevent any old person from bringing along a specially prepared UNIX filesystem and using it to compromise your machine. If you have entries in your filesystem table for removable ext2 filesystems, set these two options for them.

Setting removable device options

1. Log on as the root operator. Using your favorite text editor, such as `pico`, open the `/etc/fstab` file:

   ```
   # pico -w /etc/fstab
   ```

2. If you have a removable device, such as a Zip drive, you can make your system a bit more secure by inserting the `nosuid` and `nodev` mount options. Look for your device's entry in the `fstab` file:

   ```
   /dev/sda4   /mnt/zip     vfat
   ➥user,noauto,dev,exec,suid     0 0
   ```

3. Make sure the devices are not mounted. Then change the `dev` and `suid` options to `nodev` and `nosuid`, like this:

   ```
   /dev/sda4   /mnt/zip     vfat
   ➥user,noauto,nodev,exec,nosuid     0 0
   ```

4. Save the `fstab` and quit your word processor.

The third ignore option is also sometimes used on network servers. Some filesystems are designed to be mounted only by client machines and aren't of much use to the server itself. They might, for example, contain executables for a bunch of client machines running some incompatible version of UNIX. If this is the case, you should set the `noexec` option so that nobody can try to run the incompatible kinds of programs.

Options Useful for Fixed Devices

Most fixed devices need to be mounted at boot time, so that option should normally be set for nonremovable devices. On the other hand, this option should not normally be set for removable devices since there often is no disk in the drive at boot time.

The writable (`rw`) flag is usually set, but one might unset it for CD-ROM drives that aren't writable anyway, or for filesystems containing important archive data.

The `updateatime` option is relatively new to Linux and isn't used by most people. Normally one of the three timestamps on a file is a record of the time that it was last accessed. If a filesystem is heavily read from and rarely written to, then the endless updating of access-time timestamps can lead to an unproductive waste of performance.

Access timestamps and Linux

Although the access timestamp is an integral part of all UNIX filesystems, including Linux's `ext` filesystem, disabling usually doesn't break anything. The most significant thing that this breaks is the reporting of new mail; if the modification time for your mailbox is newer than its access time, you must have received new mail since you last read mail. Conversely, if the access time is newer, you have no unread mail. This fact is used by the `finger` program. Some specialized systems benefit from the `noatime` option, particularly Usenet News servers with a lot of clients. For most other machines, this option is usually left alone.

The `user` option is occasionally used for filesystems belonging to other operating systems; it allows ordinary users to mount Microsoft Windows filesystems (for example) and access the files on them without falling afoul of the fact that Windows (except Windows NT in some cases) does not keep track of who owns files.

Mount Options for NFS Filesystems

When you set up an NFS filesystem, the normal Options dialog box also includes an NFS Options button that allows you to customize the way the filesystem is mounted and used.

Most of the `nfs` options are concerned with what should happen if the server machine is unreachable (because, for example, either it or the network has failed). This perhaps seems unlikely but, believe me, you'll care on the day it happens.

The default options just make the system keep trying indefinitely until the filesystem can be mounted. Many filesystems are essential but some are not. For nonessential filesystems, the default options are probably too conservative. For these, you should check the Retry in Background If Mount Fails checkbox. This allows your Linux system to continue to boot if the remote filesystem is not available. If a program has to use a file on the failing server, it waits until the filesystem has been mounted (the upper limit on how long this takes until it gives up is also configurable).

The read and write sizes are configurable. Again, the defaults are conservative and should be satisfactory. The default read and write size is 1,024 bytes (this conveniently fits inside a 1,500-byte Ethernet packet), but often the system performs much better if this size is increased to 4,096 or even 8,912 bytes (that is, 4KB or 8KB). Sometimes doing this actually makes things worse rather than better, however; it depends on the server and the quality of the network cards, as well as the amount of network traffic.

Creating New Filesystems with *cabaret*

After you have configured a new filesystem entry using `cabaret`, you must create the filesystem on the disk itself. The Status button in `cabaret` provides a Format button. The resulting menu gives several options for the filesystem type with the format, but the type you already configured is preselected for you. If the filesystem you want is VFAT (Windows 95), you must format the disk as an MS-DOS disk, because the only difference between the two kinds of filesystems is the different way they handle long filenames.

The Red Hat Filesystem Manager

An easy way to set up filesystem entries in `/etc/fstab` is with the configuration tool Filesystem Manager in the Red Hat Control Panel (although you can invoke it separately as `fstool`). This program must be run during X11 sessions. The Filesystem Manager is shown in Figure 29.5.

```
cabaret 0.5                                   Copyright (C) 1997 Red Hat Software
                    Edit Filesystem Configuration

 /                   /dev/hda1                                    ext2
 /proc               /proc                                        proc
 /var                /dev/hda3                                    ext2
 /usr                /dev/hdc2                                    ext2
 /home               /dev/hdc3                                    ext2
 none                /dev/hda2                                    swap
 /mnt/bigdisk        /dev/hdc4                                    ext2
 /mnt/cdrom          /dev/hdd                                     iso9660
 /mnt/floppy         /dev/fd1                                     vfat
 /mnt/pcd            /dev/sbpcd0                                  iso9660
 /usr/src            /dev/hdb2                                    ext2
 /mnt/periwinkle     periwinkle:/                                 nfs
 /mnt/pericd         periwinkle:/mnt/cdrom                        nfs

  Edit     Add     Delete     Status     Save     Quit

  F1=Edit   F2=Add   F3=Delete   F4=Status   F5=Save   F12=Quit
```

FIGURE 29.5

The Filesystem Manager.

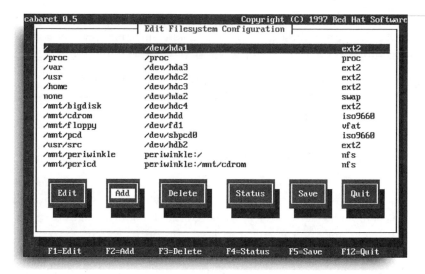

When you start `fstool`, it produces a window that contains all the entries in `/etc/fstab`. Each entry shows the device name, mount point, filesystem type, size, space used, and space available. Additionally, each mounted filesystem is marked with an asterisk. The Info button displays extra information about the highlighted filesystem (the same information as is indicated in `/etc/fstab` and in the output of the `df` command).

Filesystems can be mounted or unmounted with two buttons: Mount and Unmount. Any errors that occur are shown in a dialog box; this can happen if, for example, you try to mount a CD-ROM when there is no CD in the drive. (Go ahead and try it.) The Format button works only for hard disk partitions; for these, it runs `mkfs` (see the section "Creating New Filesystems Manually," later in this chapter). Other media (for example, floppy disks) are formatted differently.

The Check button works only for `ext2` and `minix` filesystems. If you get the error `fsck: command not found`, this just means that the directory `/sbin` is not on your path; you should be able to fix this by running `su - root`. (You might also need to do `export DISPLAY=:0.0`, if that is necessary.) Checking a filesystem can take a while, and the result is shown in a dialog box afterward. It is very unusual for errors to be shown for hard disk filesystems here because these are checked at boot time and don't get corrupted during the normal operation of Linux.

The NFS menu is used to add and remove NFS network mounts. You can exit the Filesystem Manager by selecting the Quit option from the FSM menu.

Editing */etc/fstab* Manually

The filesystem table `/etc/fstab` is just a text file; it is designed to have a specific format that is readable by humans and not just computers. `/etc/fstab` is separated into columns by tabs or spaces and you can edit it with your favorite text editor. You must take care, however, if you modify it by hand, because removing or corrupting an entry can make the system unable to mount that filesystem next time it boots. My `/etc/fstab` looks like this:

```
#
# /etc/fstab
#
# You should be using fstool (control-panel) to edit this!
#
#<device> <mountpoint> <filesystemtype> <options>    <dump>
➥<fsckorder>

/dev/hda1      /           ext2  defaults  1        1
/dev/hdb5      /home       ext2  defaults,rw     1  2
/dev/hda3      /usr        ext2  defaults        1  2
/dev/hdb1      /usr/src    ext2  defaults        1  3

/dev/hdc       /mnt/cdrom  iso9660user,noauto,ro 0  0
/dev/sbpcd0    /mnt/pcd    iso9660user,noauto,ro 0  0
/dev/fd1       /mnt/floppy vfat   user,noauto    0  0

/proc           /proc        proc       defaults
/dev/hda2      none          swap       sw
```

The first four entries are the ext2 filesystems comprising my Linux system. When Linux is booted, the root filesystem is mounted first; all the other local (that is, non-network) filesystems are mounted next.

The following three filesystems are all removable filesystems: two CD-ROM drives and a floppy disk drive. These have the noauto option set so that they are not automatically mounted at boot time. These removable devices have the user option set so that I can mount and unmount them without having to use su all the time. The CD-ROMs have the filesystem type iso9660, which is the standard filesystem for CD-ROMs, and the floppy drive has the filesystem type vfat, because I often use it for interchanging data with MS-DOS and Windows systems.

Order is important in /etc/fstab

Filesystems appear in /etc/fstab in the order in which they are mounted; /usr must appear before /usr/src, for example, because the mount point for one filesystem exists on the other. Be sure to use the proper order if you have partitioned your hard drive in order to separate parts of the Linux file system.

/proc is a special filesystem provided by the kernel as a way of providing information about the system to user programs. The information in the /proc filesystem is used in order to make utilities such as ps, top, xload, free, netstat, and so on, work. Some of the "files" in /proc are really enormous (for example, /proc/kcore) but don't worry—all the information in the /proc filesystem is generated on-the-fly by the Linux kernel as you read it; no disk space is wasted. You can tell that they are not real files because, for example, root can't give them away with chown.

The final "filesystem" isn't, in fact, a filesystem at all; it is an entry that indicates a disk partition used as swap space. Swap partitions are used to implement virtual memory. Files can also be used for swap space. The names of the swap files go in the first column where the device name usually goes.

The two numeric columns on the right relate to the operation of the dump and fsck commands, respectively. The dump command compares the number in column five (the *dump interval*) with the number of days since that filesystem was last backed up so that it can inform the system administrator that the filesystem needs to be backed up. Other backup software—for example, Amanda—can also use this field for the same purpose. (Amanda can be found at the URL **http://www.cs.umd.edu/projects/amanda/amanda.html**.) Filesystems without a dump interval field are assumed to have a dump interval of zero, denoting "never dump." For more information, see the manual page for dump.

The sixth column is the `fsck pass`, which indicates the filesystems that can be checked in parallel at boot time. The root filesystem is always checked first, but after that, separate drives can be checked simultaneously, Linux being a multitasking operating system. There is no point, however, in checking two filesystems on the same hard drive at the same time, because this results in lots of extra disk head movement and wasted time. All the filesystems that have the same pass number are checked in parallel, from 1 upward. Filesystems with a `0` or missing pass number (such as the floppy and CD-ROM drives) are not checked at all.

Creating New Filesystems Manually

When you install Red Hat Linux, the installation process makes some new filesystems and sets the system up to use them. You can format new filesystems by using `cabaret`, as described in the earlier section "Creating New Filesystems with `cabaret`," but you can also do this manually.

Many operating systems don't distinguish between the preparation of the device's surface to receive data (formatting) and the building of new filesystems. Linux does distinguish between the two, principally because only floppy disks need formatting in any case, and also because Linux offers as many as half a dozen different filesystems that can be created (on any block device).

SEE ALSO

➤ *For a list of a number of different filesystems for Linux, see Table 7.1 on page 94.*

Linux provides a generic command, `mkfs`, that enables you to make a filesystem on a block device. In fact, because UNIX manages almost all resources with the same set of operations, `mkfs` can be used to generate a filesystem inside an ordinary file! Because this is unusual, `mkfs` asks for confirmation before proceeding. When this is done, you can even mount the resulting filesystem using the loop device.

Because of the tremendous variety of filesystems available, almost all the work of building the new filesystem is delegated to a separate program for each; however, the generic `mkfs` program provides a single interface for invoking them all. It's not uncommon to pass options to the top-level `mkfs` (for example, `-V` to make it show what commands it executes or `-c` to make it check the device for bad blocks). The generic `mkfs` program also enables you to pass options to the filesystem-specific `mkfs`. There are many of these filesystem-dependent options, but most of them have sensible defaults, and you normally would not want to change them.

The only options you might want to pass to `mke2fs`, which builds `ext2` filesystems, are `-m` and `-i`. The `-m` option specifies how much of the filesystem is reserved for root's use (for example, for working space when the system disk would otherwise have filled completely). The `-i` option is more rarely exercised and is used for setting the balance between inodes and disk blocks; it is related to the expected average file size. As stated previously, the defaults are reasonable for most purposes, so these options are used only in special circumstances.

Formatting and creating a Linux floppy *fstab* entry

1. Log on as the root operator and insert a blank disk into your floppy drive.
2. Use the `mkfs` command, followed by the `-t` option, the name of a filesystem, and the floppy device name on the command line to format a floppy:

```
# mkfs -t ext2 /dev/fd1
mke2fs 1.10, 24-Apr-97 for EXT2 FS 0.5b, 95/08/09
Linux ext2 filesystem format
Filesystem label=
360 inodes, 1440 blocks
72 blocks (5.00) reserved for the super user
First data block=1
Block size=1024 (log=0)
Fragment size=1024 (log=0)
1 block group
8192 blocks per group, 8192 fragments per group
360 inodes per group

Writing inode tables: done
Writing superblocks and filesystem accounting
➥information: done
```

3. After the mkfs command creates the filesystem on your disk, you can include the disk in your filesystem's table by changing an existing line referring to a vfat filesystem on /dev/fd1, or by creating a new line.

   Log on as the root operator, and then, using your favorite text editor, open the /etc/fstab file. Type an entry for your floppy like this:

   ```
   /dev/fd1        /mnt/floppy     ext2
   ➥user,sync,errors=continue 0 0
   ```

4. You can then use the mount command to mount your new Linux disk, like this:

   ```
   # mount -t ext2 /dev/fd1 /mnt/floppy
   ```

5. Use the ls command, along with the -la (long-format and all) options, to verify the contents of the new disk:

   ```
   # ls -la /mnt/floppy
   total 14
   drwxr-xr-x   3 root     root          1024 Aug  1
   ➥19:49 .
   drwxr-xr-x   7 root     root          1024 Jul  3
   ➥21:47 ..
   drwxr-xr-x   2 root     root         12288 Aug  1 19:49
   ➥lost+found
   ```

6. Finally, you can unmount the disk with the umount command, followed by the mount point of the disk:

   ```
   # umount /mnt/floppy
   ```

The structure and creation of an ext2 filesystem on a floppy shows that there is no volume label, and there are 4,096 bytes (4KB) per inode (360 × 4 = 1,440). The block size is 1KB and 5% of the disk is reserved for root. These are the defaults (which are explained in the mke2fs manual page).

The first three columns in the floppy disk's /etc/fstab entry are the Device, Mount Point, and Filesystem type. The Options column is more complex than previous ones. The user option indicates that users are allowed to mount this filesystem. The `sync` option indicates that programs writing to this filesystem wait while each write finishes, and only then continue.

This might seem obvious, but it is not the normal state of affairs. The kernel normally manages filesystem writes in such a way as to provide high performance (data still gets written to the device, of course, but it doesn't necessarily happen immediately). This is perfect for fixed devices such as hard disks, but for low-capacity removable devices such as floppy disks, it's less beneficial. Normally, you write a few files to a floppy, then unmount it and take it away. The unmount operation must wait until all data has been written to the device before it can finish (and the disk can then be removed).

Having to wait like this is off-putting, and there is always the risk that someone might copy a file to the floppy, wait for the disk light to go out, and remove it. With asynchronous writes, some buffered data might not have yet been written to disk. Hence, synchronous writes are safer for removable media.

The `ext2` filesystem has a configurable strategy for errors. If an `ext2` filesystem encounters an error (for example, a bad disk block), there are three possible responses to the error:

- Remount the device read-only—For filesystems that contain mostly nonessential data (for example, `/tmp`, `/var/tmp`, or news spools), remounting the filesystem read-only so that it can be fixed with `fsck` is often the best choice.
- Panic—Continuing in the face of potentially corrupted system configuration files is unwise, so a kernel *panic* (that is, a controlled crash—or emergency landing, if you prefer) can sometimes be appropriate.
- Ignore it—Causing a system shutdown if a floppy disk has a bad sector is a little excessive, so the `continue` option tells the kernel to "carry on regardless" in this situation. If this actually does happen, the best thing to do is to use the `-c` option of `e2fsck`, for example, with `fsck -t ext2 -c /dev/fd1`. This runs `e2fsck`, giving it the `-c` option, which

invokes the `badblocks` command to test the device for bad disk blocks. After this is done, `e2fsck` does its best to recover from the situation.

How to Organize Your File System Tree

It is often useful to have major parts of the Linux file system on separate partitions; this can make upgrades and reinstalls easier, and it can also facilitate backup and network administration.

Good Candidates for Separate Filesystems

The best candidate for being on a separate filesystem is the `/home` tree. A separate `/home` file system means that your own data will survive unscathed even if you have to reinstall everything from scratch. If you have more than one machine, it is often useful to mount `/home` over the network so that your files can be shared between all the machines.

Other filesystems are made separate for different reasons—for example, so that they can be mounted over the network, or so that they can have different mount options.

Because the `/usr` file system is large, it is often on a separate filesystem, sometimes mounted from another machine. A separate `/usr` also allows you to have a much smaller root (`/`) partition. Having a small root partition is beneficial because this tends to reduce the chances of it becoming corrupted when the power fails. Having a separate `/var` partition can help for the same reason.

Some of the machines that I administer are security-critical. On these machines I make `/var/log` a separate, huge filesystem. There are two reasons for this. First, it means that filling up `/tmp` or `/var` will not mean that the system cannot continue to log activity. Second, making `/var/log` large means that an attacker (or "cracker") can't fill up the partition in order to prevent the logging of future activities.

Bad Candidates for Separate Filesystems

There are some directories that absolutely must be part of the root filesystem. These are listed in Table 29.3.

TABLE 29.3 **Essential Linux directories of the root filesystem**

Directory Name	Description
/bin	The mount command lives in /bin and if it is not available on the root file system, there is no way to mount any other filesystem.
/sbin	Contains programs essential to booting, such as /sbin/init, the very first program to be started (the kernel starts it in order to get the system going).
/etc	Contains many configuration files that must be present at boot time, such as /etc/inittab, and /etc/fstab.
/dev	Contains device files for all the other filesystems in /dev. The mount command needs these in order to work.
/lib	Contains libraries to which many programs needed at boot time are dynamically linked.
/root	It's a good idea to have root's home directory available even when some filesystems cannot be mounted; useful backup files may be kept there.

Almost any other directories can be on separate filesystems. Insightful users will note that the `/boot` directory is not in this list. That is because the files in `/boot` are not needed at boot time; they are needed only when you run the program `/sbin/lilo`. As long as the BIOS can read these files by sector-by-sector BIOS calls, the kernel can be loaded by the boot loader. After the kernel is loaded and the root file system is mounted, these files have done their job. Having a separate `/boot` file system allows you to ensure that it resides near the start of a large hard disk. This can be vital for some older PC-compatible machines.

Repairing Filesystems

Some disk data is kept in memory temporarily before being written to disk, for performance reasons (see the previous discussion of the `sync` mount option). If the kernel does not have an opportunity to actually write this data, the filesystem can become corrupted. This can happen in several ways:

- The storage device (for example, a floppy disk) can be manually removed before the kernel has finished with it.
- The system might suffer a power loss.
- The user might mistakenly turn off the power or accidentally press the reset button.

As part of the boot process, Linux runs the `fsck` program, whose job it is to check and repair filesystems. Most of the time, the boot follows a controlled shutdown (see the manual page for `shutdown`), and in this case, the filesystems will have been unmounted before the reboot. In this case, `fsck` says that they are "clean." It knows this because before unmounting them, the kernel writes a special signature on the filesystem to indicate that the data is intact. When the filesystem is mounted again for writing, this signature is removed.

If, on the other hand, one of the disasters listed earlier takes place, the filesystems will not be marked "clean," and when `fsck` is invoked, as usual, it will notice this and begin a full check of the filesystem. This also occurs if you specify the `-f` flag to `fsck`. To prevent errors creeping up on it, `fsck` enforces a periodic check; a full check is done at an interval specified on the filesystem itself (usually every 20 boots or every six months, whichever comes sooner), even if it was unmounted cleanly.

The boot process checks the root filesystem and then mounts it read-write. (It's mounted read-only by the kernel; `fsck` asks for confirmation before operating on a read-write filesystem, and this is not desirable for an unattended reboot.) First, the root filesystem is checked with the following command:

```
fsck -V -a /
```

Then all the other filesystems are checked by executing this command:

```
fsck -R -A -V -a
```

These options specify that all the filesystems should be checked (`-A`) except the root filesystem, which doesn't need checking a second time (`-R`), and that operations produce informational messages about what it is doing as it goes (`-V`), but that the process should not be interactive (-a). This last option is included because, for example, there might not be anyone present to answer any questions from fsck.

In the case of serious filesystem corruption, the approach breaks down because there are some things that fsck will not do to a filesystem without your say-so. In this case, it returns an error value to its caller (the startup script), and the startup script spawns a shell to allow the administrator to run fsck interactively. When this has happened, this message appears:

```
*** An error occurred during the filesystem check.
*** Dropping you to a shell; the system will reboot
*** when you leave the shell.
Give root password for maintenance
(or type Control-D for normal startup):
```

This is a very troubling event, particularly because it might well appear if you have other problems with the system—for example, a lockup (leading you to press the Reset button) or a spontaneous reboot. None of the online manuals are guaranteed to be available at this stage, because they might be stored on the filesystem whose check failed. This prompt is issued if the root filesystem check failed, or the filesystem check failed for any of the other disk filesystems.

When the automatic fsck fails, you need to log on by specifying the root password and running the fsck program manually. When you have typed in the root password, you are presented with the following prompt:

```
(Repair filesystem) #
```

You might worry about what command to enter here, or indeed what to do at all. At least one of the filesystems needs to be checked, but which one? The preceding messages from fsck should indicate which, but it isn't necessary to go hunting for them. There is a set of options you can give to fsck that tells it to check *everything* manually, and this is a good fallback:

```
# fsck -A -V ; echo == $? ==
```

This is the same command as the previous one, but the -R option is missing, in case the root filesystem needs to be checked, and the `-a` option is missing, so `fsck` is in its "interactive" mode. This might enable a check to succeed just because it can now ask you questions. The purpose of the `echo == $? ==` command is to unambiguously interpret the outcome of the `fsck` operation. If the value printed between the equal signs is less than 4, all is well.

If this value is `4` or more, on the other hand, more recovery measures are needed. The meanings of the various values returned are as follows:

`0`	No errors
`1`	Filesystem errors corrected
`2`	System should be rebooted
`4`	Filesystem errors left uncorrected
`8`	Operational error
`16`	Usage or syntax error
`128`	Shared library error

If this does not work, this might be because of a *corrupted superblock*—`fsck` starts its disk check and if the superblock is corrupted, it can't start. By good design, the `ext2` filesystem has many backup superblocks scattered regularly throughout the filesystem. Suppose the command announces that it has failed to clean some particular filesystem—for example, `/dev/fubar`. You can start `fsck` again, using a backup superblock by using the following command:

```
# fsck -t ext2 -b 8193 /dev/fubar
```

`8193` is the block number for the first backup superblock. This backup superblock is at the start of block group 1 (the first is numbered 0). There are more backup superblocks at the start of block group 2 (`16385`), and block group 3 (`24577`); they are spaced at intervals of 8192 blocks. If you made a filesystem with settings other than the defaults, these might change. `mke2fs` lists the superblocks that it creates as it goes, so that is a good time to pay attention if you're not using the default settings. There are other things you can attempt if `fsck` is still not succeeding, but further failures are very rare and usually indicate hardware problems so severe that they prevent the proper operation of `fsck`. Examples include broken wires in the IDE connector cable and similar nasty problems. If this command still fails, you might seek expert help or try to fix the disk in a different machine.

These extreme measures are very unlikely; a manual `fsck`, in the unusual circumstance where it is actually required, almost always fixes things. After the manual `fsck` has worked, the root shell that the startup scripts provide has done its purpose. Type **`exit`** to exit it. At this point, in order to make sure that everything goes according to plan, the boot process is started again from the beginning. This second time around, the filesystems should all be error-free, and the system should boot normally.

Disaster Recovery

Easy disaster recovery, in computing as in life, requires forward planning. This means making regular backups of your computer, and checking that those backups work properly.

The actual backup process is covered in Chapter 31, "System Maintenance," but here we discuss the other aspects of disaster recovery.

What's Vital and What Isn't?

There was a time when PC floppy disks were 360KB and hard disks were 10MB. A complete system backup might fit onto 30 floppy disks. A few years later, floppies were 1.44MB and hard disks were 100MB—that's over 60 floppies. Today, floppy disks are still the same size but disks are 4GB. Even if you could buy 3,000 floppy disks, system backups would be ridiculously impractical.

There are many solutions to this problem. Floppy disks are no longer viable for backups of a whole system. Tapes and recordable CDs are perfectly good in their place.

A useful backup strategy takes into account several things:

- What is the maximum acceptable downtime?
- How much data must be backed up?
- How quickly does the data change?
- What backup devices are available?

If all the data you need to back up will fit on your backup device, then the simplest solution works best—back everything up, every time.

If a complete backup every time is impractical, you have to find a balance between the risk to your data and the cost of making backups. As an example, my own system has almost 4GB of filesystems. Much of this is occupied by the operating system and could easily be restored from the installation CD-ROM. Of the rest, the majority consists of packages either from CDs or downloaded from the Internet (WINE, POV, Gnome, LCLint, and so on). These come to over half a gigabyte. All these things can either be reinstalled from the CDs or downloaded again.

SEE ALSO

➤ *For more information about doing system backups for Linux, see page 542.*

Altogether, the files on which I work actively come to under 100MB, including the intermediate compiler output files, which don't really need to be backed up. I keep these files separate from the things that I don't work on. So, for me it is practical to back up my vital data to a series of floppy disks. This is not ideal, but it's reasonable. This strategy is only possible because the filesystem is organized so as to keep the various kinds of data separate; I don't mix my own files (which I have to keep safe) with downloaded packages or documents (which I can delete).

Nontraditional backup devices

If you don't have a traditional kind of backup device, this does not mean that you cannot back up your important data. See your backup device's documentation for more information, and remember that backing up is absolutely crucial.

When to Back Up

When you have a catastrophe, you will lose everything modified since it was last backed up. So, there are two factors that determine how often you back your data up: what the capacity of your backup device is and how much suffering you can bear.

What to Do with the Backups

After you've backed up your data, the three most important things to do are as follows:

- Write-protect the media—There's nothing worse than trying to restore from backup in a panic and accidentally deleting the backup.
- Label your backup—If you can't identify the most recent backup when you need it, it's no use. Keep your backups in a safe place.
- Test your backup—Make sure you can restore from it.

This last point is particularly important. Many people have a backup routine that they follow day in and day out but find out only too late that their backups are useless. A cautionary tale that sticks in my memory is that of a vendor of backup software whose code had a bug; it would make multivolume backups, but the second and following volumes were useless and could not be read back. Unfortunately, they used their own software to back up their systems and amazingly had never done a trial restore with their tapes.

Reviewing Your Backup Strategy

Don't forget to periodically reconsider your backup strategy. Circumstances change; your data may grow, or it may suddenly be more important that you be able to recover from backup suddenly. For example, while writing this chapter I added up the size of my working data and realized it was larger than I thought. Part of my next paycheck will go on a larger backup device; probably a SCSI tape drive or (if I can afford it) a CD-ROM recorder.

Coping with Disaster

When the worst happens, it's important to be extra careful about what you do. If you've just typed `rm -rf /tmp *` instead of `rm -rf /tmp/*`, then by all means immediately interrupt this. Once you realize that data has been lost, take a moment to calm down and review your options. Determine the answers to these questions:

1. What data has been lost?
2. Where is my most recent backup?
3. Where is my system installation media (boot disk and installation CD-ROM)?

System won't boot? Don't panic!

Don't panic if your Red Hat Linux system won't start. The problem could be with your LILO configuration, or errors in your filesystem table. One fail-safe approach to try is to restart your computer with your Red Hat Linux boot disk or CD-ROM. At the boot prompt, enter the word **`rescue`**. Red Hat Linux will try to find and mount existing Linux volumes or partitions, and you can either try to fix the problem or salvage your data.

Restoring System Files

If you've just lost a few system files, you might be able to fix everything by reinstalling a few packages from the CD-ROM. People with even quite badly destroyed systems have recovered simply by booting from the installation floppy and selecting Upgrade. The Red Hat upgrade process can replace only missing files. If the destruction is more extensive, you may need to consider reinstalling from scratch.

Strictly speaking, it is quite possible to recover from losing almost everything just by booting the installation floppy in `rescue` mode and knowing how to haul yourself up by your bootstraps. However, if you're not an expert, you may find a reinstallation easier. If you do this, however, the installation process will destroy any data on partitions that the operating system installs onto. That is, if you only have one file system, `/`, then a reinstall will delete the contents of your home directory, too. If you have your `/home` file system on a separate drive, then the reinstall will not delete it (unless you tell it to format that partition by accident).

If a reinstall would destroy your own data and you have no useful backup, you're in a tight spot. The best approach is to avoid the reinstall, perhaps by recruiting the help of an expert. Lastly, if you do reinstall your system, consider putting your own important data on a separate filesystem (`/home`, for example).

Restoring User Files

After the system files are taken care of, you can restore your own data from a backup. The actual details of this are explained in Chapter 31.

CHAPTER

30

Managing Applications

By Sriranga Veeraraghaven

Managing Linux software packages with the `rpm` command

Installing, deleting, and upgrading software packages

Uninstalling software with the `rpm` command

Querying and verifying `rpm` packages

Using Red Hat's `glint` X11 client for package management

Using the X11 `xrpm` client

Package Management with *rpm*

One of the most powerful and innovative utilities available in Red Hat Linux is `rpm`, the Red Hat package manager. It can be used to install, uninstall, upgrade, query, verify, and build software packages.

A software package build with `rpm` is an archive of files and some associated information, such as a name, a version, and a description. A few of the advantages of `rpm` packages over the traditional `tar.gz` method of software distribution are as follows:

- Upgrading—A new version of the software can be installed without losing customization files.
- Uninstalling—A software package that installs files in several locations can be cleanly removed.
- Verification—After its installation, a package can be verified to be in working order.
- Querying—Information about what package a file belongs to can be easily obtained.

In addition to these features, `rpm` is available for many flavors of Linux and UNIX, making it one of the emerging utilities for distributing software packages.

SEE ALSO

➤ *To learn more about installing other Linux packages, see page 628.*

➤ *For more information about other software backup or archiving utilities for Linux, see page 542.*

The *rpm* Command's Major Modes and Common Options

Following are the major modes in which `rpm` can be run:

- Install (`rpm -i`)
- Uninstall (`rpm -e`)
- Query (`rpm -q`)
- Verify (`rpm -V`)

The options to invoke the major modes are given in parentheses. These major modes are covered in detail in subsequent sections.

All of these major modes understand the following options:

- `-vv` Prints out all debugging information; this mode is useful for seeing what exactly RPM is doing.
- `--quiet` Prints out very little information—only error messages.

In addition to these, there are a few other "minor" modes that are useful:

- `version` The `version` mode is invoked as the following:

  ```
  # rpm --version
  ```

  This mode prints out a line containing version information, similar to the following:

  ```
  RPM version 2.3.11
  ```

- `help` The `help` mode prints out an extensive help message:

  ```
  # rpm --help
  ```

- `showrc` If a message is long, it is handy to have a large `xterm` to pipe the output to `more`. To get a shorter help message, just type the following:

  ```
  # rpm
  ```

  This prints out a usage message. The `showrc` mode prints out a list of variables that can be set in the files `/etc/rpmrc` and `$HOME/.rpmrc`:

  ```
  # rpm --showrc
  ```

  The default values are adequate for most installations.

- `rebuilddb` The `rebuilddb` option is used to rebuild the database that `rpm` uses to keep track of which packages are installed on a system. Although this option is rarely needed, it is invoked as follows:

  ```
  # rpm --rebuilddb
  ```

Installing Packages

One of the major uses of rpm is to install software packages. The general syntax of an rpm install command is as follows:

```
rpm -i [options] [packages]
```

options can be one of the common options given earlier or one of the install options covered in the following list, and *packages* is the name of one or more rpm package files. Some of the install options are listed in Table 30.1.

TABLE 30.1 *rpm* install options

Option	Description
-v	Prints out what rpm is doing.
-h or --hash	Prints out 50 hash marks (#) as the package is installed.
--percent	Prints out percentages as files are extracted from the package.
--test	Goes through a package install, but does not install anything; mainly used to catch conflicts.
--excludedocs	Prevents the installation of files marked as documentation, such as man pages.
--includedocs	Forces files marked as documentation to be installed; this is the default.
--nodeps	No dependency checks are performed before installing a package.
--replacefiles	Allows for installed files to be replaced with files from the package being installed.
--replacepkgs	Allows for installed packages to be replaced with the packages being installed.
--oldpackage	Allows for a newer version of an installed package to be replaced with an older version.
--Force	Forces a package to be installed.

When giving options to rpm, regardless of the mode, all the single-letter options can be lumped together in one block:

```
# rpm -i -v -h kernel-2.0.30-3.i386.rpm
```

This command is equivalent to the following:

```
# rpm -ivh kernel-2.0.30-3.i386.rpm
```

All options starting with `--` must be given separately, however.

Now take a look at a few examples of installing `rpm` packages. The first example installs `vim` (the improved version of `vi`) from the following package:

```
vim-4.5-2.i386.rpm
```

Installing the *vim rpm* package

1. `rpm` software packages generally follow a standard naming convention:

   ```
   name-version-release.arch.rpm
   ```

   `name` is the package's name, *`version`* is the package's version, *`release`* is the package's release level, *`arch`* is the hardware architecture the package is for, and `rpm` is the default extension. This naming scheme is quite handy because some of the essential information about a particular package can be determined from just looking at its name.

2. For this example, `vim` package, `vim` version 4.5, release 2 is installed for a computer with the i386 architecture. To install this package, mount your Red Hat CD-ROM on `/mnt/cdrom` using the `mount` command, like this:

   ```
   # mount /mnt/cdrom
   ```

   The package you want to install is located in the following directory:

   ```
   /mnt/cdrom/RedHat/RPMS/vim-4.5-2.i386.rpm
   ```

3. Use `cd` to change to the appropriate directory, then install `vim` by using the `rpm` command's `i`, `v`, and `h` options, followed by the name of `vim`'s `rpm` file, like so:

   ```
   # rpm -ivh vim-4.5-2.i386.rpm
   ```

   As the package is installed, the output will look like the following:

   ```
   vim                              ###############
   ```

   When the install is finished, 50 hash marks are displayed.

SEE ALSO

➤ *To learn more about other text editors for Linux besides* vim, *see page 49.*

In this example, I used the pound character (#) to indicate the root prompt because only root can properly install packages for an entire system. If you try to install this package as a user other than root, an error similar to the following will be generated:

```
failed to open //var/lib/rpm/packages.rpm
error: cannot open //var/lib/rpm/packages.rpm
```

Occasionally, the files that one package installs conflict with the files of a previously installed package. If you had `vim` version 4.2 installed, the following message would have been generated:

```
/bin/vim conflicts with file from vim-4.2-
➥8/usr/share/vim/vim_tips.txt
conflicts with file from vim-4.2-8
error: vim-4.5-2.i386.rpm cannot be installed
```

If you wanted to install these files anyway, the `--replacefiles` option can be added to the command.

Another type of conflict that is sometimes encountered is a *dependency conflict*. This happens when a package that is being installed requires certain other packages to function correctly. For example, perhaps you try to install the following package:

```
# rpm -ivh dosemu-0.66.2-1.i386.rpm
```

You get the following dependency errors:

```
failed dependencies:
kernel >= 2.0.28 is needed by dosemu-0.66.2-1
dosemu = 0.64.1 is needed by xdosemu-0.64.1-1
```

This indicates two things. You must upgrade your kernel to 2.0.28, and if you install a newer version of `dosemu`, you must also install a newer version of `xdosemu`. Although it is usually not a good idea to ignore dependency problems, using the `--nodeps` option causes `rpm` to ignore these errors and install the package.

Upgrading Packages

`rpm`'s *upgrade mode* provides an easy way to upgrade existing software packages to newer versions. Upgrade mode is similar to install mode:

```
rpm -U [options] [packages]
```

`options` can be any of the install options or any of the general options.

Here is an example of how to upgrade packages. Suppose that on your system you are currently running `emacs` version 19.31, but you want to upgrade to the newer `emacs` version 19.34. To upgrade, use the following command:

```
# rpm -Uvh emacs-19.34-4.i386.rpm
```

The upgrade mode is really a combination of two operations, uninstall and install. First, `rpm` uninstalls any older versions of the requested package, and then installs the newer version. If an older version of the package does not exist, `rpm` simply installs the requested package.

An additional advantage of upgrade over a manual install and uninstall is that upgrade automatically saves configuration files. For these reasons, some people prefer to use upgrade rather than install for all package installations.

Uninstalling Packages

The uninstall mode of `rpm` provides for a clean method of removing files belonging to a software package from many locations.

SEE ALSO

➤ *To learn about other ways to delete files, see page 42.*

Many packages install files in `/etc`, `/usr`, and `/lib`, so removing a package can be confusing, but with `rpm` an entire package can be removed as follows:

```
rpm -e [options] [package]
```

`options` is one of the options listed later in this section, and *`package`* is the name of the package to be removed. For example,

if you want to remove the package for dosemu, the command is as follows:

```
# rpm -e dosemu
```

The name specified here for the package is just the name of the package, not the name of the file that was used to install the package. Perhaps you ask for the following:

```
# rpm -e dosemu-0.64.1-1.i386.rpm
```

The following error would have been generated:

```
package dosemu-0.64.1-1.i386.rpm is not installed
```

Another common error encountered while trying to uninstall packages is a *dependency error*. This occurs when a package that is being uninstalled has files required by another package. For example, when you try to remove dosemu from your system, you get the following error:

```
removing these packages would break dependencies:
dosemu = 0.64.1 is needed by xdosemu-0.64.1-1
```

This means that the package xdosemu does not function properly if the package dosemu is removed. If you still want to remove this package, rpm could be presented with the --nodeps option to make it ignore dependency errors.

The other useful option is the --test option, which causes rpm to go through the motions of removing a package without actually removing anything. Usually there is no output from an uninstall, so the -vv option is presented along with the --test option to see what would happen during an uninstall:

```
# rpm -e -vv --test xdosemu
```

This example produces the following output on the system:

```
D: counting packages to uninstall
D: opening database in //var/lib/rpm/
D: found 1 packages to uninstall
D: uninstalling record number 1650520
D: running preuninstall script (if any)
D: would remove files test = 1
D: /usr/man/man1/xtermdos.1 - would remove
D: /usr/man/man1/xdos.1 - would remove
```

```
D: /usr/bin/xtermdos - would remove
D: /usr/bin/xdos - would remove
D: /usr/X11R6/lib/X11/fonts/misc/vga.pcf - would remove
D: running postuninstall script (if any)
D: script found - running from file /tmp/02695aaa
+ PATH=/sbin:/bin:/usr/sbin:/usr/bin:/usr/X11R6/bin
+ export PATH
+ [ -x /usr/X11R6/bin/mkfontdir ]
+ cd /usr/X11R6/lib/X11/fonts/misc
+ /usr/X11R6/bin/mkfontdir
D: would remove database entry
```

As you can see, the files that would have been removed are clearly indicated in the output.

Querying Packages

The querying mode in `rpm` allows for determining the various attributes of packages. The basic syntax for querying packages is as follows:

```
rpm -q [options] [packages]
```

`options` is one or more of the query options listed later in this section. The most basic query is one similar to the following:

```
# rpm -q kernel
```

On my system, this prints out the following line for the kernel package:

```
kernel-2.0.27-5
```

In a manner similar to uninstall, `rpm`'s query mode uses the name of the package, not the name of the file that the package came in for queries.

Now for a few more sample queries. If you want to retrieve a list of all the files "owned" by the kernel package, you can use the `-l` option:

```
# rpm -ql kernel
```

This outputs the following list of files on my system:

```
/boot/System.map-2.0.27
/boot/module-info
/boot/vmlinuz-2.0.27
```

In addition to getting a list of the files, you can determine their state by using the -s option:

```
# rpm -qs kernel
```

This option gives the following information about the state of files in my kernel package:

```
normal          /boot/System.map-2.0.27
normal          /boot/module-infonormal          /boot/vmlinuz-
➥2.0.27
```

If any of these files reported a state of `missing`, there are probably problems with the package.

In addition to the state of the files in a package, the documentation files and the configuration files can be listed. To list the documentation that comes with the `dosemu` package, use the following:

```
# rpm -qd dosemu
```

This produces the following list:

```
/usr/man/man1/dos.1
```

To get the configuration files for the same package, use the following query:

```
# rpm -qc dosemu
```

This results in the following list:

```
/etc/dosemu.conf
/var/lib/dosemu/hdimage
```

In addition to these queries, complete information about a package can be determined by using the `info` option:

```
# rpm -qi kernel
```

This example gives the following information about the installed kernel package:

```
Name        : kernel              Distribution: Red Hat
➥Linux Vanderbilt
Version     : 2.0.27              Vendor: Red Hat Software
Release     : 5                   Build Date: Sat Dec 21
➥21:06:28 1996
Install date: Thu Jul 17 14:10:52 1997     Build Host:
➥porky.redhat.com
```

```
➥Group        : Base/Kernel        Source RPM: kernel-2.0.27-
5.src.rpm
Size          : 565900
Summary       : Generic linux kernel
Description : This package contains the Linux kernel that is
used to boot and run your system. It contains few device
drivers for specific hardware. Most hardware is instead
supported by modules loaded after booting.
```

A summary of the query options appears in Table 30.2.

TABLE 30.2 Summary of *rpm*'s query options

Option	Description
`-a`	Lists all installed packages
`-c`	Lists all files in a package that are marked as configuration
`-d`	Lists all files in a package that are marked as documentation
`-f` *file*	Lists the package that owns the specified file
`-i`	Lists the complete information for a package
`-l`	Lists all the files in a package
`-p` *package*	Lists the package name of the specified package
`-s`	Lists the state of files in a package

If any of these options, except for `-i`, are given along with a `-v` option, then the files are listed in `ls -l` format:

```
# rpm -qlv kernel
```

This example outputs the following:

```
-rw-r—r---   root   root   104367 Dec 21 21:05
➥/boot/System.map-2.0.27
-rw-r—r---   root   root    11773 Dec 21 21:05 /boot/
➥module-info
-rw-r—r---   root   root   449760 Dec 21 21:05 /boot/
➥vmlinuz-2.0.27
```

Verifying Packages

Verifying packages is an easy way to determine whether there are any problems with an installation. In verification mode, `rpm` compares information about an installed package against information about the original package, which is stored in the package database at install time.

The basic syntax for verifying a package is as follows:

```
rpm -V [package]
```

If a package is verified correctly, `rpm` does not output anything. If `rpm` detects a difference between the installed package and the database record, it outputs an 8-character string in which tests that fail are represented by a single character, and tests that pass are represented by a period (.). The characters for failed tests are listed in Table 30.3.

TABLE 30.3 Characters for failed verification tests

Letter	Failed Test
5	MD5 Sum
S	File Size
L	Symlink
T	Mtime
D	Device
U	User
G	Group
M	Mode (permissions and file type)

For example, on my system, verifying the `bash` package using `# rpm -V bash` fails:

```
.M..L...   /bin/bash
....L...   /bin/sh
```

This indicates that the size of my `bash` is different from the information stored in the database. This is okay on my system because I have recompiled `bash`.

In addition, it is possible to use the query option `-f` to verify a package containing a particular file, which is helpful when diagnosing problems with programs:

```
# rpm -Vf /bin/ksh
```

If `ksh` were behaving peculiarly, the preceding line would verify the package that `ksh` came in. If any of the tests fail, at the very least you will be closer to understanding the source of the problems.

Using Red Hat's X11 *glint* Client to Manage *rpm* Packages

The most common way most users interact with `rpm` is via `glint`, the graphical Linux installation tool. `glint` is an X-based interface for `rpm` that allows for installing, uninstalling, querying, and verifying packages via a graphical File Manager interface.

`glint` is accessible from the command line or the Control Panel application that comes with Red Hat Linux. You must be the root operator, or must use the `su` command to run `glint`. `glint` can also be accessed from the command line of a terminal window by simply typing the following at the prompt:

```
# glint
```

`glint` accepts no command-line options. When `glint` is loading, a message such as the following appears in the terminal window:

```
Glint Graphical Package Manager -- version 2.1.5 Copyright
➥1996 - Red Hat Software
This may be freely redistributed under the terms of the GNU
➥Public License
```

After `glint` has loaded, a window similar to Figure 30.1 appears.

SEE ALSO

➤ *For more information about the X Window System, see page 260.*

➤ *To learn more about how to begin a superuser, and using the* `su` *command with Linux, see page 5.*

The folders displayed in this window correspond to different groups or classes of packages. In each group, there can be subgroups as well, which are represented as folders within folders. Any files displayed in the folders represent the currently installed packages of a particular group. These are the main groups into which packages can be installed:

- Applications
- Base
- Daemons
- Development
- Documentation
- Games
- Libraries
- Networking
- Shells
- Utilities
- X11

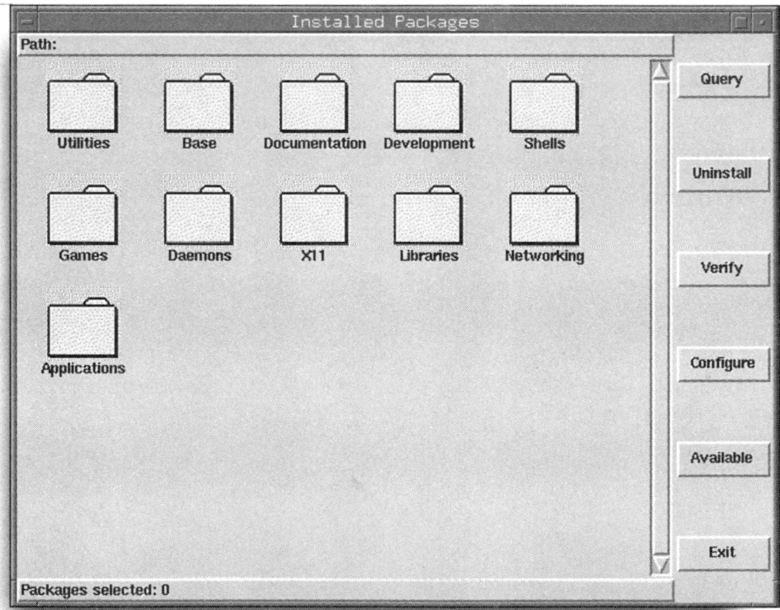

FIGURE 30.1
The primary `glint` window displays folders of installed software packages.

From the main `glint` window, different packages can be selected and queried, verified, uninstalled, or installed. When you click the Available button, all packages available for installation from the default location (`/mnt/cdrom/RedHat/RPMS`) are listed in a separate window similar to Figure 30.2.

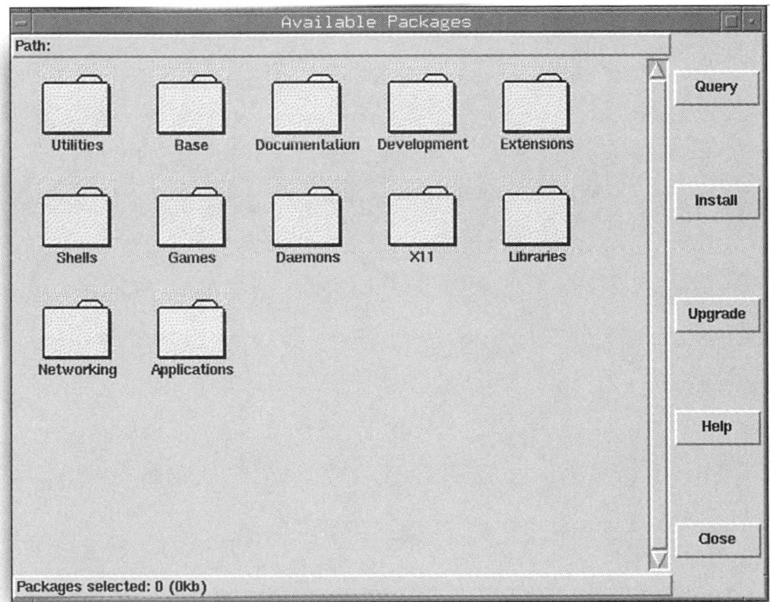

FIGURE 30.2
The Available Packages `glint` window shows software on your Red Hat CD-ROM that has not yet been installed on your system.

By navigating through the folders, you can select and install different packages. As an example, let's take a look at installing the `vim` package.

Installing the *vim* Package with the *glint* Client

1. To install the `vim` package, first log on as the root operator, and then launch `glint` from the command line of a terminal window:

   ```
   # glint &
   ```

2. Insert and mount your Red Hat CD-ROM. When `glint`'s Installed Packages window appears, click the Available button.
3. After a short period of your CD-ROM's disk activity, the Available Packages window appears. Select the Applications folder and then the Editors folder.

4. Click the package `vim-4.5-2`, which becomes highlighted (see Figure 30.3).

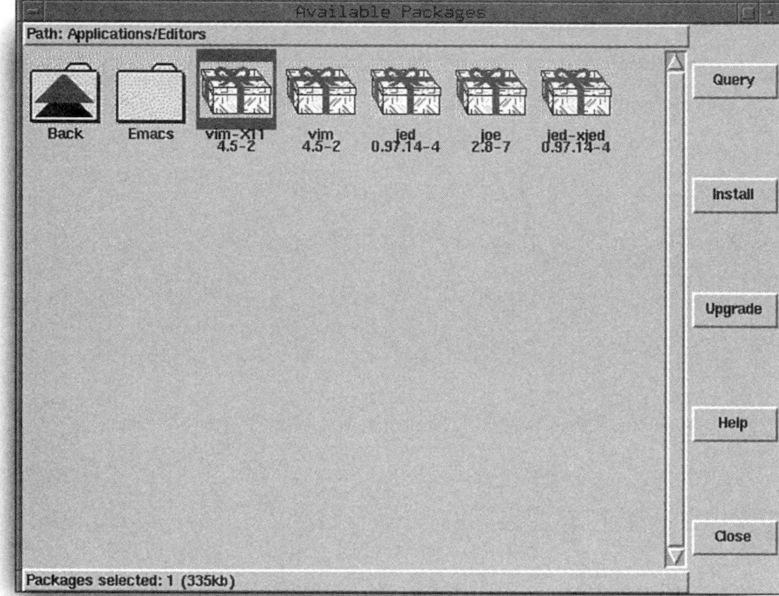

FIGURE 30.3
Available Packages with `vim` selected.

5. When a package is highlighted, it can be installed by clicking the Install button. You can install many packages at once by highlighting more than one package.
6. When you click the Install button, the Installing dialog box appears (see Figure 30.4). This dialog box shows the progress of the installation.

   After `vim` has been installed, it is removed from the Available Packages window.

In this example, I assumed that the available packages were stored in the default location mentioned earlier. Often that is not the case. You can change this location by clicking the Configure button and entering a different location where package files are located in the Changing dialog box (see Figure 30.5).

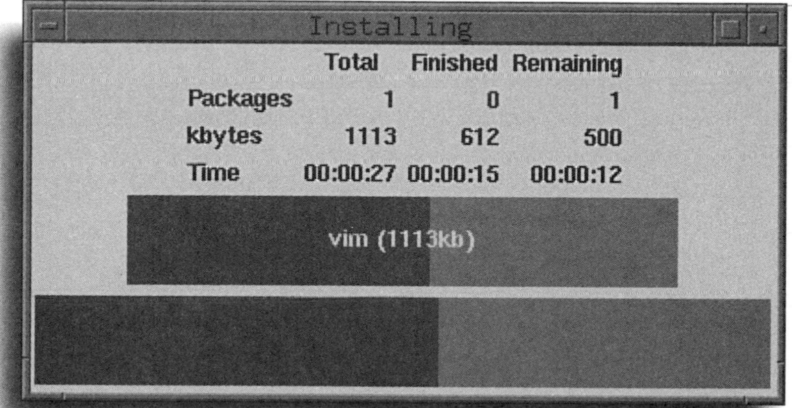

FIGURE 30.4
The Installing dialog box shows the progress of package installation.

FIGURE 30.5
Changing the package location is a convenient way to install `rpm` packages from somewhere else besides CD-ROM.

`glint` also provides a nice front end for querying packages. `glint` executes most of the queries automatically and displays the results in a tabular form. For example, a query of the `vim` package looks similar to Figure 30.6.

In this format, the description of the package and all its files marked by type are clearly visible. In some respects, it is easier to use than the command-line queries.

Installing and Using the *xrpm* Client

Another graphical X11 package management utility similar to `glint` is `xrpm`. Its interface is slightly different, but it provides many powerful features not found in `glint`.

Once the `rpm` version is downloaded, installation is as follows:

```
# rpm -ivvh xrpm-2.1-2.i386.rpm
```

Want the latest version of `xrpm`?

`xrpm` is freely available from **`http://www.gmsys.com/xrpm.html`**. It is distributed in both `rpm` and `tar.gz` formats. As of this writing, the newest version is 2.1-2.

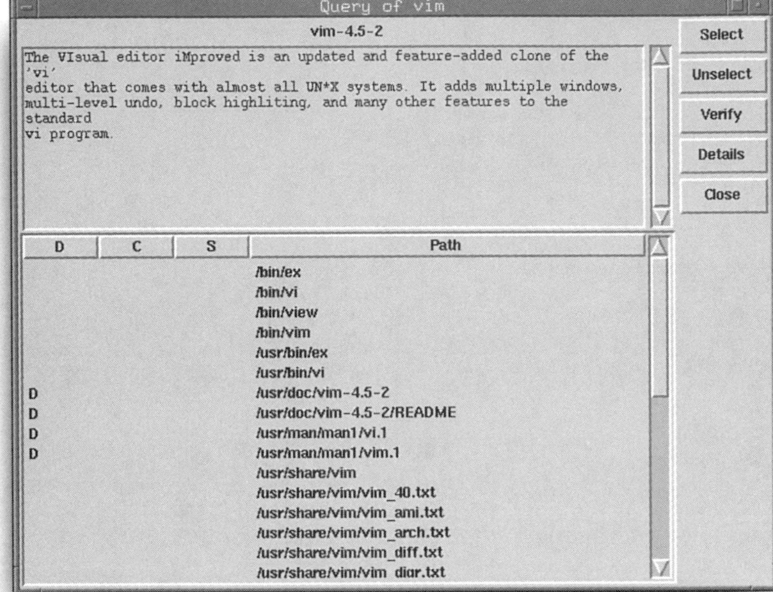

FIGURE 30.6
Query of the `vim` package.

Installation of the `tar.gz` distribution is slightly more complicated; complete instructions are given on the `xrpm` web page mentioned earlier.

Once installed, `xrpm` can be invoked from the command line of an X11 terminal window by typing the following:

```
# xrpm
```

This brings up the `xrpm` main window, shown in Figure 30.7.

The main window of `xrpm` contains a list of all installed packages at the left and the following buttons at the right:

- `Query`—Queries a package and outputs the results into a window (see Figure 30.8).
- `List Files`—Lists the files in a given package in a separate window.
- `Remove`—Removes an installed package.
- `Install`—Installs a selected package.
- `Exit`—Exits `xrpm`.

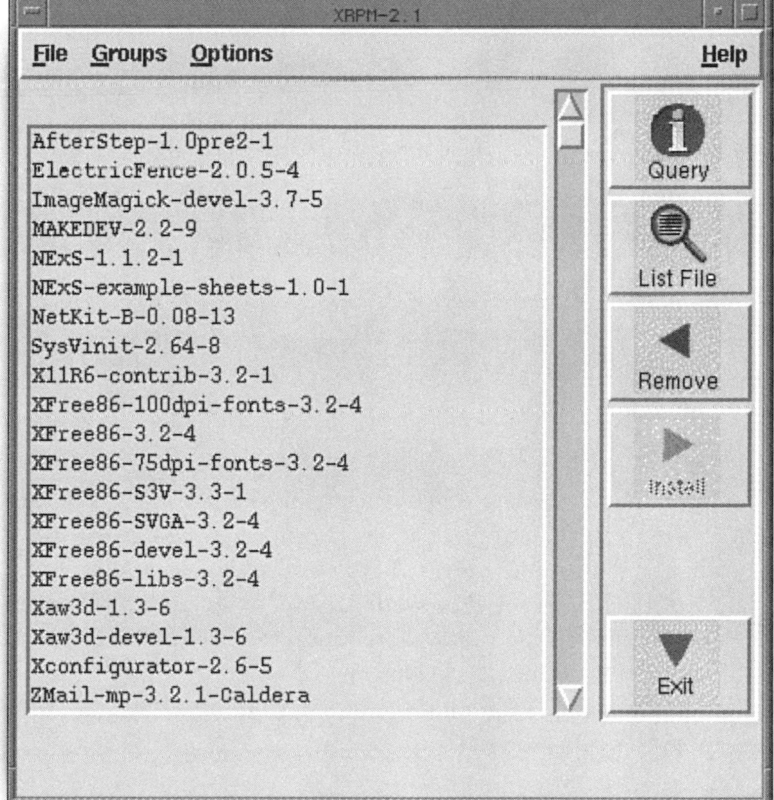

FIGURE 30.7
Main window of `xrpm`.

When `xrpm` first starts up, all the buttons except `Install` are active. Take a look at the functionality of each of these buttons.

In `xrpm`, to execute a query on a package, simply click on a package name in the list and then click on the Query button. The resulting query is slightly different than `glint`—the files included in the package are not listed. An example of a package query is given in Figure 30.8.

To list the files in a package, click on a package name in the list and then click on the List Files button. This action produces a list of files in the selected package. The listing is slightly different than `glint`, because it does not include extra information about the files.

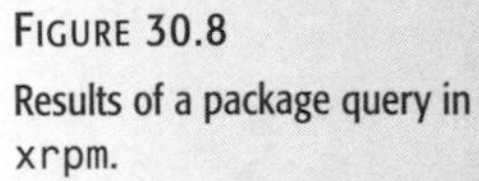

FIGURE 30.8
Results of a package query in `xrpm`.

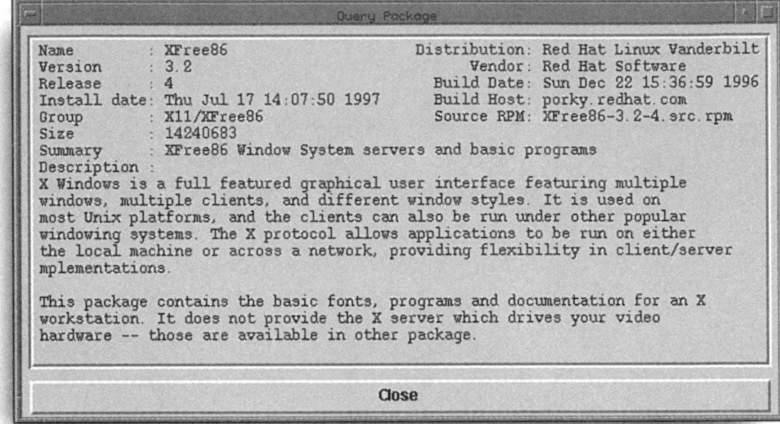

To remove a package, simply click on a package and then click on the Remove button. This action brings up the Remove RPM window shown in Figure 30.9. To remove the package you selected, click on the Remove button in this window. Any errors encountered during removal are reported in separate windows. To cancel the removal, click on the Close button. The Options button gives access to some of the more advanced options, which are not usually required.

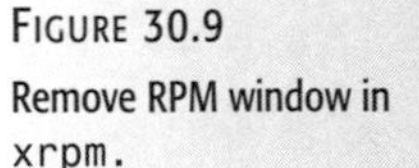

FIGURE 30.9
Remove RPM window in `xrpm`.

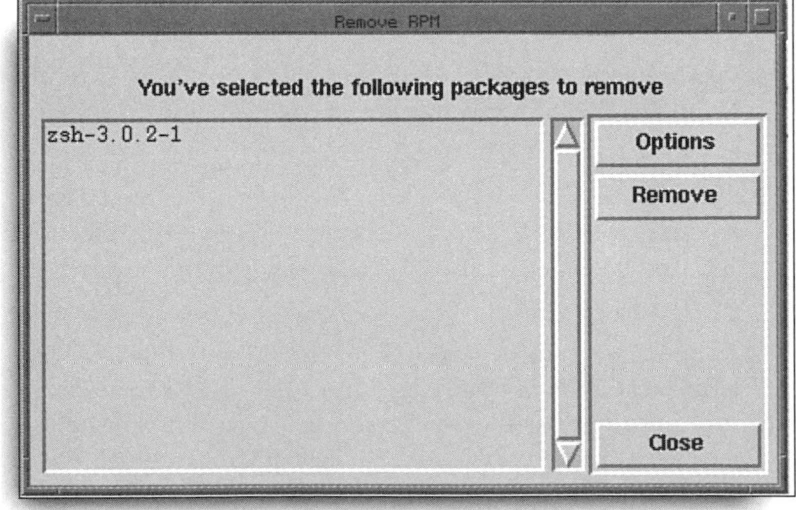

`xrpm` also provides the ability to list packages by their groups. For example, to list all the packages installed in the Applications group, select the Applications menu item from the Groups menu. A new list appears, listing each package's subgroup, as shown in Figure 30.10.

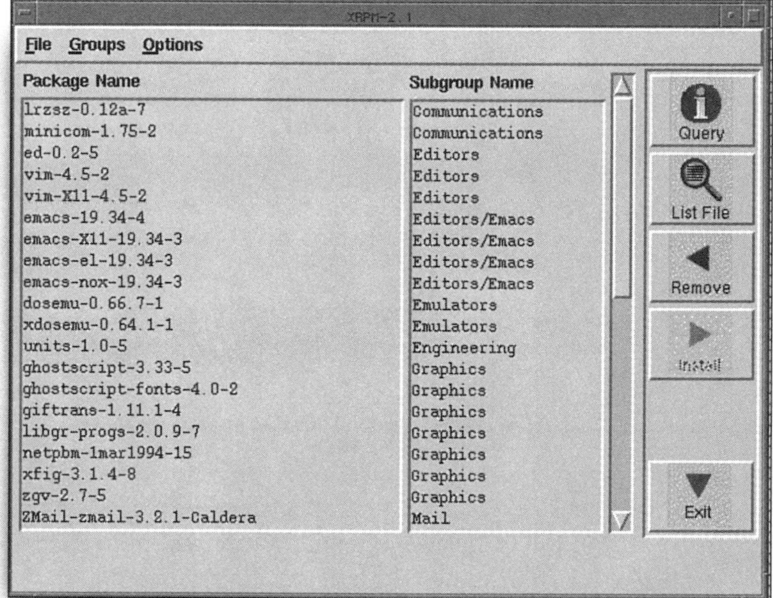

FIGURE 30.10

Application group listing in `xrpm`.

To restore the full list of all installed packages, select List Installed from the File menu.

To install a new package using `xrpm`, simply select a location containing `rpm` files. This location can be on either the local machine or an ftp site. To install packages from the local machine, select Open Directory from the File menu. This brings up a dialog box, shown in Figure 30.11, from which a directory containing `rpms` can be selected.

After a directory has been selected, the list in the main `xrpm` window changes to a list of all the available `rpms` for installation in that directory. At this point, the Install button becomes active and the Remove button becomes inactive. Figure 30.12 shows all the available `rpms` on the Red Hat Power Tools CD-ROM.

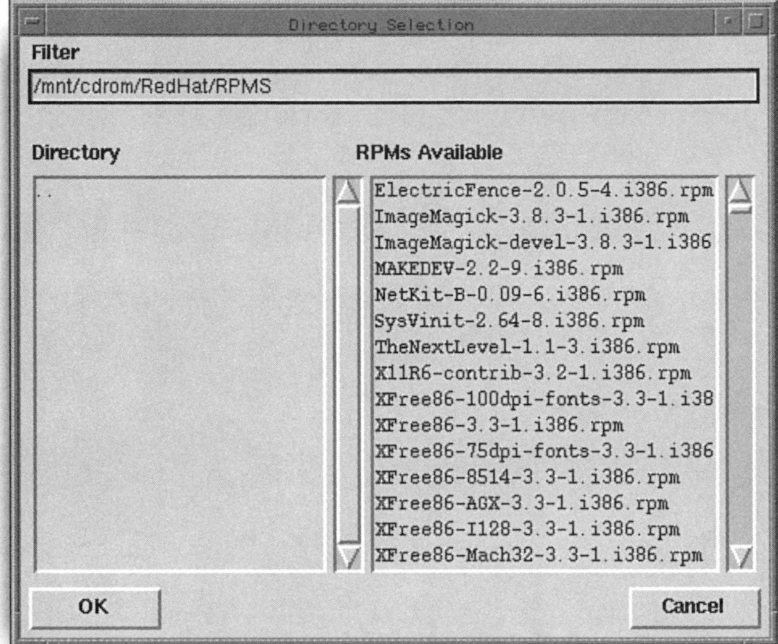

FIGURE 30.11
Selecting a directory containing `rpms` in `xrpm`.

To install a package, click on the package and then click on the Install button, which brings up the Install RPM window (shown in Figure 30.13). To install the selected package, click on the Install button. This installs the package and reports any errors in a separate window. To cancel the installation, click on the Close button. As in the Remove RPMS window, the Options button gives access to several advanced options, which are not usually needed.

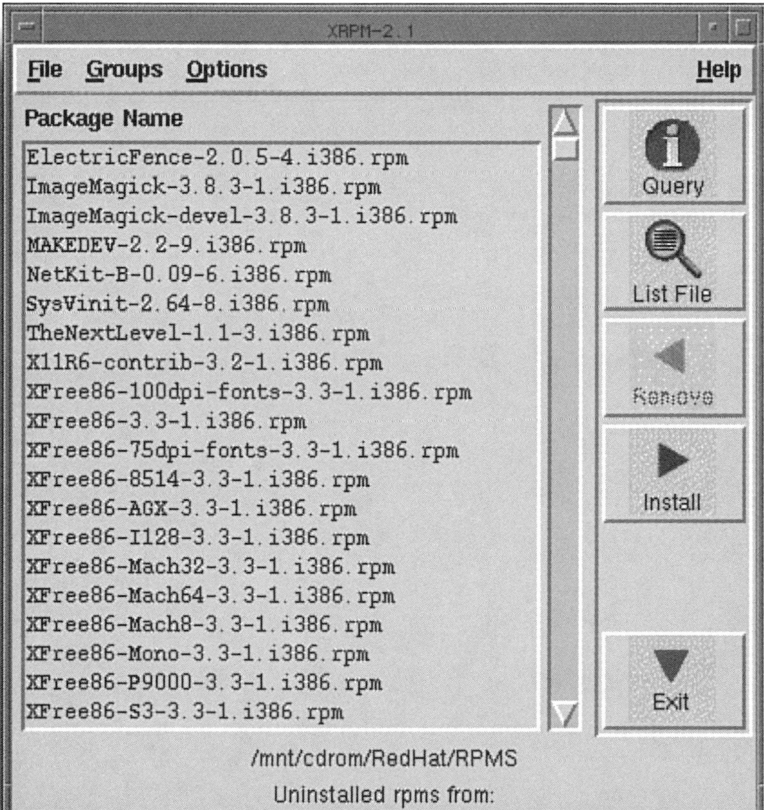

FIGURE 30.12
Available rpms for installation.

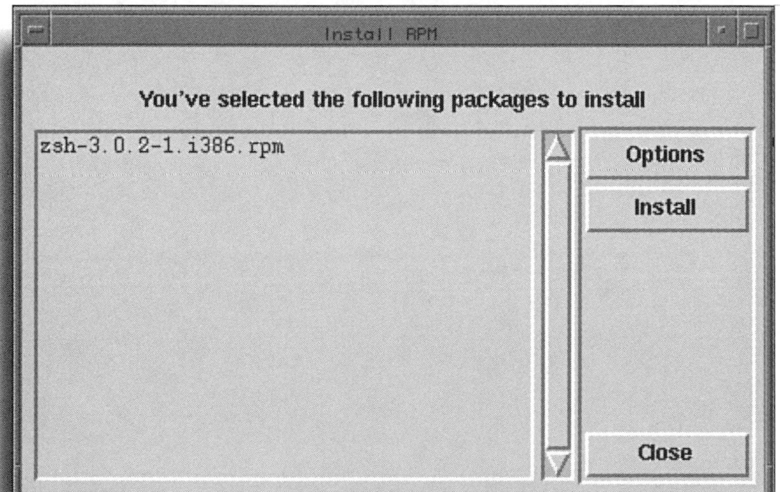

FIGURE 30.13
Install RPM window in xrpm.

CHAPTER

31

System Maintenance

By Tad Bohlsen

Performing System Backups

Making backups is the only way to ensure that you can replace files that become accidentally deleted. To get the most bang for your backup buck (if you can't back up everything), identify the most important files on your own system. If you use your Linux machine exclusively as a web server, your backup requirements are probably a little different than those of someone who tests software. Try to archive the most critical parts of your system on a regular basis. There is little need to back up applications that you loaded from another storage device (CD-ROM, floppy, and so on) unless you have made major modifications to them. If you are supporting a machine with multiple users, you should definitely set up a backup schedule for the `/home` directory tree.

Compressing and Decompressing Files and Directories

Often you will need to compress files when backing them up. Compression can also reduce the size of files you are emailing or transferring to someone on diskettes. Linux provides several ways to compress files and directories: The `gzip` (gnu zip) command is generally considered the best of the bunch for most purposes. `gzip`'s alter ego, `gunzip`, decompresses files compressed by `gzip`. `gzip`'s basic syntax is as follows:

```
#gzip filename
```

`gunzip`'s syntax is similar:

```
#gunzip filename
```

Using *gzip* and *gunzip* to compress and decompress files

1. First, choose a file to compress:

```
#ls --l frankie.txt
--rw--r----r-    1 tb  users        1425 Mar 31 09:22
➥frankie.txt
```

2. Compress the file using the `gzip` command:

```
#gzip frankie.txt
```

3. Use `ls` to check the file again (don't list a filename on the command line). You can see that `gzip` replaces the file whose filename you provide (`frankie.txt` in our example) with a compressed version whose name ends in the suffix `.gz`. The permissions, ownership, and date stamp of the original uncompressed file are retained in the compressed version.

```
#ls --l
total 1
--rw--r----r-    1 tb    users        705 Mar 31 09:22
➥frankie.txt.gz
```

4. Use `gunzip` to uncompress the compressed file we just made:

```
#gunzip frankie.txt.gz

#ls -l
total 1
--rw--r----r-    1 tb users          1425 Apr  1 09:22
➥frankie.txt
```

`gunzip` restores the original filename (removing the `.gz` suffix) and file attributes, removing the compressed file.

`gunzip` can expand files created with other Linux compression utilities, like the `compress` command. Table 31.1 contains useful command-line options for the `gzip` and `gunzip` commands. You can also use the `info` command to look at online documentation for `gzip`:

```
#info gzip
```

TABLE 31.1 Commonly used command-line options for *gzip* and *gunzip*

Option	Mnenomic	Description
h	help	Lists command line options for `gzip` and `gunzip`

continues...

TABLE 31.1 Continued

Option	Mnemonic	Description
v	verbose	When used with gzip, produces a verbose information listing, including the name of the compressed file and the degree of compression (as a percentage of the original file size)
l	list	Lists the original filename(s) of file(s) contained in a compressed file
t	test	Tests to determine the result of a gzip or gunzip command. Indicates expected results without actually executing the specified command
r	recursive	Recursively descends a directory tree, compressing or uncompressing files that match the filename(s) given on the command line
c	concatenate	Accepts input from the standard input, or places output onto the standard output (allows the use of pipes when generating filenames to be compressed or uncompressed)

SEE ALSO

➤ *To find out how to use* `ls` *to list files and directories, see page 31.*

Compressed Archiving with the *tar* Command

`gzip` does not allow you to easily compress entire directories or directory trees; to compress directories you must also use the `tar` (tape archive) command. `tar` can accept entire filesystems as its input, placing all their directories and files into one file, called a `tar` *file*:

```
#tar -cf tarfile.tar file(s)
```

This command creates (`-c`) an archive file (`f tarfile.tar`) containing all the listed files. The `file(s)` argument can be a directory in a directory tree; `tar` archives everything beneath that directory (inclusive), maintaining all the directory relationships, including links, permissions, ownership information, and date stamps. To tell tar exactly what type of archiving job to perform, specify one function as the first argument on the command line (see Table 31.1 for a list of tar's major function identifiers).

TABLE 31.2 *tar's* major function identifiers

Function Identifier	Mnenomic	Action
c	create	Instructs tar to make a new archive, putting the listed files and directories in the tar file you designate
x	extract	Instructs tar to recreate a set of original files (and directories) using the specified tar archive file
t	list	Generates a list of the listed files that are stored in the tar file (if no files are listed on the command line, lists all files in tar)
u	update	Updates an existing tar file with the files listed if they are not currently contained in the tar file, or have more recent modification times (m times) than the file(s) already contained in the tar file
r	append	Adds listed files to the end of an existing tar archive file

In addition to using functions to designate the major action it will perform, tar accepts dozens of additional options. Listed here are some of the ones most often used:

f *filename*	Designates tar filename
k	Keeps old files (doesn't overwrite with files being extracted)
v	Verbose (provides information while running)
z	Archives/extracts by using gzip compression/decompression
M	Multivolume (indicates an archive that can use several floppy disks or tapes)

continues...

V	Volume name (stored in tar file for reference)

Using *tar* to Archive Directories

tar can archive an entire directory if you use a directory name on the command line:

```
#pwd
/public/sharedfiles/me

#ls -l
total 27
--rwxrwxr--x   1 me       users       22843 Apr  1 20:40
➥README.txt
--rwxrwxr--x   1 me       me           1519 Mar 15 21:29
➥iousage
drwxrwxr--x   2 me       users        1024 Jun  8  1996
➥fileshare
lrwxrwxr--x   2 me       users           8 Dec 12 20:39
➥thtfil -> thisfile

#tar cf share.tar /public/sharedfiles/me
tar: removing leading / from absolute pathnames in the
archive

#ls -l
total 28
--rwxrwxr--x   1 me       users       22843 Apr  1 20:40
➥README.txt
--rwxrwxr--x   1 me       me           1519 Mar 15 21:29
➥iousage
drwxrwxr--x   2 me       users        1024 Jun  8  1996
➥fileshare
--rwxrwxr--x   1 me       users       46058 Apr  1 20:40
➥share.tar
lrwxrwxr--x   2 me       users           8 Dec 12 20:39
➥thtfil -> thisfile
```

tar uses relative pathnames; it creates an archive of the me directory in the preceding code without referring to the root pathname (the first slash). (That's what the tar: ... system message means.) You can place archived directories in other directories without worrying about the archive's original pathnames and parent directories.

You can think of tar as a way to graft a directory branch to another directory tree; you can use one tar file to move an entire set of directories and subdirectories from place to place on your system, or from system to system (many ftp files are tar files).

Moving and Extracting *tar* Files

After you create a tar file, anyone with read and write permissions for the directory containing the file (such as the user notme) needs to add the me directory that was archived earlier to his or her home directory:

```
#pwd
/home/notme

#ls -l
total 53
--rw--rw--r-    1 notme    users     8432 Apr  1 20:40
➥zipcode.c
--rw--rw--r-    1 notme    users    21519 Mar 14 21:29
➥stadd.o
drwxrwxr--x    2 notme    users     1024 Dec  4 20:39
➥docfiles
drwxr-xr-    1 notme    users     1024 Jan 11  1996
➥perlscripts
drw--r---r-    2 notme    users     1024 Mar 14 21:29
➥progfiles

#cp /public/sharedfiles/me/share.tar .

#tar xvf share.tar
public/sharedfiles/me/README.txt
public/sharedfiles/me/iousage
...

#ls -l
total 80
--rw--rw--r----    1 notme    users     8432 Apr  1 20:40
➥zipcode.c
--rw--rw--r----    1 notme    users    21519 Mar 14 21:29
➥stadd.o
drwxrwxr--x    2 notme    users     1024 Dec  4 20:39
➥docfiles
```

```
drwxr-xr----    1 notme    users     1024 Jan 11  1996
➥perlscripts
drw--r---r----    2 notme    users     1024 Mar 14 21:29
➥progfiles
drwxrwxrwx   2 notme    users     1024 Apr  1  1996 public

#ls -l public
drwxrwxr-x   2 notme    users     1024 Aug  17 08:42 me
```

Because the user notme ran the tar extraction command, the extracted directory public (and its subdirectories) are now owned by notme rather than me. The v (verbose) option in the last example provides a listing of relative pathnames for each file tar processes (abbreviated for space). Increasing the number of v options listed increases the amount of information tar provides (vv lists date stamps and sizes as well as pathnames, like the ls -l command).

tar command line options do not require leading dashes

Unlike most Linux commands, the initial arguments on the command line of a tar command do not require leading dashes to set them apart. This is partly because the first argument after the tar command must be one of the major tar functions (c, x, t, u, and so on), so the shell doesn't need an additional cue to determine how to parse the command line.

Compressing Archive Files with *tar*

tar can also serve double duty as an archive compression/expansion utility. When used with the z option, tar gzips (or gunzips) the tar archive file it creates (or extracts) by using gzip compression. To compress our sharedfiles tree, use the following:

```
#tar czf meshare.tar.gz me
```

tar compresses and archives in one step. If you use the filename.tar.gz naming convention for gzipped tar files, it helps you keep track of when to use the z option to extract a tar file.

SEE ALSO

➤ *For more information about file attributes, see page 43 and page 418.*
➤ *For more information about command-line syntax, see page 16.*

Using *find* to Locate Files for *tar* Backups

Often you must back up certain kinds of files based on their type, owner, creation date, or other file attributes. The find command helps you look for those files by using a large number of options.

```
#find pathname(s) to search search rule expression
```

For instance, you can use find to look for HTML files like so:

```
#find . -name '*.html' -print
```

Used this way, find locates all files in the current directory and any of its subdirectories with filenames ending in .html, and then prints a list of those filenames. (Actually, you would not have to list the . before html to indicate the current directory; find automatically searches the current directory if no pathname(s) are listed.)

find works like an inspection line in a factory. It passes each filename it finds in the specified path(s) to the first rule in the search rule expression. Each rule in the search processes the file in some way, and then either passes the file to the next rule, or excludes the file from the search.

Using *find* to Help with System Maintenance

You can use find to search using a number of different rules. When using find for system maintenance purposes, often you will need to locate files based on one of three criteria: file ownership, file size, or other file attributes (such as file access time, file type, or file permissions). find is equipped to handle most jobs simply. For instance, you can print a list of all files of type d (the directories) in /usr:

```
#find /usr -type d -print
```

```
#find $HOME -size +5k -print
```

In the preceding example, find prints a list of files with sizes larger than 5KB in your home directory. (In find test expressions, +number represents all values greater than the number, -number represents all values less than the number, and a number with no plus or minus attached stands for the value of the number itself.)

Using the atime and fprint options, you can print a list of man page files that have not been accessed within the last five days in the log file unhit_man_files.log.

```
#find /usr/man -atime +5 -fprint unhit_man_files.log
```

find uses three general kinds of search rules

Find recognizes three basic kinds of rules: tests, actions, and options. *Tests*, such as name, run tests on each file they process, and forward only those files that pass the test to the next rule in the search. *Actions*, like print, perform some action on all the files that reach them; they also can pass the file to the next rule in the search. find *options* determine how the command runs generally; they don't process individual filenames.

find can use a version of the ls command as an option. The following command prints a list of files on the current device (-xdev) belonging to the user tb in the ls -dils format to the file all_tb_files.lst.

```
#find / -xdev -user tb -ls > all_tb_files.lst
```

This last example illustrates a way to use find with tar. If the user tb were taking a sabbatical, you could round up all the files owned by that user and back them up by using the tar command.

```
#cd /

#find / -user tb -print
/usr/local/proj1/stadd.o
/usr/local/proj1/stadd.c
/home/tb/docfiles/mk2efs_notes
/home/tb/scripts/perlscripts/hform1
...

#find / -xdev -user tb -fprint all_tb_files.lst

#tar -cvz -T all_tb_files.lst -f all_tb_files.tar.gz
```

The -T option instructs tar to look for the list of files to archive inside a file, instead of on the command line.(When using the -T option with tar, you must separate command-line options with leading dashes.) If you were to delete all the tb files, and needed to reinstall them when tb returned, you would have to extract the all_tb_files.tar.gz archive from the same spot you created it (to ensure that the tar extraction replaced the files in the original spots recorded by the find command).

There are more options available for the find command than for almost any other Linux utility. See Table 31.3 for useful search rules to use with find.

TABLE 31.3 *find* command search expressions

Expression	Type	Function
-atime/-mtime/-ctime	test	Tests whether file(s) were created before (+n), after (-n) or on (n), where n is an

Expression	Type	Function
		integer representing n number of days before today. (For example, -ctime -5 would find all files changed within the last five days.)
-depth	option	Processes the files in each directory before checking the permissions of the directory itself.
-exec command {} \;	action	Executes command for each file passed to it.
-group groupname	test	Tests whether files are owned by group groupname.
-name filename	test	Tests whether filenames passed to it match filename.
-nouser	test	Tests for files with no user associated; useful for finding "orphaned" files that could be archived or deleted.
-ok command {} \;	action	Like exec, except prompts user before executing com mand on each file passed to it.
-path pathname	test	Tests whether the path of the file(s) passed to it matches pathname.
-prune	action	Skips directories passed to it (often used with -path, where -path identifies the directory to skip and passes the name to prune).
-regex expression	test	Tests whether the filename(s) passed to it match a regular expression.
-size nk	test	Tests whether files passed to it are *n* KB in size (can use +n or -n for greater or less than n).

continues...

TABLE 31.3 **Continued**

Expression	Type	Function
`-type d`	test	Tests whether files are of type `d` (directories).
`-user username`	test	Tests whether files are owned by user `username`.
-xdev	option	Instructs find to search on the current device only (for example, only on the hard drive).

Locating Files Based on Their Access Times

You've seen how `find` can locate files based on their access times (for example, the most recent time the file was accessed, or used) in Chapter 3, "Navigating the Linux File System."

```
#find /dev -atime +30 -print
```

This command prints to the screen the device files that haven't been accessed for the past 30 days. You can build a list of files to archive based on their most recent access times. However, it's sometimes necessary to change files' access times to make sure the `find` command locates them during a search.

To update a file's access times, use the `touch` command:

```
#touch $HOME/*
```

Using the `touch` command like this changes the access times of all files in your home directory to the current system time.

You can then use the `tar` command to select files based on access times when archiving.

```
#ls -l $HOME
total 2
--rwxrwxr--x    1 me       users       22843 Apr  1  9:40
➥README.txt
--rwxrwxr--x    1 me       me           1519 Apr  1  9:40
➥iousage

#tar -cvz -N DATE -f home.tar.gz $HOME
```

The N option tells tar to archive only those files with access times more recent than DATE, where the date is given in the format of the date command.

For more information about the find and tar commands, consult their respective man pages.

SEE ALSO

- *For more information about regular expressions, see page 25.*
- *For more information about file attributes (date stamps, permissions, and ownership) see page 43 and page 418.*
- *For more information about the* touch *command and file* date *stamps, see page 36.*

Using *taper* for Backups

Red Hat Linux 5.0 includes a backup utility developed by Yusuf Nagree called taper. You can use the Red Hat package manager utility, rpm, to query whether the taper package was installed on your system with Red Hat Linux 5.0.

```
#rpm -q taper
taper-6.8.0a10-1
```

If you do not have the taper package installed, you can use the rpm or glint utility to install it.

You can run the taper utility entirely from the command line, but it is made to use a menuing system. The main piece of information you must supply is the type of backup device you use.

```
#taper -T device type indicator
```

Table 31.4 lists the device types you can use with taper, and the device type indicator for each.

TABLE 31.4 Device type options to use when starting *taper*

Device Indicator	Mnemonic	Description
z	zftape	Newest floppy drive tape driver, recommended for use if you have the zftape device driver

continues...

TABLE 31.4 **Continued**

Device Indicator	Mnemonic	Description
`f`	ftape	Older floppy drive tape driver, use if the `ftape` version you use is earlier than version 3.0
r	removable	Use when backing up to floppies and other removable devices (like Zip drives)
s	scsi	Use with SCSI tape drives

`taper` works best with tape drives connected to a floppy disk drive controller. To find out if you have a version of `ftape` more recent than 3.0, you can look in your `/dev` directory. To download a recent version of the new `zftape` driver, point your browser to **`ftp://sunsite.unc.edu/pub/Linux/kernel/tapes/zftape-1.06.tar.gz`**. Or check out **`http://samuel.math.rwth-aachen.de/~LBFM/claus/ftape`** for the latest versions of `ftape` and `zftape`. For more information about the differences between these drivers, see the `taper` documentation in `/usr/doc/taper.6.8.0a10`. You can view it with a pager command such as `less`.

After you have determined which driver to run with `taper`, you can use the menu system to set up an interactive backup. Figure 31.1 shows the main `taper` menu.

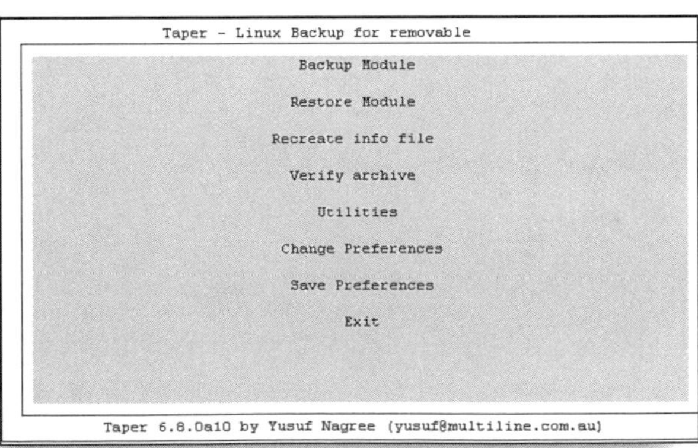

FIGURE 31.1
From the main `taper` menu, you can archive and restore files as well as change your `taper` preferences.

Selecting the backup module brings up a three-part selection menu (see Figure 31.2).

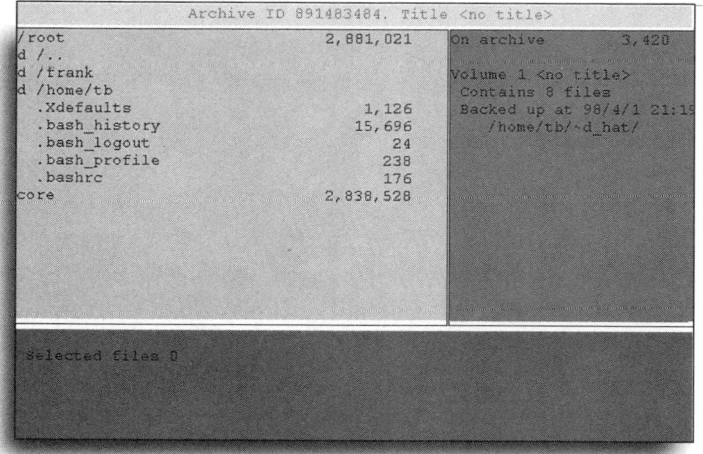

FIGURE 31.2
The `taper` backup menu lets you examine existing taper archives and select files for a new archive.

To maneuver within the `taper` menus and screens, you can use arrow, Tab, and other keys (see Figure 31.3).

```
                       Commands Available
                       ------------------
Up arrow, Left arrow          move cursor up
Down arrow, Right arrow       move cursor down
Page up                       move cursor up a page
Page down                     move cursor down a page
End                           move cursor to end of screen
Home                          move cursor to beginning of screen
TAB                           move to next panel
H, h, ?                       print this screen
U, u                          unselect
i                             select file/directory for backup
I                             select file/directory for backup
D, d                          details about entry
S, s                          Save file set
R, r                          Restore file set
L, l                          Look for entry
J, j                          Jump to a directory
Q, q, A, a                    abort
F, f                          finish selecting and start

                        Press any key ...
```

FIGURE 31.3
You can use various keys to maneuver in a `taper` menu.

Across the top of the backup module screen is the archive ID number and the title of the archive (you will be asked to enter a title for your backup when you enter this menu). The upper-left portion of the screen lists the files contained in the current directory. You can move to subdirectories by selecting their names by using the arrow keys and then pressing Enter (move into the parent directory by selecting the .. item). The upper-right portion of the screen lists current archives created with `taper` on the device you selected when starting `taper`. The bottom portion of the screen lists files that you have selected for the current backup. Select files by using the `i` command. If you select a directory, all the files within that directory are selected; you can unselect files by using the `u` command.

Now that you have some familiarity with the `taper` menu interface, you can use it to make backups. Start with a new, preformatted tape on a floppy tape drive (the process is similar for other storage devices and floppies).

Backing up with *taper*

1. Determine the backup device you want to use and ensure that you have the appropriate device driver (`taper` was developed using a Colorado tape drive, so it works well with those).
2. Start `taper` by using the appropriate command-line instruction (`taper -T z`, `taper -T f`, `taper -T r`, and so on—refer to the previous device selection instructions). After you have started `taper`, you can save this device driver information by using the Preferences menu so you do not have to enter it again.
3. After `taper` has started, enter the Utilities menu.
4. In the Utilities menu, select Test Make Tape.
5. Test Make Tape might determine that you need to run the `mktape` utility; assuming this is a new tape, it's safe to do this now.
6. Select the Back to Main Menu option.
7. Enter the Backup Module.
8. Using the menu system at the top-left of the screen, select the files and the directories to be archived. `taper` displays the list of files selected in the bottom half of the screen.

Be careful

Use the Test Make Tape option only on *new* tapes because it will erase and write some data onto the tape.

9. When you have selected all the files you need to include in this archive, press F to start the archive. `taper` creates the archive and displays some details about it.

10. You might want to make a note of the title of the archive to use to label the tape. taper records this information in an archive index file for use whenever the archive is used. You can now begin selecting files for another archive, or exit the Backup Module and exit `taper`.

If you do not have a preformatted tape, you can use a third-party application in Windows or MS-DOS (for floppies, you can use the Linux utility `fdformat`—see the man page on `fdformat` for details). Some aspects of `taper` differ from `tar`. `taper` uses a proprietary compression utility by default; you can change the compression utility to `gzip` in Preferences menu. Also, `taper` makes incremental backups by default (it only overwrites a file if the archived version is older than the selected file). Likewise, `taper` automatically restores the most recent version of a file if several versions exist in different `taper` archives. Most of these behaviors can be changed using the Preferences menu.

For more information about `taper`, including available drivers (Iomega, for example), refer to the taper documentation (`usr/info/taper.6.8.0a10`).

SEE ALSO

➤ *For more information about the Red Hat package manager* (`rpm`) *and* `glint`, *see page 520.*

➤ *For more information about setting up peripheral storage devices for use with Linux, see page 99, page 119, and page 133.*

Backing Up with Floppy Disks

`taper` allows you to use several kinds of peripherals to back up files. Standard Linux utilities also work with a number of different devices, including SCSI drives and other external hard drives. Often, though, backups use a tape drive or floppies. Floppy disks are convenient for small backups, or at times when you need to store a few files or directories for physical transport to another location.

To use floppy disks as storage devices, you must know the device name your floppy disk drive uses. Usually, this is `/dev/fd0`, but you may need to do some snooping to verify this—one way to snoop is to try the procedures for formatting or mounting floppies (described later in this section) on different device files (`/dev/fd0`, `/dev/fd1`, and so on). Then you must mount a preformatted floppy disk (you must have more than one disk handy, so format extras if you need to). You can do a low-level format (similar to the one performed by the MS-DOS command `format`) using the `fdformat` utility to preformat a floppy:

```
#fdformat /dev/fd0
```

Use `fdformat` with care

Using `fdformat` erases all data on the floppy disk. Try mounting and reading from it (using the `mount` and `ls` commands) to make sure it is empty before formatting if you're not sure.

After the floppy disk has been formatted with `fdformat`, you must configure it for the `ext2` file system. The `mkfs` command sets up the parameters for the Linux Second Extended file system:

```
#mkfs -t ext2 /dev/fd0 1440
```

The `1440` indicates that the floppy disk contains 1,440 kilobytes of storage, or 1.44 MB).

Finally, we can mount the floppy disk by using the default mount point `/mnt/floppy`.

```
#mount -t ext2 /dev/fd0 /mnt/floppy
```

Be sure to use one mount point per mounted device. Now that you have a mounted floppy disk at your disposal, you can start to back up information onto it:

```
#tar -cvfz /dev/fd0 files
```

The preceding command creates an archive on the device `/dev/fd0`. Note that in this command, you use the name of a device and not the `tarfile.tar` filename structure. `tar` recognizes that `/dev/fd0` is a device, but allows you to treat the device like an archive file. Usually, when backing up onto floppy disks, you will use the `M` option with `tar` to signify that this is a backup with multiple volumes.

```
#tar -cvzMf /dev/fd0 files
```

`tar` prompts you when you need to change floppy disks. Make sure you mark the disk order number on each floppy used, or you will have problems when you try to restore the archive.

SEE ALSO

➤ *For more information about formatting and mounting devices, see page 99.*
➤ *For more information about the* `tar` *command, see page 544.*

Backing Up with Removable Drives

If you plan to use removable tape drives connected to your floppy disk controller for backups, you must determine the device file associated with your tape drive. Usually, tape drives are divided into two types: rewindable (represented by the device files `/dev/rft0`, `/dev/rft1`, `/dev/rft2`, and so on) and non-rewindable (represented by the device files `/dev/nrft0`, `/dev/nrft1`, `/dev/nrft2`, and so on). *Rewindable* tape devices rewind the tape automatically after `tar` finishes writing an archive to the tape, so they are best used when you use a tape for only one archive file. *Non-rewindable* tape devices do not automatically rewind after `tar` finishes, so you can place several archive files, one after the other, on one tape.

Consider the following commands:

```
#tar -cvzf /dev/rft0 /usr/doc
```

When used with a rewindable tape drive, this `tar` command creates a compressed archive of all the Red Hat documentation installed on your main system. After the command has finished running, the tape rewinds automatically. Running `tar` again on the same tape overwrites this archive (so label your tapes well). Conversely, with a non-rewindable tape drive, you can put several successive archives on one tape.

```
#tar -cvzf /dev/nrft0 /usr/src
```

This command creates an archive of all the standard source code on the main system. Assuming there is enough space left on the tape, after this command runs you can run another `tar` command to create a second archive on the tape.

```
#tar -cvzf /dev/nrft0 /usr/lib
```

This command is not the same as using `tar` with the `-A` function to append files to an existing archive. This command creates a second archive, distinct from the first, on the device `/dev/nrft0`.

To restore the second archive, you must use the `mt` command to skip over the first archive file on the tape:

```
#mt /dev/nrft0 fsf 1
```

If you use another kind of drive for backups, you can substitute the device file it uses for the previous floppy tape device files. So, if you use a SCSI tape device, for instance, you'd indicate it with the nomenclature `/dev/st0`, as follows:

```
#tar -cvzf /dev/st0 /home
```

Likewise, if you use an Iomega Zip drive on a SCSI port, you would use the `/dev/sda1` drive (`sda1` usually refers to the first SCSI device that is removable, but not a tape):

```
#tar -cvzf /dev/sda1 /home
```

The device you use depends on the device that the kernel supports . To check available devices, you can run `mount` with no arguments:

```
#mount
/dev/hda5 on / type ext2 (rw)
/dev/hda7 on /usr type ext2 (rw)
/dev/fd0 on /mnt/floppy type msdos (rw)
/dev/sda1 on /mnt/zip type ext2 (rw)
```

SEE ALSO

- *For more information about formatting and mounting devices, see page 99.*
- *For more information about using tape drives and Iomega Zip drives with Red Hat Linux 5.0, see page 119.*
- *For more information about the* `tar` *command, see page 544.*

Automating Incremental Backups

You can use the `find` and `tar` commands to automatically back up files that have changed since the last time the entire system was backed up. Backing up the entire system, called a *full backup*, usually involves backing up everything that was created or changed after the initial installation. There is little need to include in a full backup most packages that can be reloaded with `rpm` or `glint`, because these packages exist on separate devices. However, if you have added some utilities via ftp from the Internet, or have lost the original disks that packages came on, you should make sure you have at least one good backup copy.

If you have enough room on tapes, a full backup can be simple:

```
#tar -cvzMf /dev/rft0 /
```

Or, you could be more selective:

```
#tar -cvzMf /dev/rft0 /etc /var /sbin /usr/local /home
```

This command archives many of the files unique to most systems.

Again, if you cannot back up everything, make sure you are backing up everything important.

The Linux Filesystem Standard describes the general layout of most Linux systems

For more information about the standard configuration of most Linux filesystems, you can review the Linux Filesystem Standard (often abbreviated FSSTND) at `http://www.pathname.com/fhs/`.

Once you have a full backup, you can begin to take advantage of the `tar` and `find` command options to make backups of files that have changed since the last full backup (incremental backups).

To track the date of the last backup, sometimes it makes sense to store it in a file:

```
#ls -l lastarchive.tar ¦ cut -f6-8 > lastarchive.date
```

If you are backing up with `tar`, the `-N` option backs up only files with more recent access times than the date provided:

```
#tar -cz -g archlog.txt -N DATE -V 'latest backup' /home
```

The `-g` option creates a log file `archlog.txt`, which contains the archive time and a list of the directories archived. `-V` electronically labels the archive `latest backup`. The `-N` option specifies that `tar` is only to back up files newer than `DATE`, where the date is entered in the same format as the date command's. So, if you know the date of the last archive, you could use this date to generate an incremental backup. (Actually, this command is a bit redundant. The `-g` archlog option looks for an existing file named `archlog` and, using the date recorded from the last backup in this file, instructs `tar` to archive only files newer than that date. So this command assumes you have not yet created a `-g archlog` file.)

If you need to archive files that could be anywhere on the system, the `find` command comes in handy:

```
#find / -atime -1 -print > /home/backuplists/todaysfiles
#tar -cvz -f /dev/rft0 -T /home/backuplists/todaysfiles
```

These commands place an archive of files accessed within the last 24 hours on the tape mounted at /dev/rft0. (Make sure to change the tape each day if you need to store more than one day's backup.)

You can use the crontab feature to avoid having to run this backup manually:

```
* 3 * * * find / -atime -1 -print > \
 /home/backuplists/todaysfiles; mt -f /dev/rft0 rewind; \
 tar -cvz -f /dev/rft0 -T /home/backuplists/todaysfiles
```

You can also use shell scripts to automate backups. A simple example would be to take the cron bash commands in the preceding example and type them into a shell script called todaysbu. You could then just add the following to crontab:

```
* 3 * * * /home/backupscripts/todaysbu
```

SEE ALSO

➤ *For more information about using dates and* crontab *with Linux, see page 429.*
➤ *For more information about using shell scripts to automate tasks, see page 365.*
➤ *For more information about* cron, *see page 435.*

Performing File System Maintenance

It's good to be in the habit of snooping around your system a little for unnecessary files. Besides keeping space free, it familiarizes you with the layout of your directories, and the way users (including you) are utilizing the system.

Deleting Unnecessary Files

In addition to using find to locate files to back up, you can use it to search for files that are no longer needed. After you have found those files, you can delete them from the command line, or use an automated process (crontab entry or shell script) to remove them. (Warning: Make sure you back up any files you may *ever* need again before removing them.)

For instance, you can search for files belonging to users who no longer have access to the system, archive them to a tape, and delete the originals (make sure your backup is good):

```
#find / -user tb -print > tbfiles
#tar -cvz -f tbfile.tar.gz -T tbfiles
#find / -user tb -print0 ¦ xargs -r0 rm
```

The last command line makes use of the `xargs` utility. `xargs` processes each argument piped to it and runs a command on that argument. The `find print0` option separates filenames with a `NULL` (`0`) character instead of a `newline`, in case some files or directories have a `newline` in their names (unlikely, but better safe than sorry). The `-r0` options tell `xargs` to expect input separated by `NULL` characters (`0`), and make sure the command doesn't run if the input is a blank line (`r`). To remove directories, use the following command:

```
#find / -user tb -print0 ¦ xargs -r0 rmdir
```

For more information about `xargs`, see its man page.

SEE ALSO

➤ *For more information about shell scripts, see page 365.*

➤ *For more information about using* `crontab`, *see page 435.*

➤ *For more information about the* `rm` *and* `rmdir` *commands, see page 42.*

➤ *For more information about the* `tar` *command, see page 544.*

Undeleting Files

The only way to undelete files with Linux is to use a backup system like `tar` or `taper`. There is no Recycle Bin or Trash icon where deleted files are kept indefinitely. To examine archives for a lost file, use the `tar` command

```
#tar -tvz -f monthlybackup.tar.gz lostfile(s)
```

`tar` lists any files in the monthly backup matching `lostfile(s)`. To restore lost files, create a lost file directory and extract the designated files there (rather than trying to place them back in their original habitat immediately). Sometimes directory permissions or pathnames may have changed, and occasionally someone will have created a new file in the same place, with the same name, as the one you are restoring. Use the following commands:

```
#cd /home/me/restored_lostfiles
#tar -xvz -f monthlybackup.tar.gz lostfile(s)
```

Then you can move the files back to the original places after you have verified that no conflicts or problems with file attributes exist.

SEE ALSO

➤ *For more information about file permissions and attributes, see page 43.*
➤ *For more information about the* `tar` *command, see page 544.*

Maximizing Disk Space

Generally, it's best not to allow free space on your hard drive to fall below 25–30 percent of your hard drive's total capacity. The following sections examine ways to keep an eye on disk space, and (more importantly) ways to reclaim parts of a shrinking hard disk pie.

Performing System Cleanups

While the kernel and other Linux processes run, they generate a number of "housekeeping" files. Often, Linux automatically disposes of these files but sometimes you must take matters into your own hands. For instance, if you are creating your own logs, use a redirect command like >> (append); the files used by that redirect will continue to grow until removed.

Linux provides two commands to check on disk usage, `df` and `du`, described in the following two command examples:

```
#df
Filesystem        1024-blocks  Used Available Capacity
➥Mounted on
/dev/hda5            128790   61203     60936      50%   /
/dev/hda7            257598  172332     71962      71%
➥/usr
/dev/fd0               1423     471       952      33%
➥/mnt/floppy
```

`df` (disk free space) reports on the total number of blocks used and free on all mounted partitions. It's good for getting an overall snapshot of the space available on the entire system. Its compatriot, `du`, allows you to examine individual files and directories for space usage, a little like `ls` with the `-l` option:

```
#du
15          ./taper_info
1          ./docs/f2
2          ./docs/x
2853     .
```

You can use these commands in shell scripts to automate monitoring of system space usage.

You can also use the `find` command with the size (`-s`) option to generate lists of large files that bear examining:

```
#find -s +1000k -print > /home/me/filemaint/bigfilelist
```

This command prints a list of files larger than 1 MB (1,000 KB) in the designated log file. You can also run this command using the `crontab` feature to receive email listing those files:

```
* 8 * * Mon find -s +1000k -print
```

This command checks for large files every Monday at 8:00 a.m. (a good way to enjoy light entertainment on Monday mornings is to see some of the gargantuan files created over the last week).

Aside from looking for files created by users, there are several places that you can check for files that need to be cleaned up. The best place to start is in the `/etc/syslog.conf` file. This file maintains a listing of all of the logs used by the `syslogd` daemon, a "system logger" started when you boot Linux:

```
#cat /etc/syslog.conf
# Log all kernel messages to the console.
# Logging much else clutters up the screen.
kern.*
/dev/console
# Log anything (except mail) of level info or higher.
# Don't log private authentication messages!
*.info;mail.none;authpriv.none                    /var/log/
messages
# The authpriv file has restricted access.
authpriv.*
/var/log/secure
# Log all the mail messages in one place.
mail.*
/var/log/maillog
```

```
# Everybody gets emergency messages, plus log them on anoth-
er # machine.
*.emerg                                                    *
# Save mail and news errors of level err and higher in a
# special file.
uucp,news.crit
/var/log/spooler
```

In this file, the lines starting with # signs are comments; the other lines instruct the `syslog` daemon how to handle log messages. The Linux system logs a variety of messages to help with everything from lost mail to system crashes. Almost every message contains a time, machine name, and the name of the program that generated it. The `syslog` daemon also categorizes messages by order of importance, ranging from simple system debugging and info messages to high-priority critical and emergency (`emerg`) messages.

In addition to being routed by severity, messages are earmarked based on the facility (`cron`, `mail`, and so on) associated with them. So, as you can see above, mail log messages are handled differently than kernel (`kern`) messages. Some of these logs can be good places to look if you're having problems with a particular feature of Linux (like mail).

You can see how, if the system were left up for some time with no other housecleaning done, some of the files might get large. Almost all of these `syslogd` logs are stored in `/var/log`, so this is a good place to check for files experiencing runaway growth:

```
#find /var/log -s +250k -print
```

It's also worth becoming a little familiar with the Linux File System Standard to help identify other likely places to clean (the Red Hat documentation contains a description of how Red Hat's filesystem structure conforms to the Linux File System Standard). Two candidates are the `tmp` directories: `/tmp` and `/var/tmp`. These directories are used as "dumping grounds" by various applications and utilities, and if the system isn't rebooted periodically, they too can become larger than you'd like:

```
#ls /var/tmp
taper00291oaa
```

```
taper00291paa
taper00420caa
taper00420daa
taper01047caa
taper01047daa
```

The /var/tmp file contains a set of taper-related files. If you're not sure whether taper still needs these (it probably doesn't), move them to another directory and run a taper backup and/or restore. Assuming taper runs satisfactorily, it should be safe to remove these files.

SEE ALSO

- *For more information about the* find *command, see page 548.*
- *For more information about the* crontab *utility, see page 435.*
- *For more information about Linux kernel management, see page 569.*
- *For more information about using the Linux* mail *utility, see page 179.*
- *For information about Linux system daemons, see page 467.*

Compressing Manual Pages

The Linux manual is divided into several sections, and many users only need information from the first section (user commands). You can compress the rest of the man sections, and even store them on a removable tape to save space:

```
#ls /usr/man
man1 man2 man3 man4 man5 man6 man7 man8 man9 manl mann
#tar -cvz -f /dev/nrft0 /usr/man[2-9]
```

You can then selectively extract sections of the manual or single commands as needed:

```
#cd /home/manextract
#tar -xvz -f /dev/nrft0 usr/man2
```

Again, it's sometimes safest to extract an archive in a directory created to do just this, in case any surprises occur. After the extraction, you can use the cp command to move the extracted files back into the /usr/man/man2 directory:

```
#pwd
/home/manextract
#cd usr/man2
#cp * /usr/man/man2
```

SEE ALSO

➤ *For more information about using the Linux man pages, see page 11.*

Compressing Unused Documents and Directories

Man pages obviously aren't the only candidates for compression when disk space gets tight. By knowing where "the bodies are buried" on your system, you can often find a way to restore underutilized space. For instance, perhaps you are engaged in a project to code a sequel to Doom: Doom B. Unfortunately, things didn't work out with the licensing, and you're ready to put Doom B on the back burner. The following command would help you move along:

```
#tar -cvz -f /dev/rft0 /projects/DoomB /home/lib/DoomB
/usr/local/DoomB_graphics,
```

This last directory, `/usr/local/DoomB_graphics`, contains graphics, which usually don't compress well. However, they are often not used by many users, and can sometimes be archived until needed.

CHAPTER

32

Managing the Kernel

By Jan Walter

Using the Red Hat `kernelcfg` tool

Editing the Linux kernel configuration files

Managing modules

Managing processes

Recompiling the kernel

The *kernel* is the core component of every operating system. The performance of the kernel determines the most fundamental properties of the operating system, as it is an application's gateway to the computer hardware. Modern kernels provide *preemptive multitasking* capability, which allows multiple programs to operate seemingly at the same time. This is physically impossible with only one system processor, but the kernel schedules the processes in such a way that they seem to be running concurrently.

While the Linux kernel is a complicated piece of software, it is one of the most simple 32-bit kernel designs in common use. Linux has always been on the leading edge of feature support, as well as performance—a truly rare combination. The simplicity of the kernel also increases the system's reliability, which is another of Linux's hallmarks.

The Linux kernel requires very little maintenance after it is set up to run correctly. It's the process of getting it that way, however, that many newcomers to Linux have complained about.

Red Hat Linux is almost completely configurable at run-time, with few reboots required. This means that networking, sound cards, file systems, and even device support can be dynamically reconfigured, added, and removed from the system as necessary to facilitate almost any configuration.

Using the Red Hat *kernelcfg* Tool

`kernelcfg` is the graphical management utility included with Red Hat Linux that manages `kerneld`. `kerneld` manages the automatic loading and unloading of kernel device driver modules—for instance, the Zip drive driver is loaded into memory only when a program needs to use the Zip drive.

In particular, `kerneld` is very useful for dcaling with filesystem drivers, since these are loaded and unloaded often in general use. `kerneld` knows about file system modules, and is usually smart enough to figure out if it needs to load one to access a file system. It gets this information from `/etc/fstab`, the file system configuration file.

As of this writing, the `kernelcfg` program has a number of problems, especially with regard to saving the configuration file. The following sections document how `kernecfg` is *supposed* to work. Keep an eye on the Red Hat Linux Web site for updates to `kernecfg`.

Adding a Module to the Kernel Configuration

Only SCSI host and ethernet device modules need to be added to the kernel configuration. Most of these devices benefit from command-line arguments, and using `kernelcfg` is a good way to keep things consistent and reduce the amount of searching the driver has to do to find your particular hardware.

Booting from a SCSI device

If your system is booting from a SCSI device, the Linux kernel must load the SCSI device driver module before `kerneld` is even running. This is achieved by using an initial ramdisk, from which the driver is loaded. By convention, this SCSI adapter is still configured for `kerneld`, but in reality it has no effect because the driver is vital to system operation.

1. Log on as root and start X Window.
2. From the Control Panel, select Kernel Daemon Configuration. You might have to start the Control Panel application yourself before doing this. Open an X Terminal window and enter `control-panel &` to open the Control Panel, shown in Figure 32.1.

FIGURE 32.1
Clicking the topmost icon in the Control Panel starts the `kernel` Daemon Configuration applet.

3. Click the topmost icon in the Control Panel to open the Kernel Configurator applet, shown in Figure 32.2. Click the Add button.
4. From the dialog box shown in Figure 32.3, choose the module type that you want to add (click the Module Types button to get a list of them). The most common additions are

ethernet devices (`eth`) and SCSI host adapters (`scsi_hostadapter`). Occasionally, a proprietary-interface CD-ROM must be configured (`cdrom`). The remainder of the additions deal with Token-Ring networks, parallel-port networking, and other more advanced configuration topics.

For this example, configure `kerneld` to automatically load and unload the device driver for our parallel port Zip drive. Choose `scsi_hostadapter`, and then click OK.

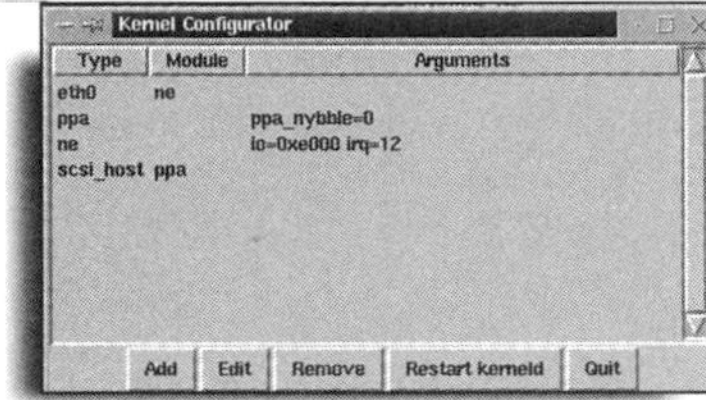

FIGURE 32.2
This is how the Kernel Configurator applet looks on the author's system.

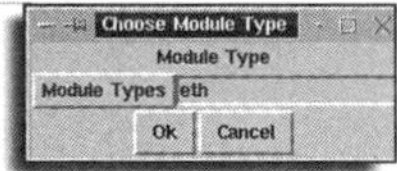

FIGURE 32.3
Click the module type you want to add to your system's configuration.

5. The Kernel Configurator now requires the exact module name. In this example, it is `ppa`. Click the Which Module? button in the Define Module dialog box (shown in Figure 32.4) to find the module you want. Click OK to proceed.

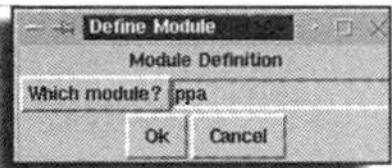

FIGURE 32.4
In this case, the `ppa` module was selected.

6. Now comes the module-specific part. Most modules accept a number of arguments, like device addresses and interrupt numbers. These depend on the device, and most device drivers are able to autodetect the device parameters.

Autodetection of device parameters is not fool-proof, however, and can cause your machine to hang, crash, or do other undesirable things. Fortunately, the Kernel Configurator seems to know about the parameters a particular module can take. Click Done when you're satisfied that everything is set up correctly.

Figure 32.5 shows the options available for the `ppa` parallel port Zip drive.

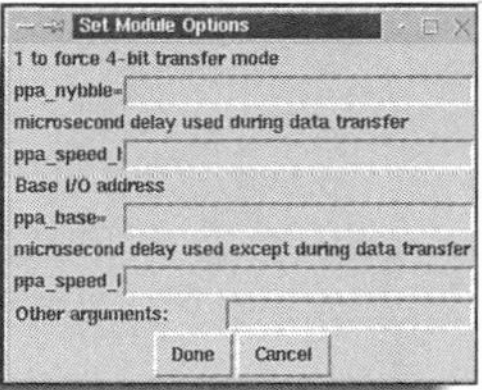

FIGURE 32.5
Entering the module options for the ppa module.

7. To get `kerneld` to recognize the changes to the configuration, click the Restart `kerneld` button.

Finding information on module parameters

Module documentation has always been something of a weak point in Linux. The most up-to-date information is always included in the kernel, but some repositories on the Internet are also starting to keep this information. (A good place to start looking is the Linux Documentation Project, at **http://sunsite.unc.edu/LDP/**.) The problem with the information included with the kernel source itself is that it is scattered in all the directories in various `Readme` files, and for some modules the only way to find out what the parameters are called is to read the source code for the module.

Editing the Linux Kernel Configuration Files

`kerneld` and other programs can do a lot more for you when they are configured by hand. Granted, this is not as nice as a graphical configuration program, but Linux's roots (in fact, UNIX's roots) are in text mode, and these systems for the most part have been run by hackers (the good ones, that is) who do not care too much for glitzy configuration tools when `vi` will do.

That being said, later revisions of the 2.0 Linux kernel sport both text-based menus and point-and-click X compile-time configuration tools in addition to the obtuse step-by-step configuration method. Recompiles are now rarely required for systems running production kernels. Only kernel updates themselves require compilation of the kernel for your system. If you're really allergic to compiling and installing kernels, a number of packages can be found that can install a later kernel for you.

Other modules take other parameters

Other modules, such as networking, ask for IRQ and IO address information.

The main file for kernel module configuration is `/etc/conf.modules`. In fact, this is the same file that is edited with the `kernelcfg` tool. The kernel daemon supports a great deal more than the `kernelcfg` tool, and manually editing the file allows for a great deal more flexibility. `kerneld` and the supporting programs know about most modules that ship with the stock Linux kernel, and attempt to take care of these automatically. The only ones that `kerneld` needs help with are network, SCSI, and CD-ROM devices. The reason for this is pretty simple—autodetection of hardware is not something that should have to happen on a running system if it can be avoided, because the PC platform is just far too complex for things to be 100% reliable in this regard.

`kerneld` comes preconfigured for the majority of modules that now come with Linux. To find out about which modules `kerneld` is currently aware of, run the following command:

```
/sbin/modprobe -c ¦ grep -v '^path' ¦ less
```

This command gives you a listing of what the `/etc/conf.modules` file would look like if `kerneld` knew nothing about the modules on your system. Fortunately this is not the case, but it is handy to be able to see how `kerneld` actually sees the world. `Kerneld` keeps some configuration information elsewhere on your system to allow it to know about the modules it listed for you, and to provide the basic functionality to keep your system running. The `modprobe` command is a tool that can be used to manually manage modules, and is documented in detail later in this chapter. As far as the preceding command goes, the call to `grep` just filters out all the extraneous information such as the actual paths of the module files, which are irrelevant to the current discussion.

Configuring Your Sound Card

As mentioned before, the Red Hat Linux kernel is almost entirely modular. Chances are that there is a module already compiled for your sound card, and that all you need to do is add the appropriate line to your module's configuration file to point the system to the right file. While it's possible to load and unload sound modules on-the-fly, it's not recommended because sound card drivers need to allocate contiguous areas of memory for buffering. At boot-up, this is easy, but it becomes increasingly difficult the longer the system has been running.

With the advent of Plug and Play PC hardware (most affectionately known by most PC support techs as *Plug and Pray*), things can get complicated with configuring sound cards at times, and the only advice I can give is *be patient*. Eventually it will work if the hardware is directly supported. Asking questions on Usenet newsgroups can be especially enlightening if you're absolutely stuck. In some cases, it's best to recompile the kernel, and make the sound drivers you need into one module, rather than a whole mess of them. You see, in my opinion the good folks at Red Hat set up their sound system to be a bit *too* modular, and the result is that it's easy to make a mistake when there are multiple modules being loaded with multiple parameters each, and which have to load in a certain order. I am trying to spare you the hours of fighting with the sound system and detail a way as to how to get only the drivers you need and the base sound functionality into one module instead of three or four. I detail this later in the section "Using `make config`."

Configuring your sound card

1. Determine what device driver module supports your sound board. The best place to start looking for information is in the Linux HOWTOs. The most up-to-date copies are kept at **`http://sunsite.unc.edu/LDP/`**, but relatively current copies of these documents are usually included with CD-ROM distributions.
2. Determine the device addresses for your audio card. The easiest way to do this on a dual-boot Windows 95/Linux machine is to look up the audio card in the device manager to get the interrupt and IO addresses. Barring that, it is possible to configure Plug and Play devices as discussed in the next section.
3. Using your favorite text editor, edit the `/etc/conf.modules` file. Make sure you have a backup of this file somewhere so

Determining the device driver module for your sound card

Determining what device driver module supports your sound card can take quite a bit of time because there is a lot of documentation to wade through for some of the weirder configurations. The Creative Labs' ubiquitous SoundBlaster series is well supported, and can even be made to work without recompiling the kernel. Even the cheaper Opti and Crystal audio chipsets can be made to work with some effort, but these are the cards in which it's best to combine all the drivers you need into one module.

Using sndconfig to configure SoundBlaster cards

If you have a SoundBlaster, SoundBlaster Pro, SoundBlaster 16, 16 Pnp, AWE 32, or AWE 64 sound card, you can use `/usr/sbin/sndconfig` to configure Plug and Play and the sound modules for you. Although these are the only cards `sndconfig` officially supports, you can use `sndconfig` to gain insight into how sound configuration works by looking over the output files (that is, the changes to `/etc/conf.modules` and `/etc/isapnp.conf` files). If all this works for you and your SoundBlaster card, you can stop reading this section right now…

you can restore it in case things go wrong. My `/etc/conf.modules` looks like this:

```
alias eth0 ne
options ne io=0xe000 irq=12
alias scsi_hostadapter ppa
options ppa ppa_nybble=0
alias sound sb
```

The key element here is the line `alias sound sb`. In this case, the `init` scripts included with Linux look for the sound alias in the `/etc/conf.modules` file and, if they find it, load the sound modules. In this case, the defaults work fine. The modules attempt to find the sound card, and in the case of common hardware, everything will work just fine.

4. If you (or the sound card's configuration program) have set the configuration to non-default settings, you might need to specify these when adding your sound card. Generally, the IO address, IRQ(s), and DMA channels must be specified. The following example tells the SoundBlaster driver to look for the card at the factory default values:

```
alias sound sb
options sound ioaddr=220 irq=5 dma=1,5
```

This tells the driver to look for the SoundBlaster card at IO address 220, interrupt 5, and using DMA channels 1 and 5. For 8-bit SoundBlaster and SoundBlaster Pros, only one 8-bit DMA channel is required.

Plug and Play Devices

ISA Plug and Play hardware is becoming more and more common. Although it is a common myth that only Windows 95 supports Plug and Play devices, PCI devices are inherently Plug and Play, and are managed (for the most part) by your PC BIOS with little operating system intervention. ISA Plug and Play is another matter altogether because the ISA bus predates the Plug and Play standard by more than a few years. Most people mean *ISA Plug and Play* when they utter the words *Plug and Play*.

Linux can be made to work with ISA Plug and Play devices. The first tool that can be used to make Plug and Play devices work with Linux is your system's BIOS. Most PC BIOSes have a setting to indicate whether a Plug and Play operating system is installed. Changing the setting to No often causes the BIOS to activate all ISA Plug and Play devices before booting the system. This means that, for the most part, these devices act as regular jumpered devices.

Some BIOSes, however, either do not have this capability, or don't support the correct Plug and Play specification. There are two specifications: the Intel one, and the Microsoft one. Each is somewhat compatible with the other, but more so in theory than in practice. If this is the case for you, all is not lost.

One ISA Plug and Play utility for Linux can be used to activate ISA Plug and Play devices. There is a good Web page that describes the process in greater detail, as well as links to the software, at **`http://www.redhat.com/linux-info/pnp/`**.

The system will use PnP if it finds a configuration file

Red Hat's `init` scripts actually look for the PnP package's configuration files, and automatically call the program to configure the hardware for you if the program is installed according to specifications.

Managing Modules

Most modules on your system are managed by `kerneld`, but there are times during which manual intervention is required. One limitation is having multiple SCSI adapters of different types in the system. The main SCSI adapter is in the `conf.modules`' `scsi_hostadapter` alias, but since `kerneld` allows only one SCSI setting in the `conf.modules` file, you have a problem. The answer is not overly complicated—the additional SCSI adapter must be managed manually. This is not as big of a deal as it seems, since the SCSI driver can be loaded with one command and then left in memory. In most cases, this is a parallel port SCSI device anyway, such as a Zip drive.

Other circumstances can occur where it is more convenient to manage modules manually. Sound driver modules should be tested by manually loading and unloading them, rather than immediately configuring them into the `/etc/modules.conf` file.

Installing Modules

To load a module manually from the command line, log on as root and issue the following command:

```
/sbin/modprobe <module-name>
```

In this case, `<module-name>` is the name of the module you want to install (for instance, use `ppa` to install the Zip driver module). `modprobe` reads its configuration from `/etc/conf.modules` as well, and it accepts aliases as well as real module names on the command line.

Listing Modules

If you're logged on as root

If you have logged on as root rather than having `su`'d from a user account, you can leave out the `/sbin` at the beginning of the command.

Listing modules is fairly easy; you simply issue the following command:

```
/sbin/lsmod
```

Output of the program on my system looks like this:

```
[root@jansmachine jwalter]# /sbin/lsmod
Module        Pages        Used by
ppa           1               1 (autoclean)
sd_mod        4               1 (autoclean)
scsi_mod      7            [ppa sd_mod] 2 (autoclean)
vfat          3               1 (autoclean)
fat           6            [vfat]1 (autoclean)
ne            2               1 (autoclean)
8390          2             ≠     0 (autoclean)
sound         19              0
```

The entries followed by `(autoclean)` are modules managed by `kerneld`. Note that the `sound` module is not followed by this designation, even though it is listed in the `/etc/conf.modules` file. This is because the module is actually loaded from an `init` script when the system boots.

Creating Module Dependencies

In many cases, loadable modules depend on one another to work—for example, the SCSI CD-ROM driver requires that a

SCSI adapter driver be loaded before the CD-ROM driver is loaded, so it can actually access the CD device. This is a critical function of the system, and the system must keep detailed information on which module requires another module to be loaded first. There is another advantage to having interdependent modules in a system—common functionality can be built into one module, and provide this functionality to other, more specific modules. Both the SCSI and sound module systems work this way, as do some file system driver modules. For instance, the Windows 95 long-filename system, `vfat`, is essentially a modified version of the standard DOS filesystem. Thus it makes sense for the `vfat` module to use the functionality found in the `msdos` file system module for most of it functions. The benefit here is that the new module can take advantage of extremely well-tested, dependable code, and if a standard (non-`vfat`) `msdos` file system is mounted, there is no code being loaded twice.

The system automatically creates the module dependencies at boot-time. Under certain circumstances, it is convenient, or even necessary, to update the dependency information. It is usually done when installing modules that are not part of the standard kernel distribution, such as the latest versions of `ftape`, the module that provides access to QIC tape drives. You also want to run module dependencies if you have changed your `modules.conf` to include additional directories where modules are kept. This prevents surprises if there are errors or problems with the modules in the directories that have been added and the system is rebooted, since you'll see any error messages while the system is still in a state at which these problems can be fixed.

To have the system generate new module dependencies, log on as root and issue the following command:

```
/sbin/depmod -a
```

The system searches the standard module directory trees and generates dependencies for every module it finds.

If you want to keep certain modules in directories outside the standard module directory tree (`/lib/modules/<kernel-version>`, where `<kernel-version>` is the current version of the Linux kernel), you must add the following to the top of your `modules.conf` file and restart `kerneld`:

```
keep
path=<path name>
```

Again, `<path name>` points to the directory where the additional modules are kept. The `keep` directive tells the module utilities to *append* the directory name to the module paths. If this directory is not there, the module path will be *replaced*, which most likely is not what you want.

Enabling Modules at Boot Time

The module management utilities can be configured to load entire directories of modules at boot time. This is not the same as using `initrd` to get the kernel to pre-load modules.

This process is a viable alternative to listing individual modules to be loaded at boot time in init scripts, or to letting `kerneld` automatically load and unload them.

In case you forget...

The kernel must be able to read the hard disk to load modules at boot time, which means that this is *not* the place to put entries for the SCSI adapter drivers that your system boots from because by the time the kernel has booted, the drivers must already be loaded and initialized for Linux to read the hard disk. These SCSI drivers that allow your system to boot are loaded from the *initial ramdisk*.

Loading a module at boot time by using *modules.conf*

1. Create a directory in which these modules should be kept. Use something like `/lib/modules/<kernel version>/boot` to keep the modules with the kernel version they were compiled for, and also within the directory tree where the rest of the world expects to see modules.
2. Copy the modules you need to load at boot time to the directory.
3. Make sure the first line of `/etc/conf.modules` is the directive `keep`. You don't want your module utilities thinking that this is the *only* thing you want them to do.
4. Add the line `path[boot]=/lib/modules/'uname -r'/boot` as the next line of `/etc/conf.modules`. If you want to make sure that you have typed this correctly before saving your changes, execute the command `echo /lib/modules/'uname -r'/boot` on another virtual terminal or `xterm`. The output should have your current kernel version in place of the `'uname -r'`.
5. Restart `kerneld`. There are lots of ways to do this, but the command `/etc/rc.d/init.d/kerneld restart` works adequately.

Managing Processes

As introduced in Chapter 28, "Managing Daemons," the Linux process model places significant importance on the ideas of process ownership and parent processes. Managing all the programs that run on a Linux system is a task that requires constant attention from the system administrator. The "mother of all processes" is called `init`, which is part of the kernel, and this process *spawns* all other processes, usually via the `inittab` file entries and the `init` scripts that define the system run levels.

Because Linux is a multiuser operating system, its processes also have other information attached to them. The user ID and the group ID, as well as a priority setting, are part of the process. You see, the process has all the rights of the user that started the process on the system. This is an important concept: the process is what prevents a user's programs from overwriting another user's home directory or reading his email. The process also makes it dangerous to run programs, especially unattended *daemon* programs, on the system as root because the program can read from and write to any file and all networks.

Rights, as specified by user and group IDs, are *inherited* by all processes spawned by any other process. For example, when a user logs on, the shell that is started to process the user commands, usually `bash`, has the same user ID as the user who has logged on, and so any process that the shell starts (such as `ls`, `pine`, and so on) has the same settings as well. When a process's parent process finishes before the child process does, the child process is *orphaned*. In this case, `init` takes over as the parent process. If the user is no longer on the system and the process has not been flagged to continue running after the user logs off, using the command `nohup` (meaning "no hang-up," or "don't send the hang-up signal to the process when the user leaves"), `init` terminates the process.

Because every process must have a parent, and many programs use multiple processes to accomplish their tasks, child programs must have a way of passing some information back to their parents. Fundamental to this is the *return code*, a number that a program returns to the system after its completion. The problem is that the parent must be ready to accept the return code of the child process. In cases when this does not happen, the child process, although having completed processing, continues to exist in the system because its parent has not accepted the return value of the child process. Such a process is termed to be in a *zombified* state. Zombie processes don't use many system resources, but an excess of them can cause problems and require intervention from the system administrator. The simplest way to clear up zombie processes is to kill their parent processes (that's quite the social policy, if you ask me...). The children then become the property of `init`, which happily accepts the return code.

Using the */proc* Directory Information

The `/proc` directory tree is a special directory structure that is a window on the running Linux kernel. This structure contains files and directories with all sorts of information that the kernel collects, and is useful for troubleshooting the system or learning about how it works. Utilities such as `ps`, `top`, and `uptime` gather information from this directory tree.

Some files in `/proc` are security sensitive—in particular, the file `/proc/kcore` is essentially a file pointing to all of the system's memory, and as such can contain passwords or other information that others should not see. As a result, this file and any other files that contain sensitive information have the appropriate permissions set on them to prevent this sort of abuse. Table 32.1 covers a few files of interest in the `/proc` directory.

TABLE 32.1 **A few files of interest in the */proc* directory**

File	Description
cpuinfo	Contains information about the processor(s) in the system, including the capabilities and bugs that Linux has detected. For example, many Intel processors contain the F0 0F bug that can cause the system to completely freeze when certain machine instructions are executed. Later kernels (2.0.33 and later, for example) can detect this and take appropriate measures to minimize the impact of these problems with the system processor. Other processor

File	Description
	problems include the Pentium floating point math bug, but the kernel also accounts for differences in how floating point coprocessors and halt instructions are handled.
version	Contains the kernel version number, the system name, and the time and date that the kernel was compiled.
pci	Contains information about the devices on the system's PCI bus, as well as the detected capabilities of the hardware that's on the bus.
interrupts	Contains a count of all interrupts the system has processed, and the device that they are attached to.

The majority of these files are used by Linux developers to debug their systems, and this material, while interesting, is not vital to any administration task. The `pci` and `interrupts` files can provide insight into system problems, however.

Viewing the System Load Average

The load on a system in the UNIX world is measured by using a number called the *load average*. This number is based on the number of processes waiting to run at a given time.

The best command for viewing the system load average is `uptime`. The output of this command also reveals how long the system has been up, along with the load average over the last 1, 5, and 15 minutes, and number of users logged on. If you'd rather gather all this information yourself, it's in `/proc/loadavg`—the first three numbers are the load average.

Viewing Processes with the *top* Command

`top` is a dynamic process-viewing utility. It essentially combines the output of several other utilities in a compact and relatively easy-to-read format. `top` provides the means to sort processes by the percentage of processor time they use, the memory they use, or the total amount of time they have run on the system.

To start `top`, simply type **`top`** from a command prompt. A screen comes up showing you the memory allocated, the system-uptime and load averages, and a list of processes sorted by the amount of CPU time they are using.

`top`'s commands are pretty simple, and are summarized in Table 32.2.

CPU time vs. how long a process has been running

CPU time for a process is a reasonable estimate of how long a process has run on the processor. This is different from how long the program has been running, from a human perspective, because there are a lot of other programs running at the same time. Time used gives an estimate on how far along the process is if it had been the only thing running on the system.

Case sensitivity with `top`

`top`'s commands are case-sensitive!

TABLE 32.2 **Command summary for the *top* utility**

Command	Usage
h	Help. This brings up a detailed help screen.
M	Sorts processes by memory used. Use this to find the program that is using the most memory on your system.
S	Changes `top`'s display from current to cumulative mode when displaying CPU time used by a process. By default, `top` displays only the CPU time a process has used from the time `top` was last checked. With this flag, `top` displays all the CPU time a process has used since the program was started. There are always some inaccuracies here—`X`, for example, always seems to display cumulative time on my system, no matter what the flag is set to.
T	Sorts by the amount of processor time the process has used, either cumulative, or since the last refresh of the `top` screen.
P	Sorts the display by the percentage CPU time a process has had since the last time the `top` display refreshed itself.
r	Re-`nice`s a process. The `nice` value of a process is the priority the process has in the system, ranging from 32 to –32. The lower the `nice` value, the higher the process's priority in the system. Only processes owned by root can have negative `nice` values. You must be the owner of the process or logged on as root to change its `nice` value.
k	Kills a process. This sends the appropriate signal to a process to indicate that it should finish processing and exit. `top` enables you to send different signals to a process—it prompts you for the one to send. Normally, the `TERM` signal `(15)` works fine to terminate a process. Processes that are hung, or those that ignore the `TERM` signal, however, may need some stronger persuasion to terminate, such as the `KILL` signal `(9)`. This signal makes Linux unconditionally terminate the process.

Viewing Processes with the *ps* Command

ps is the UNIX standard utility used to manage processes on a system. This utility provides pretty much the same functionality as top, but is command-line driven rather than using a primitive text interface.

The ps command alone produces a list of all processes owned by the current user, along with the process ID, the terminal the process is running on, the process status, the CPU time used, and the command line and name of the process itself.

At it's most basic, the output of ps looks like this:

```
[jwalter@irksome jwalter]$ ps
  PID TTY STAT  TIME COMMAND
 1296  p1 S    0:00 -bash
 1310  p1 R    0:00 ps
[jwalter@irksome jwalter]$
```

I own only two processes on this system: bash (my shell) and ps (the program that produced this data). The STAT column tells me what the processes are currently up to—whether the program is running (R), sleeping (S), stopped (T), or zombified (Z). While the Linux kernel does a good job of keeping the system clean, once in a while the system administrator should go around and clean up any remaining zombie processes.

ps Command-Line Parameters

The ps utility accepts command-line parameters without requiring a hyphen, like so:

```
ps <options>
```

ps command-line options are discussed in Table 32.3.

TABLE 32.3 ***ps* command-line options**

Option	Effect
a	Lists all processes, even those not owned by the user running ps.
x	Lists processes that don't have a controlling terminal (daemon programs and so on).

continues...

TABLE 32.3 **Continued**

Option	Effect
`u`	Prints user ID and memory usage information. This looks remarkably like the process list for `top`.
`j`	Prints job information. This lists the process user and group IDs in numerical format, along with the parent process IDs.
`f`	Prints process information in a tree format showing parent processes and their relations.
`t`	Prints only process attached to the terminal name that immediately follows. The preceding `tty` is assumed, so `ps tS1` would list all processes with `ttyS1` as the owning terminal.

Of course, there are plenty of other options listed in the man pages for `ps`. The ones in Table 32.3 are simply the ones that systems administrators use the most often.

Using the *kill* Command and Process IDs

The `kill` utility is used to send signals to processes. One of the uses, as the name of the utility suggests, is for terminating or removing unwanted processes from the system. `kill` can also send other signals to processes. For instance, the `HUP` signal by convention causes most daemon programs to re-read their initialization files.

Confusing signal names

Signal names such as `HUP` and `KILL` are often referred to as `SIGHUP` and `SIGKILL`. Either way of writing them is usually valid, but some utilities might accept only one or the other.

Another noteworthy point is that most shells, such as `bash`, contain their own built-in `kill` utilities. On some shells, this can be quite different than the `kill` that's described here, and you'd do well to check your shell's documentation to see how that behaves. In this section, you learn about `bash`'s `kill` behavior.

The `bash` shell is capable of getting a process ID for you, provided the process is running in the background of that session. For other processes, you must use the `ps` utility to get the process ID. You can kill only processes that your user ID owns—unless, of course, you are logged on as root.

This syntax of the `kill` command is as follows:

```
kill -s <signal> <process id>
```

To print a list of signals and their numbers, execute the following command:

```
kill -l
```

The default signal that `kill` sends is `TERM` signal.

Killing a process

1. Obtain the process ID by running `ps`. If the list is too long, and if you know the process name, try piping the output to the `grep` utility to find the word for you.
2. With the process ID handy, type the command `kill <PID>`, where `<PID>` is the process ID number. The command prompt returns. If `bash` complains about there being no such process, then you have the wrong number, or the process has already terminated.
3. After the next command is executed, `bash` should produce a message such as the following:

   ```
   [1]+  Terminated                  find / -name what
   ```

   If it does not produce such a message, the process is not responding to `TERM` signals. In this example, the program `find` was terminated.
4. If `bash` does not issue that message, and another look using `ps` shows that the process is still merrily gobbling up your CPU time, you'll need to do something more drastic. First make sure that the program is not doing some sort of shutdown processing that needs to be completed, and then issue the following command to kill the process:

   ```
   kill -s 9 <PID>
   ```

   This is a signal that a program cannot ignore, so the process is terminated even if it does not want to be. After the next command (or just after pressing Enter if you have nothing else to do), `bash` should print the following message to tell you that the program has been killed:

   ```
   [1]+  Killed                  find / -name what
   ```

Getting impatient when sending signals to programs

Some programs need to do some work before shutting down, such as saving open files. Be sure to give the program enough time to do this, or data loss can occur.

Recompiling the Kernel

Every once in a while, it is worthwhile to see whether a new kernel for Linux has been released. Usually new kernels provide fixes for problems that people have experienced, or provide performance improvements (usually both). The new kernels can also contain more device drivers. This section discusses how to obtain, compile, and install a new kernel on your Linux system.

The disclaimer

The process of compiling and installing kernels is not for the technically faint-of-heart: Mistakes here could leave your system in an unbootable state, or worse, could damage your hardware or disk contents. You have been warned.

The official repository for Linux kernels is the FTP site `sunsite.unc.edu`, in the directory `/pub/Linux/kernel/v2.0`. The Red Hat Linux installation program should have placed the source code to your current kernel in the `/usr/src/linux` directory on your hard disk. This is a symbolic link to the actual source directory.

Installing the New Kernel Source

After you have downloaded the kernel source, you must decompress it and extract the directories within. You must be logged on as root, as well, or at least have full permissions to the `/usr/src` directory. This assumes that you have downloaded the kernel source to the `/root` directory. Be sure to substitute the directory that the kernel was downloaded to for your system. You must also have about 10–15 MB of free space to extract and compile a new kernel.

1. Delete the symbolic link pointing to the current Linux kernel source directory. The idea is to avoid overwriting the current source directory, because it might contain modifications you have made. It's also a setup that you should be able to restore if something goes wrong. The command is as follows:

   ```
   rm linux
   ```

   If `rm` tells you you're deleting a directory, then there is something wrong. Check the directory you're in, and make sure that `linux` is a symbolic link to the current source directory.

2. Create the new directory to hold the kernel source. The reason this is being done is that the source distribution wants to extract itself to a directory called `linux`, but this is not the way it is intended to be used. Create a directory with an appropriate name, usually `linux-`, followed by the kernel version (for example, `linux-2.0.33`).
3. Create the new symbolic link to the new directory by entering the following:

```
ln -s <your directory name> linux
```

4. Extract the file to the new directory by entering the following:

```
tar xzvf <kernel file name>
```

Your new kernel source is now correctly installed and you can configure the kernel. Depending on the speed of your system, this can take some time.

Before Configuring the Kernel

Make sure that you note the following information about your system before configuring a kernel that you intend to use:

- Your processor type.
- Whether your machine is PCI.
- The type of IDE controller in your system (if there is one).
- The type of SCSI controller in your system—manufacturer, model number, chipset number, and revision are important here.
- The type of interface your CD-ROM uses.
- The type of network card that's in your system. Having the make and model number of the chipset on the network card is also quite handy.
- The make, model, and chip number of your sound card. You should also note the interrupt request line (IRQ, for short), the IO addresses the card uses, and the DMA lines the card uses.

PC hardware is a complex thing. Not only is there a myriad of possible combinations of hardware for your computer, but also many manufacturers and their products, although not officially supported by Linux, use chip sets and other components that work just fine. Sometimes it's a matter of trial and error to figure out what works, but often, the answer can be determined easily by getting the chip numbers from the cards, and looking into the appropriate directory containing similar drivers.

In fact, the writers of the drivers for Linux often go as far as to include one or more documentation files with the drivers to explain some of the "gotchas" for a particular piece of hardware. Just look in the `drivers` subdirectory of the `linux` directory. The documentation files in the `drivers/sound` and `drivers/net` are particularly detailed.

Also, I recommend that, if you have never built a Linux kernel before, you review all the sections, in particular the `make config` and the `make xconfig` sections. They both deal with the same kernel, but the material (and configuration programs) are organized slightly differently. These differences may shed some light on items that may not be apparent from reading just one section.

Using *make config*

If the descriptions in this section differ from what you see on your system

The kernel configuration examples here use a kernel that Red Hat Linux 5 did not ship with. Some additional support for devices has been added to the newer kernels, and the additional information about these devices is included in this section.

This section describes the classic way to configure the Linux kernel, and is entirely text based. I don't recommend that you use it, simply because it's inconvenient—after you make a decision, you must restart the process to change it.

To configure your kernel by using `make config`, change to the `/usr/src/linux` directory and, as root or someone with write permissions there, type the following command:

```
make config
```

You are greeted by the following friendly message:

```
[root@jansmachine linux]# make config
rm -f include/asm
( cd include ; ln -sf asm-i386 asm)
/bin/sh scripts/Configure arch/i386/config.in
```

```
#
# Using defaults found in .config
#
*
* Code maturity level options
*
Prompt for development and/or incomplete code/drivers
(CONFIG_EXPERIMENTAL)[Y/n/?]
```

The questions usually list choices of valid answers, with the default answer in capital letters. If you cannot decide, type a question mark and press Enter. Usually there is some text to help you, but sometimes the answers are quite cryptic.

In the case of the preceding code, you'll normally want to answer `Y`, especially if you have a PCI-based PC.

The configuration script continues here:

```
*
* Loadable module support
*
Enable loadable module support (CONFIG_MODULES)[Y/n/?]
Set version information on all symbols for modules
(CONFIG_MODVERSIONS)[Y/n/?]
Kernel daemon support (e.g. autoload of modules)
➥(CONFIG_KERNELD)[Y/n/?]
```

For normal configurations, answer `Y` to all of the above. If you want to turn off kernel daemon support, here is where it's done.The configuration script continues here:

```
*
* General setup
*
Kernel math emulation (CONFIG_MATH_EMULATION)[N/y/?]
Networking support (CONFI¦G_NET)[Y/n/?]
Limit memory to low 16MB (CONFIG_MAX_16M)[N/y/?]
PCI bios support (CONFIG_PCI)[Y/n/?]
   PCI bridge optimization (experimental)
➥(CONFIG_PCI_OPTIMIZE)[Y/n/?]
```

These questions should be pretty clear. The most notable is the PCI Bridge Optimization option. It's recommended, despite being experimental, and in my time I have not encountered any problems with this feature.

If you turn off kernel daemon support

Turning off kernel daemon support can cause your system to lose network connectivity because there will be nothing to load the drivers when the network cards are configured in the `init` scripts on system boot. If you turn off this support, either compile the drivers for your network card into the kernel rather than as modules, or modify your `init` scripts to manually load the modules for your network card before the `network` script is called.

The next section of script configures the binary formats the kernel supports, as well as other compatibility options:

```
System V IPC (CONFIG_SYSVIPC)[Y/n/?]
Kernel support for a.out binaries
(CONFIG_BINFMT_AOUT)[Y/m/n/?]
Kernel support for ELF binaries (CONFIG_BINFMT_ELF)[Y/m/n/?]
Kernel support for JAVA binaries
(CONFIG_BINFMT_JAVA)[N/y/m/?]
Compile kernel as ELF - if your GCC is ELF-GCC
➥(CONFIG_KERNEL_ELF)[Y/n/?]
Processor type (386, 486, Pentium, PPro)[Pentium]
  defined CONFIG_M586
```

These options allow you to set the types of binaries supported by the kernel. Respond `Y` to all options except Java support. Although the `a.out` format is the older Linux binary format, and is not technically required, it can prevent headaches when running older programs. Some kernel options can break Java compatibility, according to some sources, and in addition to this other modifications have to be made to the system to support Java binaries. As far as processor types are concerned, choose the one you have. It does not hurt too much to use a kernel built for a 386 on a Pentium system, but a kernel compiled for a Pentium will not run on a 386. If you have a NexGen processor, compile for 386, and make sure that Math Emulation (previous section) is turned on. If you have any other non-Intel processor, answer 486 here. Some processors ID themselves as Pentium processors, but some differences still exist. Besides, these processors tend to have more advanced features, such as out-of-order instruction execution, and do not need any of the more advanced optimizations to function at peak efficiency.

The next section deals with floppy and IDE devices:

```
*
* Floppy, IDE, and other block devices
*
Normal floppy disk support (CONFIG_BLK_DEV_FD)[Y/m/n/?]
Enhanced IDE/MFM/RLL disk/cdrom/tape/floppy support
(CONFIG_BLK_DEV_IDE)[Y/n/?]
```

Both questions should be answered with `Y`, unless you don't want to use either of these devices.

The next section of script assumes you have answered `Y` to IDE device support:

```
*
* Please see Documentation/ide.txt for help/info on IDE
drives
*
   Use old disk-only driver on primary interface
(CONFIG_BLK_DEV_HD_IDE)[N/y/?]
   Include IDE/ATAPI CDROM support
(CONFIG_BLK_DEV_IDECD)[Y/n/?]
   Include IDE/ATAPI TAPE support
(CONFIG_BLK_DEV_IDETAPE)[N/y/?]
   Include IDE/ATAPI FLOPPY support
(new)(CONFIG_BLK_DEV_IDEFLOPPY)[N/y/?]
   SCSI emulation support (CONFIG_BLK_DEV_IDESCSI)[N/y/?]
   Support removable IDE interfaces
(PCMCIA)(CONFIG_BLK_DEV_IDE_PCMCIA)[N/y/?]
   CMD640 chipset bugfix/support
(CONFIG_BLK_DEV_CMD640)[N/y/?]
   RZ1000 chipset bugfix/support
(CONFIG_BLK_DEV_RZ1000)[N/y/?]
   Intel 82371 PIIX (Triton I/II)DMA support
(CONFIG_BLK_DEV_TRITON)[Y/n/?]
   Other IDE chipset support (CONFIG_IDE_CHIPSETS)[N/y/?]
```

As stated here, more information on IDE peculiarities can be gleaned from the `Documentation` subdirectory of the `linux` source directory. To summarize, this section of script allows you to enable the new IDE/ATAPI device capabilities. Some IDE CD changers use a protocol similar to the SCSI Logical Units to control the several devices attached, and SCSI emulation support allows the use of regular SCSI tools to exploit this feature. Another option allows the detection of buggy IDE chipsets to be enabled along with their workarounds. Also listed is the option to turn on the Bus Mastering feature of the IDE controller included in Intel's Triton (430 series) PCI chipsets—under some circumstances the driver will work with the Pentium Pro (440FX) and Pentium II (440LX) chipsets as well.

Other IDE chipsets supported include some chipsets by QDI and others, mostly used on Vesa Local Bus add-on cards shipped with some 486 PC systems. In most cases these drivers enable bus-mastering on the controller for a performance improvement.

The following script is presented next:

```
*
* Additional Block Devices
*
Loopback device support (CONFIG_BLK_DEV_LOOP)[M/n/y/?]
Multiple devices driver support (CONFIG_BLK_DEV_MD)[N/y/?]
RAM disk support (CONFIG_BLK_DEV_RAM)[N/y/m/?]
XT harddisk support (CONFIG_BLK_DEV_XD)[N/y/m/?]
```

These devices are a bit more interesting than those in the run-of-the-mill IDE controller section. The loopback device allows the use of files as "virtual file systems" inside files. This is often used for creating disk images for writing CD-ROMs. There are some other uses for this as well—for example, this device is used by the script that makes a SCSI system's initial ramdisk. In the preceding case, the makefile recommends this to be a module. It does no harm to leave it this way, and could come in useful.

Your initial ramdisk and the loopback adapter

If your system requires an initial ramdisk (in other words, your system boots off a SCSI adapter), you need the loopback device to generate that ramdisk in the first place.

The multiple devices driver allows several partitions to be accessed as one. Additional tools and configurations are required to implement this. RAM disk support is important for systems that boot from SCSI disks with modular kernels—answer `Y` to the initial RAM disk support option that is displayed if you have a SCSI system. The last option is for those poor souls who still have hardware that predates the 286.

On to configuring your kernel's networking:

```
*
* Networking options
*
Network firewalls (CONFIG_FIREWALL)[N/y/?]
Network aliasing (CONFIG_NET_ALIAS)[Y/n/?]
TCP/IP networking (CONFIG_INET)[Y/n/?]
IP: forwarding/gatewaying (CONFIG_IP_FORWARD)[N/y/?]
IP: multicasting (CONFIG_IP_MULTICAST)[N/y/?]
IP: syn cookies (CONFIG_SYN_COOKIES)[N/y/?]
IP: rst cookies (CONFIG_RST_COOKIES)[N/y/?]
IP: accounting (CONFIG_IP_ACCT)[N/y/?]
IP: optimize as router not host (CONFIG_IP_ROUTER)[N/y/?]
IP: tunneling (CONFIG_NET_IPIP)[M/n/y/?]
IP: aliasing support (CONFIG_IP_ALIAS)[M/n/y/?]
```

```
*
* (it is safe to leave these untouched)
*
IP: PC/TCP compatibility mode (CONFIG_INET_PCTCP)[N/y/?]
IP: Reverse ARP (CONFIG_INET_RARP)[M/n/y/?]
IP: Disable Path MTU Discovery (normally
enabled)(CONFIG_NO_PATH_MTU_DISCOVERY)[N/y/?]
IP: Drop source routed frames (CONFIG_IP_NOSR)[Y/n/?]
IP: Allow large windows (not recommended if <16Mb of memo-
ry)(CONFIG_SKB_LARGE)[Y/n/?]
```

This section of script details the kernel's networking options for the base networking tool in Linux: TCP/IP. It's strongly recommended that you respond with a `Y` here even if you do not have a network card. Your system has a loopback network configured to support local programs whose operation assumes there to be a network. There are many programs (X Window, for instance) on your system that prefer to use network sockets.

The majority of cases do not need either network firewalling or aliasing. (For a more detailed description of how these options work see the Firewall-HOWTO included with your Red Hat Linux CD and available online at **http://sunsite.unc.edu/LDP/** and on many mirror sites.)

The forwarding/gatewaying option should definitely be set to `N` if you have a system on a LAN and plan to dial the Internet with it. That is, of course, only true if you don't intend to make your system the gateway. Again, the Net-2-HOWTO should shed a great deal more light on this if you're interested.

Multicasting is relatively new for the rest of the Internet, and many ISPs' equipment does not support it. Say `N` here while the rest of the world gets multicasting sorted out.

`Syn` and `Rst` cookies are designed to reduce the effectiveness of certain attacks on your system. There has been significant attention paid to "syn flooding" attacks on systems connected to the Internet in recent months, and this change in Linux networking is designed to reduce the effectiveness of the attack significantly.

IP accounting allows you to keep track of network traffic going over your system. It's really useful only if Linux is being used as a network router, a topic, unfortunately, beyond the scope of this book.

Optimizing as router not host makes some changes to the networking in Linux. It's recommended to be left off unless you're setting up a router.

IP tunneling is used similarly to Virtual Private Networks under Windows, and although the two are incompatible, it should be noted that this feature can be used to join two LANs over the Internet by using Linux. Most users can say **N** here.

IP: Aliasing is the other half of the network aliasing option, and as mentioned earlier, most people won't need it.

You should also leave the last set of options untouched, although the option Drop Source Routed Frames is recommended for better network security.

The next section of script allows you to enable support for other networking protocols and other kernel functions:

```
*
*
*
The IPX protocol (CONFIG_IPX)[M/n/y/?]
Appletalk DDP (CONFIG_ATALK)[N/y/m/?]
Amateur Radio AX.25 Level 2 (CONFIG_AX25)[N/y/?]
Bridging (EXPERIMENTAL)(CONFIG_BRIDGE)[N/y/?]
Kernel/User network link driver (CONFIG_NETLINK)[N/y/?]
```

These options are only for the technologically savvy. IPX can be used with some programs to provide services to Novell clients. The others are best left off.

The next section of script allows you to configure generic SCSI support for your kernel:

```
*
* SCSI support
*
SCSI support (CONFIG_SCSI)[M/n/y/?]
*
* SCSI support type (disk, tape, CD-ROM)
*
```

```
SCSI disk support (CONFIG_BLK_DEV_SD)[M/n/?]
SCSI tape support (CONFIG_CHR_DEV_ST)[N/m/?]
SCSI CD-ROM support (CONFIG_BLK_DEV_SR)[M/n/?]
SCSI generic support (CONFIG_CHR_DEV_SG)[M/n/?]
*
* Some SCSI devices (e.g. CD jukebox)support multiple LUNs
*
Probe all LUNs on each SCSI device
(CONFIG_SCSI_MULTI_LUN)[N/y/?]
Verbose SCSI error reporting (kernel size
+=12K)(CONFIG_SCSI_CONSTANTS)[N/y/?]
```

These options cover the common functionality for SCSI drivers and devices under Linux. The choices here depend on the hardware you have, although I recommend that verbose SCSI reporting be left off for performance and kernel size reasons.

If you have answered `Y` to SCSI support, you are now prompted to specify the actual SCSI card or chip your system has:

```
*
* SCSI low-level drivers
*
7000FASST SCSI support (CONFIG_SCSI_7000FASST)[M/n/?]
Adaptec AHA152X/2825 support (CONFIG_SCSI_AHA152X)[M/n/?]
Adaptec AHA1542 support (CONFIG_SCSI_AHA1542)[M/n/?]
Adaptec AHA1740 support (CONFIG_SCSI_AHA1740)[M/n/?]
Adaptec AIC7xxx support (CONFIG_SCSI_AIC7XXX)[M/n/?]
   Enable tagged command queueing
(CONFIG_AIC7XXX_TAGGED_QUEUEING)[Y/n/?]
   Override driver defaults for commands per LUN
(CONFIG_OVERRIDE_CMDS)[N/y/?]
   Enable SCB paging (CONFIG_AIC7XXX_PAGE_ENABLE)[Y/n/?]
   Collect statistics to report in /proc
(CONFIG_AIC7XXX_PROC_STATS)[N/y/?]
   Delay in seconds after SCSI bus reset
(CONFIG_AIC7XXX_RESET_DELAY)[15]
AdvanSys SCSI support (CONFIG_SCSI_ADVANSYS)[M/n/?]
Always IN2000 SCSI support (CONFIG_SCSI_IN2000)[M/n/?]
AM53/79C974 PCI SCSI support (CONFIG_SCSI_AM53C974)[M/n/?]
BusLogic SCSI support (CONFIG_SCSI_BUSLOGIC)[M/n/?]
  Omit FlashPoint support
(CONFIG_SCSI_OMIT_FLASHPOINT)[N/y/?]
DTC3180/3280 SCSI support (CONFIG_SCSI_DTC3280)[M/n/?]
```

```
EATA-DMA (DPT, NEC, AT&T, SNI, AST, Olivetti,
Alphatronix)support (CONFIG_SCSI_EATA_DMA)[M/n/?]
EATA-PIO (old DPT PM2001, PM2012A)support
(CONFIG_SCSI_EATA_PIO)[M/n/?]
EATA ISA/EISA/PCI (DPT and generic EATA/DMA-compliant
boards)support (CONFIG_SCSI_EATA)[M/n/?]
  enable tagged command queueing
(CONFIG_SCSI_EATA_TAGGED_QUEUE)[N/y/?]
  enable elevator sorting (CONFIG_SCSI_EATA_LINKED_
COMMANDS)[N/y/?]
  maximum number of queued commands
(CONFIG_SCSI_EATA_MAX_TAGS)[16]
Future Domain 16xx SCSI support
(CONFIG_SCSI_FUTURE_DOMAIN)[N/m/?]
Generic NCR5380/53c400 SCSI support
(CONFIG_SCSI_GENERIC_NCR5380)[N/m/?]
NCR53c406a SCSI support (CONFIG_SCSI_NCR53C406A)[N/m/?]
NCR53c7,8xx SCSI support (CONFIG_SCSI_NCR53C7xx)[N/m/?]
NCR53C8XX SCSI support (CONFIG_SCSI_NCR53C8XX)[M/n/?]
  detect and read serial NVRAMs
(CONFIG_SCSI_NCR53C8XX_NVRAM_DETECT)[N/y/?]
  enable tagged command queueing
(CONFIG_SCSI_NCR53C8XX_TAGGED_QUEUE)[N/y/?]
  use normal IO (CONFIG_SCSI_NCR53C8XX_IOMAPPED)[N/y/?]
  maximum number of queued commands
(CONFIG_SCSI_NCR53C8XX_MAX_TAGS)[4]
  synchronous transfers frequency in MHz
(CONFIG_SCSI_NCR53C8XX_SYNC)[5]
  not allow targets to disconnect
(CONFIG_SCSI_NCR53C8XX_NO_DISCONNECT)[N/y/?]
  assume boards are SYMBIOS compatible
(CONFIG_SCSI_NCR53C8XX_SYMBIOS_COMPAT)[N/y/?]
IOMEGA Parallel Port ZIP drive SCSI support
(CONFIG_SCSI_PPA)[M/n/?]
PAS16 SCSI support (CONFIG_SCSI_PAS16)[N/m/?]
PAS16 SCSI support (CONFIG_SCSI_PAS16)[N/m/?]
Qlogic FAS SCSI support (CONFIG_SCSI_QLOGIC_FAS)[N/m/?]
Qlogic ISP SCSI support (CONFIG_SCSI_QLOGIC_ISP)[N/m/?]
Seagate ST-02 and Future Domain TMC-8xx SCSI support
(CONFIG_SCSI_SEAGATE)[N/m/?]
Tekram DC-390(T)SCSI support (CONFIG_SCSI_DC390T)[N/m/?]
Trantor T128/T128F/T228 SCSI support
(CONFIG_SCSI_T128)[N/m/?]
UltraStor 14F/34F support (CONFIG_SCSI_U14_34F)[N/m/?]
UltraStor SCSI support (CONFIG_SCSI_ULTRASTOR)[N/m/?]
```

```
GDT SCSI Disk Array Controller support
(CONFIG_SCSI_GDTH)[N/m/?]
```

These options are for specific SCSI devices in your system. Particularly, if you want to support more than one or two SCSI devices, setting them as modules is a good idea. If your boot drive is a SCSI disk, and you decide to use modules, ensure that the Initial ramdisk support is enabled and that you remember to make the initial RAM disk with the SCSI driver(s) for your system.

If you do not want to use a SCSI module for your boot device, however, make sure that you delete the `initrd<kernel version>.img` file in the `/boot` directory, or that you have turned off `initrd` support in the kernel. Otherwise, the kernel's now built-in device driver will initialize the device, and then the device driver included in the initial ramdisk will try to do the same, and fail. This would not be so bad, except that the failed device driver load in this case will trigger a kernel panic. If you neglect to delete the `initrd<kernel version>.img` file, you can give to the boot the kernel image from the LILO command line with the `noinitrd` option.

The online help here is most helpful for drivers that give you additional configuration options. In general, Tagged Command Queuing is an option you should enable for the best performance, but check the other options there to ensure that there is not something else in the driver that can affect this.

The kernel configuration now takes us to the choices for network devices:

```
*
* Network device support
*
Network device support (CONFIG_NETDEVICES)[Y/n/?]
Dummy net driver support (CONFIG_DUMMY)[M/n/y/?]
EQL (serial line load balancing)support
(CONFIG_EQUALIZER)[N/y/m/?]
Frame relay DLCI support
(EXPERIMENTAL)(CONFIG_DLCI)[N/y/m/?]
PLIP (parallel port)support (CONFIG_PLIP)[N/y/m/?]
PPP (point-to-point)support (CONFIG_PPP)[M/n/y/?]
```

```
*
* CCP compressors for PPP are only built as modules.
*
SLIP (serial line)support (CONFIG_SLIP)[M/n/y/?]
 CSLIP compressed headers (CONFIG_SLIP_COMPRESSED)[Y/n/?]
 Keepalive and linefill (CONFIG_SLIP_SMART)[Y/n/?]
 Six bit SLIP encapsulation (CONFIG_SLIP_MODE_SLIP6)[N/y/?]
Radio network interfaces (CONFIG_NET_RADIO)[N/y/?]
```

This set of options is for base network device support. For anything but specialized configurations, answer `Y` to network device support, PPP, and perhaps SLIP (any of which could be needed to dial an ISP). Making these modules is your choice.

The next question really means: "Do you have a network card?"

```
Ethernet (10 or 100Mbit)(CONFIG_NET_ETHERNET)[Y/n/?]
```

Answer `Y` here for a walk-though of the choices of different network adapters. It's a pretty lengthy list, so take your time. Most network adapters require no parameters or anything, so as long as you know what you have, you should be fine.

```
*
* ISDN subsystem
*
ISDN support (CONFIG_ISDN)[N/y/m/?]
```

ISDN support for Linux is pretty new, and not that many adapters are supported. For up-to-date information about using ISDN with Linux, have a look in the `Documentation/isdn` subdirectory, where you'll find information on configuration issues and software required.

The next section of script deals with non-SCSI and non-IDE CD-ROM drives:

```
*
* CD-ROM drivers (not for SCSI or IDE/ATAPI drives)
*
Support non-SCSI/IDE/ATAPI CDROM drives (CONFIG_CD_NO_
IDESCSI)[N/y/?]
```

Answering `Y` here causes the configuration program to go through a list of non-SCSI and non-IDE CD-ROM drives. There are some issues with some proprietary CD controllers and some network cards in which the system may hang if the kernel has to probe for the CD controller's IO address. Read the documentation for the CD drivers and specify an IO address at the kernel command line if this happens.

Things will now get interesting again—the next section of script allows you to configure file system support for your Linux kernel:

```
*
* Filesystems
*
Quota support (CONFIG_QUOTA)[Y/n/?]
Minix fs support (CONFIG_MINIX_FS)[M/n/y/?]
Extended fs support (CONFIG_EXT_FS)[M/n/y/?]
Second extended fs support (CONFIG_EXT2_FS)[Y/m/n/?]
xiafs filesystem support (CONFIG_XIA_FS)[M/n/y/?]
DOS FAT fs support (CONFIG_FAT_FS)[M/n/y/?]
MSDOS fs support (CONFIG_MSDOS_FS)[M/n/?]
VFAT (Windows-95)fs support (CONFIG_VFAT_FS)[M/n/?]
umsdos: Unix like fs on top of std MSDOS FAT fs (CONFIG_
UMSDOS_FS)[N/m/?]
/proc filesystem support (CONFIG_PROC_FS)[Y/n/?]
NFS filesystem support (CONFIG_NFS_FS)[M/n/y/?]
SMB filesystem support (to mount WfW shares
etc..)(CONFIG_SMB_FS)[M/n/y/?]
SMB Win95 bug work-around (CONFIG_SMB_WIN95)[Y/n/?]
NCP filesystem support (to mount NetWare
volumes)(CONFIG_NCP_FS)[N/y/m/?]
ISO9660 cdrom filesystem support (CONFIG_ISO9660_FS)[M/n/y/?]
OS/2 HPFS filesystem support (read
only)(CONFIG_HPFS_FS)[M/n/y/?]
System V and Coherent filesystem support
(CONFIG_SYSV_FS)[M/n/y/?]
Amiga FFS filesystem support
(EXPERIMENTAL)(CONFIG_AFFS_FS)[N/y/m/?]
UFS filesystem support (read only)(CONFIG_UFS_FS)[M/n/y/?]
BSD disklabel (FreeBSD partition tables)support
(CONFIG_BSD_DISKLABEL)[N/y/?]
SMD disklabel (Sun partition tables)support
(CONFIG_SMD_DISKLABEL)[N/y/?] Kernel automounter support
(experimental)(CONFIG_AUTOFS_FS)[M/n/y/?]
```

A great number of filesystems are supported by Linux. Other filesystem drivers are available for download as well. Quota support provides a means of limiting the disk space that a certain user can use. This support must be enabled by using some programs in the `init` scripts for the system, but it seems that Red Hat Linux ships with the necessary programs to implement Quota support if you want to.

Personally, I never set `ext2fs` to be a module—it's just too much of a hassle. Trust me here. Every other file system you want can be set to be a module. I tend to not bother with Minix or the old `ext` filesystems; instead, I simply compile the MS-DOS `fat` and `vfat` file systems, `hpfs`, and `iso9660` as modules. `kerneld` is usually smart enough to pick the right file system and load the driver for you when you try to mount one.

Automounting has something to do with the system automatically mounting NFS (network file system) drives. Unless you're on a network with lots of UNIX and Linux machines, the time spent making this work is probably better spent doing other things.

On to configuring character-base devices, such as modems, and so on:

```
*
* Character devices
*
Standard/generic serial support (CONFIG_SERIAL)[Y/m/n/?]
Digiboard PC/Xx Support (CONFIG_DIGI)[N/y/?]
Cyclades async mux support (CONFIG_CYCLADES)[N/y/m/?]
Stallion multiport serial support (CONFIG_STALDRV)[N/y/?]
SDL RISCom/8 card support (CONFIG_RISCOM8)[N/y/m/?]
Parallel printer support (CONFIG_PRINTER)[M/n/y/?]
Specialix IO8+ card support (CONFIG_SPECIALIX)[N/y/m/?]
Mouse Support (not serial mice)(CONFIG_MOUSE)[Y/n/?]
ATIXL busmouse support (CONFIG_ATIXL_BUSMOUSE)[N/y/m/?]
Logitech busmouse support (CONFIG_BUSMOUSE)[N/y/m/?]
Microsoft busmouse support (CONFIG_MS_BUSMOUSE)[N/y/m/?]
PS/2 mouse (aka "auxiliary device")support
(CONFIG_PSMOUSE)[Y/m/n/?]
C&T 82C710 mouse port support (as on TI Travelmate)(CON-
FIG_82C710_MOUSE)[Y/n/?]
Support for user misc device modules (CONFIG_UMISC)[N/y/?]
```

```
QIC-02 tape support (CONFIG_QIC02_TAPE)[N/y/?]
Ftape (QIC-80/Travan)support (CONFIG_FTAPE)[M/n/y/?]
*
* Set IObase/IRQ/DMA for ftape in
./drivers/char/ftape/Makefile
*
```

The preceding script is the character device configuration section, as you can probably tell by its title. Things like mice and serial and parallel ports fall into this category. The only notable selections here are the QIC-80 drivers. There are updated drivers available for QIC-80 and Travan drivers that seem to work better, have compression support, and finally, can format tapes. If you have problems with the included driver, it might be worth it for you to look for such drivers at the `sunsite` archive, or on your Linux distribution CDs. Also note that for the `ftape` drivers to work, you must set the floppy controller parameters in the file it mentions.

User miscellaneous modules enable a device section in the kernel, intended to support other input devices. Unless you're writing or testing one, you should respond with an **N**.

The next section of script is the sound card configuration section:

```
*
* Sound
*
Sound card support (CONFIG_SOUND)[M/n/y/?]
/dev/dsp and /dev/audio support (CONFIG_AUDIO)[Y/n/?]
MIDI interface support (CONFIG_MIDI)[Y/n/?]
FM synthesizer (YM3812/OPL-3)support (CONFIG_YM3812)[M/n/?]
ProAudioSpectrum 16 support (CONFIG_PAS)[M/n/?]
Sound Blaster (SB, SBPro, SB16, clones)support
(CONFIG_SB)[M/n/?]
Generic OPL2/OPL3 FM synthesizer support
(CONFIG_ADLIB)[M/n/?]
Gravis Ultrasound support (CONFIG_GUS)[N/m/?]
PSS (ECHO-ADI2111)support (CONFIG_PSS)[N/m/?]
MPU-401 support (NOT for SB16)(CONFIG_MPU401)[M/n/?]
6850 UART Midi support (CONFIG_UART6850)[N/m/?]
MPU-401 UART Midi support (CONFIG_UART401)[N/m/?]
```

```
Microsoft Sound System support (CONFIG_MSS)[M/n/?]
Ensoniq SoundScape support (CONFIG_SSCAPE)[M/n/?]
MediaTrix AudioTrix Pro support (CONFIG_TRIX)[M/n/?]
Support for MAD16 and/or Mozart based cards
(CONFIG_MAD16)[M/n/?]
Support for Crystal CS4232 based (PnP)cards
(CONFIG_CS4232)[M/n/?]
Support for Turtle Beach Wave Front (Maui, Tropez)
synthesizers (CONFIG_MAUI)[N/m/?]
Audio DMA buffer size 4096, 16384, 32768 or 65536
(DSP_BUFFSIZE)[65536]
```

The Linux Sound System again. If you've decided that you want to re-build your kernel to support your sound card, you're in the right place. Most people with Creative Labs sound cards are well served by `sndconfig`, but the rest of us, especially those with later version Plug and Play cards, will likely need to recompile our kernels for more reliable and easier sound support.

I still compile sound as a module for my system, but do it differently from the Red Hat distribution. It took me some experimentation to get support for my sound configuration right, and I plan to spare you the majority, if not all, of the headaches I went through. The best part of doing the sound system as a module is that you can continue to rebuild the sound modules and try them until they work, usually without having to reboot. In order for this technique to work, you must use the `make xconfig` program to configure your kernel. Also note that this technique will probably stop working (or at least change significantly) in the next major Linux kernel release.

Enable `/dev/audio` and `/dev/dsp` support. Most multimedia applications for Linux depend on this. MIDI support is optional. If you enable MIDI, keep in mind that most cards come with a MPU-401–compatible MIDI controller, and that you should enable that too.

If you configure sound as a module, the sound card device drivers will also, by default, want to be made as modules. With some playing you can coax most of them to allow a **`Y`** answer instead. This results in the sound drivers being compiled into one module, rather than a whole set of modules, and should also allow you to hard-code some sane default IO address, IRQ, and DMA settings into the drivers.

I have found that this is the least painful way to get a stubborn sound card working with Linux. Once you have configured the card parameters, and if you have a Plug and Play card, I recommend that you use the `isapnp` tools to configure the card to the IO addresses and other parameters.

The configuration program asks whether you want to see additional low-level drivers. These are pretty non-standard devices, which are documented in the `drivers/sound` directory.

The last section of script has options for kernel developers:

```
* Kernel hacking
*
Kernel profiling support (CONFIG_PROFILE)[N/y/?]

The linux kernel is now hopefully configured for your setup.
Check the top-level Makefile for additional configuration,
and do a 'make dep ; make clean' if you want to be sure all
the files are correctly re-made
```

The preceding message signals the end of the kernel configuration. At this point I'll refer you to the later section "Building and Installing the Kernel."

Using *make xconfig*

Using `make xconfig` is the preferred way of configuring the kernel. In a pinch, you can use the venerable `make config`, or `make menuconfig`, which is not documented here due to space considerations, but the X configuration program for the Linux kernel is the easiest to use by far.

Starting X Window configuration of the kernel

1. Log on as—or `su` to—root.
2. Start X Window.
3. Open an `xterm` session.

4. Change to the Linux kernel source directory, `/usr/src/linux`.

5. Enter the command `make xconfig`. You are greeted by the screen shown in Figure 32.6.

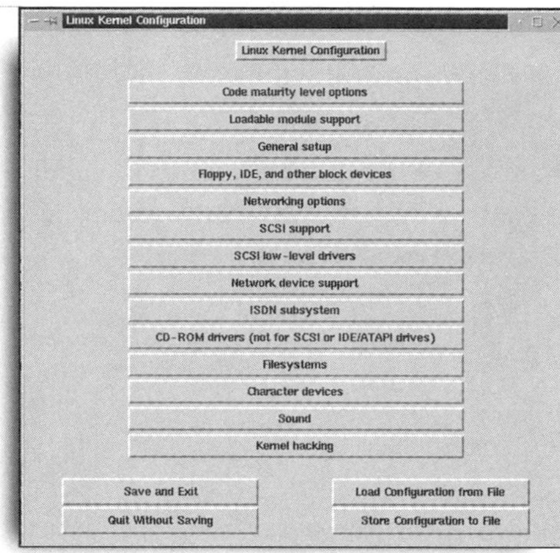

FIGURE 32.6
Configuring the Linux kernel by using `make xconfig`.

The details are the same

Most of the kernel configuration options are discussed in the previous section, and only the finer points are covered here.

Configuring the kernel

1. Start the configuration by clicking the Code Maturity Options button. This should always be your starting point when configuring a new kernel.

2. It is generally safe to answer **Y** to Prompt for Development and/or Incomplete Code/Drivers, shown in Figure 32.7. For the most part, these changes to the kernel can enhance performance, and truly experimental code will be made obvious to you. To continue, click Next.

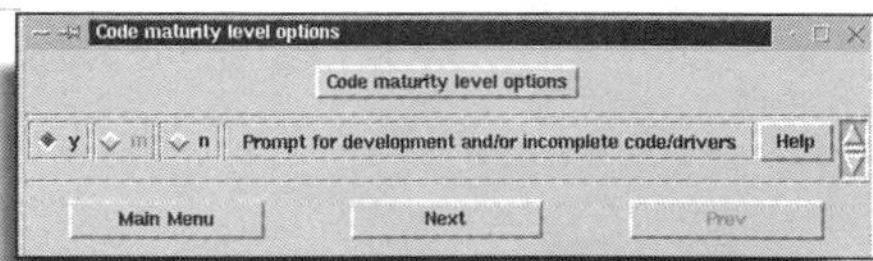

FIGURE 32.7
Selecting the Code Maturity Options.

3. The next screen, Loadable Module Support, is shown in Figure 32.8. Answering `Y` to all three questions here is recommended for Red Hat Linux, unless you really have a lot of experience with this, or are experimenting to get that experience. Click Next to continue.

4. The General Setup screen, shown in Figure 32.9, gets more interesting. Here you can choose to include support for kernel math emulation, processor type, and so on. Fresh kernel sources (ones that have not yet been configured on your system) have pretty safe defaults built in. The same caveats as in the `make config` section apply to everything here. Click Next to continue.

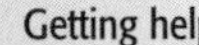

Getting help

Note the Help buttons next to the options. By now, most options are well documented in the online help for the kernel. Feel free to use this facility as you see fit. I use it often, even if only to see whether things have changed between versions.

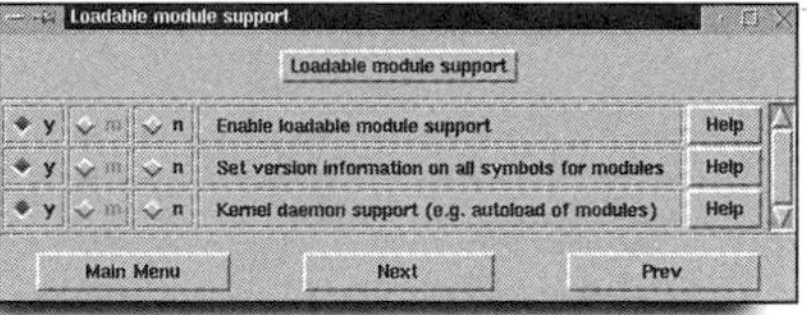

FIGURE 32.8
Configuring the loadable module options.

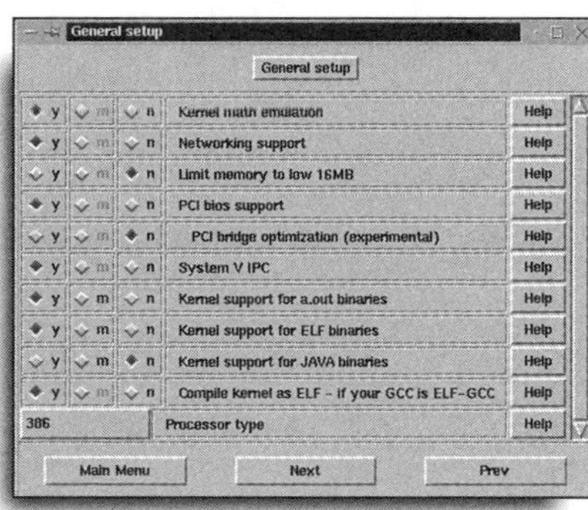

FIGURE 32.9
Configuring the general settings for the kernel.

5. The next screen, shown in Figure 32.10, configures your floppy disks, IDE drives, and non-SCSI block devices. You will probably have noticed by now that the questions are almost, if not exactly, identical as the questions that `make config` poses, but appear in a graphical format. Help, of course, is much more accessible. Note that the scroll bars on the right of the screen allow you to see the rest of the configuration options. In this section you get to set up your IDE devices and drivers for them. Click Next to continue.

FIGURE 32.10
The scroll bars on the right of the block device configuration screen allow you to see the rest of the configuration options.

6. Networking options are configured in the next screen, shown in Figure 32.11. These are covered in depth in the `make config` section above. Note that if you answer Yes to certain options, other sections become ungrayed. This makes it easy to determine which options must be enabled to allow you do what you want.

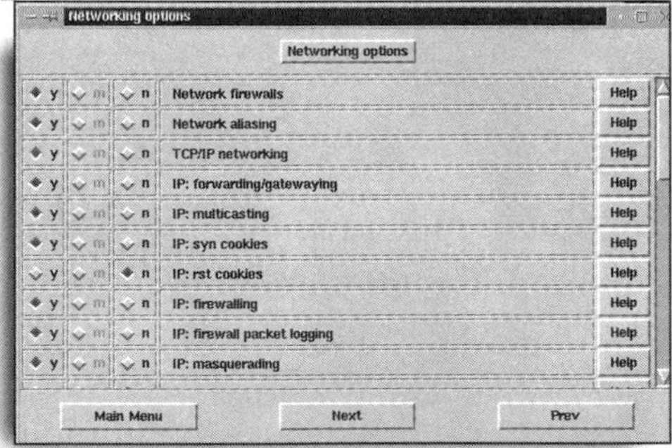

FIGURE 32.11
Configuring the network devices.

7. The SCSI configuration screen is next (see Figure 32.12). Here you can choose to support various generic SCSI devices, and how to modularize the SCSI subsystem. Note

how this kernel configuration is set up. The commonly used parts are compiled into the kernel (make sure you do this with SCSI Disk Support if you don't want to fight with `mkinitrd`), and the less commonly used parts are compiled as modules.

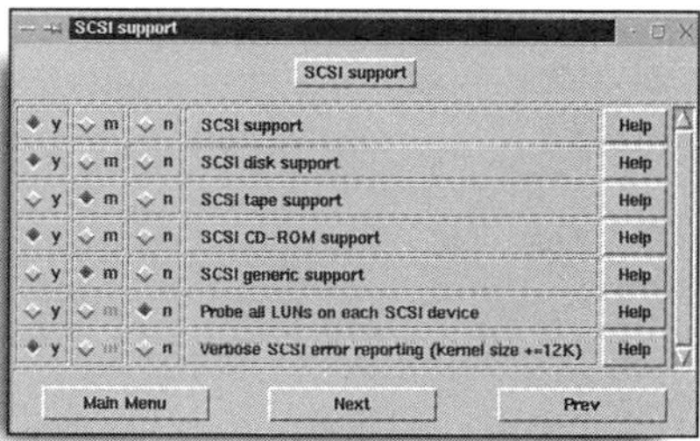

FIGURE 32.12
The Basic SCSI configuration screen is shown. Note how the modules are selected.

8. Click Next to bring up the SCSI Low-level Drivers section (see Figure 32.13). The advantage of the graphical configuration program here is that you can see which questions are coming for IO Addresses and so forth, before you get there. You can also go back and fix things easily if necessary. It's worth noting that some of the tagged command queuing options and SCB paging options have a profound impact on the performance of the system, so be sure to read the driver documentation for your card.

   Again, note that the stock system has your SCSI disk driver as a module if your system boots from it, and make sure that you disable the initial ramdisk if you decide to compile the driver directly into the kernel.

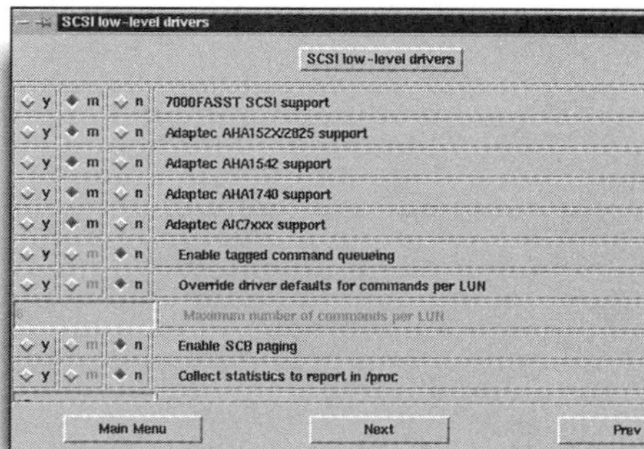

FIGURE 32.13
The SCSI Low-level Drivers selection dialog box is shown.

9. The Network Device Support screen, which allows you to configure the network cards as well as SLIP and PPP connectivity for your machine, appears next (see Figure 32.14). Again, making PPP and SLIP modules is reasonable here, since `kerneld` knows about them and automatically loads them.

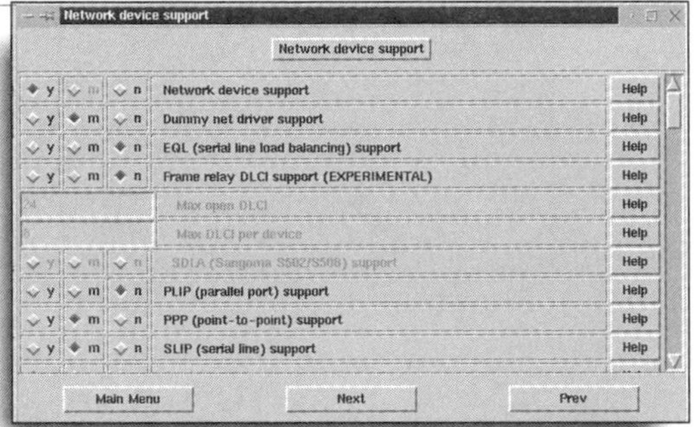

FIGURE 32.14
The Network Device Support screen probably lists the most devices, and can take some time to work though. Take your time.

10. ISDN support is next (see Figure 32.15). Choose the device connected to your computer. If you cannot find your particular device, start looking in the help screens, as well, for documentation in the `/usr/src/linux` subdirectories for any to see if your ISDN modem is compatible with something.

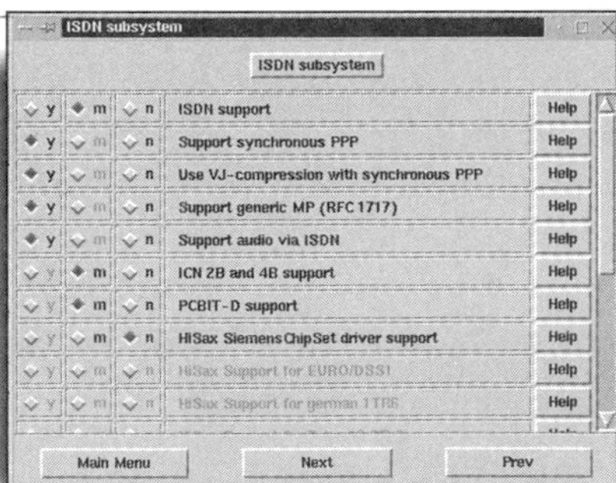

FIGURE 32.15
ISDN configuration options. Note that when experimenting with any device you're not sure of, it's best to use the driver as a module so you don't have to reboot every time you try different settings.

11. The non-SCSI and non-IDE CD-ROM device support section is next (see Figure 32.16). There are fewer and fewer of these devices around, but your system may still have one. It's particularly likely if your system has a double-spin drive, since most of these proprietary interfaces date back to that era.

FIGURE 32.16

The screen shot shows the CD-ROM configuration screen. Be prepared to give IRQ and IO Addresses for some CD-ROMs.

12. In the Filesystems screen that appears (see Figure 32.17), pick your file systems and move on. I recommend making any file system you want modular, except for `ext2fs`, because your system will need to use that to mount its initial ramdisk and the root partition.

13. Character Devices is where support for parallel ports, serial ports, and non-serial mice is configured (see Figure 32.18). If you plan to use a parallel port Zip drive, you'll want to make your parallel port driver as well as your Zip driver modular; the Zip driver does not yet support sharing the parallel port.

Modularizing drivers can be handy

It's probably worthwhile to modularize your ISDN drivers if you're experimenting. That way, device addresses and so on can be changed by unloading the module and reloading it with different parameters. It's also possible then to recompile a module and use it without rebooting the system in most cases.

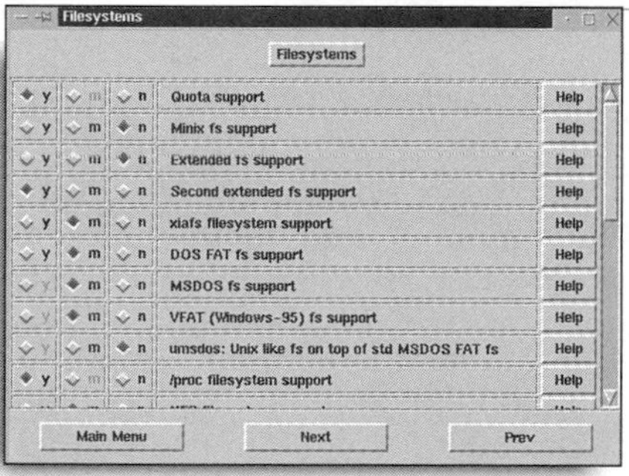

FIGURE 32.17

On the Filesystems configuration screen, make sure that you don't disable the `ext2` file system, or make it a module.

14. The sound card for your Linux system is now configured (see Figure 32.19). Everything noted in the `make config`

section applies here, but also note that it is possible to hard-set non-standard device addresses for your sound modules using `make xconfig`. It's worth noting that few of the configuration fields in this section check for "sane" values, so it's up to you to make sure that you enter correct ones. Make the sound driver static (by answering Yes), then change the option Sound Card Support back to being a module. This has the effect of producing only one module to contain sound support, which is something I have had a lot less trouble with.

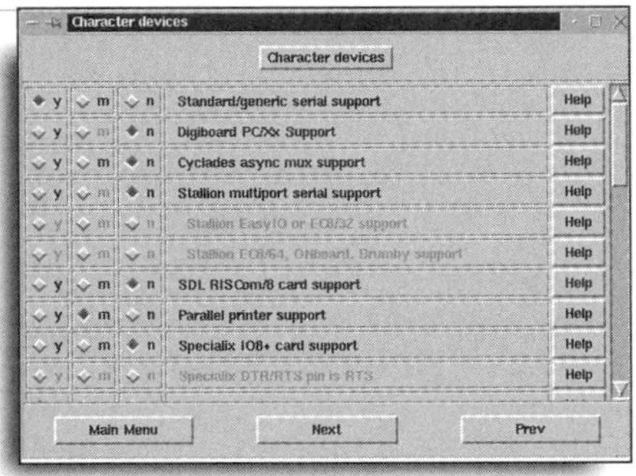

FIGURE 32.18
The Character Devices screen.

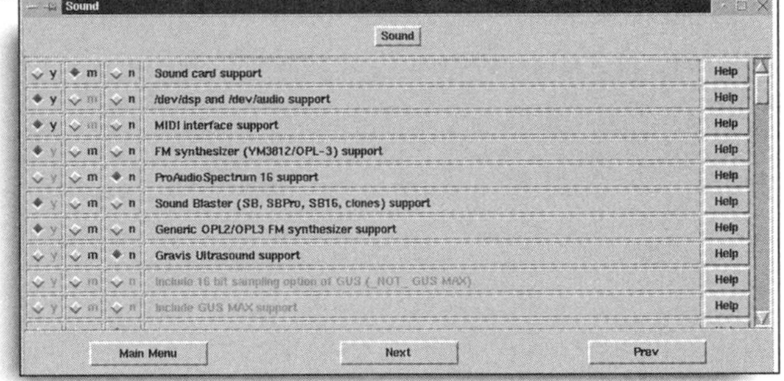

FIGURE 32.19
The Sound configuration screen.

15. The last screen allows you to enable kernel profiling. Unless you're doing some fine-tuning and development on the kernel (in which case this entire section should have put you to sleep), it's of no use, and better left set to No. Click the Main Menu button to return to the main menu.

16. Click the Save and Exit button, and you're now ready to build your kernel.

Building and Installing the Kernel

No matter which configuration tool you used to configure your kernel, now you must compile all the source files and produce the kernel itself. After building the kernel, and the modules for it, you need to create an initial ramdisk if your system is booting from a SCSI disk, and then re-run `LILO`, if you're using `LILO` to boot the system. If you're using `LOADLIN`, you must copy the kernel and the ramdisk file to a location from which `LOADLIN` can load the kernel.

Compiling the kernel and modules

1. Make sure you're in the Linux kernel directory. (You're probably already there.)
2. Issue the `make dep` command. This command causes the `make` system to generate dependency files to facilitate the correct building of the kernel.
3. Issue the `make clean` command. `make dep` leaves a lot of files lying around that can prevent the `make` program from compiling some files, and this can cause problems.
4. Issue the `make zImage` command. Note that this command is case sensitive. `make zImage` builds the kernel file. If the build process stops with an error message, run `make clean`, `make dep`, and then `make zImage` again. Any remaining error is likely to be an error in the configuration from the `make config` or equivalent script. Rerun that script, and perhaps take out some of the experimental stuff.
5. If all went well, run the `make modules` command to compile the module files.
6. If the version of the kernel you're compiling is different from the kernel you're currently running, run the `make modules_install` command. (Note the underscore in this command.) `make modules_install` copies the modules into

the correct tree in the /lib/modules directory tree. If you want to make backups of the modules you currently have, you can make a quick backup by issuing the following command:

```
tar czvf /root/modules-`uname -r`.tar.gz
/lib/modules/`uname -r`
```

This command assumes that you're going to install modules of the same kernel version that you're currently running.

You're now ready to make your initial ramdisk. You must perform this step only if you are booting from a non-IDE block device (such as a SCSI hard disk or RAID array), are using modules for your SCSI block device driver, and have switched kernel versions.

Initial ramdisks and static (non-modular) device drivers

The default installation of Red Hat Linux does use modular device drivers for SCSI hard disks, and if you have compiled drivers specific to your SCSI hardware into your kernel you must make sure that you have either disabled initial ramdisk support in the kernel as well, or edited your `/etc/lilo.conf` file to remove the initial ramdisk entry; otherwise, your system attempts to load the drivers for your SCSI card twice. Because your system will not find a SCSI device the second time the driver is initialized, the boot system will stop–this is not what you want!

Creating an initial ramdisk with *mkinitrd*

1. Ensure that the /etc/conf.modules file on your system is set up correctly. (Chances are it is, especially if your SCSI system booted from your hard disk successfully.)
2. Make a backup of your current ramdisk. The file is located in the /boot directory, usually called either initrd or initrd-<kernel-version>, where <kernel-version> is the version number of the kernel it is compiled for. Since it's probably a good idea to set up your system so that you can still boot the old kernel, rename the file to initrd.old.
3. Determine whether your system needs to preload the generic SCSI system support modules. Execute the command /sbin/lsmod to obtain a listing of the modules that your system currently has loaded. The generic SCSI modules are called sd_mod and scsi_mod. If these appear in the output listing, chances are your system needs them.
4. Issue the following command:

   ```
   /sbin/mkinitrd <--needs-scsi-modules> /boot/initrd <ker-
   nel-version>
   ```

   The option --needs-scsi-modules should be used if you have configured your kernel so that the generic SCSI disk support is modular. <kernel-version> is the version of the kernel for which you need to make the ramdisk.

If you have problems with this command, make sure that your system has support for a loopback block device, either as a module (recommended—`kerneld` will automatically load the module), or as a static device. It would also be worthwhile to check for updates for `mkinitrd` at the Red Hat Web site.

Installing the Kernel

This assumes that you have configured and compiled your kernel, installed your modules, and configured `initrd`. You should also have configured LILO (refer to Chapter 24, "Using LILO and LOADLIN") to perhaps include the old boot image and ramdisk so that you can boot those if things go wrong with your new kernel.

The following steps will save you the most typing if you are in the `/boot` directory because you can leave the `/boot` directory path out of every command.

1. Copy the kernel image, `/usr/src/linux/arch/i386/boot/vmlinuz`, to the `/boot` directory as file `zImage-<kernel-version>`. Of course, replace `<kernel-version>` with the version number of your kernel. If you have customized LILO to look for a different filename as the kernel image, make sure you use that instead.
2. Delete the symbolic link `/boot/zImage`. Create a new symbolic link using the command `ln -s /boot/zImage-<kernel-version> /boot/zImage`.
3. Type the command `lilo`. You should see output something like this:

   ```
   [root@jansmachine /root]# lilo
   Added linux *
   Added old
   ```

   The `*` character after the `linux` image is the image that LILO will boot by default. If you want to boot another image (for instance, the image `old` that was listed above), just type the image at the `lilo:` prompt that the system presents you with before it boots.

You may also want to test to see if LILO will install your configuration successfully. To do this, type `lilo -t` instead of `lilo`. This does everything but actually modify your disk to install LILO.

Enabling Advanced Power Management

Advanced Power Management provides a means to reduce the power a PC consumes, and controls features such as software power off as well. APM was around a long time before the standard was implemented, with significant 16-bit underpinnings, which makes support difficult in 32-bit operating systems. To make matters worse, desktop machines' "Green" BIOSes often don't comply fully with the established APM standard. My opinion is that it's interesting to try APM even with a desktop machine—just make sure that you have a backup kernel that does not have APM enabled in case things go awry.

The APM driver for Linux was designed specifically for notebook PCs to use the CPU's power-saving features. The driver does not provide support for hard disk spin-down (this is provided separately by the utility `hdparm(8)`), or VESA–compliant monitor power-saving, which can be enabled by editing a kernel source file. Notebooks, more so than desktop PCs, vary widely in their configuration and adherence to PC standards. This means that your mileage on this information will vary, probably not only from machine to machine, but also depending on the BIOS revision of a given line of machines from the same manufacturer.

Enabling APM is a simple case of checking the Enable Advanced Power Management under the Character Devices section of `make xconfig`. After you enable APM, there are a few additional choices to make:

- `Ignore User Suspend` turns off the code that responds to the user suspend APM signal. This must be turned off if the machine hangs or the Linux kernel panics/OOPes (you know you're there when your screen is full of hexadecimal numbers). The documentation specifically mentions the NEC Versa M series notebooks as qualifying for this special setting.

- `Enable PM at Boot Time` makes the Linux kernel turn on APM as soon as the machine boots. Most machines do this automatically, but it's worth experimenting with if power-saving does not seem to work. NEC Ultralite Versa 33/C and Toshiba 410CDT machines seem to experience problems when this is enabled, and this option is off by default.
- `Make CPU Idle` calls when Idle makes the Linux kernel call the APM CPU idle routines when not busy. This setting results in significant power savings on machines where this works; it allows the APM BIOS to do things such as slow the CPU clock after the machine has been idle or at a low load for some time.
- `Enable Console Blanking Using APM` allows the LCD backlight on your notebook PC's LCD screen to be turned off when the stock Linux screen-blanker blanks the screen. This option has known problems with the `gpm` utility, and if you're using this feature you should disable `gpm` using the command `chkconfig ---del gpm`.
- `Power Off on Shutdown` causes your machine to turn off when the system's `halt` command is issued, typically by the shutdown script. This feature is possibly of interest to owners of later desktop machines that support soft power-off, if their system has a compliant BIOS.

The main point to keep in mind here is that with the wide variety of implementations of APM in PC systems today, some or all of the features may not work with your particular PC. If you're comfortable with reading C and assembler source code, the `drivers/char/apm_bios.c` file makes for interesting reading (this is subjective, of course) and contains plenty of notes about how varying machines implement APM.

PART VI

Appendixes

APPENDIX

Installation of Red Hat Linux

By Bill Ball

- Preparing for the installation
- Defragmenting and partitioning your hard drive
- Selecting and activating swap space
- Choosing and installing software packages
- Initially configuring X11
- Setting up the system time, your printer, and your password
- Selecting system services
- Installing the bootloader (LILO)
- Booting Linux

Finding and Getting Red Hat Linux

The easiest way to install Red Hat Linux is from a CD-ROM, either from Red Hat Software, Inc., or another vendor that sells Linux distributions.

You can, however, download the required software (for Intel, SPARC, or Alpha CPUs) from the Internet from a variety of places, such as:

`ftp://ftp.redhat.com/pub/redhat/redhat-5.0`

`ftp://sunsite.unc.edu/pub/Linux/distributions/redhat`

If you have the time, patience, high-speed Internet connection, and hard drive storage space, it is possible to install Linux via FTP. In this case, all you need to do is start your Internet connection, download a couple of disk image files, and create your boot floppies. But do yourself a favor and save the time and effort—get a distribution on CD-ROM! This chapter assumes that you have a Red Hat Linux 5.0 CD-ROM and are ready to take the plunge.

If you don't have Red Hat's Linux CD-ROM, the definitive place to order one is:

`http://www.redhat.com`

There are some advantages to ordering the commercial version of Red Hat Linux. For example, the most recent version of Red Hat 5.0 includes Netscape's Communicator suite of web browsing and Internet tools, RealNetwork's RealVideo player, Enhanced Software Technologies' BRU 2000 tape backup software, and Metro-X's commercial X11 server.

SEE ALSO

➤ *For more information about using web browsers, see page 216.*

➤ *To learn more about using FTP, see page 198.*

Considering Hardware Requirements

According to Red Hat Software, Intel PC users should have at least a 386 or greater equivalent CPU (this includes the Pentium Pro and Pentium II). A little more than 40MB hard drive space is needed for a basic installation without the X Window System. To include X, you'll need an additional 60MB. A full installation will require nearly 600MB of hard drive space.

Although you can run Linux with 8MB of memory, you'll be much happier with 16MB for X11, and even better off with 32MB if you plan to use any large applications such as Netscape or Applixware. Your computer should also have a CD-ROM and a 3.5-inch floppy drive.

If you can run DOS or Windows 95 on your computer, don't worry—you'll be able to run Linux. But if you like to worry, ponder these additional questions:

- How much room on my hard drive should I devote to Linux?
- Will my video card support X11?
- Will my sound card work with Linux?
- Do I need to have MIDI support?
- Do I want to be able to use my microphone?
- Do I need PC card support?

Fortunately, most common hardware, such as graphics, sound, or PC cards is supported. If you find that your base installation does not provide the support you need, you might be able to find another Linux vendor or software company with the software drivers you need to make your hardware work. Consult the `HOWTO` documents, found under the `/usr/doc` directory, for additional information.

SEE ALSO

➤ *For more information about configuring your sound card for Linux, see page 573.*

Take care before installing!

Use a little common sense before installing Linux. Back up your important files and don't leave anything on your computer's hard drive that you will regret losing if something goes awry during the partitioning, formatting, or installation process. You have been warned!

The Installation Program's Interface

Red Hat uses a character-based interface rather than a graphical interface for installing Linux. A mouse isn't used during the installation process; instead, various keystrokes are used to select items.

If you're in a text region that has multiple choices or selections, you can usually use the arrow keys to move around. To switch between regions, you can use the Tab and Alt+Tab keys.

To choose a button to select, you normally position the highlighted area using one of the movement keys. You can then press the Spacebar or Enter key to select the button. To select check boxes, scroll through the entries, highlighting the desired option. Then use the Spacebar to select or toggle the option on or off.

The F12 key takes the values as selected on the screen and proceeds to the next screen. If your keyboard doesn't have an F12 key, the combination Shift+F2 should have the same results.

The installation program presents various diagnostic information for you to determine what might be happening in various parts of the install. To not clutter the main screen with extra data, the installation program uses a feature of Linux called the Virtual Console, which can be seen via a single keystroke. Table A.1 lists the keystrokes used to view each of the virtual consoles.

TABLE A.1 **Virtual console keystrokes**

Keystroke	Result
Alt+F1	The main installation dialog box.
Alt+F2	After the CD-ROM has been found, you get a shell prompt that can be used to execute commands.
Alt+F3	The log from the installation program.
Alt+F4	The log from the kernel and other system level programs.
Alt+F5	Messages from disk formatting and some other programs.

For the most part, you won't need to ever leave the first virtual console, unless you are curious, or trying to diagnose a problem.

Creating Installation Diskettes

To install Red Hat Linux, you must first create two installation disks—a boot floppy and a supplemental floppy. You'll need your Red Hat Linux CD-ROM to complete this step.

Creating boot disks

1. Get two blank disks and perform a DOS format. For example, to format a disk in your computer's A: drive from the DOS prompt, use the format command:

   ```
   format a:
   ```

2. Insert your Red Hat Linux CD-ROM and a formatted floppy into your computer. Then use the `rawrite` program on the CD-ROM to create the boot floppy (assuming that your CD-ROM is the D: drive on your computer) like so:

   ```
   D:\dosutils\rawrite
   ```

3. Press the Enter key. When the `rawrite` program prompts for the name of a disk image, enter the name:

   ```
   D:\images\boot.img
   ```

4. Press the Enter key. When the `rawrite` program prompts for the name of your floppy (assuming that it is in the A: drive):

   ```
   A:
   ```

5. Press the Enter key twice. When `rawrite` finishes, remove the completed boot floppy. Repeat step 2 to start `rawrite` again, but when the program prompts for the name of a disk image, enter the name of the supplemental boot disk:

   ```
   D:\images\supp.img
   ```

6. Repeat step 4. When `rawrite` finishes, remove your supplemental boot disk.

Making Room for Linux

To install Linux, you must make space on your existing hard drive. This section outlines the basic steps to do this, but before you begin, you should thoroughly read the documentation for the `fips` command, found under the `dosutils` directory on your Red Hat CD-ROM.

The `fips` command will create free space on your hard drive. But before you can begin, you should first defragment your hard drive. We'll show you how to do this for Windows 95.

Defragmenting your hard drive in Windows 95

1. Move your mouse pointer to My Computer on the desktop, and open the folder by double-clicking with the left mouse button.
2. Move your mouse pointer to your primary drive, press the right mouse button, and drag down to select the Properties menu item.
3. The properties dialog box will appear. Press the Tools tab at the top of the dialog box to show the disk tools, as shown in Figure A.1.

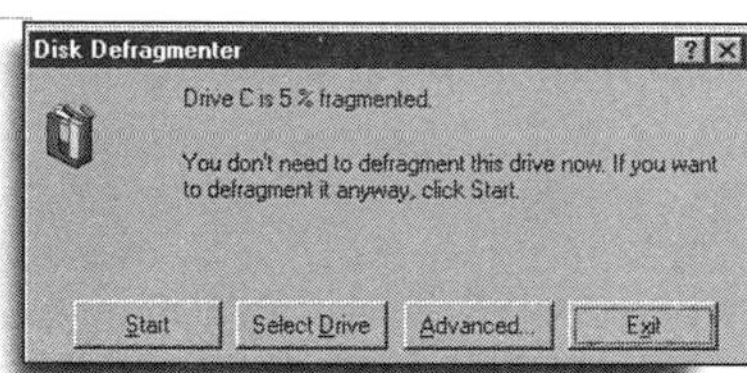

FIGURE A.1
Defragment your hard drive before using `fips`.

4. Click on the Defragment Now button to defragment your drive. Windows 95 might inform you that your drive does not need to be defragmented, as shown in Figure A.2. Click on the Start button with your left mouse button anyway to defragment your drive.
5. Click on the OK button at the bottom of the Properties dialog box to finish.

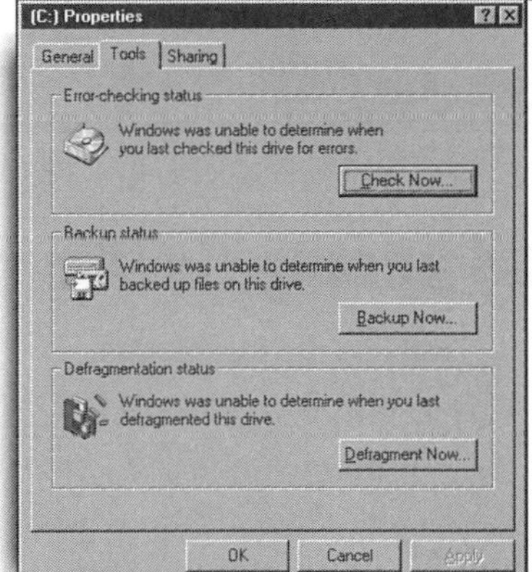

FIGURE A.2
Ignore Windows 95 and defragment your hard drive before using fips.

Creating room for Linux with *fips*

Backup, backup, backup!

Before you use **fips**, make sure to make a copy of any important files. Carefully read the **fips** documentation, in the file **fips.doc** under the **dosutils/fipsdocs** directory on your Red Hat Linux CD-ROM. You have been warned!

1. The first step in making room on your hard drive for Linux is to create a boot disk with the `fips` program. Insert a blank disk into your floppy drive. At the DOS prompt, format and make a bootable disk using the `format` command's `S` option:

```
format /S a:
```

2. After the format command finishes, copy the `fips` program to the bootable disk (assuming that your CD-ROM is in the D: drive):

```
copy d:\dosutils\fips.exe a:
```

3. Also copy the `fdisk` and `format` commands to your bootable floppy:

```
copy c:\windows\command\format.com a:
copy c:\windows\command\fdisk.exe a:
```

4. Restart your computer. Start `fips` from the DOS command line:

```
fips
```

5. Press Enter to start `fips`. The program will check your hard drive and then present a table showing the existing partition. After using your cursor keys to size your new partition, press Enter.

6. The program will then check your drive and display a new partition table. Press the **c** key. Then at the `fips` prompt, press the **y** key to save your changes and exit.

Beginning the Linux Installation

Starting the installation

1. To begin the Linux installation, insert the boot disk into the floppy drive and restart your computer. The machine should go through the normal process of booting from a floppy and then come to a screen with a `boot:` prompt.

Linux installs in two stages

The installation process occurs in two stages. In the first stage, you tell the installation program some basic information about your computer and where to find the installation files. The second stage performs the rest of the installation.

2. This initial screen contains helpful tips about starting the install and allows access to some initial help screens before the boot process. To access these help screens, press one of the following function keys, which are listed at the bottom of the screen. There is a short delay as the data is read from the floppy drive.

Function Key	Result
`F1 Main screen`	The one you initially saw at startup.
`F2 General`	Some general tips on what the boot process does.
`F3 Expert`	This screen explains the `expert` mode. This mode disables most of the auto-probing and autodetection.
`F4 Rescue`	This mode enables you to help repair a damaged system. You need both the boot and supplemental floppies for this mode.
`F5 Kickstart`	The `kickstart` is an advanced mode that uses a preconfigured text file. The use of `kickstart` mode is beyond the scope of this tutorial but is documented on the CD-ROM.
`F6 Kernel`	A help screen on some options that you can pass to the kernel at boot time.

3. You can now type any options you require at the boot prompt. Press Enter to start the install. If you do not type anything or press any function key, the install automatically begins after one minute.

   After pressing Enter, you should see the following output:

```
Loading initrd.img...................
Loading vmlinuz..........
Uncompressing Linux.......
```

   If the disk activity stops, and the initial screen doesn't appear, hardware problems or incompatibility are likely culprits.

The First Installation Stage

Proceeding with the installation

1. After a moment of floppy disk activity, you should see a black-and-white screen asking whether you are using a color monitor, shown in Figure A.3. This is the beginning of the first stage of the installation process. First, you set up some basic hardware, and the install attempts to find the installation media.
2. The default choice on the first screen is `Yes`; you should see a blinking cursor or highlight near the `Yes`. If you see the cursor or highlight option, press Enter and continue to the next step. This walkthrough assumes that you have a color monitor.
3. The next screen is a welcome screen, stating that the Red Hat installation guide also details the installation process. If you're ready to begin the install, press Enter.
4. The next screen, shown in Figure A.4, asks you to select the keyboard type you are using. If, after you have installed Linux, you want to change to a different keyboard type, the command `/usr/sbin/kbdconfig` can be used to change the keyboard type.

No boot prompt?

If you didn't get to this first screen, or if you received an error message, there might be something wrong with the floppy image. The most common causes are that the floppy disk had a bad sector, or that the floppy drive hardware has some sort of problem using the floppy. You need to re-create the boot floppy following the instructions at the beginning of this chapter.

Moving from option to option

When choosing from options on the screen, you can use Tab to move the selection. If you overshoot your selection, you can either press Alt+Tab to back up, or continue pressing Tab to wrap around to the other choices.

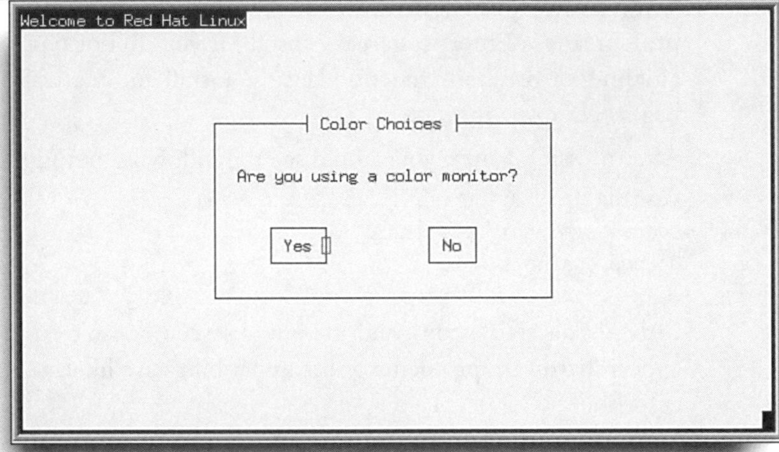

FIGURE A.3
Selecting the type of monitor you have.

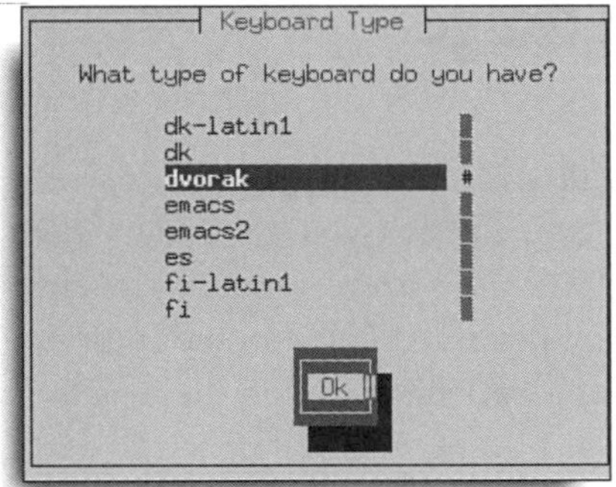

FIGURE A.4
Selecting the keyboard.

5. Most choices on this screen are for language-specific keyboards. The typical United States PC keyboard is the default choice. You can select a different choice using the arrow up and arrow down keys. To the right of the screen, you should notice a scrollbar with a # mark. This mark indicates that there are more types of keyboards than can be shown on the screen at present.

   After selecting the keyboard for your machine, Tab over to the OK button and press Enter.

6. Next, the program searches for a PCMCIA chipset in your computer. If a known PCMCIA chipset is found, then you are asked to insert the supplemental floppy. When you have

done this, you can select OK, and the program loads additional drivers from the floppy. If no known PCMCIA chipset is found, then the program quietly goes on to the next step of the install.

SEE ALSO

➤ *For more details about adding PC cards to use with Linux, see page 134.*

7. The next screen, shown in Figure A.5, asks which kind of install you want to attempt. Four methods can be used (see Table A.2). This section details installation only from a CD-ROM and a hard drive.

FIGURE A.5
Indicating where the installation files are located.

TABLE A.2 The four installation methods

Method	Description
Local CD-ROM	The default method of installing Linux to your hard drive. This method does not use the supplemental floppy.
Hard Drive	If you are unable to install from the CD-ROM, then you need to copy the \RedHat\ directory tree over to a FAT16 (DOS) partition on your hard drive. This method then loads the supplemental floppy and continues with the install.
NFS	This method enables you to install from an NFS server (a type of network file system).
FTP	This method enables you to install from an FTP server.

If you choose to install from a CD, the program asks you to insert the CD into the player. It then tries to autoprobe for an

IDE CD on the system. If it doesn't find an IDE CD, it presents a screen asking you to choose which of the following types of CD-ROM you have:

SCSI	If your CD is on an SCSI adapter, it tries to find the SCSI adapter, and if it is unable to, it asks you what kind of SCSI device it should try to load. You will be asked whether you want to autoprobe for the device or whether you want to give options to the device. In most cases, you shouldn't need to specify any options.
Other CD-ROM	If your CD isn't an IDE or an SCSI CD, it probably falls under this category. You are presented with a long list of drivers. Choose which driver matches your CD-ROM and if you need to, any special options.

After the CD has been detected, the program attempts to mount the Red Hat CD and go on to the next stage of the install.

CD-ROM problem?

If you have an IDE CD and it wasn't detected, you'll need to restart the install and at the very first screen give the kernel a special option to point out where the drive is:

```
boot: linux hdX=cdrom
Where hdX =

Channel  Jumper  hdx
==========================
ide0     master  hda
ide0     slave   hdb
ide1     master  hdc
ide1     slave   hdd

ide0 = primary channel
ide1 = secondary channel
```

The Second Installation Stage

You are now ready to begin the second stage of the installation process. In this stage, you create the necessary partitions and select which parts of the Linux distribution you want to install.

Selecting to Install Fresh or Upgrade

The next menu window, shown in Figure A.6, asks whether you are installing or upgrading an existing system. We'll assume that you're installing Linux for the first time.

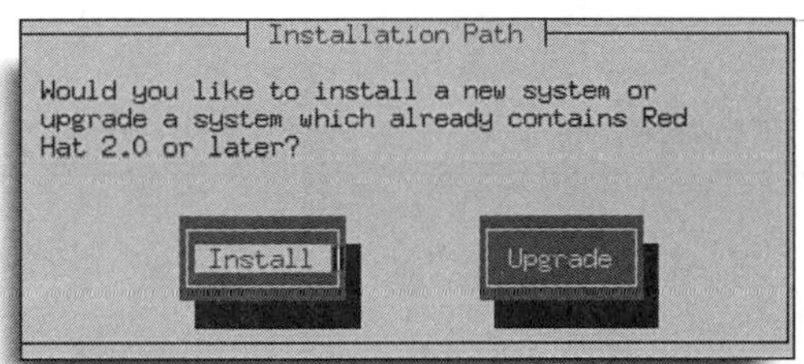

FIGURE A.6
Choosing to install fresh or upgrade an existing system.

SCSI Support

After choosing an installation option, the program tries to autoprobe for any SCSI adapters. If it cannot locate any, it asks whether you have any SCSI adapters in your machine. If you do, select Yes, and a dialog box asks which adapter you have. Choose the adapter you have in your machine, and another screen asking whether you want to autoprobe or give options is displayed. Most SCSI drivers do not need options. If you don't have an SCSI adapter, choose No and press Enter.

Want to overwrite a previous Linux installation?

If you already have Linux on your system, an install using existing partitions will overwrite all your data. Back up important files first!

Partitioning the Hard Drive

Before you partition your drive, you should understand how Linux references different partitions. In the DOS/Windows world, different partitions are given different drive letters. For example, if you have a drive with two partitions, they would probably show up as drives C: and D:. Linux does away with drive letters, and partitions show up as what can best be described as different directories. So if you have two partitions under Linux, they might show up as `/` and `/data` in the user interface.

The next screen that appears begins the Disk Setup portion of the install, shown in Figure A.7. You can choose between two partitioning tools that are shipped with Red Hat Linux. The first choice is the Disk Druid program, and the second is the `fdisk` command.

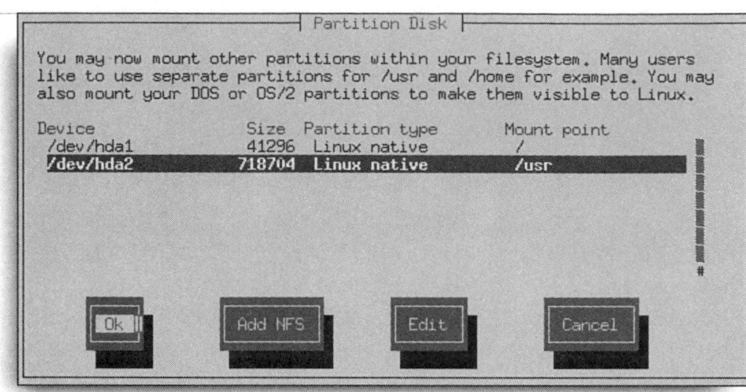

FIGURE A.7
Selecting the disk-partitioning program you want to use.

Disk Druid is a GUI-based disk management program. It can create and delete partitions, while also defining the mount points for those partitions. `fdisk` is a more esoteric partitioning tool. Although it is more flexible than Disk Druid in certain situations (dealing with disk drives having odd geometries, for example), it also is less user-friendly.

Red Hat Linux needs at least two partitions: the root mount point / and the Linux swap space. The recommended Linux swap space is usually equal to twice the amount of RAM you have, but if you have 32MB or more of RAM, you can set the swap space equal to the amount of RAM and still feel safe.

The Disk Druid Interface

The Disk Druid screen contains a lot of information about your hard drives. At the top of the screen is a section listing the Current Disk Partitions found on your hard drive. The middle of the screen is devoted to the Drive Summaries—the disk drives the installation program found. The bottom section lists the buttons and hot keys the program uses. All the sections are described more fully in the following text.

Current Disk Partitions

This section details the partitions that already exist on your machine. Each listed partition has several fields that are (left to right):

`Mount Point` The name of the directory that you will mount the directory under in Linux. Not putting anything in this field means that the partition will not be mounted.

`Device` This field gives the device name of the partition.

`Requested` This field shows the minimum size requested when the partition was defined.

`Actual` This shows how much space is currently given to that partition.

`Type` This field shows the type of partition. Commonly seen types are DOS, NTFS, Linux native, or Linux swap. You might also see that the partition has not been allocated yet. This is usually due to the fact that there isn't enough disk space for the minimum amount originally requested.

Drive Summaries

The lines in this section represent the hard drives present in the machine. Each line has these fields:

`Drive` The hard drive's device name. IDE hard drives use the device names `hdX`, where *X* is a letter indicating which drive it is. SCSI hard drives are labeled by how they appear on the chain. The first drive found is `sda`, the second `sdb`, and so on.

`Geom [C/H/S]` The hard drive's geometry as detected by Disk Druid. The geometry is separated by the number of cylinders, heads, and sectors that were found. Compare these numbers to those reported by Windows 95's System Properties (in the Control Panel), or your computer's BIOS (accessed by holding down a specific Function during startup). If they do not match up, you might need to use `fdisk`.

`Total`	This area reports the total amount of disk space the disk drive has. Compare this number to what you have already written in your inventory.
`Used`	An area that indicates in megabytes how much of the hard drive is currently allocated.
`Free`	This section shows how much of the hard drive is currently not allocated.
`#####`	The final area is a bar graph giving a rough visual guide to how much disk space is still available on the drive.

Disk Druid Commands

The bottom section contains the buttons that control Disk Druid. They can be used to Add, Delete, Change, Reset to the Beginning, or Finish the install. The following text discusses the keys and gives the hot key that is equivalent to selecting the button.

The `F1-Add` option is used to add partitions. A pop-up menu appears when selected. The fields in this pop-up are explained in Table A.3.

TABLE A.3 The *F1-Add* pop-up menu

Menu Item	Explanation
Mount Point	Used to enter the partition's mount point. Remember that the entire space of the mounted hard drives is seen as subdirectories of the `/` partition. Therefore, you need to specify one Linux partition to be the root partition `/`.
Size (Megs)	Used to enter the minimal requested size of the partition. Unless changed, the minimum size is 1MB.
Growable?	A check box to indicate that the size entered is a minimum or an exact size. If Growable is selected, the partition size tries to fit all available disk space on the drive.
Type	Used to choose the partition type to be used for the partition. This field is a highlighted scrollable section.

Menu Item	Explanation
Allowable Drives	Another check box area that tells Disk Druid on which drives to try to create this partition.
Ok	Selecting this button tries to create the partition.
Cancel	Selecting this button aborts the addition of a partition.

The `F2-Add NFS` option is used to add NFS partitions. NFS partitions are network partitions.

SEE ALSO

➤ *For more information about NFS, see the section "Enabling Network File System Service," on page 461.*

The `F3-Edit` option is used to change an already existing partition. The dialog box that appears enables you to edit various fields depending on whether the partition has been written to the disk already.

The `F4-Delete` option is used to remove the highlighted partition from the drive. A dialog box appears, asking to confirm this deletion.

The `F5-Reset` option is used to bring Disk Druid to the state it was before you made any changes. All changes that have been made are removed. Any data on the mount points also has to be reentered.

The `OK` option is used to write changes to the disk drive. A confirmation pop-up appears, and if confirmed, the hard drives partition tables is written with the new data. The mount points that have been chosen are passed on to the installation program to define the file system layout.

The `Cancel` option bails you out of Disk Druid. Any changes made will be lost, and a pop-up dialog box is displayed asking which step in the install should be done next.

Working with Disk Druid

Make sure that you know which partitions you want to delete, and which you want to keep. Select the deletable partitions and press F4 to delete them.

Think before you delete a partition!

Remember that after you have removed a partition and chosen the `OK` option, the information in the partition is gone. Make sure that you don't delete your DOS or Windows 95 partition, or other needed partitions.

Creating a Linux and swap partition

1. Press F1, and you are presented with the Adding Menu. To create your root Linux partition (`/`) in the mount point area, type:

   ```
   /
   ```

2. Press the Tab key to navigate to the size field. For the purposes of this example, enter **250** megs (change this to fit with your earlier estimates), Select `Linux Native` as the partition, double-check all your entries, and then select `OK`.
3. Press F1 to create the swap partition. Make sure to select `Linux Swap` as the partition type and then choose `OK`.
4. When you're finished selecting the new partitions for your drive, select `OK` or press F12 and confirm that you want to make the changes. The install then goes to the next stage.

Disk Druid error

If your attempt to create the partition fails, an error window pops up, explaining what the error is. More than likely the error is that Disk Druid could not allocate the disk space for the drive currently, and you will need to edit the partition to be smaller or make other alterations to accommodate the partition.

Activating Swap Space

After the partitions have been created, the install program searches for swap partitions. If it doesn't find any, it will warn you, and you can go back to the previous step of partitioning the drives and set up a section to be swapped. If one or more swap spaces were detected, a screen, shown in Figure A.8, asks which partitions you want to use for swap. Select the check boxes of the partitions you want to use, and also select whether you want to check for bad blocks when it does the swap formatting. When you are ready to continue, choose `OK`.

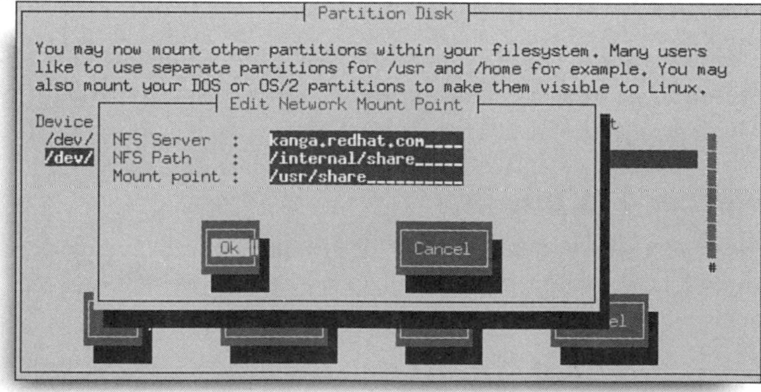

FIGURE A.8

It's a good idea to have Linux check for bad blocks during formatting.

Formatting Partitions

After the swap space has been selected, the next screen brings up a dialog box of the Linux Native partitions you need to format. You need to format any new partitions you created in the install process, and you should reformat any old partitions from previous Linux installs that do not contain data you want to keep.

Toggle the check box for each partition you want to format, and toggle whether you want to check for bad blocks during the format.

Selecting Which Components to Install

The next stage of the install is to select which packages you want on your Linux Box. A screen, shown in Figure A.9, asks which components you want to install on your machine. These components are sets of packages that work together or are similar in nature. The X Window System is all the packages that give most of the X functionality (server, basic libraries, window manager, and some clients). Adding the X Games package installs various amusements.

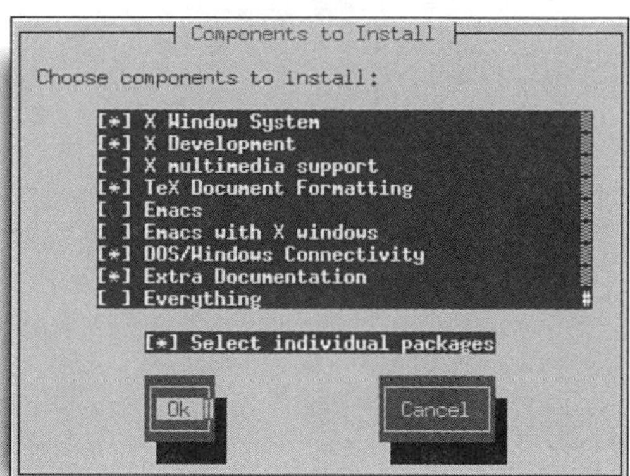

FIGURE A.9
This dialog box gives you a list of packages you can install.

To install a minimal base 50MB system, unselect everything that has been autoselected. To fine-tune the items in the component listings, select individual packages by toggling the package listing. If chosen, another screen, shown in Figure A.10, enables you to pick and choose which subpackages you want to install.

A scrolling menu of all the package groups available is displayed, and you can select or deselect any package inside a grouping. In selecting or deselecting individual packages, the install program might ask you to choose them again, or you will need to install other packages. This is due to the fact that other packages might depend on the unselected package to work properly.

SEE ALSO

➤ *For more details about installing or removing software using Red Hat Linux, see page 520.*

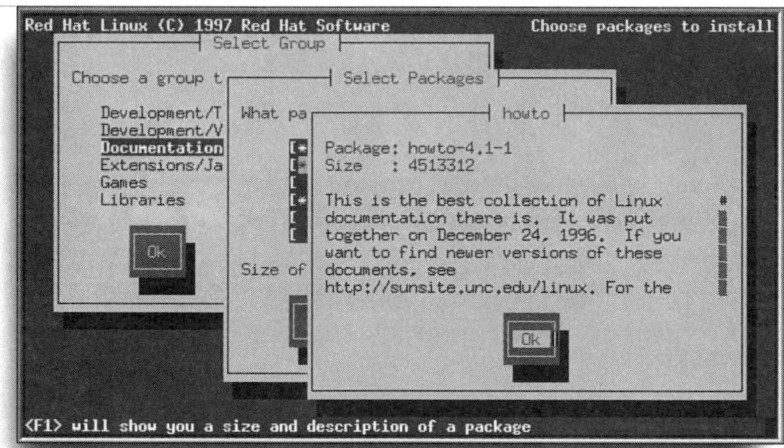

FIGURE A.10
Selecting individual packages for installation. Not recommended for beginners.

Finally, in this mode, you also can get more information on what each package contains, or is supposed to do, by pressing the F1 key. To continue on to the next stage of the install, Tab over to the OK button, and the installation begins.

Format and Install

After any dependency issues have been resolved, the installation program lets you know that a complete listing of packages installed will be put in the `/tmp/install.log` file. Press Enter to continue on to the next stage. This stage is where each of the partitions that you chose previously to be formatted will have new file systems placed on them. The packages are now installed, and you can follow the progress in the Install Status window.

Configuring Your Hardware

This final section of the chapter covers the items needed to fin ish the install and boot your Linux system.

Choosing a Mouse

After installing the Linux software, the program then probes your system for a mouse. If one is found, the install program indicates the type and port that the mouse is connected to. Depending on the mouse, you might be asked for the number of buttons the mouse has, what protocol it uses, and if you need your two-button mouse to emulate a three-button model.

SEE ALSO

- *For more information about configuring a pointing device, such as a mouse, see page 144.*
- *For information about configuring a mouse for the X Window System, see page 269.*

Choosing a mouse

Make sure to use three-button mouse emulation if you have a two-button mouse and want to use the X Window System. After choosing a mouse during the install, you can always change the values for the mouse later on with the program `/usr/sbin/mouseconfig`.

Configuring the X Window System

The next window that comes up asks you about the X Window server you want to run. Scroll down the list of video cards and try to find a card matching the one in your computer. Note that video cards, like cars, have brand names similar to one another, but the items under the hood (chipset in the case of the card) can be very different.

SEE ALSO

- *For more information about starting or configuring the X Window System, see page 260.*

If you can't find a card that matches your computer's card, choose the Generic VGA-compatible card that every video card should be able to emulate. After a card has been selected, the appropriate X server will be installed onto your machine.

The next screen tries to determine the model of monitor you have. It is important to select a monitor that exactly matches your model. If your model isn't listed, choose custom and fill in the values listed in your monitor's manual.

Having trouble fine-tuning X11?

Red Hat Linux comes with a program called Xconfigurator that may help you fine-tune your X configuration. You need to know the technical details about your computer's graphics card and monitor to properly configure X. To get help with a specific card or card chipset, look under the `/usr/X11R6/lib/X11/doc` directory for technical notes concerning many chipsets and monitors after you install and boot Linux.

Don't fry your monitor!

Entering incorrect values for your monitor can cause damage to the monitor. The author has smoked a monitor in the past for putting the wrong model's data into the settings. If you can't find the information in your monitor's manual, try searching the manufacturer's Internet web site for the information.

If you have chosen the Generic VGA card, you are asked whether you want to probe for settings using X `-probeonly`. Choose not to probe, and after a moment, you should move on to the next section of the install.

Network Configuration

Networking setup

1. If you will be installing this machine onto a local area network (LAN), and you want to set up networking now, you should choose the Yes button. Otherwise choose No. If needed, you can configure networking after the install.
2. If you have chosen Yes, you are asked what network card driver the program should try. Scroll down the selection bar until you see one that matches your card. Tab to the OK button and press Enter. You are then asked whether you need to supply any options for the card. If you need to supply arguments for the card, they will be the IO address of the card (supplied in Hexadecimal), and the interrupt that the card is using (example: io=0x330 and irq=5). In most cases, the autoprobe will find the card.
3. If the card is found, the next screen presents you with choices to set up your network. If you have a `bootp` server running on your network that sets up the IP addresses and other data for your machines, toggle `[]Configure device with bootp` and select OK. If not, you will need to input information such as the hostname, domain name, IP address, netmask value, gateway, nameserver, or NFS or FTP servers. If you're not sure, contact your network administrator.

Setting the Time Zone

You are next asked to set up your system's time zone and what your BIOS clock is set to. The first toggle area asks whether your computer's BIOS clock is set to GMT. Using the BIOS clock at GMT enables Red Hat Linux to deal with daylight savings changes but can have the effect of turning other OS's clocks off.

The next selection area on the screen asks what time zone you are in. Scroll to the zone that best matches your time zone. Select OK to continue with the install.

Selecting Which Services to Start

The next section of the install goes over the services or daemons to start when the system restarts. The dialog box for this section of the install contains a long scrollable list of check boxes linked to a service that starts when you boot the machine. You can get more information on a service by scrolling to that service and pressing F1. If a service was selected by default, it should stay on, and if it wasn't turned on should only be enabled when you have configured it later. You can change these services later on with the `ntsysv` command.

SEE ALSO

➤ *For more details about using the* `ntsysv` *command, see page 482.*

Selecting a Printer

Don't change default service settings

Certain services should only be turned off if you know what the consequences are. Otherwise, you might run into a system that is not fully bootable. These services are as follows: `atd`, `crond`, `inet`, `kerneld`, `keytable`, `network`, and `syslog`.

Configuring a printer

1. You are next asked to configure a printer. Select Yes if you want to do this now, or No if you don't have a printer or want to install it later.
2. Selecting Yes brings up a dialog box asking where the printer is. There are three selections available:

`Local`	Meaning a printer connected to the computer.
`Remote lpd`	This printer is one connected to your LAN that can communicate via `lpd`.
`LAN Manager`	Use this if the network printer is printed to via a LAN Manager or SMB printer server.

3. Choosing local printer asks you to name the printer queue (`lp` by default) and the spool directory that this printer will use. For the purposes of this install, you should probably choose the default values and select Next.

4. The computer then tries to determine what printer ports are available and asks you to match the printer to the ones found. Pressing Next sends you to the next section of the install.

SEE ALSO

➤ *For more information about configuring your printer for Linux, see page 74.*

Setting up a network printer

If you're trying to connect to a network printer, it would be a good idea to wait until you can ask your system administrator for help. You can always come back and add the printer later with the `printtool` command during an X Window session.

5. Choosing `Remote lpd` printer brings up a dialog box asking you the name of the machine you will be printing to, and the name of the queue on that machine. For example, if the printer on the `lpd` print server is called laser, you would enter **laser** and the hostname of the print server. Pressing Next sends you to the next section of the install.
6. Choosing `LAN Manager` brings up a dialog box that will set up various `smbfs` items for you. The first selection is the LAN Manager host name, the next is the IP address of that LAN Manager host, followed by the Share Name of the Printer, and finally the Username and Password needed to access the printer. Pressing Next sends you to the next section of the install.
7. The next screens complete the Printer setup. You are first asked what kind of printer you have. Choose a printer that is similar to your printer, and if not found, select a text-only printer. Select Next and press Enter to begin choosing paper sizes.
8. If the printer has multiple resolutions available, choose the one that you want to use.
9. Select the `Stair Stepping` option if your printer does not send a carriage return at the end of a line, causing your printing to look tilted as everything becomes a run-on. When finished with this screen, select Next and press Enter.
10. The next screen shows you all the values for the printer you have chosen. If you are happy with these items, select Done and press Enter. If not, choose Edit, and you will go back through the printer selection. When you're happy, click on Done, and you will go on to the next stage of the install.

Entering Your Initial Password

The next screen asks you to type a root password for your computer. This password is used to log in the administrative account as root. Your first login is as root so that you can set up other accounts and finalize setting up any other system items before bringing the machine into "production." In choosing a root password (or any password, for that matter), choose one that is at least six characters and not a word found in a dictionary, a set of numbers, or some item that is easily guessable about you (such as your birthday).

SEE ALSO

➤ *For more information about passwords and Linux, see page 422.*

Come up with a password for your machine, write it down on a separate piece of paper, and then enter it in the dialog box areas. For security reasons, what you type does not show up on the screen. For this reason, you need to enter the password twice to confirm that you are typing it the same way. When you have entered it twice, select OK and press Enter. If the two passwords match, you will go on to the next screen. If they don't, you will need to reenter them.

Remember, the root user has complete access and control over the system and can look into or change any file on the system—this is why this password should be kept secure!

What's the password on good passwords?

Good passwords have a mixture of numerals and case, or are acronyms of sentences or combined words. Examples of good passwords (at least until this is published) would be Fraz93Re, SH22puk, Iam99bal. Passwords are case-sensitive and usually have a limit of only eight characters (so Fraz93Rent and Fraz93Rex would both be considered the same password).

Selecting Boot Options

You have reached the final stretch of the installation. This is the part where you decide how you will boot Linux after the installation.

The screen you are presented with, shown in Figure A.11, gives you the choice of installing `LILO` (the bootloader) to two different parts of the system.

- Master Boot Record. This replaces the master boot record of the system, causing a LILO prompt to come up each time you boot the machine. Useful in most cases.

- First Sector of the Root Partition. This option can be used if you have another boot loader on your system (OS/2, NT, Partition Magic, or System Commander are some examples). These boot loaders are already in the Master Boot Record of the primary drive, and you don't want to replace them. With LILO installed to the root partition, you can then configure the other boot system to start that OS.

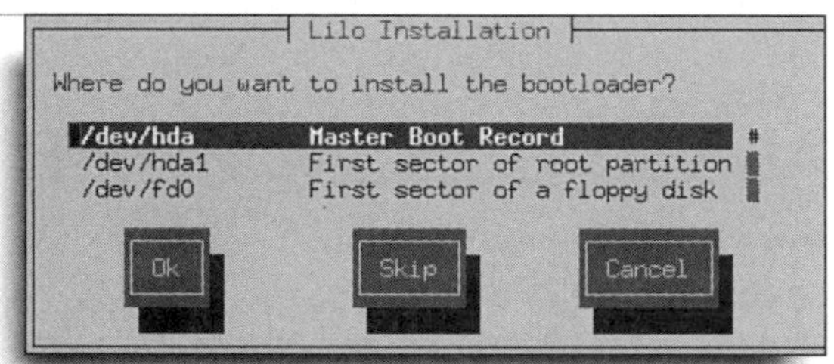

FIGURE A.11
Selecting where you want to install the bootloader. Most people should select the default Master Boot Record option.

You also can choose to skip the installation of LILO to the hard drive. This is usually done when you want to use the LOADLIN program or if you installed Linux to an IDE system on the boot floppy. Choose which of the methods you want and select either OK or SKIP.

SEE ALSO

➤ *For more information about using LILO and LOADLIN, see page 382.*

Whether you selected the First Sector of the Root Partition or the Master Boot Record, you are shown a screen asking for any boot options you need to pass to the machine or if you need to use the linear addressing mode to write to the system. For most systems, you don't have to choose anything going with the default.

When LILO has been written to the boot record, you see a screen notifying you that the install is done, to remove the floppy disk from the drive, and to press Enter. If you do not get this screen, press Alt+F3 and Alt+F4 to check related screens to see whether an error occurred during the LILO installation. In that case, you might need to skip the LILO installation and then use the alternative methods of booting.

Booting Linux

After LILO or LOADLIN has been installed, you can boot the Linux operating system. If LILO was chosen, you see the LILO prompt:

```
LILO:
```

If you don't do anything at this point, the system automatically boots into Linux after a short timeout. If you have set up your system to boot to other operating systems, you can press the Tab key to see what choices are available and then just type in your option and press Enter.

```
linux dos
LILO:
```

After a few seconds, you see a set of text as the kernel boots up for the first time. After a short while, you should see the following prompt:

```
Red Hat Linux release 5.0 (Hurricane)
Kernel 2.0.32 on an i586

login:
```

You are now ready to log in to the Red Hat Linux system. To do so, type **root**, and you are prompted for a password. Type the password you typed during the install, and you should get a `#` prompt indicating that you have successfully logged on.

APPENDIX

Resources

B

By Bill Ball

Usenet news group resources

World Wide Web Internet sites

Usenet Resources

Following is a list of current Linux Usenet newsgroups. Note that the list does not include international newsgroups in other languages, such as French, German, or Italian.

- `comp.os.linux.advocacy` Rants, raves, taunts, and flame wars between Linux's Defenders of the Faith and the minions of the Dark Side.
- `comp.os.linux.alpha` Discussions of Linux on the Digital Equipment Corporation's Alpha CPU.
- `comp.os.linux.announce` Commercial, user group, and software release announcements.
- `comp.os.linux.answers` The definitive source of new or updated Linux HOWTOs, FAQs, and other Linux documents.
- `comp.os.linux.development.apps` Discussions concerning porting software programs, and using compilers or other languages for Linux.

- `comp.os.linux.development.system` Linux kernel and other programming information, such as modules or device drivers.
- `comp.os.linux.hardware` Questions, answers, and debates concerning using different hardware with Linux.
- `comp.os.linux.m68k` News and development information about Linux on Motorola 68x000-series CPUs.
- `comp.os.linux.misc` Miscellaneous questions, answers, and debates about hardware and software for Linux.
- `comp.os.linux.networking` Discussions about topics such as communications and networking administration and configuration.
- `comp.os.linux.powerpc` News and development information about Linux on the PowerPC series of CPUs.
- `comp.os.linux.setup` Questions and answers about how to install, set up, configure, and maintain Linux.
- `comp.os.linux.x` Discussions about installing, configuring, and using the X Window System and X11 clients with Linux.

WWW Resources

There are too many Linux Web sites to list a them all. Nonetheless, you'll find most of the answers you need through the Linux Documentation Project, available through the following site:

http://sunsite.unc.edu/LDP

For a list of other computers (or mirrors) with the LDP contents, browse to the following address:

http://sunsite.unc.edu/LDP/hmirrors.html

Another site, featuring commercial Linux distributions, X software, and laptop information that may help you, is as follows:

Want to see an estimate on the number of people who use Linux around the world? Navigate to this site, and register as a Linux user! The latest estimates are 6,000,000 users worldwide:

http://counter.li.org

Looking for a certain Linux logo? This site has a link to three pages of logos for Linux:

http://pobox.com/~newt/

Have extra copies of old Linux distributions on CD-ROM you'd like to donate? Navigate to this site for more information:

http://visar.csustan.edu:8000/giveaway.html

This site features Caldera's OpenLinux distribution, which includes the StarOffice suite of applications, DR-DOS, the ADABAS-D relational database, along with various Netscape clients and servers:

http://www.caldera.com

Walnut Creek's Web site is a great starting place to get other free UNIX distributions, such as BSD or Slackware Linux:

http://www.cdrom.com

The following site is the definitive Web site for Linux laptop users. This site features many different links and documentation to solve problems and provide solutions to making Linux and X11 work correctly:

http://www.cs.utexas.edu/users/kharker/linux-laptop

Want the very latest Linux kernel? Navigate to this site to learn about up-to-the-minute changes:

http://www.cviog.uga.edu/LinuxBleed.html

The definitive site for downloading the Debian Linux distribution is as follows:

http://www.debian.org

Want to know whether your favorite Linux Web site has been updated or new software uploaded? Use this site to watch for daily changes:

http://www.emry.net/webwatcher

A long-time distributor of Linux, Infomagic offers many different sets of software collections available by FTP or on CD-ROM:

`http://www.infomagic.com`

This site not only offers the oldest and newest kernels, it also offers more than 20GB of software for Linux:

`http://www.kernel.org`

With more than 4,000,000 visitors during 1997, this site, aside from `sunsite.unc.edu`, is one of the most popular Linux Web sites, and is generally considered the Linux home page:

`http://www.linux.org`

This is the place to start looking for Linux books by Sams, Que, New Riders, and Red Hat Press:

`http://www.mcp.com`

Ken Lee's X and Motif Web site has more than 700 links to different X Window System Web pages (Ken is the maintainer of the Motif FAQ):

`http://www.rahul.net/kenton/index.shtml`

Red Hat Software, Inc.'s Web site offers links to Linux information, news, and support for Red Hat's Linux distribution, and versions of commercial Linux software, such as Applixware, Motif, and CDE:

`http://www.redhat.com`

This site is the home of the Linux Journal, a four-color, 70+-page monthly magazine all about Linux:

`http://www.ssc.com/lj`

The great folks of the XFree86 Project, Inc., provide free distributions of the X Window System not only for Linux, but for other operating systems on other computers:

`http://www.xfree86.org`

APPENDIX

Using Linux HOWTO Documents

By Bill Ball

Guide to current Linux HOWTOs

Guide to current Linux mini-HOWTOs

A massive collection of Linux HOWTO documents is usually included with each Linux distribution. Red Hat Linux 5.0 comes with nearly 200 documents, requiring more than 6 MB in compressed form! HOWTO documents are comprehensive, detailed guides to solving problems or for obtaining a quick education on specialized aspects of using Linux.

To read one of the regular HOWTO documents (compressed text, not `.html`, `.sgml`, `.dvi`, or `.ps`), use the `zless` command, followed by the path and name of the document, like this:

```
# zless /usr/doc/HOWTO/Serial-HOWTO.gz
```

Table C.1 provides a quick summary of each compressed HOWTO.

Table C.1 **Red Hat 5.0 HOWTO documents *(under the /usr/doc/HOWTO directory)***

HOWTO	Description
3Dfx-HOWTO	Using the 3Dfx graphics accelerator chip with Linux
Access-HOWTO	How to use adaptive technology with Linux to help users with disabilities
Alpha-HOWTO	Discusses Linux for the Alpha series of CPUs
Assembly-HOWTO	How to program in i386 assembly language
AX25-HOWTO	How to install and configure support for AX.25 packet radio protocol
Benchmarking-HOWTO	Discusses issues with benchmarking Linux systems
Bootdisk-HOWTO	How to create Linux boot, utility, or maintenance disks
BootPrompt-HOWTO	Covers boot time arguments at the LILO prompts
CD-Writing-HOWTO	How to write CDs under Linux
CDROM-HOWTO	How to install, configure, and use CD-ROMs for Linux
Chinese-HOWTO	How to use Chinese software with Linux
Commercial-HOWTO	Lists of commercial software for Linux
Consultants-HOWTO	Lists of companies providing commercial support for Linux
Cyrillic-HOWTO	How to use Russian language fonts with Linux
Danish-HOWTO	How to use the Danish language with Linux
Database-HOWTO	How to set up and use PostgresSQL with Linux
Disk-HOWTO	How to use multiple disks and partitions with Linux
Distribution-HOWTO	Help on how to choose a Linux distribution
DNS-HOWTO	How to administer a small Domain Name Server

HOWTO	Description
DOS-to-Linux-HOWTO	A DOS users guide to Linux
DOSEMU-HOWTO	How to use the dosemu DOS emulator with Linux
ELF-HOWTO	How to use the ELF binary format
Emacspeak-HOWTO	How vision-impaired users can use Linux with a speech synthesizer
Ethernet-HOWTO	How to set up and use different ethernet devices with Linux
Finnish-HOWTO	How to use the Finnish language with Linux
Firewall-HOWTO	Discusses the basics of firewalls with Linux
French-HOWTO	How to use the French language with Linux
Ftape-HOWTO	Discusses how to use the ftape driver
GCC-HOWTO	Setting up and using the GNU C compiler and development libraries for Linux
German-HOWTO	How to use the German language with Linux
Glibc2-HOWTO	Installing and using the GNU C library, version 2 (libc 6)
HAM-HOWTO	Assistance for Linux amateur radio operators
Hardware-HOWTO	What types of hardware and drivers exist for Linux
Hebrew-HOWTO	How to use Hebrew characters with Linux
Installation-HOWTO	How to get and install Linux software
Intranet-Server-HOWTO	How to set up an intranet with Linux
IPX-HOWTO	Using the IPX protocol with Linux
ISP-Hookup-HOWTO	How to connect to the Internet through your Internet Service Provider (ISP)
Italian-HOWTO	How to use the Italian language with Linux
Java-CGI-HOWTO	How to set up your Linux server to use Java

continues...

Table C.1 **Continued**

HOWTO	Description
Kernel-HOWTO	Configuring, compiling, upgrading, and troubleshooting your i386 Linux kernel
Keyboard-and-Console-HOWTO	Using the Linux keyboard and console
MGR-HOWTO	How to configure and use the MGR window system
MILO-HOWTO	How to use the milo loader for Linux Alpha systems
Mail-HOWTO	All you need to know about electronic mail for Linux
NET-3-HOWTO	How to install and configure Linux networking software
News-HOWTO	All you need to know about Usenet news and Linux
NFS-HOWTO	How to set up NFS clients and servers under Linux
NIS-HOWTO	Details about the Network Information System and Linux
Optical-Disk-HOWTO	Installing, configuring, and using optical disk drives under Linux
PCI-HOWTO	The latest details about Linux and PCI motherboards
PCMCIA-HOWTO	The definitive guide to using PC cards with Linux
Pilot-HOWTO	All about using the 3COM Palm Pilot and Linux
Polish-HOWTO	Using the Polish language with Linux
PPP-HOWTO	How to connect to the Internet with PPP under Linux
Printing-HOWTO	All you need to know about printing under Linux
Printing-Usage-HOWTO	How to use line printer spooling under Linux

HOWTO	Description
RPM-HOWTO	The definitive guide to the rpm command
Reading-List-HOWTO	Suggested books for Linux users
SCSI-HOWTO	Configuring and using SCSI devices with Linux
SCSI-Programming-HOWTO	How to program generic SCSI interface under Linux
SMB-HOWTO	How to use the Session Message Block (SMB) protocol with Linux
SRM-HOWTO	How to boot Alpha Linux systems using SRM
Serial-HOWTO	How to set up serial devices under Linux
Serial-Programming-HOWTO	How to program Linux serial ports
Shadow-Password-HOWTO	How to install and configure Shadow passwords under Linux
Slovenian-HOWTO	How to use the Slovenian language with Linux
Sound-HOWTO	How to configure Linux to use sound
Sound-Playing-HOWTO	How to play different sound file formats under Linux
Spanish-HOWTO	How to use the Spanish language with Linux
TeTeX-HOWTO	How to install and use teTex and LaTeX TeX packages with Linux
Thai-HOWTO	How to set up Linux to use Thai language
Tips-HOWTO	Miscellaneous tips and hints to make using Linux easier
UMSDOS-HOWTO	How to use the UMSDOS filesystem and Linux
UPS-HOWTO	Details about how to use an uninterruptible power supply (UPS) and Linux
UUCP-HOWTO	All you need to know about UUCP and Linux
User-Group-HOWTO	How to set up and maintain a Linux User Group (LUG)

continues...

Table C.1 Continued

HOWTO	Description
VAR-HOWTO	Lists of Value-Added Resellers of Linux software
VMS-to-Linux-HOWTO	A gentle introduction to Linux for VMS users
XFree86-HOWTO	How to use the XFree86 distribution of X11
XFree86-Video-Timings-HOWTO	How to create mode lines for your graphics card and monitor to use with XFree86's X11

Need to read everything at once?

You can quickly find information in the HOWTO series without listing the `/usr/doc/HOWTO` directory. First, log on as the root operator, and then use the `gunzip` command, along with its `-r` (recursive) option to decompress the entire directory tree under the `/usr/doc/HOWTO` directory, like this:

```
# gunzip -r
/usr/doc/HOWTO/*
```

Next, combine the `find`, `xargs`, `head`, and `less` commands to find and list the first 20 lines from the top of each file, like this:

```
# find /usr/doc/HOWTO/* ¦
xargs head -v -n 20 ¦
less
```

You can now peruse the contents of your HOWTO documents!

The mini-HOWTO documents, found under the `/usr/doc/HOWTO/mini` directory, provide detailed information in a short format, and usually cover specialized subjects. Unlike the regular HOWTOs, the mini-HOWTO is not distributed in compressed form with Red Hat Linux 5.0. Use the `less` pager, followed by the path and name of the file to read a mini-HOWTO, like this:

```
# less /usr/doc/HOWTO/mini/Advocacy
```

Table C.2 contains a guide to current mini-HOWTOs from the Red Hat 5.0 Linux distribution.

Table C.2 Red Hat 5.0 mini-HOWTO documents (under the ***/usr/doc/HOWTO/mini*** **directory)**

HOWTO	Description
3-Button-Mouse	Using three-button serial mice with Linux
ADSM-Backup	Using IBM's ADSM backup system with Linux
AI-Alife	Linux and artificial intelligence software
Advocacy	How to advocate the use of Linux
Backup-With-MSDOS	How to back up Linux using DOS

HOWTO	Description
Battery-Powered	How Linux laptop users can conserve power
Boca	Using the Boca 2016 serial card with Linux
BogoMips	The definitive tome on the infamous Linux BogoMips
Bridge	Creating and using ethernet bridges with Linux
Bridge+Firewall	Creating and using firewalls with ethernet bridges
Clock	Keeping correct time with Linux
Colour-ls	Using color `ls` command listings
Comeau-C++	Using Comeau C++ with Linux
DHCPcd	How to set up Linux as a DHCP client
DHCPd	Using the DHCP server daemon with Linux
Dial-On-Demand	How to set up Linux to dial on demand for Internet connections
Diskless	How to set a diskless Linux box
Dynamic-IP-Hacks	How to set up Internet connections with dynamic Internet Protocol addressing
Ext2fs-Undeletion	Tips on recovering lost data and undeleting files on `ext2` filesystems
Fax-Server	How to set up fax printer service for Linux
GIS-GRASS	How to set up a GRASS mapping system for Linux
GTEK-BBS-550	How to set up and use the GTEK BBS-550, 8-port serial card for Linux
Gravis-Ultra-Sound	How to use Gravis Ultra Sound cards with Linux
IO-Port-Programming	How to program I/O ports for Linux
IP-Alias	How to set up and run IP aliasing for Linux
IP-Masquerade	How to enable IP masquerading for Linux

continues...

Table C.2 **Continued**

HOWTO	Description
IP-Subnetworking	How to subnetwork an IP network with Linux
ISP-Connectivity	How to best use your Internet connection
Jaz-Drive	How to configure and use the Iomega Jaz drive
Kerneld	How to configure and use the Linux kerneld daemon
LBX	How to use low-bandwidth X with Linux
Large-Disk	All you need to know about large hard drives and Linux
Linux+DOS+Win95	How to configure LILO to boot Linux, DOS, or Win95
Linux+DOS+Win95+OS2	How to configure LILO to boot Linux, DOS, Win95, or OS2
Linux+FreeBSD	How to use Linux and FreeBSD on your computer
Linux+NT-Loader	How to use the NT loader to boot Linux
Linux+OS2+DOS	How to boot Linux from OS2
Linux+Win95	Discusses issues concerning installing Linux on Win95 systems
Loadlin+Win95	How to use LOADLIN.EXE to boot Linux from Win95
Locales	How to use locales with Linux
MIDI+SB	How to use a MIDI keyboard with a Sound Blaster card under Linux
Mail-Queue	Configuring `sendmail` to deliver local mail for Linux
Mail2News	How to set up mailing list and local news groups with your Linux news server
Man-Page	How to write man pages for Linux software
PLIP	How to build and use the Parallel Line Interface Protocol (PLIP) with Linux

HOWTO	Description
Modules	Using kernel modules with Linux
NFS-Root	How to boot Linux via the Network File System (NFS)
NFS-Root-Client	How to create client root directories on a Linux server
Netscape+Proxy	How to create an in-house intranet
Offline-Mailing	How to get mail for multiple users using only one email address
Online-Support	Description of the Linux Internet Support Cooperative
PPP-over-minicom	Setting up a Point-to-Point Protocol (PPP) connection using the minicom program
Pager	How to set up and use a Linux alphanumeric pager gateway
Print2Win	How to print from Linux to a Win95/NT shared printer
Process-Accounting	How to use process accounting with Linux
Proxy-ARP	How to use the proxy Address Resolution Protocol (ARP) with Linux
Proxy-ARP-Subnet	How to use ARP with subnetting under Linux
Public-Web-Browser	How to set up a public web browser using Netscape and Linux
Qmail+MH	Using qmail with Linux
Quota	Enabling disk quotas under Linux
RCS	Installing and using the Revision Control System (RCS) and Linux
RPM+Slackware	How to use the `rpm` command and the Slackware Linux distribution
Remote-Boot	Booting Linux in a network environment
Remote-X-Apps	How to run remote X clients using Linux
SLIP+proxyARP	How to connect a local area network to an Internet network using the Serial Line Interface Protocol (SLIP) and Proxy ARP

continues…

Table C.2 **Continued**

HOWTO	Description
SLIP-PPP-Emulator	How to connect to the Internet via a SLIP/PPP emulator
Sendmail+UUCP	Using sendmail and UNIX-to-UNIX-Copy
Software-Building	How to create software distributions under Linux
Software-RAID	Using RAID software with Linux
Soundblaster-16	Using a Soundblaster 16 card with Linux
Soundblaster-AWE64	Using a Soundblaster AWE64 card with Linux
StarOffice	Installing the StarOffice Office Suite for Linux
Swap-Space	How to share swap space with Linux and Windows
Term-Firewall	How to access network information through a TCP firewall under Linux
Token-Ring	How to configure Linux to use Token-Ring networks
Upgrade	How to upgrade from one Linux distribution to another
VPN	How to set up a Virtual Protected Network (VPN) under Linux
Virtual-wu-ftpd	Setting up and using virtual ftp servers with Linux
Visual-Bell	How to disable console bells under Linux
Win95+Win+Linux	How to boot multiple operating systems
Windows-Modem-Sharing	How to share a modem over a TCP/IP network under Linux
WordPerfect	How to run WordPerfect under Linux
X-Big-Cursor	How to configure large cursors under X
XFree86-XInside	How to convert XFree86 XF86Config modelines to XI modelines

HOWTO	Description
Xterm-Title	How to place titles in xterm windows
ZIP-Drive	How to configure and use the Iomega Zip drive with Linux
ZIP-Install	How to install the ppa Zip disk driver

APPENDIX

Top 50 Linux Commands and Utilities

This appendix is not meant to replace the man pages; it does not go into anything resembling the detail available in the man pages. This appendix is designed to give you a feel for the commands and a brief description as to what they do. In most cases there are more parameters that can be used than are shown here.

Most of the descriptions also have examples with them. If these examples aren't self-evident, an explanation is provided. This is not an exhaustive list—there are many more commands that you could use—but these are the most common, and you will find yourself using them over and over again.

To keep things simple, the commands are listed in alphabetical order. I would have preferred to put them in order of how often I use them, but that would make locating them quite difficult. However, I do want to summarize by listing what are, at least for me, the ten most common commands—also alphabetically. This list of essential commands could be compared to a list of the top ten words spoken by the cavemen when searching for food and a mate:

1. `cat`
2. `cd`
3. `cp`
4. `find`
5. `grep`
6. `ls`

7. `more`
8. `rm`
9. `vi`
10. `who`

General Guidelines

In general, if you want to change something that already exists, the command to do that will begin with `ch`. If you want to do something for the first time, the command to do that will usually begin with `mk`. If you want to undo something completely, the command will usually begin with `rm`. For example, to make a new directory, you use the `mkdir` command. To remove a directory, you use the `rmdir` command.

The List

The commands listed in this appendix are some of the most common commands used in Red Hat Linux. In cases where the command seems ambiguous, an example is provided. With each of these commands, the man pages can provide additional information, as well as more examples.

.

The . command tells the shell to execute all the commands in the file that are passed an argument to the command. This works in the `bash` or `pdksh`. The equivalent in the `tcsh` is the `source` command. The following example will execute the command `adobe`:

```
. adobe
```

&

The `&` after any other command tells the computer to run the command in the background. By placing a job in the background, the user can then continue using that shell to process other commands. If the command is run in the foreground, the user cannot continue using that shell until the process finishes.

adduser

The `adduser` command is used by root, or someone else who has the authority, to create a new user. The `adduser` command is followed by the account name to be created—for example,

```
adduser dpitts
```

alias

The `alias` command is used to make aliases or alternative names for commands. Typically, these aliases are abbreviations of the actual command. In the following example, the user (probably a DOS user) is adding an alias of `dir` for a directory listing:

```
alias dir=ls
```

Typing `alias` by itself will give you a list of all your current aliases. Such a list might look like this:

```
svr01:/home/dpitts$ alias

alias d='dir'
alias dir='/bin/ls $LS_OPTIONS --format=vertical'

alias ls='/bin/ls $LS_OPTIONS'

alias v='vdir'

alias vdir='/bin/ls $LS_OPTIONS --format=long'
```

apropos <parameter>

The `apropos` command literally means appropriate or regarding (others). When it is followed by a parameter, it will search the man pages for entries that include the parameter. Basically, this performs a keyword search on all the man pages. This is the equivalent of the `man -k <parameter>` command.

banner

`banner` prints a large, high-quality banner to standard output. If the message is omitted, it prompts for and reads one line from standard input. For example, enter `$ banner hi` to create the following banner:

```
##                                                    ###
##                                                    ###
#########################################################
#########################################################
#########################################################
#########################################################
#########################################################
##                           ###
                                ###
                                ###
                                ####
                                ####
                                ####
##                          #######
#################################
#################################
################################
#############################
##########################
##
##                            ##
##                            ##            ####
#################################         ########
#################################         ########
#################################         ########
#################################          ######
#################################           ####
##
```

bg

The `bg` command is used to force a suspended process to run in the background. For example, you might have started a command in the foreground (without using `&` after the command),

and realized that it was going to take a while, but that you still needed your shell. You could take that process that is currently running and hold down the Ctrl key, and, while it is held down, press the Z key. This places the current process on hold. You can either leave it on hold, just as if you called your telephone company, or you could place that process in the background by typing **bg**. This then frees up your shell to allow you to execute other commands.

bind

Used in `pdksh`, the `bind` command enables the user to change the behavior of key combinations for the purpose of command-line editing. Many times people bind the up, down, left, and right arrow keys so that they work the way they would in the Bourne Again Shell (`bsh`). The syntax used for the command is

```
bind <key  sequence>  <command>
```

The following examples are the bind commands to create bindings for scrolling up and down the history list and for moving left and right along the command line:

```
bind `^[[`=prefix-2
bind `^XA`=up-history
bind `^XB`=down-history
bind `^XC`=forward-char
bind `^XD`=backward-char
```

cat

`cat` does not call your favorite feline; instead, it tells the contents of (typically) the file to scroll its contents across the screen. If that file happens to be binary, then the cat gets a hairball and shows it to you on the screen. Typically, this is a noisy process as well. What is actually happening is that the cat command is scrolling the characters of the file, and the terminal is doing all it can to interpret and display the data in the file. This interpretation can include the character used to create the bell signal, which is where the noise comes from. As you might have surmised, the cat command requires something to display and would have the following format:

```
cat <filename>
```

cd

cd stands for change directory. You will find this command extremely useful. There are three typical ways of using this command:

`cd ..`	Moves one directory up the directory tree.
`cd ~`	Moves to your home directory from wherever you currently are. This is the same as issuing cd by itself.
`cd directory name`	Changes to a specific directory. This can be a directory relative to your current location or can be based on the root directory by placing a forward slash (/) before the directory name.These examples can be combined. For example, suppose you were in the directory /home/dsp1234 and you wanted to go to tng4321's home account. You could perform the following command, which will move you back up the directory one level and then move you down into the tng4321 directory: `cd ../tng4321`

chgrp

The chgrp command is used to change the group associated with the permissions of the file or directory. The owner of the file (and, of course, root) has the authority to change the group associated with the file. The format for the command is simply

```
chgrp <new group> <file>
```

chmod

The `chmod` command is used to change the permissions associated with the object (typically a file or directory). What you are really doing is changing the file mode. There are two ways of specifying the permissions of the object. You can use the numeric coding system or the letter coding system. If you recall, there are three sets of users associated with every object: the owner of the object, the group for the object, and everybody else. Using the letter coding system, they are referred to as `u` for user, `g` for group, `o` for other, and `a` for all. There are three basic types of permissions that you can change: `r` for read, `w` for write, and `x` for execute. These three permissions can be changed using the plus (+) and minus (-) signs. For example, to add read and execute to owner and group of the file test1, you would issue the following command:

```
chmod ug+rx test1
```

To remove the read and execute permissions from the user and group of the test1 file, you would change the plus (+) sign to a minus (-) sign:

```
chmod ug-rx test1
```

This is called making relative changes to the mode of the file.

Using the numeric coding system, you always have to give the absolute value of the permissions, regardless of their previous permissions. The numeric system is based upon three sets of base two numbers. There is one set for each category of user, group, and other. The values are `4`, `2`, and `1`, where `4` equals read, `2` equals write, and `1` equals execute. These values are added together to give the set of permissions for that category. With the numeric coding you always specify all three categories. Therefore, to make the owner of the file test1 have read, write, and execute permissions, and no one else to have any permissions, you would use the value `700`, like this:

```
chmod 700 test1
```

To make the same file readable and writable by the user, and readable by both the group and others, you would follow the following mathematical logic: For the first set of permissions, the user, the value for readable is 4, and the value for writable is 2. The sum of these two is 6. The next set of permissions, the group, only gets readable, so that is 4. The settings for others, like the group, are 4. Therefore, the command would be chmod 644 test1.

The format for the command, using either method, is the same. You issue the chmod command followed by the permissions, either absolute or relative, followed by the objects for which you want the mode changed:

```
chmod <permissions> <file>
```

chown

This command is used to change the user ID (owner) associated with the permissions of the file or directory. The owner of the file (and, of course, root) has the authority to change the user associated with the file. The format for the command is simply

```
chown <new user id> <file>
```

chroot

The chroot command makes the / directory (called the root directory) be something other than / on the filesystem. For example, when working with an Internet server, you can set the root directory to equal /usr/ftp. Then, when someone logs on using FTP (which goes to the root directory by default), he or she will actually go to the directory /usr/ftp. This protects the rest of your directory structure from being seen or even changed to by this anonymous guest to your machine. If the person were to enter cd /etc, the ftp program would try to put him or her in the root directory and then in the etc directory off of that. Because the root directory is /usr/ftp, the ftp program will actually put the user in the /usr/ftp/etc directory (assuming there is one).

The syntax for the command is

```
chroot <original filesystem location> <new filesystem loca-
tion>
```

cp

The `cp` command is an abbreviation for copy; therefore, this command enables you to copy objects. For example, to copy the file `file1` to `file2`, issue the following command:

```
cp file1 file2
```

As the example shows, the syntax is very simple:

```
cp <original object name> <new object name>
```

dd

The `dd` command converts file formats. For example, to copy a boot image to a disk (assuming the device name for the disk is `/dev/fd0`), you would issue the command

```
dd if=<filename> of-/dev/fd0 obs=18k
```

where `filename` would be something like `BOOT0001.img`, of is the object format (what you are copying to), and `obs` is the output block size.

env

The `env` command is used to see the exported environment variables. The result of the command is a two-column list where the variable's name is on the left and the value associated with that variable is on the right. The command is issued without any parameters. Hence, typing **env** might get you a list similar to this one:

```
svr01:/home/dpitts$ env
HOSTNAME=svr01.mk.net
LOGNAME=dpitts
MAIL=/var/spool/mail/dpitts
TERM=vt100
HOSTTYPE=i386
PATH=/usr/local/bin:/usr/bin:/bin:.:/usr/local/java/bin
HOME=/home2/dpitts
SHELL=/bin/bash
LS_OPTIONS=--8bit --color=tty -F -b -T 0
PS1=\h:\w\$
PS2=>
```

```
MANPATH=/usr/local/man:/usr/man/preformat:/usr/man:/usr/lib/perl5
    /man
LESS=-MM
OSTYPE=Linux
SHLVL=1
```

fc

The `fc` command is used to edit the history file. The parameters passed to it, if there are any, can be used to select a range of commands from the history file. This list is then placed in an editing shell. The editor that it uses is based upon the value of the variable `FCEDIT`. If there is no value for this variable, the command looks at the `EDITOR` variable. If it is not there, the default is used, which is `vi`.

fg

Processes can be run in either the background or the foreground. The `fg` command enables you to take a suspended process and run it in the foreground. This is typically used when you have a process running in the foreground and for some reason, you need to suspend it (thus allowing you to run other commands). The process will continue until you either place it in the background or bring it to the foreground.

file

The `file` command tests each argument passed to it for one of three things: the filesystem test, the magic number test, or the language test. The first test to succeed causes the file type to be printed. If the file is text (it is an ASCII file), it then attempts to guess which language. The following example identifies the file nquota as a text file that contains Perl commands. A magic number file is a file that has data in particular fixed formats. Here is an example for checking the file `nquota` to see what kind of file it is:

```
file nquota
nquota: perl commands text
```

find

Did you ever say to yourself, "Self, where did I put that file?" Well now, instead of talking to yourself and having those around you wonder about you, you can ask the computer. You can say, "Computer, where did I put that file?" Okay, it is not that simple, but it is close. All you have to do is ask the computer to find the file.

The find command will look in whatever directory you tell it to, as well as all subdirectories under that directory, for the file that you specified. After it has found this list, it will then do with the list as you have asked it to. Typically, you just want to know where it is, so you ask it, nicely, to print out the list. The syntax of the command is the command itself, followed by the directory you want to start searching in, followed by the filename (metacharacters are acceptable), and then what you want done with the list. In the following example, the find command searches for files ending with .pl in the current directory (and all subdirectories). It then prints the results to standard output.

```
find . -name *.pl -print
./public_html/scripts/gant.pl
./public_html/scripts/edit_gant.pl
./public_html/scripts/httools.pl
./public_html/scripts/chart.no.comments.pl
```

grep

The grep (global regular expression parse) command searches the object you specify for the text that you specify. The syntax of the command is grep <text> <file>. In the following example, I am searching for instances of the text httools in all files in the current directory:

```
grep httools *
edit_gant.cgi:require 'httools.pl';
edit_gant.pl:require 'httools.pl';
gant.cgi:   require 'httools.pl';  # Library containing
   ➥reuseable code
gant.cgi:        &date;      # Calls the todays date subroutine
   ➥from httools.pl
gant.cgi:         &date;   #  Calls the todays date subroutine
   ➥from httools.pl
gant.cgi:   &header;  # from httools.pl
```

Although this is valuable, the grep command can also be used in conjunction with the results of other commands. For example, the following command

```
ps -ef ¦grep -v root
```

calls for the grep command to take the output of the ps command and take out all instances of the word root (the -v means everything but the text that follows). The same command without the -v (ps -ef ¦grep root) returns all of the instances that contain the word root from the process listing.

groff

groff is the front end to the groff document formatting program. This program, by default, calls the troff program.

gzip

gzip is GNU's version of the zip compression software. The syntax can be as simple as

```
gzip <filename>
```

but many times also contains some parameters between the command and the filename to be compressed.

halt

The halt command tells the kernel to shut down. This is a superuser-only command (you must "be root").

hostname

hostname is used to either display the current host or domain name of the system or to set the hostname of the system—for example,

```
svr01:/home/dpitts$ hostname
svr01
```

kill

kill sends the specified signal to the specified process. If no signal is specified, the TERM signal is sent. The TERM signal will kill processes that do not process the TERM signal. For processes that do process the TERM signal, it might be necessary to use the KILL signal because this signal cannot be caught. The syntax for the kill command is kill <option> <pid>, and an example is as follows:

```
svr01:/home/dpitts$kill -9 1438
```

less

less is a program similar to more, but which allows backward movement in the file as well as forward movement. less also doesn't have to read the entire input file before starting, so with large input files it starts up faster than text editors such as vi.

login

login is used when signing on to a system. It can also be used to switch from one user to another at any time.

logout

logout is used to sign off a system as the current user. If it is the only user you are logged in as, then you are logged off the system.

lpc

lpc is used by the system administrator to control the operation of the line printer system. lpc can be used to disable or enable a printer or a printer's spooling queue, to rearrange the order of jobs in a spooling queue, to find out the status of printers, to find out the status of the spooling queues, and to find out the status of the printer daemons. The command can be used for any of the printers configured in /etc/printcap.

lpd

lpd is the line printer daemon and is normally invoked at boot time from the rc file. It makes a single pass through the /etc/printcap file to find out about the existing printers and prints any files left after a crash. It then uses the system calls listen and accept to receive requests to print files in the queue, transfer files to the spooling area, display the queue, or remove jobs from the queue.

lpq

lpq examines the spooling area used by lpd for printing files on the line printer, and reports the status of the specified jobs or all jobs associated with a user. If the command is invoked without any arguments, the command reports on any jobs currently in the print queue.

lpr

The line printer command uses a spooling daemon to print the named files when facilities become available. If no names appear, the standard input is assumed. The following is an example of the lpr command:

```
lpr /etc/hosts
```

ls

The ls command lists the contents of a directory. The format of the output is manipulated with options. The ls command, with no options, lists all nonhidden files (a file that begins with a dot is a hidden file) in alphabetical order, filling as many columns as will fit in the window. Probably the most common set of options used with this command is the -la option. The a means list all (including hidden files) files, and the l means make the output a long listing. Here is an example of this command:

```
svr01:~$ ls -la
total 35
drwxr-xr-x   7 dpitts   users        1024 Jul 21 00:19 ./
drwxr-xr-x 140 root     root         3072 Jul 23 14:38 ../
```

```
-rw-r--r--   1 dpitts   users        4541 Jul 23 23:33
   ➥.bash_history
-rw-r--r--   1 dpitts   users          18 Sep 16  1996 .
   ➥forward
-rw-r--r--   2 dpitts   users         136 May 10 01:46
   ➥.htaccess
-rw-r--r--   1 dpitts   users         164 Dec 30  1995 .kermrc
-rw-r--r--   1 dpitts   users          34 Jun  6  1993 .less
-rw-r--r--   1 dpitts   users         114 Nov 23  1993 .lessrc
-rw-r--r--   1 dpitts   users          10 Jul 20 22:32 .profile
drwxr-xr-x   2 dpitts   users        1024 Dec 20  1995 .term/
drwx------   2 dpitts   users        1024 Jul 16 02:04 Mail/
drwxr-xr-x   2 dpitts   users        1024 Feb  1  1996 cgi-
   ➥src/
-rw-r--r--   1 dpitts   users        1643 Jul 21 00:23 hi
-rwxr-xr-x   1 dpitts   users         496 Jan  3  1997 nquota*
drwxr-xr-x   2 dpitts   users        1024 Jan  3  1997 passwd/
drwxrwxrwx   5 dpitts   users        1024 May 14 20:29
   ➥public_html/
```

make

The purpose of the make utility is to automatically determine which pieces of a large program need to be recompiled and then to issue the commands necessary to recompile them.

man

The man command is used to format and display the online manual pages. The manual pages are the text that describes, in detail, how to use a specified command. In the following example, I have called the man page that describes the man pages:

```
svr01:~$ man man

man(1)                                               man(1)
NAME
       man - format and display the on-line manual pages
       manpath - determine user's search path for man pages
SYNOPSIS
       man  [-adfhktwW]  [-m system] [-p string] [-C config_file]
       [-M path] [-P pager] [-S section_list] [section] name  .
```

```
DESCRIPTION
man  formats  and displays the on-line manual pages.This
version knows about  the  MANPATH  and  PAGER  environment
variables, so you can have your own set(s) of personal man
pages and choose whatever program you like to display  the
formatted  pages.  If section is specified, man only looks
in that section of the manual.  You may also  specify  the
order to search the sections for entries and which prepro-
cessors to run  on  the  source  files  via  command  line
options  or  environment  variables.  If name contains a /
then it is first tried as a filename, so that you  can  do
```

mesg

The `mesg` utility is run by a user to control write access others have to the terminal device associated with the standard error output. If write access is allowed, programs such as `talk` and `write` have permission to display messages on the terminal. Write access is allowed by default.

mkdir

The `mkdir` command is used to make a new directory.

mkefs

The `mkefs` command is used to make an extended filesystem. This command does not format the new filesystem, just makes it available for use.

mkfs

`mkfs` is used to build a Linux filesystem on a device, usually a hard disk partition. The syntax for the command is `mkfs <filesystem>`, where `<filesystem>` is either the device name (such as `/dev/hda1`) or the mount point (for example, `/`, `/usr`, `/home`) for the filesystem.

mkswap

mkswap sets up a Linux swap area on a device (usually a disk partition).

The device is usually of the following form:

```
/dev/hda[1-8]
/dev/hdb[1-8]
/dev/sda[1-8]
/dev/sdb[1-8]
```

more

more is a filter for paging through text one screen at a time. This command can only page down through the text, as opposed to less, which can page both up and down though the text.

mount

mount attaches the filesystem specified by specialfile (which is often a device name) to the directory specified as the parameter. Only the superuser can mount files. If the mount command is run without parameters, it lists all the currently mounted filesystems. The following is an example of the mount command:

```
svr01:/home/dpitts$ mount
/dev/hda1 on / type ext2 (rw)
/dev/hda2 on /var/spool/mail type ext2 (rw,usrquota)
/dev/hda3 on /logs type ext2 (rw,usrquota)
/dev/hdc1 on /home type ext2 (rw,usrquota)
none on /proc type proc (rw)
```

mv

The mv command is used to move an object from one location to another location. If the last argument names an existing directory, the command moves the rest of the list into that directory. If two files are given, the command moves the first into the second. It is an error to have more than two arguments with this command unless the last argument is a directory.

netstat

netstat displays the status of network connections on either TCP, UDP, RAW, or UNIX sockets to the system. The -r option is used to obtain information about the routing table. The following is an example of the netstat command:

```
svr01:/home/dpitts$ netstat
Active Internet connections
Proto Recv-Q Send-Q Local Address           Foreign Address
    ➥(State)
User
tcp        0  16501 www.mk.net:www          sdlb12119.san
    ➥net.:3148 FIN_WAIT1
root
tcp        0  16501 auth02.mk.net:www       sdlb12119.san
    ➥net.:3188 FIN_WAIT1
root
tcp        0      1 www.anglernet.com:www   ts88.cctrap.com:1070
    ➥SYN_RECV
root
tcp        0      1 www.anglernet.com:www   ts88.cctrap.com:1071
    ➥SYN_RECV
root
udp        0      0 localhost:domain         *:*
udp        0      0 svr01.mk.net:domain     *:*
udp        0      0 poto.mk.net:domain      *:*
udp        0      0 stats.mk.net:domain     *:*
udp        0      0 home.mk.net:domain      *:*
udp        0      0 www.cmf.net:domain      *:*
Active UNIX domain sockets
Proto RefCnt Flags      Type            State           Path
unix  2      [ ]         SOCK_STREAM     UNCONNECTED
    ➥1605182
unix  2      [ ]         SOCK_STREAM     UNCONNECTED
    ➥1627039
unix  2      [ ]         SOCK_STREAM     CONNECTED
    ➥1652605
```

passwd

For the normal user (non-superuser), no arguments are used with the passwd command. The command will ask the user for the old password. Following this, the command will ask for the new password twice, to make sure it was typed correctly. The new password must be at least six characters long and must contain at least one character that is either uppercase or a nonletter. Also, the new password cannot be the same password as the one being replaced, nor can it match the user's ID (account name).

If the command is run by the superuser, it can be followed by either one or two arguments. If the command is followed by a single user's ID, then the superuser can change that user's password. The superuser is not bound by any of the restrictions imposed on the user. If there is an argument after the single user's ID, then that argument becomes that user's new password.

ps

`ps` gives a snapshot of the current processes. An example is as follows:

```
svr01:/home/dpitts$ ps -ef

 PID TTY STAT   TIME COMMAND

10916  p3 S      0:00 -bash TERM=vt100 HOME=/home2/dpitts
    PATH=/usr/local/bin:/us

10973  p3 R      0:00  \_ ps -ef LESSOPEN=¦lesspipe.sh %s
    ignoreeof=10 HOSTNAME=s

10974  p3 S      0:00  \_ more LESSOPEN=¦lesspipe.sh %s ignoree-
    of=10 HOSTNAME=svr
```

pwd

`pwd` prints the current working directory. It tells you what directory you are currently in.

rm

`rm` is used to delete specified files. With the `-r` option (Warning: This can be dangerous!), `rm` will recursively remove files. Therefore if, as root, you type the command `rm -r /`, you had better have a good backup because all your files are now gone. This is a good command to use in conjunction with the find command to find files owned by a certain user or in a certain group, and delete them. By default, the rm command does not remove directories.

rmdir

`rmdir` removes a given *empty* directory; the word *empty* is the key word. The syntax is simply `rmdir <directory name>`.

set

The `set` command is used to temporarily change an environment variable. In some shells, the set `-o vi` command will allow you to bring back previous commands that you have in your history file. It is common to place the command in your `.profile`. Some environment variables require an equals sign, and some, as in the example `set -o vi`, do not.

shutdown

One time during *Star Trek: The Next Generation*, Data commands the computer to "Shut down the holodeck!" Unfortunately, most systems don't have voice controls, but systems can still be shut down. This command happens to be the one to do just that. Technically, the `shutdown` call

```
int shutdown(int s, int how));
```

causes all or part of a full-duplex connection on a socket associated with s to be shut down, but who's being technical? The `shutdown` command can also be used to issue a "Vulcan Neck Pinch" (Ctrl+Alt+Del) and restart the system.

su

`su` enables a user to temporarily become another user. If a user ID is not given, the computer thinks you want to be the superuser, or root. In either case, a shell is spawned that makes you the new user, complete with that user ID, group ID, and any supplemental groups of that new user. If you are not root and the user has a password (and the user should!), `su` prompts for a password. Root can become any user at any time without knowing passwords. Technically, the user just needs to have a user ID of `0` (which makes a user a superuser) to log on as anyone else without a password.

swapoff

No, `swapoff` is not a move from *Karate Kid*. Instead, it is a command that stops swapping to a file or block device.

swapon

Also not from the movie *Karate Kid*, `swapon` sets the swap area to the file or block device by path. `swapoff` stops swapping to the file. This command is normally done during system boot.

tail

`tail` prints to standard output the last 10 lines of a given file. If no file is given, it reads from standard input. If more than one file is given, it prints a header consisting of the file's name enclosed in a left and right arrow (`==> <==`) before the output of each file. The default value of 10 lines can be changed by placing a `-###` in the command. The syntax for the command is

```
tail [-<# of lines to see>] [<filename(s)>]
```

talk

The `talk` command is used to have a "visual" discussion with someone else over a terminal. The basic idea behind this visual discussion is that your input is copied to the other person's terminal, and the other person's input is copied to your terminal. Thus, both people involved in the discussion see the input for both themselves and the other person.

tar

`tar` is an archiving program designed to store and extract files from an archive file. This tarred file (called a `tar` file), can be archived to any media including a tape drive and a hard drive. The syntax of a `tar` command is `tar <action> <optional functions> <file(s)/directory(ies)>`. If the last parameter is a directory, all subdirectories under the directory are also tarred.

umount

Just as the cavalry unmounts from their horses, filesystems unmount from their locations as well. The `umount` command is used to perform this action. The syntax of the command is

```
umount <filesystem>
```

unalias

`unalias` is the command to undo an alias. In the `alias` command section, earlier in this appendix, I aliased `dir` to be the `ls` command. To unalias this command, you would simply type **`unalias dir`**.

unzip

The `unzip` command will list, test, or extract files from a zipped archive. The default is to extract files from the archive. The basic syntax is unzip `<filename>`.

wall

`wall` displays the contents of standard input on all terminals of all currently logged in users. Basically, the command writes to all terminals, hence its name. The contents of files can also be displayed. The superuser, or root, can write to the terminals of those who have chosen to deny messages or are using a program that automatically denies messages.

who

Either the `who` command calls an owl, which it doesn't, or it prints the login name, terminal type, login time, and remote hostname of each user currently logged on. The following is an example of the `who` command:

```
svr01:/home/dpitts$ who
root      ttyp0    Jul 27 11:44 (www01.mk.net)
dpitts    ttyp2    Jul 27 19:32 (d12.dialup.seane)
ehooban   ttyp3    Jul 27 11:47 (205.177.146.78)
dpitts    ttyp4    Jul 27 19:34 (d12.dialup.seane)
```

If two nonoption arguments are passed to the who command, the command prints the entry for the user running it. Typically, this is run with the command who am I, but any two arguments will work; for example, the following gives information on my session:

```
svr01:/home/dpitts$ who who who
svr01!dpitts    ttyp2    Jul 27 19:32 (d12.dialup.seane)
```

The -u option is nice if you want to see how long it has been since that session has been used, such as in the following:

```
svr01:/home/dpitts$ who -u
root      ttyp0    Jul 27 11:44 08:07 (www01.mk.net)
dpitts    ttyp2    Jul 27 19:32   .   (d12.dialup.seane)
ehooban   ttyp3    Jul 27 11:47 00:09 (205.177.146.78)
dpitts    ttyp4    Jul 27 19:34 00:06 (d12.dialup.seane)
```

xhost +

The xhost + command allows xterms to be displayed on a system. Probably the most common reason that a remote terminal cannot be opened is because the xhost + command has not been run. To turn off the capability to allow xterms, the xhost - command is used.

xmkmf

The xmkmf command is used to create the Imakefiles for X sources. It actually runs the imake command with a set of arguments.

xset

The xset command sets some of the options in an X Window session. You can use this option to set your bell (xset b <volume> <frequency> <duration in milliseconds>), your mouse speed (xset m <acceleration> <threshold>), and many others.

zip

The zip command will list, test, or add files to a zipped archive. The default is to add files to an archive.

Summary

If you read this entire appendix, you will have noticed two things. First, I cannot count. There are about seventy commands here, not fifty as the title of the appendix states. Second, you have way too much time on your hands, and need to go out and program some drivers or something!

I hope this appendix has helped you gain an understanding of some of the commands available for your use, whether you are a user, a system administrator, or just someone who wants to learn more about Red Hat Linux. I encourage you to use the man pages to find out the many details left out of this appendix. Most of the commands have arguments that can be passed to them, and, although this appendix attempts to point out a few of them, it would have taken an entire book just to go into the detail that has been provided in the man pages.

Glossary

This is a fairly extensive glossary of terms that are related to the UNIX environment and their definitions. All the authors of this book contributed to this section.

Note: The language of the computer field is constantly expanding. If you cannot find a word in this glossary, it is because it is newer than anything the authors knew about or the authors decided is was so obvious that "everyone should already know it."

#—Octothorpe.

$HOME—Environment variable that points to your login directory.

$PATH—Pathname environment variable.

$PATH—The shell environment variable that contains a set of directories to be searched for UNIX commands.

.1—Files with this extension contain manual page entries. The actual extension can be any value between `1` and `9` and can have an alphabetic suffix (`.3x`, `.7`, and so on).

.ag—Applixware graphics file.

.as—Applixware spreadsheet file.

.aw—Applixware word processing file.

.bmp—Bitmap graphics file.

.c—C source file.

.C—C++ source file.

.cc—C++ source file.

.conf—Configuration file.

.cxx—C++ source file.

.db—Database file.

.dvi—Device-independent TeX output.

.gif—GIF graphics file.

.gz—File compressed using the GNU `gzip` utility.

.h—C header file.

.html—HTML document.

.jpg—JPEG graphics file.

.m—Objective C source file.

.o—Compiled object file.

.p—Pascal language source file.

.pbm—Portable bitmap graphics file.

.pdf—Adobe Acrobat file.

.ps—PostScript file

.s—Assembler file.

.tar—`tar` file.

`.tgz`—Gzipped `tar` file.

`.tif`—TIFF graphics file.

`.txt`—Text document.

`.z`—File compressed using the `compress` command.

`/`—Root directory.

`/dev`—Device directory.

`/dev/null` file—The place to send output that you are not interested in seeing; also the place to get input from when you have none (but the program or command requires something). This is also known as the *bit bucket* (where old bits go to die).

`/dev/printer`—Socket for local print requests.

`/etc/cshrc` file—The file containing shell environment characteristics common to all users that use the C Shell.

`/etc/group` file—This file contains information about groups, the users they contain, and passwords required for access by other users. The password might actually be in another file, the shadow group file, to protect it from attacks.

`/etc/inittab` file—The file that contains a list of active terminal ports for which UNIX will issue the login prompt. This also contains a list of background processes for UNIX to initialize. Some versions of UNIX use other files, such as `/etc/tty`.

`/etc/motd` file —Message of the day file; usually contains information the system administrator feels is important for you to know. This file is displayed when the user signs on the system.

`/etc/passwd` file —Contains user information and password. The password might actually be in another file, the shadow password file, to protect it from attacks.

`/etc/profile` —The file containing shell environment characteristics common to all users of the Bourne and Korn shells.

`/usr/local`—Locally developed public executables directory.

`/var/spool`—Various spool directories.

`[]`—Brackets.

`{}`—Braces.

ANSI—American National Standards Institute.

API—Application Program Interface —The specific method prescribed by a computer operating system, application, or third-party tool by which a programmer writing an application program can make requests of the operating system. Also known as Application Programmer's Interface.

ar—Archive utility.

arguments—See *parameters.*

ARPA—See *DARPA.*

ASCII—American Standard Code for Information Interchange. Used to represent characters in memory for most computers.

AT&T UNIX—Original version of UNIX developed at AT&T Bell Labs, later known as UNIX Systems Laboratories. Many current versions of UNIX are descendants; even BSD UNIX was derived from early AT&T UNIX.

attribute —The means of describing objects. The attributes for a ball might be rubber, red, 3 cm in diameter. The behavior of the ball might be how high it bounces when thrown. Attribute is another name for the data contained within an object (class).

awk—Programming language developed by A.V. Aho, P.J. Weinberger, and Brian W. Kernighan. The language is built on C syntax, includes the regular expression search facilities of grep, and adds in the advanced string and array handling features that are missing from the C language. nawk, gawk, and POSIX awk are versions of this language.

background —Processes usually running at a lower priority and with their input disconnected from the interactive session. Any input and output are usually directed to a file or other process.

background process—An autonomous process that runs under UNIX without requiring user interaction.

backup —The process of storing the UNIX system, applications, and data files on removable media for future retrieval.

bash —Stands for GNU Bourne Again Shell and is based on the Bourne shell, sh, the original command interpreter.

biff—Background mail notification utility.

bison—GNU parser generator (yacc replacement).

block-special —A device file that is used to communicate with a block-oriented I/O device. Disk and tape drives are examples of block devices. The block-special file refers to the entire device. You should not use this file unless you want to ignore the directory structure of the device (that is, if you are coding a device driver).

boot or boot up—The process of starting the operating system (UNIX).

Bourne shell —The original standard user interface to UNIX that supported limited programming capability.

BSD—Berkeley Software Distribution.

BSD UNIX —Version of UNIX developed by Berkeley Software Distribution and written at University of California, Berkeley.

bug—An undocumented program feature.

C—Programming language developed by Brian W. Kernighan and Dennis M. Ritchie. The C language is highly portable and available on many platforms including mainframes, PCs, and, of course, UNIX systems.

C shell —A user interface for UNIX written by Bill Joy at Berkeley. It features C programming-like syntax.

CAD—Computer-aided design.

cast—Programming construct to force type conversion.

cat—Concatenate files command.

CD-ROM —Compact Disk-Read Only Memory. Computer-readable data stored on the same physical form as a musical CD. Large capacity, inexpensive, slower than a hard disk, and limited to reading. There are versions that are writable (CD-R, CD Recordable) and other formats that can be written to once or many times.

CGI—Common Gateway Interface. A means of transmitting data between Web pages and programs or scripts executing on the server. Those programs can then process the data and send the results back to the user's browser through dynamically creating HTML.

character special —A device file that is used to communicate with character-oriented I/O devices like terminals, printers, or network communications lines. All I/O access is treated as a series of bytes (characters).

characters, alphabetic—The letters A through Z and a through z.

characters, alphanumeric—The letters A through Z and a through z, and the numbers 0 through 9.

characters, control—Any nonprintable characters. The characters are used to control devices, separate records, and eject pages on printers.

characters, numeric—The numbers 0 through 9.

characters, special—Any of the punctuation characters or printable characters that are not alphanumeric. Include the space, comma, period, and many others.

child process—See *subprocess.*

child shell—See *subshell.*

class—A model of objects that have attributes (data) and behavior (code or functions). It is also viewed as a collection of objects in their abstracted form.

command-line editing —UNIX shells support the ability to recall a previously entered command, modify it, and then execute the new version. The command history can remain between sessions (the commands you did yesterday can be available for you when you log in today). Some shells support a command-line editing mode that uses a subset of the `vi`, `emacs`, or `gmacs` editor commands for command recall and modification.

command-line history—See *command-line editing.*

command-line parameters —Used to specify parameters to pass to the execute program or procedure. Also known as *command-line arguments.*

configuration files —Collections of information used to initialize and set up the environment for specific commands and programs. Shell configuration files set up the user's environment.

configuration files, shell—For Bourne shell: `/etc/profile` and `$HOME/.profile`.

For Korn and `pdksh` shells: `/etc/profile`, `$HOME/.profile`, and `ENV= file`.

For C and `tcsh` shells: `/etc/.login`, `/etc/cshrc`, `$HOME/.login`, `$HOME/.cshrc`, and `$HOME/.logout`. Older versions might not support the first two files listed.

For `bash`: `/etc/profile/`, `$HOME/.bash_profile`, `$HOME/.bash_login`, `$HOME/.profile`, `$HOME/.bashrc`, and `~/.bash_logout`.

CPU—Central Processing Unit. The primary "brain" of the computer—the calculation engine and logic controller.

daemon —A system-related background process that often runs with the permissions of root and services requests from other processes.

DARPA—(U.S. Department of) Defense Advanced Research Projects Agency Funded development of TCP/IP and ARPAnet (predecessor of the Internet).

database server—See *server, database.*

device file —File used to implement access to a physical device. This provides a consistent approach to access of storage media under UNIX; data files and devices (like tapes and communication facilities) are implemented as files. To the programmer, there is no real difference.

directory—A means of organizing and collecting files together. The directory itself is a file that consists of a list of files contained within it. The root (`/`) directory is the top level and every other directory is contained in it (directly or indirectly). A directory might contain other directories, known as *subdirectories.*

directory navigation —The process of moving through directories is known as navigation. Your current directory is known as the current working directory. Your login directory is known as the default or home directory. Using the `cd` command, you can move up and down through the tree structure of directories.

DNS—Domain Name Server. Used to convert between the name of a machine on the Internet (`name.domain.com`) to the numeric address (`123.45.111.123`).

DOS—Disk Operating System Operating system that is based on the use of disks for the storage of commands. It is also a generic name for MS-DOS and PC-DOS on the personal computer. MS-DOS is the version Microsoft sells; PC-DOS is the version IBM sells. Both are based on Microsoft code.

`double`—Double-precision floating point.

dpi—Dots per inch.

EBCDIC—Extended Binary Coded Decimal Interchange Code. The code used to represent characters in memory for mainframe computers.

`ed`—A common tool used for line-oriented text editing.

`elm`—Interactive mail program.

`emacs`—A freely available editor now part of the GNU software distribution. Originally written by Richard M. Stallman at MIT in the late 1970s, it is available for many platforms. It is extremely extensible and has its own programming language; the name stands for editing with macros.

email—Messages sent through an electronic medium instead of through the local postal service. There are many proprietary email systems that are designed to handle mail within a LAN environment; most of these are also able to send over the Internet. Most Internet (open) email systems make use of MIME to handle attached data (which can be binary).

encapsulation—The process of combining data (attributes) and functions (behavior in the form of code) into an object. The data and functions are closely coupled within an object. Instead of all programmers being able to access the data in a structure their own way, they have to use the code connected with that data. This promotes code reuse and standardized methods of working with the data.

environment variables—See *variables, environmental.*

Ethernet—A networking method where the systems are connected to a single shared bus and all traffic is available to every machine. The data packets contain an identifier of the recipient, and that is the only machine that should process that packet.

expression—A constant, variable, or operands and operators combined. Used to set a value, perform a calculation, or set the pattern for a comparison (regular expressions).

FIFO—First In, First Out. See *pipe, named.*

file—Collection of bytes stored on a device (typically a disk or tape). Can be source code, executable binaries or scripts, or data.

file compression—The process of applying mathematical formulas to data, typically resulting in a form of the data that occupies less space. A compressed file can be uncompressed, resulting in the original file. When the compress/uncompress process results in exactly the same file as was originally compressed, it is known as lossless. If information about the original file is lost, the compression method is known as lossy. Data and programs need lossless compression; images and sounds can stand lossy compression.

file, indexed—A file based on a file structure where data can be retrieved based on specific keys (name, employee number, and so on) or sequentially. The keys are stored in an index. This is not directly supported by the UNIX operating system; usually implemented by the programmer or by using tools from an ISV. A typical form is known as *ISAM.*

file, line sequential—See *file, text.*

file, sequential—This phrase can mean either a file that can only be accessed sequentially (not randomly), or a file without record separators (typically fixed length, but UNIX does not know what that length is and does not care).

file, text—A file with record separators. Can be fixed or variable length; UNIX tools can handle these files because the tools can tell when the record ends (by the separator).

filename—The name used to identify a collection of data (a file). Without a pathname, it is assumed to be in the current directory.

filename generation—The process of the shell interpreting metacharacters (wildcards) to produce a list of matching files. This is referred to as filename expansion or globbing.

filename, fully qualified—The name used to identify a collection of data (a file) and its location. It includes both the path and name of the file; typically, the pathname is fully specified (absolute). See also *pathname* and *pathname, absolute.*

filesystem—A collection of disk storage that is connected (mounted) to the directory structure at some point (sometimes at the root). Filesystems are stored in a disk partition and are sometimes referred to as being the disk partition.

finger—User information lookup program.

firewall—A system used to provide a controlled entry point to the internal network from the outside (usually the Internet). This is used to prevent outside or unauthorized systems from accessing systems on your internal network. The capability depends on the individual software package, but the features typically include filter packets and filter datagrams, system (name or IP address) aliasing, and rejecting packets from certain IP addresses. In theory, it provides protection from malicious programs or people on the outside. It can also prevent internal systems from accessing the Internet on the outside. The name comes from the physical barrier between connected buildings or within a single building that is supposed to prevent fire from spreading from one to another.

flags—See *options.*

float—Single-precision floating point.

foreground—Programs running while connected to the interactive session.

fseek—Internal function used by UNIX to locate data inside a file or filesystem. ANSI standard `fseek` accepts a parameter that can hold a value of +2 to -2 billion. This function, used by the operating system, system tools, and application programs, is the cause of the 2GB file and filesystem size limitation on most systems. With 64-bit operating systems, this limit is going away.

FSF—Free Software Foundation.

FTP—File Transfer Protocol or File Transfer Program. A system-independent means of transferring files between systems connected via TCP/IP. Ensures that the file is transferred correctly, even if there are errors during transmission. Can usually handle character set conversions (ASCII/EBCDIC) and record terminator resolution (linefeed for UNIX, carriage return and linefeed for MS/PC-DOS).

gateway—A combination of hardware, software, and network connections that provides a link between one architecture and another. Typically, a gateway is used to connect a LAN or UNIX server with a mainframe (that uses SNA for networking, resulting in the name SNA gateway). A gateway can also be the connection between the internal and external network (often referred to as a firewall). See also *firewall.*

GID—Group ID number.

globbing—See *filename generation.*

GNU—GNU stands for GNU's Not UNIX, and is the name of free useful software packages commonly found in UNIX environments that are being distributed by the GNU project at MIT, largely through the efforts of Richard Stallman. The circular acronym name ("GNU" containing the acronym GNU as one of the words it stands for) is a joke on Richard Stallman's part. One of the textbooks on operating system design is titled *XINU: XINU Is Not UNIX,* and GNU follows in that path.

GPL—GNU General Public License.

grep—A common tool used to search a file for a pattern. `egrep` and `fgrep` are newer versions. `egrep` allows the use of extended (hence the *e* prefix) regular expressions; `fgrep` uses limited expressions for faster (hence the *f* prefix) searches.

GUI—Graphical user interface.

here document—The << redirection operator, known as *here document*, allows keyboard input (`stdin`) for the program to be included in the script.

HTML—Hypertext Markup Language. Describes World Wide Web pages. It is the document language that is used to define the pages available on the Internet through the use of tags. A browser interprets the HTML to display the desired information.

i-node—Used to describe a file and its storage. The directory contains a cross-reference between the i-node and pathname/filename combination. Also known as *inode*. A file's entry in disk data structure (`ls -i`).

I-Phone—Internet Phone. This is a method of transmitting speech long distances over the Internet in near real-time. Participants avoid paying long distance telephone charges. They still pay for the call to their ISP and the ISP's service charges.

ICCCM—Inter-Client Communications Conventions Manual.

ICMP—Internet Control Message Protocol. Part of TCP/IP that provides network layer management and control.

`imake`—C preprocessor interface to `make` utility.

inheritance —A method of object-oriented software reuse in which new classes are developed based on existing ones by using the existing attributes and behavior and adding on to them. If the base object is automobiles (with attributes of engine and four wheels and tires; behavior of acceleration, turning, deceleration), a sports car would modify the attributes: engine might be larger or have more horsepower than the default, the four wheels might include alloy wheels and high-speed–rated tires; the behavior would also be modified: faster acceleration, tighter turning radius, faster deceleration.

inode—See *i-node*.

`int`—Integer.

Internet—A collection of different networks that provide the ability to move data between them. It is built on the TCP/IP communications protocol. Originally developed by DARPA, it was taken over by NSF, and has now been released from governmental control.

Internet Service Provider —The people that connect you to the Internet.

IRC—Internet relay chat. A server-based application that allows groups of people to communicate simultaneously through text-based conversations. IRC is similar to Citizen Band radio or the chat rooms on some bulletin boards. Some chats can be private (between invited people only) or public (where anyone can join in). IRC now also supports sound files as well as text; it can also be useful for file exchange.

ISAM—Indexed Sequential Access Method. On UNIX and other systems, ISAM refers to a method for accessing data in a keyed or sequential way. The UNIX operating system does not directly support ISAM files; they are typically add-on products.

ISO—International Standards Organization.

ISP—See *Internet Service Provider*.

ISV—Independent Software Vendor. Generic name for software vendors other than your hardware vendor.

K&R—Kernighan and Ritchie.

kernel—The core of the operating system that handles tasks like memory allocation, device input and output, process allocation, security, and user access. UNIX tends to have a small kernel when compared to other operating systems.

keys, control—These are keys that cause some function to be performed instead of displaying a character. These functions have names: The end-of-file key tells UNIX that there is no more input; it is usually Ctrl+D.

keys, special—See *keys, control.*

Korn shell—A user interface for UNIX with extensive scripting (programming) support. Written by David G. Korn. The shell features command-line editing and will also accept scripts written for the Bourne shell.

LAN—Local Area Network. A collection of networking hardware, software, desktop computers, servers, and hosts all connected together within a defined local area. A LAN could be an entire college campus.

limits—See *quota.*

link file—File used to implement a symbolic link producing an alias on one filesystem for a file on another. The file contains only the fully qualified filename of the original (linked-to) file.

link, hard—Directory entry that provides an alias to another file within the same filesystem. Multiple entries appear in the directory (or other directories) for one physical file without replication of the contents.

link, soft—See *link, symbolic.*

link, symbolic—Directory entry that provides an alias to another file that can be in another filesystem. Multiple entries appear in the directory for one physical file without replication of the contents. Implemented through link files; see also *link file.*

LISP—List Processing Language.

login—The process with which a user gains access to a UNIX system. This can also refer to the user ID that is typed at the login prompt.

lp—Line printer.

`lpc`—Line printer control program.

`lpd`—Line printer daemon.

`lpq`—Printer spool queue examination program.

`lprm`—Printer spool queue job removal program.

`ls`—List directory(s) command.

man page—Online reference tool under UNIX that contains the documentation for the system—the actual pages from the printed manuals. It is stored in a searchable form for improved ability to locate information.

manual page—See *man page.*

memory, real—Theamount of storage that is being used within the system (silicon; it used to be magnetic cores).

memory, virtual—Memory that exists but you cannot see. Secondary storage (disk) is used to allow the operating system to enable programs to use more memory than is physically available.

Part of a disk is used as a paging file and portions of programs and their data are moved between it and real memory. To the program, it is in real memory. The hardware and operating system performs translation between the memory address the program thinks it is using and where it is actually stored.

metacharacter—A printing character that has special meaning to the shell or another command. It is converted into something else by the shell or command; the asterisk (*) is converted by the shell to a list of all files in the current directory.

MIME—Multipurpose Internet Mail Extensions. A set of protocols or methods of attaching binary data (executable programs, images, sound files, and so on) or additional text to email messages.

motd—Message of the day.

MPTN—MultiProtocol Transport Network IBM networking protocol to connect mainframe to TCP/IP network.

Mrm—Motif resource manager.

mtu—Maximum transmission unit.

mwm—Motif window manager.

Netnews —This is a loosely controlled collection of discussion groups. A message (similar to an e-mail) is posted in a specific area, and then people can comment on it, publicly replying to the same place (posting a response) for others to see. A collection of messages along the same theme is referred to as a thread. Some of the groups are moderated, which means that nothing is posted without the approval of the owner. Most are not, and the title of the group is no guarantee that the discussion will be related. The official term for this is Usenet news.

NFS—Network File System. Means of connecting disks that are mounted to a remote system to the local system as if they were physically connected.

NIS—Network Information Service. A service that provides information necessary to all machines on a network, such as NFS support for hosts and clients, password verification, and so on.

NNTP—Netnews Transport Protocol Used to transmit Netnews or Usenet messages over top of TCP/IP. See *Netnews* for more information on the messages transmitted.

Null Statement—A program step that performs no operation but to hold space and fulfill syntactical requirements of the programming language. Also known as a *NO-OP* for no-operation performed.

object—An object in the truest sense of the word is something that has physical properties, like automobiles, rubber balls, and clouds. These things have attributes and behavior. They can be abstracted into data (attribute) and code (behavior). Instead of just writing functions to work on data, they are encapsulated into a package that is known as an object.

operator—Metacharacter that performs a function on values or variables. The plus sign (+) is an operator that adds two integers.

options—Program- or command-specific indicators that control behavior of that program. Sometimes called *flags*. The `-a` option to the `ls` command shows the files that begin with . (such as `.profile`, `.kshrc`, and so on). Without it, these files would not be shown, no matter what wildcards were used. These are used on the command line. See also *parameters.*

OSF—Open Software Foundation.

parameters—Data passed to a command or program through the command line. These can be options (see *options*) that control the command or arguments that the command works on. Some have special meaning based on their position on the command line.

parent process—Process that controls another often referred to as the child process or subprocess. See also *process.*

parent process identifier—Shown in the heading of the `ps` command as PPID. The process identifier of the parent process. See also *parent process.*

parent shell—Shell (typically the login shell) that controls another, often referred to as the child shell or subshell. See also *shell.*

password—The secure code that is used in combination with a user ID to gain access to a UNIX system.

pathname —The means used to represent the location of a file in the directory structure. If you do not specify a pathname, it defaults to the current directory.

pathname, absolute—The means used to represent the location of a file in a directory by specifying the exact location, including all directories in the chain including the root.

pathname, relative—The means used to represent the location of a file in a directory other than the current by navigating up and down through other directories using the current directory as a base.

PDP—Personal Data Processor Computers manufactured by Digital Equipment Corporation. UNIX was originally written for a PDP-7 and gained popularity on the PDP-11. The entire series were inexpensive minicomputers popular with educational institutions and small businesses.

Perl—Programming language developed by Larry Wall. (Perl stands for "Practical Extraction and Report Language" or "Pathologically Eclectic Rubbish Language"; both are equally valid.) The language provides all of the capabilities of `awk` and `sed`, plus many of the features of the shells and C.

permissions—When applied to files, they are the attributes that control access to a file. There are three levels of access: Owner (the file creator), Group (people belonging to a related group as determined by the system administrator), and Other (everyone else). The permissions are usually `r` for read, `w` for write, and `x` for execute. The execute permissions flag is also used to control who may search a directory.

PGP—Pretty Good Privacy encryption system.

`pine`—Interactive mail program.

pipe—A method of sending the output of one program (redirecting) to become the input of another. The pipe character (`¦`) tells the shell to perform the redirection.

pipe file—See *pipe, named.*

pipe, named—An expanded function of a regular pipe (redirecting the output of one program to become the input of another). Instead of connecting `stdout` to `stdin`, the output of one program is sent to the named pipe and another program reads data from the same file. This is implemented through a special file known as a pipe file or FIFO. The operating system ensures the proper sequencing of the data. Little or no data is actually stored in the pipe file; it just acts as a connection between the two.

polymorphism—Allows code to be written in a general fashion to handle existing and future related classes. Properly developed, the same behavior can act differently depending on the derived object it acts on. With an automobile, the acceleration behavior might be different for a station wagon and a dragster, which are subclasses of the superclass automobile. The function would still be `accelerate()`, but the version would vary (this might sound confusing, but the compiler keeps track and figures it all out).

POSIX—Portable Operating System Interface, UNIX. POSIX is the name for a family of open system standards based on UNIX. The name has been credited to Richard Stallman. The POSIX Shell and Utilities standard developed by IEEE Working Group 1003.2 (POSIX.2) concentrates on the command interpreter interface and utility programs.

PostScript —Adobe Systems, Inc. printer language.

PPP—Point-to-Point Protocol. Internet protocol over serial link (modem).

`pppd`—Point-to-Point-Protocol daemon.

`printcap`—Printer capability database.

process—A discrete running program under UNIX. The user's interactive session is a process. A process can invoke (run) and control another program that is then referred to as a subprocess. Ultimately, everything a user does is a subprocess of the operating system.

process identifier—Shown in the heading of the `ps` command as `PID`. The unique number assigned to every process running in the system.

`pwd`—Print working directory command.

quota—General description of a system-imposed limitation on a user or process. It can apply to disk space, memory usage, CPU usage, maximum number of open files, and many other resources.

quoting —The use of single and double quotes to negate the normal command interpretation and concatenate all words and whitespace within the quotes as a single piece of text.

RCS—Revision Control System.

redirection—The process of directing a data flow from the default. Input can be redirected to get data from a file or the output of another program. Normal output can be sent to another program or a file. Errors can be sent to another program or a file.

regular expression—A way of specifying and matching strings for shells (filename wildcarding), `grep` (file searches), `sed`, and `awk`.

reserved word—A set of characters that are recognized by UNIX and related to a specific program, function, or command.

RFC—Request For Comment Document used for creation of Internet- and TCP/IP-related standards.

`rlogin`—Remote Login. Gives the same functionality as `telnet`, with the added functionality of not requiring a password from trusted clients, which can also create security concerns (see also *`telnet`*).

root—The user that owns the operating system and controls the computer. The processes of the operating system run as though a user, root, signed on and started them. Root users are all- powerful and can do anything they want. For this reason, they are often referred to as superusers. Root is also the very top of the directory tree structure.

routing—The process of moving network traffic between two different physical networks; also decides which path to take when there are multiple connections between the two machines. It might also send traffic around transmission interruptions.

RPC—Remote Procedural Call. Provides the ability to call functions or subroutines that run on a remote system from the local one.

RPM—Red Hat Package Manager.

script—A program written for a UNIX utility including shells, `awk`, Perl, `sed`, and others. See also *shell scripts*.

SCSI—Small Computer System Interface.

`sed`—A common tool used for stream text editing, having `ed`-like syntax.

server, database—A system designated to run database software (typically a relational database like Oracle, SQL Server, Sybase, or others). Other systems connect to this one to get the data (client applications).

SGID—Set group ID.

shell—The part of UNIX that handles user input and invokes other programs to run commands. Includes a programming language. See also Bourne shell, C shell, Korn shell, `tcsh`, and `bash`.

shell environment —The shell program (Bourne, Korn, C, `tcsh`, or `bash`), invocation options and preset variables that define the characteristics, features, and functionality of the UNIX command-line and program execution interface.

shell or command prompt—The single character or set of characters that the UNIX shell displays for which a user can enter a command or set of commands.

shell scripts—A program written using a shell programming language like those supported by Bourne, Korn, or C shells.

signal—A special flag or interrupt that is used to communicate special events to programs by the operating system and other programs.

SLIP—Serial Line Internet Protocol. Internet over a serial line (modem). The protocol frames and controls the transmission of TCP/IP packets of the line.

SNA—System Network Architecture. IBM networking architecture.

`stderr`—The normal error output for a program that is sent to the screen by default. Can be redirected to a file.

`stdin`—The normal input for a program, taken from the keyboard by default. Can be redirected to get input from a file or the output of another program.

`stdout`—The normal output for a program that is sent to the screen by default. Can be redirected to a file or to the input of another program.

sticky bit—One of the status flags on a file that tells UNIX to load a copy of the file into the page file the first time it is executed. This is done for programs that are commonly used so the bytes are available quickly. When the sticky bit is used on frequently used directories, it is cached in memory.

stream—A sequential collection of data. All files are streams to the UNIX operating system. To it, there is no structure to a file; that is something imposed by application programs or special tools (ISAM packages or relational databases).

subdirectory—See *directory.*

subnet—A portion of a network that shares a common IP address component. Used for security and performance reasons.

subprocess—Process running under the control of another, often referred to as the parent process. See also *process.*

subshell—Shell running under the control of another, often referred to as the parent shell (typically the login shell). See also *shell.*

SUID—Set user ID.

superuser—Usually the root operator.

sysadmin—Burnt-out root operator (system administrator).

system administrator—The person who takes care of the operating system and user administrative issues on UNIX systems. Also called a *system manager*, although that term is much more common in DEC VAX installations.

system manager—See *system administrator.*

system programmer—See *system administrator.*

`tar`—Tape archiving utility.

TCP—Transmission Control Protocol.

TCP/IP—Transport Control Protocol/Internet Protocol. The pair of protocols and also generic name for suite of tools and protocols that forms the basis for the Internet. Originally developed to connect systems to the ARPAnet.

`tcsh`—A C shell-like user interface featuring command-line editing.

`telnet`—Remote login program.

Telnet—Protocol for interactive (character user interface) terminal access to remote systems. The terminal emulator that uses the Telnet protocol is often known as `telnet` or `tnvt100`.

`termcap`—Terminal capability database.

terminal—A hardware device, normally containing a cathode ray tube (screen) and keyboard for human interaction with a computer system.

text processing languages—A way of developing documents in text editors with embedded commands that handle formatting. The file is fed through a processor that executes the embedded commands, producing a formatted document. These include `roff`, `nroff`, `troff`, `RUNOFF`, TeX, LaTeX, and even the mainframe `SCRIPT`.

TFTP—Trivial File Transfer Protocol or Trivial File Transfer Program. A system-independent means of transferring files between systems connected via TCP/IP. It is different from FTP in that it does not ensure that the file is transferred correctly, does not authenticate users, and is missing a lot of functionality (like the `ls` command).

`tin`—Interactive news reader.

`top`—A common tool used to display information about the top processes on the system.

UDP—User Datagram Protocol. Part of TCP/IP used for control messages and data transmission where the delivery acknowledgment is not needed. The application program must ensure data transmission in this case.

UID—User ID number.

UIL—Motif User Interface Language.

URL—Uniform Resource Locator. The method of specifying the protocol, format, login (usually omitted), and location of materials on the Internet.

Usenet—See *Netnews.*

UUCP—UNIX-to-UNIX copy program. Used to build an early, informal network for the transmission of files, email, and Netnews.

variables, attributes—The modifiers that set the variable type. A variable can be string or integer, left- or right-justified, read-only or changeable, and other attributes.

variables, environmental—A place to store data and values (strings and integers) in the area controlled by the shell so they are available to the current and subprocesses. They can just be local to the current shell or available to a subshell (exported).

variables, substitution—The process of interpreting an environmental variable to get its value.

WAN—Wide Area Network.

Web—See *World Wide Web.*

whitespace—Blanks, spaces, and tabs that are normally interpreted to delineate commands and filenames unless quoted.

wildcard—Means of specifying filename(s) whereby the operating system determines some of the characters. Multiple files might match and will be available to the tool.

World Wide Web—A collection of servers and services on the Internet that run software and communicate using a common protocol (HTTP). Instead of the users' having to remember the location of these resources, links are provided from one Web page to another through the use of URLs.

WWW—See *World Wide Web.*

WYSIWYG—What You See Is What You Get.

X

X—See *X Window System.*

X Window System—A windowing and graphics system developed by MIT, to be used in client/server environments.

X11—See *X Window System.*

X-windows—The wrong term for the X Window System. See *X Window System.*

yacc—Yet another compiler compiler.

Index

Symbols

A

D

E

G

H

I

M

N

O

Q

R

S

U

Z